I0812225

Believers Church Bible Commentary

Douglas B. Miller and Loren L. Johns, Editors

BELIEVERS CHURCH BIBLE COMMENTARY

Old Testament
Genesis, by Eugene F. Roop, 1987
Exodus, by Waldemar Janzen, 2000
Joshua, by Gordon H. Matties, 2012
Judges, by Terry L. Brensinger, 1999
Ruth, Jonah, Esther, by Eugene F. Roop, 2002
Psalms, by James H. Waltner, 2006
Proverbs, by John W. Miller, 2004
Ecclesiastes, by Douglas B. Miller, 2010
Isaiah, by Ivan D. Friesen, 2009
Jeremiah, by Elmer A. Martens, 1986
Ezekiel, by Millard C. Lind, 1996
Daniel, by Paul M. Lederach, 1994
Hosea, Amos, by Allen R. Guenther, 1998

New Testament
Matthew, by Richard B. Gardner, 1991
Mark, by Timothy J. Geddert, 2001
Acts, by Chalmer E. Faw, 1993
Romans, by John E. Toews, 2004
2 Corinthians, by V. George Shillington, 1998
Ephesians, by Thomas R. Yoder Neufeld, 2002
Colossians, Philemon, by Ernest D. Martin, 1993
1-2 Thessalonians, by Jacob W. Elias, 1995
1-2 Timothy, Titus, by Paul M. Zehr, 2010
1-2 Peter, Jude, by Erland Waltner and J. Daryl Charles, 1999
1, 2, 3 John, by J. E. McDermond, 2011
Revelation, by John R. Yeatts, 2003

Believers Church Bible Commentary

Joshua

Gordon H. Matties

HERALD PRESS
Harrisonburg, Virginia
Waterloo, Ontario

Library and Archives Canada Cataloguing in Publication
Matties, Gordon
Joshua / Gordon H. Matties.
(Believers church Bible commentary)
Includes bibliographical references and index.
ISBN 978-0-8361-9567-5
1. Bible. O.T. Joshua—Commentaries. I. Title.
II. Series: Believers church Bible commentary

BS1295.53.M38 2012 222'.207 C2011-907618-7

Library of Congress Control Number: 2011942181
Canadiana Entry Number: C2011-907618-7
International Standard Book Number: 978-0-8361-9567-5
Printed in the United States of America
Cover by Merrill R. Miller

20 19 18 17 16 15 14 13 12 10 9 8 7 6 5 4 3 2 1

To order or request information, please call 1-800-254-7894 in the U.S. or or visit 1-800-631-6535 in Canada. Or visit www.heraldpress.com.

To Jesse Gabriel

Abbreviations

*	*see* TBC
+	*see* TLC
AD	*anno Domini*, in the year of the Lord, the era since the time of Christ
ANET	*Ancient Near Eastern Texts Relating to the Old Testament*. Edited by James B. Pritchard. 3rd ed. Princeton, NJ: Princeton University Press, 1969.
art.	article
AT	author's translation
b.	born
BC	before Christ, the era before the time of Christ
BCE	before the Common Era (= before Christ)
ca.	*circa*, approximately
CEB	Common English Bible, 2011
cf.	*confer*, compare
ch./chs.	chapter/chapters
d.	died
DtrH	Deuteronomistic History: Joshua, Judges, Samuel, Kings
ed.	edition/editor
e.g.	*exempli gratia*, for example
emph.	emphasis
Eng.	versification in most English translations
esp.	especially
et al.	*et alia*, and others
etc.	*et cetera*, and the rest
HALOT	Koehler, L., W. Baumgartner, and J. J. Stamm. *The Hebrew and Aramaic Lexicon of the Old Testament*. Translated and edited under the supervision of M. E. J. Richardson. 5 vols. Leiden: E. J. Brill, 1994–2000.
Heb.	Hebrew
i.e.	*id est*, that is
KJV	King James Version of the Bible
lit.	literally
LXX	Septuagint, ancient Greek translation of the OT
ME	*The Mennonite Encyclopedia*. Vol. 5. Edited by Cornelius J. Dyck and Dennis D. Martin. Scottdale, PA; Waterloo, ON: Herald Press, 1990.
m.	masculine
MBCF 1999	*Confession of Faith: Commentary and Pastoral Application*. Winnipeg, MB: (Mennonite Brethren) Board of Faith and Life, and Kindred Productions, 2000. http://www.mbconf.ca/home/products_and_services/resources/theology/confession_of_faith/detailed_version/.
MCF 1995	*Confession of Faith in a Mennonite Perspective*. Scottdale, PA: Herald Press, 1995, http://www.mcusa-archives.org/library/resolutions/1995/index.html.

MT	versification/readings in the Masoretic Text, the standard Hebrew version of the OT, preserved by Masoretes, a group of early medieval Jewish scribes
n	note, as in 168n13 (page 168, note 13)
NASB	New American Standard Bible, 1995
NIV	New International Version of the Bible, 2011
NIV 1984	New International Version of the Bible, 1984
NJPS	New Jewish Publication Society version of the Bible, 1999
NLT	New Living Translation of the Bible
NRSV	New Revised Standard Version of the Bible
NT	New Testament
OT	Old Testament
pl.	plural
1QM	*Milḥamah*, or *War Scroll*
1QSa	*Rule of the Congregation* (1QS, Appendix a)
rev.	revised
RSV	Revised Standard Version of the Bible
sg.	singular
TBC	Text in Biblical Context, in the commentary
TLC	Text in the Life of the Church, in the commentary
TNIV	Today's New International Version of the Bible
v./vv.	verse/verses
WT	*Worship Together* [hymnal]. Edited by Clarence Hiebert et al. Fresno, CA: Board of Faith and Life of the Mennonite Brethren Churches, 1995.

Pronunciation Guide for Certain Transliterated Hebrew Consonants

'	(not pronounced)
'	(not pronounced)
ḥ	ch (Scottish *loch*)
ṣ	ts
ś	s
š	sh
ṭ	t

Contents

Series Foreword

The Believers Church Bible Commentary Series makes available a new tool for basic Bible study. It is published for all who seek more fully to understand the original message of Scripture and its meaning for today—Sunday school teachers, members of Bible study groups, students, pastors, and others. The series is based on the conviction that God is still speaking to all who will listen, and that the Holy Spirit makes the Word a living and authoritative guide for all who want to know and do God's will.

The desire to help as wide a range of readers as possible has determined the approach of the writers. Since no blocks of biblical text are provided, readers may continue to use the translation with which they are most familiar. The writers of the series use the *New Revised Standard Version* and the *New International Version* on a comparative basis. They indicate which text they follow most closely and where they make their own translations. The writers have not worked alone, but in consultation with select counselors, the series' editors, and the Editorial Council.

Every volume illuminates the Scriptures; provides necessary theological, sociological, and ethical meanings; and in general makes "the rough places plain." Critical issues are not avoided, but neither are they moved into the foreground as debates among scholars. Each section offers Explanatory Notes, followed by focused articles, "The Text in Biblical Context" and "The Text in the Life of the Church." This commentary aids the interpretive process but does not try to supersede the authority of the Word and Spirit as discerned in the gathered church.

The term *believers church* has often been used in the history of the church. Since the sixteenth century, it has frequently been applied to the Anabaptists and later the Mennonites, as well as to the Church of the Brethren and similar groups. As a descriptive term, it includes more than Mennonites and Brethren. *Believers church* now represents specific theological understandings, such as believers baptism, commitment to the Rule of Christ in Matthew 18:15-20 as crucial for church membership, belief in the power of love in all relationships, and willingness to follow Christ in the way of the cross. The writers chosen for the series stand in this tradition.

Believers church people have always been known for their emphasis on obedience to the simple meaning of Scripture. Because of this, they do not have a long history of deep historical-critical biblical scholarship. This series attempts to be faithful to the Scriptures while also taking archaeology and current biblical studies seriously. Doing this means that at many points the writers will not differ greatly from interpretations that can be found in many other good commentaries. Yet these writers share basic convictions about Christ, the church and its mission, God and history, human nature, the Christian life, and other doctrines. These presuppositions do shape a writer's interpretation of Scripture. Thus this series, like all other commentaries, stands within a specific historical church tradition.

Many in this stream of the church have expressed a need for help in Bible study. This is justification enough to produce the Believers Church Bible Commentary. Nevertheless, the Holy Spirit is not bound to any tradition. May this series be an instrument in breaking down walls between Christians in North America and around the world, bringing new joy in obedience through a fuller understanding of the Word.

—The Editorial Council

Author's Preface

I begin this commentary with a precious hope that you, the reader, will take Eugene Peterson's advice to heart: "I recommend reading commentaries in the same way we read novels, from beginning to end, skipping nothing" (2006:54). I do not think much can be gleaned from the book of Joshua by dipping into it in midplot as though somehow a gem might be extracted from the ore. The story as a whole is the thing with which I have occupied myself. The work of commentary writing, and reading, must ultimately be an act of love that is not simply interested in "a quick look, get a 'message' or a 'meaning,' and then run off and talk endlessly with their friends about how they feel" (55).

The commentary focuses on the literary and theological character of the book of Joshua. In the commentary proper, I have not paid attention to the questions, which are important for some readers, of the date of the "exodus and conquest" or of the date of composition of the book of Joshua. For general reflection on those topics, please consult the essays located near the back of the commentary *[Archaeology and Joshua; Composition of Joshua; Models of the Settlement]*. A more comprehensive introduction to the interpretive stance taken in this commentary can be found in my 2009 article.

During the revision of the final drafts, I read Chris Hedges's *War Is a Force That Gives Us Meaning*. He writes, "War is a drug. . . . It dominates culture, distorts memory, corrupts language, and infects everything around it." It raises "fundamental questions about the meaning, or meaninglessness, of our place on the planet" and it "exposes the capacity for evil that lurks not far below the surface within all of us" (3). In an age of fear and insecurity, in which ethnic nationalisms continue to give rise to conflict and war, we dare not avoid critical engagement with biblical texts that have been used to justify colonialism, conquest, occupation, and ethnic cleansing. In this commentary I suggest that the book of Joshua is not a conquest account even though it incorporates several conquest accounts into its narrative. I advocate for the book of Joshua even as I engage in a "difficult conversation" with it.

I am indebted and grateful to numerous scholars whose influence is pervasive. Especially notable are Girard, Hauch, Hawk, Mitchell, Person, Polzin, Rowlett, and Younger (see bibliography).

I am grateful to Canadian Mennonite University for a full year sabbatical leave in 2003–4, during which I was able to complete the first draft of the commentary. Revisions and the writing of the topical essays continued during the summers between teaching, administrative duties, study tours, film festivals, and other smaller writing and editing projects. My wife, Lorraine Matties, patiently read and commented on the manuscript. Doug Miller, the OT editor of the commentary series, brought wise and perceptive insights to bear in countless ways. I cannot adequately express how deeply indebted I am to his careful attention to my work. David Garber, Herald Press copy editor, paid extraordinary attention to detail. I am also grateful to Raymond Person, Doug Enns, and the members of the Editorial Council of the commentary series—all of whose encouragement and suggestions were invaluable. Of course, the shortcomings of the commentary are entirely my own.

Unfortunately, as with any work that has taken a long time, the research must end and the final product must be submitted. Because of that, I regret not having been able, at this late stage of my work, to engage excellent new books by Douglas Earl (2010a, 2010b), Daniel Hawk (2010), J. Gordon McConville and Stephen N. Williams (2010), and Pekka Pitkänen (2011).

—Gordon Matties
Winnipeg, Manitoba

Introduction to Joshua

There is a crack in everything;
that's how the light gets in.
—Leonard Cohen, "Anthem"

The book of Joshua raises so many questions that readers might well be excused for neglecting the book in favor of other less troubling biblical texts. For some readers, Jesus' command to love the enemy trumps Joshua (Matt 5:43-48), and the older story is best left in the hoary and horrible past. Others might read Joshua and conclude that God sometimes sanctions war, as horrible as that is. The matter will not go away; genocide and so-called ethnic cleansing are with us still. The theological debate simmers politely in the book *Show Them No Mercy: Four Views on God and Canaanite Genocide* (Cowles et al.). In an era in which humankind has not begun to reverse the tragedies of the bloody and brutal twentieth century, there are good reasons to reject the alliance of religious fervor and violent rivalry.

Even so, and in spite of our predisposition to hearing what we want to hear, we do well to foster an openness to the unexpected. Perhaps reading Joshua carefully will open windows into how and why we read Scripture at all. It will push us not to settle for easy answers or to give up too soon. This commentary is a plea to pay attention to a difficult text, a text we might well call a "text of terror." In a time of religious justification for terrorism and counter-terrorism, Joshua may be a book for our time.

This commentary is the result of a difficult conversation with the text, even an argument with it. In any such conversation, we try to speak the truth as we understand it, and we do our best to listen attentively so as to understand the matter from the other's perspective. We include God in the conversation because, like Abraham (Gen 18:25) and Job, we assume that there is a moral standard to which we might hold God accountable *[Difficult Conversations, p. 421]*.

Such truthfulness cannot be avoided because the book of Joshua marries the memory of violent events with assertions about God's character and the identity of God's people. Joshua's violence challenges the interpretive community's sense of moral coherence. If this story tells the truth, is faith in a loving God not in vain? Some readers try to rescue the book from its own demise. For example, some suggest that a "conquest" likely never happened as it has been described in the book *[Archaeology and Joshua, p. 389]*. Others tend to rewrite the story so that it sounds as if a peasant revolt took place among the indigenous inhabitants of the land *[Models of the Settlement, p. 448]*. Thus the book of Joshua flounders in the face of other, more acceptable stories. Yet even those reconstructions of the historical world behind the text of Joshua represent genuine attempts to rescue the text or ancient Israel or God from the charge of sacred violence and genocide.

An Intrabiblical Conversation

An alternative imagines the book as a participant in an intrabiblical conversation (also called "inner-biblical" or "intertextual"). In this process, Joshua interprets other texts, and other texts interpret Joshua. Viewed that way, the Bible itself bears witness to a lively, if painful, debate about the relationship between violence and the identity and mission of God's people. Joshua belongs to a long tradition that reflects on old patterns and archetypal events so as to make new events understandable. By linking events through time, such an interpretive tradition gives rise to the notion of a living story *[Figural Reading, p. 426]*. Because of that, the book of Joshua, as one figure in a canonical tapestry of memory and theological reflection, is not as easily reduced to "meaning" or "application" as we might wish.

A Legacy of Violence

From our vantage point, it seems clear that the church has inherited the violent legacy of Constantine and the crusades (Lynch; Collins). The church has its share of complicity in the atrocities of Nazi Germany's slaughter of millions of Jews and other "undesirables," Rwanda's "ethnic cleansing," centuries of interreligious strife in the Balkans, the mistreatment of indigenous peoples throughout the modern world, the involvement of the United States in the Vietnam war, the firebombing of German and Japanese cities, and the unleashing of nuclear weapons on Hiroshima and Nagasaki.

In telling its "truth," the book of Joshua names what needs to be named. Such naming evokes hope that the reality named might one day, be transformed. Will that transformation come by recognizing the latent violence within us all? Will it come by transposing the story into the language of spiritual warfare? Will it come by identifying our own complicity in othering (distinguishing between us and them) that so often generates rivalry, envy, and retributive justice? My hope is that this commentary will contribute to hearing the voices that need to be heard and understood, so that we can, with Isaiah's vision, begin to "beat swords into plowshares and spears into pruning hooks" (Isa 2:4) and so that God's kingdom might come on earth as it is in heaven (Matt 6:10).

Difficult Conversations: Attending to One Another

As the early church theologian Origen wrote to restore the honor of the book of Joshua against "canoniclasts" like Marcion (who sought to expunge unsavory books from the Bible), so I write to give voice to a word that transcends the limits imposed on the text of Joshua by its detractors. That does not mean I will defend the book at all costs. It means that I will take the text seriously as a conversation partner even when I disagree with it, do not understand it, or am offended by it. By doing so, I seek to interpret by being hospitable to the text (Matties 2009).

Just as it is hard to be hospitable to another person whose behavior is damaging, abusive, or violent, it is challenging to pay attention to a scriptural text that tells a violent story and that has been used to justify conquests, illegal occupations, ethnic cleansing, and killing of indigenous peoples. If we claim to be open to what God might communicate to the church through Scripture, and to how the church might continue to embody Scripture's overarching narrative, then we do well to foster receptiveness to the book of Joshua. The easier route, of course, is to ignore the text (as we might ignore a person who has offended us), or to pretend that the problem does not exist (as we might do by covering up a relational problem and hoping it will go away). A third option suggests itself in the book *Difficult Conversations: How to Discuss What Matters Most*, by Stone, Patton, and Heen. Neither avoidance nor pretense will bring healing to a relationship. The authors invite those struggling with challenging relationships to transform "the battle of warring messages into . . . a learning conversation" (xviii).

For many readers, restoring a hopeful relationship with Scripture will mean that the "warring messages" of the book of Joshua need to be brought into a "difficult conversation." Is it possible to stop focusing on who is right or wrong and begin listening again? Such attentiveness requires recognizing the text as Other, an interpretive stance I am calling "hospitable hermeneutics," and a relational honesty that is willing to engage in difficult conversations *[Difficult Conversations, p. 421]*.

The Text in Biblical Context: An Hospitable Hermeneutic

In the practice of hospitable hermeneutics, we become vulnerable by inviting the many voices in the book of Joshua to have their say. Although the book comes to us as a coherent narrative, it includes the voices of God, Rahab, Joshua, the narrator, the Gibeonites, the Transjordan tribes, the daughters of Zelophehad, Caleb, all Israel, and others. Even the genres embedded in the narrative add vocal depth to the chorus. For example, the book of Joshua includes conquest accounts, but the book of Joshua is not itself a conquest account. A hospitable hermeneutic will, therefore, recognize a variety of voices and genres that make up the whole.

An hospitable hermeneutic will also allow the book to have its say within the larger chorus of voices we call Scripture. Although we cannot be certain about the compositional history of the book of Joshua, this book is itself part of a conversation with texts that stand before and after it in the canonical ordering *[Composition of Joshua, p. 398]*. Moreover, other biblical texts take up themes from the book of Joshua and interpret them in different ways. The biblical canon as a whole, for example, does not speak in Joshua's dialect on the topic of warfare *[Theology of Warfare, p. 458]*.

Although we do well to allow Joshua to have a say, we can also ask the book to attend to the perspectives of other texts. In the process of allowing texts to attend to one another, we discover a dynamic interaction that offers a model for biblical authority in the interpreting community. Texts in conversation do not deny each other a place at the table. In conversation they are modulated, transformed, and transposed into a new key. For example, the figure of Joshua becomes a paradigm in a larger figural imagination by which we are able to recognize a trajectory, or a pattern of linkages, between Moses, Joshua, David/Solomon, Hezekiah, Josiah, Isaiah's Servant, and Jesus. How each character is depicted in the various stages of the narrative allows readers to see connections and ways in which imitation and failure to imitate shape the narrative's implicit or explicit evaluation of the character *[Figural Reading, p. 426]*.

The Text in the Life of the Church: Attentiveness Through Conversation in Community

Hospitable hermeneutics also makes contemporary readers vulnerable by extending hospitality to readers who have gone before. Modern interpreters have been tempted to view biblical texts as a source from which to derive truths or principles that can be applied in new contexts. The text is an object, a mine from which to extract precious gems, leaving the slag of the narrative behind. If, however, the text represents an Other with whom I am in a conversation, and if this Other calls a community into being, then reading the text is not simply about mining the gems or distilling the essence. And if the story is problematic, telling another story (as historical reconstructions tend to do) will not solve the problem. The only way of engaging the story is to enter its plot, follow its own dynamic trajectory. In other words, the book of Joshua is not an end in itself, but part of an ongoing telling of God's hopeful transformation of a broken world. Take that trajectory out of the plot, and the rest of the story no longer makes sense.

Joshua stands in "the middle" of a particular biblical plot—a journey from landlessness to landedness to landlessness—fulfilling the early promises to Israel's ancestors and anticipating the failures to come in the books of Judges through Kings. As part of that longer story, the book also shapes the imaginations and identities of the communities and readers who, through time, have considered it to be Scripture. Our being and becoming are bound to this story, though we may embrace some parts and dislike others. The difficult conversation continues into the life of the church as readers look for ways the story might intersect with their lives. Readers over time have mapped those continuities through discerning a trajectory of words, themes, plot elements, characters, structures, and patterns in order to identify relationships between elements of the biblical story and their own. Hence, for most of the history of interpretation, the book of Joshua has been a source of reflection on the character of the Christian life. The early church fathers were adept at such reflection, basing their interpretation on their discernment of typologies and resonances throughout Scripture. The commentary will feature conversation with Origen (b. 185 AD), who was one of the first Christians to write a commentary on Joshua *[Figural Reading, p. 426]*.

The book of Joshua contributes to the conversation about what it means to be a people in relationship with God, to be connected to land/earth, and to be faithful in the journey into and out of the land. The Bible is not a closed book but an invitation to live in the direction of God's purposes for all of creation. "Because we know something about the direction in which the world is moving, we are encouraged by that picture and guided by the shape of its depiction of the way things are now that God has redeemed the world in Jesus" (Hauerwas and Willimon: 86). The book of Joshua, then, belongs to a larger narrative, in which "a community [is] called by God to participate in an ongoing drama" (Hanson 1986: 533; Matties 2009).

In what follows, I will sketch the outline of an approach that I am commending to readers who wish to become hospitable to this strange text, and who in the process long to move from violent exclusion to embrace of the Other. Most of the topics introduced here will reappear in various ways in the commentary and in the topical essays at the end of the commentary. Readers who wish a more extended introduction to the commentary may read those topical essays before reading the commentary itself.

Joshua and the Tapestry of the Grand Narrative of Genesis Through Kings

Genre and Joshua

One of the challenges of reading the book of Joshua is to read with genre consciousness. Since many readers are unfamiliar with ancient historical narrative, they draw conclusions about the biblical text based on modern assumptions about literary types. Historical writing has always been shaped by the generic conventions of its time. In the modern world, historiography has been informed by objectivist and materialist assumptions. These assumptions are rooted in the view that it is possible to gain relatively objective knowledge about the past through scientific analysis of source data, which must be interpreted without recourse either to a transcendent point of reference or to divine providence.

Such were not, however, the assumptions of the historians responsible for the book of Joshua. The narrative bears all the marks of ancient Near Eastern historiography, including reports about divine speech and interpretation of events as shaped by the hand of God. The book includes a spy narrative that goes strangely awry, a story about outsiders who become insiders by trickery, conquest accounts that include unusual and even hyperbolic elements to emphasize their significance, distribution lists, sermonic speeches, and reports of ritual activities and covenant making. Even the covenant-making account is not a straightforward narrative: it includes an odd conversation in which Joshua cajoles and provokes the audience (Josh 24:19). The book assumes that it is God's prerogative to grant land to a people. Although Joshua does not share the stylistic conventions of modern historiography, neither does it adhere to all the standard conventions of ancient history writing. Its focus is not simply on the conquest of the land, but especially on the formation of a people faithful to divine instruction *[Composition of Joshua, p. 398]*.

That is why the framework of the book in chapters 1 and 23–24 sets the parameters for understanding the book more fully—not as a conquest narrative, but as a reflection on the covenantal journey of a people in time and place. The focus on faithfulness to divine instruction (Torah) in chapter 1 and on covenantal relationship with the Lord in chapters 23–24 places the entire story in the context of promissory covenant making initiated by God with Israel's ancestors. Israel's entry into the land is a divine act, and the land is a gift of God, but the keeping of the land is contingent upon Israel's loyalty to God and faithfulness to God's word *[Land: Gifted and Lost, p. 440]*.

That thematic relational focus should not be lost even though the commentary divides the book into two parts: "Entering the Land" in chapters 1–12, and "Distributing the Land" in chapters 13–24. As the commentary will show, these labels and divisions are inexact (for overviews of each section, see p. 40 and p. 284). Although these sections of the biblical text are approximately the same length, the commentary focuses less on the distribution accounts themselves (chs. 13–19) than on other chapters of the book where the relational and covenantal character of the narrative is more prominent.

Plot and Ideology

This covenantal context suggests that although the book may be read on its own, it only makes sense as one segment of a tragically hopeful narrative of divine involvement along a path that leads both in and out of a promised land. In that tragedy the hopefulness lies precisely in two affirmations: in God's final assertion that *it was not by your sword or by your bow* that Israel entered the land (Josh 24:12); and in the assumption based in Deuteronomy that the Lord "will neither abandon you nor destroy you; he will not forget the covenant with your ancestors that he swore to them" (Deut 4:31). The book depicts the fulfillment of promise, sets the stage for shaping the character of the faithful community, and opens the doors to the failure of attentiveness to divine instruction, which will lead to exile.

Yet questions about the function of the conquest narratives keep surfacing. We do well to be aware that conquest narratives on their own can serve the ideological interests of those in power, granting them divine right to possession of land and political control over it and its peoples. On the other hand, these same conquest narratives may serve the interests of those who understood the dangers of violent control (political hegemony by military means) and who, therefore, sought to shape a community that would attend to God's word and trust in God's agency in and through the historical process. From that perspective, the book of Joshua raises questions at a metahistorical level. Rather than shutting down interpretive options by reducing the book to one or another agenda, the book opens doors of conversation and debate about divine and human agency in history. That debate is at the heart of the covenantal tradition that both creates a community under the rule of God and offers a prophetic critique of that community. Oddly, covenantal identity also opens the door to challenging the justice of God's ways. In the same spirit that Abraham challenged God to do what is just (Gen 18:25), so readers might bring a challenge to the conversation with Joshua. Joshua's uniqueness is in how the conquest accounts have been embedded in a larger covenantal story that reframes and reimagines the conquest *[Conquest Accounts, p. 406]*.

Joshua and the Pentateuch (Torah)

Joshua shares the conventional characteristics of ancient Near Eastern conquest accounts, but it transcends the genre by placing the conquest in a covenantal drama of promise and gift, receiving and losing. In so doing, the book looks backward to the first part of Israel's grand narrative, Genesis through Deuteronomy (Torah), and looks ahead to the second part of that story of tragedy and loss in Judges through Kings. Joshua's plot belongs to both bodies of literature. It functions as a hinge, with Genesis to Deuteronomy forming one side and Judges through Kings the other.

Joshua has often been linked to the first five books of the Bible because it offers the conclusion to the promise of land initiated by God in Genesis (12:1-7). Some scholars have even spoken of the book as the conclusion to an original Hexateuch (six books). That theory is not as important as the impulse that gave rise to it. Joshua contains both implicit and explicit echoes of texts, motifs, and themes in the first five books, including the promise motif in Genesis (blessing to others, progeny, a great name, and a land); the crossing-the-sea story in Exodus; the stories in Numbers of Israel's unfaithfulness, of the twelve spies, and of the commissioning of Joshua; and, above all, the speeches, exhortations, and warnings of Moses as presented in the book of Deuteronomy. Being so rooted in the tradition of Moses, Joshua in a sense is the beginning of a prophetic commentary on identity and peoplehood in covenantal relationship within the sovereign care of God.

Joshua pushes the story ahead even as it refers back to texts in the Pentateuch by revealing the dramatic edge of the plot:

- It transforms motifs from the spy narratives in Numbers.
- It reiterates the various commissionings of Joshua in the Pentateuch.
- It highlights the weaving of outsiders into Israel's communal fabric.
- It challenges the assumption that extermination of alien Others is an inevitable consequence of faithfulness to God's instruction.
- It highlights the significance of each generation as the generation of covenantal relationship *[Covenant and Treaty, p. 416]*.
- It opens up questions about both the extent of the land and ethnic diversity of the people called Israel *[Extent of the Land, p. 424]*.

It does not idealize Israel's faithfulness, nor does it minimize the complexity by which non-Israelites came to be part of Israel. But it does all of this within the framework of covenantal relationship rooted in faithfulness to divine instruction as that is mediated through God's faithful servant leaders.

Two such leaders stand out: Moses and Joseph. The notice about the death of Moses in Joshua 1:1 and the naming of Joshua as *servant of the* LORD (24:29-31) connects the book explicitly to the end of Deuteronomy. In this way the book becomes not simply a justification for possession of land but also a story about how divine instruction takes possession of Israel *[Characterization of Joshua, p. 394]*. At the end of the book, the burial of Joseph's bones (24:32) takes the reader back to the promise theme of the ancestral narrative, which alludes to "Israel's" exile in Egypt prior to their return (Gen 15:13-21, esp. v. 16).

Joshua and the Deuteronomistic History (DtrH)

The tragedy of the narrative about life in the land, beginning with the book of Joshua, is that Israel's faithfulness is short-lived; it lasted one generation (24:31). The books of Judges, Samuel, and Kings, which follow Joshua in the Hebrew Bible, tell the story of God's care for an unfaithful and (sometimes) repentant people without consistent leadership (Judges), through the rise of the monarchy under prophetic jurisdiction (Samuel), to the fall of monarchy and kingdom (Kings). The beginning of Judges carries the story forward by referring to the death of Joshua, just as the book of Joshua refers to the death of Moses. According to the books of Kings, Israel failed because they did not attend to the words of the prophets and because they chose to serve other gods. Similarities to and dependence on Deuteronomy, which infuse the trajectory of the plot as it moves from entry to exile, have motivated the title Deuteronomistic History (DtrH) for these books.

This commentary makes six assumptions about the DtrH (adapted and supplemented from Richter: 228):

1. It makes good sense to speak of a DtrH, even though these texts are diverse in style and content. The DtrH was compiled with a serious historiographic intent, a real interest in writing about the past.

2. The DtrH is grounded in the law code and theological themes of Deuteronomy, including the notion that the relationship between God and people is a "*political* agreement" according to which "Israel will rise and fall based on its ability to keep covenant" (McConville 1993: 98). Having said that, the DtrH reflects a dynamic conversation with the Deuteronomic tradition rather than a wooden application of Deuteronomy's theology (Polzin).

3. The DtrH is marked by significant speeches by its major characters. These speeches carry much of the Deuteronomistic theological freight, as though to provide the "voice" of the narrator through the voice of the characters. Joshua 1 and 23–24 are markedly Deuteronomistic in style, content, and vocabulary.

4. Although earlier editions of the DtrH may have been compiled before the final version we now read, we cannot determine exactly which portions belong to those earlier editions. Some suggest, for example, that the DtrH was begun during the reign of Hezekiah, and others claim that it was begun during the reign of Josiah and then edited or supplemented by exilic and postexilic writers.

5. These writers/editors used ancient oral and written source material such that each book retains some of the distinctive character of those earlier sources.

6. Throughout these books individual Deuteronomic themes cannot simply be assigned to a variety of respective editors along the way. Rather, with Raymond Person and others, we do well to

think of a "Deuteronomic school," perhaps like a denomination with its distinctive theological vocabulary. Viewed that way, the DtrH is a complex work that is tied together structurally, although with unique individual parts, and thematically, although unique in the way certain themes, motifs, and vocabulary are highlighted in various places.

This historical narrative shares the theological convictions of Deuteronomy about both the gift and the responsibility inherent in life in the land. Each of the books also contributes to a larger agenda: the telling of a (hi)story that enables readers to negotiate their experience of a land gained and lost *[Composition of Joshua, p. 398; Land: Gifted and Lost, p. 440]*.

Inhospitable Readings of Joshua

Such negotiation, however, can and has led to all kinds of "rewritings" that effectively diminish or dismiss the actual narrative of the book of Joshua. Three examples point up the need for a hospitable hermeneutic that attends to Joshua as an engagement with the world of stories inherited and stories constructed for the shaping of a coherent communal identity called Israel.

The VeggieTales version of *Josh and the Big Wall* highlights "God's way of doing things," which, according to the Veggie narrator, is the most important lesson of the Jericho incident. In order to protect children from the full story, VeggieTales performs a textectomy by cutting out the offending parts, notably the violent slaughter of Jericho's inhabitants (Peterson [1989: 98] laments "psalmectomies"). No doubt there is an irony in this surgery, since "God's way" as advocated by the video is to love one's enemies.

Second, certain interpreters, who recognize that archaeological evidence and the biblical narrative do not coincide, reconstruct the sequence of events by positing a variety of "models" for the conquest to account for the archaeological data. Although such critical historical analysis confirms that the book of Joshua is theological testimony and not twenty-first-century historiography, it does not help much with explaining the actual text *[Models of the Settlement, p. 448; Archaeology and Joshua, p. 389]*.

A third example of thinly disguised inattentiveness to the text is the tendency to subject the narrative to some predetermined criteria for a verdict on its admissibility as witness to God's purpose on earth. Dismissal of the book is based on the inability to solve one problem or another, the "problem of war" being the prime example. Focusing on one problem tends to make that the major focus of interpretation, leaving the narrative as a whole stranded *[Conquest Accounts, p. 406]*.

Joshua in the Middle of Time

I include those three examples not because I disagree entirely with them but to suggest that each one highlights the need to situate the narrative of Joshua within its own narrative world. From that perspective, the book of Joshua is situated in the middle, between the promise of land (Genesis through Deuteronomy) and the loss of land (Judges through Kings). Even though the book tells of the generation under Joshua's leadership that entered the land, its story is linked to other stories and other generations "by a host of semantic and allusive cords" (Hauch: 79). The recognition of patterns and paradigms in the Joshua narrative allows us, for example, to see echoes and connections that situate this narrative in the middle of a long and complex narrative rather than as a fixed point whose "message" must be applied to our time.

From the vantage point of the end of the story in Babylonian exile, this host of reverberations is informed by a rich and dynamic theological perspective that speaks of character and identity, gift and responsibility, divine and human agency, inclusion and exclusion, reality and vision, and life in the presence of a God whose sovereignty extends to the whole earth. Such concerns may also be relevant in various ways to readers who situate themselves between the loss of exile and the promise of restoration (Fretheim's summary of those concerns is esp. apt [1983: 46–47]).

Joshua and the Diversity of Scripture

Coherence and Tension in Joshua

As I have noted above, the book of Joshua participates in the plot of ongoing identity formation and theological imagination within the dialogical drama of Scripture. That drama, situated "in the middle of time," emerges even more clearly as we bring the thematic coherences and tensions within the book of Joshua into conversation with the diversity of the biblical canon.

Some interpreters suggest, for example, that the literary linkages between Joshua and Josiah imply that the narrative provides theological and ideological justification for Josiah's political agenda in the late seventh century BC *[Characterization of Joshua, p. 394]*. Nelson, for example, thinks that "the overall intention of the book is to strengthen national identity and assert Israel's possession of its ancestral lands" (1997a: 11). Those kinds of comments are helpful if we are willing to locate the story's interests in some construct like "national identity" or "ancestral lands." Certainly identity and land are integral to the book, but other similar thematic emphases might also add to or modify such explicit statements of purpose. What if a "submerged plot" (Hauch) or "contesting plots" (Hawk 1991) might complicate matters or make things more exciting? This commentary will identify a good number of plot elements, themes, and motifs that testify to a complexity within the overall coherence of the book (identified, e.g., by Polzin, Mitchell, Hawk 1991; Hauch). The following sampling illustrates how the literary coherence of the book is nuanced by tensions within its overall presentation:

- Instead of wiping out all the Canaanites, the book presents stories of odd inclusions (Rahab and the Gibeonites), even warning that insiders might become outsiders (Achan). Then, oddly, the book affirms that *all Israel, alien as well as citizen*, will be included in the covenant ceremony (8:33) *["All Israel," p. 385]*.
- The book depicts Israel as fighting against the enemy while affirming that God alone has fought for Israel (10:14, 42; 23:3, 10).
- In chapters 10–12 the narrator affirms that the conquest has been thoroughly accomplished (10:40-42; 11:23), whereas chapters 13–22 demonstrate that the Israelites did not conquer all the peoples (13:1, 13; etc.).

Tensions such as these illustrate a kind of transposition from ethnic and geographical exclusiveness into a fuller significance for the resident alien or indigenous population. In the end, even the shape of Israel as a people in a bounded land remains unresolved (ch. 22). Only chapters 23–24 bring a kind of resolution to both incomplete conquest and incomplete distribution. That solution is not tidy: it does not offer the kind of ending that one hopes for. It points forward to failure and loss, even as it invites critical reflection on the possibilities for hope and reconstruction of a faithful community, attentive to the instruction and sovereign care of God *[Plot Tensions in Joshua, p. 452]*.

The commentary will attend to these tensions along the way so as to highlight the theological questions posed by them. For example, who is going to determine Israel's destiny? What kind of a God does Joshua invite Israel to serve? What stance ought Israel to take toward these nations that remain in the land? How will it be possible to continue being loyal to God alone? Since the DtrH seems to end in tragedy, the Joshua story functions as an idealized story of origins. Perhaps the exile is an opportunity for readers to go back, not to imitate the behavior of the first generation in the land, but to pay fresh attention to divine instruction in a new time of weakness and landlessness.

Joshua and the Diversity of the Biblical Canon

Appreciating the complexity of Joshua's thematic coherence allows us to read Joshua as participant in a drama or chorus of voices. Joshua can be read, therefore, as a text in dialogue with other texts. And it can be interpreted from the point of view of various reading contexts rather than simply as having a message derived from a single authorial context. In other words, Joshua belongs to an intra-biblical "difficult conversation."

To speak of such a conversation implies that no simple "resolution" may be found to the conflict among perspectives. Suggesting an overarching unity that encompasses the diversity minimizes the distinctiveness of the various voices. Highlighting the distinctive voices so as to eliminate any possible unity creates an unnecessary dualism. Brevard Childs's perspective is worth highlighting: "The basic hermeneutical problem of the Bible, therefore, is not adequately formulated by using terminology of unity and diversity. The oneness of Scripture's scope is not a rival to the multiple voices within the canon, but a constant pointer, much like a ship's compass, fixing on a single goal, in spite of the many and various ways of God (Heb 1:1), toward which the believer is drawn" (1992: 725).

The great variety of texts and thematic expressions in Scripture reflect, therefore, "a dialogue or debate rather than one static pronouncement that demands acceptance or provokes rejection" (Kittredge: 755). Still, there is a goal (Greek *telos*) toward which God's redemptive and re-creative impulses are yearning. The entire biblical canon strives, as it were, toward God's redemptive purposes. Scripture testifies that God has no desire to allow God's creation to run amok; rather, God wishes to restore all things to their original goodness. And all of that yearning remains visible throughout the OT. As René Girard puts it, the Bible is "a process under way, a text in travail; it is not a chronologically progressive process, but a struggle that advances and retreats" (1987a: 141). In the light of that affirmation, within biblical texts like Joshua we can discern the writers' work of discernment. As Kittredge puts it, "rather than censor, silence, or reject inherited traditions perceived to be outmoded or unedifying," scribal caretakers of the biblical tradition "preserved, reworked, and juxtaposed them with their own revised theological judgments and perspectives" (753).

Yet Kittredge suggests, counterintuitively, that we might "*resist* some texts and traditions" (760). Such resistance is critical to a commentary on Joshua—naming what is not consonant with God's redemptive purposes. Kittredge suggests that it may mean "arguing with a particular perspective to the point of saying 'no'" to a reading of the text that accepts the view that anyone could be so dangerous as to be subjected to extermination (761). In other words, reading Joshua "requires that readers distinguish between that which they affirm and that which they reject, based on their understanding of the gospel message in its entirety" (761). Concerning the book of Joshua, for example, Kittredge asks, "Do you choose to reflect the conquest tradition or the quiet, ironic note that undercuts it? . . . To proclaim the conquest tradition from the position of First-world military might and to exclude the ironic voice of critique would be an uncritical and potentially abusive reading of the text" (761).

This raises the question of the relationship between hospitable hermeneutics, which I have advocated above, and critique of the text. This commentary will seek an honest criticism in the context of hospitable dialogue with the text, the whole biblical canon, and the history of interpretation. Such reading will acknowledge that "even our Scripture and valued traditions themselves have been misused in order to afflict others" (Kittredge: 761).

Joshua and Its Transposition in the New Testament

The NT writers made sense of their encounter with Jesus' life, death, and resurrection by drawing on texts, traditions, and trajectories from the OT. As Jewish readers of their own Scriptures, they had no wish to annul the validity or authority of those Scriptures. The newness of Jesus could only be explained in the light of what God had already been doing in Israel. Since Jesus' name in Aramaic (*Yeshu'a*) is a slightly shortened form of Joshua's Hebrew name (*Yehoshu'a*), and both are spelled the same in Greek (*Iēsous*, LXX and NT), NT writers were able to imagine Jesus as a "new Joshua." A most striking example of that is in the angelic announcement of the meaning of Jesus' name: Jesus is savior (Matt 1:21). And by appropriating other aspects of the story of Israel, NT writers found themselves writing another act in what would become God's unfinished drama of healing and transformation of all creation (Matties 2009) *[Conquest and Land in the NT, p. 411]*.

From the explicit to the implicit, the book of Joshua has a significant place in the NT understanding of Jesus and of faithful discipleship. Remarkably, NT writers take up the character of Rahab as one of the most explicit connections between the NT and Joshua. Rahab is included in Matthew's genealogy as an intimation of the inclusion of the Gentiles (1:5), a major theme in Matthew's Gospel. The book of Hebrews presents Rahab as a model of faith (11:31). The letter of James notes her hospitality as an example of good works (2:25). Those writers viewed Rahab's story as paradigmatic. Rahab's story not only sets the agenda for the book of Joshua, but also initiates a figural, or typological, pattern that reverberates into the NT and beyond. Rahab, the unlikely outsider, becomes a pattern of discipleship that is rooted in the ongoing story of God's trajectory of redemptive hopefulness for all humankind *[Figural Reading, p. 426]*.

A second appropriation of the Joshua story is the NT transposition of entry into the land as an entry into God's eschatological "rest," which is partially realized in the presence of the kingdom, especially in Jesus, who offers "rest" in his presence (Matt 11:29; cf. Josh 1:13, 15; 11:23; 14:15; 21:44; 22:4; 23:1). Jesus' kingdom teaching transposes the gift of land into the gift of kingdom. That kingdom is not first of all an eschatological kingdom but an encounter with the reign of God as it impinges on life on the ground. Jesus' parables of the kingdom touch human life in all its complexity as they deal with worship, economics, poverty, justice, and hopefulness in the face of adversity and oppression. In all of this, Jesus declares that the kingdom is both a gift to be received and a treasure to be sought. The book of Hebrews also imagines this "rest" as incomplete and yet continuously available (4:8-11). Bypassing Joshua's "rest" (e.g., Josh 21:44), the author of Hebrews draws on creation's rest (Gen 2:2) and the psalmist's citation of divine disapproval (95:11), thereby not nullifying the land as a place of rest, but expanding the notion of rest from its historical rootedness (in a particular land) to its creation-redemptive intent. The point Hebrews makes is that "Sabbath rest" transcends land rest. Both kinds of rest require human agency, but more, they require attentiveness to the divine message and trust in its efficacy. The good news of God's rest and the requirements for entering that rest are "to us just as to them" (Heb 4:2) *[Rest, p. 455]*.

A third explicit, although once removed, appropriation of the Joshua narrative is the NT use of battle imagery. The battle against evil in which believers are involved is prefigured by the victory of Jesus in his death and resurrection. In John's Gospel, Jesus even says, "I have conquered the world!" (16:33; cf. 1 John 2:13; 4:4; 5:4-5). Such a conquest theme is not about land or human enemies but about the cosmic darkness that has launched a guerrilla movement against God's reign (cf. Rev 3:21; 5:5; 12:11; 15:2; 17:14; 21:7). Paul describes Christian discipleship as a contest/victory over evil and adversity (Rom 8:37). This life is a struggle, not against flesh and blood, but against cosmic powers and spiritual forces (Rom 8:38; Eph 6:12). Such appropriation and transposition of the conquest motif expands the battle to the cosmic realm. Human beings are no longer the object of the struggle. That is left in the hands of God (Rom 12:21) *[Conquest and Land in the NT, p. 411].*

A Vision of Warfare Transformed

Thus the biblical narrative as a whole is rooted not so much in a warfare worldview that justifies ongoing human violence as in a hopeful vision that transposes and transforms that worldview. The biblical drama provides what Swartley calls "the structural perception" for the Christian life: "Pacifist believers especially can learn much from Scripture's warfare imagery. Not only will it save them from passivism, but it will [also] anchor pacifist belief and action firmly within the biblical witness" (2003a: 173).

Such anchoring is rooted in the Gospel narratives themselves, which depict Jesus' life, death, and resurrection as a journey of exodus, conquest, and life in the kingdom (see Swartley 1994). The Gospels' figural (typological) appropriation of the journey of Israel as depicted in the OT carries on the tradition present already in the book of Joshua, with its appropriation of the exodus crossing to the crossing of the Jordan River (Josh 3–5). The linking of exodus and conquest in other biblical texts (Ps 114:1-2; Exod 15) confirms that the NT reading of Jesus' life, death, and resurrection stands in continuity with the OT itself *[Figural Reading, p. 426].*

Biblical writers understood such events not simply as historical events but as "a remanifestation of divine redemptive power" (Fishbane: 360). Fishbane suggests that later writers do not draw on typological analogies because the earlier story fails to have a significance of its own. Rather, "by means of retrojective typologies, events are removed from the neutral cascade of historical occurrences and embellished as modalities of foundational moments in Israelite history" (360). The Gospel writers' kingdom journey of Jesus places him into that same stream of "foundational moments" as another embodiment, even incarnation, of God's redemptive purposes on earth. In such a redemptive purpose, the meek are the ones who "inherit the earth" (Matt 5:5). Such inheritance (a central theme in Joshua) is based on Jesus' victory, which in Mark's Gospel is linked to his conquest as "Son" (Mark 1:11), an allusion to God's granting him, in the light of Psalm 2, the "ends of the earth [as] your possession" (2:8).

The NT's transposition of Joshua's conquest and inheritance narrative comes full circle in the victory of his resurrection. As Stephen Davis puts it, "In the resurrection of Jesus from the dead, we see God's decisive victory not only over death but over all God's other enemies as well. In that one climactic event, we see the certainty that someday, in the kingdom of God, there will be no more violence, war, jealousy, or death. . . . These forces are still alive and at work in the world, but because of the victory that God won at Easter, their doom is certain" (200–201).

Discerning God's Redemptive Goals Within Canonical Debate

Such attentiveness to the figural and transformative dynamics of the biblical drama is significant because narratives like Joshua are not straightforwardly didactic. Nor is it always transparent how the Bible, and a text like Joshua in particular, might shape the self-understanding and self-identity of those seeking to be faithful readers of the text. A description of an event does not automatically endorse the assumptions underlying that description. A depiction of violence, even if divinely sanctioned, may not require readers to embrace violence against enemies. Wise readers will not be fooled by the surface of a narrative. They will listen to the gaps, to the voices that speak around the fringes, and to the intratextual interpretation that focuses attention away from the violence and toward the cosmic purposes of God for the nations. In other words, a story may reveal more than it tells on the surface.

To say that the narrative shapes the community's self-understanding, however, means that we must ground that understanding not in the particularities of individual texts but in the direction of the narrative as a whole, beginning with a nonviolent creation through to a blessing for the nations and eventually to a reconstitution of God's hope for cosmic transformation. Such a reading of Joshua, grounded in a hospitable, dialogical interpretive strategy, will resist transforming landedness into colonization, or landlessness into an idealized permanent exilic existence *[Narrative Theology and Communal Identity, p. 451]*.

Thus our reading of Joshua within the entire canon of Scripture suggests that the Bible bears witness not to a two-faced God, but to two paradigms: one reflects the rivalry implicit in ethnic nationalism, and the other is a critique and even renunciation of violence and sacrifice. These two paradigms become interpretive options that debate one another within the Bible, a debate that is ultimately transformed by the vision of the peaceful reign of God (in the OT) and the kingdom of God (in Jesus' life and teaching).

This transformation is not an example of some texts trumping other texts. Rather, such a reading acknowledges that in some way all biblical texts share in the struggle toward transformation. Even in the book of Joshua—with its explicit evidence of covetousness and rivalry (e.g., in the Achan story of Josh 7 and in the intertribal conflict of Josh 22), and with its struggle to include the outsider, the one devoted to destruction (e.g., in Rahab of Josh 2 and 6, and the Gibeonites in Josh 9)—there is evidence of a "text in travail, . . . a struggle that advances and retreats" (Girard 1987a: 141) *[Theology of Warfare, p. 458].*

Colliding Narrative Theologies

Three observations point to the fact that Joshua's story all too readily collides with our notion of story-formed identity and mission. First, although we may choose to read Joshua as a slice of the open-ended drama of Scripture, the theological portrait of a God who sanctions sacred violence leading to extermination of entire towns and villages, along with the human perception that sacred violence is a mandate from God, creates an awkward, if not impossible, contradiction with the teaching of Jesus. I argue that the conquest accounts in Joshua do not define the entire book. Even so, the accusation of genocide remains either to be accounted for or to be argued with *[Theology of Warfare, p. 458; Genocide and Sacred Violence, p. 430].*

Second, in one way or another, Jewish identity is bound up with land and with Israel. Just how the relationship of peoplehood, faith, and land is understood remains contested among both Jews and Christians. To negate the relationship between peoplehood and land would be to succumb to the very problem with which we are struggling: the challenge of inhospitable readings. Ancient Israelite othering and exclusion of Canaanites cannot be corrected by excluding the Jewish vision for life in the land. On the other hand, embracing the relationship of peoplehood and land uncritically all too easily dismisses other concerns. For example, exclusive focus on the election of a people (Abraham and his descendants through Jacob) misses God's promises to Hagar (Gen 16:10; 21:18) and God's participation in the life of all peoples (e.g., Amos 9:7-9; Isa 19:19-25). And the focus on land as the essence of the promise all too easily manages to equate the ancient promises (and the book of Joshua) with the modern state of Israel, thereby refusing to embrace the necessity for pluralism and multiethnic identities in contemporary nation-states *[Land: Gifted and Lost, p. 440]*.

Third, the colonial enterprise continues to trade on old hostilities, many of which are analogous to the ancient biblical fear of the Other. Contemporary globalization seems to introduce another incarnation of colonization within which certain groups vie for identity, power, and even survival in the face of nearly impossible odds. And the ongoing conflict between Jewish Israelis and Palestinians (in Israel and in the Palestinian territories) is exacerbated by claiming biblical texts (like Joshua) as precedents for exclusive rule of one group over others *[Conquest and Colonialism, p. 410]*.

I raise these concerns because at its heart the book of Joshua is concerned with leadership and political community, concerns that become ever more pressing in our time as ethnic nationalisms and corporate interests vie for human loyalty, and as disenfranchised groups exert their will against either powerful minorities or overpowering imperialisms. These concerns intersect and even conflict with one another, as, for example, sacred violence becomes the basis for the particularism of modern Israel's claim to the land as *Jewish* land. My brief reflections in this commentary do not do justice to the complexity of these problems.

Even if these matters can be adequately resolved, and if the violence in the book of Joshua can be explained, the particularity of the association of God, people, and land remains a stumbling block that cannot altogether be removed. Perhaps the offense of particularity is the path that God treads on the way to restoration of all things.

Subversive Particularity

The book of Joshua begins with the promise and instruction of God. That emphasis provides the interpretive key signature to the entire book of Joshua, which is confirmed at the end of the book. There, both in Joshua's address to the Transjordan tribes (22:2-5) and in his charge to Israel (23:6, 8, 11), the Lord's promise (cf. 1:3, 6) and the people's love for God's instruction (Torah) stand at the center (cf. 1:7, 8). God's instruction shapes Israel's identity and is the ground for Israel's gaining, keeping, and losing the land *[Torah, p. 462]*. From the several occurrences of the "giving" motif in Joshua (1:2, 15; 2:24), we may assume that one of the main purposes of the Joshua narrative as a whole is to tell the story of how God "gives" this land to this people. Along the way we discover that the gift is both unqualified and conditional. God intends to give the land, an intention that will not be shaken. Israel's responsibility is both to receive that gift and to honor the covenant loyalty with God so as to retain the gift.

Although such particularity implies that the God of the OT is a mere tribal deity, the narrator of the book of Joshua imagines a larger theological vision that can be characterized as prophetic and theopolitical (Buber 1967: 57) *[Composition of Joshua, p. 398; Theology of Warfare, p. 458]*. One may read the book of Joshua as fostering imperialistic illusions of grandeur like those of Josiah *[Characterization of Joshua, p. 394]*; however, the motif of universal recognition of God's sovereignty in Joshua 3–4 anticipates the hope for a wider, more compassionate sovereignty. In the light of Exodus, Isaiah, and Matthew—along with Paul's concern for Gentile inclusion into the olive tree of God's grand story of redemption, and Revelation's hope that people from every language and nation might acknowledge the Lamb—the purposeful comment of Joshua 4:24 is good news for all nations: *so that all the peoples of the earth may know that the hand of the LORD is mighty, and so that you may fear the LORD your God forever.* This text belongs to the intrabiblical theological struggle to foster a healthy conversation between the particular character of God's redemptive gifts to Israel and the universal hope for humankind and all creation. Measured against the larger canonical context, God's activity among the peoples of the world concerns the doing of justice (Ps 82; Amos 1–2; Matt 25:31-46). Moreover, God's creating and saving work among the nations is analogous to God's work in Israel (Deut 32:8-9; Isa 2:2-4; 19:19-25; Amos 9:7-8).

The commentary pays most attention to the NRSV and NIV (2011 and 1984) versions. All translations of Joshua are given in italics, including those of the author (AT). Unless otherwise noted, translations of the Bible will appear as NRSV (not flagged). English versification of the OT occasionally differs from that of the Hebrew (MT). Generally only English versification is indicated.

Part 1

Entering the Land

Joshua 1–12

OVERVIEW

The book falls into two roughly equal parts (chs. 1–12 and 13–24), lending the book an inexact literary and structural coherence. Chapter 1, with its focus on divine instruction (Torah), highlights the covenantal themes taken up in chapters 23–24. And the focus on the two and a half Transjordan tribes in Joshua 1 can be brought to bear on the conflict between those tribes and "all Israel" in chapter 22 [*"All Israel," p. 385; Transjordan Tribes, p. 464*]. Moreover, the narrator's summary at the end of the book about Israel as having served the Lord (24:31) echoes the promise of faithfulness by the Transjordan tribes in chapter 1. The notices of Moses' death at the beginning (1:1) and Joshua's death at the end (24:29) frame the book.

More specifically, the summaries in 10:40-43 and 11:16-23 mirror the summary in 21:43-45. The mention of Moses' giving land to the Transjordan tribes (12:6) is taken up in the recapitulation of his distribution to those tribes beginning in 13:8. The summary of Joshua's action in 12:7 is taken up by his distribution *in the land of Canaan* in 14:1. The narrator's conclusion in 11:16, 23 that *Joshua took all that land/the whole land* stands out for its obvious tension with the ambiguous motif of 13:1 that *very much of the land still remains to be possessed.* Moreover, 13:1 marks a transition in its reference to Joshua's age, as though anticipating his death in 24:29. Joshua 11:23 looks forward to Joshua's distribution of "Canaan," west of the Jordan, beginning in 14:1. Thus the accounts of the entry into the land in the first half are mirrored in the distribution accounts in the second half.

More significant than those formal elements is the odd collection of so-called outsiders in the first part of the book (Rahab,

Gibeonites, and assorted indigenous peoples) who are mirrored in the second part of the book. They are the ones whom Israel could not or did not drive out, who *live within Israel to this day* (e.g., 13:13). They are also reflected in the assortment of Canaanite personal and place names that have been absorbed into the distribution lists in various places (e.g., Caleb and Othniel, both Kenizzites in 15:13-19; places/people like Shechem, Tirzah, and Hepher in 12:17, 24; 17:3; and even Gilead in 17:1-6).

On the surface, chapters 1–12 tell the story of how Israel entered the land and, against all odds, took the land from the indigenous population. If that were all we were to expect, however, the first twelve chapters could easily be characterized simply as a conquest account. But already in the first chapters of the book, it becomes clear that the book is not a conquest account. Rather, it is a story of God's engagement with Israel, a people in formation, in the context of conquest and settlement in the land. These chapters include exhortations, dialogue, intrigue, betrayal and deception, ritual acts, compromises, and theological reflections.

The first part of the book of Joshua presents the conquest in a kind of telescoped time. Near the end of this half of the book, we hear that although *Joshua took all that land/the whole land* (11:16, 23), and that *Joshua made war a long time with all those kings* (11:18), ultimately *it was the LORD's doing* (11:20). In the end, the narrator asserts, *the land had rest from war* (11:23). Chapter 12 provides a list of conquered kings as though the conquest were easily summarized.

The stories of chapters 1–12 set the stage for the second half of the book by presenting us with particular stories of particular people, along with a representative sampling of conquest stories told in the traditional style for cultures of the ancient Near East. The prominent themes in chapter 1, including God's instruction through the *book of the law*, gift of land, word of Moses, rest, strength and courage, and crossing the Jordan—all conspire to imply that the book has an agenda not bound to the conventions of generic conquest accounts *[Conquest Accounts, p.406]*.

Key characters and moments in the story stand out as interpretive keys or paradigmatic figures: Rahab, the man with the sword, Achan, the Gibeonites. Central actions like circumcision, Passover, and reading the words of the book of the law set the stage for the formation of a people who are called, at the end of the book, to exclusive allegiance to Yahweh, the God whom the Transjordan tribes vow to obey and whom Rahab confesses as *God in heaven above and on earth below* (2:11). Outsiders become insiders; insiders become outsiders. God's ways in the world appear to nourish genocide, but various clues in the text lead us to recognize a motif for inclusion of the "other," even as Israel is called to acknowledge the Lord's action in giving Israel nourishment from the land. The overarching warning of the book is that so-called insiders must be vigilant in attending to divine instruction (Torah) and in discerning the idols, those loyalties that prevent exclusive allegiance to the God who calls a people into a hopeful future.

Joshua 1:1-18

The Promise and the Preparation

PREVIEW

Joshua 1 has been the sermon text for at least two Christian college presidential installation services that I have attended. Each one saw in God's instructions to Joshua a model for faithful leadership in the ministry of educational administration. Considering the prominence given to Scripture instruction in Christian colleges and universities, an emphasis on the importance of the Bible for those in leadership is not surprising. The first chapter of Joshua is among the first biblical texts to highlight the importance of being faithful to the written "word" (cf. Deut 8:3). Not only that, it also sets the reader on the way to recognizing that obedience involves attentiveness to Another, to a Thou, to a relationship. Attentiveness to the text thus becomes a listening and respectful conversation that begins within Scripture itself.

Joshua 1, as an "overture" to the book (Lohfink: 237), presents its main motifs and themes: the promise, instruction, and encouragement of God; and human leadership and responsibility. Joshua's story is bound up with the story of Moses. God's presence with Joshua is likened to God's presence with Moses. The divine instruction to Moses (Torah) is commended to Joshua. And the promise of land looks backward not only to Deuteronomy but also to Israel's story beginning with the ancestors in Genesis *[Composition of Joshua, p. 398]*.

Verses 1-9 introduce the entire book and set the stage for recognizing Joshua as *servant of the Lord* in 24:29-33. Verses 10-18 prepare for the plot developments and complications that lie ahead, with the crossing sequence that ends in chapter 4 and the conquest narrative that concludes in chapter 12. The prominence of the two and a half Transjordan tribes here looks ahead to the distribution narrative, which begins with a reiteration of the Transjordan tribes' inheritance (13:8-31) and ends with a sending and conflict story concerning "Israel" and the Transjordan tribes (ch. 22). The book begins with an assurance of what the Lord promises to do and ends with a note about Israel's recognition of the Lord's work on Israel's behalf (24:31).

The chapter also imagines the hoped-for unity of the people, even while it foreshadows the risk of fall and failure (Winther-Nielsen: 297-99). God's promises are mentioned in various ways throughout the chapter (vv. 2, 3, 4, 6, 11, 13, 14, and twice in 15), beginning with the declaration *I am giving* in verse 2. That promise of land is linked explicitly to God's promise to Moses (v. 3), and to the assurance of divine presence (v. 5). Joshua's responsibility to be faithful to God's instruction is at the heart of God's first speech to Joshua (vv. 7-8). And the response of the people in verses 16-18 affirms their willing obedience to God and to God's chosen leaders. The speeches of Joshua 1 look forward to an end of warfare through the motif of "rest."

Speeches and conversation initiate the story's action. God speaks first: God will take the primary role in the drama by giving the land. Joshua speaks next: he will carry out God's instructions. And the people speak last: they promise faithfulness. But readers who know both the beginning and the end of Israel's story may wonder about the promises and commitments. Not all had gone well under Moses' leadership. Nor does the end of the story in Babylonian exile leave much room for hope (2 Kings 25). The chapter, therefore, invites questions about how the story will turn out. Will we discover that indeed we are participating in a drama in which God fulfills promises, people respond to God's gift, and land has rest from war?

OUTLINE

A Joshua Commissioned for the Task, 1:1-9

- 1:1-5 God's Promise to Joshua
- 1:6-9 God's Charge to Joshua

B Joshua's Preparation of the People, 1:10-11

B′ Joshua's Preparation of the Transjordan Tribes, 1:12-15

A′ Response of the People, 1:16-18

The chiastic structure of the chapter (A, B, B′, A′) is suggested by the role of Joshua as listener in the two A sections and as speaker in the two B sections. Significantly, the speech of the Transjordan tribes in A′ echoes the first speech of God in A (Hawk 1991: 58–59). Verses 1-9 are linked to verses 10-18 through verses 1 and 13, in which Moses is named *servant of the Lord*; through the repetition of *strong and courageous* in verses 9 and 18; and through repetition of the motif of "crossing" (vv. 2, 11).

EXPLANATORY NOTES

Joshua Commissioned for the Task 1:1-9

This section's central focus is not the task itself, but the promise and instruction of God. That emphasis provides the interpretive key to the entire book of Joshua, which is confirmed at the end of the book. There, both in Joshua's address to the Transjordan tribes (22:2-5) and in his charge to Israel (23:6, 8, 11), the Lord's promise (cf. 1:3, 6) and the people's love for God's instruction (Torah) stand at the center (cf. 1:7, 8). God's instruction shapes Israel's identity and is the ground of Israel's gaining, keeping, and losing the land *[Torah, p. 462]*. These motifs are woven throughout the fabric of the book. The promise, initiated by God (1:2-5), is repeated by Joshua to the people (1:11, 13, 15), by Rahab (2:9), by the two spies (2:24), and by the Gibeonites (9:24). And in good Deuteronomic language, the narrator even reminds readers of God's promise (5:6).

The book begins with a speech by God. Readers familiar with the stories in the Pentateuch know that reporting God's speaking voice is not unusual in biblical narratives. This speaking voice ties the book of Joshua to that same word of promise in Genesis 12, to God's "gift" of land and presence, and to God's assumption and command that God's people are to act with justice and righteousness (Gen 18:19). In Martin Buber's terms, God's speech in Joshua 1 reveals an ultimate encounter of an "I" and a "Thou." As the first chapter unfolds, it becomes clear that the "Thou" has a spokesperson, Moses, and that God's voice continues to instruct through a *book of the law* (1:8). The text now comes to us similarly as an invitation to an encounter of an "I" and a "Thou," inviting readers to be attentive to God's word now mediated through the narrative (Kepnes).

Repetition of key words and phrases highlight the central themes of this section: the figure of Moses (vv. 1a, 1b, 2, 3, 5, 7); give (vv. 2, 3, 6); all (vv. 2, 3, 4, 5, 7a, 7b, 8, 9); will be with you (vv. 5, 9); strength and courage (vv. 6, 7, 9). The notions of success (vv. 7, 8), invincibility (v. 5a), and lack of fear (v. 9); God's promise of presence (vv. 5b, 9b) along with the first person "I" who promises (vv. 2, 3, 5, 6) and commands (v. 9a)—all draw us into the story's heart. This is no ordinary story of human achievement. Not only does God speak to Joshua in the first person; the speech also ends with a third-person reminder to all who read that the Lord is a living and active presence (v. 9).

1:1-5 God's Promise to Joshua

Joshua has already been featured as the successor to Moses (Num 27:12-23; Deut 1:37-38; 3:21-22, 28; 31:1-8, 14-15, 23; 34:9). Now Moses' death marks a turning point in the story. After verse 1, Joshua is no longer Moses' assistant but the one to whom God speaks and whom God commissions for a new task. Joshua does not replace Moses (Deut 34:10-12). Yet a kind of succession links the two figures through literary and theological connections between the books of Deuteronomy and Joshua. What we expect in the story that follows, therefore, is that God is about to use another servant to bring God's promises to reality (cf. 5:14; 24:29-33).

It comes as no surprise that the book of Joshua begins with God's addressing Joshua. Joshua has already been commissioned and was declared capable of wise leadership (Deut 34:9). The twice-repeated mention of Moses' exalted position as God's servant (vv. 1, 2), however, emphasizes the central place of Moses in the narrative that follows (see also 1:7, 13, 15; 8:31, 33; 9:24; 11:12, 15; 12:6; 13:8; 14:7; 18:7; 22:2, 4, 5). But Moses is not revered as a cult figure; he is servant and prophet (vv. 1, 7, 13, 15; cf. Deut 34:10). His role as God's agent is to mediate God's instruction. Joshua is above all a listener, for as successor to Moses he becomes *servant* as he fulfills the commission to attend to the divine instruction (cf. 24:29). But before he becomes *servant*, he is witness to and mediator of God's salvation. The transition from Moses' leadership to that of Joshua marks a transition symbolized by Joshua's name. In the book of Numbers we read that Moses changes Joshua's original name, Hoshea (salvation), to Joshua, which means "the LORD is salvation" (Num 13:8, 16). Joshua's name itself reflects the central theological affirmation of the book of Joshua.

Although Moses is important, the Lord is the one who promises to act (note the pronoun "I"). The Lord is about to give the land, as promised to the ancestors (e.g., Gen 12:7), a promise that is reiterated throughout Deuteronomy (e.g., 1:8). The motif of "giving" occurs eight times in Joshua 1 alone and numerous times throughout the book *[Land: Gifted and Lost, p. 440]*. The Hebrew forms of the verb "to give" highlight a dynamic tension in the theology of a gifting God. On the one hand, God is in the process of *giving* the land (participle, v. 2). On the other, God has already given the land even though no one has yet crossed the river. Although God is speaking to Joshua (v. 1), all the "you" pronouns in verses 3-4 are plural. Joshua attends to God on Israel's behalf. He is the conduit of God's words to them.

Joshua 1 sets the stage: God's word of promise places the people at the threshold of a new world. At stake is the veracity of the Lord's word, which is the starting point for theological reflection on the book of Joshua and on the entire history as told by the prophet-historians of Israel. The speech makes the point that Joshua is as much a recipient of God's gracious presence as was Moses. Ultimately the divine "I" defines the shape of the future: *as I was with Moses, so I will be with you; I will not fail you or forsake you* (v. 5). God's promise of presence repeats Moses' words to all Israel (Deut 31:6) and to Joshua (Deut 31:8). God's negative promise of not failing or forsaking also echoes Deuteronomy's affirmations (11:25; 31:6, 8).

Even though the Lord begins with assurances of presence and promises fulfilled, the declaration that *no one shall be able to stand against you all the days of your life* (v. 5a) also alerts the reader that surely some will take a stand against Joshua. The expression "to take a stand against" reminds readers of the folly of such presumption as expressed in Psalm 2:2. They also bring to mind God's similar words to Moses (Deut 7:24; 11:25). The promise of divine presence recalls the promises to Israel's ancestors (Gen 26:3; 31:3; Exod 3:12), which are even echoed by Moses to Joshua (in Deut 31:8, 23) and repeated by the Lord (31:23).

The description of the extent of the land (v. 4) reflects traditional Egyptian descriptions of Canaan during the fourteenth and thirteenth centuries BC (Weinfeld 1983: 65–66) *[Extent of the Land, p. 424]*. The phrase *all the land of the Hittites*, which does not occur in other depictions of the extent of the land (Gen 15:18-21; Exod 23:31; Num 34:1-12; Deut 1:7; 11:24), reflects memory of an even older imperial power that held sway in the ancient Near East west of the Euphrates before Israel's arrival on the scene. Such traditional ancient imperial boundary descriptions seem to have become the basis for describing the land of promise, a larger-than-life depiction that extends from the Jordan River to the Mediterranean and from the Brook of Egypt to the Euphrates (cf. Gen 15:18). Although this old description extends far to the east, Joshua 1:2 states that the crossing of the Jordan marks the entry into the land of promise. The grand scope of the promise (all the way to the Euphrates) hints that God's promise here (and in Deuteronomy) is a divine appropriation of imperial claims. Territorial descriptions normally included as bragging rights of the great powers, Assyria/Babylon and Egypt, have now been taken over by the Lord, who is Sovereign over all empires. An even greater imperium now holds sway, that of God's sovereign rule over all nations and all lands. This Sovereign has the prerogative to assign land and to take it away *[Land: Gifted and Lost, p. 440]*.

One small detail makes clear that this text does not define actual boundaries of Israel's land. The expression *this Jordan* (MT, KJV, NASB, RSV) marks a boundary that is confirmed in the crossing motif throughout Deuteronomy and in the first four chapters of Joshua (the phrase occurs only in Josh 1:2 and Deut 31:2). Although Solomon is said to have dominion as far as the Euphrates (1 Kings 4:21, 24), the area east of the Jordan was contested by imperial powers (cf. 2 Kings 23:29; 24:7; and the words of King Mesha of Moab) *[Mesha Inscription, p. 447]*. In the light of that, Solomon fulfills the geographic promise of Joshua 1, but he fails to be faithful to God alone and to God's instruction.

The ambiguities inherent in this boundary description invite reflection on how geographical boundaries and peoplehood are related. Perhaps verses 1-5 introduce the seeds of tension between the tribes east of the Jordan and those west of the Jordan (Josh 22:9-34). The narrator's summary that *Joshua took the whole land* (11:23; cf. 11:16) restricts interpretation of the promise of 1:3-4 to lands west of the Jordan (not surprising, given Deut 2-3; Josh 1:12-15; 12:1-6). Similarly, the promise of 1:5 that *no one shall be able to stand against you* also stands in tension with the partial occupation reported in Joshua 13:1, and the picture of people who remain in the land *to this day* (6:25; 9:27; 13:13; 15:63; 16:10; 17:12-13; cf. Deut 7:22-24; Josh 23:5). Could it be that all the land was promised, but not all was settled? Both boundary descriptions and settlement patterns will contribute to questions that arise for readers several times later in the book. Which people ought to be considered part of the people "Israel"? Who can be considered "in" or "out"? What is the relationship between geography and peoplehood? *[Plot Tensions in Joshua, p. 452]*.

In spite of that potential ambiguity, the first words of promise set the stage for the book. Land is a gift from the One who promises to fulfill a word spoken earlier to the ancestors and to Moses, and who promises to be an unfailing presence with the one to whom that One speaks: Joshua. Because the essence of land theology here is its character as a gift, Israel's own claims of ownership may well be limited *[Land: Gifted and Lost, p. 440]*. "The homeland comes from God, not from natural rights nor from human claims of possession or power" (Butler 1983: 12). Therefore the first command in the book, *Now proceed to cross the Jordan* (v. 2), makes sense only in the light of the gift of land and the promise of divine presence. Yet the book of Joshua may not be a straightforward narrative of success. The narrator will affirm that all of God's good promises come to pass (21:45), yet Joshua will cajole the people by suggesting that they *cannot serve the Lord* (24:19-20).

1:6-9 God's Charge to Joshua

Now God addresses Joshua with an invitation to act on the truth of what has already been spoken. God commissions Joshua with a twofold task: to lead the people across in order to possess the land, and to distribute the inheritance. Three times in these verses Joshua is called to *be strong and courageous* (vv. 6, 7, 9; note *very* in v. 7), a charge that is picked up later by the Transjordan tribes (v. 18). The repetition is significant because it frames the central command to be faithful to *torah/book of the torah* (1:7b-8) and because it prefaces three distinct sayings.

First, verse 6 focuses on the task with which Joshua is commissioned. Although the land is given by God, Joshua is clearly named as God's agent who will bring the people into the reality of the gift. God reminds Joshua that this task places him into the larger story of the ancestors, to whom God has spoken a word of promise about land. Thus, although Moses is preeminent, he is not the first nor the last recipient of the promise.

Second, verses 7 and 8 include a double encouragement to be faithful to the Lord's instructions through Moses *[Torah, p. 462]*. Such diligent action will bring both prosperity and success. Faithfulness to Torah, however, is not a prerequisite for the presence of God. God is already present and speaking to Joshua. There is already a relationship characterized by gift giving. Torah faithfulness is Joshua's response to the initiative of God. The words for success and prosperity are often used in the wisdom tradition to describe the positive effects of a character formed in keeping with morally upright conduct, even in the face of evil. God's admonition to Joshua to be *strong and courageous* is therefore an encouragement to live in the light of God's instruction, which is a life-giving orientation (cf. admonitions in Deut 30:19-20 to "choose life" by loving and obeying the Lord). That way leads to a good life in the good land. Joshua's "prosperity" and "success" have little to do with financial success and economic prosperity. Joshua's success is linked to his receiving the gift, which ultimately is contingent upon his (and Israel's) attentiveness to God's instruction.

The twofold emphasis on being *careful to act in accordance with* God's instruction complements the encouragements to strength and courage (vv. 7, 9). The two verbs used to form this common expression (lit., "to keep/observe" and "to do/obey") occur together in the OT only in Deuteronomy, as a stereotypical way of encouraging faithfulness to God's instruction (e.g., Deut 6:25; 7:12; 8:1; 11:22, 32). Although the NRSV translates this word pair in Deuteronomy as "diligently observe/observing," in Joshua 1:7 it reads *being careful to act*. God exhorts Joshua to pay deliberate attention to *all the law* (v. 7), to *this book of the law* (v. 8a), to *all that is written in it* (v. 8b). Through attentiveness to the written Torah (perhaps an early version of the book of Deuteronomy), Joshua will get his bearings in this new endeavor *[Composition of Joshua, p. 398]*. This emphasis on God's written instruction stands out at critical moments in the book (see also 8:31-34; 22:5; 23:6; 24:26). The threefold mention of the written instructions in verses 7-8 stands at the center of the Lord's speech, highlighted by two mentions of divine presence and of encouragement to strength and courage on either side (vv. 5-7a, 9). The book begins by acknowledging a kind of "canonical" status to Moses' words, through which Moses' authority continues (Creach: 22) *[Characterization of Joshua, p. 394]*.

The emphatic word *only* (*raq*, v. 7; also in 1:17, 18) highlights the connection between the gift of land (v. 6) and the admonition to obedience. This instruction, given through Moses (v. 7) and written (v. 8), is to provide Joshua with an orientation that will serve him in trying times. Joshua is not first commanded to conquer but to obey. Verses 7-8 therefore introduce the notion that God's initiative and human responsibility are intertwined. God promises to be present and to give the land. Joshua is commanded to live in and meditate on the instructions of God. It seems clear from verses 5 and 9 that God's presence and promise cannot be thwarted. What is not as clear is whether Joshua's obedience is the condition on which God will act or the qualification for keeping the land for the long run (about which we learn in 2 Kings). Deuteronomy implies that keeping Torah is a prerequisite for keeping the land (11:8, 22-23; 19:8-9; 28:58-63).

Two word pictures in the text may clarify the ambiguity. One is that God's instruction is like a path from which Joshua ought not depart (v. 7; cf. Ps 119:105). This is a path of confidence and a source of strength and courage. In the story of God's presence with the ancestors, and in God's instructions, Joshua will find the patterns of divine initiative and human response that will guide him into the unknown but promised future. If Joshua continues to live by that story, he will discover the reality of God's promise. The divine promise is unequivocal; Joshua's faithfulness is not.

The other picture is of Joshua's being encouraged (even commanded) to meditate on God's teachings (v. 8). This is not simply a silent intellectual exercise, but especially a ruminating on Torah through vocal recitation. The Torah is always to be in his *mouth* (v. 8). The image has two connotations. One is of internalization: God's instructions are to be a source of constant meditation that nourishes all of life (cf. Deut 11:18-19; Ps 1:2, where the same expression is used). The other is of the mouth as the origin of communication. As God has spoken to Moses, and as Moses has spoken God's teaching to the people, so now Joshua is to repeat Torah aloud and to impart God's instruction to all who might hear. In doing so, Joshua fulfills the requirements for the human king (Deut 17:19) *[Characterization of Joshua, p. 394]*.

These two word pictures suggest two implications. First, Joshua must pay diligent attention to the way, to the journey informed by God's instruction. In this action Joshua becomes the model for all listeners to the narrative. The shape of life lived in God's presence, with strength and courage, can only flourish if nourished by paying attention to the word, which "requires more than a . . . casual acquaintance, . . . but also an intimate knowledge" (Hauch: 82). Second, there must be integrity between words and actions. Both are grounded in promise and presence, which are prior to hearing and obedience. The *book of the law* illuminates the path because it is accompanied by God's presence.

In the third saying (v. 9), therefore, Joshua can only be convinced of the possibility of strength and courage by being reminded again of the living presence of God. Without that assurance as he moves into an unknown future, Joshua's only options are fear and dismay (cf. Pss 27:14; 31:24; Jer 1:8; Isa 43:5). *Be strong and courageous* occurs again in the mouth of the Transjordan tribes (1:18), and later by Joshua when offering encouragement to the people (10:25). The phrase occurs in Deuteronomy (31:6, 7, 23; cf. 31:8), with variations of it in instructions regarding Joshua's pending leadership (Deut 1:38; 3:28). Except for Deuteronomy 31:6 and Joshua 10:25, the technical sense of these words suggest "a kind of installation in office"

(Lohfink: 241). Joshua had already been commissioned as leader of the people even while Moses was alive (Num 27:18-23). Now he is commanded to carry out his responsibility as leader, and in Joshua 13 he is commissioned to distribute the inheritance. In that way, the divine speech actually introduces the two main structural parts of the book of Joshua—the possession (chs. 2–12), which he initiates immediately, and the distribution (chs. 13–22; Lohfink: 244).

The encouragement to be *strong and courageous* introduces the challenge to be faithful to *torah* (1:7). In verse 9 it introduces the contrast, assuring Joshua that he need not be frightened. Strength and courage require trusting fully in God rather than in human ability. Joshua will embody such trusting as he walks the path of God's instruction and meditates on it day and night.

Joshua's Preparation of the People 1:10-11

Joshua now speaks for the first time. Addressing *the officers of the people*, Joshua's speech echoes God's command in 1:2, illustrating that Joshua faithfully passes on the commands of God. But the setting of the speech belongs with the action that begins in 3:1. Before that action resumes, the interaction with the Transjordan tribes (1:12-18) and with Rahab (ch. 2) pauses the action and allows reflection on two paradigmatic encounters that will shape the story.

The verb *cross over* (*'abar*) ties these verses together, looks forward to the crossing episode in chapters 3 and 4, and evokes memory of the exodus (the verb is used twice in v. 11: *pass through* and *cross over*). Since Joshua follows Moses according to God's intention, and since God will be with Joshua as God was with Moses, so also will the people cross the Jordan as the previous generation has crossed the sea.

Joshua's command is exercised through *the officers of the people*, illustrating again that Joshua is following the tradition established by Moses (Exod 18:24-25; Num 11:16; Deut 1:15). His command includes concern for provisions. Although God is giving the land, the people must prepare for the journey into the land. The verb *to possess* (*yaraš*, twice in v. 11), understood in the context of the speech of God in 1:2-9, indicates receipt of a gift rather than a taking. The same word is used in Genesis 15:7 to indicate that the land is an inheritance gift (cf. context of Gen 15:3-5). The people appear as tenants, receiving land from their owner (Hamlin 1983: 9).

The verb *to possess* has often, however, been understood to signify military conquest. It has become customary to read it as emphasizing the human participation in and responsibility for the conquest (Butler 1983: 17). To this point in the narrative, however, crossing the Jordan initiates the fulfillment of God's promise and God's gift. As I shall note below, in Deuteronomy "possession" is linked most often with faithfulness to covenant instruction, and "dispossession" with covenant disobedience. "Possession," therefore, is about more than military conquest in the book of Joshua.

Perhaps this speech itself provides a clue to the tension inherent in gift and possession. First, the exodus stands out as a model of God's action through the twofold use of the verb "to cross." Second, the double use of "to possess" surrounds a statement that the land is theirs only by divine gift (v. 11b). From the first words of the Lord (v. 2) to Joshua's initial instructions to the leaders (v. 11), the land comes to Israel by God's initiative (gift) alone. But only the narrative ahead can lead us into the full meaning of Israel's possession of the land.

Joshua's Preparation of the Transjordan Tribes 1:12-15

Joshua turns now to the Transjordan tribes and reminds them of the command of Moses at the time when God gave them their territory (Num 32; Deut 3). Here we have the first instance of boundary confusion. Whereas 1:2 clearly identifies the Jordan as the boundary of the land that God gives, here these tribes are granted land east of the Jordan *[Transjordan Tribes, p. 464]*.

Joshua begins his speech (v. 13) by emphasizing the *word of Moses*, which he now passes on to the people, thereby fulfilling his charge from God *[Characterization of Joshua, p. 394]*. In this speech Joshua reiterates the essence of Moses' words (Deut 3:18-20), emphasizing the theme of *rest*. He begins by focusing again on God's activity in providing and giving. This gift is called *a place of rest* and *this land*. Significantly, the only other occurrence of the theme in Deuteronomy is in the Sabbath commandment (5:14). Even more striking is the echo of God's words to Moses in Exod 33:14, "My presence will go with you, and I will give you rest." In the double occurrence of *rest* in Joshua's speech (1:13, 15), we see the beginning of fulfillment both of God's promise of presence and of Moses' earlier word to the Transjordan tribes. In several places in the middle of the book, the narrator summarizes, saying that *the land had rest from war* (11:23; 14:15). And at the end of the book, the narrator reminds the reader three times that rest has become a reality according to the promise (21:44; 22:4; 23:1). Implicit in the emphasis on gift of land and promise of rest in verses 13 and 15 is the charge to Joshua at the end of Moses' speech to the Transjordan tribes in Deuteronomy 3:22, "Do not fear them, for it is the LORD your God who fights for you." To be at rest is for wars to have come to an end. And for readers in the context of Israel's future dispossession in the postexilic era, this rest becomes a hope for a life without fear and without oppression *[Rest, p. 455]*.

In the very context of that promise, therefore, the Transjordan tribes are charged to *cross over armed before your kindred and . . . help them* (v. 14b). For the first time, we read explicitly that the people are armed for war. Their *help* will certainly involve battle; for that we are prepared *[Theology of Warfare, p. 458]*. The language of verse 14 does not lead us to expect passive participants. That may be the point: our expectations play an important role in how we hear the story. The question, however, is whether our expectations will be confirmed, challenged, or modified as we read on.

Response of the People 1:16-18

The Transjordan tribes now respond in a way that sets this generation apart from the previous, unfaithful generation. This new generation is intent on faithfulness to divine instruction; the previous generation was not. We might have expected Joshua himself to have responded earlier to God's instruction (after God's speech of 1:2-9). But he does not. Remarkably, he makes his own confession of faith only at the end of the book (24:15b). Instead, the first to reply are the tribes located "outside" the boundary of the Jordan. Throughout the book *all the people* or *all Israel* interact with Joshua (see Howard 1997). And in chapter 24 *the people* make a covenant with the Lord *["All Israel," p. 385]*. Yet here the Transjordan tribes serve a rhetorical purpose of resolving a conflict that is associated with them in the narrative of Numbers 32 and that points forward to another conflict in Joshua 22.

The response of the Transjordan tribes is powerful for its simplicity. The Transjordan tribes reiterate several motifs from verses 1-9: divine presence (vv. 5, 17) and *strong and courageous* (vv. 6, 7, 9, 18). They seem to be repeating God's words even as they commit themselves to Joshua's commissioning of them in verses 12-15. They promise to do all that Joshua commands and to go where he sends (v. 16). They too draw a parallel with Moses and, in particular, with their obedience to him (v. 17a) *[Characterization of Joshua, p. 394]*. Although the promise here is commendable, we remember that obedience to Moses has not been consistent. In particular, the Transjordan tribes, in another context, are chastised for discouraging Israel from entering (Num 32:7, 14, 15). And the "sin at Peor" (Josh 22:17; cf. Num 25) comes to be associated with the Transjordan tribes. Thus the response here poses a question for the reader and creates a tension that is not resolved until Joshua, without qualification, commends the Transjordan tribes near the end of the story (22:1-3). The strong affirmation by these tribes in chapter 1 and the conflict story in chapter 22 deliberately frame the sequence of conquest stories (chs. 2–12) and distribution stories (chs. 13–22). In addition, the promise to *obey* (v. 17) echoes throughout the dialogue between Joshua and people in the debate about "serving" the Lord (24:19, 24).

The Transjordan tribes, therefore, are representatives of larger concerns in the story. The contrast between the old generation—reflected in the wilderness stories in the book of Numbers—and this new generation is typified by the response of the Transjordan tribes to Joshua. "If the old broke faith by engaging in harlotry with the daughters of Moab at Shittim[,] the new will keep faith when engaging a harlot west of Shittim" (Hauch: 96).

Their affirmation is followed by a qualification voiced in the second half of verse 17, which highlights again the motif of divine presence. The wish for, or conviction of (so Howard 1998: 96), God's continual presence qualifies the vow of obedience by acknowledging that divine empowerment is integral to the possibility of obedience. The parallelism in verse 17 emphasizes that link: we-Moses-we-you // the LORD-you-the LORD-Moses. In other words, the hyperbole of verse 17a is justified by the confidence in God expressed in verse 17b. Thus verse 17 creates a tension that needs to be resolved. The people's vow will have to be tested, and the Lord's promise will need to be confirmed. Their affirmation of the presence of *your God* (v. 17) becomes, in chapter 22, *our God* as the Transjordan tribes assert their loyalty not only to Joshua but also to the *God of gods* (22:22) whom *we serve* (22:27 AT). Their confession in Joshua 1:16-17 also places limits on obedience to human leadership. If Joshua is a royal figure, then obedience to him must depend on divine presence and blessing (1:9; Nelson 1981b: 539) *[Characterization of Joshua, p. 394]*.

The tribes' final words transfer allegiance from Moses to Joshua, whose *words* are now equivalent to Moses' *word* (v. 13). Moreover, verse 18 for the first time introduces the reality that actions have consequences. In keeping with the ancient tradition, the tribes affirm that rebellion and disobedience will result in death. The story of Achan in chapter 7 comes to mind (cf. Num 16). But "death" also comes in other forms in the covenant curses of Deuteronomy 28. The warning at the end of the book of Joshua frames the death warning in terms of *perish[ing] from this good land that the LORD your*

God has given you (23:13b). Will Israel be faithful to the covenant instruction of God or not? More particularly, will the Transjordan tribes confirm their vow by their actions? Finally, does life come to those who obey, whether or not they are located in the physical boundaries of the promise? *[Plot Tensions in Joshua, p. 452].*

The final words of the Transjordan tribes reiterate God's threefold charge to *be strong and courageous.* Even as the tribes' obedience depends on God's living presence, so their vow of faithfulness invites firm faithfulness from Joshua. In God's mouth the same words are a command. Here they reflect an acknowledged dependence on Joshua's own integrity. They call for a response from him—a response that will be demonstrated throughout the book and then confessed at the end.

But their statement is not simply a wish for correspondence between actions and consequences. Because of the repetitions from God's speech in verses 2-9, these last words provide an ironic twist that creates tensions for the reader. It is not obvious that they have *obeyed Moses in all things* (v. 17a). And yet the Transjordan tribes, judged as disobedient in Numbers 32, are vowing obedience in the same language as the speech of God to Joshua; in so doing they acknowledge their history and emphasize their final obedience. The irony is heightened by the idiom condemning anyone who *rebels against your orders* (v. 18a). The OT has used the expression only three times previously, each time referring to Israel's refusal to obey the command to enter the land (Deut 1:26, 43; 9:23; Hawk 1991: 59).

Joshua's story may have a more complex plot than a surface reading suggests. Just as our expectations are reversed regarding the Transjordan tribes, or just as tensions are raised in Joshua 1 that call for resolution, so we enter the action of Joshua 2 with eyes open to the possibility of further reversals of fortune and expectation. Even more, as we explore the intrabiblical conversation reflected in and evoked by this chapter, we discover layers of significance that add depth to our understanding of the text.

THE TEXT IN BIBLICAL CONTEXT

Joshua 1 as Hinge Text

We have already seen glimpses of how Joshua 1 echoes the ancestral narratives, the exodus story, and particularly the book of Deuteronomy. In the first chapter of the book, we discover how Joshua is a "second volume" that refers the reader back to Deuteronomy, the "first volume" (Lohfink: 237). (The Explanatory

Notes have identified similarities between Josh 1:3-5a and Deut 11:24-25; Josh 1:4 and Deut 1:7; Josh 1:5a and Deut 7:24; Josh 1:5b, 6, 9 and Deut 31:6-8, 23; Josh 1:7-9 and Deut 5:32-33; 17:14-20.) Joshua's words to the Transjordan tribes (1:12-15) echo Moses' words to them (Deut 3:18-20), and their response to Joshua (1:18) echoes God's words to them (Deut 31:17). The correspondence between Joshua 1 and Deuteronomy can also be seen in how the speakers reiterate other voices. What Moses says to Israel, God says to Joshua (Deut 11:24-25; Josh 1:3-5). What Moses says to Joshua, God says to Joshua (Deut 31:7-8; cf. Deut 17:18-20; 29:28; Josh 1:6, 9). And what Moses says to the Transjordan tribes, Joshua says to them (Deut 3:18-20; Josh 1:12-15). Even the notice about the "death of Moses" draws Joshua 1 back to Deuteronomy and looks forward into the book of Judges, where Joshua's death is announced in the same way (Judg 1:1) *[Characterization of Joshua, p. 394]*.

This echoing of textual voices reinforces Moses' importance as a mediator of God's instruction as written in Deuteronomy. That God, Joshua, and the narrator can take up the same language in Joshua 1 suggests that both the content and the messengers of the Torah are important. Like Moses, Joshua and the narrator are capable transmitters of the tradition (Polzin; Hauch: 84). Similarly, the same themes of instruction (Torah), obedience, God's presence, promise, leadership, and the gift of land also reverberate throughout Scripture, particularly through Deuteronomy and the DtrH. In many respects, therefore, Joshua 1 presents a biblical theology in miniature.

The chapter's canonical position strengthens that observation. Joshua 1 opens the second part of the Hebrew canon (the Prophets) in the same way that Psalm 1 opens the third part of the Hebrew canon (the Writings). Both chapters highlight faithfulness to God's instruction (Torah). And they do so by using exactly the same expression: meditating on God's teaching *day and night* (Josh 1:8; Ps 1:2). Such an attentive stance is the orientation around which the community of Scripture readers shapes its identity as listeners who *serve* and *obey* (1:17; 24:24) *[Torah, p. 462]*.

Gift of Land

Besides the emphasis on God's instruction, the gift of land stands out because of the explicit reference to the promises to Moses (v. 3; cf. Exod 3:7-8; 6:8) and to the ancestors (v. 6; cf. Gen 12:1, 7; 13:14-17; 15:7, 18). Since Joshua's connection with Deuteronomy is most immediate, and since the story inaugurated by the book of Joshua ends with Israel in exile at the end of 2 Kings, we do well to begin the intrabiblical conversation by noticing how the gift of land is set within the exhortations of Deuteronomy. Joshua 1 cites Deuteronomy 11:23-25, with its emphasis on the Lord's actions to give the land to Israel. This divine initiative is set within context of exhortations to fear, love, and serve the Lord, and to keep the Lord's commandments (Deut 10:12-13; 11:1, 13). The exhortations are intended specifically for the generation listening to Moses (11:2). Strength, obedience, and long life in the land are all bound together in Deuteronomy 11, where the "crossing over" motif is mirrored in Joshua 1 (Deut 11:8-9, 11, 31). Indeed, loving and serving the Lord are prerequisites to fruitfulness of the land (11:13-17). Therefore "diligent observance" (11:22, 32) in the land is a significant prerequisite to the Lord's "driving out all these nations" (cf. 11:23).

That conditional promise stands before the grand scope of the land described in Deuteronomy 11:24, which is framed by two references to "every place/the land on which you set foot" (11:24a, 25b), a promise reiterated by the Lord in Joshua 1:3a. Clearly, however, that "every place" is west of the Jordan even though the description of the extent of the land seems grander *[Extent of the Land, p. 424]*. Since Joshua 1 emphasizes the crossing of the Jordan as a kind of boundary event, and Joshua 1:12-18 includes a significant theological conversation with the Transjordan tribes—all this suggests that Joshua 1 is about more than drawing a line in the sand. Both parts of Joshua 1 affirm that the divine gift of land includes both sides of the Jordan (1:2, 14-15). Both parts mention the instruction of the Lord through the book of the law/word of Moses. And both parts include exhortations to faithfulness. That the Transjordan tribes are highlighted as the first who vow their faithfulness suggests that those outside the Jordan-boundary are as capable of covenant loyalty as those inside. And that becomes the critical nub of the conflict in Joshua 22. If these can be loyal, in whose territory Israel was once unfaithful, then might it not also be possible for "all Israel" to be faithful while in Babylonian exile east of the Jordan or in the Diaspora among the nations?

That possibility also resonates with the tension between complete and incomplete possession of the land. Joshua 1 assumes both loyalty and success, premised on divine gift, presence, and empowerment. Israel will cross into gifted land and, obedient to divine instruction, will *possess* the land (1:11). Although land that is promised is received, the book reflects only a partial fulfillment. At 13:1 we become aware that *very much of the land still remains to be pos-*

sessed. That partial realization of the promise is significant not only for the book of Joshua. In Deuteronomy, and within the history that follows the book of Joshua (DtrH), the theme of land loss stands out in stark contrast to the certainty of the gift of land. Thus the gift of land is enigmatic. From the perspective of the end of the story in 2 Kings, Israel stands outside "the land," just as it did at the beginning of the book of Joshua. Read from the other end of the story, Joshua 1 emphasizes the possibility of the gift even after disobedience and expulsion from the land (according to the covenant curses of Deut 28 and the intimations of exile in Deut 4:25-31; 28:36-37, 62-64; 29:22-28). The tribes ready to cross the Jordan are homeless, as is Israel in Babylonian exile.

Such a reading helps us to understand several other emphases within the chapter and their resonance with other biblical texts. First, the gift of land to Israel, along with the hints of exile in Deuteronomy, must be viewed in relation to the larger biblical notion that God has also given land to other people groups, and in doing so has dispossessed other indigenous peoples as well (Deut 2, esp. vv. 5, 9, 12, 19, 22-23, 31, 36; cf. 32:8-9; Gen 15:16; Deut 9:4; 18:12; Amos 1–2; 9:7-8). Although some of those texts include a judgment of the nations, the "gift" of Joshua 1 does not include an explicit critique of the nations.

Second, the chapter calls for renewed obedience to covenantal instruction. We do well to remember that even in some of the ancestral promises, the gift is provisional (Gen 18:19; Deut 11, 28), even as God's compassionate presence remains certain (Deut 4:31 in context). Third, the tension between divine commitment and human obligation (with the implied condition of keeping/losing the land) underscores the theme of divine presence in Joshua 1.

In other words, this promise reminds readers that the *human* threat of death upon the disobedient (1:18) must be interpreted alongside the *divine* announcement of the consistent gracious presence of God (1:5). Gift and responsibility are united, not simply to underline a pattern for success of the community of faith, but as a way of being in the world for the world. But the "blessing to the nations" theme in Genesis raises a question for readers of the book of Joshua (Gen 12:3; 18:17-19; 26:3-5; 28:13-15). Is the killing of the Canaanite population punishment for their wickedness, as Deuteronomy suggests (9:4-6) and Genesis implies (15:16)? Or is the call for obedience to God's written instruction in Joshua 1 the beginning of an alternative to violence? Deuteronomy 9:4-6 repeats three times that the gift of land is "not because of your righteousness." In this text, entry into the land is not conditioned upon Israel's obedience to God's instruction. Such faithfulness does, however, play a role in the larger story of Israel. Since the book of Joshua stands "midway" between the promise (Gen 12) and loss of land (2 Kings 25), it marks a kind of hinge point at which gift and responsibility coincide. Up to this point land is anticipated as a gift (see also Josh 21:43-45; 24:13, 18). After this point land is maintained on the basis of loyalty to the Lord and obedience to God's instruction (Torah) *[Land: Gifted and Lost, p. 440]*.

Presence, Promise, and Royal Faithfulness

The book of Joshua is rooted in a tension between the Lord's promise/presence and human faithfulness to God's instruction (see "Gift of Land" above). As Lawson Stone writes, "For the Deuteronomists, the saving actions of God in history are conveyed by the normative word of the written Torah, and the alternative to Canaanite intransigence and hostility emerges as the choice to serve Yahweh faithfully." In this way "the story of the occupation of the land becomes a massive metaphor for Israel's 'occupation' of the law" (36). And if "Joshua represents a Deuteronomistic type for Josiah, the archetypal champion of Deuteronomistic lawbook piety" (36), then the book of Joshua also begins to shape a theopolitical vision for the requirements of royal power, as noted in Deuteronomy 17:14-20. There the king is counseled not to increase military strength, but rather to pay attention to the reading of the Torah, "diligently observing all the words of this law" and turning neither "to the right or to the left" (Deut 17:19-20) *[Characterization of Joshua, p. 394]*.

The Lord's instructions in Joshua 1:6-9 sound strangely reminiscent of those words in Deuteronomy 17. Thus, as Stone continues, "For the reader, holy war cannot ultimately be a matter of territory or warfare; it is about uncompromising obedience to Yahweh's law understood as a normative text" (36). And since Joshua is the paradigmatic figure in the book of Joshua, we do well to consider how Joshua (and the call that he attend to God's instruction) echoes throughout Scripture *[Characterization of Joshua, p. 394]*.

Joshua as Model

In the NT, Joshua stands out because of the explicit use of typology in Hebrews 4:8 *[Figural Reading, p. 426]*. There his incomplete "rest" is interpreted as caused by disobedience (4:11). Israel's negative example therefore ought to encourage believers not to disobey.

Hebrews reverses the obedience image in Joshua 1 and focuses on disobedience. Joshua himself is only incidental to the comparison. Yet even in the book of Joshua, Joshua's obedience is only part of the whole in which *Israel's* faithfulness is ultimately in view (24:31). The emphasis on daily faith(fulness) in Hebrews also echoes the divine promise "I will never leave you or forsake you" (Heb 13:5), where that promise from Joshua 1:5 is set in the context of concern about the "love of money" and its corollary, contentment. Hebrews is steeped in a theology of rest, in which the gift of God's presence actually empowers the believers to say no to the allure of prevailing idolatries. That concern shapes the book of Joshua, especially chapters 23 and 24 *[Rest, p. 455]*.

In other parts of Scripture, however, Joshua is a model in different ways. That is not surprising, given that a parallel has already been established between Joshua and Moses in Joshua 1. At least four other parallels have been observed. First, in the Chronicles history, David is portrayed as a second Moses and Solomon as a second Joshua. Specifically, Joshua is the model for Solomon for he too is charged to "be strong and of good courage" (1 Chron 22:13; cf. Deut 31:6; Josh 1:7, 9). Like Joshua, he too will prosper by obeying the instruction of the Lord (1 Chron 22:13). Second, the book of Joshua presents Joshua as a royal figure who is told to meditate on *torah* day and night (1:8; cf. Deut 17:18-19; the *torah* in the mouth becomes eating the scroll in Ezek 3:1-3; Rev 10:8-11). Both Joshua and the king are to turn from it neither right nor left (Josh 1:7; Deut 17:20). Third, the parallels between Joshua's commissioning and David's commissioning of Solomon are strikingly similar (1 Kings 2:2-4). Both Joshua and Solomon are commissioned to be faithful to Torah (Porter 1983). The DtrH shows that there are two paths: the way of Joshua and the way of Solomon. Fourth, the model of Joshua as leader and ideal royal figure is also reflected in the emphasis on King Josiah in 2 Kings 22–23 (Nelson 1981b: 531-40). Josiah's model obedience is described in the same terms as Joshua's (on not turning to the right or to the left: Josh 1:7; 23:6; 2 Kings 22:2; Deut 17:20). And related to that, the "book of the law" is mentioned eleven times in 2 Kings 22–23. Similar emphasis is found only in the book of Joshua (Josh 1:8; 8:31, 34; 22:5; 23:6) *[Characterization of Joshua, p. 394]*.

That ongoing call for obedience has also been reinterpreted by the prophets of Israel. The combination of verbs "be successful" (*yaśkil*) and "prosper" (*yiṣlaḥ*; Josh 1:7-8) occurs elsewhere in the OT only in the Suffering Servant poem of Isaiah 52:13–53:12 (specifically, *yaśkil*, 52:13; *yiṣlaḥ*, 53:10). The poet who reflects on the exile in Isaiah 40–55 suggests by this parallel that "the picture of Joshua/ Josiah has been reinterpreted as the one who 'succeeds' by his death!" (Hamlin 1983: 8). This combination, along with the emphasis on renewal of faithfulness to God's instruction in those chapters of Isaiah, suggests that the prophet envisions a new entry into the land, based on a renewed faithfulness. But the hope for faithfulness goes beyond Israel; God's instruction is now to be welcomed by the nations (Isa 51:4-5). And the prophet opens the way to see suffering as a path through which redemption may come. In that way victory is interpreted in a new way—a way that welcomes all (cf. the use of Isa 42:1-4 in Matt 12:18-21).

Joshua and Jesus

Joshua is a model by which biblical writers portray royal figures (see above). That reinterpretation continues in the NT with Jesus, whose Aramaic name is based on the same root as Joshua. One might even say that Jesus is a "new Joshua," whose life and work transposes the Joshua story into a new key. He is the one who offers "rest" to those who are weary. His law is not burdensome (Matt 11:28-30; cf. Deut 30:11-14). And his way of the cross is a suffering path that leads to life within God's kingly rule and that vanquishes the enemies of sin and death. The inheritance that Jesus offers is entry into a community of love and service, sharing life with brothers and sisters of all nations. Jesus is the new Joshua, who leads all who follow to the land of promise—a land not taken by sword or bow, but given by the Spirit (Zech 4:6; Rom 8:37). These texts continue the conversation begun in the Deuteronomic tradition (Deut 3:20; 12:9-10; 25:19), continued into Joshua (21:44; 22:4; 23:1), and reimagined by the prophets and NT writers *[Conquest and Land in the NT, p. 411; Rest, p. 455]*.

THE TEXT IN THE LIFE OF THE CHURCH

Gift and Responsibility

The dual emphasis on gift and responsibility is the central motif in Joshua 1. Perhaps more than any other issue, the church has wrestled with the balance between God's initiative and human responsibility. Joshua 1 states with brazen assurance that both are necessary. God is a covenant partner, one who has chosen to work with human beings but not to manipulate them. This God calls a people into existence and assures them of divine presence. The wonder is that the promise persists even when we raise questions about the reliability of the Transjordan tribes' promise of obedience. And the promise persists even in exile in Babylon. The promise of God, however, does not nullify the consequences of covenant disloyalty (see Josh 7 and 23). Still, the rhetoric of command and consolation (gift), evident from God's first words in Josh 1:2, suggests that presence and possibility complement command and responsibility.

Yet in that context of potential and real disloyalty, Joshua 1 offers a model of loyalty that is worth emulating. The Transjordan tribes, outside the boundary and hardly dependable (from other testimony), offer a commitment that is truly "the assurance of things hoped for, the conviction of things not seen" (Heb 11:1). Against expectation, the Transjordan tribes are the first in the book of Joshua to declare their allegiance. Geographically they are "outside," yet by confession of commitment, they sign on to God's project and, with their fellow Israelites, prepare to receive the gift of land (see Polzin on the insider/outsider dynamic in Joshua, which I will explore in more detail in the reflections on Josh 2). The emphasis on the Transjordan tribes begins to open the door to risking inclusion of those who previously have proved unreliable and to venture opening a way for those outside the established boundaries of the community.

Obedience

The believers church tradition has been noted for its emphasis on obedience (Murray: 186-202; Ollenburger 1984). For Peter Riedemann, true faith makes one live in God's righteousness, "ardent in love, and in keeping his commandments" (Klaassen 1981: 64). Menno Simons suggested that "true faith or true knowledge begets love, and love begets obedience to the commandments of God" (Menno Simons: 307). Certainly the early Anabaptist writers did not expect Christians to follow the OT laws. But their view of obedience rooted in love of God is completely in keeping with Deuteronomy's great admonition to love God (6:5), which is followed immediately with the admonition to pay constant attention to God's instruction. The church does well to continue calling one another to obedience, since "obedience is the primal form of biblical faith" (Brueggemann 1982: 101). Still, in the sequence of priorities in the divine speeches in Joshua 1, God's gift is prior to the response. Thus, while obedience may be a primal expression of faith, God's promise of presence and active gift giving is antecedent to and independent of human faithfulness (as Deuteronomy affirms, e.g., in 4:31).

Yet the reality of the believers church tradition has not kept pace with its reputation even as surely as Israel's reality fell short of

Deuteronomy's hope. Brueggemann reminds us that no one has a monopoly on obedience. Jewish theologian Abraham Heschel offers this way of seeing the heart of biblical faith: "I am commanded—therefore I am." John Calvin also affirms the formative power of obedience: "But not only faith, perfect and in every way complete, but all right knowledge of God is born of obedience" (both cited in Brueggemann 1982: 102).

Obedience is what creates space for knowledge of God's living presence. But the word of God's gracious presence even in exile, even after the loss of land because of disobedience, must also be heard today. Grace comes to us who have failed just as it came to those who first read the historian's account in Joshua 1. It comes to us with an invitation to imitate the Transjordan tribes in their affirmation and to stand in the position of Joshua, hearing the word of command that orders our existence in terms of God's instruction.

That command to pay deliberate and constant attention to God's instruction has often been compared to our paying attention to the word of Scripture. Although the full content of either Joshua's or Josiah's "book of the law" is unknown, drawing an analogy to our Bible is commonplace today. The principle is certainly similar: as Deuteronomy (or part of it) served as normative for Hezekiah's or Josiah's reforms, and the "book of the law" served as Joshua's guide, so the Bible is the source that authorizes and shapes the church's life.

But God's promised presence in Joshua 1 is not simply equated with the words of the book. God's presence is most assuredly experienced in the congruence of the external word embodied in the transformed life, which makes "the book of the law" in Joshua 1 significant for the church. To pay attention to the "book of the law" is to heed the voice of God, or of Moses. First of all, one must give an attentiveness to a Thou who stands over against the self and the community, one who commands and who invites a response. Obedience is possible only if there is a conversation. And the book of Joshua points up specific challenges to obedience when the conversation and the commands are difficult or even immoral.

The fact that the Transjordan tribes respond together suggests also that obedience is not simply a private matter. The community is where God's presence is known. And through the gracious initiative of God, together with the grateful response of the community's obedience, "rest" is granted.

Remarkably, the boldness of the community's challenge to Joshua (v. 18b) and its wish that God be present (1:17b) offer a glimpse into this chapter's realistic appraisal of the future. The outcomes of success and prosperity are not automatic. The Transjordan tribes pick up God's own admonition and offer their leader a challenge. At the same time, the community affirms the leadership of the one who follows in Moses' footsteps. The leader whom the church follows is the one who submits to God's instruction—who follows as did Joshua, Josiah, and Jesus. But that following does not preclude setting out certain criteria for the faithfulness of those who lead. For Calvin, such exhortations are not onerous, for if Joshua, who was a faithful leader, needed to be encouraged in his faithfulness, "how much more necessary must it be that we who labor under so much sluggishness should be spurred forward" (31). After all, "many, by talking and discoursing, have the Law in their mouth, but are very bad keepers of it" (33).

Land and Abundant Life

The concreteness of the gift of land eludes easy appropriation. The church has always had difficulty with the promise of land. Within the Bible we find clues for both a literal and a typological or figural interpretation (Brueggemann 2002: 2). Land is both "soil" and "symbol." As a symbol, land represents, for NT writers, "life abundant" (Martens: 354). Origen, like the Gospel of Matthew, understood the related notion of "rest" as the experience of believers who gain the upper hand in struggling against vices through the strength of God (34; Matt 11:29; see also discussion at Josh 11:23). Throughout the Bible, however, we find concern for the real lives of people—especially those on the fringes of power, those at the margins, and those who are weak and disenfranchised. Land, the earth on which people live, is the Lord's (Ps 24:1; Lev 25:23). Land is given as a gift to all who derive their nourishment from it *[Figural Reading, p. 426]*.

The biblical teaching on land is not limited to the particular piece of land that has been given to Israel (see Brueggemann 2002; W. Janzen 1992). Yet drawing analogies between the particular gift to Israel and a modern people's or nation's experience has been common (Noll). Unfortunately, those who claim their land as God's special provision for them have most often not recognized the association in Joshua 1 between gift and covenantal responsibility. Loss of land (Deut 28) comes to those who go their own way by grasping for possession on their own terms rather than by submitting to the instruction of the Lord *[Land: Gifted and Lost, p. 440]*.

The church may discover similar experiences in its history, but the mode of existence called for by Joshua 1 is always the gracious obedience that listens for the summoning word from God. The invitation, the command, and the gift are expressions of life within the rule or kingdom of God. Those who live by the gracious obedience offered in Joshua 1 will inherit the earth (Matt 5: 5) and will know the saving presence of God.

Joshua 2:1-24

Testing the Water: The Story of the Spies

PREVIEW

This well-known story about the prostitute Rahab and the Israelite spies interrupts our expectations after the speeches of chapter 1. Instead of gathering *all* the people to cross the Jordan, as he has been commanded to do (1:2; cf. 3:1), Joshua sends two men *secretly* to spy out the land, where they encounter a prostitute. Rahab is a collaborator, the Benedict Arnold of her people. Today she would likely be hunted down by nationalists. Although sworn to secrecy, she risks exposure as a collaborator by identifying with the other side.

What do we make of this woman and her confession? How do we allow her story a voice in the conversation? Is she an opportunist or a convert? Does she represent the narrator's attempt to vilify Canaanite culture by highlighting her departure from it? Is she a symbolic character whose story stands as the first significant and archetypal narrative in the book of Joshua? Could her story highlight the main point of the book?

Likewise, we may wonder about Joshua's actions. How are we to view this diversion in the light of the story as a whole? Does Joshua disregard the command to cross the river? Does the narrator present the story of Joshua's initiative as an ominous sign or a serendipitous opportunity?

The introduction (v. 1) and conclusion (vv. 23-24) set the text off from its context. The story that begins here continues in chapter 6, where the Jericho story reaches its conclusion and Rahab's story concludes (6:22-25). Although chapter 2 contains its own plot and tensions, it also helps us to understand the entire book.

As the first narrative after the book's introduction, this story serves notice that the Lord is the central character in the book. It depicts a Canaanite as responding to the Lord's initiatives in the land. And it invites readers to reflect on the significance of Rahab's acknowledging the Lord's actions. In those ways the story, together with Joshua 1, becomes the book's key signature, indicating how the music of the rest of the narrative might be played out and interpreted. This story offers a voice in the theology of conquest and land, and it begins to explore the subtle complications involved in identifying insiders and outsiders.

We do best to read this story in conversation with other texts, especially those about hospitality (Gen 19; Judg 19), about the original twelve spies (Num 13–14), the sin at Shittim (Num 25), and Moses' negotiations with the Transjordan tribes (Num 32). Joshua 2 (along with the response of the Transjordan tribes in Josh 1) sets up the possibility of a new beginning by deliberately opening up an intrabiblical dialogue that begins the "unweaving of the tapestry of sin and judgment that the previous generation had woven in the wilderness" (Hauch: 98). The juxtaposition of *prostitute* and *Shittim* in Joshua 2:1 recalls Israel's apostasy (just east of the Jordan River to the northeast of the Dead Sea; Num 25:1-3; Deut 31:16-17) and sets the stage for us to ask, "What happens next?" (Hauch: 99).

OUTLINE

Setting the Stage, 2:1
A Royal Search, 2:2-7
Confession and Covenant, 2:8-14
The Escape Plan and Counterconcessions, 2:15-21
Return and Report of Findings, 2:22-24

Various elements of structure are important for understanding the implicit message of the chapter. The form of ancient treaties is evident in (1) preamble (v. 11); (2) prologue (vv. 9-11); (3) stipulations by Rahab (vv. 12-13); (4) stipulations by spies (vv. 18-21); (5) sanctions (vv. 18-20); (6) oath (vv. 14, 17); and (7) sign of the treaty, the scarlet cord (vv. 18-21; Campbell). The overall direction of the story is also apparent in the alternating descriptions of action and dialogue (McCarthy 1971: 170). The dialogue sequence allows readers to enter the conversation by identifying with various participants in the plot, which moves from a complication (vv. 2-7), to a climax (vv. 8-14), and then unwinds to an odd resolution *[Covenant and Treaty, p. 416].*

EXPLANATORY NOTES

Setting the Stage 2:1

Given the way Moses and Joshua are juxtaposed in chapter 1, it is not surprising that the narrative continues by telling about Joshua, who like Moses sends spies to view the land. This telling introduction invites several questions.

Why, after being instructed to cross the Jordan (1:2), does Joshua send spies? Why has the narrator deliberately placed this story here between the command of 1:2 and its being carried out in 3:1? It is significant that Joshua's action mirrors an earlier action of Moses. In addition, readers who are familiar with other spy stories (Num 13–14; Deut 1:19-46; Judg 18) will recognize that one of the aims of similarly composed narratives is to awaken commitment and call forth decision. But the similarity also reminds us that in the earlier spy story only two of the twelve spies returned with a positive report. The overwhelmingly negative response turned the trust of the people away from the Lord's gift, with the corresponding result: "The LORD will not be with you" (Num 14:43). Sending spies, therefore, may well entail a risk. Sending two spies may be a subtle nod to the two faithful spies (Joshua and Caleb). And after the Transjordan tribes have (uncharacteristically) declared their allegiance (1:16-18), the spies' positive report recalls the complaints and "rebellion" following the negative report of the ten spies (Num 14; Hauch: 97).

Some have suggested that Joshua acts inappropriately because, unlike Moses, he does not act on a specific command of the Lord (cf. Num 13:1; Eslinger: 35). The point could also be made that Joshua is not fully confident and hence "gropes cautiously for the gift" (Gunn: 110). Nowhere, however, does the narrator judge Joshua's action. The impact of the story as a whole suggests a guardedly positive evaluation of Joshua's action in sending the spies.

Yet the specific mention of Shittim, as the first geographical reference in the book, raises an ominous concern. Shittim reminds us of the gruesome story of Israel's apostasy and the judgment of God (Num 25:1-5). It is the place where Israel "began to play the harlot" (25:1 RSV). It may also be the same place as Abel-Shittim, where Moses noted that the inhabitants of the land who remain would cause trouble (33:48-56).

These allusions highlight a final concern raised by verse 1. The spies *spent the night* (or *slept there*) at the home of Rahab, a prostitute. Her name means "wide," the same word as is used for the public square in other stories in which strangers enter towns and seek lodging (Gen 19:2; Judg 19:15). In Ugaritic literature the word is used occasionally for female genitalia (Barstad; Spina 1997: 1124). In biblical poetry, the name Rahab comes to represent the mythical monster of chaos, whom God has subdued (Job 26:12; Ps 89:10; Isa 30:7; 51:9; yet in Ps 87:4 "Rahab" is named along with imperial powers who are now said to be born in Zion). "In a symbolic sense, Rahab is a synthesis of all that is most threatening to Israel, a point which the narrator underscores by the names given her: woman, prostitute, Rahab" (Hawk 1991: 61).

According to some biblical texts, foreign women are considered dangerous and are to be avoided (Deut 7:3; cf. Judg 3:6; 1 Kings 11:1-8; Prov 2:16; 5:3, 20; 7:5; 22:14; 23:27). Prostitution is often a metaphor for covenant violation (Exod 34:14-16; Num 25:1; Deut 31:16-18; Judg 2:17; Hos 4:10-15; Isa 1:21; Jer 3:1). The added note that *they slept there* (AT) heightens the tension from the very beginning (Bird: 127). The NRSV's *spent the night* or the TNIV's *stayed there* hides the double meaning. Although Wiseman has suggested that Rahab's house is an inn, the emphasis on Rahab's occupation and the ambiguity of the verb *šakab* (*to sleep/lie down*, vv. 1, 8) focuses our attention on the potential threat that Rahab poses for the Israelites. The Moabite Ruth's proposition to Boaz in Ruth 3 may represent a similar (perceived) threat.

At the beginning of the story, those ominous signs are precisely what make it so remarkable in this setting. The narrative begins by offering readers, through its literary allusions, both the prospect of deliberate trust in the purposes of God and the threat of compromise, leading to the eventual demise of Israel. Whatever other questions lie hidden between the lines, the spies have chosen a place that allows them access to the city and its people and gives them cover by means of anonymity.

A Royal Search 2:2-7

Without explanation, we hear that the king of Jericho has been made aware of the spies' identity and motive. More than that, the sexual insinuation that continues throughout the entire dialogue exposes the threat that Rahab represents. The language used for entry into the city and into Rahab's house (*to come to*, four times in vv. 1-4) is also used for sexual intercourse. The king's messengers demand sarcastically, *Turn over the men who've entered you* (lit.; Spina 1997: 1124). The repetition of the verb raises questions about Rahab's motives (Bird: 128–29). The NRSV translates the same verb in 1:18 as *invade*. And three times Rahab uses the verb *to know*, which is used in other contexts as a euphemism for sexual intercourse (vv. 4, 5, 8; e.g., Gen 4:1). Harlotry, a metaphor for apostasy, and the sexual connotations suggest that "Rahab symbolized everything that was opposite to Israel's best religious self" (Spina 1997: 1125).

We are not surprised that a king should have an interest in maintaining state security, nor that he is able to discover the spies' presence. Imperial powers have eyes and ears in unlikely places. What is unexpected is that Rahab protects her guests. Or is it? Is she not acting out of respect for the laws of hospitality to strangers, a common ancient Near Eastern custom? Twice in these verses we read that she hid the men (vv. 4a, 6). The scenario of verses 3-6 unfolds like this: (1) the king sends messengers, who ask Rahab about the men (v. 3); (2) verse 4a can be read two ways. It could be a flashback: "But the woman had taken the two men and had hidden them" (McCarthy 1971: 170–71; similarly in NIV/TNIV, NLT, NJPS). Or perhaps there is a gap in the narration, since Rahab must go and (pretend to) look for the men. While "looking," she hides the men (v. 4a); (3) returning to the messengers, she tells them that the men were indeed there but have already left (vv. 4b-5); (4) the narrator adds an aside to the reader, lest verse 4a slipped by the first time (v. 6). However we read verse 4a, the reader cannot miss the fact that because of Rahab's hospitality and foresight, the men have been preserved from immediate danger.

Ancient readers of this story, however, might not as readily have given Rahab the benefit of the doubt. Nor might they have looked favorably on the spies' choice of Rahab's house (cf. Jer 5:7-9). By all conventional standards, Rahab's act is contrary to expectation. Negative expectations make the story work as well as it does to provoke thought and stimulate the imagination. Rahab, the unlikely ally, outwits the king's intelligence and foils their hopes of maintaining a position of privilege and power. In stark contrast to the king's fear, Rahab risks protecting unknown agents of a threatening power. "In her display of loyalty, courage, and altruism, she acts out of keeping with her assumed character as a harlot and thus reveals her true character as a person" (Bird: 131).

But the spies are not safe. Twice the point is made that the gate has been closed (vv. 5, 7). They are virtually locked inside the enemy camp. Rahab is confident in lying to the king's agents and in assuring them that the spies can be caught. Thus far Rahab is the only character to demonstrate any independent action. She directs all the action, both of the spies and of the king's agents. Do we trust her judgment? Can the spies rest assured of her protection?

Confession and Covenant 2:8-14

Our curiosity is aroused as the scene changes with the notice that before the men go to sleep (*šakab*; cf. v. 1), she goes up to them on the roof. The Hebrew text, translated *she came up to them on the roof*, heightens our suspicion by emphasizing her action with alliteration (*'aletah 'alehem 'al-haggag*). But totally uncharacteristic of the expected sexual encounter, Rahab makes an orthodox confession of Israelite faith (vv. 9-11) in words reminiscent of Moses' exhortations and of Deuteronomistic theological vocabulary (Deut 4:39; 1 Kings 8:23). Even more, she practically quotes Exodus 15, with its mention of the nations' hearing (15:14; cf. Josh 2:10-11; 9:1; 10:1; 11:1) and its claim "All the inhabitants of Canaan melted away" (15:15, exchanging "land" for "Canaan," cf. Josh 2:9). The verb "to melt" is used prior to this chapter (where it occurs in vv. 9 and 24) only in Exodus 15:15. Quoting the Song of Moses and echoing Deuteronomistic theology, she is the first person in the book to make such a confession, which is remarkable, given her status as a Canaanite, a woman, and a prostitute. Not only does she speak for herself; her use of "we" language also suggests that she speaks for the entire Canaanite population (vv. 10-11; Ottosson 1989: 420–21). But the confession of God's cosmic lordship in verse 11b is hers alone. She is a most unlikely candidate to foreshadow Joshua's call to commitment in 24:14-15.

The progression of Rahab's confession in verses 9-11 also highlights her own commitment. She speaks first in verse 9 of acknowledging God's gift of the land (in contrast to her *I do not know* of vv. 4b and 5) and of the inhabitants' fearful response. In her explanation, beginning in verse 10, she speaks of *we* who have *heard* of God's mighty acts. God's action in Israel's experience stands at the heart of the confession. Her description of her people includes melting of the heart and loss of courage (cf. Josh 5:1). Rahab's own response, however, does not betray fear or lack of courage. She cleverly finds a way to make an alliance with Israel. In contrast to all the fearful responses to hearing that follow (5:1; 9:1, 9; 10:1; 11:1), Rahab takes a risk, acts with courage, and makes an alliance with Israel (Stone: 28–29).

Although Rahab confesses to having *heard* what *the* LORD has done, that is juxtaposed with *what you did*, namely, *you utterly destroyed* the two kings in Transjordan (v. 10). The word translated *utterly destroyed* is the important Hebrew word *ḥerem*. The word is used in Deuteronomy and (primarily) in the first half of the book of Joshua, in both noun and verb forms, to specify the complete eradication of the indigenous population (Deut 2:34; 3:6; 7:2, 26; 13:16, 18; 20:17; Josh 6:17, 18, 21; 7:1; 8:26; 10:1, 28, 35, 37, 39, 40; 11:11, 12, 20, 21). For further exploration of the word, see the commentary at chapter 6 and the essay *Ḥerem, p. 433*. Since this word occurs for the first time in the book within the Rahab story, and in her own words, its use is especially significant. One could conclude that she knows the narrative of Deuteronomy 2–3, which summarizes Israel's victory over Sihon and Og, as well as the instructions concerning warfare in Deuteronomy 20. And since she shows such familiarity with the vocabulary of warfare, she and her people have good reason to fear. Such action, along with divine empowerment, must surely mean that Israel's God is *God in heaven above and on earth below* (v. 11). Acknowledgment of God's cosmic sovereignty may not be an unprovoked "conversion." Some might argue that her confession seems more like the forced conversions that have always followed invading imperial armies. Even so, her words are also used elsewhere only by Moses (Deut 4:39) and Solomon (1 Kings 8:23; cf. Jehoshaphat in 2 Chron 20:6-7).

Yet Rahab's motivation in protecting the spies is not answered simply by her confession and recitation of Deuteronomic theology in verses 9-11. In the following scene, Rahab reveals the purpose of her actions. The transition in verse 12, *Now then*, indicates that she is about to state her terms. She shifts her focus from the cosmic to the personal (v. 11b), which reveals either that she has invented a clever ploy to protect herself or that she is making a deliberate move to identify with the community of the Lord.

Rahab's description of her actions as having *dealt kindly* [*ḥesed*] *with you* suggests that her understanding is more profound than self-preservation. That she and the spies understand each other at all suggests that they may share more in common than we usually imagine. She speaks the most theologically significant Hebrew word for "loyalty" within the covenant community, *ḥesed* (often translated as "loving-kindness," "covenant love," or "loyalty"). The term is often used together with the word "covenant/treaty" to indicate God's loyalty to the terms of the covenant with God's people *[Covenant and Treaty, p. 416]*. Every occurrence of the words for "covenant/treaty" and "loyalty" speak of God's characteristic actions (e.g., Deut 7:9, 12; 1 Sam 20:8; 1 Kings 8:23; 2 Chron 6:14; Neh 1:5; 9:32; Pss 25:10; 89:28; 106:45; Isa 54:10; 55:3; Dan 9:4). In Deuteronomy the word *ḥesed* is used exclusively to describe God's loyalty to those who love God and keep the commandments (5:10; 7:9; 7:12; cf. Exod 15:13; 34:6-7; Num 14:18-19; 1 Kings 8:23). Thus, Rahab recognizes that her actions have been consistent with covenant loyalty, which binds her to the spies. And in Deuteronomic terms, she borrows language used for God's loyalty to describe the interaction between her and the spies (2:12; cf. Ruth 1:8 for similar reciprocity between people). Even more striking is the proximity of the word *ḥesed* to the cosmic language of God's sovereignty at the end of verse 11, which mirrors a similar combination in Solomon's prayer (1 Kings 8:23).

Rahab's cleverness, cloaked in careful theological phrasing, keeps us interested in what happens. The incongruence between her perceived character and her confessional integrity makes her story significant. Rahab is a paradigmatic figure. As the first Canaanite in the book, she is "not faceless" (Davis 2000: 741). She represents an inversion of expectation in which "the stock notion of Canaanite wickedness is ironized and radically relativized, if not demolished altogether" (742). She, as the first witness to God's cosmic sovereignty, stands in judgment on Israel, whose first named character after Joshua, Achan (ch. 7), becomes the paradigmatic sinner of the narrative.

Like Joshua and Achan, Rahab helps us understand the larger concerns of the story. As is evident elsewhere in Joshua, the warfare texts must be interpreted in terms of how they are placed within the book of Joshua and in the light of the motif of land acquired and lost in Deuteronomy and the DtrH. Rahab responds to God's gift-giving initiative by offering a voluntary confession. The first two chapters of Joshua, therefore, set the stage for the rest of the book by interpreting the entry into the land in the light of two great themes: faithfulness to God's instruction and voluntary commitment and confession *[Torah, p. 462]*.

Rahab now reveals the intent of her action and states the terms of her bargain (2:12-13). She wants a *sign of good faith* (*'emet*). On the basis of the "bond of obligation" she has initiated with the men, she requests life for life: their protection for hers. Although the spies try to turn the situation to their own advantage (v. 14), their oath returns to the heart of the matter: *when the Lord gives us the land*.

Having noted Rahab's confession of faith and her concession from the spies, we also observe that her terms include protection for her extended family. The men acknowledge her request by responding with plural pronouns: *Our life for yours* [pl.]. Consistent with ancient Israelite practice, faith is not assumed to be simply an individual matter. Rahab's identity hinges as much on her inclusion within a human family as within a faith family. This fact of her ready inclusion of her family may also contradict our expectations of her as a prostitute.

The response of the spies echoes both theologically freighted words that Rahab uses: *ḥesed*, covenant loyalty; and *'emet*, relational faithfulness or integrity (v. 14b). In spite of the potential for interpreting the spies' behavior throughout the story as either bungling or completely passive, their response indicates thorough acquaintance with Israel's theological and moral obligations within the confessional community.

The Escape Plan and Counter-concessions 2:15-21

If the density of theological language indicates that we have reached the heart of the narrative in verses 9-14, the narrator does not allow us to pause for a moment. The action continues immediately in verse 15: *She was about to let them down* (AT; NRSV and NIV: *she let them down*; on tenses and translation, see McCarthy 1971: 170–71). Instead of immediate action, the dialogue continues until "she sent them away" (v. 21). The narrator wants to keep the reader immersed in the action until the conclusion of the espionage mission has been reached.

But more is involved. The spies receive their escape instructions from Rahab (v. 16), yet before they make their getaway, they launch into an extended response to the oath with which they are bound. Although they have placed a condition on their oath (v. 14b), it is not verifiable. They are willing to comply with the terms of the treaty arrangement, but will Rahab live up to her end of the bargain? The spies' counterproposal is an attempt to verify Rahab's reliability. But it may also represent a sign of public confirmation of Rahab's confessional commitment. They obligate her to tie a crimson cord in the window *and* to gather her family into her house (vv. 18-20). They also reiterate their previous demand for silence (v. 20).

The scene ends with Rahab's affirming the spies' requirement and then tying the crimson cord in the window. The interchange should not be seen as exacting concessions from Rahab, but as a common pattern of negotiation involving mutual obligation and assurances. Rahab begins to confirm her commitment by her action. Confirmation of the spies' promise, however, remains open. Rahab makes that point in her emphatic final statement: *According to your words, so be it* (v. 21a).

That openness to the future fulfillment of the treaty entails risk. The spies have confessed their intentions in their final speech and risk being betrayed. Yet Rahab has already sided with Israel by refusing to cooperate with Jericho's king. Her hope lies entirely in her confession that *The LORD your God is indeed God in heaven above and on earth below* (2:11). Her allegiance is now with the divine king. Her life is completely in God's care.

The twice-mentioned crimson cord (vv. 18, 21) has been likened to the blood of the Passover lamb, so that Rahab's deliverance parallels that of the Israelites (Hauch: 104). The blood on the doorposts and the red cord may reflect a typological connection between Rahab and the Israelites. There is also a pun reflected in the Hebrew words: "The cord (*tiqwat*) is a sign of Rahab's waiting or hope (*tiqwat*). And it is scarlet (*shani*) because it is a signal to the two (*shney*) men who have made the oath" (Hawk 1991: 70).

Return and Report of Findings 2:22-24

The report continues by describing the departure of the spies and the unsuccessful search by the king's troops. The three-day span corresponds to Rahab's instructions (v. 16), suggesting her foresight and wisdom in giving instructions. It also highlights the thoroughness of the search (v. 22b). The spies are in the hill country, *the land* of verse 1, but the story is not interested in reconnaissance there. All that matters is what they have seen and heard in one place, from one woman. And that is what they report back to Joshua (v. 24). Although verse 23b states that they *told him all that had happened to them*, what they are reported as saying (and what is important for the story) is a direct quotation from Rahab's speech in verse 9. Like the earlier responses of the spies, this speech echoes Rahab's words for a reason. She is the central character in the story. This fact underscores the ironic elements in the story and focuses our attention on the reversals of expectation within the story.

The conclusion of the story confirms the conviction that the Rahab narrative (in which the spies play a minor role) depicts a model of divine operation. An alien prostitute makes a public confession of faith and is willing to risk a public declaration of that faith. The supposed threat, Rahab, ironically becomes the model of faithful confession. Her confession acknowledges the Lord's initiative in Israel's experience, but it also recognizes the cosmic lordship of Israel's God. This God does not have a limited perspective or purpose; the divine interests include the entire cosmos (heaven and earth). Although the spies' mission is to include viewing the land, they view only Rahab's home, and from that vantage point they frame a bold statement of trust in God. Yet that response to Joshua is couched completely in Rahab's own words. She, although an outsider, is the vehicle for conveying the pattern of all that follows. Her confession models the call to covenant faithfulness charged to Joshua, particularly in the charge to be faithful to the treaty book (1:7-8).

In recounting the great mercy and judgment of God in Israel's experience, Rahab speaks as one who knows and owns Israel's story as articulated in Deuteronomy. But she is also a challenge to a one-dimensional interpretation of that book. Although Deuteronomy demands extermination of all the inhabitants of the land, the first narrative of the book of Joshua depicts one of the inhabitants placing her hope in the story of God's faithfulness recorded within that same book. Rahab, we begin to suspect, is also one on whom the Lord may have mercy, not because of her strength or numbers (cf. Deut 7:7-11). By depicting an unlikely and ironic scenario, the story offers an alternate model for faithfulness in covenant and challenges narrow and limited perceptions of God's character and purposes.

THE TEXT IN BIBLICAL CONTEXT

The story of Rahab and the spies finds echoes in many biblical texts, some of which have already been cited above. Through explicit reference, allusion, and thematic similarity, this narrative shares in a larger biblical conversation about God's purposes and the identity of God's people. Most remarkably, Rahab has found her way into Matthew's genealogy of Jesus (Matt 1:5), into the roster of those who lived by faith in the book of Hebrews (11:31), and into an example of being justified by works (James 2:25).

Gentiles in the Family Tree

In Matthew's genealogy, Rahab shares company with Tamar, Ruth, and Bathsheba (see Nowell). All four are Gentile "outsiders." Jesus is born into a line that repeatedly "crossed" or "transgressed" the boundaries stipulated in Deuteronomy about not marrying foreign women. Their inclusion in Matthew's genealogy makes them part of his "key signature" announcing a larger concern in that Gospel for the inclusion of Gentiles (e.g., Matt 8:10-11; 12:15-21; 15:21-28; 21:43; 24:14; 28:16-20) and the welcoming of "the tax collectors and the prostitutes" (Matt 21:31; cf. 9:10). Only in Matthew's Gospel is the Syro-Phoenician woman called a Canaanite (Matt 15:22; cf. Mark

7:26). Rahab's presence in Matthew 1 comes to mind when reading about the so-called judgment of the nations (Gentiles) in Matt 25:31-46. As one who welcomes strangers (Matt 25:35, 43), she is "blessed by my Father" to "*inherit* the kingdom prepared for you" (Matt 25:34). In Hebrews (11:31), she is contrasted with the "disobedient" (who could that be but Achan?). Her faith is concretely described not as words alone, but as actively having "received the spies in peace." And James (2:25) tells us that she was "justified by works when she welcomed the messengers and sent them out by another road." James's concern is like that of Matthew: those who do the will of God share in the blessings of the kingdom (Matt 7:21, 24; 12:49-50). None of these references hint that her "faith" is somehow related to her orthodox confession.

The story affirms that God is the one looking after the interests of God's people. The real spy is God, who has already spied out a place (cf. Num 10:33; Ezek 20:6). The spies simply receive hospitality and hear a confession of faith. Because they gain no significant information on their own initiative, God's action, as identified by Rahab's confession, is the key to the text.

Yet in contrast to the "harlotry" depicted in Numbers 25, this harlot protects the two spies. In contrast to Israel's bowing to foreign gods in the wilderness, a foreign prostitute trusts Israel's God. And in contrast to the foreign women who have compromised Israel's faith in the wilderness, a foreign woman becomes a model of faithful confession about God's great deeds. Rahab as a "sinner" has proved to be more "righteous" than the "saints." The report of the ten spies (Num 14) "melted the hearts" of the people (cf. Deut 1:28); the two spies in Joshua report of the melting hearts of the Canaanites (Josh 2:9-11, 24; Hauch: 101–2). Rahab, contrary to expectation, risks an action without knowing the outcome. Her confession suggests that she trusts that outcome to a God about whom she has only heard. Whether by political strategy or wily courage, Rahab (as NT writers interpret her) is an example of living by faith.

Understanding Rahab's story in its larger biblical context creates a problem, however, when compared to Deuteronomy's instructions to utterly destroy the inhabitants of the land (Deut 7:2; ch. 20). According to Deuteronomic treaty obligations, the covenant with Rahab and the promise to spare her family seems to have been prohibited. Several suggestions have been offered. One option is that the narrator is a "critical traditionalist" for whom Deuteronomy forms the theological foundation for the narrative (Polzin). The writer, in contrast to Deuteronomy, wishes to suggest that strict legalism is not how Israel's story was actually lived out. Another suggestion is that the covenant with Rahab represents a "sinful covenant," since it violates the commandment in Deuteronomy *[Torah, p. 462]*. As such, this covenant foreshadows the ultimate demise of Israel since it has begun to allow foreigners in its midst (Eslinger: 42).

This impulse also emerges in the reading of the book in Ezra's time, only there the reading presents a literalistic, even xenophobic, interpretation of Deuteronomy 7:3, which entrenches the ethnic identity of Israel in the postexilic era. In Ezra, outsiders are excluded. In Deuteronomy, while they may not be considered "full members," they live as Israel, with Israel, and in Israel, as "People of the Book." That option seems not to be available to the foreigners in Ezra (contrast Chronicles: 1 Chron 22:2; 29:15; 2 Chron 2:16; 30:25; cf. Josh 20:9).

The book of Isaiah not only includes foreigners in its eschatological vision (2:2-4; 19:23-25; 56:6-8; 60:3; 66:18-20); it also bears witness to considerable tension between groups and emphasizes lack of faithfulness (which 63:17 blames on the Lord!). The prophet Jonah finds his lack of compassion for Nineveh challenged by God's decision to preserve the city and its inhabitants. And Ruth, a Moabite, marries Boaz, an Israelite. Even though she does not belong to the excluded seven nations of Deuteronomy 7:1-3, she is certainly marginalized by Deuteronomy 23:3, which states that no Moabite may be admitted to "the assembly of the LORD" (same word for "assembly" as in Josh 8:35). The Psalms include invitations for all nations to join in the worship of God (see Matties 2003).

Deuteronomic law served to protect Israel's exclusive loyalty to God. One of the ways of trying to assure such loyalty was to frame the problem as a danger arising from the indigenous Canaanite population. When the first such Canaanite actually appears on the scene in the person of Rahab, the law loses its cutting edge. A wedge has been inserted, and the narrative can proceed with the assumption that even those so-called outsiders have a place at the table. After all, even Deuteronomy encourages care for aliens "in your midst" (1:16; 5:14; 24:14-21).

The apostolic community of the first century worked hard at discerning which biblical laws continued to be valid for Jesus' followers. As the book of Acts reports, Gentile followers came to be welcomed into the fellowship (11:1-18) and were required to observe a limited range of laws (15:19-20). Of particular interest to the Rahab story (and later to that of Achan in Josh 7) is the encouragement "to abstain only from things polluted by idols" (Acts 15:20; cf. Col 3:5).

Hospitality, the Enemy, and Hope for the Nations

Rahab's confession of God's cosmic sovereignty echoes Deuteronomy: "So acknowledge today and take to heart that the LORD is God in heaven above and on earth beneath; there is no other" (4:39). This is the same confession that Solomon makes in his prayer at the dedication of the temple (1 Kings 8:23). The goal of this exclusive monotheism is that all peoples and all nations would recognize the Sovereign of all creation. Rahab is the first and most unlikely example of this hope. Her confession is more significant within the larger story of God's intentions than the destruction of Canaan's inhabitants.

Yet ironically, Rahab welcomes strangers. She is an improbable example of one who keeps the covenant obligations that follow from the confession of God's sovereignty (cf. Deut 4:39-40). In contrast to other stories in which strangers are welcomed, but with devastating consequences (Gen 19; Judg 19), Rahab protects as though she is thoroughly responsible to her covenant relationships (Hawk: 1992). The entire episode is structured, moreover, around the practice of hospitality, in which the host risks her life for her guests, thereby exhibiting the practice of loyalty (*ḥesed*). Rahab negotiates an arrangement of reciprocity. Her hospitality will surely be returned to her (Josh 2:12). In Genesis 19, Lot considers the help of the messengers an act of *ḥesed* (Gen 19:19). "As a true host, Lot was ready to sacrifice everything for his guests. As loyal guests, they came to his assistance" (Glueck: 44). The reciprocity of Rahab's guests is only realized in Joshua 6, which rounds out the host-guest paradigm. Hospitality to strangers is initiated by an unlikely woman, and it is offered in return against expectation and against the grain of Deuteronomic instruction regarding alliances with people of the land (Deut 7:2).

The parallel is more starkly drawn by several other similarities. In both Genesis 19 and Judges 19, the declaration of the guests that they will spend the night in the square (*reḥob*) corresponds to the name of Rahab, with the same Hebrew consonants (Judg 19:20; Gen 19:2). In Genesis 19, Lot's daughters had not "known" a man, whereas Rahab declares she *does not know* the men or where they have gone. In Genesis 19, the people of the city, like the messengers of the king in Joshua 2, call to bring out the guests. The similarities serve to emphasize the ironic plot of Joshua 2. "The correspondences elicit a mood of sinfulness, wrath, and doom" (Hawk 1991: 64–65). Rahab's story, however, evokes a sense of hope.

Similar hopes are offered in the history that follows the book of Joshua. Both Solomon and Hezekiah offer prayers that reflect the expectation that "all the peoples of the earth may know that the LORD is God; there is no other" (1 Kings 8:60; 2 Kings 19:19). Other confessions in the DtrH reflect a similar interest in acknowledging God's sovereignty: the Israelites on Mount Carmel in contrast to the worship of Baal (1 Kings 18:39); and Naaman the Syrian (2 Kings 5:15). Earlier Jethro, the Midianite, offered such a confession (Exod 18:11; cf. the many references to the acknowledgment of God's cosmic sovereignty in Exod 6:7; 7:5, 17; 8:10, 22; 9:14, 29; 10:2; 14:4, 18). The book of Isaiah, in reflecting on the problem of God's people living in exile, offers the hope that foreigners and eunuchs (56:3-7) as well as Egyptians, Ethiopians, and Sabeans will recognize the one Lord (45:14-15; cf. 44:5; 45:22-23; 49:7; 55:5; Hamlin 1983: 18–20). And Ezekiel, imagining a redrawing of the boundaries of the land, has "aliens who reside among you" sharing the "inheritance" with Israel (47:22-23). In the NT, the letter to the Ephesians echoes a welcome of Gentile "aliens" as "citizens with the saints" and "members of the household of God" (2:12, 19). Although some of those texts, like Isaiah 45:14-15, depict this recognition of God in language that is imperialistic and triumphalistic, the critical thread by which we contextualize these hopes is the promise that blessing is to flow to all peoples (Gen 12:1-3). The election of Abraham's family is an election of service, not of domination.

Rahab is not the only biblical model of unlikely trust and faith. Besides Ruth and Naaman, consider the widow of Zarephath in Sidon (1 Kings 17:9), the Ninevites (Jon 3:6-9), and Roman soldiers (Matt 8:5, 10; 27:54; Acts 10). God's hope is for all peoples of the earth to imitate Rahab's hospitable action, join her confession, and become a partner in God's peoplehood (Zech 8:20-23; Matt 8:11-12; Rev 7:9-17). These examples throughout the Bible, and even within the documents that comprise the DtrH, suggest that God's faithfulness to Israel is a means through which God intends all people to acknowledge God's cosmic sovereignty.

A New Way of Seeing

Even as Rahab's confession of a new God with a new story represents a new basis for shaping identity and for understanding power, the spies represent a reversal of sorts as well. The spy narrative, we have observed, raises suspicions because of the memory of failure to perceive the Lord's purposes. In Numbers 32 the negative response of the spies is associated with the request of the Gadites and

Reubenites for land east of the Jordan (Num 32:5, 7-15, 23). Could it be that the positive report of the spies in Joshua 2 is to be read alongside the positive promise of obedience by the Transjordan tribes in Joshua 1? In that way we recognize a reversal in two dimensions: the sin of the former spies is reversed in Joshua 2 just as the negative request of the Transjordan tribes is reversed in Joshua 1.

The reversals and ironic elements of Rahab's story lead us to ask whether this story, along with the preparatory first chapter, provides clues to the central focus of the book. The Transjordan tribes, the spies, and Rahab all represent ambiguous characters in the larger biblical narrative. Just as Joshua 1 invites us to reflect on the theme of faithfulness by an unlikely group of *Israelites* who have chosen to reside *outside* the land, so Joshua 2 invites us to reflect on the faithfulness of an *outsider* who dwells *inside* the gifted land (Polzin). Joshua 1 and 2 together suggest that peoplehood is constituted by commitment (Josh 1) and confession (Josh 2). Peoplehood is not constructed simply by ethnic identity and geographical location. Reading Joshua 2 in the light of its own literary and theological context, and in the context of the entire canon of Scripture, we find patterns for response and models for identity that correspond to a larger vision of the purposes of God.

Joshua 2 offers readers a way of seeing that shatters expectations. Foreigners are not simply those whom God will destroy for their wickedness, but also those who may confess the cosmic sovereignty of Israel's God. Israel is not simply a people who fails to recognize the purposes of God, as did spies of a previous generation, but a people who can also confess that God is the giver of the land and the one who can be trusted. Israel may even learn to trust again in exile as it sees foreigners embracing Israel's cosmic Sovereign. And just as Rahab's story reminds readers of the earlier account of how Israel came to be constituted by various groups of peoples (a "mixed crowd," Exod 12:38), she now becomes a paradigm of faith for later readers. But more, Israel is invited to make its confession of faith in imitation of her, even as the spies, who use her very words, do. Yet her *action*, not simply her confession of faith, has become paradigmatic for writers of the NT.

THE TEXT IN THE LIFE OF THE CHURCH

Early church fathers interpreted the chapter focusing on Rahab as one of the most important parts of the book (see Origen; Daniélou; Drucker; Auld 1999). As Auld declares, "She was saved by her faith and her hospitality; the scarlet cord given her by the messengers of Joshua/Jesus was a sign of salvation by the Lord's blood; and her example is endorsed by Jesus' statement to religious leaders of his time that publicans and courtesans proceed them into the kingdom" (1999: 626).

Rahab Still Speaks

The church does well to reflect on how we draw lines of inclusion and exclusion in God's community, whether those lines are drawn ethnically, geographically, or by notions of purity. That Rahab the outsider becomes an insider by confession of faith is surely instructive even as her hospitality before her confession illuminates her faith and indicates the integrity of her character. Her actions are ironic in the light of Deuteronomy, where Canaanites are to be exterminated, yet "aliens" are to be treated with respect. She therefore represents the radical change of loyalty to which Joshua, at the end of the book, invites Israel. Her story is paradigmatic for she, an unlikely outsider, is the first to make a commitment to the radical monotheism of Deuteronomy. She represents the motif "that they may know," which courses through the first fourteen chapters of the book of Exodus.

John Howard Yoder suggests that the church is a voluntary community made up of people who have freely chosen to become part of the community that seeks "to be an instrument of the will of God." This understanding of the church as "a voluntary community" is rooted in the sixteenth-century Schleitheim Confession, in which baptism "shall be given to all those who have been taught repentance and the amendment of life" (Yoder 2003: 126). Yet in some strange way, Rahab's action and confession of faith defy convention. No community approves her qualifications for entry and guards the boundaries of inclusion. Although Yoder in another place speaks about the "good news" of "Abrahamic particularity" (1984: 55), Rahab's action and confession of God's cosmic sovereignty is the "good news" that transcends that particularity. By giving Rahab a paradigmatic position in the book of Joshua, the narrator has made her a shaper of communal identity. Rahab is not only an ideal figure (to be emulated), but also a figure who stands as a perpetual critique of established ways of defining inclusion and exclusion.

Of course, many contemporary readers of the Rahab story may be reluctant (unlike NT writers and most premodern readers of Joshua) to view Rahab as prototypical in that way. By contrast, her story continues to challenge our memory of what kinds of community boundaries are worth upholding. Rahab's story invites us to consider whether the church is defined by boundaries, or whether the church is defined by a clear center with porous boundaries. At least the story begins to call into question the validity of ethnic and geographical boundaries; it offers the option that generous hospitality and single-minded loyalty to one cosmic Sovereign are the center toward which the community strives as it knows itself to be embraced by the love of God.

In the contemporary conflict between Israelis and Palestinians, Rahab would be considered a "collaborator." Like many such collaborators, Rahab may act in order to save her life. But the story confirms that her action and confession constitute the first paradigmatic "moment" in the larger story of the conquest. Because of their paradigmatic character, both Rahab's story and that of the Gibeonites (Josh 9) imply that inclusion into Israel, either by confession or collusion/trickery, is the better alternative to wholesale warfare and extermination. In both stories ethnicity, geography, and nationalism are subverted in favor of God's cosmic sovereignty, the priority of covenant loyalty, and a vision of radical hospitality (for a similar reading from a Palestinian Christian perspective, see Isaac). Neither Rahab's ethnicity nor the Gibeonites' geographic origin determines their identities nor, in the end, are adequate criteria for exclusion from the people of God.

In our own identification with the Rahab story, we might create space for unexpected actions and words, confessional and prophetic, from unexpected and unlikely sources. We might align ourselves with her in saying yes to radical monotheism and no to our contemporary allegiances that tend to shape our identity more than we might like to admit. We might identify ourselves with the helpless and hapless spies who, being powerless, are welcomed and protected by an unlikely host. Her hospitality—welcoming enemies—is about as risky a venture as one could engage. We are reminded of Corrie ten Boom and many other Gentiles who harbored Jews and others during the Second World War. Even today Jews recognize their actions as "righteous." There is an Avenue of the Righteous Gentiles at *Yad VaShem*, the Holocaust memorial in Jerusalem, and an online index at the memorial's website (see, e.g., Hellman).

If Rahab is indeed a model for the ancient narrator, we can conclude that her story, with its skillful irony, reversals of expectation, and intrabiblical allusion, offers us insight into the trajectory of

God's purpose. Her story registers a prophetic protest, offering us criteria by which to evaluate difficult aspects of Joshua's narrative. The story leads us into reflection on the identity of God's people and on the shape of God's purposes for humankind *to this day*.

Joshua 3:1–4:24

Crossing into the Promise: Holy Lord and Holy People

PREVIEW

This episode has been etched in Israel's memory even as it has become the source for countless hymns and folk songs that borrow the motif of "crossing Jordan." Anyone who has visited the banks of the Jordan River knows that it is not "chilly and cold." It could be, however, that a return to the "other side" is a kind of death, with its memory of return to wilderness or the experience of exile in Babylon. But in the biblical imagination, the Jordan River was never the equivalent of the Greek river Styx, across which the land of the dead was said to lie.

The biblical story was told time and again to remind Israel of God's actions in the past, to challenge Israel's faith and commitment in the present, and to generate hope for the future. In the book of Micah, for example, the prophet reminds Israel of "what happened from Shittim to Gilgal" (6:5). Why is it that Micah invites the people to reflect on this sequence of events as Israel has remembered them? As the prophet continues, we find the answer: "that you may know the saving acts of the LORD." These acts are, in Israel's memory and confession, past, present, and future.

The narrative about the crossing of the Jordan is therefore about more than movement across the boundary of the Jordan River. The story reaches back to the exodus for its typological allusions; it is grounded in the confidence of God's presence, and it marks a significant transition from the wilderness era. By joining the theme of God's cosmic sovereignty (begun in ch. 2) with the instruction theme, the narrative takes on a distinctly catechetical flavor (3:7, 10; 4:6, 14, 21).

The story of the crossing is not, however, a matter-of-fact account. The people do not simply cross the river and begin to settle down in the land in whatever way they deem convenient. As we shall see, the entire narrative reflects a thoughtful compilation that resembles a liturgical, or worship, event. This emphasis is a clue that not all is ready for the crossing and the receiving of the land-gift. The story begins with notices about the procession of the ark of the covenant and the command to sanctify the people (3:3-5) and concludes with the summary catechetical statement (4:21-24). Within the text we often find ourselves puzzled by the sequence of events and the overlapping descriptions of action. Why is the crossing recounted so many times? Where are the stones placed? Where are the priests standing? From which vantage point is the narrator telling the story?

All of this suggests that the crossing of the Jordan is a highly theological enterprise. As a conclusion to the larger story of exodus-wilderness-gift of land sequence, this story not only echoes the exodus event in many of its details; it also presents a dramatic contrast between the chaos symbolism of the wilderness and the order/fertility symbolism of the land (cf. 5:12; Thompson: 356; Hawk 1991: 95). But the narrative not only looks back; it also ripples forward in its exaltation of Joshua as the model of leadership, its anticipation of recognition of the universal dominion of God, and its emphasis on the holiness of the worshiping community in the holy place of God's gift.

OUTLINE

Setting the Stage: Camping at the Jordan, 3:1
Instructions for Preparation, 3:2-5
Instructions for Crossing the Jordan, 3:6-13
The Crossing, 3:14-17
Memorial of the Stones, 4:1-10
Conclusion of the Crossing, 4:11-14
Coming Up out of the Jordan, 4:15-18
Encampment at Gilgal, 4:19-24

This outline focuses on transitions within the text that convey the movement across the Jordan River (the verb "to cross" occurs twenty-two times). This text shares in a unifying seven-day symbolic chronology depicted in the first five chapters, culminating on the fourteenth day (5:10), a seven-day sequence that is repeated in the Jericho incident (Josh 6). These seven days may be linked in this way: Day 8 (1:11; 2:1); Day 9 (3:1); Day 10 (3:2; 4:19; implying that Joshua sets out without waiting for the spies; cf. 2:16, 22); Days 11-13 (at Gilgal; 4:20-5:9); Day 14 (5:10; Boling 1982: 190; Wilcoxen 1968: 60–64; Winther-Nielsen: 173). In addition, the sequence of events in chapters 3–4 include "flashbacks" (Winther-Nielsen: 176; see Explanatory Notes). Thus, although there is a movement forward in the story as a whole, chapters 3–4 fold back in the telling.

EXPLANATORY NOTES

Setting the Stage: Camping at the Jordan 3:1

After hearing a positive report from the spies and without losing time, Joshua moves *all the Israelites* from Shittim to the Jordan and sets up camp. The expression *all the Israelites* is repeated deliberately throughout the text (3:7, 17; 4:14; also *the entire nation*, 3:17; 4:1). The repetition emphasizes the unity of the people under Joshua's singular leadership *[All Israel, p. 385]*.

Joshua's action takes up the narrative thread initiated in 1:10-11. He is now in a position to act on God's initial command to cross the Jordan with "all this people" (1:2) into the land that God has given (1:2, 11; 2:9, 14, 24). As the story is told, Joshua moves the people from Shittim to the Jordan (3:1), apparently without waiting for the spies' report (cf. 1:11; 3:2). After the alleged response of the inhabitants of the land, nothing stands in the way. Or so we are led to expect.

The crossing of this important boundary signifies the crossing from wilderness and chaos to gifted land of promise and blessing. That blessing is symbolized in 5:12, the last verse of the next unit, which tells of eating the crops of the land that year. But the crossing may also be ominous, for this is a crossing into the land of other gods. Since the same verb can be translated "to cross" and "to transgress," depending on the context, the threat represented by Rahab (ch. 2) is heightened by the danger of another kind of transgression—that of worshiping the deities of the land. Joshua highlights this very risk in 23:16, where he raises the possibility that they might *transgress the covenant* and *serve other gods* (cf. Josh 7:11, 15; see Hawk 1991: 72).

Instructions for Preparation 3:2-5

Instructional speeches follow the narrative introduction. The reference to the passing of three days and the mention of the officers takes us back to Joshua's command in 1:10-11 and implies the return of the spies (cf. *three days* in 2:16, 22). Both the officers and Joshua speak in the sequence that follows (3:3-6). The officers prepare the people to follow the ark of the covenant across the Jordan and to keep their distance from the ark (3:3-4). In only one other biblical text does the ark have the role of leading the people (Num 10:33). As the portable throne of Israel's divine king, the ark fulfills the promise of divine presence (1:9). *Ark* is a key term in chapters 3–4, occurring twelve times (again in Josh 6:4, 6, 7, 11, 12, 13; 7:6; 8:33; see also 1 Sam 4–6; 2 Sam 6; and a few other times until 1 Kings 8, after which it does not appear in the DtrH).

The complete expression *ark of the covenant of the Lord your God* (3:3) is found elsewhere in the OT only in Deuteronomy 31:26. The context in Deuteronomy reaches back as far as Deuteronomy 27, which begins with instructions for an altar at Mount Ebal "when you have crossed over" (27:3). The importance of "the words of this law" (27:3) anticipate Joshua 8:30-35 and the altar building and reading of Torah in that scene.

The ark's prominence in Joshua, therefore, corresponds to its role as the "keeper of the book." Identified as the *ark of the covenant*, it contains the stipulations of the relationship between God and people, the Ten Commandments. In addition, the ark is identified in Joshua 3:11, 13 with *the Lord of all the earth.* This reference to the ark as symbolizing the cosmic King echoes Rahab's confession of *God in heaven above and on earth below* (2:11) and accounts for the required distance from the ark (3:4). Since the people *have not passed this way before* (3:4), they must rely only on their divine guide, now represented by the divine instructions embodied in the written Torah. Israel is to cross into a land and be guided, not by a moveable box, but by that which it contains divine instruction. The Hebrew word order in verses 3b-4 places the instruction about keeping *a distance* immediately after the command to *follow*, after which comes the *so that* clause, emphasizing the fact that the ark will empower Israel to *know the way you should go* (emph. added). That phrase introduces a word picture often used in the OT for the divine instruction (cf. Pss 86:11; 119:1; Jer 7:23). Significantly the *levitical priests* are the ones who carry the ark. According to some OT traditions, they are responsible for the tabernacle (Num 1:50) and for guarding Torah (Deut 17:18; 24:8; 27:14; 31:25-26; 33:8-10; cf. Aaron as teacher, Lev 10:10-11).

Although following the ark will involve obedience to Torah, it will also involve a certain theopolitical risk. The ark was certainly used and misused later in Israel's story as its leaders thought of the ark as a talisman, or a guarantee of victory and imperialistic expansion. Yet the ark also presents an implicit critique of military power (cf. 1 Sam 4:1–7:2; 2 Sam 6). This becomes evident in 1 Samuel 6. As soon as the ark returns on its own (1 Sam 6), Samuel calls on the people to "put away the foreign gods . . . from among you. Direct your heart to the LORD and serve him only, and he will deliver you out of the hand of the Philistines" (1 Sam 7:3). Thus the call in Joshua 3 to follow the ark requires trust in God alone and ultimately leads to Joshua's call to *put away the foreign gods* and choose to serve God alone (Josh 24:14, 23-24). The ark represents the divine actor in history: the living God and cosmic Lord (Josh 3:11, 13; Exod 15:8, 11, 18).

At this point Joshua speaks for the first time. He tells the people, *Sanctify yourselves.* The Lord is about to *do wonders among you* (3:5). The story begins, therefore, by focusing on Israel's real leader, God. The ark moves well ahead of the people not only because of the danger of their polluting the sphere of divine holiness, but also because this God is to be followed without human attempts to manage the path to be taken. Israel's leader is a servant of Israel's divine King and obeys God's instructions.

Joshua's instruction to the people in 3:5 is important, therefore, since it implies an ethical counterpart to the Lord's holiness. Joshua gives no instructions about ritual activity but commands them, *Make yourselves holy* (lit.). That includes taking care that all activity corresponds to the laws of ritual purity. This purification is intended to prepare the people for an encounter with their holy Lord (cf. Exod 19:10-15, 22; Num 11:18; Deut 23:9-14). By crossing the Jordan and following the ark, the people are about to experience the work of the Lord, who "travels along with your camp" (Deut 23:14). According to Deuteronomy, Israel's ritual purity (holiness) corresponds to the purity of divine presence. This traveling Lord is present "to save you and to hand over your enemies to you, therefore your camp must be holy, so that he may not see anything indecent among you and turn away from you" (Deut 23:14).

Ritual and moral purity permitted Israel to dwell in God's presence. P. D. Miller suggests that the holiness Joshua calls for is required "because the war was sacral, a sphere of divine activity in which Israel's God was present" (1973: 157). Yet the text does not identify holiness with the act of warfare itself. The narrative emphasizes the *wonders* that the Lord will do. God's presence and actions alone call for ritual and moral integrity. This observation need not blind us from recognizing that Israel did fight its enemies. But the stress in this statement lies elsewhere, as it does in the hinge text Joshua 5:13-15. The liturgical and instructional motifs in the narrative suggest as well that the Lord's wonders are to be celebrated in the community that is receiving the gift of land. Part of that celebration involves the response of ritual and moral integrity. The worshiping community is therefore invited to be a holy community (cf. 5:15; 7:13; 24:19).

Instructions for Crossing the Jordan 3:6-13

Although the sequence of speeches continues to 3:13, verse 6 makes a transition, having Joshua initiate the crossing by instructing the priests to make their move (cf. v. 3). Then verses 7-8 interrupt Joshua's speech to the priests and the people (vv. 9-13), with God's speaking only to Joshua (vv. 7-8). Including the speech would not have been necessary if the text's purpose were simply to report the events. But it highlights the theme of God's presence with Joshua and the parallel with Moses from the Lord's speech in 1:5. The emphasis on Joshua as the one who will give orders to the priests and people suggests a parallel not often recognized between the two men. Joshua, like Moses, will be a spokesperson for God and one who acts on God's initiative (Boling 1982: 163; cf. other references to God's speeches to Joshua in 1:1; 4:1, 15; 5:9; 6:2). In that role Joshua too carries out a prophetic function. Joshua's exaltation does highlight his accomplishments or establish the validity of hierarchical leadership in the faith community. It confirms him as an instrument for recognizing God's presence through the word. Joshua's theologically freighted speech to the people (vv. 9-13) bears that out.

Joshua introduces his speech by inviting the people to *Draw near and hear the words of the* L*ORD* *your God* (v. 9). The motif of hearing the words of God is drawn from Deuteronomy. This motif continues in the book of Joshua (5:6; 8:30-35) up to Joshua's closing admonitions to *observe and do all that is written in the book of the law of Moses* (23:6). God is the One who leads, who commands, and who, through Joshua, speaks (cf. Deut 4:13; 10:4) *[Torah, p. 462]*. It seems as though this *word* is not only the written word of Moses' book (1:8), but also a spoken word that continues to direct and guide along the way (3:4). Joshua is exalted as mediator of the divine word. The goal of that exaltation, although mediated through human figures like Joshua and Moses, is *that they may know that I will be with you* (3:7). The text is thoroughly theocentric: God is the truly exalted one.

In Joshua, the emphasis on divine presence is especially significant not only because God is *with* Israel, but also because this God who is *among you is the living God* (3:10), who is also *the Lord of all the earth* (3:11, 13). This intimation of cosmic sovereignty reaches its climax at the end of chapter 4, in the second catechetical statement: *so that all the peoples of the earth may know that the hand of the* LORD *is mighty* (4:24; cf. 3:7). This dual motif of "know" and "hand" occurs throughout the exodus story, culminating in the question and answer in Exodus 15 concerning Yahweh's rank among the gods (15:11, 18).

The double reference to *the Lord of all the earth* (vv. 11, 13) provides the theological context for the list of seven peoples (v. 10). These seven represent the symbolic completeness of the groups that have set up independent city-states in the wake of the Egyptian failure to maintain political control of the land (cf. Deut 7:1; Josh 12:7-24, mentioning thirty-one kings; and the Amarna letters, found at Amarna, Egypt, reflecting initial losses of Egyptian control of Canaanite city-states in the fourteenth century BC). In the context of the declaration of *the living God* in verse 10a, and the cosmic sovereignty of God in verses 11 and 13, the list of seven people groups highlights God's sovereignty, not only over Israel, but also over all people groups (cf. Deut 2–3; 32:8-9) *[Dispossessed Peoples, p. 424]*.

The specificity of this list prompts a look ahead at the rest of the book of Joshua, where similar lists appear (9:1; 11:3; 12:8; 24:11). Although the promise is that the Lord will give the land (1:2-4), we know that in many cases the indigenous population continues to live within the gifted land (13:1-7, 13). In 13:6 the Lord is reported as saying again, *I will myself drive them out*. Of the list of seven in 3:10, only the first and the last are specifically mentioned in the land-allotment as remaining (Canaanites in 17:12, Jebusites in 15:63).

Why then do we read in 3:10 that the Lord will *without fail* drive out these seven peoples? How is this divine speech to be understood in the context of the entire book? Clearly the book presents a tension between promise and reality *[Plot Tensions in Joshua, p. 452]*. We know from history, as well as from archaeological research, that Israel always lived in a world of mixed peoples *[Archaeology and Joshua, p. 389]*. Jerusalem, for example, seems still to have been occupied by Jebusites when it was captured in King David's time (2 Sam 5:6-9; cf. Judg 1:8; 1:21; and 2 Sam 5:7).

Perhaps the narrator depicts the settlement in the land as a tension between promise and reality because the indigenous population, like Rahab, represent a threat. The threat is not ethnic difference, but the worship of other gods (cf. the Rabshakeh's speech, 2 Kings 18:25, 33-35). This notion comes through in other such lists of peoples in the OT (see Gen 15:18-21; Exod 3:8, 17; 13:5; 23:23, 28; 33:1-2; 34:10-16; Num 13:29; Deut 7:1; 20:17; Judg 3:5-6; 1 Kings 9:20; Ezra 9:1-2; Neh 9:8. For an analysis of these lists, see Hostetter). A good number of those lists are set in contexts of divine promise of land, of assurance of God's help, or of the danger of worshiping the gods of those peoples. Of particular interest is the tension between divine agency and human action. Several texts mention exclusively the divine agency in the process of driving out the indigenous inhabitants (e.g., Exod 14:14; 15:15-16; 23:27-28; 33:2; 34:11-16; Deut 1:30; 20:4; Josh 3:10), especially those set in the context of promise (e.g., Gen 15:18-21; Exod 3:8, 17; 13:5; 33:1-2; but cf. Deut 7:19-24; Neh 9:8, 24-25). The opposite seems to be the case in other texts (e.g., Num 13:30; 33:52-53; Deut 2:24; 20:17; Josh 12:7; see Hostetter: 128–31).

More significant than the question of divine or human agency, however, is the concern about worship. These lists are set in contexts where covenant with these inhabitants is prohibited (Exod 23:32; 34:12, 15; Deut 7:2). Israel is not to worship their gods (Exod 23:24; 34:13; Deut 7:5). Intermarriage is forbidden (Deut 7:3; cf. Gen 24:3; 28:1-9; contra Gen 38:2; 46:10). Counter-examples illustrate that it is not intermarriage in itself that is the problem (even Joseph and Moses married Egyptian women), but worship (cf. 2 Kings 11:4). Related to these prohibitions, however, is the assumption that the indigenous population is immoral (Gen 15:16; Deut 9:4). According to the priestly concern for land, abominable behavior would lead to the land's vomiting out its inhabitants, whether indigenous or Israelite (Lev 18:28; 20:22-24; Hostetter: 129–30). OT texts assume a universal moral reality accessible to all (e.g., Amos 1–2). The DtrH falls back on the moral argument as well as on the practice of idolatry for its explanation of Israel's expulsion from the land (Deut 9:3-5) *[Idolatry, p. 438]*. According to Deuteronomy, Israel's displacement of indigenous peoples is part of a metahistorical impulse in which earlier peoples also displaced others (Deut 2–3). Such displacement stands in some tension, however, with the notion that people groups and their lands have been apportioned according to Yahweh's allotment of the gods, an allotment that has reserved Israel and its gifted land for Yahweh alone (Deut 32:8-9; cf. Gen 10) *[Land: Gifted and Lost, p. 440]*.

The list of seven nations also prompts us to look back to Deuteronomy. There, in a different order, we find with a list of seven a note that the Lord will "clear away" the nations (Deut 7:1). These nations are described as "mightier and more numerous than you," which emphasizes the impossibility of human means to accomplish the task and calls to mind the need for God's own activity (Deut 1:30; 20:4; 31:6). Although Deuteronomy 7 does not rule out human battle (v. 2), it does make it clear, from the Deuteronomic perspective, why the nations are a dangerous presence in the land. They will turn God's people "to serve other gods" (v. 4; cf. Deut 6:14). Although Deuteronomy 7 refers to driving the inhabitants out "little by little" because of potential increase in the wild animal population (Deut 7:22; cf. Exod 23:29-33), the book of Joshua, even in referring later to the incompleteness of possession of the land-gift, does not mention that motive. In dispossessing the indigenous population and in stopping the flow of the Jordan, Joshua 3 puts the emphasis on the wonders performed by God, the Lord of all.

This accent leads us to refrain from providing a naturalistic explanation for the stopping of the water, first mentioned in Joshua's instructions to the people (v. 13). Although such an explanation may well be compatible with God's activity in human experience (e.g., a collapsing riverbank upstream), this text takes pains to emphasize that God's presence alone accounts for the crossing and the receiving of the land-gift. The note in verse 15 about high water (see below) heightens the miraculous element in the story, since *the Lord of all the earth* is about to act (vv. 11, 13).

The Crossing 3:14-17

The narrative of the crossing in verses 14-17 bears out what Joshua has said. The report reiterates the words of God and Joshua. By repeating words and phrases from verses 8-13, the story illustrates that God's words through Joshua become reality. The special mention of the high water level heightens the miraculous element in the story. Yet it is not so much a flood (as NRSV and NIV assume), but high water (implied by NJPS *flowing over its entire bed throughout the harvest season*), since the river remains high during harvest (late spring, early summer), but diminishes during the summer itself (cf. 4:18). Verse 17 summarizes the story of the people's crossing and provides a bridge to the next major section. Joshua's command for the people to select *twelve men* (3:12), however, seems to presuppose the Lord's command in 4:2. The twofold use of the word *dry ground* in verse 17 (and again in 4:18; cf. synonym in 4:22) links this text to the exodus story (Exod 14:21) and the Elijah story (2 Kings 2:8). The crossing is punctuated by the word *finished* (3:16, NIV *completely*; 3:17; 4:1, 10, 11; cf. 5:8), which later in the text is linked specifically to the motif of having done what *the LORD commanded Joshua to tell the people, according to all that Moses had commanded Joshua* (4:10). The narrator's summary here makes it clear that the crossing is taking place by divine directive, not at Joshua's initiative.

Memorial of the Stones 4:1-10

Just as 3:17 summarizes the previous section and provides a bridge to what follows, 4:1 summarizes and looks forward. Again the initiative comes from God to Joshua. Joshua is to select twelve men and have them pick up twelve stones from the middle of the Jordan. They are to set the stones down at the place where they camp for the night. God commands, and Joshua repeats the command, yet not in a word-for-word repetition. Joshua actually cuts short the details of God's instruction in order to add his own reflections on the significance of the stones (vv. 4-7). Hence, instead of repeating God's words, Joshua interprets them. Only in the report of verse 8 do we read that the twelve have done as they were instructed, including placing the stones at the camp. In spite of a clarification of that action in 4:20, we find an odd and unexplained reference in 4:9 to a second heap of stones in the middle of the river.

Instead of giving the men instruction about where to place the stones, as we might expect, Joshua suggests that the stones *may be a sign among you* (4:6a; cf. 4:21). Verses 6-7, therefore, mark a teachable moment within the sequence of command and action. In this case the *sign* (*'ot*) is to be an aid to historical memory and a motive for asking questions about the meaning of the past. Setting up memorial stones was common in the ancient world. The stones are to spark interest in children (cf. Deut 6:2, 7, 20-25; Exod 12:26-27; 13:14-15) and presumably also in adults of future generations. But the stones are important only in their function to generate an occasion for storytelling *[Twelve Stones, p. 465]*. The use of the expression *memorial* (*zikkaron*) *forever* (v. 7) reinforces the instructional theme. Over time, centuries after the composition of this text, the stones would no longer be visible, and thus the story of the crossing takes the place of the stones. This transformation of the memorial stones into narrative allows future generations to identify with the crossing (cf. Deut 5:2-3). The story becomes the testimony to later readers of the *wonders* that *the Lord* will perform (3:5).

Conclusion of the Crossing 4:11-14

The hope in the story is found in how the instruction of the Lord corresponds to the obedient responses of Joshua and the people. Although the action-command sequence makes the text appear repetitive, it serves to highlight the motif of hearing and obeying. The twelve men have done as they were told (vv. 8-9). The priests stand in the middle of the Jordan (v. 10), and the people cross over *in haste* (v. 10). Verse 11 then begins the summary, beginning with people (v. 11a), ark and priests (v. 11b), and Transjordan tribes (v. 12a).

The duplication in the text emphasizes that all has been done according to the instruction of the Lord and of Moses (vv. 10, 12), a motif that highlights the results of attending to *the words of the* LORD *your God* (3:9). The action has been *finished* (vv. 10, 11) in keeping with what God has commanded (vv. 10, 12). This double mention of the completion of action and Moses as mediator of divine instruction "reinforces and advances the plot of obedient Israel as it enters the land to obtain Yahweh's promise" (Hawk 1991: 71). The mention of the Transjordan tribes ties the story to 1:12-18, reminding readers of the continuing obedience of these tribes, and looks ahead to 22:7-34 and the ominous events there. Obedience to the Lord's instruction stands out as the central theme. Even so, the reader recalls earlier narratives about murmuring in the wilderness and is aware of the ambiguity of obedience as criterion for keeping the gift of land *[Land: Gifted and Lost, p. 440]*.

The summarizing in verses 12-13 reminds us of Joshua's instructions in 1:14. The fact that the Transjordan tribes are prepared for battle stands in tension with the overall thrust of the passage, which highlights the acts of God. Although the narrator may be using older narrative sources that recount battles more freely, in this context he wishes to downplay the element of human participation in order to present a model for thinking about God in relation to human action and responsibility. More specifically, verse 12 shares the language of Exod 13:18, where the same word is used for battle readiness (*ḥamušim*). There the battle equipment proved unnecessary, so it has an ironic function (cf. Exod 14:14). By noting it again here, the narrator invites wonder about whether human battle preparation is of any value. The fact that both Joshua's instructions (1:14) and the narrator's summary report (4:12-13) instruct the Transjordan tribes to be *armed* indicates an ideology of human participation in divine judgment (cf. Num 31:3; 32:20-22a; Deut 3:18) *[Theology of Warfare, p. 458]*. The allusion to the narrative in Numbers is striking. There Moses tells the Transjordan tribes that after crossing the Jordan, they will go "before the LORD for the war . . . until he has driven out his enemies from before him and the land is subdued before the LORD" (32:20-22a). The reminiscence of that narrative here in the story of the crossing is significant for understanding Joshua because the text of Joshua 4:12-13 emphasizes that the Transjordan tribes are *armed* even though it is clear that all Israel is also *armed for war . . . for battle* (4:13). Israel will fight. But the story does not stay there long.

The pause in the narrative at verse 14 indicates that God's announcement of 3:7 has become a reality. The people stand in awe of Joshua *as they had stood in awe of Moses.* God has demonstrated God's presence with Joshua, as God had been with Moses (3:14; cf. 1:9). And that divine presence has been made known for the benefit of the entire community. Readers will be reminded of the expression *all the days of his life*, which recurs in modified form in 24:31. Joshua's exaltation serves the larger purpose of making known—to *all the peoples of the earth* (4:24) and to Israel—*all the work that the* LORD *did for Israel* (24:31).

Coming Up Out of the Jordan 4:15-18

Verse 15 introduces God's final command of the crossing episode. As God commands, Joshua reiterates and the priests obey. The result is that the Jordan returns to its place as before (v. 18; see above at 3:15). The crossing is complete. The words *finished* and *dry ground* also occur in this section, which remind the reader of 3:14-17 and 4:10-11.

Encampment at Gilgal 4:19-24

Verse 19 marks a transition in the narrative by summarizing the previous sequence and by adding new information. The narrative that follows refers back to the twelve stones (4:8), the instructional theme of the children's questions, the motif of recognition of the Lord (4:6), and the theological meaning of the twelve stones (4:7). As a response to the children's question about the meaning of the stones (4:21), the "memorial" stones of 4:7 are now interpreted in 4:24 in rich theological language. The unit ends in marked contrast to the response of the kings in 5:1, whose "hearing" brings about a different kind of fear from that hoped for in 4:24.

Now we learn that Gilgal is the place of encampment and the location of the twelve stones (v. 19) *[Twelve Stones, p. 465]*. The place itself might be unimportant, except that it implicitly situates the people in Benjaminite territory. Also noteworthy is its significance as a cultic site during the monarchy. Here both Saul's and David's kingship was recognized (1 Sam 11:15; 2 Sam 19:15, 40). Ironically, the prophets identify Gilgal as one of the places associated with great transgression (Hos 9:15; 12:11; Amos 4:4; 5:5; but cf. Mic 6:5) *[Archaeology and Joshua, p. 389].*

The addition of the date, *the tenth day of the first month* (v. 19), confirms the interest of the story in depicting the crossing in terms of a worship event in which God leads people in a procession that culminates in recognizing God's grandeur. The date connects the crossing with the celebration of Passover, as recounted in 5:10-11. The tenth day of the first month (the beginning of spring in the biblical calendar) would have been the day for choosing the lambs for the Passover meal (Exod 12:3; Butler 1983: 50). These details help us to recognize that the story aims not simply to report history, but also to establish a model of the faithful worshiping community, responding to the fulfillment of promise and divine presence.

That response appears again in the reiteration of the catechetical question *When your children ask* (v. 21; cf. 4:6). The context of the question this time is the home, even though the setting of the story is the cultic site of Gilgal. Parents are specifically instructed to teach their children. If the festival setting of the story suggests that instruction has once belonged to the priests in public contexts, the emphasis on the parental role offers a way of instructing future generations even in times when such institutions no longer exist (Boling 1982: 186).

The simple answer to the children expands in a style typical of Deuteronomic teaching (vv. 23-24). Joshua continues Moses' role in shaping the theological memory and identity of the people. The story draws a parallel between Red Sea and Jordan River. Storytelling forms the identity of the next generation by establishing correspondences that will become paradigmatic not only for shaping the memory of Israel's relationship to God, but also for articulating a grand theological vision.

The meaning of the confession, therefore, explodes dramatically in verse 24, where Joshua states the double hope that *all the peoples of the earth may know that the hand of the Lord is mighty* and that *you may fear the Lord your God forever.* This high point in the confessional instruction connects *the people* of v. 19 with *all the peoples* of verse 24 (Boling 1982: 186). We are reminded of Rahab's confession (2:9-11) and of her subsequent incorporation into Israel (cf. 6:25). She also "knows" what the Lord has done. The double theme of knowing and fearing in verse 24 also echoes the exodus narrative (cf. "know" in Exod 6:7; 7:5, 17; 8:10, 22; 9:14, 29; etc.; "fear" in 1:17, 21; 9:20, 30; 14:31).

The narrative suggests that the peoples of the earth will, in and through Israel's storytelling confession, come to acknowledge God alone. Perhaps like Rahab they will make the same covenantal confession. Confessing the Lord's active presence in the past aims to generate active faithfulness in the present. The fact that the *fear* of the Lord belongs in a covenantal context here suggests that the desired response (and the meaning of "to fear") is complete allegiance, or "single-minded and exclusive loyalty" (Boling 1982: 187) to the Lord of all the earth (3:13; cf. 2:11).

Summary

The narrative of the crossing portrays a God who leads and who commands. The story depicts the crossing as a reverse image of the exodus narrative. Israel's existence is shaped by a characteristic kind of memory, which looks back in order to move into the future. The story invites readers, whatever their time and location, to continue the pattern of an obedient, holy community with a faithful leader under the direction of their cosmic Lord.

This story has raised some concerns, however, about Israel's identity and future. Although it portrays the crossing as a patterning of cultic events, the note about the obedience of the Transjordan tribes (4:12) leads us to think about questions of place. Must these memories be enacted in the place where they have first occurred? Or is "the other side" of the Jordan also the arena where God's guiding presence can be known? Similarly, the battle readiness is ironically out of place, not because battles in ancient times were not accompanied by cultic rituals, but because of the allusion to the exodus narrative, where battle becomes unnecessary even though the warriors are fully armed (Exod 13:18).

The shape of the narrative thus far begins to break apart a static notion of the God-people relationship. By echoing and developing the cosmic lordship theme of Rahab's confession, this narrative presents the faithful worshiping community as one that reveres and follows its cosmic Lord and its obedient leader. This people's transforming memory and obedient actions are developed in the sacred time of the liturgical year for two reasons: (1) as a model for future faithfulness, identity formation, and education; and (2) as a pattern to be recognized by the peoples of the earth.

That liturgical dimension of this text is filled out in the texts that follow: in circumcision, in celebrating Passover (5:1-12), and in the Jericho episode (ch. 6). All of these stories, including Joshua's encounter with the man with the drawn sword (5:13-15), suggest that the Joshua story is modeled after the exodus story. Perhaps, like that narrative, Joshua will also develop the motif that "the LORD will fight for you" (Exod 14:14; cf. Deut 1:30; 20:1-4). But even without that, the people will already have tasted the food of the future and the provisions of the promise (5:12).

THE TEXT IN BIBLICAL CONTEXT

Echoes of the Red Sea Crossing

The text's most explicit echoes and allusions correspond to the story of the exodus and the Red Sea crossing in the book of Exodus. The entire sequence of chapters 3–5 echoes the exodus narrative, but not in the same order. In Exodus the sequence is Passover, crossing, wilderness (landlessness). In Joshua it is wilderness (landlessness), crossing, Passover. Thus the entire sequence is completed not in the taking of the land itself (or even in the divine encounter of 5:13-15), but in the celebration of the Passover (Wilcoxen 1968). At the heart of both stories is the knowledge of God's presence, highlighted in the hope that Israel, along with *all the peoples of the earth*, will acknowledge God's active presence (3:7, 10; 4:24).

For Israel, the crossing is the first act of obedience, which is then celebrated in the circumcision and Passover. The new generation hears the command, obeys and crosses the river by following the ark, and then marks its identity as covenant community and as recipients of God's active presence. That the Joshua narrative includes echoes of the creation/flood and exodus/wilderness stories suggests a patterned storytelling tradition. Events remembered are like one another. This likeness is confirmed by further echoes and allusions.

First, the word *wonders* (3:5) echoes the same word used three times in the exodus story (Exod 3:20; 15:11; 34:10 NJPS). These "wonders" are celebrated in the worship tradition reflected in the Psalms, including learning by children and youth (71:17; 78:4). Several psalms refer to God's wonders as done alone (72:18; 86:10; 136:4) or among all peoples (96:3; 98:1; cf. 77:14; 106:22; five times in 107; 111:4; 145:5).

Second, the reference to *dry ground* (3:17; 4:18, 22) echoes rare uses of two Hebrew words for *dry ground* in Israel's primary narrative from Genesis to Kings. In Genesis the two words occur, respectively, in the creation account (1:9-10) and the flood story (7:22). In the exodus story, both words appear, echoing the Genesis narratives (Exod 14:16, 22, 21, 22, 29; 15:19). And in the Elijah story, Elijah and

Elisha reverse the journey of the Joshua story when they travel from Bethel to Jericho and the Jordan, where they cross the Jordan on dry ground (2 Kings 2:8) before Elijah is taken up by a whirlwind in the company of the divine chariot and horses (2 Kings 2:11). Divine horses and chariots appear later in the Elisha story, which also echoes Joshua's words emphasizing God's agency rather than human swords and bows (2 Kings 6:17, 22; Josh 24:12) *[Horses and Chariots, p. 434]*.

Third, the word *heap* (3:13, 16) echoes the use in Exodus 15:8, which is significant since the word is used otherwise with this meaning only in Psalm 78:13, again to refer to the exodus event.

Fourth, the story echoes Deuteronomy with its frequent use of the verb "to cross over" (e.g., Deut 3:28; 4:14, 21, 26; 6:1; 9:1, 3; 11:8, 31; 12:10; 27:2-4, 12; 30:13, 18; 31:2-3, 13; 32:47; 34:4). The verb "takes on theological connotations in Deuteronomy, where it signifies action that must take place if Israel is to achieve the divine promise of the land at the end of their wilderness march" (Dozeman: 64). Not surprisingly, therefore, this verb occurs twenty-two times with various related meanings in chapters 3–4 (thus also echoing the divine command in Josh 1:2, 11, 14), telling how "the ark, the people, the leaders of the tribes, the tribes east of the Jordan, and even the cultic stones are described as crossing the Jordan River for conquest" (64). The question remains: What kind of "conquest" is imagined? The book of Exodus depicts that crossing as an escape-from-oppression story, where warfare is left in the hands of God (14:14), and where "entering" the sea is emphasized rather than "crossing" the sea (Dozeman: 64–65). Deuteronomy's focus on crossing over into the land provides the backdrop for the transition from wilderness to land, just as Exodus depicts transition from slavery to wilderness. Both Exodus and Deuteronomy highlight divine agency, human trust, and recognition of God's power. In the overall story of Israel, therefore, "the wilderness is presently framed by parallel events which accentuate Yahweh's power over sea and river and that this framing is providing the backbone for an interpretation of salvation history" (Dozeman: 65). Joshua 4:21-24 crystallizes that interpretation, in which events are perceived as like one another since they reflect the purposes and sovereignty of God.

Certainly other biblical motifs also intersect with this text, including the ancient Near Eastern mythic motif of God's victory over the chaotic power of the river (*Nahar*) and the sea (*Yamm*; Cross; Dozeman: 64). Part of that intersection involves a reimagining of victory by transposing earthly battles into the cosmic and moral spheres. Such transpositions occur, for example, in Psalm 46, where the poetic motif imagines the river of God (v. 4) as divine presence that assures the universal end of warfare (v. 9). And in John's Gospel, the Word is the river/water of life, a Word that also announces peace (14:27). (On the motif of the river as representative of chaos, against which God does battle to bring order and peace, see Ollenburger 1994.)

In the biblical context, those details may be interesting, but they do not evoke the imaginative transpositions that accompany the crossing motif itself. Isaiah, for example, hopes that the God who created Israel will, even in the context of Babylonian exile (east of the Jordan!), redeem Israel: "When you pass through the waters, I will be with you; and through the rivers, they shall not overwhelm you. . . . For I am the Lord your God" (43:1-3). Within the biblical tradition itself, the river crossing, although a fearful thing, becomes a paradigm of divine rescue and hope. Yet even Isaiah 43 includes a theopolitical dimension: God "gives up" Egypt, Ethiopia, and Seba in order to save Israel (43:4b). The language here reflects God's sovereignty over creation and over the nations, with Israel as Yahweh's own.

Both the book of Joshua and Isaiah 43 reflect on the possibility that this beleaguered people can survive the onslaught of slavery and empire to settle in their own land. Though the dispossession of peoples is not acceptable today, history in the ancient world is the arena of the gods (or of one God). In Israel's monotheizing literature (James Sanders 1984), all that transpires on the stage of international events must be explained not as a competition among the gods, but as an affirmation (or assertion) that one God is Sovereign over all, yet this one God loves Israel as his own people. In this monotheizing talk, the nations often get lost and the universal sometimes disappears. Yet the universal motifs show up in due time, as in Amos 9:7-8, where God's superintending care and judgment applies equally to all peoples, and in Isaiah 19:19-25, where God's "work" includes Egypt and Assyria. God's decimation of the seven groups of people (3:10) is balanced somewhat by the hope that *all the peoples of the earth* may acknowledge God's sovereignty. In Matthew's Gospel, with its explicit concern for the Gentiles, the risen Jesus announces that because he has "all authority in heaven and on earth," he commissions his disciples to "go therefore and make disciples of all nations, baptizing them . . . and teaching them to obey everything that I have commanded you" (Matt 28:19-20; cf. Josh 2:11; 3:11, 13). Even here baptism is linked with obedience, and people of all nations are invited to learn and to obey.

The Earth Belongs to the Lord

The explicit reference to the Red Sea in the catechetical summary of Joshua 4:22-24 includes two prominent motifs of the larger Exodus story—the power of God's "hand" (7:5; 13:3, 9, 14, 16) and the recognition of the Lord by the peoples of the earth (see, e.g., 5:2; 6:7; 7:5; 8:10; 9:14, 29; 10:2; 14:4, 18). After all, "the earth is the LORD's" (9:29; cf. Lev 25:23) and "the whole earth is mine" (i.e., all peoples, Exod 19:5; cf. Pss 24:1; 47:9). The "hand" motif appears in Exodus 13 in the same catechetical context as it does in Joshua 4:24. And the motif of recognizing God's cosmic sovereignty appears in Rahab's speech (Josh 2:11) and several times within the crossing narrative (Josh 3:11, 13; 4:24). In both the Exodus and Joshua crossing stories, Israel crosses armed for battle (Exod 13:18; Josh 4:12-13). Yet the paradigmatic first battle scene in Joshua is depicted as a liturgical march in Joshua 6, picking up the Deuteronomic motif of the Lord's fighting for Israel (Deut 1:30; 3:22; 20:4), which confirms Moses' exclamation of praise, "What god in heaven or on earth can perform deeds and mighty acts like yours!" (Deut 3:24). The Lord's fighting for the land is paradigmatically linked to the exodus narrative: "as he did for you in Egypt" (Deut 1:30; cf. 20:1, 4).

God's action, as reported in Israel's historical memory, becomes the basis for acknowledging the divine sovereignty that governs the earth and all nations. The acknowledgment by the nations, articulated in Exodus, finds prominent echoes in both Isaiah and Matthew's Gospel. In chapters 40–66, Isaiah depicts this hope in terms of "justice to the nations" (42:1) or "light to the nations" (42:6). This outward vision (along with its centripetal force of bringing the nations to Zion: 55:5; 60:3) is rooted in a cosmic vision of the divine sovereignty that excludes all possible ultimate allegiances, and in which "all the ends of the earth" are invited into the saving sphere of God (e.g., Isa 45:22; 49:6). The vision reaches so far as to welcome "foreigners" to the "holy mountain," to the temple, which "shall be called a house of prayer for all peoples" (Isa 56:6-8). Instead of violence accompanying the interaction with the nations (60:3), "violence shall no more be heard in your land" (60:18). Isaiah even signals the end of warfare altogether when all peoples hear the instruction of the Lord and beat their swords into plowshares (Isa 2:2-4). In later Isaianic texts, the nations (unlike the plunder of the Egyptians in Exodus) bring their treasures to Jerusalem (49:22; 60:5, 11; cf. 60:16). The motif of the nations' gifts is interwoven with an imperialist vision. The nations will submit to Israel's supremacy or perish (60:12). Israel will itself enjoy the "wealth of nations" (61:6; 66:12; cf. Zech 14:14). The goal of these texts is for the nations to see God's glory (Isa 66:18-20), an acknowledgment of glory that is gained through willing submission to God's imperial power.

Other Isaiah texts pick up a countertheme. Rather than violence against the nations, the servant in Isaiah brings justice and light (42:1, 6; 49:6). God's salvation has been made known among all the nations (52:10). Called out by Israel, nations shall come (55:5; 60:3). This is the hope upon which Matthew's Gospel draws for its extensive interest in "justice to the Gentiles" (12:18-21). Matthew transforms the ambiguity inherent in the biblical trajectory of conquest by interpreting the nations/Gentiles according to the key signature of blessing to the nations of Gen 12:1-3. In Matthew "a transformation of almost paradigmatic proportions occurs" (Swartley 1994: 70).

Yet this raises the question of what remains of the Joshua story. Here, as in Joshua 2, there are hints that the narrator imagines a larger theological vision than that implied by accusations that the God of the OT is a mere tribal deity. Still, the ambiguity of power in Isaiah and the possibility that the book of Joshua fosters imperialistic illusions of grandeur—these elements could lead to the conclusion that the motif of universal recognition of God's sovereignty merely undergirds Israel's claim to the land *[Characterization of Joshua, p. 394]*. Such a reading is possible. Still, the anticipation of universal recognition of God's cosmic sovereignty in Joshua 3–4 resonates more powerfully with the hope for a wider, more compassionate sovereignty. In the light of Exodus, Isaiah, and Matthew—along with Paul's concern for Gentile inclusion into the olive tree of God's grand story of redemption (Rom 11:17-24) and Revelation's hope that people from every language and nation might acknowledge the Lamb (Rev 5:9; 14:6)—the concluding hope of Joshua 4:24 belongs to the intrabiblical theological struggle to foster a healthy conversation between the particular character of God's redemptive gifts to Israel and the universal hope for humankind and all creation.

A Covenant for the Next Generation

At the heart of Deuteronomy's covenantal theology is the assumption that this covenant is "not only with you who stand here with us today before the LORD our God, but also with those who are not here with us today" (29:14-15). These are "the next generation, . . . as well as the foreigner who comes from a distant country," who will "see the devastation of that land" (29:22; cf. the Gibeonites, who also *come from a far country*: Josh 9:6). Deuteronomy 29 ends with the nations' asking why God has devastated the land and sent the Israelites into exile, and concludes that "they turned and served other gods" (29:26). Therefore "the LORD uprooted them . . . and cast them into another land, as is now the case" (29:28). Set in the context of those warnings, with the intimation of exile, Deuteronomy 31 announces that the Lord will "cross over before you" and will "destroy these nations before you" (31:3; cf. Josh 3:10). Deuteronomy 31:7-8 finds echoes in Joshua 1, including a promise of presence: "He will be with you; he will not fail you or forsake you" (31:8). Yet the chapter continues by commissioning Joshua (31:14-23). But before continuing with that commissioning, God warns Moses of Israel's impending apostasy in "turning to other gods" (31:18), on account of which God will "hide my face from them" (31:17). The divine speech announces that after God brings them into the land, they will eat their fill and "turn to other gods" (31:20-21). Then Joshua's commissioning continues (anticipating Josh 1 in 31:23) with Moses' writing words in a book (31:24), placing the words in the ark (31:26), and making another ominous statement about impending apostasy (31:27). Then the opening words of the book of Joshua, *After the death of Moses*, serve notice to the reader to ask whether Moses' words are prescient or not.

The irony of Moses' insight into Israel's future apostasy is that Joshua's final speech also includes such a negative statement (Josh 24:19-20). Moses reminds his audience that after his death "you will surely act corruptly, turning aside from *the way* that I have commanded you. In time to come trouble will befall you, because you will do what is evil in the sight of the Lord, provoking him to anger through the work of your hands" (31:29, emph. added). That is the context of the unique expression "the ark of the covenant of the LORD your God" (31:26), which elsewhere occurs only in Joshua 3:3. Notice now why that connection to Deuteronomy is significant.

In Joshua 3:3-4, Joshua tells the people to follow this ark *so that you may know the way you should go, for you have not passed this way before* (emph. added). Now it is no longer fire and cloud (Deut 1:33), but the ark that guides them. We ought not assume that the ark, although carried by Levites, is literally the guiding mechanism, since we do not find it functioning that way in the conquest stories of Joshua. The ark is not a magical talisman. Rather, the ark is representative of divine presence and, in particular, of the divine word, the Torah, that it holds. This divine presence, described in Deuteronomy as the God with no form (4:12, 15), is known in the declaration of his words: "I will let them hear my words," through which the people "may learn to *fear* me as long as they live on the earth, and may teach their children so" (Deut 4:10, emph. added; cf. 31:12).

This word/Torah is what Joshua reads in the ceremony of Joshua 8:30-35, in the *assembly of Israel*, including children, women, and resident aliens *[Torah, p. 462]*. And Joshua 3:9 alludes to Torah: Joshua invites the Israelites to *Draw near and hear the words of the LORD your God*, which upon hearing, we presume, will lead them to *fear the LORD your God forever* (4:24). Although in Joshua 3–4 we do not actually hear divine words after 3:9, Joshua alludes to the Deuteronomic "when the children ask" episode of Deuteronomy 6:20 (Josh 4:6, 21; cf. Deut 4:9-10; 6:7; 11:19; 32:46; Exod 12:26). But exactly what is to be told the children? Two things: the commandments and the story. These go hand in hand in the Deuteronomic theology. According to Deuteronomy, Israel is to be faithful "so that it may go well with you and with your children after you forever" (12:28; cf. 29:29).

The divine words are first of all enshrined in the ark and serve as Israel's guide for life. These will guide Israel on the way (Josh 3:4; Deut 31:29). But just as Moses is skeptical of their ability to do that, Joshua is positive (at least until Josh 24:19-20). Thus the exhortation *Follow it* in Joshua 3:3-4 states the criterion for entering and keeping the land even though Deuteronomy ominously anticipates a failure of that enterprise.

Still, Joshua 3–4 highlights—in the midst of or in spite of that tension between Moses' words and Joshua's words—that God, who is *Lord of all the earth* (3:13), is present and acts *so that all peoples of the earth may know that the hand of the LORD is mighty, and so that you may fear the LORD your God forever* (4:24). That is the emphasis in the text of Joshua 3–4, which is rooted in the exodus story. But the text also makes clear that it is not Joshua and the Israelites whom the nations will fear (as in Deut 28:10 and Josh 2:9), but the Lord. The text focuses on Israel's response to the wonders of God: they are to devote their exclusive allegiance to this God alone.

Hear the Words

The significance of Joshua's invitation to hear the words is related to Deuteronomy's understanding of the ark not as the "holy habitation" of God (which is heaven, Deut 26:15), but as repository of God's words (Deut 10:1-6), for God is present in God's words (Deut 4:12; 5:24; 8:3; 11:18). We do well to pay attention, since Joshua 3:9 is the only place in the OT where the full expression occurs (with imperative and pl. noun): *Hear the words of the LORD your God* (emph. added). And in only two other places does the expression *Hear* [pl. imperative] *the words* occur (Isa 36:13; Jer 11:2; cf. Jer 11:4, 6). The similarity of these expressions in their respective contexts suggests that

Joshua's invitation is to exclusive allegiance and loyalty, which reflects the theopolitical character of Israel's relationship with God. Behind the expression in Joshua and Jeremiah is the Deuteronomic call, "Hear, O Israel" (Deut 6:4), and the ubiquitous call throughout Isaiah, Jeremiah, and Ezekiel (only once by Hosea, in 4:1) to "Hear the word of the LORD." But Joshua's plural, *words*, is more particular. Like the "words of the LORD" in Jeremiah, these words are often related to words in a scroll/book (Jer 36:4, 6, 8, 11; 37:2). The expression refers not only to the words that God has just now spoken, but also to the words of the Torah that Joshua is to heed (Josh 1:8), to the words that Joshua reads during the ceremony at Gilgal (8:34), and to *the words in the book of the law of God* (Josh 24:26–27). These are words of immediacy, the like of which Amos longs for in his lament for "hearing the words of the LORD" (8:11).

All of this is related to the Deuteronomic words, the hearing of which will lead to fearing the Lord as they teach their children (see Deut 4:10; 31:11-12; Josh 3:9; 4:6, 21, 24). The expression "words of the LORD" does not appear in Deuteronomy itself (in MT), although the idea is clear from the singular "word of the LORD" (Deut 5:5 NIV), "these words the LORD spoke" (5:22), and "words that the LORD had spoken" (9:10). Deuteronomy emphasizes that there was only the "sound of words" at the mountain, no divine form (4:12). The king would need to fear God by observing "all the words" (17:19). The emphatic expression "words of the LORD" is rare enough in the DtrH to bear some significance when it does occur. *Words of the LORD* in Joshua 24:27 reflects a slightly different idiom to refer to *the book of the law of God* (24:26). The next occasion in the DtrH concerns Samuel's reporting "all the words of the LORD to the people who were asking him for a king" (1 Sam 8:10). Samuel also announces the "words of the LORD" to Saul at his anointing (1 Sam 15:1). After that, such "words" appear only with the rise of Josiah and the discovery of the "book of the law" (2 Kings 22:11, 13, 16; 23:2, 3, 24), which highlights again the parallel between Joshua and Josiah (see Josh 1 and the essay *Characterization of Joshua, p. 394*).

Since "words" represent the active presence of God in Deuteronomy, and hence also in Joshua, the sanctity called for in Joshua 3:4 is linked to divine presence in 3:9-10 and covenant faithfulness and acknowledgment of the cosmic sovereignty of this God (3:11, 13; 4:24). In the NT, and particularly in the Gospel of John, the motif of divine presence implies both a dwelling among the people and a commanding word. And in continuity with Deuteronomic tradition, where the ark represents both name and word, John's Gospel affirms both the immanence and the transcendence of God in Christ (John 1:14). The promise of presence finds expression in Jesus' saying "I am [will be] with you" (John 7:33; 13:33; cf. Matt 28:20; Heb 8:10; 2 Cor 6:16). That is, though "no one has ever seen God," the Son, as the Word, has revealed the Father (John 1:18; cf. Ecclesiasticus 24:8-12). This trajectory, the continuity between word and divine presence, is what Joshua invites the people to regard.

As the people become attentive to that commanding and leading presence, they also are a type, or a figure that is echoed in the NT notion that the church becomes a dwelling place of the Lord (note pl. subject throughout: 1 Cor 3:16-17; 2 Cor 6:16; Eph 2:22; cf. 1 Cor 6:19). Although these texts refer to OT temple traditions, the notion of the people's sanctity remains a vital aspect of divine presence. And if the ark represents the throne of God, then the apocalyptic vision of the Lord's cosmic reign imagines a world in which God reigns and who, by means of a word-sword, brings warfare to an end forever as God also dwells among humankind in a new way (Rev 21:3-4).

THE TEXT IN THE LIFE OF THE CHURCH

Nurturing the Next Generation

Highlighting the motif of *dry ground* (3:17) echoes the crossing of the Red Sea (Exod 14:22). Joshua's specific reference to the Lord's action *for us* includes the present generation in the past event, even though they have not been there. Exodus, crossing the sea, and crossing the Jordan belong to a sequence of events in the memory of Israel that are always contemporary. Israel confesses its present faith as though the past belongs to today's experiences. The story of the crossing thereby becomes the story of every generation. Each generation is invited to begin here again. The focus of the story, therefore, is not the beginning, but the future. The questions of the children (4:6) imply not only an explanation of the past, but also invitation to create hope for the future. The future, however, is not simply a repetition of the past, either for Israel, for the nations, or for the church. Rather than establishing a conquest paradigm for later readers (with its victors and victims), the text offers another kind of paradigm, that of attending to God's actions and commandments. Drawing on this text, Menno Simons encourages readers to "teach our children rightly in the Word" so that, through example and instruction, they may be "furnished to all manner of good works" (Menno Simons: 388–89). Through attending to Scripture and the presence of God's Spirit in the body of Christ, the church continues to experience God's presence and to live into God's promised future.

Crossing a Threshold

"Crossing Jordan" has always been about more than a physical transition from one land to another. The story represents a threshold, a liminal moment for Israel between promise and fulfillment, between wilderness and fruitfulness, between homelessness and landedness. As such, the story's focus on children's questions reminds me of the popular song "Teach Your Children" by Crosby, Stills, Nash, and Young. The story offers a paradigmatic image "that they can live by" because it tells of the wonders the Lord has done. It generates a narrative memory that shapes identity through remembrance, and therefore through theological imagination. Although the story is thoroughly focused on divine agency, it also offers several theological handles for shaping that imagination and identity. It gives a clear image of the inseparable character of divine action and human response. It presents a vision of divine sovereignty whose reach encompasses and embraces all peoples. And it invites the human community to be attentive and to follow the divine word, which calls them into the uncertainty of promised reality. Hearing God's instructions and obeying become characteristic of peoplehood. Both the exodus and the Jordan crossing reverberate together throughout Scripture; in so doing, they suggest that God continues to lead and invite people to follow the path of the promise-making and promise-keeping God, for they "have not passed this way before." Several illustrations will show how this paradigmatic and evocative text has borne fruit in the interpretive tradition and life of the church.

I have been in a good many worship services where the symbolic act of taking up small stones and setting them down at a designated place allows the congregation to commemorate significant moments in their experience of God's grace. The text lends itself to metaphorical interpretation and symbolic actions of remembrance. Taking up Joshua 3–4 in a very different way, David Dueck produced a feature-length film *And When They Shall Ask*, which tells the story of the Russian Mennonites and memorializes the past for another generation that has crossed the water to a new land. The film takes its title from the motif found in Joshua 4:6, 21 (cf. Deut 6:20).

A classic of Christian spiritual writing, John Bunyan's *Pilgrim's Progress* (1678), transposes Israel's crossing the Jordan into a figurative individual believer's crossing the river of death. After traveling to all of the places described in the book, Christian finally arrives in Beulah Land, the beautiful land that borders the Celestial City. John Ripon's publication of the hymn "On Jordan's Stormy Banks" (1787) sets the metaphor to music. As in the Joshua story, neither in Bunyan's *Pilgrim's Progress* nor in Ripon's hymn is there a struggle against Jordan's waves. The Pilgrim in Beulah Land waits for the trumpets to sound from the other side and makes a triumphant crossing of the watery barrier between him and the Delectable Country. Eschatological interpretations like those of Bunyan take the crossing as a type of initiation into the heavenly, eternal land. The well-known hymn "Guide Me, O My Great Redeemer" contains the line "cross the Jordan, . . . land me safe on Canaan's side" (*WT* #606). Such eschatological transpositions seem to have much in common with the Egyptian idea that the Pharaoh, after his death, crosses the Nile from the east (the land of the living) to his tomb on the west side of the Nile. Yet such a crossing of the "river of death" is a significantly different, although related, typology from that of the early church's understanding of the crossing as a figure of baptism. The early church affirmed that what happened there continues to happen in believers' experience. Linked by Jesus' baptism, the Jordan crossing becomes a type of believers baptism.

Crossing and Baptism

Although the *Epistle of Barnabas* 6.13 already links the promised land with the kingdom of God (Daniélou: 262), Origen highlights the crossing of the Jordan and links it to baptism (and to 2 Kings 2:1-8 and to Naaman in 2 Kings 5). For Origen, the crossing of the Red Sea was an entry into the Christian faith, with the crossing of the Jordan a type of baptism (52–53). According to Daniélou, "Joshua crossing the Jordan, with the dove of the Spirit resting on him, is a type of the humanity of Jesus assumed by the Word and dwelt in by the Holy Spirit: the theme of Joshua and that of Baptism harmonize to form a great theological symbol" (269).

Cyril of Jerusalem borrows from Origen but adds the dragon from the book of Job: "The dragon, according to Job, was in the waters, and swallowed the Jordan in his mouth. That is the reason why, in order to break the dragon's head, Jesus went into the waters and bound the strong man, so that we should receive power to walk over dragons and scorpions" (cited in Daniélou: 270). For Gregory of Nyssa, crossing the Jordan means leaving the desert, the life of sin, thus to "hasten to the life according to the commands of Christ" (*De baptismo*, cited in Daniélou: 271). Jordan also takes on a mythic resonance as a river that "spreads over the whole earth and flows into Paradise," for it is "the river of grace [that] flows everywhere" (271).

Even here, however, Origen transposes the text of Joshua 4:13, about crossing the Jordan "armed for war." Taking his cues from his reading of Ephesians 6:14 ("Let your loins be girded with truth"), he suggests that "truth is the belt by which we are girded for the army of Christ" (*Homilies* 60). For Origen, the preservation of truthfulness, both in words and in the heart, is the essence of the battle we engage: "Let us go forth to the war, so that we may subdue the chief city of this world, malice, and destroy the proud walls of sin. . . . Within you is the battle that you are about to wage; on the inside is that evil edifice that must be overthrown; your enemy proceeds from your heart" (61–62). Origen argues this way because, as he declares, "All these things happened to them figuratively, but they were written for us, for whom the fulfillment of the ages has come." (61; citing 1 Cor 10:11) *[Figural Reading, p. 426]*.

If the crossing of the Jordan is a figure for the believer's baptism, it is also a revelatory moment when Christ, at his baptism, is revealed as the divine Son, even as Joshua was *exalted in the sight of all Israel* (4:14; cf. the revelatory dimension of Jesus' baptism texts, which is prominent esp. in John 1:32-34).

Crossing into Freedom

A rather different interpretive tradition emerges from the music of the blues, and its cousin the gospel spirituals, which echo the biblical hope of a new land. In Martin Scorsese's *The Blues* project, the segment on gospel and blues suggests that the longing for freedom and the crossing of the Jordan into the land of promise are rooted in the slave experience of crossing over into freedom, either to the north or into Canada. The crossing of the Jordan is not first of all a longing for heaven, but a longing for a place to be where slavery and oppression are no more. One song exemplifies this hope: "We Are Crossing Jordan River" (*Joan Baez Song Book*, Ryerson Music [1964/1971], 140). Other such songs reflect a similar context of oppression and hope for a transformed experience (e.g., "There Is a Fountain"; "On Jordan's Stormy Banks").

Another popular song is worth citing at some length: "Wade in the water. Wade in the water, children. Wade in the water. The Lord's gonna trouble the water" (cf. also John 5:7). The southern slaves sang this song, which was also used by those along the Underground Railroad. "The river Jordan is chilly and cold" gives directions for fleeing slaves crossing the Ohio River in winter: "Chills the body but not the soul." The spirituals offered hope that "crossing the Jordan" would bring a new freedom and a new identity as free people. They offered hope that God would get them through.

In a baptismal sermon from 1999, Walter John Boris says that although he thought "Wade in the Water" referred only to the slave movement, he learned that "in the Civil Rights Movement, it took on . . . added significance. In addition to riding buses or sitting at lunch counters, there were also wade-ins at public beaches." In the song, those crossing the Jordan are also the "children Martin Luther King led." The waters of the Jordan and of baptism, claims Boris, came to be understood as "not so much a special blessing or protection, but a call to challenge and a call for us to stand up for truth and justice. It's a call to make our way through the difficulties of life so that we may give testimony to our faith."

Another song, "Down by the Riverside" (study war no more), sung by Peter, Paul, and Mary, among others, associates the biblical motif of the river with antiwar protest. In this song the river motif is transposed by the Zion tradition (Ps 46) so that, as in the thinking of Origen, the river becomes a sign of the wonder of God's transforming presence in word and spirit.

The motif of crossing the river is also memorialized in the story of Mennonites leaving Russia by crossing the Amur River into China. I heard a story, probably apocryphal, about a woman who had crossed that river and who, many years later, met a Russian man who had been on military guard duty at the time of her crossing. She asked the guard why her group was not stopped. The former guard responded by saying that they had seen too many soldiers protecting them. Oddly, the Mennonites had not seen any soldiers. The crossing story in this example blends the Jordan crossing imagery with that of Elijah's crossing and Elisha's vision of a heavenly army (2 Kings 2:8; 6:17).

Crossing and Instruction

Perhaps it is in keeping with the early Christian interpretation of the Jordan crossing as a figure of baptism that the crossing narrative in Joshua is accompanied by the exhortation to *hear the words of the Lord your God* (3:3-4, 9). Living the baptized life requires attentive listening to God's instructive word. Baptism is an initiation into a covenant loyalty in which the believer affirms one's partnership with God in the project of transforming the world. Faithful obedience, in response to divine grace and empowerment, run hand in hand in the crossing story. The *words* are needed because *you have not passed this way before* (3:4).

Yet the motif of instruction and of listening to the words of the Lord has been used and abused in many ways. I remember how we as youngsters were taught Bible memory verses, many of which were singled out by their ability to create a sense of neediness and failure, as well as hopeful transformation. By the selection of verses, children were carefully groomed into the experience of lostness and deliverance. More hopeful are the curricula that emphasize not only the divine commands but also the story of God's wonders. Instead of learning to live out of guilt, we can be invited and drawn into the whole story, thereby learning to embody the divine words in our lives as a response of gratitude.

The neediness that the story presents is precisely the need for divine presence and divine instruction. Not having gone this way before opens the way for a kind of guidance that has not been experienced in the wilderness before. Now that the cloud and the pillar of fire have disappeared, the story of the Jordan crossing presents the word as the divine presence (in keeping with Deuteronomy's concept of the divine word). Contemporary Christians continue in various ways to shape their lives by the divine word. Yet even though our future is like Israel's (we have not traveled there before), reading Scripture is one of the main ways in which we come to know the guiding of God's Spirit.

Joshua's call to *draw near and hear the words of the* Lord *your God* (3:9) invites us to reflect on how Scripture (as divine word) guides our lives by the Spirit (see examples of reflection on formation through Scripture in the books by Work and Mulholland). Most Christians continue to read Scripture as a deliberate practice of faithful living and for guidance along the way. Even as we recognize the divine Word as a guide, we know that Word in at least three senses: as expressed in Scripture, as embodied in Jesus, and as embodied and articulated in the community of faith through the Spirit's witness. These three go hand in hand; in all three the divine and the human intersect uniquely. In Joshua the human element is in the form/genre of the story, with its ancient warfare codes and conventions of writing. The divine element remains, not as a seed to be separated from the chaff of the text, but as a source of life within which, even in the very human vehicle, is a possibility of encounter with the divine presence (signified by the ark) and transformation into a people who fear the Lord. Oddly, the nations are driven out by *the* Lord *of all the earth* (3:10-11) even as the story ends by asserting that the nations themselves may come to acknowledge *that the hand of the* Lord *is mighty* (4:24). Does this mean a conversion of the nations? Or a grudging respect? Or are they, like their archetype Rahab, to become those who acknowledge that *the* Lord *your God is indeed God in heaven above and on earth below* (2:11)?

Joshua 5:1-12

From Preparation to Passover to Produce

PREVIEW

In team sports, a ritual is sometimes practiced to help focus the group as they prepare for their upcoming contest. This may take simple and unpremeditated forms, such as when a men's squad agrees to let their beards grow until they win the title. In other cases, the ritual is more elaborate, such as the *haka* practiced by New Zealand rugby (and some other) teams before an international contest. The circumcision and Passover rituals practiced by the people of Israel, though they had greater significance and motivation, may have also served something of this focusing purpose. In chapter 5, the story of the crossing is also highlighted by a transition from the gift of God's manna for the wilderness to the nourishment that comes from the land itself. The good gifts of the land, exemplified in the classic line *land flowing with milk and honey* (v. 6), are now the provisions of the Lord.

We might expect the narrative of the fall of Jericho (6:1) to follow immediately after 5:1, where the kings' paralysis echoes Rahab's statement in 2:9-10. There is a reason, however, for the interlude begun at 5:1. The two short units (5:1-12, 13-15) that follow chapter 4 serve as a bridge between the crossing narrative and the Jericho story. The first of those begins with a new motif of "hearing" (5:1), which follows naturally from 4:24 and is picked up later in the book at narrative transition points (9:1, 3; 10:1; 11:1). It ends with the people eating the produce of the land (5:12). The second (5:13-15) continues the transition into the Jericho story by picking up the divine encounter motif from the book of Exodus. In this way, chapters 3–5 are linked by a common narrative trajectory and thematic threads.

The entire sequence from 3:1 to 5:12 echoes the exodus narrative, but not in the same order. The giving of the law at Sinai is symbolized in Joshua by the ark of the covenant, by which God is present as one who leads and commands by God's word. Joshua 5:2-12, therefore, is a hinge section that forms a transition between the crossing narrative (chs. 3–4) and the Jericho/Ai/Achan narrative (chs. 7–8). Circumcision and Passover in 5:2-12 introduce the latter sequence, and altar building, sacrifice, and reading the Torah close the sequence in 8:30-35.

The narrative of 5:2-12 reports events that take place *at that time* (v. 2), which ties these reports to the other time expressions in the previous narrative (cf. 3:7; 4:14, 19). The entire sequence echoes the preparation for the departure from Egypt in Exodus 12. As the Israelite slaves leave Egypt "prepared for battle" (Exod 13:18), having been circumcised and having celebrated the Passover, *all* Israel (Josh 5:5, 8) is now depicted as prepared to do battle in the same way.

The community that has gathered at Gilgal obeys the treaty instructions of Moses in confirming the covenant through the sign of circumcision. Then the community remembers its story in a sign-action of Passover on the fourteenth day (cf. Exod 12:18), which suggests that the present experience of the people is a redemptive experience like that of the slaves in Egypt. The entire Gilgal scene reflects the continuation of a liturgical-instructional context *[Covenant and Treaty, p. 416]*.

The circumcision and the Passover are themselves symbolic memorials of the Lord's *wonders* exhibited in the exodus event (3:5). The entire crossing sequence ends with a note about enjoying the produce of the land. The promise of blessing to the ancestors is being fulfilled.

OUTLINE

Introduction, 5:1

Remembering in the Gifted Land, 5:2-12

5:2-9	Circumcision and Covenant Commitment
5:10-12	Passover and Covenant Fulfillment

EXPLANATORY NOTES

Introduction 5:1

The response of the kings in 5:1 echoes Rahab's speech (2:9-10) and the spies' report (2:24), and it brings some closure to the episode of the crossing even as it anticipates the conquest narratives that follow. This verse, with its "hearing" motif, introduces the entire sequence that follows from 5:2–8:35, just as the "hearing" motif in 9:1-2 introduces the conquest accounts of 9:3–11:23.

Verse 1 is a hinge between the previous narrative of the crossing and the following reports of ritual activities. The verse summarizes the main action of chapters 3–4 (crossing) and, for the first time since the Rahab story in chapter 2, mentions kings of the land. There is a contrast between this verse and 4:24, although the "hearing" here is not a full recognition of God's cosmic sovereignty. Hearing of the Lord's powerful presence with the Israelites has immobilized the will of the kings of the land: their *hearts* and their *spirit* have been disarmed. Verse 1 echoes the "hearing" that Moses anticipated (Deut 2:25).

This is the second time that we have heard about kings. Although Rahab announces that *our hearts melted and there was no courage left in any of us*, the king of Jericho was determined enough to send out an expedition looking for the intruders. In this text, however, *all the kings* of the Amorites and Canaanites (reportedly from the entire land from Jordan to the sea) have been affected by what they have heard. *Kingdoms* have fallen without the help of those *armed for war* (4:13; cf. 1:14). Like the Egyptian Pharaoh, they are immobilized by God alone (5:1a). Here, in addition, they do not even have *the courage to face the Israelites* (v. 1b NIV; NRSV: *because of the Israelites*).

The perspective of the narrator in verse 1 adds a final clue to the significance of the crossing. The narrator makes a point of saying that these kings are *beyond the Jordan to the west*. The expression *beyond the Jordan* is used in two ways in the book of Joshua. It means both west of the Jordan (5:1; 9:1; 12:7; 22:7; cf. Deut 3:20, 25; 11:30) and east of the Jordan (1:14, 15; 2:10; 7:7; 9:10; 12:1; 13:8, 27, 32; 14:3; 18:7; 20:8; 22:4; 24:8; cf. Deut 1:1, 5; 3:8; 4:1, 46, 47). Because of that ambiguity, the clarifying phrase *to the west* makes sense. But the comment here seems to place the narrator on the east bank. Does this alternation suggest that Israel is to be on both sides, including the two and a half tribes? (Hawk 1991: 97). Or does the writer intend for the readers to hear the story from the point of view of someone situated east of the Jordan? Is the story told so as to place the reader in exile, homeless in wilderness, beyond the Jordan to the east? If the double use of *beyond the Jordan* comes to represent both being "at home" in the land and "in exile" outside the land, then the tension between the eastern and western tribes in Joshua 22 can be placed in a theological context. The book of Joshua affirms being in the gifted land west of the Jordan, but it does not exclude the possibility of authentic life with the Lord outside the land. Even as Rahab, an outsider in the land, can confess faith in Israel's God and become part of the covenant community, so also Israel outside the land can continue as covenant community "outside" the land. In other words, since both sides of the Jordan belong to *the Lord of all the earth*, then Israel could be at home in both places.

Remembering in the Gifted Land 5:2-12

5:2-9 Circumcision and Covenant Commitment

Verses 2-3 are framed as a command-action sequence. Joshua carries out the command explicitly. The verses (4-7) that follow present an extended explanation for why the circumcision ritual is necessary. Clarification is necessary because of the reference in verse 2 to a second time. The narrator explains that none of the children were circumcised along the way. This is the sense if we read verse 7 immediately after verse 4. But verses 5-6 add a theological reflection, reminding readers that the wilderness generation had *not . . . listened to the voice of the Lord*. That emphasis on disobedience contrasts with this text's repeated examples of obedience to the Lord's words. Thus verse 6b makes it clear that the promise of God can be compromised if they fail to heed divine instruction. By implication, the contrasting promise of *a land flowing with milk and honey* will be realized by the next generation. Such is the hope, and even the anticipation, implied in Joshua's commissioning in chapter 1, in Joshua's invitation to attend to the divine word (3:9), and then later in Joshua's reading in 8:30-35. The *warriors . . . who perished* (5:6), therefore, are a warning that this story may also go awry (cf. Deut 2:14-16). Even so, God's change of mind does not diminish the fact of the promise (v. 6b). God begins again with the next generation.

The phrase *a land flowing with milk and honey* occurs here for the first time in Joshua. It echoes imagery found throughout the Pentateuch (Exod 3:8, 17; 13:5; 33:3; Lev 20:24; Num 13:27; 14:8; 16:13, 14; Deut 6:3; 11:9; 26:9, 15; 27:3; 31:20). Its use in Jeremiah (11:5; 32:22) and Ezekiel (20:6, 15) suggests that in the exilic period the expression came to be regarded as part of Israel's envisioning a new and fruitful future.

The first step toward faithful attentiveness to the divine word is the rite of circumcision. This act, whatever its historical origins may have been, is depicted here as a covenant rite. As such, "it was to be a reminder of ethical obligation; only the circumcised could celebrate the Passover. One might speak of an 'uncircumcised heart' (Jer 9:25[-26]), meaning that one does not comprehend. An 'uncircumcised ear' (Jer 6:10) is one that is not good at listening. And 'uncircumcised lips' (Exod 6:12, 30) are inarticulate" (Boling 1982: 194). In that light, for the males to be circumcised (given the patriarchal context) means that the community not only can partake in the ritual meal but that they also are acting out a sign of their covenant commitment. Unlike the wilderness generation, they are agreeing to be a holy people who live by the Lord's words.

This transformation from a *nation* (*goy*) to a *people* (*'am*) is the concern of the story. Butler notices the wordplay between the two words "nation," referring to the disobedient generation (vv. 6, 8), and "people," identifying the faithful first (vv. 4, 5a) and, in hope, the second (v. 5b) generations. But Israel's tendency was to become like the nations (Deut 17:14-20; 1 Sam 8:5; Butler 1983: 59). Thus the word *nation* may be deliberately used in Joshua (e.g., also 4:1) to refer to the people who are in process of becoming the Lord's people. As Deuteronomy states concerning the covenant ceremony upon entry to the land, Abraham became a great "nation" (Deut 26:5), but those who enter the land and obey the Lord will be "his treasured people," and "a holy people" (Deut 26:16-19; Boling 1982: 172; cf. Exod 19:6). But the implicit question that remains here is whether this newly circumcised people will not also become like the first generation, which perished in the wilderness. That question will be answered only in the final text unit of the book.

The synopsis in verse 8, with the explanation of Gilgal's name in verse 9, completes the first episode of preparation. In a play on words (Gilgal is related to the verb *galal*, meaning "to roll"), the Lord announces that the transformation is complete. The disgrace of Egypt has been rolled away. Perhaps Israel is to be identified no longer as a slave community, but as the Lord's people, committed now to a master who liberates rather than oppresses. Or perhaps Israel is identified by its obedience to the Lord rather than through military might or political identity (cf. Butler 1983: 59).

5:10-12 Passover and Covenant Fulfillment

Celebration of Passover signifies identification with the people who came out of Egypt. But more, it marks this newly formed "people" as having been shaped by a particular memory. This people knows its identity by remembering and enacting the story it tells. And it knows its God in the same way. In other words, this God has a story and is known by that story. To participate in Passover, in memory of the exodus experience, is to learn from that story, to identify with it, and above all to embody commitment to the God celebrated in that story.

In other words, Passover is not simply a reminder of the past; it re-presents the past in order to imagine a viable future. The text in Joshua orders the future by making explicit that the story of the crossing and the celebrations associated with it belong to the annual ritual calendar of the believing community. This pattern suggests that the entire sequence including Joshua 3:1–5:12 has become, in the literary context in which it has been placed, part of the story that orders Israel's identity in the readers' present experience, wherever that might be. This is an ongoing celebration of the land-gift and the land-giving God.

The gift motif continues in the comments on eating the produce of the land. God provides even though the people have not yet come into possession of the land. Four times in verses 11-12, eating the *produce* and *fruit* of the land is underlined by time references: three references to *the day* of eating and the expansive perspective of *that year* anticipate the narratives that follow. Thus, with the final reference to manna in verse 12, the crossing story comes full circle. God continues to nourish God's people. The entire crossing story, analogous to the Exodus account, is more than a report of a past event. Israel continues to live in the presence of a promise-making and promise-keeping God. The crossing, celebrated as a liturgical event encompassing an entire year, becomes a pattern for every year.

THE TEXT IN BIBLICAL CONTEXT

Circumcision

Circumcision is a sign of covenant relationship, seldom mentioned in the Bible prior to this text: with respect to the ancestors (Gen 17:10-14, 23-27; 21:4; 34:15-24), with respect to Moses (Exod 4:26), with respect to the Israelites prior to the Passover in Egypt (Exod 12:44, 48), and in the priestly instructions regarding circumcision on a child's eighth day (Lev 12:3). According to Genesis 17:14, the uncircumcised male "shall be cut off from his people; he has broken my covenant." In Exodus 12:44, 48, we read that all who have been circumcised may participate in Passover, including slaves and aliens. Remarkably, Deuteronomy mentions no literal circumcision ceremony, only twice a "circumcision of the heart" (Deut 10:16; 30:6; cf. Lev 26:41). In Deuteronomy such circumcision will empower Israel to "love the LORD your God with all your heart and with all your soul, in order that you may live" (Deut 30:6). ("The uncircumcised" is a derogatory term used primarily in the DtrH outside of Joshua: Judg 14:3; 15:18; 1 Sam 14:6; 17:26, 36; 31:4; 2 Sam 1:20.)

Apart from that, in the OT only Jeremiah, Ezekiel, and the second part of Isaiah mention circumcision in connection with God's people. Jeremiah's references speak only positively of circumcision of the heart (4:4; 9:25-26). In Isaiah, mention of the uncircumcised not entering Zion (52:1) reimagines a return from exile as a new exodus/entry, a hope for redemption from bondage in Babylon. Ezekiel makes the prohibition stronger: "No foreigner, uncircumcised in heart and flesh, of all the foreigners who are among the people of Israel, shall enter my sanctuary" (44:9). In Ezekiel's thinking, this prohibition is part of a critique of the Levites who have been hiring noncovenantal outsiders to look after the duties in the temple (44:5-8). Ezekiel's interest is in protecting the sanctity of divine presence. The text is not simply a critique of foreigners since other texts in Ezekiel permit foreigners to have partnership and inheritance with Israel (47:22-23). Moreover, the sanctity of divine presence has an outward focus, which will result in the recognition of God by the nations (37:27-28; 38:16, 23; 39:7).

Ezekiel, though he does not mention circumcision in his renewal-of-Israel passages, emphasizes a new heart as a prerequisite to a new obedience (11:19-20; 36:26-27), which is linked to fruitfulness of the land (36:29-30). The new heart is also linked with living in the land (36:28) and becoming "my people" (11:20; 36:28). Ezekiel's entry into the land parallels Joshua's entry, except that the "conquest" in Ezekiel 38–39 is accomplished by the divine hand alone, and the distribution of the land in Ezekiel 47:13–48:35 equalizes the allotments (47:14) and allows an "inheritance" for aliens who "shall be to you as citizens of Israel" (47:22-23). Supporting such equalization, political life in the new era will be marked by a ceasing of "violence and oppression" (45:9).

Here we find two strands of thinking about circumcision. One strand defines inclusion into the covenant community; the other radicalizes the sign to a purification of the heart. According to the more radical tradition, foreigners may partake of Passover if they have been circumcised, whereas Israelites also do well to learn that external circumcision must be accompanied by a transformed heart.

Several NT writers take up the metaphorical sense of the act (Acts 7:51; Rom 2:25-29; 3:30; 4:9, 11). In the earliest churches, inclusion into the community was symbolized by the reception of the Spirit, not by circumcision (Acts 10:45; cf. 11:2-3), a conviction that gave rise to considerable controversy in the church (Acts 15:1, 5; 16:3; 21:21; Gal 2). Paul's argument in Romans is that the faithfulness of Christ (not circumcision) is the ground of relationship with God, which is followed by the believer's responsive faithfulness (Rom 2:25-4:12; see Toews: 84–87).

Paul allows that Gentiles who are not circumcised but who obey God could well be considered circumcised (Rom 2:26). So also for the Jews, Paul argues, "true circumcision" is not "external and physical" but "a matter of the heart" (2:28-29). Even Abraham's faith and righteousness preceded his circumcision (4:11). For Paul, circumcision or uncircumcision are irrelevant in the light of the much greater importance of "obeying the commandments of God" (1 Cor 7:19) or "faith working through love" (Gal 5:6). Indeed, circumcision is meaningless in the light of the "new creation" that is underway (6:15). Circumcision for Paul has become a spiritual reality of incorporation into Christ (Col 2:11). In none of these references does Paul substitute baptism for circumcision. For Paul, baptism indicates an eradication of difference in the Abrahamic family where Jew and Greek, male and female, slave and free—all are "heirs according to the promise" (Gal 3:27-29; cf. Eph 2:11; Col 3:11).

Milk and Honey

Eating from the produce of the land resonates with Deuteronomy's exposition of the gift of land and eating the land's produce (8:9-10), and the instructions for Passover (16:1-7). The problem with eating in the land flowing with milk and honey is the risk of becoming complacent and forgetting the Lord "by failing to keep his commandments" (8:11). Eating one's fill may lead to exalting self, forgetting the Lord's gracious provision, and serving other gods (8:12-19). Such action will lead to perishing should Israel not "obey the voice of the LORD your God" (8:20; cf. the similar phrase in Josh 5:6, and the invitation to *hear the words* in Josh 3:9). The same sentiment comes through in Deuteronomy 31:20, where all the motifs of eating and turning to other gods occur in one verse together with the motif "land flowing with milk and honey."

The fruitfulness of the land, captured in the phrase "a land flowing with milk and honey," reflects a widely used biblical motif (Exod 3:8, 17; 13:5; 33:3; Lev 20:24; Num 13:27; 14:8; 16:14; Deut 6:3; 11:9;

26:9, 15; 27:3; 31:20; Josh 5:6; Jer 11:5; 32:22; Ezek 20:6, 15). God's gift of land, both in Joshua and in the eschatological vision of the prophets, is for full sustenance from God. For Jeremiah, this gift is contingent upon listening, doing, and receiving the divine gift (11:4-5). Loss of land follows Israel's refusal to "obey your voice or follow your law" (32:22-23). Ezekiel highlights the divine promise as fragile and dependent on human participation in the divine intention (20:6, 15).

The NT writers use various images of divine feeding, including the feeding stories in the Gospels, banquet practices of Jesus, and the Last Supper/Passover analogy of ingesting the body and blood of Christ. The most striking contrast between wilderness manna and food in the land is Jesus' description of himself in John's Gospel as "bread from heaven" in contrast to the manna of the wilderness (John 6:22-59, esp. 6:31, 48-51). Eating of this heavenly bread is eternal life (6:54, 58). John's "eternal life" is, for the synoptic Gospels, participation in the kingdom of God, a sharing in the abundance of the new land where God is Sovereign over all.

THE TEXT IN THE LIFE OF THE CHURCH

Circumcision and the Lord's Supper

The force of the account of circumcision and Passover in Joshua is the reconstitution of the community of Israel after the wilderness experience. For many Christians, baptism is the equivalent rite to circumcision, and the Lord's Supper is the equivalent to Passover. These equations, however, are debatable and betray an ignorance of historical development. For male Jewish followers of Jesus in the early church, circumcision continued to be practiced alongside baptism; the latter grew in importance as the act of circumcision was transposed (through apostolic teaching) into the image of a transformed heart (a notion already found within the OT prophets; see TBC above). This was also true because baptism, as an initiation event, applied to believers of all backgrounds and genders. The Lord's Supper, with its celebration of Jesus' resurrection as well as his death, became the primary act that formed and constituted the community on an ongoing basis. A recognition of these developments does not require a strict equivalency between the older and the newly established rituals.

Origen's exegesis is consistent with both OT and NT perspectives on circumcision of the heart. His focus is illustrated in his explanation of the circumcision *a second time* (v. 2). He cannot understand how this is possible, literally, unless one resolves the conundrum by referring the reader to Paul's dictum "The Law is spiritual" (63). The first circumcision is through the law; the second through "the rock who is Christ" (63). Origen's interpretation is rooted in the NT, where Paul refers to Christ as the rock who followed them in the desert (63–65; referring to 1 Cor 10:4 and Exod 17:6).

When Origen explains the relationship between circumcision and Passover, his intrabiblical exegesis becomes quite clear. Citing 1 Corinthians 5:7-8, he makes the dual rite in Joshua 5 a moral act that is linked to the Passover allusion there, with its "unleavened bread of sincerity and truth" (1 Cor 5:8; Origen: 68). This ties his argument to the motif of being "armed for war" (Josh 4:13) with the weapon of truthfulness and to the ceasing of the manna (Josh 5:11-12).

The *produce of the land* that the Israelites ate *that year* is "the third fruit" (after unleavened bread and manna), which "we receive now from the holy land" (69). Here Origen shifts into an eschatological mode. The food of the desert is what we eat during this life, which is "what we learn by the instructions of the divine law" (by which he apparently means Scripture). But the food of the land is for those who, after conquering the enemy, "enter the land of promise," which we will see "when the enigma is over" (69). Origen is worth attending to because he illustrates a serious grappling with how various biblical texts relate to one another. What the OT tells, the NT retells, and both together are the narrative of the Christian life. They tell of the *Pilgrim's Progress* (as by John Bunyan [1678]).

Calvin offers us another grappling with the interface between the literal text and the Christian journey. Circumcision "was the symbol of the adoption to which they owed their freedom" (77). Calvin chastises Israel for failing to circumcise during the wilderness period and alludes to Moses' violent incident (Exod 4:24-26) as God's threat "to be an avenger against anyone" who failed to circumcise (78). Then Calvin resolves the tension between the text and life by suggesting, "as if God were making it manifest that he had put off circumcision for a time lest it should be profaned, but was waiting for an opportunity of renewing it" (79). Therefore this circumcision of the wilderness generation prepares them for Passover, "for none were admitted to the Passover and the sacrifices save those who were initiated into the worship of God; just as in the present day the ordinance of the Supper is common only to those who have been admitted into the Church by baptism" (79–80). Although Calvin does not equate circumcision with infant baptism here, the analogy of circumcision/Passover and baptism/Lord's Supper suggests as much.

Among churches that practice believers baptism, the question of children's participation in the Lord's Supper is still under discussion. The brochure "Children and Communion" (John Neufeld), published by the Canadian Mennonite Brethren Church, assumes that unbaptized children may, upon proper instruction and understanding, participate in the Lord's Supper. As I have stated above, the NT does not unambiguously equate baptism with circumcision. Hence, to draw the analogy between the circumcision/Passover sequence in Exodus and Joshua with the baptism/Lord's Supper sequence in the church may not be warranted. Rather, the NT voice in the conversation takes up the Deuteronomic and the prophetic metaphor of circumcision of the heart (see TBC above).

Joshua 5:13-15

Holy Ground, Holy Presence

PREVIEW

The political and economic realities of our time have generated a climate of fear and insecurity. We become desperate to know who our allies are, who can be trusted, and whom to name as the enemy. In particular, the so-called war on terror has generated a massive campaign of protectionism and patriotism. Joshua's encounter with the commander of the Lord's army suggests at least two responses: divinely sanctioned violence will solve the problem, or there must be another way of thinking about the issues at hand. The striking event told in these few verses is one of the most important in the book of Joshua. It marks a theological focal point through which the entire book may (even must) be read and evaluated. From this text springs the book's theological vision, as well as one of its most gripping ambiguities. The encounter reported here invites readers to take a stance on what is at stake in the book of Joshua.

Joshua 5:13-15 is a fitting conclusion to the ritual activities of chapters 3–5. Shaped almost entirely in question-answer format, it provides the final panel in Joshua's commissioning that began in chapter 1. And it offers an appropriate preface to the longer story of the conquest of Jericho, which continues in chapter 6. These verses form a hinge between two significant sections: they draw to a close the ritual preparations described in chapters 3–4; they take up the motif of holiness from 3:5; and they begin the sequence of narratives that continue from 5:13 to 12:24. Here, as in 1:1-9, God takes initiative. Although we can see a clear connection to what follows (both 5:13 and the parenthetical 6:1 begin with a reference to Jericho), the short episode recounted in 5:13-15 serves a larger purpose in the book. Besides setting the stage for the Jericho incident that follows, it also sets in motion a divine strategy that reverberates throughout the book and is highlighted at the end of the book in the repeated emphasis on God's activity (23:3, 9-10; 24:12).

Although this short text tells of an apparently random occasion (*Once*, v. 13a) when Joshua encounters a man with a drawn sword in his hand, its motifs reverberate through Scripture in a way that suggests this is the key to the book of Joshua. Not until we hear the command of this man in verse 15 do we hear the echo of Moses' encounter with the Lord at the burning bush (Exod 3:1-12). But we think also of the angel of the Lord in the Balaam story (Num 22:23, 31) and the cherubim and the sword placed "at the east of the garden of Eden" (Gen 3:24). Having eaten of the crops of the land (Josh 5:12), Joshua now faces one who bars his way forward. On what condition does this man allow Joshua entry into "the garden" of the fruitful land of milk and honey?

OUTLINE

The Setting, 5:13a
The Question, 5:13b
The Answer, 5:14a
The Response, 5:14b
The Command, 5:15a
The Response, 5:15b

EXPLANATORY NOTES

The Setting 5:13a

In this short episode we find Joshua near Jericho. The text does not tell us how long Israel has been at Gilgal. From the perspective of the narrator, that does not seem to matter. The previous verse marks *that year* as though to emphasize the first harvest after entry into the land (5:12). The marking of the cultic and agricultural year has served its purpose by setting the entire narrative within Israel's liturgical memory bank. We hear simply that on one occasion when Joshua was in the vicinity of Jericho, *he looked up and saw a man standing before him with a drawn sword* (Heb. *ḥereb*) *in his hand*. The exact expression *he looked up and saw* occurs only a few other times in the OT, one of which is in the story of Abraham's encounter with "three men" whose identities are not revealed to Abraham and Sarah (Gen 18:2; cf. 24:63). Although the wording is slightly different following that introduction, the three men are also "standing near." One wonders if the narrator might have that incident from Genesis 18 in mind. In two other biblical texts we find an angel with a drawn sword in his hand (Num 22:23, 31; 1 Chron 21:16; cf. 2 Sam 24:16-17).

The persistence of such a literary motif in various texts makes us wonder both about this man's identity and about the meaning of the sword. The fact that Joshua asks a question makes one wonder whether this man is friend or foe, helper or threat. Is the man coming to do battle or to prevent one? Is this a prelude to a promise of victory, or a not-so-subtle hint about the conspiracy of Deity and warrior? If there is any parallel to the two other OT stories in which a messenger from God (angel) appears with a drawn sword in his hand (the same words as in Josh 5:13), then we might conclude that this *man* whom Joshua encounters is not benign. As Hess observes, "He is the one who threatens divine judgment" (1996: 126). In the Balaam story, the angel of the Lord stands before Balaam, blocking his way (Num 22:23, 31). In 1 Chron 21:16, the angel is even more menacing with "a drawn sword stretched out over Jerusalem." Although later readers of Scripture may conclude from these textual similarities that Joshua's man is a threat, Joshua's perspective is more focused on the immediate. He sees a man with a weapon in his hand. And so he asks, very crisply and no doubt very quickly, about the man's allegiance. He does not yet know who this man is. He may or may not be a threat.

The image of a man standing with a drawn sword in his hand occurs often in ancient Near Eastern artistic and literary representations. Keel's extensive survey of such images shows divine beings standing behind or in front of a human being, usually a king. Keel concludes that in Egyptian iconography the outstretched sword in the hand of a god is a symbol of divinely ordained victory (77). Joshua himself stands with a raised weapon (*kidon*, not *ḥereb*) in his hand in a later story (Josh 8:18, 26). If the uplifted weapon in both of these texts has the same symbolic significance, then, as Nelson puts it, "The point is to assure Joshua (and the reader) of impending victory and Yahweh's participation in the upcoming battle" (1997a: 81). Since 5:13-15 simply includes a dialogue that begins with an ominous question, the reader may not assume that these verses imply a straightforward assurance of confidence. In this case the text calls into question the assumed significance of the iconic image. The dialogue questions a straightforward assurance of victory.

That the man may represent God, however, remains significant and may be illustrated from an ancient Near Eastern text. In a campaign (against Elam) account from the Assyrian king Ashurbanipal (ca. 668–627 BC), we read of a vision that was told to the king by a seer: "The goddess Ishtar who dwells in Arbela came in. Right and left quivers were suspended from her. She was holding a bow in her hand, and a sharp sword was drawn to do battle. You [the king] were standing in front of her and she / spoke to you like a real mother. Ishtar called to you, . . . giving you the following instructions: 'Wait with the attack; (for) wherever you intend to go, I am ready to go.'" (*ANET* 606; see also 451; cited in Van Seters; Niditch: 58). According to Van Seters, "The text goes on to indicate how the goddess gave additional words of comfort to the king and then proceeded to defeat his enemies without the king needing to do anything" (10–11). If the parallel is instructive, we may imagine that Joshua 5:13-15 depicts a divine encounter. The reader knows this, but Joshua does not. So he asks about the identity of the stranger. It seems as though Joshua's lack of clarity about the stranger's identity marks this story as different from the Balaam and David stories. The man's ambiguous identity is actually the heart of Joshua's encounter.

The Question 5:13b

Joshua's question in verse 13b seems direct and clear. He asks, *Are you one of us, or one of our adversaries?* The challenge of translating the question depends on how the Hebrew preposition *le* is understood. The NIV reads, *Are you for us or for our enemies?* Is Joshua asking, "Which side are you on?" Or is he asking, "Will you act on our behalf or on theirs?" The fact that Joshua does not know the man's identity suggests that he is asking not only what the man will do but to whom the man owes his allegiance. The answer to the latter question will determine how Joshua should treat this stranger.

The Answer 5:14a

The stranger's inexact answer tells it all. His reply begins with a simple "No" (NJPS; Heb. *lo'*). The NRSV and NIV read *neither*, which removes the ambiguity of the simple "no" and assumes the answer implies that the man is not on either side. There may be some truth to that, especially since the answer does not clarify the man's identity.

In other words, as the reply continues, we learn that this stranger is none other than the *commander of the army of the* LORD. He is the general in charge (in the OT, *śar-ṣeba'* is often used to designate "the commander of the army," as in Judg 4:2, 7). Note the wordplay here: Joshua asked whether he is aligned with *ṣarenu* (*our adversaries*; from *ṣar*, sg.); the commander answers that he is *śar* (different *s*), *commander.* Although he is the general in charge, he is accountable to someone else: the king. This stranger identifies himself in two clauses: a clause lacking a verb, followed by a terse clause with a verb. First he states his identity and then his arrival. A literal translation of the first clause reads, *No. For I [am] commander of the host of Yahweh.* In the second clause the man announces his arrival, as the NJPS puts it, *Now I have come!* That announcement of his arrival may anticipate what is about to take place in the Jericho incident that follows. But the man does not complete the sentence with an infinitive clause that fills out the intended action: to do what?

What is important, rather, is his identity as stand-in for the Lord's presence and power. God's title implied here can often be translated either as "LORD [Yahweh] of hosts" or as "LORD [Yahweh] of armies" (two hundred thirty-five times in the OT, as in Pss 46:7, 11). This commander's words resonate with the common biblical image of God as Sovereign of the cosmic forces (cf. the "host of heaven" that Micaiah sees; 1 Kings 22:19). Yahweh is the Creator of the heavens, often named "host" (Isa 40:26). Occasionally these hosts, along with other named entities, participate with God in battle (e.g., Judg 5:20; 2 Sam 5:24). Sometimes the "host" refers to angels, or divine messengers (Ps 103:19-21; cf. Job 1:6). In only one place is Israel described, in the plural, as "all the hosts/armies of the LORD" (Exod 12:41 NASB/AT; Howard 1998: 157).

The commander's response suggests a God-centered (theocentric) orientation rather than an Israel-centered (ethnocentric) perspective. Does the commander's answer allow Joshua some sense of relief? Not at all. For the reader who knows the fuller story of Israel's devastation at the hands of conquering Assyrians and Babylonians, and the prophetic interpretation of those losses, this answer is fraught with ambiguity. This military man does not represent one who can be rallied onto one ideological side or another. Nor does this one come simply to fight for Israel, as one might surmise if this text is a narrative exposition of Deuteronomy 1:30-31: "The LORD your God, who goes before you, is the one who will fight for you." Although we might read the incident in Joshua 5 in the light of that text, the Joshua story implies that this commander comes representing an independent power. He comes as an agent of the one whom Rahab had confessed as *God in heaven above and on earth below* (2:11). He comes as one who represents *the* LORD *of all the earth* (3:11, 13), the one whom *all the peoples of the earth* will acknowledge (4:24).

Victory, therefore, is not to be taken for granted. We are not dealing with warfare as usual. Howard takes a different position, assuming that the man is "'for' Israel, not 'against' it." Howard then asks, if that is the case, "Why, then, did he not speak more forthrightly with Joshua and tell him that he was indeed for Israel?" (1998: 158). Howard suggests, "It appears to have been to teach Joshua a lesson about priorities" (158). I am not convinced that this commander is "for Israel," even though God's presence is promised to Joshua. Presence is one thing; unequivocal military victory is another. Howard is at least partly right when he says, "The more important lesson was about God's holiness, not about the coming conflicts" (159). Consider again the "cosmic" scope of the vision reflected in Joshua 2:11; 3:11, 13; 4:24. The more important lesson was the sovereignty of God, which gives rise to the call for holiness (3:5) and transforms ordinary places into holy places.

The Response 5:14b

Joshua does not compel the man to change his mind. He does not ask, "Please, join us." Rather, he falls to the ground and invites a command. Another biblical text describes an encounter between two men that includes the only other exact sequence of Hebrew words found here. When before King David, "Joab prostrated himself with his face to the ground and did obeisance" (2 Sam 14:22). It is possible, given that Joshua now knows the identity of this man, that, upon falling on his face, *Joshua . . . worshiped* (NRSV). But that need not be the case. The story in Gen 18:2 describes Abraham as "bowing to the ground" (NJPS) upon meeting the three men. It seems most likely that Joshua's falling to the ground indicates either a gesture of hospitality and welcome, or a gesture of submission and reverence (NIV reads *in reverence*; NJPS has a neutral expression, *prostrating himself*). The fact that Joshua has already asked a question and received an answer suggests that a welcoming gesture (like that of Abraham) may not be in view here. Rather, Joshua's posture indicates that he, like Joab, is acknowledging his commanding officer and putting himself under his command.

That is exactly what Joshua's words in verse 14b confirm. Joshua invites the commander to speak (*command* in NRSV, NLT, NJPS). The NIV *message* assumes too much that the man is some kind of intermediary with a word from God. The sense may rather be reflected in a stance taken by Samuel, who replies, "Speak, LORD, for your servant is listening." Joshua's response, like Samuel's, is an invitation to being addressed (1 Sam 3:9, where the same verb is used). As in Samuel's situation, Joshua identifies himself as *servant* of this commanding officer, referring to himself in the third person, *his servant* (NIV, NJPS). This self-identification is significant since the word *servant* is used for the first time since its fivefold repetition in Joshua 1, where *servant* is used exclusively of Moses (1:1, 2, 7, 13, 15). This personal affirmation seems to complete the exaltation of Joshua, as noted in 3:7 and 4:14. Oddly, not until the end of the book (24:29) is Joshua fully "exalted" by being named *servant of the LORD.* In 3:7, however, the intent of the exaltation of Joshua's reputation among the people is *that they may know that I will be with you as I was with Moses.* Divine presence then gives way to reverence for Joshua in 4:14. The encounter with the commander in 5:13-15, however, makes it clear that Joshua must defer to another.

The Command 5:15a

With the command to remove the sandals and the qualification that *the place where you stand is holy*, we hear explicitly the echo of Exodus 3:1-5. This text now completes the commissioning of Joshua begun in Joshua 1, and it does so in ways reminiscent of Moses' encounter with God. Both Moses and Joshua ask questions, both are asked to remove their sandals, both respond by turning away (Joshua falling on the ground), and both episodes are followed by narratives that tell of the partial fulfillment of the commission. The texts also present a theological pattern: "The one who brings the people in [Joshua] is not only like the one who led them out [Moses,] but the one who led them out [also] becomes typologically the one who brings them in" (Hauch: 117). Now it remains for Joshua's generation to obey wholeheartedly and enter God's rest. In these ways, Joshua 5 rounds out the extended parallel between Joshua and the Exodus narrative *[Characterization of Joshua, p. 394]*.

Further, the fact that the place is *holy* (*qodeš*) needs some explanation. The reader may also wonder how the holiness of this place relates to the curse on Jericho in 6:26. The analogy with Moses' encounter in the desert suggests that it is not Jericho that is holy. It is not "holy land." The ground (Exod 3:5) or the *place* (Josh 5:15) is holy because of the encounter, not because of the intrinsic holiness of the land or the place. As such, this short unit rounds out the entire sequence of ritual activities begun in 3:1. A narrative sequence that begins in 3:5 as Joshua's command to *sanctify yourselves* (3:5, with the same root *qdš* as the word *holy* in 5:15), now ends with the commander of the host of the Lord declaring *the place* holy, a place set apart for God.

That *this* place is holy indicates that Joshua, and Israel, may not presume to have privileged access either to the Lord or to the land. According to Deuteronomic teaching, although the land itself is a "good land" (Deut 1:25, 35; 3:25; 4:21, 22; 6:18; 8:7; 9:6; 11:17), it is not a land that Israel may presume is theirs as an unqualified right. Deuteronomy 11:16-17 even assumes the possibility that, if Israel worships "other gods," they will "perish quickly off the good land that the LORD is giving you." The expression "good land" occurs in the DtrH outside the book of Deuteronomy only in Joshua 23:13, 15, 16, in warnings about Israel's perishing and being destroyed; and in 1 Kings 14:15, in a judgment speech by Ahijah against Jeroboam I, king of Israel, where the warning comes to graphic fruition in Israel's being scattered beyond the Euphrates (cf. Judg 18:9, with its allusion to Gen 1:31).

I mention these references to "good land" here because the book of Joshua does not refer to this *place* on which Joshua stands as "good land" until the warnings in chapter 23. Rather, the *place* is an echo of Joshua 1:3, which emphasizes the land as "gift." Thus Joshua stands on a gifted place, given only because God is the giver, here represented by the commander, who represents God's cosmic sovereignty. Joshua stands, as it were, empty-handed and barefooted before an Other whose prerogative it is to give and to take. The responsibility is Joshua's, and hence Israel's, to hear and obey (Deut 6:4-5) *[Land: Gifted and Lost, p. 440]*.

The Response 5:15b

A final short sentence completes the sequence in this unit. The episode begins with Joshua's questioning the commander; it ends with him obeying. Thus Joshua, in this simple gesture, embodies the implication in the exhortations in Joshua 1 to be faithful to the instruction of the Lord *[Torah, p. 462]*. Not only is Joshua faithful; his symbolic action is also an act of worship par excellence. Whereas Joshua's prostration in 5:14 is an act of submission, removing his sandals is an act of both obedience and worship.

This text prepares the reader for what is to follow even as it provides a culmination point for everything that has happened until now. This confirms that God has been the historical agent in both the Rahab story and in the crossing narrative. Joshua now stands before Jericho as Moses stood before Egypt. Joshua and the people have already eaten the Passover meal. Now all that remains is for God to act. So is the commander on Joshua's side after all? Not without qualification, as we will discover in chapter 7. And not in the way warfare is conventionally practiced, as we shall see in chapter 6. What unfolds after this encounter is an example, rather, of an entirely different assumption regarding human participation in warfare. Although the book of Joshua depicts human participation in warfare, a reading through Joshua from the beginning sets in place a paradigmatic emphasis on trusting and attentive listening (and hence obedience) to divine instruction. With this emphasis the book of Joshua also ends.

The passage prepares readers for Jericho, which we will discover is paradigmatic for the entire narrative of Joshua, and which the Lord summarizes in retrospect at the end of the book: *It was not by your sword or by your bow* (24:12). The sword in the commander's hand and the bared feet on holy ground, therefore, represent the kind of war that readers should anticipate. They "become signs of the kind of muster, the kind of arms to be employed in this war. Human weapons, like human instrumentality, will play a minor role, if any, in the battles to follow" (Hauch: 124). This episode suggests that not even Joshua will be the military leader, but Yahweh. The human role will be obedience and trust (Hauch: 125). Richard Nelson puts it nicely: "The narrative ends with a barefoot Joshua—like Moses at the burning bush (Exod 3:1-6)—who has been given nothing to do" (2003: 60).

To this point nothing has gone wrong. Readers have noticed only reversals of earlier stories: of the Transjordan tribes and of the episode at Baal Peor. *The Israelites did as Joshua commanded* is the keynote of obedience in 4:8. Joshua does as the stranger has commanded (5:15). But a subplot remains. Will the Transjordan tribes be authentic paradigms of all-Israelite faithfulness, as Rahab is a paradigm of the acknowledgment of *all the peoples of the earth* (4:24)? Or will obedience and trust be compromised? It all depends on how Israel models itself after Joshua's response to the divine messenger. Will all Israel, like Joshua and Moses, take off their shoes? Or will they, like the impatient people at the foot of Sinai, make gods for themselves?

THE TEXT IN BIBLICAL CONTEXT

The Encounter with the Other

The encounter with the other has been reflected in the book of Joshua: in the Israelite other represented by the Transjordan tribes (ch. 1), the Canaanite other represented by Rahab (ch. 2), and now in the divine Other, the commander of the army of the Lord (5:13-15). The divine Other transcends human constructs and confounds human attempts to domesticate God.

The encounter in Joshua 5:13-15 suggests that theological reflection about God's involvement in warfare (let alone in history generally) may well remain a mystery that we cannot fully comprehend.

Joshua is not the only biblical character who meets a mysterious and even dangerous stranger. Sometimes the biblical characters come to understand the encounter as a meeting with God (e.g., Gen 18:1-15; 32:22-32). And in two other stories, which include drawn swords, the meeting seems fraught with danger. In the Explanatory Notes we have already noticed how the messenger with a sword challenged Balaam (Num 22:23, 31) and David (1 Chron 21:16). The messenger comes to correct or to judge or to set things right. In the NT, messengers appear for various reasons; in each case the encounter intends to bring God's perspective to bear on a particular situation, or to reveal God's purposes within the current reality, or to announce God's initiative (Matt 2:13; Luke 1:11-20, 26-38; 2:9-14; Acts 12:7-10).

Yet the indication that the Israelites cross the Jordan *armed for war* (4:13) implies a military engagement. Is this military man going to bar their entrance into the gift? Although Joshua makes sure to assess the situation quickly, he is also quick to respond in submission and with an open ear. This suggests that Joshua is able to hear divine instruction as *the warriors who came out of Egypt* had not, *not having listened to the voice of the Lord* (Josh 5:6). Unlike Balaam and David, Joshua's encounter seems not to be motivated by a deed deserving judgment. Even so, the sword is menacing. Contrary to ancient Near Eastern iconography, this stranger does not simply empower the human warrior, but actually stands over against him and negates his militaristic assumptions.

The allusion to the story of Moses' encounter at the burning bush is most instructive. Since (1) the sword motif implies divine authority, justice, and victory; and since (2) the *army/host of the Lord* (NRSV/NASB) implies that the battle is not determined by human means; then (3) the words that echo the voice from the burning bush, along with Joshua's response, are most important for understanding this encounter. Not only is this commander not the commander of any human army; he also announces that the *place* (not "ground" or "earth" or "land") on which Joshua stands is *holy*. And therefore it is *not* a land belonging to one side or the other. The land belongs to the Lord (3:11, 13). Whereas Moses wants to pin down the divine name, Joshua wants to discern whether the man is on one side or on the other. The man, however, wants to protect the divine prerogative as cosmic Sovereign. Since the sword symbolizes action for/against (in)justice, it could fall either way. This man's actions and words suggest "I am above this": I am in higher command than both sides.

Joshua is like Moses, however, only on the surface. The emphasis on Joshua's willingness to be commanded and his immediate obedience stands in contrast to "Moses' repeated hesitancy and reluctance to accept his charge (Exod 3:11, 13; 4:1, 10, 13)" (Hauch: 119). This event marks a new divine initiative for a new generation and a new leader. Whereas the first leader and the first generation were barred from entry into the gifted land, we readers trust that this second leader and second generation will trust and obey, and thus enter and embrace the gift (Hauch: 119–21).

Joshua's encounter with the divine Other has revealed that there is *another* army, *another* commander besides Joshua, *another* Sovereign besides the king of Jericho, and *another* place determined off-limits to ordinary human transgression. That Joshua listens is surely a good sign in an otherwise terrifying moment. His response is first of all an acknowledgment of transcendence and of God's cosmic sovereignty. As Redekop describes it, "Transcendence is about opening oneself to new, previously unimagined realities—about opening one's Self to the Other. It is an openness to new meaning systems, relationships, and actions. It means letting go of control over the means of security" (282). His response also acknowledges the incapacity of Israel's own war-making tools, a recognition that begins in the next episode (Josh 6) and that comes to a conclusion in Joshua's speech at the end of the book, in which he affirms allegiance to God (24:15).

Since the book of Joshua has this stranger with the sword at the beginning of the conquest narrative proper, and has God say at the end of the book that the entrance into the land was accomplished *not by your sword or by your bow* (24:12; cf. 2 Kings 6:22), the narrator's perspective on the many other occurrences of the word *sword* throughout the conquest section (sixteen times, including eleven times in chs. 10–11) could well be read through the lens of that narrative framework. In that light, there are two interpretive options: (1) the sword that Israel wields is not their sword but God's, and (2) as Sovereign of all nations, God may well use Israel's weapons, or any other nation's weapons for that matter, but in the end God preserves the prerogative of wielding the sword. The commander with the sword in his hand implies that the course of human history is not an autonomous human endeavor. The Sovereign of the cosmos, the one who is *Lord of all the earth* (Josh 3:11, 13), shapes the future in response to the human community. This protecting of divine prerogative is part of the narrative's monotheizing of history. Do not presume to trespass on that divine prerogative.

Leviticus depicts the consequences of that trespass (covenant violation) as a relentless divine sword, setting in motion both the exile of Israel and a Sabbath rest for the land (Lev 26:25, 33-35), resulting in Israel's "perish[ing] among the nations" (26:38) even though Yahweh continues to "remember" that he is "their God" and will not "break my covenant with them" (26:44-45). According to the prophetic vision, God's cosmic sovereignty allows him to summon "a sword against all the inhabitants of the earth" (Jer 25:29; cf. 50:35-37), against Israel (Ezek 5:17; 21:3-4; Amos 7:9; Zech 9:13) and an unrepentant church (Rev 2:16). This divine sword becomes identified later as the prophetic word (Isa 49:2; cf. Heb 4:12), which the book of Revelation transforms by calling it the sword of the word that comes from the mouth of the rider on the white horse (Rev 1:16; 2:16; 19:15, 21).

Joshua's commander also reminds us of the divine promise in Exodus 23:20-33 and 33:2-3, where God promises to "send an angel in front of you, to guard you on the way and to bring you to the place that I have prepared." If the narrator of the book of Joshua understands this commander in Joshua 5:13 to be that angel/messenger, then the remainder of the Exodus passage is worth attending to. There God instructs Israel to "be attentive to him and listen to his voice" (23:21). The meeting with this commander in Joshua 5 is not, therefore, a benign encounter. Much is at stake. He could lead or he could bar the way, depending (like the Balaam story) on whether Israel heeds the voice of the Lord.

Joshua's story thus far is a fully theocentric text, which asserts God's promise, invites covenant loyalty, establishes a paradigmatic perspective, and culminates in an encounter with a divine delegate who declares a divine "No" to partisanship. The problem in all of this is that the juxtaposition of biblical texts leads us to a completely different conclusion from the one gleaned from a straightforward reading of Joshua 5:13-15. And so some readers may be suspicious of such a reading, as is Gil Bailie, who offers us another way of hearing the voice of the text.

Bailie writes that a great gulf separates Moses' theophany at the burning bush from Joshua's encounter. The Moses event "had reverberated with genuine transcendence. The armed angel of Joshua's vision is purely and simply a specter of sacred violence expressed militarily" (159). A common unity emerges in warfare that is analogous to the vicarious unity achieved in sacrificial ritual" (160). Bailie confirms that it is possible to read Joshua with the grain of a militaristic and imperialistic ideology. My attempt to read it against such a grain recognizes that "sacred violence" is embedded in the text, but in the larger conversation with the whole book of Joshua in its biblical and theological context, violence is put in its place and circumscribed by the even more prominent themes of sacred trust and loyalty to a divine other who is Sovereign over all nations and to whom the whole earth belongs. Hearing another voice that offers a universal and transcendent perspective keeps the conversation dynamic. The text is not simply the assertion of one ideology but itself reflects a dynamic debate about competing options for human-divine relations.

The Army of the Lord / The Lord of Hosts

Joshua's divine diplomat represents the army of the Lord. Such military language implies a political theology, whether that be an ideological militarism, an antipartisan theopolitics, or some other nondualistic alternative.

That the Lord has an army/host implies that God is a warrior. This metaphor is grounded in the exodus story and celebrated in the victory poem of Exodus 15, where we read, "The LORD is a warrior; the LORD is his name" (15:3). The Exodus poem, like the narrative that precedes it, celebrates the victory of Yahweh over the forces of Pharaoh (Exod 14:13). On the other side of that liberation, God announces the creation of a people with a new identity and mission (19:5-6).

Their missional vocation requires attentive listening, which in Hebrew also implies obedience (Exod 19:5a). Exodus 15 grounds that attentiveness in an identification of Yahweh as King. It does so, after recounting the victory against Pharaoh, by asking, "Who is like you, O LORD, among the gods?" (15:11). The poem does not deny the existence of other gods. Rather, it elevates Yahweh to the highest position as Sovereign of the cosmos (as does all of Exod 1–15). This is the cosmic sovereignty that Rahab's confession (Josh 2:11) and the story of the crossing of the ark have already affirmed (Josh 3:11, 13; 4:24).

That the Lord's commander in Joshua 5 is commander of Yahweh's army suggests that the Lord has cosmic resources at his disposal. This army, and the ark that goes before it, is not first of all a human army. That Israel crosses the Jordan after the ark "armed for war" (4:13) highlights the fact that the first victory that follows in chapter 6 is entirely the Lord's doing. Like the ark story in 1 Samuel 6 and 7, the ark needs no human help to free Yahweh from Philistine hands or to demonstrate Yahweh's supremacy over the Philistine god.

In other texts, God is said to be riding or enthroned on the cherubim (Pss 18:10; 80:1; 99:1). Because God has vanquished the forces of chaos, God is Sovereign over all powers that threaten to undo the fabric of creation (Ollenburger 1994). That God is Sovereign of the cosmic forces is significant for our discussion because, as Ollenburger puts it, "The order wrought by Yahweh in vanquishing his cosmic foes is at the same time an order wrought among the earthly forces with which Israel was confronted" (1987: 57).

At the same time, the cosmic dimension of divine conflict does not automatically validate all human warfare. For example, in 2 Kings 6, Elisha asks God to open the eyes of his servant to see that "the mountain was full of horses and chariots of fire all around Elisha" (v. 17). When Elisha leads the Aramean army into Samaria, the king asks whether he should kill them. But Elisha says, "No! Did you capture with your sword and your bow those whom you want to kill?" (v. 22a). With that he instructs the king to feed the enemy and let them go (vv. 22-23). Notice the exact repetition of "your sword" and "your bow," which we also find in God's summary evaluation reported by the narrator in Joshua 24:12 *[Horses and Chariots, p. 434]*.

The motif of the army/hosts of the Lord continues into the NT *[Conquest and Land in the NT, p. 411]*. To confirm that this army is not automatically one that models human moral behavior can be surmised also from several NT expressions of this motif. In the story of Jesus' temptation in Matt 4:6 and Luke 4:11, Satan challenges Jesus with the line from Ps 91:12 about the protecting power of the angels. Jesus flatly rejects such use of the cosmic powers as a means of gaining the land/kingdom (cf. Deut 6:16-18). One of the other temptations is sovereignty over all the kingdoms of the earth, to which Jesus responds that only God must be worshiped (Matt 4:10; Luke 4:8). Jesus' kingdom reflects a different kind of politics, based on a different kind of allegiance. This too is the emphasis in Joshua, which tells of a people's journey through impassable barriers and formidable foes to come out on the other end as a people faithful to God in time and space. Yes, Joshua is political, but its emphasis is prophetic and therefore theopolitical (Buber 1967: 57).

Allegiance and Political Theology

Not only does this text echo Moses' encounter with God at the burning bush and share in the theopolitics of Yahweh as Lord of hosts; it also resonates with Deuteronomic admonitions to single-hearted loyalty to God. Throughout the first chapters of Deuteronomy are significant statements like the one in Deuteronomy 6:4, called the Shema because it begins with the call "Hear [*šemaʿ*]." Deuteronomy assumes that the covenantal conversation between the Lord and Israel involves loyalty and faithfulness. Moses declares that the Lord "will neither abandon you nor destroy you; he will not forget the covenant with your ancestors" (4:31). At the same time, Deuteronomy calls for thoroughgoing reciprocal loyalty on Israel's part (6:4-5). Joshua's submission and then worship/obedience resonate with the paradigm of exclusive allegiance enjoined on Israel in Moses' exhortations in Deuteronomy.

In the NT, Jesus affirms, as noted above in the reference to the temptation story, that only God must be worshiped/served. Similarly, "No one can serve two masters" (Matt 6:24; Luke 16:13). The christological hymns of Ephesians and Colossians assert that Christ is supreme over all other powers (Eph 1:21; Col 1:16). The book of Revelation may well make the boldest claim of all, that those who endure in times of political and economic turmoil and persecution do so by affirming the victory of the reigning King of the cosmos, not by taking up weapons against the enemy. The only weapon against the enemy is the sword of the word (Rev 1:16; 2:16; 19:15, 21; Heb 4:12; Eph 6:17; cf. 2 Cor 10:4-5). In this way these writers transform the moral potency of the sword motif.

One must not mistake the divine sword as a pretext for human violence. The sword in the hand of this commander in Joshua 5, along with the command to remove Joshua's sandals, suggests that Joshua is standing before the Other against whom no power can prevail. This ground on which Joshua stands is not holy because it is intrinsically different from all other lands but because of the presence of the God who promised it to Israel and who governs the peoples of the earth and gives them their lands as well. The biblical affirmation that "the earth is the LORD's" (Exod 9:29; 1 Sam 2:8; Ps 24:1; 1 Cor 10:26) is rooted in the notion of God's cosmic sovereignty (cf. Josh 2:11; 3:11, 13; 4:24).

THE TEXT IN THE LIFE OF THE CHURCH

Wielding the Word

In the extremely polarized context of the 2004 U.S. presidential election campaign, *Sojourners* magazine placed a full-page advertisement in *The New York Times* declaring, "God Is Not a Republican. Or a Democrat." Such a bold public assertion is surely in keeping with the Commander's "No."

A well-known hymn in the church affirms the association of the word and the sword. The first line of its second verse begins, "Come, thou Incarnate Word, / Gird on thy mighty sword" (*WT* #8). The hymn invites God, the "Almighty King," who is "o'er all victorious" to "give thy Word success." This image comes from both Isaiah's notion of the prophetic word that goes out and succeeds in its task (49:2; 55:11) and the NT writers' affirmation of the word as a powerful and effective weapon against the powers of evil (Eph 6:17; Heb 4:12; Rev 1:16; 2:16; 19:15, 21). Although the sword in Ephesians seems benign to many readers since the "struggle is not against enemies of blood and flesh" but against "cosmic powers" and "spiritual forces of evil" (Eph 6:12), the sword in Hebrews is more threatening because it addresses believers who refuse to enter God's rest. Hebrews likens believers' "disobedience" with the failure of Joshua to give rest (4:8, 11). The sword wielded against those who are disobedient is the "word of God," which is "piercing until it divides soul from spirit, joints from marrow; it is able to judge the thoughts and intentions of the heart" (4:12).

Taking a figural sense that the sword is the word, Origen reads from the Greek Bible, "when Jesus was in Jericho" (Josh 5:13 LXX, with *Iēsous*) *[Figural Reading, p. 426]*. Origen understands Joshua's question to be analogous to the advice given in 1 John 4:1 to "test the spirits to see whether they are from God." This man, according to Origen, must be Jesus, for "who else is chief of the army of the powers of God except our Lord Jesus Christ?" (70–71). Calvin follows in Origen's steps by affirming "that when Christ anciently appeared in human form, it was a prelude to the mystery which was afterwards exhibited when God was manifested in the flesh." But Calvin makes sure to clarify that this man was not Christ because it is not yet the "fulness of the times" (88). Tension arises between Origen's and Calvin's readings because of different understandings of the nature of reality. In Origen's figural interpretation, past events may be repeated in future events without undermining the integrity of either. For Calvin, Jesus' incarnation must be unique, since time is linear in the divine purpose, and even more, because events themselves are unique. Origen sees God's participation in human affairs as a continual repetition of like events. Calvin focuses on the textual time rather than future time and thereby limits the commander's significance to "the combats which were about to be waged" (88).

Visionary Encounters

Although Christians have always been "People of the Book," they have also assumed that alongside their commitment to be faithful to Scripture is a similarly strong conviction of the presence of the Spirit. Although not always practiced, this divine presence has meant that the One/Other who is with them is stronger than those arrayed against them. Perhaps like Joshua's commander, or like the angel in the fiery furnace (Dan 3), they are surrounded by grace both when victorious as well as when suffering.

Philip Wiebe's book *Visions of Jesus* recounts many claims of visionary encounters with Jesus. These visionary experiences do not provide proof that Joshua really did encounter a divine messenger, but they illustrate that visionary experiences do occur at significant transitional moments. Some have called these moments *liminal experiences*, which are experiences "on the threshold" or "limen." Those threshold experiences, however, need to be tested, a testing that Origen suggests is implied in Joshua's question to the commander. Such experiences reflect a common hope that we are both nourished by and accountable to an Other who stands over against us and who cannot be domesticated by our ideologies.

Although the book of Joshua includes human violence against the human other, a reading against the grain of the narrative suggests that the commander's "No" allows us to imagine an alternative to human violence. That reading still leaves us with the theological question of how to understand both divine and human violence in the book *[Theology of Warfare, p. 458]*.

Bob Dylan's gospel song "You've Gotta Serve Somebody" illustrates what the commander of the army of the Lord might represent to contemporary readers. Many Christian and Jewish readings of this short passage have emphasized the figural, or typological, trajectory in front of the text. As Joshua's encounter echoes that of Moses' encounter at the burning bush, so the ongoing interpretive trajectory has focused on the otherness of the divine and on obedience to the divine word called forth in response to that presence.

Strange as it may seem, that obedience is fleshed out in the next chapter, in which warfare takes a decidedly odd turn.

Conversation about Joshua's encounter, however, has also been put to oppressive use. And this too is part of attentiveness to the interpretive conversation. Through the website "Jewish Jericho" (www.jewishjericho.org.il/english/) a group of people are claiming Jericho as a holy place (Josh 5:15) that now lies in the hands of the enemy. The problem is that such groups highlight only one phrase or one part of a text and do not also recognize that the holiness of the place is tightly bound up with the holiness, obedience, and exclusive loyalty of the people. Such holiness includes, oddly enough, Deuteronomy's concern for the alien and the motif of inclusion of the outsider in Joshua.

Joshua 6:1-27

A Battle like No Other: Transforming Otherness

PREVIEW

The popular spiritual "Joshua Fit the Battle of Jericho" extols Joshua's bold faith and obedience. The story has also been transformed into a Nintendo game and a VeggieTales video. Such popular expressions of this paradigmatic story of divine intervention rely on textectomy—cutting out the violence against Jericho's inhabitants, who come under the sword, as *devoted to the* Lord *for destruction* (v. 17). This is the reader's first encounter with the unspeakable horror of such religious devotion in the course of Joshua's narrative. The story is worthy of close attention not only because it is a text of terror, but also because, when read against the grain of its violence, a crack opens through which some light may come.

Although Joshua is the central figure in this story, the Lord is the One who takes the initiative, who brings down the walls, and whose reputation (along with Joshua's) is proclaimed through this story. When attending to this text, the reader has three options. One could reject the text outright as an expression of misplaced sacred violence. One might perform a hermeneutical trick so as to gloss over the violence that follows the collapse of the walls. Or one could engage in a sustained conversation between this text, other biblical texts, and our theological traditions and moral convictions. For those engaged in peace-building in particular, Jericho is more than a conundrum; it is an outrage. How shall we be honest about what this story proclaims and listen respectfully to it at the same time? Is there room to speak back and to protest? Perhaps the book of Joshua itself begins to offer clues to the possibility that violence might be transformed. Or perhaps it reflects a vestige of religiously grounded communal (and sacrificial) violence that the Bible itself suspends in the death and resurrection of Jesus.

Although the Jericho episode is to be interpreted in the light of what happens in 5:13-15, the clear introduction of God as speaker in chapter 6 suggests a shift in perspective. Chapter 6 also makes explicit connections back to the story of Rahab in chapter 2 and implies connections forward to the story of Achan in chapter 7. The backward and forward look stands in tension with the devotion-to-destruction motif (*ḥerem*) (cf. 2:10) *[Ḥerem, p. 433]*.

The narrative action in Joshua 6 proceeds by a sequence of instructions and actions that create a series of literary tensions *[Plot Tensions in Joshua, p. 452]*. Israel is armed but passive, and the enemy is removed rather than defeated (Culley: 33–36). Moreover, the announcement and sequence of ritual actions transforms the reader's expectations so that by the end one is impressed not only by "a sense of order and inevitability" (Culley: 37) but also by the potential of redemption in the context of a bloody sacrificial act.

Whatever our initial reaction to the notion that people might be *devoted to destruction* (Heb. *ḥerem*, vv. 18, 21) or *devoted to the Lord for destruction* (v. 17), we do well to engage in conversation with Joshua 6 in the light of how the narrative participates in the common conventions of ancient conquest accounts and yet invites readers to reflect on this action retrospectively. Perhaps reading Joshua 6 against the grain of its obvious violence and in the context of warfare narratives in the ancient Near East will allow us to see how this story "thwarts expectations" (Creach: 61) *[Conquest Accounts, p. 406]*.

OUTLINE

God's Instructions to Joshua, 6:1-5
Joshua Instructs and the People Comply, 6:6-11
Action on Days Two Through Six, 6:12-14
Action on the Seventh Day, 6:15-20b
The Walls Collapse and the People Act, 6:20c-21
The Rescue of Rahab, 6:22-25
Joshua's Oath Against Jericho, 6:26
Hinge to Chapter 7, 6:27

The chapter can also be divided by the speech (S) / narrative action (A) sequence, beginning with two speeches, one by God and one by Joshua: S: vv. 1-5; S: vv. 6-7; A: vv. 8-9; S: v. 10; A: vv. 11-15; S: vv. 16-19; A: vv. 20-21; S: v. 22: A: vv. 23-25; S: v. 26; with the narrator providing an interpretive summary in v. 27 (McEntire: 66).

EXPLANATORY NOTES

God's Instructions to Joshua 6:1-5

Verse 1 sets the stage by describing the people of Jericho as under siege inside the fortified city walls. They are expecting an attack. This introductory comment takes the reader back to the spies' report in 2:24, which describes the fear among the city's inhabitants. This verse also highlights the apparent impossibility of Israel's breaching the city wall (Howard 1998: 168).

The story begins, therefore, by alerting the reader to an enigma signaled in the first words of God in verse 2: *See, I have handed Jericho over to you* (sg.). These words suggest that the deed has already been accomplished (NJPS: *I will deliver*). The NASB preserves the Hebrew idiom with the expression *given . . . into your hand*, which we see echoed in Joshua's anticipatory comment in verse 16b. The expression is common in texts where military engagement and victory is expected and where the assurance is announced by God or a prophet (e.g., Deut 2:24; 21:10; Josh 8:1; 24:8, 11; cf. Deut 2:30; 1 Sam 23:4; 1 Kings 20:28; 22:6). Even in the Joshua examples, Israel engages in battle, but the Lord wins the victory (24:8, 12). But in Joshua 6 neither verse 1 nor verse 16 alludes to a battle even though we might expect that. The story begins with an even more radically theocentric perspective than we find in the Gideon story, where God declares that Gideon has too many men and might be tempted to take credit from God by saying, "My own hand has delivered me" (Judg 7:2).

Joshua 6 begins the conquest account proper with a paradigmatic narrative that does not negate the later militaristic conquest narratives, nor does it deny the fact that Israel is reported to have fought against the indigenous inhabitants of the land. But both here in 6:2 and at the end of the book in 24:11, God speaks a word that interprets the events narrated in the entire book. In chapter 6 it is a word of promise; in chapter 24, a word accomplished. And that is said after twice noting that fighting did occur (24:8, 11). The effect of framing the conquest this way may depict a synergistic notion of warfare (God and humans work together to accomplish God's purposes in history). More likely, it calls into question the presumption that human effort is the driving force in history. The chapter therefore "functions as a prototypical conquest, and thus serves as a paradigm in the light of which all the conquest materials are to be interpreted," a conclusion confirmed by the summarizing note of Joshua 24:11 in which "the entire conquest could be spoken of in terms of what happened at Jericho" (Fretheim 1983: 62).

The instructions to Israel include six discrete actions: the *warriors* are to march around the city once each day for six days (v. 3); *priests* carrying trumpets (rams' horns) are to accompany this march as they process ahead of the ark (v. 4a); on the seventh day they are to march around the city seven times while the priests blow the horns (continuously? v. 4b); the priests are to blow a long blast of the horn (v. 5a); the *people*, on hearing the blast, will shout (v. 5b); and when the walls fall down, the *people* shall charge ahead (v. 5c).

The divine instructions make it clear that no military strategy is involved. First, soldiers are not stationed around the city; they are to walk around and return to their starting point. Second, this is not strictly a siege but a ritual procession. The seven days parallel the seven days of the Passover celebration in chapters 3–4 (Creach: 63). Moreover, the ark has a role in the march around the city just as it did in the crossing of the Jordan River (3:3, 6, 11, 13, 14, 15, 17; 4:5, 7, 9, 10, 11, 16, 18). On the walk around the city, priests accompany the ark even as they are prominent in the crossing episode (3:3, 6, 8, 13, 14, 15, 17; 4:9, 10, 11, 16, 17, 18). The emphasis on the ark and the priests, along with the six-plus-one pattern of days, reminds us of the pattern of creation and Sabbath in Genesis 1. The number seven indicates the ancient notion of completeness. Thus, just as the seven days of the Passover celebration indicated the complete preparation of the people, here the seven days of walking around the city gives the sense that this task too will be completed.

Joshua's role as agent of divine instruction is anticipated in verses 2-5 as God's instructions echo throughout this story of repeated command and the people's obedience to those instructions (Culley: 36). The command to walk around is repeated in verse 7 and acted on in verses 8-9. The command to shout is emphasized by a negative command in verse 10 instructing the people to remain completely silent until the word is given (v. 16b), at which time the action may begin (v. 20). One surprising twist in the command-obedience sequence that begins in verses 2-5 is Joshua's command in verse 17a concerning the *ḥerem* (devoted to destruction), the intention of which is interpreted in verses 18-19 and applied in verse 21 [*Ḥerem*, *p. 433*]. Similarly, Joshua's command to spare Rahab does not come from the initial divine instructions in verses 2-5, but occurs first in verse 22, where it is commanded and acted upon (vv. 23-25; Winther-Nielsen: 203).

These verses (1-5), which serve as an introduction to chapter 6, do not reflect the traditional literary conventions of ancient Near Eastern conquest accounts *[Conquest Accounts, p. 406]*. Hence, when we read the instructions regarding the *ḥerem* in verses 17-19, we might wonder about the relationship between the liturgical or ritual character of this story and the warfare elements (see the discussion below on 6:15-20b).

Joshua Instructs and the People Comply 6:6-11

The sequence reported in this section alternates instruction (vv. 6-7, 10) and action (vv. 8-9, 11). Although slight variations occur, these are best interpreted as stylistic variations. The instructions are not precise prescriptions about who (priests or people) should stand where in relation to the ark; rather, they describe the mustering of the people in a kind of literary slow motion. The entire mini-episode is framed by the taking up of the ark (v. 6) and the ark's circling around the city on the first day (v. 11). Given the significance of the ark, it is odd that the summary in verse 13 is the last reference to it . No mention is made of the ark in the report about the seventh day's activities (v. 15). But the repetition is not required, since the pattern is established in verses 6-11, and verse 15 reports that the pattern is repeated *in the same manner* on the seventh day. Moreover, verse 11 highlights Joshua's role (in the subject of the Hiphil-causative form of the verb), which makes it clear that Joshua *had the Ark of the* L*ORD* *go around the city* (NJPS). After the ark comes *the rear guard*, which should probably be translated to convey the sense that "the remainder" of the people follow the ark (Winther-Nielsen: 198–99).

In this impressionistic picture of the activities, why does Joshua command that the people be completely silent (*nor shall you utter a word*) until he calls for a shout (v. 10)? The silence certainly emphasizes the solemnity of the ritual event, with only the sound of seven trumpets punctuating the march. The word used for *shout* is mentioned in other biblical texts as a victory shout (in relation to God's kingship, in Pss 47:1-3; 60:8; 95:1, 2; 98:4, 6; or victory over enemies, in Pss 60:8; 108:9; cf. Jer 50:15). Whereas a military attack might include a similar shout, here the shout is not accompanied by an attack. The only human activity involved in bringing down the walls is a *word* (Heb. *dabar*), prohibited in verse 10, and articulated only in the shout of victory.

Action on Days Two Through Six 6:12-14

As expected, the narrative continues the next morning, day two: in a terse rehearsal of the pattern presented on day one, the walk around the city continues for six days. These two verses present, in straightforward reporting prose, what has been stylistically varied in the speeches and responses up to verse 11. Without any descriptive detail about the city, the text simply reports a single march around the city each day. These verses mark a transition to the seventh day (v. 15), which is the most important day (both here and in Gen 1:1–2:4a).

The focus on the ark in the first part of the chapter emphasizes the divine presence, just as the narrator's summary interpretive comment in 6:27 underlines that same presence as the capstone of the chapter.

Action on the Seventh Day 6:15-20b

Verse 15 marks the transition to the seventh-day activity by reporting twice that the people make seven circuits around the city, as instructed in verse 4b. Verse 16 begins Joshua's instructions (vv. 16-19) by reiterating the command to shout, mentioned earlier, in verses 5 and 10. Within those instructions, beginning at verse 17, we encounter a new element not mentioned before: the instruction that *the city and all that is in it shall be devoted to the Lord for destruction*. Immediately following that command in verse 17a comes the restriction in verse 17b: *Only Rahab . . . and all who are with her in her house shall live*. Those instructions are not part of the earlier divine instructions to Joshua at the beginning of the chapter. The horror of the initial instruction now becomes clear. *The city and all that is in it* is not referring merely to flattening the city, but to killing all the people who live in the city. The phrase "to devote to destruction," which we find again in verses 18 and 21, translates the Hebrew word *ḥerem* (or its cognate verb). It refers to a common practice reported in ancient Near Eastern conquest accounts: killing the defeated enemy in a ritualistic slaughter and offering in a sacrificial manner all of the spoils, including the enemy themselves, to the god(s) who enabled the army to win the victory *[Conquest Accounts, p. 406; Ḥerem, p. 433]*.

The NJPS translation softens the impact of verse 17 slightly by omitting the phrase *to destruction* and by translating the Hebrew word *ḥerem* as "proscribed for the Lord." This is significant only because it highlights the fact that *ḥerem* does not always involve killing all the human beings. The NRSV adds "for destruction," which is not necessarily always so, as we shall see in the case of Rahab, who remains *ḥerem* but is not doomed "for destruction."

That Rahab is spared takes us back to Joshua 2, to which 6:17 refers when Joshua reminds listeners/readers that *she hid the messengers we sent.* This episode completes the story of Joshua 2 by illustrating how Israel is to honor the covenant that Rahab has made with the two spies (here called *messengers,* which adds to the intertextual echo with Gen 19:1; see TBC on Josh 2).

Joshua sharpens the focus of his instructions in verses 18-19, where he tells Israel to *keep away from the things devoted to destruction.* The rationale given in verse 18 in NRSV is *so as not to covet and take, because such action would make the camp of Israel an object for destruction.* The problem with the NRSV rendering of verse 18 can be highlighted by observing the NIV, which reads, *But keep away from the devoted things, so that you will not bring about your own destruction by taking any of them.* In this case the NRSV has followed the LXX, which either reflects an earlier Hebrew original or has imported the word *covet* from Joshua 7:21, where Achan explains his actions: *I coveted them and took them.* Or it reflects a harmonization with Deuteronomy 7:25, which warns against coveting, taking, and being ensnared. Besides its use in Deuteronomy 7:25, the Hebrew verb *covet* occurs with this meaning in the Pentateuch only three times (Exod 20:17; 34:24; Deut 5:21; in Gen 2:9; 3:6 the same Hebrew verb means "to be pleasing/delightful"). The point of Deuteronomy 7:25 is clarified in naming things "abhorrent" (a word not used in Joshua). They are not to be brought into one's house or "you will be set apart for destruction [noun *ḥerem*] like it" (Deut 7:26). The point of Joshua 6:18 is to emphasize the danger of taking the devoted things, the *ḥerem,* which would render the one who takes as *ḥerem.* Something designated *ḥerem* becomes contagious (Deut 7:26). Hence, although covetousness may be implied, especially given the link between this text and the story of Achan in chapter 7, that is not the point here. The allusion forward to Joshua 7:12 is significant, but Joshua 7 will develop the motive of covetousness independently and consonant with Deuteronomy 7:25-26. Here in Joshua 6:18, the boundary between *ḥerem* and everything else is established. If Israel itself becomes *ḥerem* (a dreadful thought), the persons (v. 18 addresses pl. "you") responsible will be said to be *bringing trouble* on the camp. In the three other uses of this expression in the DtrH, the main characters are responsible for leading Israel away from wholehearted devotion to the Lord (Achan in Josh 7:25; Saul in 1 Sam 14:29; Ahab in 1 Kings 18:17-18).

In order to prevent such disloyalty, the *ḥerem* relegates these objects to *the treasury of the* LORD (Josh 6:19). They are *sacred* to the Lord. Just as the people are to be *sanctified* (3:5), so the place is *holy* (5:15), and now these objects are identified as *sacred*. In each case the Hebrew root is the same (*qdš*).

Several other characteristics of verses 17-19 deserve special attention. First, mentioning Rahab in verse 17b—between two uses of the word *ḥerem* in verses 17a and 18a—highlights the fact that Rahab is an exception to Deuteronomic instructions regarding warfare (Deut 7; 20). Second, all the instructions in verses 17-19 fall between Joshua's instruction to shout in verse 16b and the people's shouting in verse 20a. Third, verses 17-19, flavored by Deuteronomic vocabulary, are inserted in the sequence of events, the effect of which is to create a pause to reflect on the real danger ahead. Verses 17-19 emphasize, therefore, that the danger lies not with the enemy, but within Israel. That which belongs to the Lord is the Lord's. Any crossing of boundaries constitutes a challenge to life itself. That is why the instructions about sparing Rahab (*all . . . shall live*, v. 17b) are and yet are not out of place. According to Deuteronomic instruction, Rahab ought to have been among those killed, but she is not because the spies have already transgressed the letter of the law in Deuteronomy by making a covenant with her and sparing her life. Yet the narrator in Joshua 6 remembers the technicality that Rahab too is *ḥerem* and reminds us that after her rescue, she was placed *outside the camp* (see below on v. 23).

The sub-unit ends with the brief announcement that *the people shouted and the trumpets were blown* (v. 20ab; note the chiastic reversal of order from v. 16).

The Walls Collapse and the People Act 6:20c-21

The final action reported in verses 20c-21 reiterates the trumpet blast and the shout (now in proper sequence), then describes the fall of the wall, the charge of the people to capture the city, and the terrifying action of killing all its inhabitants *by the edge of the sword*. All of the actions reported here and in the previous verses have been ordered by God in verses 2-5 except for the slaying of all Jericho's inhabitants. That act is commanded only in Joshua's instructions in verse 17, where the *ḥerem* is commanded, but only in verse 21 is the means articulated: *by the edge of the sword*.

Now we read not simply about a theoretical dedication of the spoils to God. The narrator, using merism (opposites to represent the whole), makes it clear who *all in the city* are: *men and women, young and old*, plus animals. This action corresponds to the instructions in Deuteronomy 20:16-17: "You must not let anything that breathes remain alive" (Deut 20:16b).

We come now to ask again about the relationship between the apparent liturgical or ritual character of Joshua 6 and the "warfare" that the text depicts. That the walls should fall down after seven days of walking around the city is a wonder to imagine. It makes us think of the world of fantasy literature. But that every living thing should be destroyed is more the stuff of horror than fantasy. This description is so theologically problematic that it requires separate attention *[Archaeology and Joshua, p. 389; Conquest Accounts, p. 406; Theology of Warfare, p. 458]*. Here, however, we need to reflect on how and why this text makes sense in this context. According to McEntire, "The primary theological issue for Joshua 6 is the nature of God's presence within all of the activity which occurs in and around Jericho" (70). McEntire reports that in the history of interpretation concerning Joshua 6, "there seems to be a tendency to avoid theological interpretation. . . . When theology is considered, the most common conclusion to which interpreters struggle to arrive is that what took place in Jericho was worship, not warfare" (70). For example, Longman writes: "Indeed, it is not too strong to say that *ḥerem* warfare is worship. The battlefield is sacred space. To be involved in warfare is a holy activity analogous to going to the temple" (Cowles et al.: 164). Hamlin also suggests that Joshua 6 is "history remembered through liturgy" (1983: 46). Butler declares concerning the priests, "Their role has been to transform the narrative from battle story to cultic drama" (1983: 86). Similarly, Nelson comments: "To extol Yahweh as the Divine Warrior was to engage in doxology" (1997a: 17).

To all of this McEntire responds by suggesting that these are attempts to ignore the violence of war: "The story ends with a city full of dead bodies" (71). Even Wink states, "Jericho's walls collapsed after ritual, not military action." Yet Wink suggests that this story reflects "the depth to which the myth of redemptive violence had penetrated Israel's theology and politics" (1992: 188). Although McEntire acknowledges the liturgical elements in the text, these, he says, "fade away as the story progresses" (71).

To say that the text depicts the initial entry into the land as worship has several consequences. It may highlight the sacral character of warfare, which may make sense in our world only to those who continue to use religion to justify violence and ethnic warfare. Having said that, however, we have substituted all kinds of other ways of ascribing meaning to war (Hedges). For that reason we do well to pay more attention. The effect of sacralizing warfare this way allows us to see how warfare in the ancient world (and in ours as well) participates in a ritual of sacrificial or redemptive violence. At least in the memory preserved in the text (and in the Mesha Inscription as well), the victims of war are treated as belonging exclusively to the divinity *[Mesha Inscription, p. 447]*. A second consequence of recognizing the priority of worship over warfare in the story is an acknowledgment that God's universal sovereignty stands at the paradigmatic heart of the book *[Theology of Warfare, p. 458]*.

The problem must be dealt with not on its own, but through two parallel considerations: (1) the way the story shares the traditional conventions of ancient Near Eastern conquest accounts raises questions about the normative theological vision in *these* texts that ascribe such violence to a divine command; and (2) the way the story as a whole works to undermine or to call into question the necessity or inevitability of total destruction. In other words, this text, as well as the book of Joshua as a whole, works within the generic conventions—what one would expect of an ancient warfare account, including language, metaphor, hyperbole, structure, and so forth (Younger 1990). It uses the language and forms of communication that are available to speak about divine and human involvement in warfare. Yet the book of Joshua, including this chapter, creates an opening for theological reflection that challenges the cultural assumptions hidden in the genre and vocabulary of the text *[Conquest Accounts, p. 406]*. And that sense of calling into question comes into focus in the next subunit of the text.

The Rescue of Rahab 6:22-25

Joshua's instructions continue in verse 22, picking up the notice about Rahab from verse 17b. Remarkably, the instructions here are not to a generic plural audience, but specifically *to the two men who had spied out the land* (v. 22a). The echo of Joshua 2 comes through in the details recounted in verse 22, including the swearing of an oath (2:12-14). Verse 23 reports the action of the two men, reporting also that Rahab and her family are placed *outside the camp of Israel*. The identification of her family members, emphasized by the addition of *all her kindred*, suggests an irony: this woman, a Canaanite and a prostitute, brings many from her web of relationships along with her. That Rahab is an insider by confession (ch. 2) has not yet resolved the question of whether there might be another way in which she is "inside" Israel. The point here is not to juxtapose confession with geography or ethnicity, but to highlight the fact that she continues her status as *ḥerem* (*outside the camp*) and yet has remained alive.

The report of Rahab's rescue includes a cutaway to another scene, that of burning the city and placing the valuable objects *into the treasury of the house of the* Lord (v. 24). That this *treasury* is in the *house of the* Lord is not unusual, since in the ancient world temples often functioned as royal treasuries (cf. 2 Kings 18:15). The expression *house of the* Lord seems not to be connected to a prominent usage in Deuteronomy, where the expression occurs in a negative command only once (Deut 23:18). But it may be linked to the law about firstfruits in Exodus 23:19; 34:26, where the first or choice harvest is to be brought to the house of the Lord (Creach: 63). That this *house* is the place where the ark is located can be inferred from a poetic text like Psalm 27:4-6 and the several references in Judges and Samuel (Judg 19:18 NIV; 1 Sam 1:7, 24; 3:15; 2 Sam 12:20; cf. 2 Sam 6:17). After that, beginning with the reign of David, the house of the Lord refers to a shrine in Jerusalem (2 Sam 12:20) or to the temple (1 Kings 3:1). In this scene, the firstfruit of the Lord's victory over Jericho is presented to the *house of the* Lord.

The subunit concludes with the narrator's summary about the sparing of Rahab (v. 25). Especially prominent is the notice that Rahab (with *her family and all who belonged to her*) *has lived in Israel ever since* (NIV: *lives among the Israelites to this day*; NJPS: *She dwelt among the Israelites—as is still the case*). The NJPS is clearer in its separation of past time from present time, whereas the NIV collapses narrated time into present time. Several things may be said about this brief but important notice. First, in verse 25b the NRSV has substituted the wider "her family" for the Hebrew "she" (in *She has lived in Israel*). It is clear from verse 23 that "she" includes her family. But the "she" in verse 25b suggests even more: Rahab has become like one of the other ancestors; her name has come to represent the group. She (the woman from the distant past) now stands for all who continue to carry her name and who continue, even at a much later date, to live *in Israel*. Here the narrator finally takes Rahab from *outside the camp* (v. 23) to *in Israel* (v. 25). The process of inclusion is not mentioned, but the passing of time seems to have looked after that.

One final aside is worth noting. The Hebrew word for "in" (NRSV, NIV) or "among" (NJPS) in verse 25 is *beqereb*. Being "among" is significant in this paradigmatic story, especially since Joshua later will say that others live among Israel (13:13; 16:10), and in Judges,

Israel will live "among" others (Judg 1:32, 33; 3:5). Rahab's case is unique, however, because she has made an agreement, has entered into a relationship, and has confessed God as Sovereign of the earth. Rahab's presence is an anomaly and an irony, testifying against literal application of Deuteronomy's warfare laws. She becomes a symbolic double for Israel who, as noted in the book of Judges, also lives "in the midst" of the indigenous population.

Moreover, Rahab is "within"; she is a *ḥerem*-designated person who has been saved from the sword. Looking ahead to 7:12, we notice that some of the things designated *ḥerem* are now "within" Israel, which becomes a problem. Israel there becomes *ḥerem* (Eslinger: 44). Yet this story shows how *ḥerem*-designated persons become non-*ḥerem* persons. Creach suggests that the sparing of Rahab may be an attempt to show how "the ban's barbaric character is mitigated" or softened (65). He points out how "each command concerning the devoted things is followed immediately by a reference to Rahab's salvation (vv. 17b, 22-23, 25)" (65). That she is spared offers an alternative voice to the instructions in Deuteronomy 7 or 20, where no examples of exceptions can be found (similarly Lev 27:28-29).

Joshua's Oath Against Jericho 6:26

The story ends with an ominous curse, taken up in 1 Kings 16:34, which suggests not only that Joshua is a spokesperson for God, but more, that the word of God is the driving force in history. This is the first text in the DtrH that corresponds to the larger vision of prophecy-fulfillment in the books of Kings, where at least ten times the narrative emphasizes that events occur because they have been directed by a prophetic word (1 Kings 12:15; 14:18; 15:29; 16:12, 34; 2 Kings 1:17; 7:16-18; 9:36; 15:12; 23:16-18, 30; 24:2). This saying, therefore, marks a significant moment in the narrative: like other ancient Near Eastern conquest accounts, it ascribes the victory to a god.

But it does more. This saying makes Joshua the first of the post-Moses prophets whose word continues to impinge on the future in such a way that it cannot be mistaken that God is the primary agent in shaping Israel's future. Human choices have significant consequences, but those choices are always made within the scope and sphere of God's universal sovereignty. In other words, God does not arbitrarily "make things happen," but things happen as humans so choose under the watchful eye and purposive direction of God. The narrator, by including Joshua's statement here, is not simply saying that Joshua is making a prediction, but is surely asserting that Joshua is a prophet, and that the prophetic word, not imperial and military might, drives Israel's future.

Hinge to Chapter 7 6:27

Verse 27 is both the capstone verse of chapter 6 and a hinge verse that provides the transition between this narrative and the next. It highlights the presence of the Lord in the events surrounding the taking of Jericho and celebrates the fact that the Lord is with Joshua (cf. 3:7; 4:14). The only ambiguous aspect of the verse concerns the pronoun referent in the phrase *his fame* (lit., *the report of him*). In Joshua 9:9 the *report of him* (same noun and pronoun suffix), meaning the Lord, has reached the Gibeonites. It seems likely, therefore, that the *fame* is first of all of Joshua, which becomes in the story of the Gibeonites the fame of the Lord. The cumulative witness of both texts underlines that *the LORD was with Joshua* (6:27a). Thus the theocentric focus of the Jericho story is punctuated at the end by this interpretive comment by the narrator. And it leads us into the story of Joshua 7, which focuses on the human failure in the face of divine action.

THE TEXT IN BIBLICAL CONTEXT

A "Warfare Worldview"

In spite of the affirmation in the book of Hebrews that the walls of Jericho fell *by faith* (11:30), the slaughter of Jericho's inhabitants creates the most challenging point for conversation with and among biblical texts. The violence reported here cannot be denied any more than can the twentieth-century murder of Jews in Nazi Germany. Both contexts were shaped by a religious or ideological worldview *[Conquest Accounts, p. 406]*. Nor may the rhetorical impact of this text be legitimately toned down, either by rewriting the story (e.g., by claiming that the *ḥerem* was never practiced consistently in ancient Israel), or by claiming that this is a late idea inserted or read back into a narrative about the origins of Israel in the land. We may be able to place the composition of Joshua into one or other historical context and then argue that the book of Joshua was written to buttress that era's claim on the land. But attempts to locate the book of Joshua in a particular time remain debatable *[Composition of Joshua, p. 398]*. We are still left wrestling with a text that reflects a warfare worldview and, over time, has been in dialogue with other texts that challenge that worldview.

Some interpreters (e.g., Lind 1980) suggest that Joshua's narrative of conquest can be relativized by noting that a text like Exodus 15, which was certainly written earlier, provides the paradigmatic lens through which Joshua may be read. Exodus 15, a poetic text, asserts with poetic hyperbole that God alone did battle against the opponent: "I will draw my sword, my hand shall destroy them" (15:9b). The Exodus poem, claims Lind, presents an ethical paradigm. Israel ought to have allowed God to wage the battle alone (thus the term *monergism*, "working alone"). Whether we can accurately determine which biblical texts came first is partly beside the point. The book of Joshua itself shares some of the same lively hyperbole as the Exodus poem *[Conquest Accounts, p. 406]*). The point of such hyperbole is to affirm an imperialistic worldview. But is it God's imperium or Israel's that is being celebrated? The Exodus poem celebrates God's victory against overwhelming odds to rescue an enslaved people. This same perspective shapes the narrative of the book of Joshua (and other texts like the Gideon story in Judg 7). The narrative of Joshua, like that of the exodus story as a whole, does not advocate an ethic for imperialists. It includes, rather, a conquest narrative that subtly undermines itself by using the generic conventions of ancient conquest accounts (including victory provided by the god) in order to make a theological assertion that Yahweh is greatest among deities (cf. Exod 15:11a). God's universal sovereignty is at stake in the narrative of Joshua. And if that can be demonstrated, then why would Israel worship any other gods? That question is at the heart of Joshua's speeches in chapters 23–24.

The story of the Assyrian siege of Jerusalem in 2 Kings 18–19 celebrates the answer to the question. The Assyrian diplomat asks whether "any of the gods of the nations ever delivered its land out of the hand of the king of Assyria?" (18:33). "Who among all the gods" (18:35) would be capable against such imperial might? As the narrative concludes, the reader discovers that "the angel of the LORD" accomplishes the impossible (2 Kings 19:35). Is this "angel of the LORD" to be likened to the one who appears and who "goes before" Israel (Exod 3:2; 14:19; 33:2) and who, we presume, appears to Joshua (Josh 5:13-15)? If these intertextual allusions emphasize the divine presence, then this narrative in Joshua 6 is first of all about who is *with* Joshua and Israel (6:27). In Joshua 6, therefore, the Lord stands with Israel. In Joshua 7, as we shall see, the Lord stands against Israel. These two paradigmatic stories in Joshua, therefore, open up the heart of the narrative. The story highlights not so much what Israel does, but rather the implications of divine presence and divine instruction.

Joshua 6, therefore, begins to open up the question of whose "word" shapes history. The chapter begins with a divine word and ends with Joshua announcing a prophetic word. And in the context of Deuteronomy and the DtrH, that is ultimately what matters. The divine word shapes the future, and human response to the divine word creates the conditions within which the divine word bears fruit or not. Still, the divine word will not be thwarted: God's purposes will prevail.

Placing the Joshua narrative into a conversation with other biblical texts suggests that Joshua 6 has been understood within Scripture as one example among many of the attempt to "make sense of war and killing in war" (Niditch: 151). The tendency in Scripture and in the history of interpretation has been to transform the violence of the Jericho story in one way or another. To claim that God is ultimately the Sovereign One in all the earth relativizes Israel's self-importance.

Having acknowledged the centrality of the theological concerns in Joshua, it will nevertheless also be important for us to allow the narrative of Joshua 6 a voice of its own. In the conversation that follows, it will be tempting to conclude, simply, that since other biblical texts subvert Joshua 6 or rewrite it, there is no longer anything to hear. We run the risk of silencing the voice of this text because of its terror. Still, it may be possible to reject some aspects of the text and receive others.

Rahab and the Warfare Laws in Deuteronomy

The intimate connections between Joshua 6 and the laws governing warfare in Deuteronomy 7 and 20 are unmistakable. Both chapters highlight divine action but do not exclude human involvement (7:1-2; 20:4; cf. 1:30, 42). Deuteronomy 7 begins with a mention of the seven nations that God will "clear away . . . before you" (7:1). Deuteronomy 7:2 states that the conquest will be a divine gift and that Israel's role will be to "defeat them." They are to "annihilate them" (*ḥerem*; 7:2; 20:17) and "not let anything that breathes remain alive" (Deut 20:16) [*Ḥerem, p. 433*]. Moreover, they are instructed: "Make no covenant with them and show them no mercy" (7:2; "no pity" in 7:16; for a provocative dialogue on this theme in Scripture, see Cowles et al.). Both Deuteronomy 7 and 20 are concerned that the involvement with indigenous people might "turn away your children from following me, to serve other gods" (7:4), which "would be a snare to you" (7:16). The word "snare" is used in this way only three times in the DtrH (Josh 23:13; Judg 2:3; 8:27). In Deuteronomy 20 the danger of the indigenous Other is expressed this way: "so that they may not teach you to do all the abhorrent things that they do for their gods" (20:18). We have discovered in Joshua 2 the ironic fact that Israel has already made a covenant with Rahab. Hence her rescue in chapter 6 has the potential of becoming such a snare.

The argument in Deuteronomy concerns the danger of intermarriage and the worship of other gods (7:3-4), or of behavior endorsed by the worship of those gods (20:18). Clearly Rahab's living *in the midst of Israel to this day* has created the reality of intermarriage (Josh 6:25 NASB), but her confession of faith in Israel's Lord has eliminated the danger of worshiping other gods (cf. 23:12-13). Yet her rescue is the key that opens the interpretive door on Deuteronomy's warfare laws and calls into question a static understanding of divine law *[Torah, p. 462]*.

Since the story does not depict a wooden application of Deuteronomy's warfare laws, Stone looks for textual clues in the book of Joshua itself that "explain, mitigate, and reinterpret the portrayal of Israel's slaughter of the Canaanites" (28). In focusing on the literary structure of the book, Stone deals with six texts (Josh 2:9-11; 5:1; 9:1-2; 9:3-4; 10:1-5; 11:1-5) and a pattern of report-response within those texts. "The six recurring similarly formulated statements . . . function as a structural feature which both organizes Joshua 9–11 internally and relates that unit to Joshua 6–8. Moreover, chapters 6–11 move within the expectations created by Joshua 2–5. These units frame the Jericho-Ai section with events focusing on Israel's presence in Canaan as an action of God to which the Canaanites must respond" (33). Joshua 6 is related to Joshua 2, therefore, by drawing the reader back to Rahab's confessional response in 2:9-11.

The book of Joshua is not concerned with the abhorrent behavior of the indigenous population. Instead of Deuteronomy's fear that the nations will "teach you" (20:18), Joshua focuses on that other "teach you" of the Torah (Deut 4:5, 14; 6:1). That Rahab "knows" Torah is implied in her Deuteronomic confession (Josh 2:9-11). In this way Rahab is more than an "exceptional outsider" (Polzin); she is an outsider who not only knows the exodus story and Deuteronomic language but also models a response to Israel's God. Even though Genesis 15:16 announced judgment for "the iniquity of the Amorites," Rahab demonstrates that judgment is not inevitable. Rescuing Rahab, therefore, not only introduces a crack of light into Deuteronomy's laws of warfare, but also into the notion of redemption through violence (sacrifice). She stands out in this story not as an aside, or a literary link back to the story in Joshua 2, but as the key note in the narrative. Her rescue, along with her family of refugees, signals an end to strict adherence to the prohibition on rescuing human beings from being sacrificed as part of *ḥerem* (Lev 27:29) *[Conquest Accounts, p. 406; Ḥerem, p. 433]*. Here now is one who, apart from race, culture, or status, stands for all the marginal whom God's story embraces.

The Seven-Day Procession and Rest

The seven-day procession around Jericho, with its sevenfold march around on the seventh day and the blowing of seven trumpets—all this alerts the reader to the familiarity and significance of the number seven in the OT. The patterning that signifies completeness is also part of the weekly repetition of six and one, which recalls the first creation story in Genesis 1. The seven-day pattern is also reflected in the Passover celebration and implied seven-day eating of unleavened bread in Joshua 5:10-11 (cf. seven days in Exod 12–13; Deut 16). Dauphinais and Levering suggest that this story, in which "soldiers are to fight not by violence, but simply by solemnly circling the city in harmonious liturgical procession," is thus the beginning of a "new creation" story (85; cf. the liturgical character of warfare in 2 Chron 20:20-22). Here, perhaps, is an example of the universal (cosmos: creation) embodied in the particular (history: land).

Although the same word for "rest" is not used in Joshua as in Genesis 2:2-3, the motif of rest occurs at the beginning and the end of the book of Joshua (1:13, 15; 21:44; 22:4; 23:1). In addition, the narrator notes twice that Israel *had rest from war* (11:23; 14:15). This notion of rest is echoed in the NT, especially in the book of Hebrews, where entering God's rest is a significant motif. Joshua is even mentioned in Heb 4:8-11, where the seventh day surely alludes to the victory of the Sabbath rest. I mention this here, even though we will return to it in Joshua 21–23, because the motif of disobedience (Heb 4:11) is also implicit in the juxtaposition of Joshua 6 and 7. Perhaps this is why 6:27 is so laden with implicit tragedy in the light of what is to follow. Whereas the Jericho story is a paradigm of the seventh-day rest on which no one labors, Joshua 7 is the paradigm story of the day of disobedience that nullifies the promise of rest. Hence the narrators in Joshua and Hebrews are working within a figural worldview in which both texts may be unique and typical at the same time *[Rest, p. 455]*.

Joshua as Prophet/Agent of the Divine Word

That Joshua 6:26 is cited practically word for word in 1 Kings 16:34 is as important as anything else in the chapter. The citation in Kings is set during the reign of Ahab. The narrator recounts how Ahab took Jezebel as his wife, how he "served Baal, and worshiped him," and how he "did more to provoke the anger of the LORD . . . than had all the kings of Israel who were before him" (1 Kings 16:31-33). Immediately after that report, we read an apparently unrelated brief account of a man named Hiel of Bethel, who during Ahab's time built Jericho "at the cost of Abiram his firstborn . . . and of his youngest son Segub, according to the word of the LORD, which he spoke by Joshua son of Nun" (16:34). Two observations may be made.

First, the reference to Joshua 6:26 in 1 Kings 16:34 belongs to the theology of God's involvement in history as presented in the books of 1 and 2 Kings. Throughout Kings, the expression "according to the word of the LORD" occurs fifteen times (1 Kings 12:24; 14:18; 15:29; 16:12, 34; 17:5, 16; 22:38; 2 Kings 1:17; 4:44; 7:16; 10:17; 14:25; 23:16; 24:2). God is actively present in history through the prophetic word, which brings about God's purposes for Israel and against Israel. Joshua's only "prophetic announcement," cited here, is important for understanding not only Joshua's role in the narrative, but also for the implied sense of the purposefulness of God's actions. Joshua's "curse" is not a magical pronouncement but rather a prophetic judgment saying that (cryptically) warns against Israel's participation in the indigenous practice of child sacrifice (cf. the story of the king of Moab who offered his firstborn son in 2 Kings 3:27; cf. 2 Kings 17:17). Although it is not clear that *at the cost of* alludes to child sacrifice, Joshua 6:26 and 1 Kings 16:34 seem to imply that.

Second, the brief note in 1 Kings 16:34 may well serve as an introduction to the Elijah story that follows in 1 Kings 17, where Elijah announces in his first speech that there will not be any rain "except by my word." Since the emphasis on the "word of the LORD" coming to fruition is a prominent theme in Kings, Joshua's curse of Jericho, as it apparently comes to fruition in Ahab's time, is symptomatic of a larger problem: the loss of life of the children on the one hand, and Baal worship on the other. At the heart of the text, however, is the power of the divine word uttered through God's agents. For the Deuteronomic school of writers, therefore, Joshua becomes a paradigmatic figure who, like Moses, speaks an effective word. The only time Moses is so mentioned in a similar manner in Kings is in Solomon's blessing on the people after his prayer of dedication of the temple (1 Kings 8:56, which echoes almost exactly Josh 23:14; cf. Josh 21:45).

In the DtrH, events transpire "according to the word of the LORD," thereby affirming the primacy of the prophetic word over the political and military initiatives of kings. The irony of that, however, is that even though Joshua is obedient servant of God's word, he does not fully obey the word of the Lord as provided by Moses in Deuteronomy: Rahab is spared even though there are no "loopholes" in the Deuteronomic law (Creach: 67). Joshua spares Rahab. The *word* of Deuteronomy is circumvented by Rahab and the spies, Joshua and Israel keep the word of the spies, and the letter of the law is bent. Joshua disobeys and in so doing demonstrates the dynamic freedom of the law to generate life within the sovereignty of God. As in the case of the daughters of Zelophehad, the law needs fine-tuning (Num 27; 36; Josh 17:3-6). The Jericho story thus shares in ancient conventions of warfare, but adds an odd and merciful twist. Disobedience in this case gives life *[Characterization of Joshua, p. 394]*.

Bringing Trouble

The threat of bringing trouble on the camp (6:18) finds echoes in the stories of Achan (Josh 7:25), Saul and Jonathan (1 Sam 14:29), and Elijah and Ahab (1 Kings 18:17-18). The only other place where the Hebrew verb for "bring trouble" occurs in the context of a narrative about a threat to the people is in Gen 34:30, where Jacob tells Simeon and Levi, "You have brought trouble on me by making me odious to the inhabitants of the land, the *Canaanites* and the *Perizzites*" (two of the people groups mentioned in Josh 3:10; 9:1; 11:3; 12:8; 24:11). And this "trouble" was caused, as Jacob understands it, by the indiscriminate slaughter of all the males in Shechem. That action avenges the "taking" and (possible) rape of Dinah (Gen 34:2 NIV), whom the brothers claim was treated like a prostitute (*zonah*). Yet their plunder of the city (34:27-29, cf. "took," v. 28) could be seen as contributing to the "trouble" (34:30). By contrast, in the Joshua story *Rahab the prostitute* (*zonah*) is spared by a similar act of annihilation. In both cases the "taking"—or in the case of Joshua 6, the possibility of taking—threatens to "bring trouble" on the group as a whole.

Joshua 6 and the Jubilee

Besides Joshua 6:4-16, the only other place in Scripture where the trumpet (*šopar*) and ram's horn (*yobel*) are used in the same context is in Leviticus 25 (in Josh 6 *yobel* is used nine times and *šopar* seventeen times; *šopar* is used in Lev 25:9; *yobel* is found in 25:10-12 and many following verses). It cannot be said with any certainty that the taking of Jericho is being portrayed as similar to the Jubilee year (the view originates in medieval Jewish interpretation; see Drucker: 177). It could be that Jericho as *ḥerem* is offered to the Lord as a firstfruit of the new year (e.g., following the harvest reported in Josh 5:12). This would correspond to the use of the word *ḥerem* in Lev 27:28, which refers to things that are designated *ḥerem* to the Lord outside of wartime, or as a portrait of the return of the land to its rightful owners (as in Lev 25). This notion of the land and the Jubilee year ties this narrative to the motif of the justice of God, the rightful owner of the land, who gives it to whom God pleases, and who judges all nations for their bloodshed, violence, and idolatry (e.g., Amos 1–2; 3:2; 9:7-8) *[Idolatry, p. 438]*.

Jericho in the Book of Hebrews

The book of Hebrews classifies the fall of Jericho as an act of faith akin to the people's passing through the Red Sea (11:29-30). Remarkably, the sparing of Rahab is also an act of faith (11:31). Her faith saves her, since "by faith" is contrasted with "those who were disobedient" and perished. Yet her faith is not her confession (Josh 2:9-11), but her action of having "received the spies in peace" (Heb 11:31). The only other use of the word "disobedient/unbelieving" in Hebrews refers to those Israelites who were not allowed to enter God's rest (3:18). These two uses of the word in Hebrews suggest that Hebrews makes no significant distinction between disobedient Israelites and disobedient residents of Jericho. And therefore Rahab enters God's rest, yet she, like the Israelites, "did not receive what was promised" (11:39). The promise was not exhausted, according to Hebrews 11:40, by the faithfulness of the former generations. Thus, even though the book of Joshua will say later that every promise of God was fulfilled (Josh 21:45; 23:14), later readers and interpreters will read the book of Joshua as though the fulfillment of the promises is not unique, but typical. The fulfillment in Joshua 6 is figural since Rahab's rescue, allied with her faithfulness, becomes a kind of salvation that becomes a reality again and again (hence her appearance in Matthew's genealogy, in Hebrews, and in James) *[Rest, p. 455]*.

All that has come before strives toward that which God is yet to do (Heb 11:40). Thus the examples in Hebrews 11, including those of warfare and the fall of Jericho's walls, are but partial expositions of

God's purpose within the limited sphere of human experience—expositions of a longer hope in what is not yet seen. This hoped-for existence stands in the middle of time. It is not the beginning nor the end of the story. Life in the middle of time must be a life of faith—faith to see through and to discern faithful action in the midst of horrific circumstances. That is what the book of Joshua highlights about Rahab, and what the book of Hebrews affirms as faith.

THE TEXT IN THE LIFE OF THE CHURCH

Appropriating the Story

There have been times in the life of the church, represented by the example of the First Crusade (1096 AD), when the crusaders "acted out Old Testament scenes" like that of Joshua 6. "Just as the ark of the covenant had been carried into battle, . . . so the Holy Lance, discovered at Antioch and purportedly the very lance with which the centurion pierced Christ's side, was carried into battle" (Lynch: 28). The anonymous knights who wrote their stories tell of spending days in preparation for battle and of shaping the battle event as a liturgical event (26).

Unlike such militaristic appropriation of the Joshua narrative, the interpretation of Joshua 6 in the early church builds on a reading such as we have in Hebrews. For example, Origen's interpretation of Joshua 6 reflects his figural reading, in which everything is related to Christ in three ways: "in his historical life, in his mystical Body, and in his final parousia" (Daniélou: 277). Origen begins his appropriation of the "conquest" of Jericho by noting the means employed. A trumpet sounds; "the sword is not drawn against it" (Origen: 72). For Origen, building on earlier interpretive tradition, Jericho is "a figure of this world," and the fall of Jericho is a type of the eschatological conquest of evil (Daniélou: 238). And if such a consummation is to take place, by what means, he asks, will it happen? Here he takes us to 1 Corinthians 15:52 and Paul's image of the trumpet as sounding at the resurrection. As Daniélou puts it, "The fall of Jericho is accomplished through Christ's passion" (278) *[Figural Reading, p. 426]*.

In his interpretation, Origen's focus on the Christian life is similar to Jewish biblical interpretation beginning with books like *Jubilees* in the first century AD. Jewish interpretation includes a similar transformation of the conquest-land narrative. Like the NT writers, the author of *Jubilees* saw that "spiritual regeneration and total repentance, not Land retention, is the crucial issue in the author's present situation. From the perspective of the past, Land promise, acquisition, and retention are the markers of Israel's history. From the author's present, purity of heart and fidelity to the covenant become the new eschatological markers" (Halpern-Amaru: 51). In the eschatological perspective of *Jubilees*, "Satan and the power of evil will be destroyed, God's servants will be empowered to 'drive out their enemies,' and, thereafter, will 'rejoice forever and ever with joy' (23:29-30)" (53). Return to land is understood "in mythic, cosmic proportions" (53). The authors of texts like *Jubilees*, the *Testament of Moses*, *Pseudo-Philo*, and Josephus retell the ancient biblical story so as "to deemphasize the theological significance of land" (116). For writers like these, "the imminent threat is loss of faith, not loss of the Land" (94). Later medieval Jewish interpreters encouraged worshipers to pray "that *evil behavior*—not evil people—will be destroyed" (Drucker: 183).

Hence Rahab's "faith," read through the lens of Hebrews, James, and Jewish interpretation, is not simply a spiritualizing of the story even though such a reading attends only to Rahab's hospitable action and her rescue. Yet to fix our attention only on the violence and disregard all else may be an equally complicated omission. Origen and others like him read Joshua as we read Tolkien's *The Lord of the Rings*. The violence is real within the narrative world, but in the world of the reader, it represents a different kind of struggle. We find ourselves limited by our modern notion of genre and thus end up amid two or three different conversations when we read Joshua 6.

The Power of Story

Is the traditional interpretation, which transforms the Jericho story into a contemporary struggle against evil, a wrong interpretation? Or rather, does that interpretation actually acknowledge that stories have a power that can be both dangerous and helpful, depending on the reader's use of the story? The conquest story can be used to justify illegal occupation (see Prior 1997; and www.jewishjericho.org.il/english/), and it can be used to refocus the questions or reframe them in other terms.

Ironically, most of the use of Joshua's conquest themes has been by Christians living in the post-Constantinian West, either in the medieval period of "Christian" political control, or in the modern period of "Enlightenment" and colonial conquest (see Prior 1997; Hawk 2010). Jewish interpreters, like those of the early church fathers, reinterpreted the stories of violence in the OT by transforming them rather than appropriating them for ideological purposes.

Early Christian interpretation, and most Jewish interpretation, has denied that Joshua 6 justifies human warfare. But most Christian interpretation since the sixteenth century has not questioned the divine right to kill. If the ban is understood as divine judgment (see Niditch), Calvin's interpretation of Joshua stands in such continuity when he writes about the killing in 6:21: "The indiscriminate and promiscuous slaughter, making no distinction of age or sex, but including alike women and children, the aged and decrepit, might seem an inhuman massacre, had it not been executed by the command of God. But as he, in whose hands are life and death, had justly doomed those nations to destruction, this puts an end to all discussion" (97). Thus these Israelites were "executing the command of God, who was pleased in this way to purge the land of Canaan of the foul and loathsome defilements by which it had long been polluted" (97; in his exposition Calvin alludes to Gen 15:16). Calvin's perspective is reflected in one of the views presented in the book *Show Them No Mercy: Four Views on God and Canaanite Genocide* (Cowles et al.) *[Theology of Warfare, p. 458; Genocide and Sacred Violence, pp. 430].*

In spite of all of those attempts either to transpose the Jericho story into a new key or to plunder it for ideological purposes, is it still possible both to be honest about the violence, to reject it, and also to hear a word for the church that is not insipid or insulting? Is it possible to acknowledge what the text actually says and to reject its ideological appropriation and even its theological portrayal of a God who commands *ḥerem*? Following are four ways of responding positively to those questions.

First, if the word we need to hear is linked to the sparing of Rahab, the story's focus becomes not the destruction of Jericho's inhabitants but the miracle of Rahab's rescue, contrary to all expectation. She is a type of God's concern for the Gentiles, for the outsider, for the marginal. This text, therefore, serves to undermine its own premise, so that even God's instructions can be transcended or superseded (see the exposition of God's concern for the outsider in Spina 2005).

Second, we might focus on how the human element of Scripture helps us here. The conquest narrative participates in ancient conventions like *ḥerem* that spring out of a worldview in which the gods were involved in human battles. Joshua 6 is a reflection of that divine condescension in human language (on the nature of Scripture, see Work 63–67, 97–100, 120–22, 169, 320; he refers to the *kenōsis*, or divine self-emptying, of God in the Bible). Recognizing the generic language of warfare used in all ancient conquest accounts allows us to distinguish between the God *depicted* in the text, and the hopeful and peaceful goal that God desires for his people (see Seibert) *[Conquest Accounts, p. 406; Theology of Warfare, p. 458].*

Third, we can focus on Joshua's dynamic modification of Moses' instructions in Deuteronomy 7 and 20 and suggest that the Jericho story, and within it the sparing of Rahab, reflects a dynamic reinterpretation of divine instruction that leaves Israel both open and vulnerable (Hauch) and yet embracing the new possibility of breaking down barriers between so-called insiders and outsiders (Polzin).

Fourth, we can affirm the transposition of figural readings of Joshua 6 by Jewish and Christian interpreters for whom, as for the NT writers, the conquest is a battle against either cosmic powers or the violence within *[Conquest and Land in the NT, p. 411; Figural Reading, p. 426].*

I find all of those suggestions fruitful. Many of them are fully in continuity with contemporary attempts to relate Joshua 6 to the life of the church. For example, Hess writes: "For the Christian, the story of Rahab is the story of the shepherd's search for the one lost sheep. . . . It is the concern of Jesus for the despised of the world. . . . It is the transformation of values to which Christianity calls disciples. Those rejected by the world are precious to God" (1996: 134–35). "For the Christian, the fall of Jericho represents an example of the power of faith in God. Without this faith, nothing can happen. With this faith, however, and the faithful obedience that it brings about, the Christian can overcome any obstacle in life, no matter how great" (137).

John Hamlin develops a completely different analogy: "Jericho as the doomed city is a paradigm of a society which can no longer survive as it is" (1983: 48). "In our day we may see in the walls of Jericho the political, military, and economic defenses which give an illusion of security to the rich and powerful, but which must fall down in the day of God's coming" (49). For Hamlin, the story emphasizes God's victory, stresses an alternative social order, and opens windows of welcome to all the families of the earth. He suggests that the story also warns against fatalism, which gives up on hope, and fanaticism, which assumes "a quick and final solution on one's own terms." Hence "we may have to wait and suffer in quiet action with appropriate 'weapons of our warfare,' or proclaim God's coming to judge and save" (54–55).

Each of those examples imports to the text an extratextual perspective that governs where the trajectory of the story might lead. Each one, like early Jewish and Christian interpretation, finds in the story a testimony to the ongoing judging and saving work of God. And each one invites further conversation about the *telos*, the ultimate purposes of God for humankind and for all creation. The story of Jericho's fall is an archetypal story that does not diminish the terror of its retelling—in the hope that such genocide will not happen again. The story shocks us into imagining that there must be an alternative to violence. If one family can be spared, perhaps that is a beginning. Perhaps the end of sacred and sacrificial violence may come into view if we can see through this story into the hopefulness of Rahab's faith-affirming existence in Israel *to this day*, even into the genealogy of the "Prince of Peace" (Matt 1:5; Isa 9:6), whose violent death offered the hope of an end to sacrificial violence once and for all. The sad reality remains: after thousands of years the human race has not eradicated genocide. A text of terror like this one ought to provoke us to say, "No more!"

Joshua 7:1–8:29

Ai and Achan

PREVIEW

Stories about spies and espionage, desire and deceit, get good ratings at the box office. This well-known biblical adventure also tells a spy story, yet it is ultimately not a story about winning in the end, but a story of human failure. Not many biblical stories tell a tale more horrifying than this one, which includes the execution of Achan and his family, the slaughter of all the citizens of Ai, and the public exposure of the king's body. Even more disturbing is the way the story, on the surface, seems to instruct concerning the requirement of absolute obedience. Is this a story of the failure to heed the divine word, which amounts to a violation of covenant relationship? Is the incident at Ai central to that agenda or peripheral to it?

The fact that Achan's story loops back into the story of Jericho in chapter 6, and the earlier spy story of chapter 2, suggests that the public and the private realms are intimately related to one another, and that the stories of individuals (Rahab and Achan) intersect significantly in the public actions of Israel and God. This double-edged overlapping narrative is a story of success and loss, of victory and transgression, interpreted within a worldview in which moral mathematics of retributive justice brings a tragic and unexpected twist to the tale the book tells.

Joshua 7 is a complementary panel to chapter 6 and is integral to what follows in chapter 8. Joshua 6 is a story of a divine strategy. Human participation is liturgical, a sacrificial act of setting the spoil apart for God. By contrast, Joshua 7, full of human strategy and action, imagines the possibility that Israel itself might become devoted to destruction *[Ḥerem, p. 433]*. Chapter 7 begins with a mention of Achan and ends with a note about the name of the place: Valley of Achor, meaning "Valley of Trouble" (or as Nelson 1997a: 99, puts it, "Taboo Valley"). And since the LXX identifies *Achan* as *Achar*, verses 1 and 26 form a verbal inclusio (see also 1 Chron 2:7).

Although Achan is not mentioned in chapter 8, chapters 7–8 present two interwoven plots: one that deals with the attack on Ai, which begins in 7:2 and ends in 8:29; and another that deals with Achan's violation of the command of 6:18, which begins in 7:1 and ends in 7:26. Joshua 7 therefore stands as a transitional narrative between two stories of victory. Though beginning with an attack on Ai, chapter 7 focuses primarily on the violation reported in 7:1. Joshua 8 picks up the "positive" strand of the narrative that one might expect to follow 6:27, with the Lord's addressing and instructing Joshua on the next step he should take, and comes to a conclusion in 8:29, with the report about the death of the king of Ai. Chapter 7 and the subunit that follows (8:1-29) each end in a similar way, with a reminder to the reader of something that remains in effect *to this day* (7:26; 8:29).

Chapter 7 is also linked to chapter 22 through the term *broke faith* (7:1; 22:16, 20, 22, 31), where Achan is mentioned in 22:20 as one who *broke faith* with respect to the *devoted things*. The story of Achan is likely included here to present "an archetypal figure of the dark side of Israel, which was first hinted at in 1:18" (Hess 1996: 57). This "dark side" raises questions about how we should read the narrative of Joshua as a whole. Rahab the outsider becomes an insider by confession and covenant; Achan the insider becomes an outsider (*ḥerem*) by covetousness and disobedience.

OUTLINE

Narrative Introduction: Israel and Achan, 7:1
The Defeat at Ai, 7:2-5
The Problem with Ai and Achan, 7:6-26

- 7:6-9 Joshua's Cry to the Lord
- 7:10-15 The Lord's Response
- 7:16-23 Joshua's Action
- 7:24-26 The Consequences

Divine Initiative and Command, 8:1-2
Joshua's Strategy, 8:3-9
The Action, 8:10-13
The Ruse Works, 8:14-17
Divine Intervention and Victory, 8:18-23

Summary and Flashback, 8:24-27
Death of the King, 8:28-29

EXPLANATORY NOTES

Narrative Introduction 7:1

In movie review language, verse 1 is a "spoiler" that gives the story away, and that raises an important question. Both *Achan* and *the Israelites* are intertwined in the plot. Who *broke faith*? Is Achan singled out as a sacrificial victim from *the Israelites*, many of whom *broke faith*? Or are *the Israelites* implicated because Achan's actions had consequences for all? The chapter is framed by an inclusio (vv. 1, 26) by allusion to Achan and the "Valley of Trouble" (*Achor*, *'achor*), along with the mention of *the anger of the* Lord. The LXX even identifies Achan as Achar, meaning "trouble." The trouble of "breaking faith" preoccupies not only this chapter, but also the entire book of Joshua.

Reading verse 1 in the light of chapter 6 allows us to link key words from 6:18, where both *devoted things* (*ḥerem*) and *take* are mentioned. Further, the awkward *but* (NRSV, NIV) emphasizes the contrast between Joshua in 6:27 and the Israelites in 7:1. Israel *broke faith*. Joshua 7:1 shatters the expectation of continuing and active divine presence. Thus 6:27–7:1, as a hinged pair of verses, concludes the previous story and sets up the story that follows. The contrast may be better preserved with this translation: *So the* Lord *was with Joshua. . . . The Israelites, however, violated the proscription* (cf. NJPS).

That proscription in verse 1 (like 6:17) reflects the absolute commands of Deuteronomy (7:2, 25-26; 13:16-17; 20:17). In Joshua 6:19, however, the people are allowed to take certain valuable things for the Lord's treasury even though Deuteronomy 7:25-26 does not allow keeping the silver and gold on the idols. But Deuteronomy 20:16-18, which describes the taking of towns nearby (as opposed to 20:10-15, "towns that are very far from you"), is ambiguous about whether one may take the spoil. It stipulates only that nothing "that breathes remain alive" (20:16). But is disobedience of the command the main concern here?

The first half of verse 1 may run counter to our assumptions since it begins with *the Israelites* rather than with *Achan*. The expression *broke faith* includes a plural verb. Most of the time elsewhere in the OT, the object of the verb is God. In 7:1, however, the object of the verb is the *ḥerem*, those things devoted to destruction. The narrative that follows will therefore deal with a corporate problem, not an individual one. Breaking faith with the *ḥerem* is the consequence of a breach of trust in a relationship (Wakely: 1022), a violation in which the people are also implicated. In the story of the so-called illicit altar of Joshua 22, in an echo of Joshua 7, the Israelites and the Transjordan tribes debate about what constitutes "breaking faith" when the Israelites from the west side of the Jordan accuse the Transjordan tribes of imitating Achan, who perished along with his family (22:20, 22).

That emphasis is corroborated by observing that "broke faith" (*ma'al*) occurs primarily in so-called "priestly" contexts in Leviticus and Numbers (never in Genesis and Exodus, and in Deuteronomy only in 32:51). It reflects not so much a Deuteronomic notion of disobedience as a violation of relational integrity (purity) that must be restored by confession and restitution (Wakely: 1021). It is a favorite word in Chronicles (eleven times), where it is used for the first time in 1 Chron 2:7 to describe the action of Achan (called Achar). The word also appears seven times in Ezekiel, where the NRSV often translates it as an act of treachery or treason against God. The Chronicler has incorporated the public *Israel* (from Josh 7:1) into *Achar* in 1 Chron 2:7 and imported the notice that Achan "brought trouble" (from Josh 7:25; cf. 1 Kings 18:17-18).

The second half of Joshua 7:1 focuses the reader's attention on Achan. That he is *of the tribe of Judah* is important in the light of Judah's prominence as the tribe of David, as the locus of the Southern Kingdom after Solomon's death, and as the victim of conquest by Nebuchadnezzar. Is Judah also going to be implicated in Achan's act?

The final motif in verse 1 is *the anger of the Lord*, the object of which is *the Israelites*. The motif sets the tone for Achan's story at the beginning and end of the chapter (vv. 1, 26). Verse 1 begins and ends with *the Israelites*. The expression *anger of the Lord* occurs forty times in the OT *[Anger of the Lord, p. 386]*. The references in Deuteronomy link the divine anger with the threat of the people's destruction or of their perishing from the land (6:15; 7:4; 11:17; 29:27). There are two other references to divine anger in Joshua. Joshua 23:16 echoes Deuteronomy 11:17 (but not the more extreme "destroy you from the face of the earth" in Deut 6:15). Joshua 22:18, 20 threatens divine judgment on the Transjordan tribes for building an altar. That text mentions Achan as a model of divine judgment, using the same words as 7:1 for *broke faith* and *devoted things* but a different word, *wrath*, for the divine response. Joshua 22:20 makes it clear that this *wrath fell upon all the congregation of Israel*. Moreover, *he did not perish alone for his iniquity.* This notion of consequences of one person's action falling on the group (Israel or family) recurs throughout Scripture (see TBC below).

God's anger is a response to the violation of Joshua's command in 6:18. Not until 7:10, in God's speech to Joshua, do we discover the full motivation for the anger. This anthropopathism (divine emotion expressed with human imagery) reflects a complex theological understanding. We recoil at the thought of divine anger because our experience of human anger often has violent consequences. Yet in the text, divine anger arises because relational integrity has been violated. In this respect God is like a human being. Human anger, as a secondary emotion, masks a more serious loss or fear. Here, although God's anger is a response to a loss of covenant relationship, it exposes a dark side in our understanding of the divine character.

All of the significant terms in verse 1 anticipate motifs that will be developed in the narrative that follows. After being found out, Achan confesses that he *took* (v. 21). But before that, God has notified Joshua that Israel has sinned and has taken of the devoted things (v. 11). Thus, the chapter continues throughout to juxtapose the corporate (Israel) and the individual (Achan). *The Israelites broke faith*, and *Achan . . . took* (v. 1). So *Israel has sinned* (v. 11) and Achan *took* (v. 21).

Furthermore, "all Israel" is not only implicated by, but also participates in and experiences, the consequences of Achan's action [*"All Israel," p. 385*]. Thus the resolution of the story executed by divine command (the defeat of Ai in ch. 8) initiates a new beginning after a decisive loss. And both stories together participate in a larger biblical pattern of the intersection of human failure, divine judgment, and new divine initiative.

The Problem with Ai and Achan 7:6-26

7:2-5 The Defeat at Ai

As he did in the first action sequence in the book (2:1), Joshua sends men to spy out the land (7:2). This time the starting point is Jericho and the goal is *Ai, which is near Beth-aven, east of Bethel.* The location of Ai is uncertain. The meaning of the place names may be more important than the locations. The Hebrew word *Ai* (*'ay*) means "ruin." The name always occurs in the Hebrew text with the definite article (*ha*, as in *ha'ay*): "the ruin." It could be that Ai was a long-abandoned site, and this story came to be attached to it in the oral traditions associated with settlement in the land. Or Ai may be a symbolic name that represents the tragedy of disobedience reflected in this story and that prefigures Israel's own ruin or demise.

That the place name *Beth-aven* is associated with the story may also add an ominous note. Besides being mentioned in the boundary descriptions of Joshua 18:12, Beth-aven is mentioned in only two other OT books. In 1 Samuel 13:5 and 14:23, Beth-aven is associated with a battle against the Philistines when Saul offered a sacrifice in violation of Samuel's explicit command for Saul to wait seven days until Samuel arrived (13:8-15). In judgment speeches and warnings, Hosea identifies Beth-aven (4:15; 5:8; 10:5). Hosea 5:8 precedes a warning that "Ephraim shall become a desolation in the day of punishment" (5:9). And 10:5 is a mourning cry for the calves of Beth-aven (perhaps an allusion to the calves set up at Bethel by Jeroboam I), with the notice that "its glory . . . has departed from it." That Bethel is named in Joshua 7:2 may therefore be a cryptic allusion to the setting up of Jeroboam's calves in Bethel, which, according to the DtrH, became a stumbling block for Israel. Moreover, since *'aven* means "iniquity" in many other biblical texts, this place name, associated in 1 Samuel and Hosea with questionable activities, has become ruinous and troubling. What began as a "house of God" (Bethel; cf. Gen 28:10-22) became a house of iniquity, Beth-aven.

In verse 2d the description of the action uses the same verbs as in Joshua's command. Doing as Joshua commands is important. The advice of the spies in verse 3 is based on their evaluation of the situation. The irony here is that this word for *toil* (or *weary*, NIV), used in historical and narrative literature only once outside of Joshua (2 Sam 23:10), is also used in Joshua 24:13, in God's speech to the people, *I gave you a land on which you had not labored* (emph. added). Reading the book of Joshua from beginning to end allows us to catch the irony at the end. But it is worth noticing here that the spies wish not to labor or weary the people, which is exactly the point of God's speech at the end of the book. Yet here their toil is wearisome because it confounds the entire mission.

The report of the ensuing action is completely unexpected (vv. 4-5c). Joshua has sent the spies. The spies do as they are told. They evaluate the situation as the spies in the Jericho mission have done. Perhaps we ought to be surprised that the spies recommend any troops at all. Or should we imagine that the battle would require any *toil* at all? After all, Jericho's walls fell after their walking, blowing trumpets, and shouting. The text reports no battle, even though we cannot imagine it actually having happened that way (i.e., the slaughter of the people would certainly have been accompanied by fierce fighting if that story had been a literal battle report, as Josh 24:11 claims). Yet here, out of character with the previous story, we find a recommendation to send soldiers (and either three thousand go up or three troop units) *[Hyperbole, p. 437]*.

That thirty-six of Joshua's troops are killed is the first indication that Achan's act has repercussions. Or to put it another way, the casualty number is the first sign that the corporate act of breaking faith (by *the Israelites* in 7:1) leads to corporate consequences. Achan's action affects not only his family (who are implicated by connection to him in 7:24), but also unsuspecting Israelites who had nothing to do with him. This notion of corporate consequences pervades Deuteronomy and the DtrH and is, ultimately, the explanation for the exile of Israel and Judah.

The disaster can only be narrated as a devastating blow to the *hearts* of the people (v. 5d; the sg. Heb. words for *heart* and *people* are used here, implying a collective response). Since *heart* is not simply the seat of the emotion, but primarily the source of the will, the concluding remark in this subunit uses the image either of ice or wax melting (see Ps 22:14; cf. Deut 20:8; 2 Sam 17:10; Pss 68:2; 97:5). The narrator employs the same words as appear in Rahab's description of her people's response (Josh 2:11) and in the narrator's report of the Amorite and Canaanite kings' reaction (5:1). The expression is used in Deuteronomy 1:28, in the report about Israel's response to the spies' evaluation of the situation in the land. There God's response to the melting hearts of the people is a word that challenges Israel not to fear; it affirms that God goes before and will fight for them and guide them all along the way (Deut 1:29-33). Now the same scenario appears to be echoed in the language of 7:5d, which prompts Joshua to respond in desperation.

7:6-9 Joshua's Cry to the Lord

Joshua's first response to this news is to initiate an act of mourning. Or is it an act of repentance for sending spies instead of consulting the Lord? (Culley: 39). Such actions as putting dust or ashes on one's head, tearing one's clothes, and falling down to the ground are widely reported actions accompanying mourning at someone's death or some other terrifying experience (Gen 37:34; 44:13; 2 Sam 1:2; 13:19; Job 2:12; Lam 2:10; Ezek 27:30). The contrast between this falling on his face *to the ground* and the same action in Joshua 5:14 could not be starker.

Joshua's verbal response to God recalls Moses' intercession after the golden calf incident (Exod 32–34) and the complaints of the people when Moses reports their refusal to enter the land after the report of the first spy mission: "It is because the LORD hates us that he has brought us out of the land of Egypt, to hand us over to the Amorites to destroy us" (Deut 1:27; cf. Moses' intercession in Deut 9:25-29). Like the Israelites in the wilderness, Joshua wishes they had stayed, not in Egypt (e.g., Exod 16:3; 17:3; Num 11:18; 14:2), but *beyond the Jordan* (for the phrase in Joshua, see 1:14-15; 2:10). He wishes the people had stayed with the two and a half Transjordan tribes—which sounds very much like a wish to reverse the entire sequence of confidence-building speeches of Joshua 1, in which the two and a half tribes vow their allegiance to Joshua and promise to cross over the Jordan, leaving their allotted territory behind so as to help the other tribes.

Although Joshua has a good number of words to say to God, he uses an expression that one might expect to hear of an exasperated partner in an argument: *What can I say?* (v. 8 NIV). What can he say to whom? To Israel? To God? Has he lost honor before his people? Or has he lost confidence in God? The speech of Joshua, as placed in the narrative, assumes that Joshua does not know about the narrator's introduction in 7:1. In this way the reader is set up to know more than the characters. In Joshua's address to God, on the other hand, the narrator juxtaposes the announcement of Achan's violation and the anger of God (7:1) with Joshua's loss of confidence. Because of that experience, Joshua places the blame on God.

Joshua's complaint introduces motive clauses as he tries to convince God to do something (v. 9). The *Canaanites and all the inhabitants of the land will hear*, which will have devastating consequences, not only for Israel (they will *cut off our name from the earth*), but even more significantly for God's reputation. The question Joshua asks, *Then what will you do for your great name?*, approaches the heart of the matter. It is not simply that *Israel has turned their backs to their enemies!* (v. 8; cf. Exod 23:27), but that God's reputation has been maligned among the nations. Although Israel's action is the initial cause of Joshua's mourning cry, a different tragedy is on his mind. No longer is it true that *we have heard* (Josh 2:10) what God has done. Now the nations have the opportunity to hear the opposite: God has failed. It will now be impossible to affirm *that all the peoples of the earth may know that the hand of the Lord is mighty* (Josh 4:24).

Is Israel the culprit? Is Israel responsible for the failure of the divine reputation? Or has God somehow failed? Is this story the first indication that Moses' covenant curses in Deuteronomy 28 may not be too farfetched? Is this an example of defeat occasioned by not obeying the Lord (28:15)? And is there a premonition that "the LORD will bring you . . . to a nation that neither you nor your ancestors have known, where you shall serve other gods" (28:36)? Will "the LORD scatter you among all peoples" (28:64)? These questions are implicit in Joshua's concern that Israel's name might be *cut off . . . from the earth* (v. 9a).

The Lord's reputation is at stake, as signified by this use of the word *name.* Joshua's lament concerns both the agency and the responsibility for the actions. Is God's reputation dependent on what happens in the sphere of human activity, in human history?

7:10-15 The Lord's Response

God's reply to Joshua is a thoroughgoing rebuttal of Joshua's lament (vv. 10-12), along with a series of instructions about how to deal with the situation at hand (vv. 13-15). We might have hoped for a gentler response.

The command *Stand up!* (v. 10) implies that the actions reported in verse 6 are inappropriate. The *Why?* question is rhetorical, implying that Joshua's evaluation of the situation is wrong. That, however, remains to be seen, since the problem that God identifies is not related to a specific action by a specific person. In every phrase of verse 11, the violator is *Israel* and *they* (cf. 7:1). God discloses the real problem in a sequence of accusations that are rich with theological/ethical language: *They have sinned; they have transgressed my covenant* (v. 11a). That statement underscores the seriousness of the accusations that follow. Here, although "sin" is the specific action of disobeying a divine command, the more important consequence of the action is violation of covenant relationship.

"Transgression of the covenant" forms an inclusio around God's speech (*my covenant* in v. 11; *covenant of the LORD* in v. 15). The verb *transgressed* could be translated *violated* (NIV) or *broken* (NJPS). It means, literally, "to cross a boundary." In other words, Israel has overstepped the boundary, or the terms of the agreement (covenant). The expression occurs again in chapter 23, where Joshua sounds an ominous note, warning that, if Israel does *transgress the covenant*, they will *perish quickly from the good land that he has given you* (23:16). One wonders about the relationship between the transgression in chapter 7 and the warning of 23:16. For Joshua 7, the similarity to Deuteronomy 17:2-7 is also striking (although in Deuteronomy there is no mention of the family, perhaps in keeping with Deut 24:16; see TBC below). There a man or woman who is discovered to have done "what is evil in the sight of the LORD," "transgresses his covenant," "going to serve other gods"—such a person shall be stoned to death (cf. Judg 2:20; 2 Kings 18:12; Hos 6:7; 8:1; Jer 34:18).

The second half of Joshua 7:11 includes a list of prohibited actions, each one introduced by the emphatic word *also/even* (Heb. *gam*), which does not appear in most English translations (but cf. KJV). The first of those accusations reminds us explicitly of Joshua's command in 6:18 not to *take* any of the *devoted things* (cf. Achan's confession in v. 21). Second, the action is then described as stealing. And third, the word translated *acted deceitfully* probably refers to the secretive nature of the act, resulting in a denial (cf. Gen 18:15; Lev 6:3; 1 Kings 13:18) and of hiding these proscribed things among their own possessions. That same word is used only one other time in Joshua (24:27), where Joshua renews Israel's covenant with God and warns them not to *deal falsely with your God*. Achan's act therefore becomes paradigmatic for Joshua's speeches in chapters 23–24. His story becomes "Israel's story," both in its potential outworking and in reality (in the light of the end of 2 Kings).

God's response to Joshua's assessment in verse 8, then, is to offer an alternative assessment, again with words that echo Joshua's instructions in 6:18. Israel has become *a thing devoted for destruction themselves* because of the *devoted things* that must be removed *from your midst* (7:12, lit.; cf. 6:25 and the irony of Rahab, who is said to live *in the midst* [AT]). The language of accusation and accountability continues to be plural (the three *you* pronouns of v. 12b are all pl.). The action of *Israel* has jeopardized the divine presence (in a way that the presence of Rahab does not). *I will be with you no more* is a terrifying prospect. The only way out is to destroy the proscribed objects (cf. Num 33:52-56). Since *Israel* has now become *ḥerem*, they are vulnerable to destruction. The Hebrew word translated in verse 12 as *destroy* occurs in contexts where both the other nations/peoples (Deut 7:23-24; 9:3; Josh 9:24; 11:14, 20; 24:8—and 11:20 also includes the verb related to *ḥerem*) and Israel (Deut 7:4; 9:8; 28:20; Josh 23:15) are subject to destruction. The implications of the Achan story are monumental if his story were to become a reality for all Israel (and for that we have only to read the book of Judges to gain a glimpse into that world of possibility). Perhaps the terror of this thought is enough to motivate a change in readers.

God's speech takes a turn from threat to solution. As in the narrative of the crossing of the Jordan, Joshua is again commanded *to sanctify the people/sanctify yourselves* (v. 13; 3:5). This act is to prepare for the removal of the *devoted things among you* (repeated twice in v. 13). Because of the presence of *devoted things*, God repeats that they are *unable to stand before your enemies* (cf. v. 12). Verses 14-15 spell out the details. Now the pronouns change for the first time, bringing us back to verse 1 and the tension between individual and community. The one responsible for taking the devoted things will be "taken" by lot, suggesting divine insight into even the secret places of human activity (cf. Num 32:23). It may be either reassuring or oppressive to know that God knows who has done wrong, and that God supervises the discovery process. Surely wrongdoing will be found out. Unfortunately reality is often more complex. Yet if this story is paradigmatic within the larger story (DtrH), it may assure readers that actions have consequences, and those consequences play themselves out in history.

The word used alongside *transgressed the covenant* in verse 15, *an outrageous thing*, is found in other contexts (Gen 34:7; Judg 19:23-24; 20:6, 10; 2 Sam 13:12). The complete phrase *done an outrageous thing in Israel* occurs in Deuteronomy 22:21 and Jeremiah 29:23. Except for four occurrences where the word means something like "folly," the word is used in the context of sexual violation. Here in Joshua 7:15, together with the transgression of the covenant of the Lord, the word implies that a violation of intimacy of some kind has occurred. In Deuteronomy 22:21 the aim is to "purge [lit., 'burn'] the evil from your midst" (as in Deut 13:5; 17:7, 12; 19:19; 21:21; 22:21, 22, 24; 24:7; cf. Deut 7:25). In some texts the motif of purging is a deterrent, intended to generate fear (Deut 17:13; 19:19; 21:21). The DtrH wants to show that certain practices, either "outrageous" or "abhorrent," are linked with Canaanite religious practices and are a threat to Israel's existence (Deut 7:25-26, where "coveting" the proscribed things is the object; 12:31; 13:14; 14:3; 17:1, 4; 18:9, 12; 20:18; 22:5; 23:18; 24:4; 25:16; 27:15; 32:16; cf. 1 Kings 14:24; 2 Kings 16:3; 21:2, 11; 23:13).

The retributive character of the consequence is that the person taken will be burned (cf. Jericho in 6:24) *together with all that he has.* Achan is a counterpoint to Rahab who, *with her family and all who belonged to her*, were *spared* (6:25). Rahab and Achan are counterparts in this story of inclusion and exclusion (Hubbard: 17).

7:16-23 Joshua's Action

Although Joshua follows God's instructions, Achan, the one *taken*, is given a prominent place in the narrative. His conversation with Joshua opens up the story and punctuates its paradigmatic role in the book.

After carrying out the lot-taking, Joshua asks Achan to speak. What appears to be an invitation to worship God turns out, in Achan's words that follow in verses 20-21, to be a confession. Joshua asks him (1) to *give glory to the* LORD (*pay honor* NJPS) and (2) to *praise* (v. 19 NIV 1984, RSV) or to *give thanks* (AT; Heb. *todah*), even though most translations render that word *make confession* (NRSV, NJPS; probably based on the content of vv. 20-21 and the only other such meaning of the word, in Ezra 10:11). Joshua's parental (*my son*) or priestly demeanor invites Achan: *Do not hide it from me* (v. 19). Perhaps the problem of grasping, of allowing these things to stick to his hand (cf. Deut 13:17), is one that can only be resolved by thanksgiving. Achan's own words that follow identify misplaced desire as the problem to which thanksgiving is the antidote.

Achan's thorough revelation recounts the entire process from *I saw* to *I coveted* to I *took* (v. 21). The details are significant, including mentioning the beauty (lit., *good*) of the mantle and the weight of the silver and gold. The temptation is substantial. Naming the hiding place relates this text to the hiding of the spies (2:6).

The confession maps the experiential route that Joshua has already named in 6:18. If the word "covet" is not in the text of Joshua's instructions ("covet" is in 6:18 LXX), then Achan's confession adds important information. Achan names what can happen between the seeing and the taking. One form (Niphal) of the Hebrew word for "covet" also bears the meaning of "to desire" or "to find desirable" (as in Gen 2:9 and 3:6, where NIV translates it in the idiom "pleasing to the eye"). In Deuteronomy the prohibition against coveting is found in the admonition not to "covet the silver or the gold" of the idols of Canaan; these "images of their gods" are to be burned "with fire" (Deut 7:25). The final commandment of the Decalogue lists coveting as the capstone of them all (Exod 20:17; Deut 5:21). Sadly, Achan did not find God's instructions "more desirable than gold" (Ps 19:10 NJPS).

Most puzzling about the story is the gap between Achan's act and his being found out. In the meantime thirty-six men have been killed. What is implied about God's participation in human affairs? Is God not willing (or not able) to intervene directly to stave off tragedy? Or does the story imply that God works inside the reality of Israel's experience? Only the tragedy of the thirty-six exposes the problem, which flies in the face of expectations after the positive outcome of the previous story. In this case, redressing wrongdoing involves a communal act of sacrificial violence. Things do not work out naturally or obviously in ordinary life, nor does God intervene immediately to prevent tragedy or to punish the sinner. The community must deal with this event, which Achan describes as an offense against God (Clements 2000: 115).

The situation is as Achan has described it. The verbs increase the pace of the action, with the running and the taking and the laying out before the Lord. That *all the Israelites* witness the recovery of the loot along with Joshua is not only because *Israel* was participant in the loot-taking (7:16), but also because they are the object of God's anger (7:1) and they will be the agents of God's judgment (7:24-25). The goods that are *sacred to the* Lord (6:19) have now been returned to their rightful owner.

7:24-26 The Consequences

Just as *Joshua and all the Israelites* have witnessed the recovery of the stolen goods, so now they *take* (cf. 6:18; 7:11, 23) not only Achan and the loot, but also his family, animals, and tent. Thus *all that he had* becomes *ḥerem* (7:24). It is not clear from the pronouns *him* and *them* (v. 25) whether the stolen goods are burned or not. According to Joshua 6:18-19, as objects designated *ḥerem*, these belong in *the treasury of the* Lord (6:18-19). The story probably echoes the instruction of Deuteronomy 7:26, according to which they are "set apart for destruction." The fact that his wife is not mentioned explicitly is part of the story of invisibility common in narratives in the OT. The woman may or may not be an accomplice (given the fact that the stolen goods were hidden in the family tent), but she, along with the sons and daughters, all belong to the man. They are part of the *all that he had.*

They are taken to the *Valley of Achor.* This place, whose name is repeated in verse 26, means "Valley of Trouble," a wordplay on Achan's name. What has been an act of misdirected desire that turned into theft from the Lord now becomes a sacrificial act that cleanses the entire community of the trouble, the contagion of *ḥerem.*

Before the "outrage" is reversed, however, Joshua holds a mock investigation. Earlier he has instructed Achan to *give glory to the* Lord (7:19), but now he wants to know why Achan was tempted to *bring trouble on us.* But the questioner has no time for an answer. He moves quickly to the sentencing: *The* Lord *is bringing trouble on you today.* The double assertions of *trouble* echo the instructions of 6:18 and other biblical accusations of "troubling" events and persons (Gen 34:30; Judg 11:35; 1 Sam 14:29; 1 Kings 18:17-18). In other words, Achan's act has threatened the life of the entire community. As "troubler," Achan becomes responsible for God's anger against the Israelites (7:1). The wordplay on the name of Achan highlights the "troubling" nature of this act (the verb "to trouble," *'akar*, may also account for the name change from *Achan* in MT to *Achar* in LXX throughout Josh 7 and in 22:20; as already in 1 Chron 2:7 MT).

Achan's death mollifies God's anger by making the guilty scapegoat preserve the life of the community. That *all Israel* becomes the executioner and raises a lasting memorial to his memory (*to this day*) suggests more than capital punishment. Achan's death, along with the demise of his family, reflects a worldview that needs to be explored and exposed. The problem corresponds to the killing of Jericho's inhabitants in chapter 6. The two stories are linked by the assumption that when the dangerous Other is eliminated via a sacrificial death, the community becomes safe and secure. The narrative of the mound of stones assures that all will remember that Israel "made peace" with its own dark and dangerous tendencies to become like the Other. Lest that not be enough, the naming of the place "Valley of Trouble" assures perpetual memory of the peacemaking act. Yet that naming is itself a troubling act, which reminds readers that all kinds of violence can easily be justified by religious conviction.

Most troubling, however, is the assertion that *the LORD turned from his burning anger.* Although anthropomorphic (anthropopathic) language may well be appropriate (see 7:1), here the full brunt of that language becomes evident. Because of the death of a whole family (who had stolen what was rightfully God's), God's anger is assuaged *[Anger of the Lord, p. 386]*. Are the things themselves the problem? Or is it that Achan disobeyed the instructions of Joshua (6:18)? It is difficult to comprehend why Achan's thorough confession (7:20-21) was not adequate for restoration.

Understanding the larger biblical-theological drama may engage the challenges presented by this text (see TBC below). Achan represents the "cleansing" of all Israel from its own tendency both to imitate and to detest the Other. Israel overcomes this tension by destroying the Other. Achan and his family become the corporate scapegoat. In other words, retributive violence purifies, but it is not at all clear that it solves the problem.

Divine Initiative and Command 8:1-2

The continuation of the Ai narrative in 8:1 returns us to the plotline that was left hanging at 7:5. The interwoven story of Achan in 7:6-26 accounts for the devastating loss in the skirmish at Ai. This second speech of God in the narrative sequence (the first is in 7:10-15) addresses directly the fear and lack of courage reflected in the narrator's evaluation of the situation in 7:5.

God's call, *Do not fear or be dismayed*, is like a new beginning as it echoes the words of assurance to Joshua (1:9). The very common *do not fear* (second person m. sg.) occurs forty times in the OT, commonly in reassurances of divine presence in contexts of danger or battle (Conrad). In Joshua the expression occurs again in 10:8 and 11:6. But the full expression with both verbs occurs only here, in Moses' exhortation to take the land (Deut 1:21; 31:8), and in David's exhortation to Solomon (1 Chron 22:13; 28:20; where Chronicles also echoes Josh 1:9; cf. Jer 23:4; 30:10; 46:27). The speech provides assurance of success as determined by God's presence and based on God's promise.

In keeping with that, God's instruction in 8:1b begins with the divine "I," who reasserts a prominent position in the narrative as historical agent. *See, I have handed over to you* (lit., *I have given into your hand*) also occurs in 6:2 at the outset of the Jericho episode. The only other place in the OT where the exact wording occurs is in God's command to Moses in Deuteronomy 2:24, followed there by the command "Begin to take possession by engaging him in battle" (Deut 2:24b; cf. other expressions of the idiom in Exod 23:31; Deut 3:2-3; Josh 10:8; 24:8).

Joshua therefore assumes, like Deuteronomy, that Israel will be involved in the battle. As God clarifies in verse 2, Joshua is to do to Ai and its king what he has done to Jericho and its king. We must presume that "Ai" and "Jericho" mean only their inhabitants, since 8:2b allows for the taking of spoil and livestock as booty. Although the *ḥerem* is assumed (it appears only in v. 26), the instructions of Deuteronomy 20:16 are not followed to the letter. Ai is to be treated as though it were a town "very far from you" (Deut 20:14-15). Thus the divine instructions for the capture of Ai in Joshua 8:2 modify the instructions for towns that are nearby (Deut 20:16). That is odd, given that Achan has just been executed for taking things allowed in Joshua 8:2 (cf. 6:17-18; ch. 9).

The instructions about Ai differ, therefore, from those concerning Jericho. No longer is there a hint of liturgical procession. Here the only battle instructions concern an ambush to be set up behind the city. The narrative that follows will expose both divine and human agency.

Joshua's Strategy 8:3-9

Although verse 3 begins with an echo of *all the fighting men* of verse 1, Joshua chooses thirty fighting units *[Hyperbole, p. 437]*. He communicates his full strategy to them. The end of his instruction, like the beginning, includes a link to the divine speech of 8:1 in his notice that *God will give it into your hand* (lit., *your hands*, v. 7b). All of this is to be done *as the Lord has ordered*, which means *as I have commanded you* (v. 8; cf. Joshua's *command* in 8:4a). The Lord's instructions are *according to the word of Yahweh* (v. 8, lit.), a phrase that occurs twice in Joshua and only in this chapter (also v. 27). The phrase is followed by Joshua's appropriation of the word *command* (common in Deuteronomy as the command of Moses). *According to the word of Yahweh* occurs for the first time here in the DtrH, and it occurs seventeen times in the books of Kings. There the word of Yahweh focuses on the prophetic word that drives history. Joshua's linking of Yahweh's word (*debar yhwh*) with his own *command* is not necessarily a usurpation of the divine prerogative but an indication that what Yahweh says, so Joshua says. Joshua is God's messenger (Josh 6:26), which is why the book of Joshua is the first of the prophets in the Hebrew canon (MT).

Joshua's words in verse 8 expose the possibility that the entire narrative is a play on seeing, which becomes clear only later in the story as we recognize the repetition of the word "see" (8:1, 4 NASB, 8, 14, 20, 21).

Joshua now sends them to the place, which is *between Bethel and Ai, to the west of Ai* (8:9; cf. 7:2). Beth-aven need not be mentioned here (cf. 7:2), for there is no indication that anything might go wrong. The narrative makes a transition at verse 9b (as it does in v. 13b) with the report about where Joshua spends the night, *among the people* (lit.; NRSV: *in the camp*). Those two transitions are interesting because the last clause in verse 9 is identical to the last clause in verse 13, except that the last word in verse 9 (*camp* or *people*) becomes *valley* in verse 13 simply by adding the consonant *qop* (*'am* becomes *'emeq*). The frequent mention of Ai in verses 9-12 begins with the expression *west of Ai* in verse 9, which becomes *west of the city* in verse 13. The difference between the words *Ai* (consonants *'y*) and *city* (consonants *'yr*) is the addition of a final letter *resh*. The wordplay reflects the story: the "city" has become a "ruin."

The Action 8:10-13

Although Joshua leads what appears to be a procession of all the people, the focus is his taking charge of *all the fighting men* (see 8:1, 3). Joshua's actions include setting an ambush to the west of the city (v. 13), which verse 14 explains as *behind the city*. Joshua 8:4 includes the same expressions *against the city, behind the city* (lit.), as 8:14, *against him behind the city*. Joshua 8:12, therefore, repeats exactly

Joshua's instructions for the ambush earlier in the chapter, thereby assuring the reader that Joshua's commands are carried out exactly. The narrative makes note of the main fighting group's geographical movement by reporting where Joshua spends the night in a vulnerable place, *in the valley* between the main camp and the city (8:9, 11-13), and then the point of view shifts to the king of Ai (vv. 14-17).

The Ruse Works 8:14-17

The king of Ai does not see the ambush, which has been sent out at night. But he does see the movement of the Israelites (and Joshua in the valley) north of the city. He *sees* but does *not know* (8:14). So *he and all his people* rush out to engage in battle. The double mention of *all his people* and *the inhabitants* emphasizes that the city was left unprotected. The narrative that follows reports what we expect: Joshua's ruse is successful, just as he has said in verses 5-6. The only thing to note is that 8:17 mentions, or repeats, not only that the men had vacated the city, but also that both Ai and Bethel *pursued Israel.* Ai and Bethel are apparently to be associated closely with one another (vv. 9, 12, 17). But that does not help us to understand how 8:9, 12 describe the ambush as being set *between Bethel and Ai.* In any case, the king of Ai comes across either as naive and without experience in warfare strategy, or as overly confident and unsuspecting because of his previous victory.

The irony in this portion becomes clear when we notice that the first time Bethel and Ai are mentioned before this is Gen 12:8. There Abram pitches his tent and builds an altar to the Lord between Bethel and Ai (cf. Gen 13:3), the very location of the ambush against Ai. Bethel, which was once Jacob's place of divine encounter and his dwelling place (Gen 28:19; 35:1-15), is now allied with Ai, against whom Israel does battle.

Divine Intervention and Victory 8:18-23

Just when the reader expects the battle report to continue, verse 18 breaks the sequence with another divine speech. There seems to be no need for what follows except, perhaps, to indicate that Joshua does not actually know what might happen next. The verses prior to this one do not indicate how the forces in hiding will know when to approach the city. We have already been assured that God has *handed over to you the king of Ai with his people* (8:1). And along with that assurance, we have the confidence that at least most of Joshua's strategy is divinely sanctioned (8:2). It comes as a surprise, therefore, that God should give Joshua more specific instructions regarding this particular battle. The divine instructions confirm that it is God, not Joshua, who is guiding the battle as it proceeds.

Perhaps we should not be surprised since this introduction, *Then the LORD said to Joshua*, appears exactly this way eleven times in the first eleven chapters of Joshua (1:1; 3:7; 4:1, 15; 5:9; 6:2; 7:10; 8:1, 18; 10:8; 11:6), and then never again in the book (for why that might be, see ch. 12). The image of a director of a movie comes to mind. Many individuals participate in the making of the movie, but the director coordinates their efforts.

What God says, however, is significant not only for that reason but also because the narrator, like many good filmmakers, borrows a scene from elsewhere with which viewers/readers might already be familiar. Othmar Keel, who has studied ancient Near Eastern images (iconography), has noticed that the image of the uplifted short sword is common in the art world of the time. He reproduces many Egyptian images that depict the god standing with upraised sword behind the king or over against the enemy (204-43). The image represents the divine assurance of victory (77).

In biblical texts, however, the image is slightly altered. Joshua 8 echoes the story of Exodus 17:8-13. There Moses lifts up his hands, and Joshua commands the troops on the field. Moses takes the initiative in that story, with the result that "Joshua defeated Amalek and his people with the sword." That the story was to be remembered "in a book" and recited "in the hearing of Joshua" (17:14) makes Joshua 8 a natural echo of Exodus 17. In both cases, unlike in the Egyptian iconography, the role depicted by a god in the Egyptian images is played by a human being in Israelite literature (Keel: 145). In the Joshua story the instruction to raise the sword is joined with a repeated assurance that *I will give it into your hand* (8:18b).

After reporting God's command and Joshua's compliance, the narrative returns to the expected outcome: *As soon as he stretched out his hand* (v. 19). The Hebrew word order mentions the action of the troops at the beginning of the sentence and notes Joshua's raised hand as a temporal clause indicating that their action was initiated by the raised hand. Thus the troops, who had already been sent out to set up the ambush, are able to act, as Joshua acts, in accord with the divine word that came to Joshua. They too are being directed by God.

By twice mentioning that things were done in a hurry, the narrator makes sure readers know that all of this happened very quickly. The carefully executed plan left the people of Ai with no options (lit., *there is not in them hands*, where *hands* is in the unusual dual form, giving us a picture of a person holding out both hands empty). The metaphor of hands signifies *no power* (v. 20 NRSV) or "no option," of fleeing one way or another. The use of the hand metaphor contrasts with the upraised hand of Joshua (8:18), and the divine giving *into your hand* (8:1, 18). The people of Ai are vanquished. None but the king *survived or escaped* (8:22-23).

Summary and Flashback 8:24-27

The gruesome ending of the story is captured by the word *slaughtering* (8:24), a word used also for slaughtering animals. Verses 24-25, when read slowly to allow the picture to form completely in one's imagination, depict a devastation and a brutality that cannot be fully grasped except by analogy to a movie like *Braveheart* (1995).

That Israel turns back to the city and kills the remaining people (old people, women, children) to the sum of twelve thousand *that day* (8:25) is incomprehensible. Yet this action is in keeping with the divine command of 8:2, and as the verb *utterly destroyed* (*ḥerem*) confirms (8:26) *[Conquest Accounts, p. 406; Ḥerem, p. 433]*. Israel has cleansed the land of a second group of victims. And that too is according to the command and direction of God. The summary ends with a reiteration of sparing the livestock and taking the spoil (in reverse order from 8:2), forming an inclusio around the battle narrative, which is capped off with the somber notice that all of this has happened *according to the word of the Lord* spoken to Joshua (8:1, 18, 27). The expression occurs in the DtrH only in Joshua 8:8, 27 and seventeen times in the books of Kings (see comments above at 6:26 and 8:8).

The reader may either cringe at the thought or celebrate God's ability to direct such dire situations to Israel's advantage. But after the scare narrated in chapter 7, victory may come as a welcome relief. In spite of failure, with measures to restore order, God can continue to assert sovereign control. The question arises, Is God's sovereignty dependent on human faithfulness? The tension inherent in that question has already surfaced at 7:9, when Joshua asks whether God's reputation might not be maligned by this battle loss.

Death of the King 8:28-29

The story ends with a graphic summary. The narrator explains that Ai, in keeping with the meaning of its name, is a perpetual ruin. The expression *a perpetual ruin* occurs elsewhere only in Deuteronomy 13:16, in the context of the total destruction of a town that has succumbed to the worship of "other gods." The dangerous allusion to the Achan story is clear. Deuteronomy 13 also emphasizes the risk involved in allowing "anything devoted to destruction stick to your hand" (13:17). As this heap of ruins stands *to this day*, so also the cairn of stones raised over the body of the king stands *to this day* (cf. Josh 4:9; 5:9; 7:26; 8:28-29; 9:27; 13:13; 14:14; 15:63; 16:10; 22:3; 23:8-9). The phrase *to this day* in the book of Joshua is a figurative expression connoting permanence. As this heap of stones remains a permanent marker of the event, readers of the story would surely wonder whether the conditions and consequences depicted in this narrative continued to their time.

The king was killed, either by being *hanged . . . on a tree* (NRSV, NIV 1984) or *impaled on a stake/pole* (NJPS, NIV; cf. Gen 40:19). That he remained exposed to public view until sunset provides the final gruesome punctuation in the reader's imagination before the narrator swallows up the violence in the distant memory enshrined in stone. There remains only a memorial to a dark day in the distant past. As Hedges documents, that kind of public humiliation has always been part of war. With the availability of electronic media, such reminders are now broadcast for the whole world to see.

THE TEXT IN BIBLICAL CONTEXT

Covetousness and Its Consequences

Is this story about the revealing and punishment of secret sins? If so, then "Achan is assumed to have 'stolen' from God. The story is a paradigmatic illustration of the priestly admonition: 'Be sure your sin will find you out' (Num 32:23)" (Clements 2000: 117). But even that assertion lives in tension with other biblical texts that depict God as one who removes sin from his children "as far as east is from west" (Ps 103:12).

More significantly, however, Achan's story mirrors Genesis 3. The desire that Achan confesses (7:21) is like the desire we find in the story of the garden, where Eve construes something inherently good and "pleasing to the eye" (Gen 2:9; 3:6 NIV) as something to "take" and appropriate for herself (Gen 3:6). And Achan's confession echoes the last and capstone of the Ten Commandments against coveting (Exod 20:17; Deut 5:21). Viewed this way, Achan is an ordinary person. He "is not labeled as strange, corrupted or evil but . . . a person who cannot resist temptation." He is like "one of us" (Latvus: 53). Already within the biblical world, this story can be read as participating in an extended metaphor.

Taking the story of desire further leads us to ask whether the *ḥerem* in this story might also be interpreted in the light of the larger sacrificial worldview with which, or against which, the Bible as a whole struggles. David too sees, desires, and takes Bathsheba (2 Sam 11:2-4). Although David wonders if the Lord might "be gracious to me" (2 Sam 12:22), the story of misplaced desire echoes back on the taker. And prior to David, Saul justifies his disobedience by accusing the people of violating the *ḥerem* command (1 Sam 15:21). In response, Samuel says that the Lord's delight is "in obedience to the voice of the Lord." Saul has "rejected the word of the Lord" (1 Sam 15:22-23). And, like Achan, Saul brings "trouble" on Israel (Josh 7:25; 1 Sam 14:29).

Even in the NT we find a shocking story of judgment against Ananias and Sapphira (Acts 5:1-11). Although the story does not explicitly allude to the story of Achan, the "keeping back" and the consequence of the deception is analogous. Can we account for such divine actions as they are reported in these biblical texts? Ought we to transpose them into another theological key? Or ought we protest them as Joshua does in Joshua 7:6-9? Our conversation with other texts and interpreters will begin to sort out the interpretive options.

Like those stories, Joshua 7 is a story that repels and warns. It does not advocate that about which it tells. It tells a story of the sacrifice of some for the salvation of all. It depicts a pattern that draws its inspiration from deep within the human condition. To read the story that way, we may have to ask, as Gil Bailie does, "Why would such booty have been forbidden?" Perhaps it is not simply because Joshua forbade it (Josh 6:18), or because Deuteronomy 20 is not consistent about whether Israel could take the spoil, but because the spoil in Joshua 7 reflects that which is contagious about the Other, and that would make Israel like the Other. Bailie suggests that bringing the booty into the camp would have introduced new conflicts as imitative (mimetic) desire would have provoked new violence among the Israelites who sought to possess it (161).

However we explain the prohibition of booty, readers will likely find this story "morally offensive" since, as Bailie puts it, the Bible as a whole awakens "an empathy for victims and a skepticism about the judgment of mobs" (163). Whether Achan deserved the punishment or not, this is one example among many of a kind of salvation by violence with which the entire Bible wrestles until the violence itself is overcome in the cross and resurrection of Jesus.

In summary, when something is declared *ḥerem* (as in Josh 6:17a), "it means that the object is consecrated or dedicated in an almost sacrificial manner" (Kaminsky 1995: 80; cf. Deut 13:17; Lev 27:28b) *[Ḥerem, p. 433]*. Moreover, this "sacral character" of the dedicated things "extends to the effect it has on those who misuse it" (80), as we see in Deuteronomy 7:25-26 and Joshua 6:18. This is very much like the contagion of ritual impurity one finds in texts like Num 19:14: when a man dies in a tent, everything that comes into the tent is declared unclean. Similarly, Achan and all connected with his tent have taken on the status of *ḥerem*. The essence of the matter is not in touching the proscribed objects (cf. Josh 7:23), but in the taking so that it will "stick to your hand" (Deut 13:17). Other texts in the DtrH imply that coveting was one of the causes of Judah's downfall. Not only Manasseh's sins (2 Kings 21:10-16; 23:26) but also Hezekiah's exposure of the temple treasury (2 Kings 20:12-19), which highlights his pride (20:13), "conveys some similarities with Achan's covetousness, perhaps suggesting that Achan was looked upon as a prototypical precursor of this Judahite king" (Clements 2000: 124).

In other words, the Achan story is an embodied illustration of the commandment against coveting, an idea that Paul reiterates precisely in his dictum "Greed . . . is idolatry" (Col 3:5). And idolatry, we recognize from Deuteronomy, is Israel's greatest temptation *[Idolatry, p. 438]*.

God's Reputation

Like the Israelites' complaint in the desert (Exod 16:3; Deut 1:27) and Moses' intercession with God (Exod 32:11-12; Deut 9:25-26), Joshua complains that God has brought this people into the land in order to destroy them (Josh 7:6-9). Joshua's initiative raises several questions that deserve exploration.

Joshua is not the only biblical character to challenge God. As part of Abraham's vocation of "doing righteousness and justice" (Gen 18:19), it falls to him to challenge God's justice in the case of Sodom (18:25). Both Abraham and Joshua assume that it is appropriate to ask "Why?" So also the prayers of lament accuse God of acting without integrity (Pss 74:10, 18; 102:15). Does Joshua's encouragement that Achan *give glory to* God fit the pattern of glorifying God in the context of such laments (Josh 7:19; cf. Ps 86:9, 12)? God is right about Israel's (Achan's) violation of the relationship and about the importance of obedience. God is also right about the human tendency to take what belongs only to God, to steal, and to lie. But surely Joshua is also right about thc apparent arbitrariness he perceives in the loss of thirty-six Israelites and the defeat of the Israelite army.

Whether or not those questions can be answered, the real challenge to God comes in Joshua's final question: *What will you do for your great name* once the Canaanites find a way to *cut off our name from the earth?* The relationship between *your name* and *our name* is critical. It highlights the theological challenge to God, which may well be one of the most difficult in the Bible. Throughout Scripture we find texts like Joshua's (some of them lament prayers) that call on God to act for the sake of the divine name or that announce that God will act for the sake of the divine name.

In Deuteronomy the "name" represents the presence and character of God. God makes God's name dwell in a place that remains unnamed (Deut 12:5). The place of worship is the place where God's name dwells (Deut 12:11; 14:23). God chooses to "put his name there" (Deut 12:5, 21; 14:24; cf. 1 Kings 8:16, 29). "This naming is a mark of ownership indicating that the land is God's own possession" (Burge 2003: 76).

The name is also associated with the people in Deuteronomy 28. There, in a series of covenant blessings, Moses announces that Israel's enemies "shall come out against you one way, and flee before you seven ways" (28:7). Ironically, Israel in Joshua 7 flees before the men of Ai (7:4). The challenge of Deuteronomy 28 is in the "if" of obedience (28:1) and keeping the commandments (28:9). If that happens, then "all the peoples of the earth shall see that you are called *by the name of the Lord*, and they shall be afraid of you" (28:10, emph. added). The threat of being defeated continues in Deuteronomy 28:25, 36, 49, 64. Joshua's raising the possibility that *the inhabitants of the land will hear of it . . . and cut off our name from the earth* (7:9a) has serious consequences not only for the existence of this people, but also for God's very reputation among the nations, which seems dependent on Israel's life in the world. If the Israelites are *cut off*, so also would God's reputation be sullied. Hence, the last question in Joshua's repertoire: *What will you do for your great name?* (7:9b).

Ezekiel also reflects on God's reputation, which has been tarnished by Israel's actions (20:39; 36:20). Time and again, and now in a situation of desperation, God has determined to act for the sake of his reputation even though Israel has been recalcitrant (36:22-23). Thus God determines not to allow Israel to profane God's reputation among the nations any longer (39:7). The restoration of Israel, therefore, is for God's sake alone (39:25).

Still, by juxtaposing two starkly different speeches (one accusing God and one accusing Israel), the narrative points up the fragility of

Israel's life in the world and of God's reputation, which is anticipated in cosmic language in Joshua 3:24. Much is at stake for both God and Israel, given the background of Deuteronomy 28, the lament tradition that calls on God to act for the sake of God's name, and Ezekiel's assertion of divine initiative. Joshua is surely right: it is not enough to make Israel solely responsible. But God is right as well: it is not enough to make God the guardian of the divine reputation. Israel and God are inextricably linked.

Individual and Community

The sacrifice of Achan's family violates the prescription of Deuteronomy 24:16, which states that children are not liable for their parents' crimes (cf. Ezek 18). Yet according to other texts, the merciful God also sees to it that actions have consequences (cf. Exod 34:6-7; Pss 86:15; 103:8-14; 145:8-9; Jer 32:18-19; Joel 2:13; Jon 4:2). Does the complex web of consequences in Joshua 7–8 reflect retributive or restorative justice? Who is punished? What is restored? How do we make sense of the way divine judgment and corporate consequences play themselves out in these chapters?

Within the DtrH, Amaziah applies the principle of Deuteronomy 24:16 to those who murdered his father. Only the murderers, not their children, are killed (2 Kings 14:6). Joshua 7 does not draw on that legal principle, but on a more thoroughly corporate, and perhaps priestly, notion of accountability (see Kaminsky 1995). Although Deuteronomy 24:16 attempts to safeguard family members from the consequences incurred by an errant parent, the Achan story seems oblivious to the principle articulated there. Similarly the Achan story does not take up the expected Deuteronomic theme of "purging the evil from Israel," a motif that occurs nine times in Deuteronomy but never in Joshua.

The Achan/Ai story clearly poses the problem as an Israel problem and pinpoints Achan as the cause. There are limits, however, to how far the consequences can reach. His act threatens to destroy Israel and to remove the divine presence. But the sacrifice (as it appears to be in 7:23-24) of Achan and his family removes the problem of contagion. Some, therefore, are sacrificed for the sake of the whole. In this way we may understand the *ḥerem* and holiness as part of a bundle of intersecting concepts. "The concept of holiness in the Hebrew Bible cuts across the Western dichotomy of the spiritual versus the physical; one's physical state is part of one's spiritual state" (Kaminsky 1995: 88). When Israel fails to maintain its sanctity, God will leave and abandon the land (Ezek 8–11). This loss of holiness could be effected by the people as a whole or by individuals. "It is on this basis that ancient Israel recognized and accepted a type of communal responsibility that held individuals responsible, at least at some level, for the misdeeds of other Israelites. Israel was held communally accountable for maintaining a fit environment in which God could manifest himself, and through this manifestation could radiate blessing to the rest of the terrestrial world" (Kaminsky 1995: 89; see also Clements 2000).

The community was therefore responsible for not "polluting" the land. The aim of purity regulations was not for the sake of the people, but to allow for God to "dwell among" the people (e.g., Exod 25:8; 29:45; Lev 16:16). Violations of purity, according to Ezekiel, have forced God to depart. It is almost as though God acted "for his own protection" or to guard his reputation (Levine: 78; quoted in Kaminsky 1995: 91). Even so, the problem of sacrificing a part for the whole (and of the action of one effecting the consequences borne by the whole) needs to be read against the backdrop of the dynamic relationship between individual and community and the larger background notion of sacrificial cleansing from the threat of communal desire and violence.

In Ezekiel 18, an extended reflection on "It is only the person who sins that shall die," the individual corresponds figurally to the "house of Israel." The "individual" in Ezekiel 18 is a literary fiction representing the options for Israel in exile. Ezekiel seeks to recover a new vision of generational responsibility and possibility (cf. Jer 31:27-30). Each generation, in other words, may begin again (see Matties 1990).

Ezekiel speaks both to individuals and to the community ("house of Israel") in assigning responsibility for Israel's predicament. The prophet affirms both that human beings are capable of sound moral judgment and that they are incapable of choosing to do what is good. And Ezekiel invites Israel to repent, to turn from their wicked ways, as well as to embrace God's gift of a transformed heart (11:19; 36:26). In wrestling with these tensions, Ezekiel affirms both human responsibility and divine initiative, both human culpability and divine justice, both human possibility and divine gift.

Like Ezekiel, the book of Joshua presents representational individuals. Achan represents Israel as Rahab represents the Gentiles (or foreigners). As Achan finds himself outside the covenant community even though he is an ethnic insider, Rahab finds herself inside even though she is an ethnic outsider (Polzin). Hubbard describes the contrast this way: "Rahab, the ultimate 'outsider,' becomes an 'insider' in Israel by submitting to Yahweh's authority, while Achan, 'the exemplary insider,' makes himself an 'outsider' by rejecting it" (17). This sequence of paradigmatic narratives sets up both figures as patterns of loyalty and disloyalty, of allegiance and rebellion in rather surprising ways. It could be, as Hubbard suggests, that "Yahweh reckons obedience more important than ethnicity" (17; see also Stone: 34-36; Rowlett 1992: 20, 22).

In those ways the larger biblical drama continues the conversation about the place of and hope for Gentiles in God's mission in the world (see TBC for Josh 2, "Gentiles in the Family Tree"; and TBC for Josh 3–4, "The Earth Belongs to the Lord"). This hopefulness for the inclusion of the Gentiles and the end of strife infuses NT texts like Matthew's Gospel and Paul's letter to the Romans. The sacrificial exclusion of Achan and the sacrificial othering of Ai is ultimately transformed through an explosion of inclusion in the covenantal vision of the Bible. In that covenantal vision, the nations will be blessed and hearts will be transformed.

THE TEXT IN THE LIFE OF THE CHURCH

Achan: Paradigm of Disciplinary Action?

The church's reading of Joshua 7–8 has almost always focused on the Achan incident as a paradigm of communal discipline of erring members. Early church theologian Origen laments when church leaders fail to deal with sinners in the church. Drawing on NT texts (e.g., 1 Tim 5:20; 1 Cor 5:5, 13; Matt 18:15-17), Origen counsels that such persons ought to be "expelled from the Church" (81). Origen urges pastors to keep an eye on the flock and to call back those who stray, for "when they spare one, they set in motion the destruction of the whole Church" (81). Origen assumes that this story has been preserved not only to report on a battle, but also to teach the church that "battles of this kind" must be waged "with the sword of my mouth" (92–93).

Over time, the church has practiced a discipline that expelled or shunned people from the congregation for real or imagined immoral practices. Appeal is often made to 1 Corinthians 5 where the community is advised, "Drive out the wicked person from among you" (5:13). The context links disciplinary action with the Day of Atonement rituals (Lev 16). In 1 Corinthians 5, Christ has become the goat for the sin offering, and the evildoer has become the goat sent out into the wilderness (see Shillington 1998). Exclusion from the community of faith by avoidance and by shaming came to be associated, by verbal similarity to Achan's story, with a purifying of the community of faith.

An early Anabaptist statement of faith, the Schleitheim Confession (1527), "calls for the conscientious and faithful use of the ban to maintain a united and faithful church" (*ME* 5:239). This confession springs from a dualistic worldview, which separates things into good and evil, darkness and light. The Schleitheim Confession continues by asserting that believers have nothing to do with such things, including "diabolical weapons of violence." Menno Simons applied the Achan story to the practice of excommunication or expulsion (Menno Simons: 723–34; further in Menno, pp. 409–18, 457–85, 959–98).

Although the ban was intended by the Anabaptists as an admonition (cf. Menno Simons: 724), it was often a punishment (*ME* 5:239), as exemplified in Patrick Friesen's play *The Shunning* (Winnipeg: Turnstone, 1980). Aware of the dangers of exclusion as a means of protecting the "purity" of the community, recent confessions of faith have clarified the practice of church discipline. As a result of fear of abuse, however, many churches have not recovered a healthy discipline. In a study of five Mennonite denominations, Kauffman and Harder (1975) found that thirty-five percent of the respondents agreed with this statement: "The way to work with members in the church who have lapsed from the standards is never to exclude them from the church but rather to keep them on the membership roll, hoping they will mend their ways by heeding the advice of the minister or following the example of upright members" (*ME* 5:240).

The *Confession of Faith in a Mennonite Perspective* (MCF 1995: art. 14) focuses on the redemptive dimension of discipline with a goal of "forgiveness and transforming grace." The Commentary on the Confession recognizes that "the misuse and the neglect of discipline" compromise "the church's life and witness." Under certain circumstances, therefore, the church may act in recognition that a person has rejected or left the body of Christ (J. H. Yoder 2003: 126).

The Mennonite Brethren Confession of Faith (MBCF 1999: art. 6) affirms that accountability among church members allows them to "admonish and correct one another." Focusing on NT texts (Matt 16:13-20; 18:15-20; 1 Cor 5:1-8; chs. 12–14; 2 Cor 2:5-11), this confession advises using "the practice of redemptive church discipline," which focuses on correction, forgiveness, and restoration.

The problem of distinguishing between prophetic correction and priestly separation and reconciliation has been addressed of late by the increasing awareness of restorative justice, which aims to restore the integrity of persons, communities, and relationships among them (Jeschke 1990: 240). When someone has violated the covenantal terms of the community that seeks to live by a rule of life under the instruction of Christ, the community acts so as to restore that which has been broken, or relationships that have been violated—to restore them to health and well-being. The aim is to re-create wholeness through a redemptive process, without denying the reality of the harm that has been done. Although there is no straight line between the story of Achan and these confessional reflections on discipline, the heart of the matter remains similar. The integrity of the community's life and witness has been violated.

In most cases restorative justice, however, does not encompass a concern for the reputation of God, as OT texts seek to do. Jeschke's goal statement comes close, for it implies the notion of holiness ("sanctified church") and divine reputation ("church's witness"; 1990: 240). It would be helpful to rethink discipleship, and healthy discipline, as not so much about the self or the individual or even about the community, as about the holiness that creates a space for the presence of God in the world.

But that deserves more conversation, especially since it is precisely in Jesus that the divine has come to dwell among those who are not holy and not clean. Jesus is depicted in the Gospel texts as transgressing (violating) the boundaries of sanctity in order to welcome even the most unclean into the table fellowship of God. If God has indeed removed our sin far away (Ps 103:12), and if Rahab has become part of Jesus' genealogy, perhaps we might find another way of dealing with the Achans among us and the Achans that we are. Each of us, and all of us, may well be those who desire and take, thereby putting not only our own integrity at stake, but also that of the entire community, and ultimately God's reputation. Yet it is important that, like Joshua, we retain the freedom to argue with God and to act against the purity code as Jesus did when he associated with, healed, and shared meals with those excluded by ritual purity codes (e.g., Luke 5:12-39; 7:36-50).

The Possibility of Arguing with God

Calvin, commenting on Joshua's lament in 7:6-9, suggests that Joshua acted according to what he knew: God promised success. But unfortunately "Joshua oversteps the bounds of moderation when he challenges God for having brought the people out of the desert" (107). Calvin even accuses Joshua of "greater intemperance" when he wishes the people had stayed east of the Jordan. Calvin represents a perspective long practiced in the church, which denigrates the power of lament and protest before an apparent injustice in God's action or failure to act (see Billman and Migliore, who explore Calvin's denigration of lament).

Unlike Calvin, we do well to consider joining Joshua in his argument with God. Such conversation, however heated it may become, toughens our faith and calls on God to act with justice. Although Achan's story is reported as an act of divine justice, it is surely excessive under any circumstances at any other time. Surely those who "trouble" and disrupt the health of the community of faith should enter a discipling/disciplining conversation. But a great gulf appears between the killing of Achan and restorative justice practices.

Whether human beings like Abraham, Joshua, Ezekiel, or the psalmists call on God to act in keeping with God's character and thereby preserve God's own reputation, or whether God calls on human beings not to besmirch the divine reputation among the nations, there is always a need for a conversation. The conversation may be a disputation, an argument, a lament, a cry for justice, or an accusation. As with Abraham, God is pleased to engage in conversation and become vulnerable by allowing us to call on "the Judge of all the earth [to] do what is just" (Gen 18:25).

The Nature of Desire and Its Relationship to Violence

Coveting and taking remain a serious problem in our time. It is difficult to live with enough. Desire for more often precludes contentment and gratitude (see Leddy). Perhaps Joshua's invitation for Achan to "give thanks" or "praise" is not far off the mark, since to do so requires a letting go of what has stuck to his hands (Deut 13:17).

Even if we are not living in a world where the contagion of holiness makes sense, we may still take the confession seriously that "the earth is the LORD's, and the fulness thereof" (Ps 24:1 KJV). Those of us who continue to take without considering to whom all things belong may well bring devastating consequences along the way. No doubt we think, like Hezekiah, that these consequences can come in the future, so long as they do not affect me and my family (2 Kings 20:19). But the insatiable desire for more (even though the things in themselves are good) may affect the well-being of entire communities. The so-called developed world takes more than it gives back. This taking creates violence because it grasps rather than receives or gives. And above all, desire can lead to independence from the Giver. Land in the OT, and even the kingdom of God in the NT, are gifts, to be received without fear (Luke 12:32).

The Anger and the Gracious Mercy of God

Is God an angry God who punishes transgression? Or is God a merciful and forgiving God? Since Achan confesses, why does God not forgive? The question continues to be alive in the church's theological reflection. Latvus suggests that "the God of the crucified and powerless Jesus cannot be the same as the Deuteronomistic God of anger" (91). Yet Latvus acknowledges that the God of the NT is also a God who is sovereign over the powers and over evil. Rather than holding anger (judgment) and mercy together in dynamic tension, Latvus suggests that we understand the theological motive that lies behind the language of God's anger as a concern for "justice, major disasters of life, and questions about hope and love" (92).

We cannot, however, imagine God's anger in the same way as those OT texts by identifying God's anger with the consequences of human action in the realms of politics and communal life. Having said that, Latvus acknowledges the principle of responsibility: "In one way or another people or society have to pay for injustice even if there is no clear connection in one's life between reason and event" (93). Somewhere, sometime, somebody experiences the consequences of injustice and especially structural injustice. At the same time, hope remains, for all of life is a gift, even in Deuteronomistic theology: "life, land, people around, food, and so on, are a gift from God, totally given by grace without being earned" (94).

The Holocaust offers us another lens through which we might consider the Achan story. David R. Blumenthal asks, "Is not speaking of God's anger blasphemous in the context of the Holocaust?" (29). And yet, Blumenthal suggests, one cannot abandon God, nor can we avoid speaking of God in human terms. One must continue to speak of a personal *and* holy God "even as one must remain aware of the darkness that encompasses and threatens humanity" (31).

Blumenthal calls such theological reflection "personalist," referring to the traditional language of Scripture that speaks of God in personal or anthropomorphic language, which is fundamentally the language of relationship. Among the personalist attributes of God he includes both "God gets angry" and "God chooses; God is partisan." At the same time, however, we also speak as though "God must be fair" (15–20). Interpreters of Scripture, he suggests, must first of all speak the truth about the tradition, and especially about the difficult texts (237).

Garret Keizer, in *The Enigma of Anger*, suggests that "the wrath of the Old Testament God is of a piece with the resurrection of the New: It is the will and the power to change the normal or customary course of things. Furthermore, it is the source of, and in some cases the sanction for, our human power to do the same" (18). Certainly God is also depicted as "slow to anger," but still, not without anger (Exod 34:6-7; Pss 86:15; 103:8-14; 145:8-9; Jer 32:18-19; Joel 2:13; Jon 4:2).

So George Herbert's poem speaks against God: "Throw away Thy rod, / Throw away Thy wrath: / O my God, / Take the gentle path!" (d. 1633; cited in Keizer: 19). These days, in our concern to avoid images of God that smack of abusive relationships, we do well to remember that God's anger "is partly, even mostly, figurative" (20). That said, Keizer suggests, "The God who never gets mad for fear of offending the abuser must sooner or later be construed as the God who never gets mad at the abuser" (20). Keizer's wit sharpens when he continues to suggest that "to divest God of wrath" makes God "so benign as to be indifferent, so slow to anger that he is always late to save" (21). What both abused and oppressed need to hear, suggests Keizer, is not a change in the metaphor, but a new way of identifying with the metaphor. The wrath of God "is not the wrath of the abusive parent or of power abused. It is the absolute claim of personhood asserting itself in the face of power and chaos alike" (21). Even Jesus' cleansing of the temple may allow a way into our hearts for the cleansing and healing fire of divine anger *[Anger of the Lord, p. 386]*.

Joshua 8:30-35

The Altar on Mount Ebal: People of the Book

PREVIEW

Among my childhood memories are the overheard theological debates in which adults used the expression "It is written." I even remember the German original "*Es steht geschrieben*," said as though such a declaration might settle the debate. The Mennonite Brethren Confession of Faith declares that confessional statements are a distillation of our best understanding of Scripture. We would therefore expect debates about the meaning of the Bible. Even though there will be the inevitable controversy now and then, the Bible is also said to bind us together, both in covenant relationship with God and with one another.

It might, similarly, be appropriate to understand this brief episode as a report of unification and identity formation under the rubric of what we might call "People of the Book." The text stands in stark contrast to the immediately preceding stories. It takes us back to narratives in which the ark features prominently: the crossing of the Jordan and the Jericho episode. It takes us out of the warfare context and incongruously back into the world of communal worship. Joshua is the main actor. Although his name frames the unit (8:30, 35), the heart of the episode is its repetition of Moses' name. Everything from the building of the altar to the reading of the Torah is subsumed under the commanding presence of Moses. And Joshua, as faithful leader, carries out all of Moses' instructions and reads all of Moses' words [*Torah, p. 462*].

Based on Moses' instructions in Deuteronomy 27:1-10, building an altar is what one might have expected after crossing the Jordan and eating the first produce of the land in Gilgal (Josh 5:12). Instead, this altar-building episode comes after two paradigmatic conflict stories: Jericho and Ai. And now, instead of another conflict story at Shechem (the ancient site at the base of Mt. Ebal), we have a story of sacrifice and "Scripture reading."

As significant as Moses and Torah is the mention of those gathered as *all Israel, alien as well as citizen* (8:33, 35) *["All Israel," p. 385]*. This emphasis connects the episode to Joshua 1 and the motif of Torah faithfulness there. It reminds readers that the faithfulness required of Joshua is intended for all Israel. Moreover, the mention of both Mount Gerizim and Mount Ebal implies a reading of the blessings and the curse (Deut 27–29), which is especially poignant in the light of the first "transgression" in the land.

Hence, "Joshua 7–8 is only theologically complete by 8:30-35" (Winther-Nielsen: 168n13). And since Mount Ebal is at the doorstep of Shechem, this episode also reaches forward to the covenant renewal of chapter 24, the only other place where Shechem is mentioned as a gathering place in the book of Joshua. Thus Joshua 8:30-35 and Joshua 24 echo Deuteronomy 26–29, thereby affirming both that transgression does and will occur *and* that covenant reaffirmation along the way is not a onetime event. Just as Moses offered instructions for covenant renewal "when all these things have happened to you, the blessings and the curses" (Deut 30:1), so Joshua begins here, and concludes in Joshua 24, to invite all Israel to "choose life" and "live in the land" (Deut 30:19-20).

OUTLINE

Narrative Setup: Building the Altar, 8:30-31
Writing on Stone, 8:32-33
Reading the Words of the Law, 8:34-35

EXPLANATORY NOTES

Narrative Setup: Building the Altar 8:30-31

After the two paradigmatic events at Jericho (Rahab) and Ai (Achan), Joshua builds an altar on Mt. Ebal, which stands as a twin to Mt. Gerizim, next to the ancient site of Shechem (Gen 12:6; 33:18). Since there is no story here or elsewhere about a conquest of Shechem, this episode is set in "unoccupied territory." It is the site of the fiasco of Genesis 34, but it is not the place where Jacob chooses to build an altar

(35:1-5). Rather, Shechem is the place where his household gives up their foreign gods (35:2). Shechem is therefore not a sanctuary set apart by the tradition. Oddly, Shechem, a "foreign" city, is considered one of the clans of Manasseh (Josh 17:2). It is also one of the cities of refuge (20:7), the site of Joshua's final speech and covenant renewal (24:1), and the place where Joseph's bones are buried (24:32). Although 8:30-35 does not mention Shechem, readers know the proximity of Mount Ebal to the site of Shechem.

Moses is mentioned five times in 8:30-35, twice as *servant of the Lord* (8:31, 33) and the first such mention since the three occurrences in chapter 1. Moses is mentioned exactly this way fourteen times in the book of Joshua, two of which occur in this text unit (1:1, 13, 15; 8:31, 33; 11:12; 12:6 twice; 13:8; 14:7; 18:7; 22:2, 4, 5; cf. 9:24; 11:15). Even more important than his designation as *servant* is his role as one who commands (cf. 1:7, 13; 4:10) *[Characterization of Joshua, p. 394]*.

Joshua's building of the altar is significant even if it is only one aspect of his, and Israel's, carrying out Moses' instructions. Oddly Joshua's action does not follow the instructions in Deuteronomy 27:1-10. The summary in Joshua 8:31 is a more or less accurate rendering of that text. Although the sequence (unhewn stones, sacrifices, writing) is the same, the plastering of the stones is missing. Why this event does not take place "when you have crossed over" (Deut 27:3-4) is not clear. Instead, the event of Joshua 8:30-35, which seems naturally to follow 5:12, has been broken by two stories of encounter with Canaanites. One depicts carrying out the divine plan and success. The second depicts failure to observe the instructions along with solutions for purging the evil from Israel so that life can go on in God's presence. It is as though these two paradigmatic stories are set within the framework of the liturgical acts of Passover and the altar of sacrifice *[Twelve Stones, p. 465]*.

More important than that, however, is the motif *the book of the law of Moses*, which appears in 8:31 for the first time since 1:8. This *book* is referred to as *book of the law* (8:31, 34; cf. 1:8), *law of Moses* (8:32), or *words of the law* (8:34), which correspond with what Moses commanded (8:31, 33, 35). The expressions show up in Joshua again only at the end of the book, in Joshua's final speeches (23:6; 24:26). In Deuteronomy the expression *book of the law* appears only in the final chapters of the book (28:61; 29:20, 21; 30:10; 31:26), but the entire book is understood as Torah (1:5; 4:8, 44; 17:18, 19; 27:3, 8, 26; 28:58, 61; 29:29; 31:9, 11, 12, 24; 32:46). Within the DtrH it appears again only in three places (1 Kings 2:3; cf. 2:1-3, with its echoes of

Joshua 1; 2 Kings 14:6; 2 Kings 22:8, 11). In the last of those references, we read of Josiah: after carrying out cultic reforms "by the book," he is evaluated as having kept "all the law of Moses" (2 Kings 23:25; cf. Josh 1:7) *[Characterization of Joshua, p. 394; Torah, p. 462].*

Why bother with those details? First, this "book" is always associated with the experience of "life" (Deut 8:3; 30:19) within the covenant community. Disregarding the book leads to death. At its worst, death includes alienation from God and loss of land. Second, this book is associated with Moses and the prophets (2 Kings 17:13) and comes into play as an explanation of the exile of Israel (2 Kings 17). Third, the Torah terminology here, in Joshua's commissioning by God (Josh 1), and in Solomon's commissioning by David (1 Kings 2:1-3), suggests that the Deuteronomic school of writers sees typological or figural relationships among the characters at the heart of Israel's story. Whereas Joshua is the faithful disciple and keeper of Torah, Solomon is the unfaithful one (Schäfer-Lichtenberger). The typology of Moses/Joshua/Josiah fills out the faithful leader (king) paradigm that both Joshua and Josiah fulfill (Nelson 1981b). In particular, both Joshua and Josiah *read* the Torah, and Joshua both *wrote* and *read* the Torah as stipulated for the king in Deuteronomy 17:18-19. Joshua is therefore depicted as a protoroyal figure *[Characterization of Joshua, p. 394; Torah, p. 462].*

Unlike at the reading of the "book of Moses" in Nehemiah 8–9, which resulted in the separation "from Israel all those of foreign descent" (13:1-3), Joshua 8:30-35 pictures the covenant community in which *alien as well as citizen* are listening to the words of the book and share in the *burnt offerings to the Lord* (v. 31, 33). Although Achan and his household are burned for their having transgressed the sphere of holiness, here even outsiders share in the sacrifice and hear the word. This juxtaposition of the sacrifice of Achan/Ai with this motif of inclusiveness at the altar must not be missed. Where one sacrifice excludes and eliminates, another welcomes and includes.

Writing on Stone 8:32-33

Following the instructions of Moses (Deut 27:1-10), Joshua writes *a copy of the law of Moses* (8:32). The Hebrew word for *copy* (used normally to mean "second") with this meaning is used only here and in the instructions for the king in Deuteronomy 17:18. Again, this is an indicator that the narrative depicts Joshua not only as able successor to Moses, but also as paradigmatic precursor to Israel's kings. The text adds *which he* [Moses] *had written* to make it clear that

Joshua is not making this up. He is a faithful mediator of the tradition just as he is the faithful obedient one *[Characterization of Joshua, p. 394]*.

That he writes *in the presence of the Israelites* (v. 32) is filled out in v. 33 by a long description specifying who stands where in relation to the ark and in relation to the two mountains, Ebal and Gerizim. Two groups are standing opposite each other, perhaps with the valley between them. Each represents either blessing or curse (Deut 11:29; 27:12-13). Deuteronomy 11:27-28 makes the function of this recitation clear: "the blessing, if you obey the commandments of the LORD your God; . . . and the curse, if you do not obey the commandments of the LORD your God." The ceremony probably depicts a symbolic action, not a liturgical reading. Where Israel stands is important, either in the curse or in the blessing (cf. Ps 1:1).

Most curious and interesting in this unit is the mention of *alien as well as citizen* (vv. 33, 35). In the Hebrew text the word order is significantly different. Verse 33 begins with *All Israel*. Immediately after that, the verse names various officials and notes where they ought to stand. In the middle of the verse, just before the mention of *half of them* on one side and *half* on the other, the narrator adds *alien as well as citizen*, as though assuming a paradigmatic reality that *all Israel* is made up of *alien as well as citizen ["All Israel," p. 385]*. Consulting Deuteronomy, we learn that *ger* (NRSV: "resident alien," CEB: "immigrant"; perhaps AT: "indigenous person") is part and parcel of Israel and subject to special care (1:16; 10:18-19; 14:29; 16:11, 14; 24:14, 17, 19, 20, 21; 26:11-13; 27:19). They are even to be included among those whom Moses has included in the covenant renewal and who are to heed the Torah (29:10; 31:12). Hence also in Joshua 20, the cities of refuge are for both Israelites and aliens (Josh 20:9).

Reading the Words of the Law 8:34-35

Like the king in Deuteronomy 17:19, Joshua reads before *all the assembly of Israel* (see also Deut 31:30; 1 Kings 8:14, 22, 55; Lev 16:17). The texts of Deuteronomy 31 and 1 Kings 8 bear comparing in relation to Joshua 8:30-35. Deuteronomy 31 is part of a longer series of speeches: covenantal blessings and curses (Deut 28); covenant renewal ceremony (Deut 29), which ends ironically with a mention of the people being uprooted "from their land in anger, fury, and great wrath, . . . as is now the case" (29:28); and instructions for covenant renewal after unfaithfulness (Deut 30). Almost all of Deuteronomy 31 concerns entering thc land, including the commissioning of Joshua, with language reiterated in Joshua 1. The chapter includes dire warnings (31:16-19, 27) and instructions to sing a song (31:19). After he "had finished writing down in a book the words of this law to the very end" (31:24), Moses muses, "For I know well how rebellious and stubborn you are. If you already have been so rebellious toward the Lord while I am still alive among you, how much more after my death!" (31:27). He then calls the elders and officials (the same groups as in Josh 8:33), reads what he has written (as does Joshua), and warns them that they "will surely act corruptly, turning aside from the way that I have commanded you" (Deut 31:29).

One can hardly imagine more sinister last words. It may not be surprising, then, to recognize that both Joshua and Solomon, as they gather *all the assembly of Israel, . . . bless the people of Israel* (Josh 8:35, 33; 1 Kings 8:55), just as Joshua, like Moses, reads both the blessings and the curses. The hearing of the covenant document by aliens (including indigenous persons), women, and children occurs in the case of Moses (Deut 29:11) and Joshua (Josh 8:33, 35). And Solomon's prayer includes a hope that strangers may come and pray because they "hear of your great name" (1 Kings 8:42). His hope is that "all the peoples of the earth may know your name and fear you" (8:43; cf. Josh 3:11, 13; 4:24).

Thus Moses and David are followed by the two disciples, Joshua and Solomon. In both contexts we find the reality of failure and hope of restoration. Deuteronomy implies both exile and restoration (esp. Deut 30). Solomon assumes that Israel will "sin against you" and be exiled (1 Kings 8:33-34, 46), but he also assumes repentance and forgiveness (1 Kings 8:33, 48-50). In the book of Joshua, the episode about the altar and the reading of Torah, however, presents us with an incomplete narrative. We have read a story of obedience (Josh 6) and a story of recovery from failure (7:1–8:29). Whereas Joshua 1 commissions Joshua to pay attention to the *book of the law*, only in 8:30-35 does this same *book of the law* (8:31) become public in the hearing of *all the assembly of Israel* (8:35). Readers have to wait until Joshua 24, at the next gathering of *all the tribes of Israel* (24:1), to hear the covenant commitment of the people (24:16-18). There Joshua calls on Israel to choose *this day* (24:15), even as Moses in Deuteronomy spoke about "today" as the day of faithfulness (Deut 5:2-3; 29:14). But even then, Joshua, like Moses (Deut 31:27), is doubtful (Josh 24:19-20). His rhetorical doubt spurs the people to an even stronger statement of commitment. Israel, having heard the Torah, and having experienced the realization of God's promises, can do no other. The interim between the hearing of the Torah in Joshua 8:30-35 and the call to ongoing and exclusive loyalty in chapter 24 is preceded by a reiteration of all the good that God has done in the meantime (ch. 23). Thus Joshua 8:30-35 makes public what was private in Joshua 1 and restores communal integrity after the first two paradigmatic narratives in chapter 6 and 7:1–8:29.

Having said that, it is important to notice that in the book of Joshua it is *Israel* whose identity is both questioned and established. It is the hearing of the Torah that shapes the identity of the congregation. The narrator reminds us that the *aliens* are those who have *resided among them*. That is significant in the light of the fact that later in the book we discover that many of the indigenous inhabitants continue living among Israel *to this day*. Moreover, verse 35 also mentions *the women, and the little ones* as comprising a part of this assembly of *all Israel*. None are excluded: all constitute the *all Israel* of verse 33, and all are listeners *["All Israel," p. 385]*.

This text has its home in the context of worship. Although divine instruction is a matter of personal faithfulness in Joshua 1, here the private has become public in a worship event. Attention to Torah (instruction) and thanksgiving go hand in hand. Joshua is faithful to the tradition as embodied by Moses. He demonstrates that he is a worthy successor to Moses because he carries out all that Moses has commanded and reads all that Moses has written *[Characterization of Joshua, p. 394]*. Yet how a text can strike an inclusive note amid stories that exclude and execute remains a mystery. Perhaps the next story adds a comic twist in an otherwise gruesome sequence of conquest accounts, which explains how such *aliens* come to be *among them* (v. 35).

THE TEXT IN BIBLICAL CONTEXT

People of the Book

The Explanatory Notes have illustrated how this text resonates with a wider biblical conversation about Torah in the context of worship, and how that instruction, as textual artifact, constitutes Israel as a people that includes aliens, women, and children (see also TBC for Josh 2) *[Torah, p. 462]*.

Deuteronomy emphasizes the role of the king in reading Torah (Deut 17:18-20). After giving the Torah to the priests and the elders, Moses commands that Torah be read every seventh year (31:10-11) in the hearing of "the people—men, women, and children, as well as the aliens residing in your towns—so that they may hear and learn to fear the LORD your God and to observe diligently all the words of this law" (31:12). Even children are to ask questions about the meaning of the Torah (Deut 6:20). The only other reading of the Torah in the DtrH occurs in Joshua 8:30-35 and 2 Kings 22, where Josiah reads aloud to all the people, "both small and great" (2 Kings 23:2).

The larger history regards *the book* as that which constitutes Israel as a people. Its narrative and instruction shapes the identity and life of this mixed community, including the alien (*ger*). This book itself does not enforce; it is read, heard, and taught (Balentine: 186). Especially when it has been recognized that a grave wrong has been done, or when the people have gone astray by worshiping other gods and failing to heed the instructions of the Lord, the book is understood as that instrumental means of setting things right. It offers a reorientation by identifying a new direction or by setting the parameters of faithfulness. It teaches both how to live with undivided loyalty to God and how to live in the world and in the community according to God's intentions. In other words, *the book* is a narration in how "to love God, and to live as people who love God" (Balentine: 186). With its paradigmatic characters and events, the book of Joshua begins Israel's journey toward that goal, which we find embodied in the early communities of Jesus followers *[Torah, p. 462]*.

There certainly was conflict in the Jesus movement about how Gentile believers ought to be faithful to Torah (e.g., Acts 15). Just as in the OT, Torah is not the means of entering covenant relationship: it is a gift that shapes the community as covenant relationship is expressed in life. In the context of first-century ethnic nationalism (where Torah functions as a boundary marker), the NT recovers a notion of Torah as a gracious and good gift of the Lord that is not binding on Gentile believers in the same way as it is for Jews. Luke–Acts pictures an expansive community of Jews and Gentiles (Luke 2:32; Acts 9:15; 10:45; 11:1: Gentiles "accepted the word of God"; 13:46-48; 14:27; cf. Rom 9:24; 15:10-12; Eph 2:11-12; 3:6). All now submit to the law of Christ, which is the law of love.

Having said that, the OT continued to be read by early Christian communities as it was read in synagogues (Acts 13:15; 15:21). Public worship included singing, praise, and reading of the Scriptures (1 Tim 4:13). Matthew is very interested in the "fulfillment" of Scripture (4:4, 6, 7, 10; cf. 11:10; 21:13; 26:24, 31), and his encounters are often punctuated with "Have you not/never read?" (12:3, 5; 19:4; 21:16, 42; 22:31). Near the beginning of his public ministry, Jesus reads Scripture in the synagogue (Luke 4:16). Although Paul thinks that the people's interpretation of Scripture is obscuring their vision (2 Cor 3:14-15),

Scripture remains the source of the divine promise to bring Jew and Gentile together (cf. "scripture says" in Rom 9:17; 10:11; 11:2). Paul brings both worship and word together in his admonishing, "Let the word of Christ dwell in you richly" (Col 3:16).

In the NT, "the book" is the source confirming that the promises of God are becoming a reality among Jews and Gentiles. "The book" does not mark inclusion or exclusion. It nourishes and guides a relationship already established, as Jesus clarifies in his discourse with opponents who are teachers of Torah (John 5:39). According to Jesus (and perhaps Deuteronomy), the book is not the source of life. Life is bound up in relationship with God as that relationship is continually chosen (by rejecting other allegiances) and shaped (by living according to the instructions corresponding to this exclusive relationship) and articulated by "the book." The book is only a mediator, a charter of the relationship. It lives most fully in the context of the community (assembly of Israel) and in the context of worship (altar, sacrifice, thanksgiving). It provides substance to the worship, identity, and mission of the community as God's people embody the word that they have heard.

A reciprocal relationship exists between community and text. Community is born by God. Community, in reflection and conversation with God, produces texts that become Scripture. Scripture in turn calls out and shapes a community that lives out of its relationship with God as articulated and understood (interpreted) in Scripture.

THE TEXT IN THE LIFE OF THE CHURCH

Shaped by Scripture

No Christian traditions affirm that the faith of believers is formed by Scripture alone. Nor does the notion of *sola scriptura* have to do with establishing the relationship of believers to God. It serves rather as a challenge to other authorities if they are considered to have equal status to Scripture. But even within that debate, which emerged with Martin Luther in the sixteenth century, all Christian denominations see themselves as shaped by Scripture in one way or another and understand that Scripture is inescapably interpreted through the lens of experience and tradition (see Hays; Work; Mulholland). Still, it remains a challenge to understand what it means to be shaped by our hearing of the word. And more, if Scripture is heard by insider and alien alike, it is a challenge to grasp how Scripture ought to be read to create a space for the Other.

Perhaps Scripture is the story that offers a mirror for our common identity as that adopted story shapes our lives and finds embodiment in our days.

The "book of the law" in Deuteronomy, Joshua, and 2 Kings is in some ways a precursor to a larger notion of Scripture, which formed within Judaism and Christianity. "The Books," which is what "Bible" means (from Greek *biblia*), have become the source through which the Spirit of God invites a people to relationship with God. Scripture thus nurtures and shapes the identity and mission of the people of God and offers a theological orientation that underlies all of life in the world and in the presence of God. Many reform or renewal movements within the church have been rooted in a reading (or more accurately, a rereading) of Scripture.

Not surprisingly, therefore, most denominational confessions of faith include a statement on Scripture, even though the early Christian creeds do not. The Mennonite Brethren Confession (MBCF 1999: art. 2), for example, states that Scripture is "the authoritative guide for faith and practice." But it says little about how Scripture actually functions in life. "Faith and practice" may mean "things to believe" or "things to do." Yet for Deuteronomy, "faith and practice" may well mean something like "trust and obey." If that is so, then Scripture functions much like Deuteronomy's vision of Torah. It invites and persuades to exclusive allegiance to one Lord, and it offers the basic contours of what life in the world ought to look like because of allegiance to that Lord.

Yet "hearing" or "being in the audience" (as was *all Israel* in Josh 8) is likely not enough. The disciples in Mark's Gospel hear everything, but they do not understand what they hear because their assumptions and self-interest get in the way (Mark 4:9, 15-20, 23-24, 33; 6:11; 8:18; 12:29). Jesus challenges his listeners to have "ears to hear." Origen finds an analogy between Joshua's writing and reading of the *second law* (as the LXX puts it in Josh 8:32) and Jesus' opening up Scripture to the disciples on the way to Emmaus (Luke 24:27-32), showing how those Scriptures spoke about himself. In the book of Acts, Philip finds himself with an Ethiopian who is reading Isaiah. To the question of whether he understands what he is reading, the Ethiopian replies, "How can I, unless someone guides me?" (8:31). In each of these cases, reading requires an understanding that moves the reader through the literal understanding of the words to the relational faithfulness to which Joshua is called, and to which he will invite the people in Joshua 24. It will not do simply to quote the text and say, as I heard often in my childhood, "*Es steht geschrieben*" (lit., "it stands written"). Joshua's reading is only a beginning.

Unfortunately, sometimes the church excludes some people from hearing the words of the book, even as it announces boldly a plan to bring the good news to the nations. During the early years of evangelism among Japanese Canadians in Alberta, Canada, some Christians in southern Alberta closed down the ministry for fear that new Japanese believers might come to worship in their churches. We trust that the question of who is allowed to hear the story is no longer an issue. Even so, we do well to be vigilant as we attend to the "aliens" among us.

Some time ago I discovered a web page about how one congregation interprets the Bible. Most striking was the parenthetical note after their first sentence: "A basic tool for interpreting the Bible is the concept of the life setting of the passage (*Sitz im Lieben*)." The irony is in the naive spelling error in the German. *Sitz im Lieben* means "setting in love," instead of the usual phrase *Sitz im Leben*, which means "setting in life." This unintended intersection of life/love suggests that reading in conversation means that the text cannot be reduced to an object to be analyzed, or a problem to be solved, or an answer to be received. It comes to us as participants in a conversation in a community that bridges time and space. If that conversation is grounded in a setting in love, then interpretation will not be driven merely by a competitive drive to get it right, but by the transformative possibilities that are part of any healthy conversation. If our interpretation is relational, we avoid the pitfall of Jesus' opponents, who seemed to have a very good grasp of the Scriptures as source of "eternal life" (or so they thought), but not a very deep awareness that, more than anything else, Scripture invites us into relationship with Jesus (John 5:39-40).

Conversation governed by love can allow church members to disagree on a variety of interpretive issues and still remain committed to working together as a congregation or conference. After all, the church has been having such conversations for two thousand years. Some of those conversations have led to confessional clarity; others have not. In other words, we can forgive ourselves if we do not get it all right all the time. Jesus' opponents in John 5 practiced interpretive consensus. But they did not recognize that loving Scripture is only a tool in the service of a higher good: loving Jesus and following him in life. Attentiveness to the word (Josh 1) and hearing that word in the covenant community (Josh 8) set the stage for the inclusion of the Gibeonites in the next chapter and, eventually, to the call to exclusive loyalty in Joshua 24.

Joshua 9:1-27

The Gibeonites' Ruse: From Trick to Treaty

PREVIEW

Trickster stories are commonplace in the folktales of peoples around the world. From Jacob as Israel's most prominent trickster figure to Bugs Bunny and the Roadrunner in Warner Brothers cartoons, tricksters represent the weak but clever one who survives by cunning in the face of impossible odds. In this story, however, the trickster motif is turned on Israel as the one being tricked.

This humor-tinged story highlights the Gibeonites' clever ploy to avoid conflict and to become part of Israel. Following the reading of Torah with the aliens (8:33, 35), Joshua 9 is a poignant reflection on the problem of welcoming the outsider. Interrupting the reader's expectation after 9:1-2, the story is a paradigmatic (and counterintuitive) introduction to the stories that follow. It engages the conversation with other texts that touch on Israel's relationship to the nations (Gen 12:1-3; Josh 2; 1 Kings 8; Isa 56). Moreover, Gibeon will become a significant Israelite worship site for some 250 years. The narrator of Solomon's story reports that Gibeon was "the principal high place" at the time, and the place where "the LORD appeared to Solomon in a dream" (1 Kings 3:4-5). Thus the story also explains how a Canaanite cultic site becomes a place for worshiping God (in spite of Deut 12:2).

The story can be read in three ways: as an affirmation of the kind of inclusive impulse that constitutes Israel; as an explanation for the second-class status of Gibeonites in Israel; or as an ideological narrative that supports colonial conquest and the subservience of indigenous populations. Something may be said for each of those interpretations. Those options invite readers to listen to Joshua 9 in the context of the larger conversations about otherness/exclusion and embrace/inclusion in the biblical drama.

Joshua 9 begins a new sequence of conquest stories that extends from 9:1 to 12:24 (the first extended from 5:1 to 8:35 [Winther-Nielsen]). The introduction (vv. 1-2) sets the stage for that sequence of stories as it highlights *all the kings* (v. 1) who *heard* (see also 9:3; 10:1; 11:1) and who now stand in opposition after the paradigmatic events at Jericho and Ai. One of those was a story of success, the other of a failure redeemed. Joshua 9 is also paradigmatic: it stands in contrast to the expectation generated by 9:1-2 and the following stories of conquest in chapters 10–12. Like the unit before it, Joshua 9 includes significant echoes of Deuteronomy 7 and 27, which highlight the anomaly of Gibeonites' becoming part of Israel.

OUTLINE

Introduction, 9:1-2
The Gibeonites' Trick, 9:3-6
Dialogue: From Trick to Treaty, 9:7-15
Discovery and Decision, 9:16-21
Joshua's Negotiation/Compromise, 9:22-26
Gibeon's Servanthood, 9:27

EXPLANATORY NOTES

Introduction 9:1-2

This story begins in the same way as 5:1, which introduced the sequence of stories that follows through chapter 8. Similarly, the general introduction in 9:1-2 is followed by three subordinate stories, each of which begin with the same words, *when [name] heard* (9:3; 10:1; 11:1).

All the kings . . . heard. The introductions in 5:1 and 9:1 depict these people groups as client kingdoms of Egyptian imperial control, or as independent city-states governed by chieftains or kings who gather together to defend or attack as the need arises (cf. 10:1). As Younger confirms, such notices about hearing of a coming army are common in ancient Near Eastern conquest accounts (1990: 200). Younger cites Assyrian texts similar to the Gibeonite story in Joshua 9 and the Adoni-Zedek and Jabin stories in Joshua 10 and 11. In one text the opponents prepare for war against the Assyrian aggressor, and in the other they submit and, like the Gibeonites, "become integrated into its society" (200).

Rahab, speaking for all her people, also reports that they have heard about what God has done (2:10-11). Although she says of all the inhabitants of Jericho, *Our hearts melted*, Rahab's own response is to confess, *The Lord your God is indeed God in heaven above and on earth below.* Another story of hearing has the Israelites discovering what the two and a half Transjordan tribes have done by building an altar (22:11-12). Their response is to prepare for war against fellow Israelites. In the story of the Gibeonites, the "hearing" becomes more than prelude to battle: it is part of the intrigue (9:3, 9, 16). The story subverts the genre.

We discover that *all the kings* of the region west of the Jordan have heard a report *of this.* Apparently word travels fast. Perhaps the narrator wants us to understand that they have heard about what was told in chapters 5–8. Very likely the report in 9:1 contrasts the two previous reported hearings, both of which include the phrase *hearts melted* (2:11; 5:1). This one leads to a gathering *with one accord* (lit., *with one mouth*) *to fight Joshua and Israel* (emph. added). Now that they have discovered that the interlopers are not invincible, they choose to initiate action against them to defend their homeland from the aggressors. It is not possible to argue that the narrative now depicts Israel as taking a defensive stance. Justifying the violence here does not do justice to the fact that in the previous stories about which these kings supposedly *heard*, Israel is in first-strike mode. What the kings of 9:1 do, therefore, is to defend against the aggressor, Israel.

The geographic location and identity of these kings is limited to those west of the Jordan even though the phrase *beyond the Jordan* describes their location. That designation is used in Deuteronomy and Joshua to signify either east or west of the Jordan, depending on the context (see Explanatory Notes for 5:1). In the context of the "hearing" of the kings and the tradition of the list of dispossessed peoples, the story of the Gibeonites (beginning in Josh 9:3) offers us both an anomaly (it goes against the grain) or an ironic twist in the assumptions of what is and is not possible in this process of God's gifting the land to Abraham's descendants (Gen 15:18-21) *[Dispossessed Peoples, p. 424].*

The Gibeonites' Trick 9:3-6

The Gibeonites also *heard* about the events at Jericho and Ai, but their response is markedly different from that of the kings. The *kings* heard and planned for war; *the inhabitants of Gibeon heard* and *acted with cunning* (vv. 3-4a). The word order in verse 3 suggests a contrast (disjunctive *waw*) clause, which is reflected in most translations with the word *but* or *however*. Verse 4 includes an emphatic pronoun *also/even they*, again highlighting their unique take on the situation (AT). This disjunctive introduction reminds us of the contrast set up between the success reported in 6:27 and the tragic violation of covenant loyalty reported at the beginning of the Ai/Achan story in 7:1 (Winther-Nielsen: 243). And the emphatic pronoun *also they* (9:4 AT) implies an "ironic twist" insofar as "the Israelites, who had used trickery and deception to conquer Jericho and Ai, are themselves now the victims of deception" (Younger 1990: 377n6). Thus the passage carries a double comparison: the Gibeonites are like Israel in their trickery but unlike the kings in their plotting for war. As Stone puts it, the passage "focuses entirely on their different response: rather than fight, they concede [that] God will give Israel victory and try to save their own lives" (30). The Gibeonites are mentioned again in chapter 10, when Adoni-zedek intends to gather a coalition to do battle against Gibeon. Since the Gibeonite story is set before two stories of hearing (10:1; 11:1), the "intrigue in chapter 9 is introduced as a contrasting response to Israel, thus transforming that story's function. No longer a story about Gibeonite craft or Israelite carelessness, it contrasts their response directly with that of Adoni-Zedek and Jabin, construing it as a positive . . . response to Israel's presence in Canaan" (Stone: 32).

The *inhabitants of Gibeon* act without mention of a king. *Elders and all the inhabitants of our country* are responsible for the decision (v. 11). Hess suggests that this social arrangement may be typical of Hittite governance, with local government administered by elders (1996: 179). There were cities ruled by oligarchies before the Amarna period (fourteenth century BC) in Palestine. This difference in governance structure may account for the conflict between Saul and the Gibeonites reported in 2 Samuel 21 (Blenkinsopp 1972: 31). According to Blenkinsopp, the political situation is similar, with shifting alliances, as that mentioned in the Amarna Letters. "States were bound together between themselves singly and with the Pharaoh by treaties, implying the taking of oaths and acceptance of responsibilities, such as we find described in Joshua ix" (32). Even so, the contrast between the Gibeonites and the kings is striking because the story itself shares in the generic conventions of ancient history writing. Because of the similarities, including the use of deception, Younger claims that the narrative shares in the generic conventions of ancient conquest accounts (1990: 201–4).

The Gibeonites appear to be tricksters, but the word used here to describe their action, *with cunning*, is used seldom in the OT. Once it means "treachery" (Exod 21:14) and three times it means "shrewdness" or "prudence" (Prov 1:4; 8:5, 12). It is related to the Hebrew root used in Genesis 3:1 to describe the serpent. Hamlin thinks this is an allusion, together with the word *cursed* in Joshua 9:23, that implies a warning about the "fatal attraction" of Canaanite culture (1983: 80). The details of their actions that follow in verses 4b-6 suggest that they are embarking on a risky venture by confronting the enemy of whom everyone else is afraid or against whom everyone else is planning to fight. They dress up as though they have just completed a long journey. The fourfold repetition of *worn-out* highlights not only the distance from which they allegedly have come (vv. 4-5; cf. v. 13), but also adds a note of humor through exaggeration. They have supposedly come so far that one cannot imagine a neighboring *country* from which they may have originated (v. 6). They must have come from even further away than that. The verbal form of *worn-out* also occurs in Deuteronomy to describe Israel's experience in the wilderness when clothes or sandals did not wear out (Deut 8:4; 29:5). So the fact that the Gibeonites should be described this way allows the reader an ironic wink at the Israelites' expense.

And so they approach Joshua in Gilgal, looking like vagabonds. In the book of Joshua, Gilgal, located not far from Jericho, is the main encampment of Israel after the Jericho incident (4:19-20; 5:9-10), and it is a main cultic site until the time of Samuel and King Saul (up to 1 Sam 15). Gibeon is probably to be associated with the modern site of el-Jib, about six miles northwest of Jerusalem (the Arabic name still reflects part of the Canaanite/Hebrew name) *[Archaeology and Joshua, p. 389]*.

The Gibeonites' remarkable request echoes Deuteronomy 7 and 20 so closely that it seems as though the Gibeonites have read Deuteronomy. With Deuteronomy 20:10-15 they say that they have come from far away (with the "very far" of Deut 20:15 echoed a few verses later in Josh 9:9), even though they are "Hivites" (Josh 9:1; 11:19), who according to Deuteronomy 20:17 ought to be annihilated rather than being offered terms of peace. Depending on the route, the distance between Gibeon and Gilgal might be seventeen to twenty miles, only a day's walk. Based on their claim, the reader can assume that they expect to be offered terms of peace (*šalom*, Deut 20:10) even though Deuteronomy never defines what constitutes "far away" *[Extent of the Land, p. 424]*. In addition, they ask, even demand (with a pl. imperative), that Joshua and the Israelites make a treaty (*berit* = covenant) with them (on *covenant* in Joshua, see 7:11, 15; 23:16; 24:25). Covenant language in Joshua 9 also echoes Deuteronomy 7:2 *[Covenant and Treaty, p. 416]*. There Moses commands that the "seven nations mightier and more numerous than you," including the Hivites, shall be destroyed and devoted to destruction (7:1). They are to "make no *covenant* with them and show them no mercy" (7:2). Whether from near or far, they are perceived by Deuteronomy as a danger if they entice Israel to "worship other gods" (13:6). Israel "must not yield to or heed any such persons. Show them no pity or compassion and do not shield them" (13:8) *[Covenant and Treaty, p. 416]*.

Even more remarkable is the parallel between the Gibeonites' claim to have come from *a far country* and the exact wording of Solomon's prayer in 1 Kings 8:41 ("distant land," NRSV/NIV). The hope there in verses 41-43 that foreigners might come to the new temple adds poignancy to the Gibeonites' story. They also "hear" about God's "great name" and come from a "distant land." Like Solomon's foreigners, the Gibeonites represent the wish that "all the peoples of the earth may know your name and fear you" (1 Kings 8:43). And yet the actions of Israel in Canaan so far are ambiguous in this regard: Rahab and her family are saved, but entire cities have been wiped out. In the light of the echoes that embrace those outside Abraham's family, it feels as though the Gibeonites are making a risky, but not altogether surprising, move. Since Rahab's story, we might expect a surprise like this (note *aliens* already present in 8:33, 35).

The fact that they ask for a treaty is not unusual in the light of historical evidence from the Amarna letters. The proposed covenant seems similar to Abraham's treaty with Abimelech (Gen 21:27). That they call themselves *servants* in the next unit (v. 8) may be a way of "defining the kind of treaty they had in mind," called by Blenkinsopp "protectorate treaties" (1972: 36).

Dialogue: From Trick to Treaty 9:7-15

The Israelites' response confirms suspicions that the story subverts Deuteronomy. The Israelites question the integrity of the travelers by recognizing the possibility of the opposite: what if they actually live *among us*? If that is the case, we cannot *make a treaty with you* (v. 7).

Addressing Joshua directly, the Gibeonites declare themselves *your* (sg.) *servants*. As though testing their earlier story (v. 6), Joshua asks them to identify themselves and their place of origin (v. 8). The Gibeonites' answer (v. 9) is the heart of this dialogue. Again identifying themselves as *servants* (*subjects*, NJPS), they add that they have come *from a very far country* and that they have come *because of the name of the* LORD *your God*. The *name* refers to the reputation of this God (the same two expressions occur in 1 Kings 8:41). And that reputation has been established for the Gibeonites, as it has for Rahab (Josh 2:10) and the other kings (5:1), by the *report* about what this God did in Egypt and in Transjordan (9:9b-10; cf. 9:24). The Gibeonite delegation reports what they have been instructed by their *elders* and fellow citizens to do (9:11; as planned in 9:4-5). They again establish themselves as *your* (pl.) *servants* and ask (with an imperative pl.) for the second time that Israel make a *treaty* with them (9:11). To corroborate this story, they show their bread, wineskins, clothing, and sandals, claiming that these are all *worn out from the very long journey* (9:12-13). Again, their description echoes the description of the plans almost exactly (9:4-5).

The Gibeonites offer their meager and stale provisions to the Israelites for sampling, to be sure, but the action is ironic because the offer is also a sign of hospitality. The Israelites (lit., *the men*) *partook*, believing the evidence. The ruse has worked: *Joshua made peace with them, guaranteeing their lives by a treaty* (v. 15a). This treaty is confirmed publicly by an *oath* sworn by *the leaders of the congregation* (on *congregation*: 9:15, 18 [twice], 19, 21, 27; 18:1; 20:6, 9; 22:12, 16, 17, 18, 20, 30; and *leaders/chiefs*: 9:15, 18 [twice], 19, 21; 13:21; 17:4; 22:14, 30, 32). In both Joshua 9 and 22, *leaders* and *congregation* are involved in the negotiation process. Both texts concern definition of relationship with the "outside." Moreover, the *peace* that this *treaty* guarantees (v. 15) is an ironic allusion to Deuteronomy 7:2 and 20:10-11. And as Blenkinsopp points out, it is usual in treaty documents for the inferior party to swear the oath "whereas here it is the Israelites who swear" (1972: 40). The irony is confirmed by analogy with the Rahab incident, in which the spies make an oath with Rahab (2:12, 17, 20; 9:18-20).

All of this seems oddly humorous. Is it likely that stale and moldy bread would have been evidence for a long journey *and* offered as part of a covenant ritual? Could they not have found fresh bread along the way (Blenkinsopp 1972: 35)? These ironies, humorous twists, and anomalies in the story suggest that a deliberate storytelling tradition has been at work. This story, told over the centuries, might have brought both a tear and a chuckle. It may have been told to explain the inclusion of this ethnic group and to explain the origin of temple personnel. In this sequence of narratives, however, the story illustrates that inclusion/exclusion of Others is a complex reality that is not so easily managed as Deuteronomy's laws suggest.

From the Gibeonite perspective, all has gone according to plan. But in verse 14b the narrator observes that the Israelites *did not ask direction from the Lord*. This is the only occurrence of the expression in Joshua. If there is a criticism here, it is implicit: if they had asked the Lord, would they have discerned the matter differently? Is the contrast between the leaders and Joshua (v. 15a)? The questions cannot be answered except by noticing that, except for casting lots in 7:14-18, nowhere in the book of Joshua does anyone ask direction from the Lord (see Boling 1983: 246). In Judges, the expression is used three times to refer to an inquiry into whether Israel ought to go into battle (1:1; 20:18, 23, 27). David is said to have inquired of the Lord (1 Sam 23:2, 4; 30:8; 2 Sam 2:1; 5:19; 5:23; cf. 1 Sam 28:6).

Asking of the Lord is also associated with a priestly or prophetic decision (e.g., Num 27:21; 1 Sam 28:6). Since it concerns Joshua's commissioning, Numbers 27:21 is relevant here as one of several places in the Pentateuch where inquiry of the Lord is found (the same Heb. word is used each time; cf. Deut 18:16). Is Joshua's commissioning the focus, or is it the manner by which Israel should discern the Lord's will? Eleazar the priest "shall inquire for him by the decision of the Urim before the Lord; *at his word* [lit., 'by his mouth'] they shall go out, and *at his word* they shall come in, both *he* and all the Israelites with *him*, the whole congregation." Whose word is operative? To whom do the pronouns refer? If "his" refers to the priest, then Joshua 9:14 simply notes that the protocol for discernment was not carried out. If "his" means Joshua, whose "mouth" is now commissioned to lead Israel, then 9:14-15 makes the point that Joshua is acting in Moses' stead: having been discerned and commissioned by the priest, his "mouth" now determines Israel's "going out and coming in." Since that expression is used most often for engaging in and returning from battle, Joshua here acts on his vocation as Moses' successor. Joshua's word now authorizes Israel's going out and coming in, or in this case, making treaties with the outsider.

Even if that is so, there is humor in the fact that a covenant meal is offered while using stale food. In other words, an inquiry was unnecessary because, based on common sense, the evidence was clear. To discern whether a people are from near or far is not a matter with which to trouble the Lord. And since the narrative offers no word of judgment, nor do any untoward consequences befall Israel because of this action, we ought to read this as the narrator's skill at intentionally prodding the reader's inquisitive mind. Still, Joshua's *treaty* (v. 15) violates the instruction of Deuteronomy 7:2 and 20:17. As the story unfolds, we discover that the consequences are quite different from what we might expect.

Discovery and Decision 9:16-21

Three days later the Israelites discover that the Gibeonites are actually *living among them* in four cities (vv. 16-17; also 9:7, 22; 10:1). Gibeon is at most a day's walk from the Israelite camp at Gilgal near the Jordan (*three days* is an indeterminate short period of time; Josh 1:11; 2:16, 22; 3:2). The expression *living among them* is used of Rahab and her family (6:25). Other texts use the same or similar expressions to describe other peoples whom Israel is not able to dispossess (13:13; 15:63; 16:10; 17:12; cf. Judg 1:27, 29-33; 3:5). Especially noteworthy is the fact that even *aliens* (*immigrants*, CEB) who *resided among them* are brought into the hearing of Torah (Josh 8:33, 35). *Living among* is not necessarily a negative evaluation.

The story line that begins with the *when* of verse 16 continues in verse 18 with a comment about not attacking these cities because of the oath *the leaders of the congregation had sworn to them* (the *treaty* of vv. 14-15). That *all the congregation murmured against the leaders* suggests that they had not been part of the negotiation and also were not pleased with the present state of affairs. The word for "murmur" occurs elsewhere in the OT only in complaints against Moses, Aaron, and the Lord (Exod 15:24; 16:7; Num 14:2, 36; 16:11, 41). There is irony in the fact that in those wilderness stories, the complaining happens after a victory, or in the case of Joshua 9, after a Torah reading ceremony in the land (Younger 1990: 378–79n10). The narrator does not explain the reason for the complaint. Perhaps the people are afraid of *their neighbors . . . living among them* (v. 16), or they wish they could have attacked the deceptive Gibeonites. In either case, *the Lord, the God of Israel* is the court of appeal (framing the complaint in vv. 18a, 19). Once the treaty has been negotiated, it is in God's hands. Only at the end of the narrative (9:26) do we find out what the complaint is really about. There we also discover the significance of Joshua's role in mediating between the making of a covenant and the people's intent to kill.

The naming of God as *the Lord, the God of Israel* occurs twice in verses 18 and 19 (fourteen times in Joshua; fifty-seven times in the DtrH, although not at all in Deuteronomy, out of a total of one hundred nineteen times in the OT; see Josh 7:13, 19, 20; 8:30; 9:18, 19;

10:40, 42; 13:14, 33; 14:14; 22:24; 24:2, 23). The repetition of the phrase emphasizes covenantal language of exclusive loyalty, as expected in the treaty-making context here. Complaint finds its proper context within the covenantal relationship with God. The newly crafted covenant with the Gibeonites, in the context of Israel's covenant with God, establishes a sphere of protection and peaceable relationship that cannot be broken.

The leaders justify their actions by referring back to the oath, with an explanation of why *we must not touch them* (v. 19). Instead, they come upon an alternative plan of action that, in their own words, is motivated so as to avoid *wrath* on account of their oath (v. 20). In Joshua the word *wrath* is used elsewhere only in the summary statement about Achan in Joshua 22:20 *[Anger of the Lord, p. 386]*. The twofold declaration *Let them live* (vv. 20-21) violates the instructions in Deuteronomy regarding nearby towns: "You must not let anything that breathes remain alive" (20:16). Instead, they treat the Gibeonites like inhabitants of distant towns who must submit to "forced labor" (20:11; see also Josh 16:10; 17:13; Judg 1:28, 30, 33, 35). Apart from Joshua 9:21, 23, 27, only in Deuteronomy 29:11 do we read about *hewers of wood and drawers of water*. There, in Moses' covenant renewal ceremony east of the Jordan, the Gibeonites are mentioned along with others, including aliens, who "enter into the covenant of the LORD your God, sworn by an oath, which the LORD your God is making with you today" (Deut 29:10-13). Moses goes on to say that this covenant is being made "not only with you who stand here with us today before the LORD our God, but also with those who are not here with us today" (29:14-15). With its emphasis on the oath and the inclusion of aliens into the covenant, this text seems to assume the inclusion of the Gibeonites, even though it does not name them (see the Midrash *Tanḥuma*, in Drucker: 231).

The combination of participants, including those "not here today" (29:15 NIV), creates an opening in the tradition that allows for the inclusion of Others into covenant relationship (as in Solomon's prayer at the dedication of the temple in 1 Kings 8:41-43). Perhaps these intertextual clues suggest that the story explains how a group of indigenous people came not only to work in and around the temple precincts but also became partners in the covenant with the Lord. This suggestion is confirmed by the notice *to this day* in verse 27. In other words, these people are no longer outsiders, but according to the covenant renewal text of Deuteronomy 29, they are full participants in the covenant with God. Not only that, but Gibeon also becomes a significant cultic site for Israelite worship.

Joshua's Negotiation/Compromise 9:22-26

Joshua now becomes the interrogator. Not only does he ask them, *Why did you deceive us?* (v. 22), but he himself announces that they will become *hewers of wood and drawers of water* (v. 23). Joshua repeats, adds to, and changes the leaders' declaration of the Gibeonites' job description. His statement seems to be pronounced as a curse, declaring them to be servant/slave (sg.) and working *for the house of my God* (v. 23). Note, however, that the Gibeonites have already declared themselves *servants* in verses 8-9. His words seem harsher than those of the leaders. Or is he deliberately modifying the job description from work *for all the congregation* (v. 21) to service for *the house of my God*? In any case, Joshua adds the ominous word *cursed* (v. 23), with its reminiscence of Genesis (3:14, 17; 4:11). But the word is also a play on the word *cunning* (*'ormah*) of Joshua 9:4 and its echo of the serpent's craftiness in Genesis 3:1 (*'arum*). This wordplay and literary allusion does not mean that the Gibeonites are serpent-like *and* cursed like the characters in Genesis 3. Rather, just as those who were tempted by cunning in Genesis 3 were spared but forced to work, these in Joshua 9 were allowed to live as servants of the Lord's house. Surely the irony is in the covenantal inclusion of foreigners as temple employees.

The Gibeonites' response to Joshua (vv. 24-25) affirms his declaration and confirms that they are aware of the story of God's actions on behalf of Israel. They use Deuteronomistic language, citing Moses, the gift of *all the land*, the verb *destroy*, the phrase *all the inhabitants of the land*, and the motif of *fear*. Fear language is not explicit in their earlier statements in verses 9-10. In the first encounter they do well not to express their fear. In v. 24, however, by adding the motif of Moses' command to *destroy all the inhabitants of the land*, fear strikes a significant chord. Their words come close to echoing Rahab's words (2:24). Both Rahab and the Gibeonites acknowledge the divine hand in recent events.

The Gibeonites' words connect the story with Deuteronomy by showing how their covenant with Israel foils readers' expectations of how the plot must unfold if it were based solely on Deuteronomic law. In particular, they place themselves at the mercy of Joshua (*in your hand*) and suggest that Joshua do *as it seems good and right in your sight* (v. 25). The Gibeonites thereby acknowledge Joshua's royal status. A partial form of that expression occurs several times at the end of the book of Judges to depict the moral chaos of an Israel without kings (Judg 17:6; 21:25). The combination of *good* and *right* occurs only twice in Deuteronomy, to describe obeying all of the words that Moses is commanding, which will lead to things going well, "because you will be doing what is good and right in the sight of the LORD your God" (12:28; see also "right and good" in Deut 6:18; cf. 12:25; 13:18; 21:9). The two words "good and right" describe two kings' actions in Chronicles (2 Chron 14:2; 31:20; cf. Jer 26:14; 40:4). Similar to the evaluation at the end of Judges, David and other kings are evaluated in the books of Kings according to whether they did "right in the sight of the LORD" (1 Kings 11:33, 38; 14:8; 15:5, 11; 22:43; 2 Kings 12:2; 14:3; 15:3, 34; 16:2; 18:3; 22:2). By using these words, the Gibeonites implicitly acknowledge Joshua's royal status as one fully qualified to do what is *good and right in your sight*, which may well also be "good and right in the sight of the LORD"; but they do not say that. Only the reader familiar with the historians' judgments on Israel's kings knows this in retrospect. Joshua is a royal figure whom the Gibeonites trust to make appropriate judgments in keeping with the Lord's ways.

The narrator concludes this unit by summarizing Joshua's action as a work of salvation (v. 26). The Israelites *did not kill them* (9:26; the Heb. word for "kill" is used elsewhere in Joshua, in 8:24; 10:11; 13:22; and in Deuteronomy only in 13:9, where Israel is instructed to "kill" those who tempt them to worship other gods). The Hebrew word used in Joshua 9:26 for *saved* is used also by Rahab (2:13) and by Phinehas of saving Israel *from the hand of the LORD* (22:31). It also describes the saving work of God in rescuing Israel (24:10; on God's saving/liberating work: Exod 3:8; 6:6; Judg 6:9; 8:34; 1 Sam 17:37; on a human being saving Israel: 1 Sam 14:48; 2 Sam 19:9). This kind of rescue, or salvation, cannot be presumed upon, as the Assyrian diplomat argues in 2 Kings 18. The Rabshakeh boasts that neither Hezekiah nor God will be able to rescue Israel (the word is used eleven times in 2 Kings 18–19, where 18:33 delivers the devastating rhetorical question). In Joshua 9, however, the narrator tells us that Joshua "rescues" the Gibeonites from Israel's rash assumption that all foreigners ought to be eliminated.

Joshua is not only a royal figure but also, in the opinion of the narrator, a savior of the outsider. In this way Joshua stands in for God's saving work. Joshua "saves" the ones whom Israel stands against (contra Beek, who views Joshua's failure to seek the Lord as an anomaly for Joshua, who is otherwise totally obedient to the Lord). It is precisely in this anomaly that Joshua is savior. As one devoted to Torah, he also violates Torah in saving the Gibeonites.

Gibeon's Servanthood 9:27

The episode ends by reiterating the main elements of the story and by adding two additional elements. First, this work is *to continue to this day*, the time of the story's much-later telling. The formula *to this day* is etiological: it answers a question (from Greek *aiteō*, "to ask"), explaining why the Gibeonites continue to be covenant partners with Israel. Second, this work is not outside the sphere of God's supervision, since it will be done *in the place that he should choose*. This final phrase of the chapter is an allusion to the instructions regarding the place of worship where the Lord's name dwells. The point is that God is the one who directs where worship takes place (in Deuteronomy twenty-two times, as in 12:5, 11, yet never again in the OT) and that place is the place of divine presence. The place is never named in Deuteronomy. Although many later Israelites considered it to be Jerusalem, it is possible that, since the ark was housed in a moveable shrine, there could be more than one place. Since Gibeonites hew wood and draw water specifically *for the altar*, it is in the Lord's presence where they work and for whom they have become *servants*. Ironically, Gibeon becomes a primary worship site for Israel, and therefore the place of God's name (1 Kings 3:4-5)! The story transforms the Gibeonites from those who declare themselves to Joshua as *your servants* (v. 9), into being God's servants in the holy precincts. God has validated the treaty with the Gibeonites, which has transformed them into God's people *[Covenant and Treaty, p. 416]*.

In that light, Joshua's "curse" is not the rhetoric of colonial subjugation, but a story of how an indigenous population group becomes incorporated into the covenant loyalty and service of God alone. What began as a trick to enter a treaty became an ironic story about inclusion of outsiders. Now not only Rahab (ch. 2) and unnamed aliens (8:30-35; cf. 20:9) but also four entire towns have become participants in the covenant community. "We must therefore reckon with the strong possibility that this is one case, not the only one, of groups later to form part of Israel which established initially peaceful relationships with much stronger and better established political entities in the early stages of penetration into Palestine" (Blenkinsopp 1972: 40). Or to put the matter more theologically, "Yahweh shows his acceptance of Gibeon's survival and . . . imputes no guilt to Israel" (Hubbard: 22). Moreover, the acceptance of the Gibeonites reflects a rather comic example of how Joshua's "when your children ask" speech of 4:21-24 might become a reality. There Israel is told that the crossing of the Jordan was God's action, analogous to that of the Red Sea crossing, the intention of which is *so that all the peoples of the earth may know that the hand of the* L*ORD* *is mighty, and so that you may fear the* L*ORD* *your God forever* (4:24). In this way the story of the Gibeonite inclusion into Israel implies that the book of Joshua "may quietly advocate them as divinely-sanctioned exceptions to the Deuteronomic mandate" to destroy the other (Hubbard: 24).

THE TEXT IN BIBLICAL CONTEXT

The Gibeonites as Israelites

That the Gibeonites, and their ancestor Gibeon, make it into the larger biblical drama in various places may seem like a divine trick. It is not incidental that the narrator of the next story describes Gibeon as *a large city, like one of the royal cities, and larger than Ai* (10:2). One might ask, How is it possible that Israel could have negotiated a treaty with a city that had a reputation like that? The result, however, is clear. Gibeon has been included in the Benjaminite city list (18:25) and in the list of Levitical cities within the tribe of Benjamin (21:17). The other cities mentioned in Joshua 9:17 include Chephirah (Josh 18:26; Ezra 2:25; Neh 7:29), Beeroth (Josh 18:25; 2 Sam 4:2-3; Ezra 2:25; Neh 7:29), and Kiriath-jearim (Josh 18:14, 28). The ark is associated with Kiriath-jearim (1 Sam 6:21; 7:1), which is depicted in the genealogy of Chronicles as a descendant of Caleb, Ephrathah, and Bethlehem (1 Chron 2:50-53). Nehemiah 7:29 mentions returned exiles from the three cities. And in Psalm 132:6, the "fields of Jaar" (related to "Jearim") is identified, along with Ephrathah, as the place where the ark was found (cf. 1 Chron 2:50-53). "Kiriath-jearim is the only Gibeonite city attributed to Judah in the lists and the only one which plays a part in the Jerusalemite narratives about the ark in 1 Samuel" (Blenkinsopp 1972: 11). This is significant since the genealogies in Chronicles do not indicate literal descendants, but identify social boundaries of diverse groups that came to be understood as Israel. This indicates either complete assimilation or annexation into Israel (see commentary on Josh 21).

Outside Joshua, Gibeon is mentioned in texts describing the reigns of Saul, David, and Solomon. Gibeon is central to the conflict between Saul and David (2 Sam 2:12-32; 3:30). Solomon offered sacrifices at the "principal high place" at Gibeon, where he encountered the Lord in a dream (1 Kings 3:4-5). Chronicles reports that the main sanctuary, where the place of the tabernacle and altar of burnt offering were located, was in Gibeon (1 Chron 16:39; 21:29). The closest resonance with Joshua 9 is a story about this time period that concerns David and the Gibeonites (2 Sam 21:1-9) in which David restores the honor of the Gibeonites after Saul has killed some of them and even "tried to wipe them out" (21:2). It seems as though Saul had thought to cleanse the land of Gibeonites since they are reported to have said that Saul "planned to destroy us, so that we should have no place in all the territory of Israel" (21:5). David is concerned to reestablish harmony (here portrayed as the ability to bless) between Gibeonites and Israelites. Blenkinsopp thinks that David might even have consulted a written form of a treaty deposited in the sanctuary at Gibeon (1972: 37). In the light of this story, we might ask why Saul appears in the Gibeon genealogy of 1 Chronicles (8:33; cf. 8:29-40).

We hear further of the Gibeonites in the reports about rebuilding the gates of Jerusalem after the return from exile (Neh 3:7). Ninety-five Gibeonites are numbered among the returnees (Neh 7:25). Their inclusion in those lists parallels the identification of Gibeon within the genealogies of 1 Chronicles. There Gibeon (1 Chron 8:29) is ancestor of the line of Kish, Saul, Jonathan and other sons of Saul (8:33). Chronicles has transformed (or clarified) Saul's origin from a geographic location, Gibeah (1 Sam 10:26; etc.), to a familial lineage related to ancestor Gibeon—a "marriage" that represents either the results of "racial symbiosis or the resettling of groups in a different locality" (Blenkinsopp 1972: 25).

This genealogical inclusivity implies that the Israelites set up their main shrine in Gibeon because the Gibeonites already had a shrine in place, including wood and water resources (cf. in Jer 41:12, "great waters" [lit.] may be the large cistern uncovered there). They knew how such a site might be operated and, therefore, naturally became managers of the physical plant. This operational management continued when Solomon built his temple in Jerusalem (Gibeonites/Hivites in Josh 9:7; 1 Kings 9:15, 20-21; cf. Solomon's "forced labor" in 1 Kings 5:13-18; 12:4; 2 Chron 2:2). By the time of Jerusalem's demise in 587 BC, the Gibeonites were thoroughly Israelitized and Yahwehized (see Blenkinsopp 1972, ch. 2 on "The Ethnic Identity of the Gibeonites").

THE TEXT IN THE LIFE OF THE CHURCH

Welcome the Outsider

The story of the Gibeonite trick tells a humorous incident on Israel, and in the process it tells how Joshua *saved* them. Both Joshua and the Gibeonites "broke the rules." Joshua violated the Deuteronomic instruction about what to do with peoples in the near vicinity of the land (inside the so-called boundaries), and the Gibeonites acted deceptively in order to avoid the fate of the people of Jericho and Ai. The narrator does not seem to criticize them. The two narratives that follow imply that God is with Joshua (and Israel) and honors the treaty with the Gibeonites. If chapter 9 is a paradigmatic story introducing the next two stories, the compromise of chapter 9 offers an alternative to the conflict with kings introduced in 9:1-2.

Along with the trajectory of biblical conversation we have considered in our reflection on Joshua 2 and 8:30-35, this story invites God's people to welcome the outsider and not worry too much about how those outsiders have entered in the first place. We find such stories in the book *Why I Am a Mennonite*, which tells not only of Mennonites who claim a genealogical heritage to the sixteenth century but also of those who have become part of the stream of the Anabaptist tradition in odd and wonderful ways (Loewen).

In some circles, for example, it matters whether one's ancestors are Swiss Mennonite or Russian Mennonite, Swedish Lutheran or Swedish Baptist. It is common, and often alienating, to hear questions like, "Is that a Mennonite name?" Such may have been the case with the Gibeonites as well, but over time those names became part of Israel, as we see in the lists later in Joshua, in genealogies of 1 Chronicles, and in the lists of workers in Nehemiah. To be "Israelite" comes, over time, to incorporate families from all kinds of ethnic backgrounds, even as is currently the case with Jews (e.g., the Ethiopian Jews) and Christians since the time of the earliest churches, as reported in the book of Acts.

The Gibeonite episode does not indicate that there are stipulations for entering the relationship treaty with Israel and with God. The motivations that they offer focus on only two things: their having heard the story of God's reputation (9:9) and their fear of extermination (9:24). In the history of the church, some have entered the kingdom for similar reasons. Some converted because of the fear of the judgment of hell, as it was proclaimed at the time by the church. For others, drawn in through mission activity, the church offered both tasks and privileges analogous to those of the Gibeonites, yet later generations in those families stay in the church for very different reasons.

Origen's figural reading of the Gibeonite story begins this way: "In my father's house are many mansions" (John 14:2). Although the Gibeonites are *saved*, they continue in their old ways and therefore do "not escape a note of infamy" (110). Origen does not view the Gibeonites' role as servants positively. One might as easily, however, have drawn an analogy between the Gibeonites' servitude and Jesus' instructions on being last of all and servant of all (Mark 9:35; 10:43-45) or his call to downward mobility in Mark 8–10. As in the story of the Gibeonites, there will always be those who grumble when leaders or the community do not tightly preserve the boundaries. But in the end, the narrator interprets Joshua's acceptance as an act of salvation *[Figural Reading, p. 426]*.

Although we might interpret this story as a paradigm of inclusiveness, or figurally as an analogy of less-than-ideal entry into the community of faith, it is also possible to read the text from a postcolonial point of view. Many indigenous peoples were subjected to forced labor in much the same way that Joshua and the Israelites subjected the Gibeonites and others. Even though such practices have been common throughout the world since ancient times, slavery and forced labor were particularly devastating during the colonial era in the West. Perhaps we all need to hear a word about the significance of making and keeping covenants, as Joshua and David did with the Gibeonites. Although such relationships with so-called outsiders are not often valued from a human point of view, solidarity with those who have become partners in the Lord's project is a kind of "salvation."

Joshua 10:1-43

Retaliation by the Kings of the South

PREVIEW

Well-written stories will often introduce surprises in their plot development. In Flannery O'Connor's powerful story "A Good Man Is Hard to Find," whimsical and humorous interchanges switch dramatically to violent and deadly accounts. In a similar fashion, this story of the defeat of King Adoni-zedek, his coalition, and other kings and cities of the south comes as a shock after the somewhat humorous story about an altogether unexpected peace treaty with the crafty Gibeonites, whom Joshua *saved from the Israelites* (9:26). The Gibeonite story stands over against the two stories that follow, all three being responses to the "hearing" of kings in the region who learned that Joshua had defeated Ai (9:1-2; 10:1; 11:1). The series of three narratives concludes with the notice that *the land had rest from war* (11:23; cf. *rest* in 1:13).

Before arriving there, however, chapter 10 returns to the *ḥerem* (10:1, 28, 35, 37, 39, 40) and to the brutal killing of enemy kings [*Ḥerem, p. 433*]. Even so, oddly juxtaposed with its gruesome violence, the chapter presents the consequences of covenant with the Gibeonites and the evaluation that these stories are about God's exploits, since *the LORD fought for Israel* (10:14, 42).

The text begins with the fearful and aggressive stance by King Adoni-zedek of Jerusalem, along with his allies, against the encroaching Israelites (10:1-2). The unit includes the narrator's two climactic summary comments about the Lord's fighting for Israel, followed by a return to the camp in Gilgal (10:14-15, 42-43). The first two verses connect the following stories back to the stories of chapters 8–9. The remainder of the narrative falls into four episodes. The narrative closes with a highly theological and stereotypical summary of the conflicts in the south (10:40-43).

The overall battle report proper is a series of three scenes, an initial battle in which God is the main actor, followed by two flashbacks: verses 16-27 take the reader back to verses 10b-11, and verses 28-39 to some time before verse 27.

OUTLINE

Transition: Adoni-zedek's Response to the Treaty with Gibeon, 10:1-2
Adoni-zedek's Coalition Attack and Gibeon's Response, 10:3-6
Joshua's Response and Defeat of the Coalition, 10:7-15
The Execution of and Memorial to the Southern Kings, 10:16-27
Summary of Various Victories in the South, 10:28-39
Theological Summary, 10:40-43

EXPLANATORY NOTES

Transition: Adoni-zedek's Response to the Treaty with Gibeon 10:1-2

The narrative introduction begins with a note about Adoni-zedek's hearing of the previously narrated stories (cf. *heard* in 9:1-2, 3; 11:1). Fear is the natural response to hearing such news (cf. 9:24). Adoni-zedek's awareness of the *peace* between Gibeon and Israel is not unusual. The Amarna letters provide examples of treaties with city-states in the region during Egyptian dominance. The narrator introduces this story by telling not only of Adoni-zedek's fear but also of the outcome of the previous story. The Gibeonites' ruse has resulted in peace between the two groups (cf. 9:15). Thus, when the narrative actually quotes Adoni-zedek (v. 4), we can assume that the narrator is strengthening his own evaluation from verse 1 by having Adoni-zedek actually say that the Gibeonites have *made peace with Joshua and with the Israelites*. With its twofold repetition of the word "make peace" (*šlm*, verb form) in verses 1 and 4, the narrative highlights the treaty between the two parties. The related noun appears in the Deuteronomic instructions about engaging towns "very far from you" (Deut 20:15): they shall "offer it terms of peace" (Heb. *šalom*, 20:10, 11). Thus the mention of making *peace* in Joshua 10:1, 4 makes clear that Joshua has violated the instruction of Deuteronomy 20, but also that this situation, although an anomaly, has resulted in a relationship of mutuality, as the story will demonstrate.

The narrator states at the outset that the hearer and initiator of the events to follow is Adoni-zedek, king of Jerusalem. His name (My lord is righteous) reminds us of Melchizedek (My king is righteous), who is called "king of Salem" (Gen 14:18). These are the only two names in the Bible that end with *zedek* (*ṣedeq*, righteousness), and both are non-Israelites (cf. Zedekiah). Moreover, this is the first time that Jerusalem is mentioned by name in the Bible. Interestingly, *the place that the Lord will choose* occurs only in Joshua 9:27, but twenty-one times in Deuteronomy. It is significant, therefore, that Jerusalem is mentioned here, especially since this king was captured and killed (10:23-27; cf. 12:10) even though Jerusalem is not mentioned in the list of cities conquered by Joshua later in chapter 10. Jerusalem does not actually become part of Israel until David conquers the city several centuries later (2 Sam 5). Thus the note at the end of Joshua 10:1 carries two connotations. First, making peace resonates with the name of Jerusalem, which also includes the same Hebrew root (*šlm*). Second, that the Gibeonites *were among them* not only reiterates what was said about the Gibeonites earlier (9:7, 16, 22) but also about Rahab (6:25) and aliens (8:35). The danger *among* Israel for Israel are devoted things (7:13) and foreign gods (24:23). Although the Gibeonites do not pose a threat to Israel, the treaty of *peace* seems to have posed a threat to Adoni-zedek. Perhaps the narrator wants to show, by juxtaposing *the place that he [the Lord] should choose* (9:27) with Jerusalem (10:1), that Jerusalem would be preserved for David and for the purposes of God in establishing that city.

In the previous story, the Gibeonites are the ones who are perceived to take initiative to make peace. And they, unlike Adoni-zedek, find a creative way of transcending their fear. This is ironic because the narrator makes special note here of Gibeon as *one of the royal cities*. This, together with the list of kings in chapter 12, suggests a city-state system within which alliances were common. The narrator mentions that the city of Gibeon is *larger than Ai, and all its men were warriors* (10:2), which highlights two things: the oddity that these *warriors* should have made peace with Israel, and the threat that this new coalition poses for Adoni-zedek and others (cf. 2:11; 5:1; 7:5; 9:24).

Adoni-zedek's Coalition Attack and Gibeon's Response 10:3-6

The sending of two messages frames this episode. In the first, Adoni-zedek invites his coalition to join him in battle against the Gibeonites, who had *made peace with Joshua and the Israelites* (vv. 3-4; cf. v. 1b). In the second, using a different and even more common word for "save/rescue" from the one used in 9:26, the Gibeonites ask Joshua to *save* them. The Gibeonites, who again call themselves *your servants* (v. 6; cf. 9:9), come with a fourfold request: *do not abandon* (lit., *do not let your hands drop*), *come up to us quickly, save us* (verb *yaša'*, which is the root of Joshua's name), *help us* (a word *'azar*, often used to describe God's help). As Adoni-zedek invites his coalition partners to *come up* in verse 4, the Gibeonites ask Joshua to *come up* (Gilgal is ca. eight hundred feet below sea level, whereas Gibeon is ca. two thousand four hundred feet above sea level). Found only twice in Exodus (2:17; 14:30) and once in Numbers (10:9), the verb "to save" occurs five times in Deuteronomy (20:4; 22:27; 28:29, 31; 33:29) and often in Judges, Samuel, and Kings—telling of God's saving acts or of the work of those who save or rescue others. Ahaz invites his treaty overlord, Tiglath-Pileser, using the same verbs, "Come up, and rescue me" (2 Kings 16:7). "Saving" is one of the responsibilities of those in covenant relationship. The Gibeonites expect their treaty partner to save them from the threat of the enemy *[Covenant and Treaty, p. 416].*

They perceive that *all the kings of the Amorites* have come against them (v. 6b) even though only five are mentioned: two of the cities are Philistine, located in the coastal plain (Eglon and Lachish), one is on the western edge of the hill country (Jarmuth), one is in the central Judean hill country (Jerusalem), and one in the south (Hebron). Whereas *all the kings* is an exaggeration, such use of the word *all* is part of the rhetoric of ancient conquest accounts *[Conquest Accounts, p. 406]. Amorites* is a generic word for Canaanites (contrast its use in 9:1). These kings represent a coalition among whom a previous treaty has now been broken by the Gibeonites, or a coalition united by their common bond to Egypt as a sworn overlord (Amarna letters).

Joshua's Response and Defeat of the Coalition 10:7-15

This episode appears to fall into two parts. Verses 12-14 are "a type of flashback" to what seems to belong between verses 9 and 10. In this way "the biblical writer relates the principal incident which is connected to the battle (namely, the hailstones) first, before he then proceeds to the special point to be cited from the book of Yashar" (Younger 1990: 211).

The episode opens and closes with a mention of both Joshua and Gilgal (vv. 7, 15). The opening presents those accompanying Joshua (*with him*) in strong military language as *all the fighting force* and *all the mighty warriors*. The unit closes by noting that *all Israel* is *with him* [*"All Israel," p. 385*]. The narrator emphasizes that this victory is not merely a military victory, but an event in which *all Israel* has experienced the victory of God even though the grand military troops detailed in verse 7 have no role in the story.

Indeed, God appears first by taking initiative in the story proper. The Lord's speech (v. 8) begins with language typical of conquest accounts. Joshua 10:8 parallels the ancient Zakkur text (ca. 805–775 BC) in which the god consoles Zakkur with similar language: "Do not be afraid. . . . I will deliver you" (cited in Younger 1990: 229). The *Do not be afraid* exhortation occurs also in 11:6 (and in 8:1 with a fuller expression: *Do not fear or be dismayed*; cf. Deut 1:21; 31:8). In contrast to Adoni-zedek and others who fear (Josh 9:24; 10:2; cf. Deut 2:4), Joshua is not to be afraid (Josh 10:8, 25; 11:6; cf. Deut 1:29; 3:2, 22; 7:18, 19, 21; 20:1, 3, 8; 28:10; 31:6, 8). The only one to be "feared" is Yahweh (Josh 4:24; 22:25; 24:14; cf. Deut 4:10; 5:29; 6:2, 13, 24; 8:6; 10:12, 20; 13:4; 14:23; 17:19; 25:18; 28:58; 31:12, 13) and his servants Moses and Joshua. Neo-Assyrian war oracles, like the one concerning Esarhaddon (680–669 BC), with their exhortations to courage and "fear not" (Conrad; *ANET* 449–50), corroborate the language of Joshua. The expression there derives from the seventh century BC, when it likely became part of the conquest account repertoire (Younger 1990; Rowlett 1996: 116).

The motive clause that follows the command not to fear is grounded in the promise *I have handed them over to you* (v. 8; cf. 6:2; 8:1; 11:6, 8; 24:8, 11; cf. Deut 3:2; 23:14). God speaks in typical Deuteronomistic language, concluding with a notice that *not one* of their coalition *shall stand before you* (also Josh 1:5; in OT elsewhere only in Deut 7:24; 11:25).

After God's motivational speech, the narrator describes Joshua's action (v. 9), carefully noting details of the attack after an all-night march up from Gilgal. There is no clear battle account. Although Israel *inflicted a great slaughter* and *chased them* and *struck them down* (v. 10b), the Lord is the main actor, the one who *threw them into a panic before Israel* (v. 10a) and who *threw down huge stones from heaven* (v. 11). Making sure readers understand the import of the day's events, the narrator notes that *there were more who died because of the hail than the Israelites killed with the sword* (v. 11b). God does not do all the fighting. Although Israel participates, Israel is not the victor. God's intervention defines the victory. The *panic* that results occurs typically when the Lord acts (v. 10; cf. Exod 14:24; 23:27; Judg 4:15; 1 Sam 7:10).

Joshua does not need to ask for directions (cf. 9:14), since he is covenant partner with Gibeon. Yet the Lord's initiative (v. 8) challenges Joshua's straightforward assumption. It is God's, not Joshua's, prerogative to protect Gibeon. God honors Joshua's treaty with the Gibeonites and utters not a word about it. And God acts to defeat the coalition forces so that what Joshua and his mighty troops (v. 7) have to do is only a small part of what God does (v. 11b).

Interpreters have debated whether the language of divine assistance here is literal or figurative. The motif of *stones from heaven* or *hailstones* (v. 11) is found in several ancient conquest accounts *[Conquest Accounts, p. 406]*. The Hittite storm god "hurled his meteor" (Younger 1990: 208). And the Assyrian king Sargon (721–705 BC) was aided by "the stone from heaven" (210). The motif of help from the sky and weather can be found in other biblical texts (e.g., Exod 9:13-35; Judg 5:19-21; Isa 30:30; Hab 3:10-11). These generic descriptions of help from the sky may well be rooted in historical memory and given a literary expression by using stereotypical language of divine assistance (208–11). The help provided by God is the narrator's real concern here. *The LORD fought for Israel* (v. 14b). That assertion, although not unique to the biblical worldview, has become a basic theological building block in ancient Israelite historiography and in Israel's theological conversation about the character of its God *[Theology of Warfare, p. 458]*.

If verse 15 belongs to the narrative framework that corresponds to verse 7, then this second subunit begins and ends in a flashback by mentioning the *day* on which the Lord *gave* the enemy over to Israel (v. 12) and the *day* unlike any other on which *the LORD heeded a human voice* (v. 14). This emphasis in verse 14 is more significant than explaining the technicalities of the sun and the moon in verses 12-13. Thus the motif of the Lord's heeding, or listening to, also contributes to the framing of the subunit, for verse 12 has Joshua speaking to God and verse 14 has God heeding Joshua. This framing emphasizes the interaction between Joshua and God, not Joshua and the sun/moon. The importance of this motif in verse 14, therefore, corresponds to the anomaly of the idiom in this place, since virtually everywhere in Deuteronomy where listening or obeying the voice occurs, it has to do with Israel's obeying God (Deut 8:20; 13:18;

15:5; 26:14; 27:10; 28:1, 2, 15, 45, 62; 30:8, 10; cf. Josh 5:6; 1 Sam 12:15; 15:19, 20, 22; 28:18; 1 Kings 20:36; 2 Kings 18:12). Since the Hebrew word for "listen" most often means "obey" in similar contexts (esp. when followed by the word "voice"), it is odd here that the Lord should "obey" Joshua. The expression *the LORD listened to the voice* (lit.; found only here in v. 14, in Num 21:3, and in 1 Kings 17:22) suggests that the narrator in Joshua 10 wants to highlight the unique relationship between Joshua and God, setting up Joshua as model leader. But more, it depicts God as one who is responsive. That God should "obey" Joshua is the heart of this chapter, for the Lord's obedience is confirmed twice in the repetition of the causal clause *for [because] the LORD fought for Israel* (vv. 14, 42).

That the Lord should respond again to Joshua's initiative is so remarkable that the narrator chooses to draw on an ancient poetic fragment from a source named *the Book of Jashar* (v. 13b; meaning "Book of the Upright"). This "book" makes one other appearance in the OT (2 Sam 1:18). There it includes David's poetic lament over Saul and Jonathan, which suggests that it may be an ancient collection of poetry as old as the reign of David. This poetic fragment about the sun and the moon (vv. 12b-13a) has driven interpreters to distraction. However, the quotation is not the most important part of this text. It functions here as an alternate account that speaks hyperbolically about the event, as Exodus 15 and Judges 5 serve to offer a "second look" at their respective "battle scenes." The use of poetry implies that a straightforward prose telling does not say enough. Poetry and narrative are dance partners that negotiate the complexity of explaining or understanding the event.

Before considering interpretive options for this poetic fragment, we do well to pay attention to the syntax and translation. Verse 12b includes only one verb (an imperative), found most often in poetry, which means to be silent, to wait, or to be still. Verse 13 reports that sun and moon were obedient to the command. That verb is repeated in verse 13 along with an additional verb reporting that the moon *stood* (AT; NRSV *stopped*). Whatever the sun and moon actually did, the final poetic line describes the effect of their obedience. The Hebrew text reads, literally, *until he avenged / nation / his enemies.* The traditional translation, *until the nation took vengeance on their enemies* (NRSV), is possible but not the best rendering. The narrative makes it clear that *the LORD* is the main actor in the episode (vv. 10-11, 14). The verb *naqam*, often translated "take vengeance," in many cases conveys a divine intervention on behalf of God's people (cf. Isa 35:4). The verb is rarely used with human beings as the subject. In keeping with the theological tradition reflected in Deuteronomy 32:35 and 43, this text depicts God as agent, even though the subject is not explicitly named. That reading, however, requires us to understand the Hebrew word *goy* (RSV: *nation*) as "force" or "army" (as it can be translated in texts like Deut 28:49-50; Jer 5:15; 50:3; Joel 1:6; Amos 6:14). That understanding leads to this translation: *until he [the Lord] defeated his enemies' force* (Boling 1982: 284–85). This is also the sense of the LXX, which has *until God repelled their enemies* (AT).

The complexity of the text's poetic imagery has been explained in at least four ways. First, a naturalistic explanation suggests that the poem depicts an eclipse dated perhaps to September 30, 1131 BC (Sawyer). According to another popular naturalistic explanation, the event depicts the summer solstice, the longest day of the year when the sun appears to stop, if only briefly. Second, the poem may offer a figurative description of a military strategy in which the enemy is unable to see because it must look into the sun. Third, the citation reflects an astrological sign in which the positioning of the sun and the moon is a bad omen for the enemy or a good omen for Israel (Holladay). Fourth, the poem reflects the mythological notion that the sun and moon are deities who participate in human affairs. None of these explanations do justice either to the significance of the interplay between narrative and poetic descriptions, which I have mentioned above, nor to the genre of warfare accounts from the ancient Near East (Younger 1990; Rowlett 1996; Van Seters 1990; Weinfeld 1986).

According to that research, ancient conquest accounts include many of the same thematic and stereotypical elements as Joshua 10. The Comprehensive Annals of the Hittite king Muršili (ca. 1321–1295 BC) reads: "And the gods stood by me: the proud storm-god, my lord, the sun-goddess of Arinna, my lady, the storm-god of Hatti, . . . the storm-god of the army, Ištar of the field, and Yarriš. And I destroyed the enemy" (cited in Younger 1990: 207). That text illustrates the analogy of divine participation in warfare, as does Joshua 10 with its double mention of God's fighting for Israel.

The hailstones and the sun/moon also have ancient parallels. The Ten Year Annals of Muršili state: "So I marched, and . . . the mighty storm-god . . . showed his godly miracle. He hurled a meteor" (cited in Younger 1990: 208). Weinfeld understands this as a thunderbolt (1986: 139n34). The text goes on to describe the effect of the divine intervention and the ongoing battle: "And I, my sun, fought with him. The sun-goddess of Arinna, my lady; the mighty storm-god, my lord. . . . And I conquered Piyama-KAL, . . . together with his troops and charioteers. And I defeated him. Then I pursued him. . . . The whole country of Arzawa fled. . . . And I did (all) this in one year" (cited in Younger 1990: 208–9). As Younger notes, in such stereotypical writing "the national deity could fight on behalf of his people and this might involve the employment of natural phenomenon [*sic*]" (210).

In another ancient Near Eastern text, the Assyrian king Sargon (721–705 BC) describes a battle scene in which he defeats Mettati and a coalition of kings, the "wicked enemy, together with its allies." Part of the description states, "The rest of the people, who had fled to save their lives, whom he had abandoned that the glorious might of Aššur, my lord, might be magnified, Adad, the violent, the son of Anu, the valiant, uttered his loud cry against them; and with the flood cloud and hailstones [lit., 'the stone of heaven' . . .] he totally annihilated the remainder." The text continues by describing the flight of one of the princes, who "hid in the recesses of his mountain." Of the conquest we read, "I established the glorious might of Aššur, my lord, for all time to come upon Urartu. I left behind a terror never to be forgotten in the future" (210). Both this story and the story in Joshua 10 include a battle on the hills, a divine intervention, hiding in a cave, and a summary of completeness and thoroughness of the conquest (Josh 10:14, 40-42).

Such similarities may also account for the apparent "long day" that is surmised by the narrator in the prose of verse 13b. The poem itself does not draw the long day conclusion from the "standing" of the sun/moon. It is the narrator who goes on to interpret the poem's *until* (v. 13a) by suggesting that the sun *did not hurry to set for about a whole day*. The prose interpretation follows neatly from the poetry but is clearly an extension of its meaning. Some even suggest it is a misreading of the poem. Again, the solution to the enigma is to compare this motif with ancient conquest accounts.

Particularly relevant is the option that the sun and the moon might be good or bad omens. Several ancient astrological texts refer to the phenomenon of the sun and moon appearing together on the fourteenth day as a favorable omen: "the land will be satisfied; the gods intend Akkad for happiness. Joy in the heart of the people." On another day such an appearance might be a bad omen: "the enemy will seize the land" (cited in Younger 1990: 213). The Jashar poem may imply a request for a favorable omen like that. The Assyrian texts do not indicate that the omen has significance for the day on which it appears, but for the future, which is not the case in Joshua (P. D. Miller

1973: 126). And since the prose of verse 13b is consistent with the poetry of verse 13a, the motif requires a different interpretation. Younger suggests that the omen could be construed as a polemic. "If the Canaanites viewed the appearance of the sun and moon together on the fourteenth day in their 'stations' as a favorable sign, then it would truly be ironic that Yahweh fighting for Israel answered Joshua's request" (1990: 219). Weinfeld refers to the similarity of this text to the *Iliad*, where Agamemnon states: "Zeus, most glorious, most great, the one of the dark clouds, that dwellest in the heaven, grant that the sun set not, neither darkness come upon us, until I have cast down in headlong ruin the hall of Priam, . . . burned with consuming fire" (2:412–15; cited in Younger 1990: 215).

It was also common in ancient Near Eastern campaign reports to ascribe the battles to a single day. Such is the case in the Annals of Tiglath-Pileser I (ca. 1115–1077 BC; 5.44–53; cited in Younger 1990: 215–16): "I plundered from the edge of the land of Suhu to Carchemish of Hatti-land in a single day. I massacred them. I carried back their booty, possessions, and goods without number." Younger also cites an inscription of Puzur-Inšušinak (ca. 2120–1990 BC), king of Elam with its capital at Susa, who is said to have conquered seventy towns: "In one day, he subdued [these towns] to his feet." Similarly, the Egyptian Pharaoh Seti I (thirteenth century BC) protects his holding of Beth-shean against the army of Hammath: "In the space of a single day, they had fallen to the power of his majesty!" (216). Again, from the Gebal Barkal Stela of Thutmose III (fifteenth century BC): "There were two hour-watchers; then a star came from the south of them. The like had never happened. It beamed towards them from its position. Not one remained standing there" (217). Some kind of unique celestial phenomenon helps the Egyptians against the enemy (cf. Josh 10:14).

In the light of those ancient Near Eastern analogues, we do well to illustrate how other biblical texts draw on the celestial bodies to refer to the Lord's victory on Israel's behalf. Habakkuk's poem bears a striking resemblance to the poem from the Book of Jashar. We find images of lightning (Hab 3:4), earthquake (3:6), and responses of the rivers and seas (cosmic powers of darkness, 3:8-9). The closest parallels to Joshua 10 are Habakkuk 3:10-13, where we read that the sun "raised high its hands" and the moon "stood still" as God "came forth to save your people." Similarly, Judges 5 depicts the stars fighting from heaven against Sisera (5:20).

Younger concludes: "According to Israel's understanding[,] cosmic elements were involved in her wars as 'Yahweh fought for

Israel'—just as the star was involved in warfare of the Egyptians in the Gebal Barkal Stela" (219). With Younger, we may draw five conclusions. First, both biblical and other ancient conquest accounts include divine intervention by means of celestial phenomena. Second, the configuration of the sun and moon in the sky at the same time could be an omen favorable to Israel (even an ironical polemic). Third, hyperbolic language may depict the battle as having taken place in one day. Fourth, the text includes a common literary motif by which the god is asked to preserve the daylight. And fifth, all texts testify that divine intervention comes as a miracle or a sign. The texts bear witness to an experience that cannot be easily explained except this way (Younger 1990: 219–20). This is one of the clearest examples within Joshua of how the biblical narrator was able to construct historical meaning out of the resources at hand. In other words, he gave significance to the event through his interpretation, which required using the available signifiers in that culture. In the ancient world, that is how people wrote about divine intervention. Israel too uses the same linguistic tools and literary conventions. The narrator cannot invent a new language. But he does make clear what happened: *The Lord fought for Israel* (vv. 14, 42).

The Execution of and Memorial to the Southern Kings 10:16-27

After the battle scene, the narrator returns to *these five kings* (see vv. 3, 5). The episode is marked by an introduction to the scenario (vv. 16-19) followed by three smaller sections, each opening with the same Hebrew narrative introduction (vv. 20-23, 24-26, 27). Although the Lord steals the thunder in the previous episode, here Joshua and the Israelites dominate the episode. The narrator takes backward glances, however, as Joshua repeats in verses 19 and 25 what God had spoken earlier in verse 8. Although Joshua is the initiator in the episode, and Israel's warriors are the military agency, God is the key player, without whom nothing would have occurred.

Verses 16-19 set up the scenario either as another flashback (since vv. 14-15 appear to close off the narrative), or as a subsequent event to the one in verses 7-15. A flashback is more likely because there is no long march required from the *camp at Gilgal* (v. 15), and because verse 21 refers to another *camp at Makkedah*, nearer the field of battle (Makkedah is the end point of the pursuit reported in the previous episode in v. 10).

Upon hearing the news about the kings (v. 16), Joshua gives instructions to turn their hiding place into a temporary cell. While some guard the prisoners, others carry on by giving chase to the enemy. The pursuit motif (v. 19) reiterates the flight and chase scene of verses 10b-11, where Israel *inflicted a great slaughter on them*, and *the LORD threw down huge stones from heaven on them*. Repetition is characteristic of Hebrew narrative. The two scenes (vv. 7-15 and 16-27) are likely to be understood as running parallel rather than sequentially. The present sequence separates out the essential first—the Lord's victory—and then focuses on the appropriation of the divine assurance of verse 8 by focusing only on the fate of the five kings. This scenario is concrete evidence (with the kings captured) that *the LORD your God has given them into your hand* (v. 19b). The motif is common in Deuteronomy and the DtrH (Deut 7:24; cf. 20:13; Josh 6:2; 8:1, 7, 18; Judg 3:28; 4:7, 14; 7:7, 9, 15; 20:28; 1 Sam 23:4; 24:4; 26:8; 2 Sam 5:19; 1 Kings 20:13, 28).

Joshua 10:20-23 summarizes the implications of giving the enemy *into your hand*. The sense of verse 20 is not captured well by the NRSV's *a very great slaughter . . . wiped out*. The hyperbole is better rendered by this dynamic translation: *the Israelites' massive military strike finished them off, except for a few survivors who made it into the fortified cities* (AT). Verse 21 emphasizes *all the people*, a characteristic of the books of Joshua and Deuteronomy (5:5; 6:5; 8:5, 16; 24:2, 27; cf. 4:1) *["All Israel," p. 385]*. The words *returned safe* reflects the Hebrew expression "in peace," which is an idiomatic expression for the state of affairs after battle. There may be peace or safety, but it is fragile. The last part of verse 21 suggests in no uncertain terms that this victory silences potential detractors. The expression literally reads, *No one sharpened his tongue*. Dissent, either within or without, has been squashed. The narrator asserts that the Israelites have been acknowledged as undisputed victors. This fact is confirmed by Joshua's command that the kings be brought to him. The people obey. The cave is opened, and the five kings (now identified as in v. 3) are brought out.

Verses 24-26 bring us to the climax of the episode. Joshua gives an instruction to do a symbolic act of putting feet on the necks of the captors. This image is found everywhere in ancient Egyptian artistic representations of victory after battle (cf. Ps 110:1; 1 Cor 15:25-28). In the Annals of Tukulti-Ninurta I (ca. 1244–1207 BC): "I captured Kaštiliaš. . . . I trod with my feet upon his lordly neck as though it were a footstool" (cited in Younger 1990: 317n86). Joshua reiterates the Lord's words of assurance (v. 25a) and interprets the symbolic action as a victory of the Lord (v. 25b). Those words of assurance echo the Lord's words to Joshua in the first chapter (1:6, 7, 9, 18) and Moses' words of assurance to Joshua (Deut 31:6-7; cf. David's similar words to Solomon in 1 Kings 2:2). The words *strong and courageous* appear exactly as here in both Moses' speech to Joshua and the Lord's commissioning of Joshua in Deuteronomy (31:6-7, 23; see also 1 Kings 2:2; 1 Chron 22:13; 28:20; 2 Chron 32:7). The expression *Do not be afraid or dismayed* appears together with the affirmation to *be strong and courageous* in Moses' final speech to the Israelites and to Joshua (Deut 31:5-8, 23; see TBC below). Joshua's story exemplifies the truth that it is "the LORD your God, who goes before you" (Deut 1:30; cf. 20:1-4; 31:23; Josh 1:9).

After his highly allusive Deuteronomic speech, Joshua announces that what he is about to do, the Lord will do the same *to all the enemies against whom you fight* (v. 25b). The odd juxtaposition of that affirmation with the brutal killing and public humiliation depicted in verse 26 is both shocking and terrifying. The scene is a most brutal demonstration of ethnic violence: no war crimes trial, no prison term, only execution. A defensive strike by the southern coalition against a coalition member (Gibeon), who had likely violated a previous treaty, has turned into a military debacle.

The episode draws to a close, ironically, with Joshua's command, *at sunset*, to bury the kings in their own hiding place (v. 27). The cave is marked by *large stones*, which remain *to this very day*. As in previous stories, a physical memorial has been transformed into a narrative (4:9; 7:26; 8:28, 29; cf. 5:9; 9:27). The site's location has been forgotten, but the memory and the tragedy linger.

Younger's analysis of ancient conquest accounts confirms the generic conventions adopted by the narrator. He cites numerous reports in which kings who, after their defeat in battle, flee to the hills or hide in caves (1990: 221–22). Assyrian and Egyptian annals describe in detail the pursuit and killing of fleeing enemies, the hanging of kings' corpses on poles (cf. Josh 8:29), and heaps for memorials (223–25).

Summary of Various Victories in the South 10:28-39

This episode is a long flashback report and fits into the chronological sequence that ends before the sunset of verse 27. This makes the overall battle report proper into a series of three episodes, a main episode (vv. 7-15) followed by two flashbacks: verses 16-27 take the reader back to verses 10b-11, and verses 28-39 to some time before v. 27 (Winther-Nielsen: 247). The episode itself falls into seven subepisodes (vv. 28, 29-30, 31-32, 33, 34-35, 36-37, 38-39). Each draws on the figurative, hyperbolic, or stereotypical language characteristic of ancient Near Eastern conquest accounts that describe complete destruction and no survivors. For example, the Gebal Barkal Stela of Thutmose III states, "The great army of Mitanni, it is overthrown in the twinkling of an eye. It has perished completely, as though they had never existed." In the Stela of Merneptah, "Yanoam made non-existent; Israel is wasted, his seed is not." In the Mesha Inscription, "Israel has utterly perished forever. . . . I killed all the inhabitants of the town. . . . I killed everyone in it, seven thousand men and women, both natives and aliens, and female slaves." And Sennacherib writes: "The soldiers of Hirimme, dangerous enemies, I cut down with the sword; and not one escaped" (cited in Younger 1990: 226–28) *[Mesha Inscription, p. 447]*.

With a range of stereotypical and hyperbolic expressions, the narrator of Joshua summarizes the capture and decimation of each area. Every episode uses the word *struck* (fourteen times in ch. 10). Six (except Gezer) have *edge of the sword and as he had done to X*. Five (except Lachish and Eglon) have *left no one remaining*. And four (except Libnah, Lachish, and Gezer) use the word *ḥerem*. Two, Lachish and Eglon, mention *laid siege, . . . and assaulted it* *[Conquest Accounts, p. 406]*.

Verse 28 returns to mention Makkedah (as in vv. 10, 21), which is not one of the five cities. For the first time since the beginning of this text unit, the narrator mentions that Joshua *utterly destroyed* (*ḥerem*) all the inhabitants *as he had done to the king of Jericho* (the same language as in 10:1). The hyperbole emphasizes the thoroughness of the military strike: *he left no one remaining*.

Verses 29-30 report the battle for Libnah (not one of the five cities), this time emphasizing *all Israel*'s participation. Along with the stereotypical motifs from verse 28, verse 30 adds a Deuteronomic phrase: giving *into the hand*. The report on the battle for Lachish (vv. 31-32) adds *on the second day*, which signals that the sequence of summary victories in verses 28-39 is not to be understood as all taking place before the nightfall noted in verse 27. Although the first two subepisodes (vv. 28, 29-30) begin there, the summary sequence reports a longer succession of military engagements. Verse 33 mentions Gezer with *no survivors*. Oddly, Joshua 16:10 reports, *They did not, however, drive out the Canaanites who lived in Gezer* (cf. Judg 1:29). This is not so much a historical discrepancy as a proof that chapter 10 uses hyperbole to make a point. Verses 34-35 report on the battle at Eglon with a few additional variations. Verses 36-37 tell of the battle at

Hebron, adding notices that Hebron *and its towns* were taken. Two stereotypical hyperbolic elements are included: all were *utterly destroyed* (*ḥerem*), with a twofold mention of *every person in it*. Hebron is located ambiguously in Israel. It is described as part of Judah (14:13-15). After his victory against Hebron, the city is given to Caleb (14:6-15; 15:13), and then later to the sons of Aaron (21:11, 13). It is also a city of refuge (20:7). Hebron becomes significant as the first seat of David's monarchy (2 Sam 2–5). Verses 38-39 report on the battle at Debir, with similar stereotypical language as for Hebron. The hyperbole here stands out by comparison with other biblical texts that ascribe the conquest of Hebron and Debir to Caleb and Othniel (Josh 15:14-17) and to the tribe of Judah (Judg 1:10; cf. 1:20).

Only three of the five coalition cities are mentioned in this summary report: Lachish, Eglon, and Hebron. Two coalition partners, Jerusalem and Jarmuth, are not mentioned in the summary report. None of these cities have destruction layers that can be dated confidently to the Late Bronze Age *[Archaeology and Joshua, p. 389]*.

Theological Summary 10:40-43

The final episode summarizes by reporting more than the previous episodes describe. In stereotypical hyperbole, Joshua defeats *the whole land*. That expression is important not only because it corresponds to similar hyperbolic statements in ancient Near Eastern conquest accounts, but also because it appears first in the OT in God's promise to Abraham (Gen 13:15) and is repeated with this meaning only in the DtrH (Deut 19:8; 34:1; Josh 2:3, 24; 9:24; with 2:3 and 9:24 spoken by "foreigners"; 11:16, 23; 21:43; cf. Deut 11:25; Josh 3:11, 13).

According to verse 40, every geographic region is covered. Not only that, but in typical ancient hyperbolic style, *all their kings* are taken with *no one remaining*, and Joshua devotes to destruction *all that breathed* (cf. Deut 20:16; Josh 11:11, 14; 1 Kings 15:29). All this is *as the Lord God of Israel commanded* through Moses (presumably Deut 20:16). The geographic range continues all the way south to Gaza and Goshen, which may well be the border region of Egypt. Thus the entire land south of the midpoint (Gibeon) has been captured. Hyperbole here can be confirmed by comparing later chapters in Joshua where similar descriptions occur (Josh 11:11-15; 18:1; 21:43-45; 23:14), and yet, oddly, where *very much of the land still remains to be possessed* (13:1), and the indigenous population continue living among Israel *to this day* (13:13; 15:63; 16:10; 17:13). Such statements limiting the extent of the conquest reflect realities depicted in the book of Judges *[Hyperbole, p. 437]*.

Verse 42 presents the most significant statement in the entire chapter, where *all these kings and their land* are said to have been taken *at one time* because *the Lord the God of Israel fought for Israel.* In chapter 11, after a report about the northern campaign, the narrator summarizes the sequence of encounters that begin in 9:1-2 by framing the last subunit with the notice that Joshua took *all the land* (11:16, 23), the exact phrase as in 10:40. Yet amid that final episode of chapter 11, the narrator also adds, *Joshua made war a long time with all those kings* (11:18). These statements are not so much contradictory as they are indicators of a narrative strategy that combines a hint of realism with an ideological or theological emphasis that everything the Lord has commanded has now been accomplished (10:40; 11:9, 15, 23). After all, it is *the Lord God of Israel* who has *fought for Israel* (10:42).

THE TEXT IN BIBLICAL CONTEXT

God as Warrior: Transforming the Tradition

In Joshua, the motif of the Lord's fighting (Heb. vb. *laḥam*) for Israel occurs only in 10:14, 42 and 23:3 (cf. 24:12). Exodus describes the defeat of Pharaoh and his army this way: "The Lord will fight for you, and you have only to keep still" (14:14; cf 14:25). Deuteronomy, anticipating entry into the land, modifies the motif: "The Lord your God, who goes before you, is the one who will fight for you, just as he did for you in Egypt before your very eyes" (1:30). A similar divine participation is testified in the war instructions of Deuteronomy 20: "It is the Lord your God who goes with you, to fight for you against your enemies, to give you victory" (20:3–4).

Outside of those passages, the notion of God's "fighting (*laḥam*) for Israel" occurs elsewhere in the OT only in 2 Chronicles 20 and 32. Chronicles is worth considering in some detail because of its transformation of Joshua's warfare language. In 2 Chronicles 20:15-17 a Levite announces a word of the Lord that echoes the phraseology of Joshua 1 and Deuteronomy 31:7-8. During the worship (!) that follows, "the Lord set an ambush, . . . so that they were routed" (2 Chron 20:22). Chronicles modifies the realism of Deuteronomy and the hyperbole of Joshua by placing the entire battle scene (the only one like it in Chronicles) into a liturgical context along with singers and processionals. This stereotypical scene suggests that worship is the real place of battle.

Second Chronicles 32 is also one of the Chronicler's paradigmatic moments. Like the scene in chapter 20, this one also echoes Joshua in

Hezekiah's affirmation, "*Be strong and of good courage. Do not be afraid or dismayed*; . . . with us is the LORD our God, to help us and to fight our battles" (2 Chron 32:7-8, emph. added). The four Hebrew verbs represented by the italicized words occur in the OT in one sentence only in Joshua 10:25 and three times in Chronicles (1 Chron 22:13; 28:20; 2 Chron 32:7; Josh 1:9 presents a slight variation). All three appearances in Chronicles reverse Joshua's order; where *fear and dismay* appear before *strong and courageous*. Chronicles seems explicitly to be drawing only on the word group that is found in the four verbs of Joshua 10:25, virtually quoting the verse and using a common quotation device in Hebrew of reversing the order from the original quotation. The conclusion of the story in 2 Chronicles 32 tells of the Lord's sending "an angel" to the Assyrian camp, with the result that God "gave them *rest on every side*" (32:22). None of those emphases within Chronicles appears in the parallel, and earlier, history in the books of Kings even though they all echo the language of Joshua.

Chronicles transforms the language of Joshua by minimizing or eliminating human fighting. Chronicles' added speeches reinterpret the tradition of divine and human warfare, implying that warfare is best left to God. Although this still leaves a theological problem, we can see how the historian works at the ethical problem of the earlier biblical tradition. By using explicit language from Joshua, Chronicles brings another paradigm to bear. It suggests that although the Chronicler's new community in a colonial context finds its identity and mission in the ancient story, it need not include in its self-understanding the mandate to fight for or alongside God. The surface tension we find in Deuteronomy and Joshua between divine engagement in warfare and human fighting is more or less resolved in Chronicles' retelling of the stories.

Although Deuteronomy assumes that Israel will engage the enemy in battle, and that God is the one who either does the fighting or empowers Israel to win the battle, Chronicles takes the motif of the Lord's fighting literally. Deuteronomy and Joshua employ the common generic conventions for writing conquest accounts *[Conquest Accounts, p. 406]*. Although Chronicles seems to move from metaphor and hyperbole to theological literalism, both Joshua and Chronicles emphasize that God is Sovereign over all human power. That sovereignty is not even hostage to God's commitment to Israel, for the book of Jeremiah turns the motif so that Yahweh "will fight against" Israel (Jer 21:2, 4-5). And when others "fight" against Jeremiah, Yahweh fights on his behalf with echoes of the exodus, "to deliver" and "to save" him (Jer 1:19; 15:20) *[Theology of Warfare, p. 458]*.

Thus the motif of the Lord's fighting for Israel becomes part of a living tradition that does not remain static. Joshua uses the conventional expressions common in ancient Near Eastern battle accounts. Chronicles adapts the expression to suit its interest in establishing the temple of *David* (not Solomon) as the place where Israel's true energy ought to focus. The Chronicler is concerned with David, therefore, as a type of Joshua. Joshua and David are to the Chronicler what Moses and Joshua are to the DtrH (cf. Deut 31; Josh 1; 1 Chron 28:20; 2 Chron 20). Moreover, Chronicles portrays Israel as active in worship and passive in combat against the powers that threaten.

Although the notion of divine participation in human warfare as we see it in Joshua is not unique to Israel *[Conquest Accounts, p. 406]*, the OT is a sustained conversation in which Israel's thinkers and writers both draw on the "language game" (cultural-linguistic literary currency) that is available to them in their culture and offer critical reflection on it. Unless we are able to sort the matter out, we are left with having to take the position of several of the four authors of *Show Them No Mercy* (Cowles et al.) who assume that what the biblical text of Deuteronomy and Joshua say, God must also say. Rather, our exploration of the linguistic motifs of Joshua 10 and its echoes in other texts allows us to discern a deliberate transformation within the biblical canon itself. This transformation either relativizes Joshua or, better, places Joshua into a larger conversation about these things. That conversation continues on into the NT, where the church's fight is "not against enemies of blood and flesh, but . . . against the spiritual forces of evil in the heavenly places" (Eph 6:12). In the Gospel narratives, the divine warrior vanquishes the foe. And victory in Revelation comes by the sword of the word *[Conquest and Land in the NT, p. 411]*.

THE TEXT IN THE LIFE OF THE CHURCH

Wait for the Lord

Hebron, one of the cities highlighted in the report of Joshua 10, continues to be a site of significant conflict. Although Hebron is considered by Jews and Muslims to be a sacred city, burial place of ancestors, it has also been the site of ongoing violence. On August 23, 1929, following rumors that Jews had killed Palestinians, a mob killed sixty-seven Jews in Hebron. On February 26, 1994, a Jewish man, Dr. Baruch Goldstein, killed twenty-nine Muslims while they were praying in the mosque above the ancestral burial caves. On November 15, 2002, Palestinian men killed twelve Israeli soldiers stationed in Hebron. The city continues to be a conflicted place as Jewish and Palestinian residents live in tension with one another, each claiming rights that all too easily exclude the other.

Contemporary political conflicts, however, cannot begin to comprehend the focus of the Joshua narrative: the Lord is fighting for Israel (Josh 10:14, 42). We do well to consider the larger biblical conversation sketched above. Like the psalmists, for whom trust in the Lord's help and saving power is a hallmark of the life of faith, we might confess, "Wait for the LORD; be strong, and let your heart take courage; wait for the LORD!" (Ps 27:14), or "Be strong, and let your heart take courage, all you who wait for the LORD" (31:24). Or, like the Chronicler, we might transform Joshua's call to courage (Josh 10:25) into a stance of trust that "there is one greater with us than with him" (2 Chron 32:7). Scripture itself invites that kind of appropriation, grounded in confidence in God's struggle against the forces allied against us. Such reading becomes part of a larger pattern of confidence in God as the Deliverer and Savior from all of life's "enemies."

It is not a long step from there to how the early church contextualized this story *[Conquest and Land in the NT, p. 411]*. In a setting of persecution and loss, rather than landedness, the early church transforms conquest, a transformation that has ongoing vitality in the early church fathers.

Origen is instructive for the church today because he illustrates, based on figural reading in the context of the entire canon of Scripture, that this text has no imitative power. He begins by retelling the setting of the story and then focuses on the poem of 10:12b-13. He explains "until I subdue this people" (likely working with 10:13b LXX) as "until the LORD completely defeated their enemies" (115). On the literal level, Origen is clear that in this story "these deeds . . . do not need interpretation from without." Still, he asks whether there may be a "spiritual interpretation" (116). Origen follows the trajectory of the psalmists, the Chronicler, and the NT writers in transforming warfare when he appeals to the NT assumption that persecution is the lot of the one who lives in Christ (1 Thess 5:15). Since according to Psalm 2:8 the nations and the ends of the earth are the goal of "your inheritance" and "your possession" (NIV), Origen suggests that the day is lengthened until both "the whole fullness of the nations" as well as "all Israel may be saved" (117). And since the day is prolonged, "'let us walk becomingly as in the day' and let us perform the works of light" (117). Citing Ephesians 6:12, Origen affirms the NT transformation of the warfare motif, allowing that some who are weak continue to struggle "against flesh and blood" when they are "assaulted by carnal faults and frailties" (118). Conquering these faults prepares believers to serve in God's living temple, as did the Gibeonites (119) *[Figural Reading, p. 426]*.

Although Origen is troubled by the violent image in Joshua 10:24, he transposes the image there into the key suggested by Luke's "set your feet upon serpents and scorpions and upon every hostile power" (cf. Luke 10:19) and the psalmist's "tread underfoot the dragon and the lizard" (cf. 91:13), which Origen considers a "petty king" of the "kingdom of sin" (119). In this way, with the dark rulers of sin destroyed, "Christ Jesus our Lord alone will reign in you" (119).

If we were to continue the trajectory of conversation along the lines of Origen, we might link Joshua 10:40 with the assurance of victory that was accomplished in Christ and to which Paul testifies in Rom 8:37: "We are more than conquerors" *[Conquest and Land in the NT, p. 411]*. In other words, in the life of the church, God continues to fight on our behalf. Yet the kingdom he establishes needs neither weapons nor lands and therefore invites love of enemies.

A Text That Provokes

Although the text highlights divine participation, it also assumes human violence against the enemy (no matter how Josh 10:13b, 14 and 42b are to be translated). Even if the weight of the story falls on God, is it too large a weight for God to carry? And is destroying all that breathes a burden no human community should wish on itself? I suggest that we live inside the conversation generated by this text, not inside this text alone. The text is part of a conversation within which the church wrestles, argues, and challenges. It is a text of terror that we dare not emulate; yet if we refuse conversation with it, we run the risk of repeating the violence of which the text tells.

This is a text that provokes and that evokes. It opens up a conversation that wanders through time, and in the process it acknowledges with Ephesians that with enough debate, with enough listening, with enough attentiveness, the dividing wall between those who are enemies might come down. Perhaps reading Joshua 11 leads us all to affirm that we were "excluded from citizenship in Israel and foreigners to the covenants of the promise, without hope and without God in the world" (Eph 2:12 NIV). Even so, "he is our peace; in his flesh he has made both groups into one and has broken down the dividing wall, that is, the hostility between us" (2:14).

Is it possible to affirm the theological emphasis in the text, which places the victory squarely into God's hands? Is it possible to affirm that the Lord hears and heeds the human command to vanquish the foe, even as the human being learns at the same time to love the enemy and beat swords into plowshares? Is it possible to affirm that the cry of the Gibeonites, *Save us, and help us,* is a cry both to God and to us? Is it possible to step in on behalf of those whose cry we also hear in their distress, and at the same time to recognize God's hand in granting that salvation and that help? Perhaps some of our conflicts also require cosmic intervention. Perhaps "making peace" with our own Gibeonites will generate conflict with those who seem threatened by such unorthodox peacemaking. The work of figural interpretation continues even as we lament the violence of the text itself *[Figural Reading, p. 426].*

Joshua 11:1-15

The Coalition of Northern Kings

PREVIEW

During a recent Stanley Cup playoff hockey game, one team scored a goal in the final seconds of regular play, tying the game and forcing an overtime period, which led to a second overtime period, until one of the teams finally scored the winning goal. Not unlike such a game, this chapter resonates with the old adage "It's not over till it's over." Kings are back, this time with *horses and chariots.* This short narrative about King Jabin of Hazor and a coalition of northern kings forms the last of three stories that begin with "hearing" (9:3; 10:1; 11:1), all three of which are introduced by the general introduction that describes the hearing of *all the kings* (9:1). Like the account of chapter 10, this story includes both a conquest account and a summary that paints the landscape of the conquest with sweeping generalizations. This third story in the sequence is followed by the most significant theological summary and interpretation of the warfare narratives in the book (11:16-23), and by two lists of conquered kings east (12:1-6) and west (12:7-24) of the Jordan.

OUTLINE

King Jabin and His Coalition Partners, 11:1-3
A Very Big and Well-Equipped Army Gathers, 11:4-5
God's Initiative and Joshua's Obedience, 11:6-9
Joshua's Conquest of Hazor, 11:10-11
Synthesis and Theological Summary, 11:12-15

EXPLANATORY NOTES

King Jabin and His Coalition Partners 11:1-3

The story begins by naming a character and a place, *King Jabin of Hazor*, who like Adoni-zedek (10:1) and the Gibeonites (9:3) *heard of this* (11:1). The narrator creates a sequence of "hearings" that begin in 9:1 (9:3 and 10:1 identify what was heard). The effect of the four "hearings" is to give the reader a sense of the spreading reports that are being relayed throughout the land. The NJPS conveys that sense well in its translation, *When the news reached King Jabin*. It may be the news of the entire story or news of what happened at Jericho and Ai (as noted in 9:3 and 10:1). Like Adoni-zedek, he gathers a coalition against Israel.

The coalition includes three named kings (v. 1), unnamed kings throughout the four main geographic regions (northern coastal plain, low foothills region, hill country, and the rift valley [NRSV *the Arabah*]: v. 2; cf. 9:1; 12:8), and the six people groups identified elsewhere in Joshua and other OT texts (Josh 3:10; 9:1; 24:11; cf. Gen 15:1-21; Deut 1:7; 7:1; 20:17). The King of Hazor takes initiative, planning for a pre-emptive strike, which may imply that he represents either a colonial power base for Egyptian control or the lead city of a group of city-states who are bound together in a treaty relationship (cf. 10:3-5). Neither description of coalition partners (ch. 10 or 11) implies the existence of "nations" in the modern sense. These are people groups linked to cities and their outlying villages and lands.

A Very Big and Well-Equipped Army Gathers 11:4-5

The narrative depicts this coalition as even more intimidating than the *forces* and *all their armies* of the southern coalition (10:5). The description here emphasizes not only *all their troops, a great army*, which would be reason enough to be nervous, but also adds that this coalition includes so many soldiers, including horses and chariots, that the effect of the description is hyperbolic: they are *like the sand on the seashore* (cf. Gen 22:17; 1 Sam 13:5; 1 Kings 4:29). The allusion to Abraham is not to be missed, since in Gen 22:17 the divine promise is that "your offspring shall possess the gate of their enemies." The irony here, however, is in the size the enemy's army, which underlines Israel's relative weakness.

Moreover, this first mention of *horses and chariots* in the book (again in Josh 11:6, 9) is significant because they represent a shorthand for the power differential between Jabin's coalition and Joshua's army. Horses and chariots typically belong to imperial power (Exod

14:9, 23; 15:19; Deut 11:4; Josh 24:6; see esp. Isa 30:1-2; 31:1-3). The text sets up the conflict in such a way that the reader cannot help but see that Joshua is up against something that is far too big for him to handle. The *horses and chariots* represent "the strength and monopoly of arms that are necessary and available for the maintenance of the economic and political monopoly" (Brueggemann 1986: 11). The other way of framing the conflict is to understand these kings as legitimate representatives of power in a city-state system that is asserting its independence against the incursions of Joshua and his forces. Although the Israelites have few weapons, their reputation as fierce and destructive fighters has preceded them. In either case, the military advantage is clearly on Jabin's side because he has the superior weaponry. He represents the state, or the empire, and his weapons are the instruments of his control of the region *[Horses and Chariots, p. 434]*.

The language is reminiscent of the war rhetoric used by government spokespersons and media reports, which tend to suggest that a war might come to a quick and decisive end because of superior weapons systems. The rhetoric in this text has the opposite, and ironic, effect. Here it is not Israel who has the superior military technology, but the enemy. Perhaps that is why the narrator does not note that Jabin is afraid (cf. Adoni-zedek, Josh 10:2). The assault force poised to take on Israel is overwhelming.

The episode opens with a notice that *all their troops, a great army* came together, and it closes with a reminder that *all these kings . . . camped together* to engage Israel in battle (v. 5). The Hebrew verb for *camped*, with its consonants *ḥnh*, anticipates the transformation at the end of the chapter with the notice that *the land had rest* (*šqṭ*) *from war* (Josh 11:23).

God's Initiative and Joshua's Obedience 11:6-9

This episode is framed by an inclusio that repeats the Lord's words in his initial instructions to Joshua and in the report that Joshua has done as God has commanded. Whether Jabin's coalition is simply defending its territory or represents an oppressive city-state system, God speaks in typical Deuteronomic confidence (cf. Josh 1:9; 10:25): *Do not be afraid, . . . for . . . I will hand over* (lit., *give*) the enemy *to Israel* (cf. Deut 7:18; 20:13). But how will this be possible in the face of such military capacity? God's assertion gives Joshua time, until *tomorrow at this time*, but that is little consolation. He has a full day to ponder his fears. And that the Lord should *hand over all of them, slain* seems an impossibility. Even though it may be God's victory, Joshua does not wait around.

After those words of assurance, God commands Joshua to *hamstring their horses, and burn their chariots with fire* (vv. 6, 9). The verb "to hamstring" is used again of David's action against Hadadezer's forces (2 Sam 8:4; 1 Chron 18:4; cf. Gen 49:6). The command to act in this clandestine way confirms, as Brueggemann puts it, that this is a "hopeless mismatch." The narrator emphasizes *horses* and *chariots* by placing the direct object first in Hebrew text: *Their horses you will hamstring, their chariots you will burn in fire* (AT). Brueggemann observes that the only action God mentions he will do is "giving," but he actually does nothing. God simply instructs Joshua to engage in a guerilla tactic against the weapons system of Jabin's forces (1986: 15–16).

From one vantage point, God gives "permission for Joshua and Israel to act for their justice and liberation against an oppressive adversary" (17). From another, Jabin and his forces are trying to defend their territory against an incursion by outsiders who had recently wrought havoc on the population of the south. Is it possible to be sympathetic to Jabin? Or must the reader take sides with Joshua against the coalition's massive military system? Although the narrator seems to invite identification with Joshua, we may turn the tables on our point of view as readers. But we are not allowed to stay there long. The text focuses our attention on Israel's fear and on the military advantage of the other side, which is poised to unleash all of its military fury on virtually defenseless Joshua and his men.

God's word to Joshua echoes similar expressions found throughout ancient Near Eastern conquest accounts. In the Zakkur inscription (ca. 800 BC), for example, we read: "And Ba'alshamayn spoke to me through the hand of seers and the hand of envoys and Ba'alshamayn said to me: 'Do not be afraid because I have made you king, and I will stand with you, and I will deliver you from all these kings who have raised a siege against you'" (cited in Younger 1990: 229).

The text offers no explanation for how Joshua and his *fighting force* made the journey from Gilgal (in the Jordan valley not far from Jericho) to Merom, slightly north and west of the Sea of Galilee. Jabin's forces do not move southward to ward off Joshua's incursion. Joshua, by contrast, is moving into Jabin's territory. He acts *suddenly* and *fell upon them* (v. 7). Joshua engages in a preemptive strike, catching Jabin's forces off guard. The narrator makes it clear, however, that this is all in the plan. God *handed them over to Israel* (v. 8) just as he had said (v. 6). That Joshua *fell on them* (v. 7) and *attacked them and chased them* (v. 8b) frames God's act of "giving" the enemy over to Israel (v. 8a; cf. v. 6). Joshua's forces pursue those who flee in panic in all directions, some all the way to the coast. In language we see elsewhere in Joshua, they *struck them down* and *left no one remaining* (v. 8b; cf. 8:22; 10:28, 30, 33, 37, 39, 40; same language in Num 21:35; Deut 3:3). Such reflections of total conquest with "none remaining" occur also in ancient Near Eastern conquest accounts *[Conquest Accounts, p. 406]*.

The final narrative summary (v. 9) tells us that *Joshua did to them as the LORD commanded him*, which reminds us of God's speech in verse 6. Both verses 6 and 9 mention hamstringing horses and burning chariots with fire. The Hebrew narrative structure is not linear. If we were to reconstruct the narrative action, which is not the narrator's intent, we would begin with verse 9, describing Joshua's immediate act of obedience following upon God's command of verse 6b. The guerilla tactic would leave the coalition forces on the ground without the advantage of their military strength. And unless they were on foot, Joshua's forces could not have *attacked and chased them* (v. 8). The narrative technique is a reverse telling. First the narrative describes the defeat, and then, so as not to lose sight of how they overpowered the enemy in the first place, the narrator reminds us of the Lord's command and Joshua's exact carrying out of the action. It would be too repetitive to have verse 9 follow immediately after verse 6. Instead, the narrator creates a dramatic tension by separating the (presumed) nighttime action of hamstringing the horses from the subsequent attack on the troops, and by reversing the order. All of that sets up the scenario for Joshua to shift locations from the waters of Merom (vv. 5, 7) and turn his attention on Hazor (vv. 10-15).

Joshua's Conquest of Hazor 11:10-11

Hazor is one of the largest Middle Bronze Age sites in the region. Situated just north of the Sea of Galilee, it was *head of all those kingdoms* (v. 10). The story line flows from the previous verses. Presumably King Jabin of Hazor was not at the battle scene (unlike the action of the kings in ch. 10). This story assumes that Jabin has remained in his capital city, just as military leaders continue to do to this day.

Verse 11 draws the battle scene to a close by emphasizing, in stereotypical and hyperbolic language, that *all* are *put to the sword*, that they *utterly destroyed them* [*ḥerem*], and that there was *no one left who breathed*. These are all Deuteronomic expressions that we have encountered before in Joshua (see ch. 10) and that express total conquest in hyperbolic terms, as do all ancient conquest accounts *[Conquest Accounts, p. 406]*.

Synthesis and Theological Summary 11:12-15

Like the final verses of the previous narrative (10:40-43), these verses widen the scope of the outcome. Not only Hazor, but *all the towns* and *all their kings* are destroyed; Joshua and his force *struck them with the edge of the sword, utterly destroying them* (v. 12a). The language of *mouth of the sword* (lit.) and *ḥerem* repeats verse 11. The double occurrence of *all* adds hyperbolic emphasis. That this has been done *as Moses the servant of the Lord had commanded* (v. 12b) is odd in this context because we expect "as the LORD had commanded," following verses 6 and 9. That is why this subsection is best understood as a final summary that reflects not on the immediacy of the previous episodes, but back to Deuteronomy and forward to the books of Kings. The only other time in the book of Joshua where this expression occurs is in the altar episode in Joshua 8:30-35, and there it occurs twice (vv. 31, 33; cf. 1:7, 13; 4:10; 8:35). In 2 Kings 18:12 the expression occurs again in an explanation for why Israel, the northern tribes, were conquered and deported to Assyria. That happened "because they did not obey the voice of the LORD their God but transgressed his covenant—all that Moses the servant of the LORD had commanded; they neither listened nor obeyed." This motif of obedience to what Moses commanded frames the book of Joshua, first in Joshua 1:13, and finally in Joshua 22:2, 5. That motif links the book of Joshua to the *book* of Deuteronomy, thus verifying Joshua as the authoritative voice of Moses. But as we have already seen in Joshua 2, 6, and 9, "obedience to Moses" is not literalistic but reflects a dynamic conversation within the Deuteronomic tradition *[Characterization of Joshua, p. 394].*

Verse 13 highlights the burning of Hazor and reports that the other towns were not burned. Like the story in chapter 8, the Israelites take the spoil after capturing the towns (v. 14). Again the three motifs of verse 11 are repeated in verse 14b, followed by a repetition and elaboration of the obedience motif in verse 15. Thus, Joshua 11:10-11 functions in this story as did 10:28-39, and 11:12-15 functions as did 10:40-43 in that unit.

The entire scenario ends by reiterating and expanding the obedience motif (cf. v. 12b). The narrator makes it clear (in case anyone missed it earlier) that *as the LORD had commanded his servant Moses, so Moses commanded Joshua, and so Joshua did* (v. 15). The hyperbole sharpens the point: *he left nothing undone of all that the LORD had commanded Moses* (v. 15). The sequence of three "hearing" stories come to an end in verse 15 by asserting that the conquest is a combination of divine initiative and human response. The polarity in the text is not "divine initiative—human participation in warfare," but rather "divine initiative—human obedience." The narrator cannot imagine Israel's historical origins as anything other: God commands; Israel obeys. That is how the last episode in the conquest sequence puts it in 11:16-23, which provides a theological synthesis in the next text unit.

THE TEXT IN BIBLICAL CONTEXT

Texts Echoing Texts

Through a mixture of stereotypical and hyperbolic language common to ancient conquest accounts, motifs in this unit echo back and forth among biblical texts as in a tapestry. This text echoes a variety of sources, particularly Deuteronomy 20:16-20, mirroring expressions like "not let anything that breathes remain alive," "annihilate them" (*ḥerem*) *[Ḥerem, p. 433]*, and the list of six people groups *[Dispossessed Peoples, p. 424]*. This unit also draws on a long tradition of reflection on the validity and value of weapons *[Horses and Chariots, p. 434]*, on the theme of obedience/disobedience as it is linked to promise and exile *[Land: Gifted and Lost, p. 440]*, and on the injunction to obey Moses the servant of the Lord (cf. Josh 1:7, 13; 8:31, 33) *[Characterization of Joshua, p. 394]*. Such echoes illustrate the narrator's theological method by which intrabiblical allusion creates a dynamic tradition through the trajectory of interpretation.

The Problem with Horses and Chariots

Both Joshua and Josiah represent the willingness to obey the divine word mediated by Moses (Josh 8:30-35; 11:15; 2 Kings 23:25). Second Kings depicts Josiah as one who obeys even though history will not turn out right in the end. He knows what he must do and does it in spite of the prophetess Huldah's declaration (2 Kings 22:16-20). That, according to the larger story for whom Joshua, David, and Josiah are paradigmatic followers of Moses, is at the heart of being the people of God *[Characterization of Joshua, p. 394]*. To follow God's instruction is more important than guaranteeing the outcome. Still, a troubling motif lurks. What if the instruction advocates violence? The book of Joshua is not a pacifist document. Its expressions, its narrative structures, and aspects of its worldview share the conventions of ancient conquest accounts *[Conquest Accounts, p. 406]*. It reports divine speech in the only way that makes sense given the available literary conventions and genres. Yet wedged into the stereotypical and the hyperbolic elements of this ancient conquest account is this odd emphasis on "horses and chariots," which casts a measure of doubt on the obviously brutal concluding summary *[Horses and Chariots, p. 434]*.

These textual affinities suggest another conversation, therefore, about the significance of *horses and chariots* in this text (vv. 4, 6, 9; cf. 24:6). God "authorizes" a guerilla action against the military hardware of the coalition partners, but does not intervene as he did in the previous story (Brueggemann 1986: 19). *Horses and chariots* evokes a memory of the exodus story of liberation, in which horses and chariots are Pharaoh's primary weaponry, and which God defeats without human help (Exod 14:9, 18, 23; 15:19). The description of the coalition forces (Josh 11:4b), God's promise and command (11:6), and Joshua's action (11:9) suggest that this text reinforces that "old memory of liberation" (Brueggemann 1986: 21). What is different here, however, is that God promises (v. 6) but does not act as he does in the exodus event. Yahweh speaks a word that authorizes human action to undermine the military power of the coalition forces representing the system of city-state power. God's action in the exodus narrative now authorizes human action. And the story as a whole presents "a *more harsh* destruction than is authorized in verse 6" (27). Although verses 11-15 refer the reader back to the *ḥerem* of Deuteronomy 20:16-20, God speaks in verse 6 about human action only with respect to horses and chariots. The entire text, therefore, appeals to Moses and thereby bypasses or goes beyond the explicit divine instruction in verse 6, thereby modifying Moses' Torah in Deuteronomy 20. God's command to Moses is "contextualized by Israel" (Brueggemann 1986: 30).

There is another way of understanding the story. God's speech in verse 6 is "reported speech" that, together with the description of the army and Joshua's action, belongs to a larger bundle of texts that do not so much justify the human violence, but rather represent a subplot of critique against "horses and chariots." Although the warfare terminology of verses 11-15 belongs to a long ancient Near Eastern tradition of stereotypical and hyperbolic language *[Conquest Accounts, p. 406]*, those verses also highlight obedience, a theme that belongs to the larger narrative framework of Deuteronomy and 2 Kings. There the story is framed in terms of east of Jordan (Deuteronomy) and exile in Babylon (2 Kings). David's "empire," as described in the larger story, is subservient to the notion that David is faithful to the Torah of Moses *[Torah, p. 462]*.

One of the most significant connections to Moses' Torah concerns his instructions concerning kingship in Deuteronomy 17:14-20. There Moses instructs, "When you have come into the land that the LORD your God is giving you, and have taken possession of it"—which sounds very much like the scenario of the entire book of Joshua—"you may . . . set as king over you." He "must not acquire many horses for himself, or return the people to Egypt in order to acquire more horses." This king is to "have a copy of this law written," and he shall diligently observe "all the words of this law," not "turning aside from the commandment, either to the right or to the left." As we have already noticed in Joshua 1:7; 8:31, 35 and will notice again at the end of the book, Joshua fulfills the royal paradigm. His action as reported in Joshua 11 against "horses and chariots" implies a subtle subversion of the general assumptions embedded in the narrative concerning Moses' instructions concerning *ḥerem* and an affirmation of Deuteronomy's limitation of weapons for purposes of imperial expansion and control. But that cannot be demonstrated by referring only to Deuteronomy 17 and Joshua 11. We need to look outside those texts for further examples of "horses and chariots."

Based on a larger biblical-canonical conversation, God has no particular fondness for horses and chariots, "which are instruments of domination used by kings and states. They represent advanced technology, they are financed by surplus wealth, and they serve a political purpose of oppression" (Brueggemann 1986: 37). In particular, several stories in the books of Kings, in offering a critique of horses and chariots, also present a vision of another kind of power (1 Kings 20:23-30; 2 Kings 6:8-22; 7:3-8; 18:23-35).

Although we might like to know more about what happened, these stories tell Israel much about its God. The prophets are God's agents who carry out his work by means of the power of prophetic vision and speech. Since God shapes the historical process, horses and chariots are irrelevant. The world is governed by an authority that stands over kings. In other words, Israel has an alternative way of interpreting the historical process. Israel knows that it should not, or need not, imitate royal ways of being. Alternatives, therefore, must be possible for a marginal people whose experience of royal power has led to their demise, and for whom faithfulness to God's instruction becomes the only way of imagining an alternative future.

The intrabiblical conversation also takes us to a number of prophetic texts that testify to God's power over horses and chariots. For example, in a judgment speech Micah announces that "in that day . . . I will cut off your horses from among you and will destroy your chariots" (5:10). And concerning Israel's release from

Babylonian captivity, Isaiah speaks of the action of the Lord, "who brings out chariot and horse, army and warrior; they lie down, they cannot rise, they are extinguished, quenched like a wick" because "I am about to do a new thing" (43:17, 19). Zechariah announces that the coming one "will cut off the chariot from Ephraim and the war-horse from Jerusalem," and in the process the "battle bow shall be cut off," and "his dominion shall be from sea to sea, and from the River to the ends of the earth" (9:9-10). The prophetic imagination here modifies the boundary description from Joshua 1 and rejects the bow (weapons) of Joshua 24:12.

For further reflections on horses, chariots, and weaponry in the prophetic and poetic imagination, see the essay *Horses and Chariots, p. 434*. These contrasts emphasize the need not only to acknowledge the intrabiblical conversation, but also to keep that difficult conversation alive in an ongoing and dynamic interpretive process in the church.

THE TEXT IN THE LIFE OF THE CHURCH

The Trajectory from War to Peace

Several general observations arise from the intrabiblical conversation thus far. First, the texts evidence a tension between human fighting and divine hope for transformation of warfare and weaponry. God is the governor of the historical-political process even in the face of overwhelming odds. Yet that governance is bound up with Israel's covenantal responsiveness. Thus not even in Joshua are we permitted a boasting in military strength. Second, the larger biblical reflection on the efficacy of superior weaponry may lead us to lament our dependence on weapons of all kinds. Third, if we were to identify with Jabin instead of Joshua, we might see ourselves as the ones wielding horses and chariots. The much boasting by the Western "coalition partners" in 2003 before the invasion of Iraq, and before that in the Balkans, suggests that such rhetoric is designed to keep the military trusting in its might and the people at home secure in thinking that nothing will touch them "at home," as U.S. American President George W. Bush said when he visited troops in Iraq on Thanksgiving Day 2003 (Michael Moore's documentary *Fahrenheit 9/11* [2004]).

Although NT texts do not explicitly reflect on the motifs and themes of Joshua 11:1-15, the trajectory of transformation continues there (e.g., Eph 6; Yoder Neufeld 1997; Zerbe 1993). While Christian interpreters have appealed to the synergistic paradigm in texts like Joshua 11, in which God commands and humans carry out God's commands, there is no precedent in the NT or the history of the church for divine commands to engage in guerrilla warfare against a technically superior military force. Still, many Christians have understood by implication that it may well be legitimate in God's sight to protest undue reliance on weapons and warfare for security against known and supposed dangers.

Origen begins his Homily 14 on Joshua 11 by assuming that Jesus himself subverts the warfare texts by becoming our peace (Eph 2:14), and thus by returning peace to the soul through expelling its enemies, "sins and vices" (130). Origen's interest is in preserving the full canon for the church when the church does not advocate war. The wars of the church are against "spiritual wickedness in the heavens" (138-39, citing Eph 6:12).

Origen does not resort to typology to avoid the letter of the text. He reads the text and then suggests textual affinities that transpose it into another key. In doing so, he is continuing a trajectory of interpretation from within Scripture itself. Origen's reading of Joshua's obedience is not far from the narrator's, in light of the overall (DtrH) plotline that ends in exile outside the land. Joshua has accomplished all that Moses has commanded, which is what Origen suggests Jesus does with us. But whereas Moses commanded the extermination of enemies, so "Jesus fulfills in us and is himself the one who destroys vices in us and overthrows the most vile kingdoms of sin." Therefore, Jesus fulfills the law (Matt 5:17) by conquering the power of sin and all that hinders the peaceful reign of God in us (145).

Contemporary readers may disparage Origen's inner warfare. Activists who affirm civil disobedience (e.g., protests against weapons of mass destruction) may transpose Joshua's action into a symbolic hamstringing of nuclear weapons, land mines, and depleted uranium. Yet such transposition raises larger interpretive questions. Such analogous and anthropomorphic language may serve us well, but it must not be stretched too far. That God commands Joshua to hamstring horses is the narrator's way of speaking about the complexities of the human historical experience. We cannot imitate this text naively without careful attention to its voice within the larger biblical vision for cosmic peace and the eradication of weapons.

Joshua 11:16-23

Conquest Summary: The Whole Land at Rest from War

PREVIEW

The entrance-into-the-land narrative has now officially come to an end. *Rest from war* is its outcome (11:23). But the text does not mince words as to its tragic journey to this point. Struck down, utterly destroyed, no mercy. These are the images of *Apocalypse Now* (1979). Film critic Roger Ebert invites us to imagine "the helicopter attack on a Vietnamese village, led by Col. Kilgore, whose choppers use loudspeakers at top volume to play Wagner's 'Ride of the Valkyries' as they swoop down on a yard full of schoolchildren." Similarly, Joshua's summary statement is not a pretty picture; yet this action, as the text states, *was the LORD's doing* (v. 20).

The summary in 11:16-23 is bracketed by a report that *Joshua took* either *all that land* (v. 16a) or *the whole land* (v. 23a), with an additional note at the end about the land having *rest from war* (11:23b). Two summaries stand between those notices: one describes the taking of *all that land* (vv. 16b-20); another seems like a footnote to the whole story, reporting Joshua's conquest of a group called *the Anakim* (vv. 21-22). Within this unit are several easily missed notices that alert us to the point of view of the narrator. We find several references to the hill country of Judah (v. 21) and the hill country of Israel (vv. 16, 21). Although *the whole land* is indeed the focus (v. 23a), the narrator's point of view lets us know that the narrative is aware of the division of the kingdoms into Israel (north) and Judah (south) after the death of Solomon. The juxtaposition of this historical division with the twofold reference to the entire land (vv. 16a, 23a) may also suggest a theopolitical agenda in the book as a whole.

At the center of this text is a theological assertion that occurs for the first time in the book. The *hardening* of the *hearts* of the kings makes it clear that these stories reflect a divine act (v. 20). This theological affirmation is not unique to Joshua (cf. the Pharaoh of the exodus). The end of the unit also highlights the motif of *rest*, a significant motif in Deuteronomic texts (v. 23b). That motif recurs in the summary at the end of the division of the land (21:44), where an even more robust theological synthesis appears (21:43-45).

The note that *Joshua took the whole land* (11:23) brings a closure to the entire conquest narrative proper. It closes a double narrative sequence of chapters 6–8 and 9–11: thus 5:2-12 sets the stage for chapters 6–8 (Jericho and Ai) as 9:3-27 sets the stage for chapters 10–11 (Adoni-zedek and Jabin; Winther-Nielsen: 251). Moreover, 5:1-2 includes the motif of "hearing," which recurs in 9:1-2.

The closure of 11:23 also provides an enigmatic opening into 13:1, with its comment about Joshua's age and the Lord's notice that *very much of the land still remains to be possessed.* The notion of "possession" appears in Joshua 1:11 and echoes an expression found throughout Deuteronomy. It is as though 13:1 takes us temporally to the beginning, since we find an ending like 11:23, with similar theological motifs, at the conclusion of the distribution of the land in 21:43-45. There, in 21:43, the motif of *rest* appears, just as it does in 11:23. Hence 11:23 draws to a close what 13:1 begins, returning to an end again in 21:43-45. Chapter 12 then becomes a hinge between the two main sections of the book.

OUTLINE

Joshua Took All That Land, 11:16-20
A Footnote about the Anakim, 11:21-22
The Whole Land Had Rest from War, 11:23

EXPLANATORY NOTES

Joshua Took All That Land 11:16-20

Joshua is the key figure in the overall summary (vv. 16, 18, 21, 23). Two terms are distinctive in this subunit. The verb *took* marks the closure of the entire conquest sequence that began in 5:13. And the phrase *all that land / the whole land* in verses 16a and 23a indicates a fulfillment of a divine promise (found with this specific meaning of "land" rather than "earth" only in Gen 13:15; Deut 19:8; 34:1; and then also in Josh 2:3, 24; 9:24; 10:40; 21:43; and never again in the DtrH).

The extent of Joshua's "taking" (v. 16) is from the far south (*the Negeb*) to the far north (*below Mount Hermon*), and from the rift valley (*the Arabah*) to the rolling hills near but not including the coastal plain (*the lowland*, Shephelah). The extent of the taking is matched by *all their kings*, whom Joshua *struck down* and *put to death* (v. 17).

In a cautious aside in the report about taking *all the land* and *all their kings*, the narrator is careful to observe that *Joshua made war a long time with all those kings* (v. 18). The idiom *a long time* (lit., *many days*) suggests a realism about the process, but the point of view of a total conquest overrules the realism. As a summary statement drawing the entire conquest narrative to a close, there is less interest in the length of time than in the one to whom it should be ascribed. The narrative names that one in verse 20, but not before mentioning the Gibeonites, who had *made peace* with the Israelites (v. 19; cf. 9:15; 10:1, 4). The odd feature of this note is that it reminds us again of how Deuteronomy 20:10-18 offers the option of "terms of peace" to towns far away, but not to towns nearby (see discussion at 9:6 and *[Extent of the Land, p. 424]*). Does verse 19 read as though all of the others mentioned here and in chapter 12 might have done the same, given that they belong to *all the land*? After all, consider the example of the Gibeonites. Yet here it says they did not (implying that they could have).

Yet the narrative moves on by explaining that *it was the* L*ORD's doing to harden their hearts* so that *they might be utterly destroyed* (*ḥerem*) and that they *might receive no mercy, but be exterminated* (v. 20; cf. 11:11, 12, 21). Surely these are among the hardest words in the book of Joshua. Before dismissing them, we do well to engage in a vigorous debate with them and about them. But first a few preliminaries. The same combination of themes and words occurs in Deuteronomy 7:2. There the Lord "clears away many nations before you" (7:1) and warns about not making treaties or engaging in intermarriage, since those "would turn away your children from following me, to serve other gods" (Deut 7:2-4). All of this is surely what *the* L*ORD had commanded Moses* (Josh 11:20b). In the light of these textual allusions, the unexpected motif of the Lord's hardening of hearts is a striking explanation of the war's duration. Although the Gibeonite episode is confirmed and affirmed, it is not the norm. In order to confirm the divine intention to give Israel the land, the historical process must be superintended by the Lord. The length of time is irrelevant if the Lord's agency in Israel's experience is to be trusted. From the perspective of the end of the story in exile, this insight may well offer hope in the long haul.

That divine agency finds expression in *It was the* LORD*'s doing* (lit., *from the* LORD *it was*). The exact phrase is found in the OT only here and at Psalm 118:23. God's agency in history places *all those kings* (11:18) into the situation in which Joshua is able to take *the whole land* (11:16, 23), according to the divine word spoken through Moses (11:23), presumably as recorded in Deuteronomy 7:1-3.

The link to Deuteronomy 7 is reflected in the noun translated *mercy* in Joshua 11:20, which appears here for the first time in the OT. Most often it means "plea" or "supplication for favor" (appearing elsewhere in the DtrH only in Solomon's prayer; eight times in 1 Kings 8:28-54; and once in God's reply, 1 Kings 9:3; cf. Pss 6:9; 55:1; 119:170). A related form (*Qal*) of the verb occurs fifty-five times, often in statements about or requests for God's mercy (Exod 33:19; Num 6:25; cf. different forms in 1 Kings 8:33, 47, 59; 9:3). Deuteronomy 7:2 commands not to "show mercy" (NASB: "no favor") in conjunction with the command not to make covenants with the "seven nations." Joshua 11:20 reflects Deuteronomy 7:2 but substitutes a noun for the verb. The irony, however, is that this mention of "no mercy" comes in the context of the mention of the *peace* with the Gibeonites (11:19), a direct violation of the command not to make covenants with peoples in the land of Canaan (Deut 20:10-18).

A further irony occurs in the hardening-of-the-heart motif, which in the DtrH concerns divine sovereignty in both process and outcome. The verb traditionally translated "to harden" (*ḥzq*), when used in a military context, means "to strengthen." Used with the word "heart," which is primarily the seat of the will (the intellectual rather than emotional center), the full expression means something like "to strengthen the resolve." It is as though God is the director who guides all the components of making a film such that he takes responsibility for the whole even though he does not, and cannot, participate in or control every aspect of the process. It is telling, therefore, that in this pivotal passage in Joshua 11, the narrative interprets the events as analogous to the liberation from Egypt. But here the Lord does not engage in battle alone, as in the exodus story. Israel under Joshua obeys a modified or reinterpreted Deuteronomic code to exterminate with *no mercy*. Moreover, in the opening and closing speeches in the book of Joshua, the same verb also has a slightly different meaning. Although in Joshua 1 the word is used in the context of impending warfare, it also means a strengthening to obey God's instructions (Josh 1:7; 23:6).

The "strengthening" of Joshua 11:20, therefore, concerns the divine empowerment of *all their kings* (v. 17) to carry out what is in their minds to do. God does not control the events, since the narrator makes clear that the Gibeonites have exercised a different and creative option. In a sense verse 19 not only tempers verse 20 but also places it in its proper context, that of human freedom to oppose the divine purpose. The narrator highlights this willed opposition in verse 20 by focusing on the divine command to Moses, yet reframing that command not as prediction or predetermination of history but as response to the initiative of the kings. The narrative implies that all could have *made peace* (v. 19), but only one did. Instead, they suffered defeat.

The phrase *in order that* (twice in the Hebrew text of v. 20) makes it clear that God intends a specific outcome. Whereas earlier theological summaries emphasize that *the LORD fought for Israel* (10:14, 42), they also make it clear that Joshua and his forces have participated in both disabling and exterminating the enemy (throughout chs. 10–11). Now in the final summary, the Lord's participation moves beyond throwing hailstones down from heaven and instructing Joshua to hamstring horses and burn chariots. The Lord also empowers *all the kings* to make war on Israel so that the Deuteronomic instruction of extermination might be fulfilled. The will of *all the kings*, like the Pharaoh of the exodus, was directed by God so that God's intentions would be carried out. The mysterious governance of God is at the heart of this unit, just as the outcome is in God's "hand" in the exodus narrative. Joshua 11:20 therefore brings together the notion of divine direction of the historical process and the human action that makes that outcome tangible.

Such an outcome of total devastation is characteristic of other summary expressions, some of which also include the motif that all of this is *as the LORD had commanded Moses* (Josh 10:40-42; 11:12, 15; on Moses' commands, see Josh 1:7, 13; 8:31, 33; 11:12, 15; 22:2, 5; 2 Kings 18:12; 21:8). This carries much theological freight. Complicity with that instruction means life in the land. Failure to live by what Moses has commanded results in loss of land *[Land: Gifted and Lost, p. 440]*. Although Israel's ongoing story takes a good number of dark turns, Israel is never abandoned by the Lord (Deut 4:31).

Would readers of the book of Joshua perceive the narrative as advocating a universal pattern of divine-human synergism? The answer cannot be gathered entirely from this text unit, although it begins to address it in the next subunit.

A Footnote about the Anakim 11:21-22

The narrative includes an aside that begins with *at that time.* The phrase is a typical transitional expression in historical and prophetic literature (see Josh 5:2; 6:26 NJPS; 11:10, 21; in all of DtrH, eighteen times). The plural form *Anakim* appears in only two books in the OT (Deut 1:28; 2:10-11; 9:2; Josh 11:21-22; 14:12). They are *descendants of Anak* (15:14, lit.; Num 13:22, 28, 33), apparently related to the gigantic Nephilim (Gen 6:4; Num 13:33). In Deuteronomy they are "tall" people (2:10, 21; 9:2). Joshua 14 describes Caleb's inheritance as belonging to the Anakim (14:12, 15; 15:13, 14). Joshua 21:11 states that Levites were given Hebron, which Joshua 15 says was given to Caleb. References to Anak/Anakim disappear after their final appearance in Judg 1:20. It is interesting that in Joshua 11:21-22 Joshua is said to have *wiped out the Anakim* from everywhere, including Hebron, except for *in Gaza, in Gath, and in Ashdod* (all Philistine cities). But are there not discrepancies between Joshua's and Caleb's conquests of Hebron (14:6-15), and between Caleb's and the Levites' inheritance (21:13)?

The Whole Land Had Rest from War 11:23

The concluding summary reiterates verse 16a by emphasizing the "taking" of *the whole land.* The verse also repeats the emphasis on Moses from verse 20b. And the word *inheritance* appears for the first time in Joshua, where it anticipates the land distribution in chapters 13–21 (forty-nine times after 11:23, beginning in 13:6). Verse 23 also introduces a structural motif that distinguishes the first part of Joshua from the second. It draws the first half of the book to a close as it picks up the opening bracket of the *rest* motif from Joshua 1:13, 15. It also looks forward to the so-called distribution of the land in chapters 13–21 and the recap of the *rest* motif in the final chapters of the book (21:44; 22:4; 23:1). Although rest implies a cessation of warfare (11:23; 21:44), it is juxtaposed with obedience (22:4; 23:1; cf. 22:2, 5; 23:6), as in Joshua's commissioning of the Transjordan tribes (1:13, 15). Rest becomes characteristic of life lived in obedience to God *[Rest, p. 455].*

Verse 23 functions as a proleptic notation. Like verses 21-22, it anticipates the distribution mapped out in chapters 13–21. Verse 23a begins by looking back (*Joshua took*) and then forward (*gave it for an inheritance*) to the following chapters as though the action of distribution described there had already occurred. The last sentence, *And the land had rest from war* (v. 23b), is a punctuation mark in the middle of the book between these two actions. Verse 23, therefore, forms the final chorus, as it were, that allows the story to fold back on itself after the hinge chapter 12, to begin again in chapter 13 with the "distribution" and come to a close with another chorus in 21:43-45.

The *rest* motif in verse 23 needs a brief explanation in relation to how it is used in other places (see Rad 1966; Roth). In Deuteronomy the "rest" motif appears in contexts that speak of inheritance. There, for example, Moses addresses people who "have not yet entered the rest and the possession [lit., 'inheritance'] that the LORD your God is giving you" (Deut 12:9). "Rest" (*menuḥah*) is related to one of the commonly used verbs meaning "to rest" (Deut 3:20) and the noun "rest" from your enemies (Deut 12:10; 25:19). The first chapter of Joshua (1:13, 15) picks up on that word, as do texts at the end of the book of Joshua (21:44; 22:4; 23:1). But Joshua 11:23 uses a different verb (*šqṭ*). The full expression *the land had rest from war* occurs only here and in Joshua 14:15, where Caleb is allotted Hebron, and where Anakim are again mentioned. The verb means to be at peace or to live quietly. The verb, used only twice in Joshua and never in the Pentateuch, occurs four times to speak of rest after "oppression" (Judg 3:11, 30; 5:31; 8:28) and twice to describe the tranquil life of the city of Laish (Judg 18:7, 27) or the quietness of the city after Athaliah's assassination (2 Kings 11:20; cf. Jer 30:10-11). Joshua 11:23 and 14:15 are referring to a specific kind of *rest*, which is the kind of life experienced after the cessation of warfare. Only within this kind of rest, in a postwar reality, can the other kind of rest noted at the beginning and end of the book of Joshua become a reality. That may be why the distribution of the *inheritance*, beginning in Joshua 13, has been separated from the so-called conquest narratives in chapters 6–11. Warfare and inheritance are incompatible realities, according to the book of Joshua. Although the *rest* of the opening and closing of the book is contingent on the rest that is a quietness without war (11:23; 14:15), it is juxtaposed with obedience (22:4; 23:1; cf. 22:2, 5; 23:6), as we find it in Joshua's commissioning of the Transjordan tribes (1:13, 15). True rest is characterized by life lived in obedience to God *[Rest, p. 455]*.

We could, however, read that motif differently through ideological lenses. Perhaps only after extermination or subjugation and colonization of the indigenous population is it possible for the Israelites to divide up the land into administrative districts of their own choosing. But that is not the main interest of the narrative as a whole. The overarching hyperbole in this unit, the conventional ancient warfare language, and the realism of verse 18—all these are subordinate to the several theological assertions in the unit. First, *it was the LORD's doing* (v. 20). Second, all that has come before is a result of divine instruction to Moses (vv. 20, 23). And third, the *inheritance* comes when war has ceased, when the land is quiet (v. 23). The intersection of those themes will become the conversation partners in the intrabiblical conversation below.

THE TEXT IN BIBLICAL CONTEXT

Land as Gift and Inheritance

Israel's inheritance of land is a divine gift, resulting in rest in that gifted land. The theme of land as gift and inheritance echoes throughout Scripture. In particular, land themes in Leviticus, Numbers, and Deuteronomy resonate with motifs of *inheritance* and *rest* found in Joshua 11:23. In Deuteronomy, land is granted to all peoples of the world, with a special relationship between "the Most High" and the *people* of Israel (Deut 32:7-9). Although "rest" in the land results in land as "inheritance" in Deuteronomy (3:20; 12:9-10; 25:19), land is also a "conditional grant" that brings with it covenantal responsibility (Habel 1995: 36–53). In Leviticus, when land and rest are mentioned in the same context, the concern is for the land's Sabbath rest in the Sabbatical Year (25:4-5). When the people are exiled from their land, the land will again rest (26:34-35). Although the book of Joshua does not speak of that kind of rest, it is the only other place in the OT where land is said to have rest (cf. 2 Chron 36:21). In neither Deuteronomy nor Leviticus is land considered a commodity, as it is in our time. For further reflection on these themes, see the essays *Land: Gifted and Lost, p. 440; Rest, p. 455.*

A specific parallel to Joshua in the book of Numbers is worth paying attention to here. In Numbers, the Lord announces to Moses that the land shall be divided as an inheritance to the tribes, with large tribes receiving a large inheritance and small tribes receiving a small inheritance (26:52-56). The language used is exactly like that of the book of Joshua, and the narrative that follows includes exactly the same content as the distribution narrative in Joshua. Numbers 27 mentions the daughters of Zelophehad (27:1-11; Josh 17:3-6) and the appointment of Joshua as Moses' successor (Num 27:12-23). Numbers 32, about the conquest of Transjordan and the first conversations with the two and a half tribes, looks forward to that conversation continuing in Joshua 1. Numbers 33–36 continue with divine instruction to Moses about the conquest (33:50-56), boundaries of the land (34:1-15), instructions for distribution

(34:16-28), cities for the Levites (35:1-8; Josh 21), cities of refuge (Num 35:9-15; Josh 20), and inheritance by the daughters of Zelophehad (Num 36:1-13; Josh 17:3-6). The intersection of these texts on inheritance not only sets the book of Joshua in a larger narrative context, but also illustrates that Joshua reflects an intersection of Deuteronomic perspectives and those found in Leviticus and Numbers (often described as priestly perspectives).

This intersection of Joshua and Numbers is particularly interesting in comparison with Ezekiel, where the allotments are divided equally instead of by the size of the tribe (47:14; 48:29). In his eschatological vision, Ezekiel transforms the potential inequity. So also, in the preceding scenario, Ezekiel's cosmic war to end all wars is accomplished without human intervention (Ezek 38–39). Ezekiel transforms the Joshua paradigm of warfare followed by distribution of inheritance. This connection between Joshua and Ezekiel is significant for one other reason.

The allotments announced in Joshua 11:23 are spelled out in Joshua 13–21 (with echoes in Num 32–36). The word *allotments* occurs three times in Joshua (11:23; 12:7; 18:10). Remarkably, only Ezek 48:29 includes both words, "inheritance" and "allotments." This double allusion to Joshua 11:23 (and not to Numbers, where "allotments" does not occur) suggests either that Joshua 11:23 echoes the Ezekiel text, or the Ezekiel text echoes Joshua. If the latter, then Ezekiel implies an equalization and an eschatologization of the tradition. Perhaps by the time of Ezekiel, and into the postexilic period, Joshua had come to be understood not in a literal sense but in a figurative or metaphorical sense. God's distribution transforms inequity so that the Deuteronomic notion of all having enough (Deut 15:4) is imagined even more thoroughly.

A Conversation about "Rest"

The specific notion of rest (*šqṭ*) in Joshua 11:23 (and 14:15) needs to be explored further in relation to other words for rest in the OT. As mentioned in the Explanatory Notes above, the expression refers to cessation of warfare. But this "rest/quietness" to which Joshua 11:23 refers is developed further in the prophetic literature and Chronicles (for further exploration, see the essay *Rest, p. 455*).

First Chronicles 22:9 (NRSV) is illustrative:

> See, a son shall be born to you; he shall be a man of peace [*menuḥah*]. I will give him peace [*nwḥ*] from all his enemies on every side; for his name shall be Solomon, and I will give peace [*šalom*] and quiet [*šqṭ*] to Israel in his days.

Here the noun translated *rest* in Joshua 11:23 (*šqṭ*) is used in God's promise for Solomon along with *šalom* in the expression "peace and *quiet*." Chronicles also uses a verb for "rest" (*nwḥ*), which is more common in Deuteronomy and Joshua, in God's promise to "*give* him *peace* (*nwḥ*, NJPS "rest") from all his enemies" (Deut 3:20; 5:14; 12:10; 25:19; Josh 1:13, 15; 21:44; 22:4; 23:1). In the expression "man of peace" (NJPS "man at rest"), the related noun "peace" (*menuḥah* from the root *nwḥ*) is translated in Deuteronomy 12:9 as "rest" (KJV, NRSV) or "resting place" (NIV). Thus Chronicles' description of God's promise for Solomon weaves together linguistic elements that are common in Deuteronomy and Joshua (root *nwḥ*) and that appear in Joshua 11:23 and 14:15 (*šqṭ*). Chronicles also uses the same verb for "rest" (*šqṭ*) as in Joshua 11:23 to describe the peace during the reigns of Asa and Jehoshaphat (2 Chron 14:1, 5; 20:30). Chronicles, therefore, seems to have blended the vocabulary of rest in Deuteronomy and the DtrH with a clearer and more consistent nonmilitarization theme. Peace and rest are part and parcel of the same divine gift.

This understanding is common also in the so-called Zion tradition. Psalm 76 celebrates God's victory over horse and rider (76:6), an act of judgment with the effect that "the earth feared and was *still* when God rose up to establish judgment, to save all the oppressed of the earth" (76:8b-9). Isaiah uses the word in oracles recommending a stance to take in relation to the threat of the Syro-Ephraimite war: "Take heed, *be quiet*, do not fear, and do not let your heart be faint" (7:4, emph. added). The oracle about the downfall of Babylon celebrates in advance God's victory against "the oppressor" (14:4), resulting in "The whole earth is at rest and *quiet*" (picking up both words in one phrase; 14:7, emph. added). Similar combinations of rest, quietness, peace, and trust are reflected in Isaiah's political vision (30:15; 32:17). Jeremiah's hope for a peaceful return of God's people includes "quiet and ease, and no one shall make him afraid" (Jer 30:10; 46:27).

The lack of finality implied in many texts anticipating rest may be reflected in the narrator's note that Joshua's conflict went on for *a long time* (11:18; cf. Exod 23:30-33). This reflects the reality depicted in the book of Judges (1:1–3:6). There the story begun in the book of Joshua includes summary narratives about Judah, Joseph, Manasseh, Ephraim, Zebulun, Asher, Naphtali, and Dan (Judg 1:1-36). In almost every case there is a similar reference: "could/did not drive out the inhabitants of *x*" (cf. Josh 13:1, 13; etc.). What Joshua 11:18 leaves cryptic, Judges fills out with detail.

Hardening the Heart

The motif of hardening the heart (11:20) occurs most often in the story of the exodus. It appears first in Exod 4:21 and nineteen times before 14:17, using three different verbs translated in NRSV as "to harden" (*ḥzq* in 4:21; 7:13, 22; 8:19; 9:12, 35; 10:20, 27; 11:10; 14:4, 8, 17; *qšh* in 7:3; *kbd* in 7:14; 8:19, 32; 9:7, 34; 10:1). The expression does not mean that God makes Pharaoh exhibit "some sort of emotional insensitivity" (Gilbert: 80). Hence the Lord's "hardening the heart" of Pharaoh allows him to remain "firm in the face of Yahweh's threats and actions. Pharaoh takes courage! He remains strong in the face of this formidable enemy" (Gilbert: 81). Exodus reflects a divine direction for history, but not a control of history. The hardening of Pharaoh's heart is a strengthening of Pharaoh's resolve, not a control of his will. God gives him the ability to carry out his own intentions to the end (Gilbert). In the context of a mythic warfare among the gods, God empowers Pharaoh to do what he wants to do in order that God's strength might be demonstrated fully in his liberation of his people from slavery. The matter turns around the theme of idolatry *[Idolatry, p. 438]*.

Similarly, Boyd suggests that "while Yahweh must genuinely battle with spiritual cosmic rivals, this 'must' is itself something Yahweh himself has brought into being. It need not imply that Yahweh secretly controls his rivals, only that the very power of his rivals to resist him is given by him" (121). According to Boyd, "What is at stake in such wars is not simply earthly territories or the dominion of earthly governments; . . . [it] is the kingly rule of the one true God. The struggle of nations to dominate, or at least to resist, Israel is also, even more fundamentally, a struggle of other gods, with whom these nations are in league, to resist Yahweh" (134). And when Israel aligns itself with other gods, God goes to battle against them (135). "Wherever and whenever a people turn from the Creator God to serve other gods, they and their gods become inextricably linked together as Yahweh enacts judgment against this type of concrete actualization of earthly/cosmic rebellion and chaos" (135; Boyd cites Ollenburger 1994). Israel engages in conflict not primarily through human fighting, but especially by Yahweh's action, a paradigm that is picked up in the final speeches in the book of Joshua (e.g., 24:12; also ch. 6). "In the end," suggests Boyd, "their earthly battles were not really theirs at all: the battle, rather, belonged to the LORD" (135).

In light of such weighty significance, it is odd that only one passage in Deuteronomy refers to the Lord's hardening of the heart

(2:30). The only other place where "hardening the heart" occurs in the DtrH is 1 Sam 6:6, but without mentioning the Lord's initiative in that endeavor. Such sparse usage hardly constitutes a strong thematic element in the history as a whole. But it is telling that in this pivotal passage in Joshua 11, the narrative interprets the events as analogous to the liberation from Egypt.

In Joshua 11:20 the role of divine liberator is supplemented with that of divine judge. God's hardening the hearts of the indigenous population becomes the impetus for carrying out a judgment against the population, as noted in Genesis 15:16: "for the iniquity of the Amorites is not yet complete." That Genesis text also resonates with the book of Joshua in its reference to a return to the land ("They shall come back here in the fourth generation"), in its inclusion of boundary descriptions (15:18), and in its list of ten people groups (15:19-21). The judgment on those nations announced in Genesis 15:16 becomes a warning also to Israel, whose keeping of the land depends on similar criteria of moral judgment (Exod 23:23-33; Lev 26:3-13; Deut 28:1-68). (For in-depth exploration of "hardening the heart," see Meadors.)

Even so, Deuteronomy holds out the hope that even in exile Israel might find that God "will neither abandon you nor destroy you" (4:31). That theological vision allows Israel's theologians to revise the hardness-of-heart motif and apply it not to the action of God but to the recalcitrance of Israel (e.g., Ezek 3:7; 2 Chron 36:13; Ps 95:8; Isa 63:14, 17-18).

Several NT writers develop more extensively the motif of the hardened heart. Mark's Gospel raises the question of whether Jesus' audience has hardened their own hearts and become unresponsive to God (Mark 3:5; 10:5) or whether somehow their hearts have become hardened (passive in Mark 6:52; 8:17). John's Gospel cites Isaiah to imply that God has hardened the hearers' hearts (John 12:40). Paul includes both human and divine hardening (Rom 2:5; 9:18; see Toews; cf. Eph 4:18; Yoder Neufeld 1997). The book of Hebrews uses the hardening motif as a warning by alluding to the wilderness stories (Heb 3:8, 15; 4:7).

THE TEXT IN THE LIFE OF THE CHURCH

Conquest or Rest from War?

The combination of themes in this short textual unit makes for a disturbing conversation in the life of the church. For a Palestinian Christian or Muslim or a North American aboriginal person reading this summary today, the text certainly evokes a sense of horror (Ateek 1995; Warrior). Several observations help us out with this text. First, the narrative uses hyperbolic and stereotypical language rooted in a common ancient Near Eastern theology of divine participation in warfare. Second, as this text and Judges make clear, the process of settlement must have taken hundreds of years. Third, the book of Joshua itself begins to lay out alternatives for redefining the meaning of insider/outsider. Fourth, the emphasis on divine agency in Joshua 11:20, culminating in the end of warfare in verse 23, is part of a larger intrabiblical conversation about how God and people participate together in the ongoing drama of their experience and the ongoing interpretation of that experience in the writing of historical memory like the DtrH.

Ultimately "rest from war" is the goal of the divine trajectory in history. This text cannot, therefore, be read as a justification for conquest or as a basis for action. Yet it is a serious reflection on God's participation in Israel's history from Israel's point of view. It can be labeled "ideological" because the text justifies the killing and dispossession of other peoples. In the context of the larger narrative, however, we do well to remember that Israel was also dispossessed and conquered, first by Assyria and then by Babylon. That too was *the Lord's doing*. Unless we are prepared to remove God entirely from the historical process (which contemporary historiography does), then we do well to linger, however painfully, with this text and others like it. We may disagree with it. We may find ways of explaining its ideology. We may also transform it or render it less harmful by positioning it within a larger conversation so that this text does not have the last word. Yet it cannot be ignored. It remains important for the church to reflect on the character of divine agency in history, and on the related notion that God's aim is restfulness—rest from war as well as rest for obedience (Roth).

Reframing a Difficult Conversation

The divine agency that makes such rest possible for believers (either present or anticipatory) includes coming to terms with divine hardening of the heart. The exodus motif of strengthening Pharaoh's resolve suggests that, even as the narrative reflects a conflict between the gods (Yahweh and Pharaoh), God does not simply control by predetermining Pharaoh's choices (see TBC above). The church, too, does well to reframe the notion of *It was from the Lord* (Josh 11:20 AT) as we reflect on divine agency in history. We should simply acknowledge Israel's historicosymbolic worldview, using common ancient generic literary conventions, sought to account for Israel's survival in a hostile world. The argument may appear to shift the blame for warfare onto God, but it actually recognizes that a subversion of language fuels the imagination to resist a warfare paradigm and offer an alternative vision of divine agency in conversation with human faithfulness. Israel's historians ascribed the battle to the Lord because they perceived their warfare as participating in God's cosmic battle against evil (Boyd: 133–35).

Subverting warfare language by following Ephesians and other NT texts that refer to "spiritual warfare," the church does well to embrace prayer as the Christian's weapon. Practiced with the conviction that Christ has defeated the powers of evil, prayer is the Christian's primary mode of resistance against evil. As Boyd puts it, "You are defeated" is the verbal proclamation "wherever there is destruction, hatred, apathy, injustice, pain or hopelessness, whether it concerns God's creation, a structural feature of society, or the physical, psychological or spiritual aspect of an individual" (254–55). Transposing the text in this way does not preclude other nonviolent modes of resistance against evil. It allows the church, however, to recognize that Israel's discourse about warfare is embedded in *their* ancient warfare worldview, and then to transpose it as the book of Chronicles and the NT writers have begun to do.

The conversation continues only by exposing the complexity of Israel's worldview and the struggle for monotheizing—for claiming Yahweh as the only God and Lord of all, who seeks wholeness and peace on earth. As in Deuteronomy 32:7-9, the nations are assigned either "sons of God" or "angels/messengers of God" (depending on the textual versions), and God (Yahweh) has Israel as his "portion/inheritance." As Boyd puts it, "The members of his heavenly council rule other nations, but it is ultimately Yahweh who rules the whole earth through them" as a kind of "delegated authority" (135–36). The role of these "gods" "was to oversee the welfare of the nation assigned to them, not to become surrogate objects of devotion in place of the Lord himself. When they fail in this duty, they become evil and are judged" (136; cf. Pss 82; 103:21; 148:1-6) *[Idolatry, p. 438]*.

All of this should be folded into understanding the extermination of the nations in Joshua, for the book includes the polemic against the gods, which is transferred to warfare against the people governed by those gods. All of that is grounded in a cosmology—a worldview—that assumes a certain way of reading how the gods interact with the world. If the people are exterminated, the gods will not be a threat *[Conquest Accounts, p. 406]*. Yet the book of Joshua also includes a countertheme that undermines (but does not soften) the harshness of the extermination. God's direction of history (Josh 11:20) is mirrored by the call for Israel to be faithful to God's instruction in the speeches at the beginning and end of the book. The book of Joshua therefore also warns that it may become *the Lord's doing* to strengthen Israel's resolve to depart from faithfulness to God and thereby to bring judgment on Israel (24:19-20). Exile becomes the flip side of the coin of possession of land.

Thus the book of Joshua does not support the conclusion that "God is in control" in the sense that God predetermines peoples' and nations' and individuals' actions. The aim of the book is to foster a faithful people, and to do so by affirming that God is responsive to the choices all peoples make in their world. Joshua 11:20 can be understood to suggest God's judging role as that role is exercised in partnership with Israel. But partnership with Israel in warfare is not the normative and prescriptive way of God for the nations in other parts of the Bible. It is so presented here because the narrative participates in the Deuteronomic language game and in the common fund of theopolitical vocabulary available in the ancient world. The book of Joshua as a whole modifies that vocabulary by setting it into the larger context of God's instruction and in the reality of later exile from the land. Measured against the larger canonical context as well, God's judging activity concerns the doing of justice (e.g., Ps 82; Amos 1–2; Matt 25:31-46). In addition, we might consider the Lord's initiative (Josh 11:20) as part of the tradition to which Paul refers in Romans 1. Human choices have consequences. And the Lord will honor, will not thwart, and will even strengthen human resolve to oppose divine sovereignty in history.

In Romans as in the context of Deuteronomy and the DtrH, the struggle is primarily against the worship of other gods. This can be read as a tragic limitation of the biblical warfare narrative if we read flatly from the text that God continues to wage war against people of this world who worship differently. Transposing this language into a pure "battle against evil" is difficult since in human experience evil is almost always embodied and ambiguous. Hence God's battle against evil is a battle against people, even though we realize that the struggle against evil begins first of all in every human heart. Thus it seems fair to say, with Boyd, that God is "at war with evil" (291), without assuming that God is in control of the war. Evil is a "hostile alien intrusion" (291).

We must add, however, that the Canaanites are slaughtered because Israel can only express divine sovereignty and the struggle against evil in terms of the conventional language and genre of ancient conquest narratives. Shall we go as far as Fretheim does when he claims that because God is fundamentally a relational God, God is present "in every event, no matter how heroic or Hitlerian," at work for "the best possible future for all creation" (1999: 346)? If so, then God's self-limitation means that the historical process is also a "continuing grieving of the heart" of God (348).

We do well to adopt a less historical and more eschatological solution. As Fretheim suggests, the Bible does not offer "the hope that God has a higher, all-encompassing plan that secretly governs every event, including the evil intentions of malicious angelic and human beings, and that somehow renders these evil wills 'good' at a higher level" (292–93). Rather, "the ultimate hope that the New Testament offers is eschatological" (293). The book of Joshua moves in that direction by bringing the land to a place of rest from war so that obedience might be fostered. In that light, the eschatological vision is visible as a crack of light beginning in those places where human beings live in the light of God's instruction because God strengthens their hearts to do so (Jer 31:33; Ezek 36:26). That is the goal of the eschatologization of the Joshua story that continues on in the interpretive tradition of the early church and beyond. Eschatology becomes ethics in hope of divine transformation of all things. The new heart supplants the hardened heart even though, ironically, God is the agent of both transformations. The first is not an end, but a beginning. The first shares in Israel's warfare; the second transforms it into peaceful sharing in the divine kingdom of peace and "rest from war." Origen understands the trajectory from Joshua to Jesus, affirming rest from war in Jesus Christ, but not without engaging in conflict through the spiritual sword of the word (149–50).

Joshua 12:1-24

Kings Conquered East and West of the Jordan

PREVIEW

On arriving at chapter 12, readers may feel like hikers who need to stop to catch their breath, take stock, look back, and look ahead. In literary terms, it might be said that chapter 12 is a hinge that binds the main parts of the book together. It looks backward by presenting a list of kings who governed the various regions taken by Israel, both east and west of the Jordan. In doing so, it says more than the previous chapters tell. Many more kings are listed here than are included in the previous conquest accounts. And it looks ahead by providing the rationale for the distribution or the allotment of the land in chapters 13–21. Chapter 12 is at the heart of the book since it gives notice that these "kings" no longer govern. Rather, it is *Moses, the servant of the Lord* whose instructions shape a different kind of political entity. The chapter makes explicit that what Moses began east of the Jordan, Joshua has completed west of the Jordan. The chapter also reminds readers of the promises made in Joshua 1 and recalls the stories of the Transjordan tribes in the book of Numbers *[Transjordan Tribes, p. 464]*.

The temporal location of the entire chapter seems to belong after Joshua's distribution of the land, yet it stands as an anticipatory summary that links conquest (chs. 1–11) with distribution (chs. 13–21). Just as 11:23 ends the entrance-into-the-land narrative with a notice about *rest*, so 21:43-45 summarizes again the giving and possessing that results in *rest*—all based on the *good promises* of God having come to fruition. Just as 11:20 establishes God as the one who has jurisdiction in the region, chapter 12 identifies *kings* as having *ruled* (12:2, 5).

This hinge chapter allows us to fold the book in half so that the end of chapter 11 corresponds to the beginning of chapter 13. And the interaction of the two and a half tribes (ch. 22), the speeches of Joshua, and the covenant commitments in chapters 23–24—all correspond to God's initial speeches and the interaction with the two and a half tribes in Joshua 1.

OUTLINE

Moses' Victories over Kings East of the Jordan, 12:1-6
Joshua's Victories over Kings West of the Jordan, 12:7-24

EXPLANATORY NOTES

Moses' Victories over Kings East of the Jordan 12:1-6

The stories of the kings who *ruled* (vv. 2, 5) east of the Jordan are told in Num 21:21-35 and Deuteronomy 2–3. In the book of Joshua we find no conquest narrative that describes those events. Joshua 12:1-6 is a simple summary that highlights *Moses, the servant of the* Lord, who along with the Israelites *defeated them and . . . gave their land for a possession* to the two and a half Transjordan tribes (12:6; for reflection on the motif of *Moses, servant of the* Lord, see Josh 1). All the references to Moses as servant deal with what Moses said or did east of the Jordan (Josh 1:1, 2, 7, 13, 15; 8:31, 33; 9:24; 11:12, 15; 13:8; 14:7; 18:7; 22:2, 4, 5). In the book of Joshua, Israel hears instructions from the Lord as those were mediated earlier by Moses. Moses is a key figure in marking transitional moments, especially in Joshua 1; 8:30-35; and chapter 22. That Joshua 12:1-6 mentions Moses as the one who *gave* the land to the two and a half tribes east of the Jordan is odd. In Deuteronomy 2–3 this same land is said to be "given" by the Lord. Now in Joshua 12, Moses takes on the role of governor-general (or vice-regent), as God's stand-in, who now *gives the land* to them (v. 6). That motif is repeated in the threefold reference to Moses in Joshua 22 (vv. 2, 4, 5), where the two and a half tribes' connection to Moses may be part of the conflict between them and the tribes west of the Jordan. In any case, Joshua 12 confirms the transfer of authority to Joshua as God's governor-general west of the Jordan, a fact that is confirmed later by the naming of Joshua as *servant of the* Lord in Joshua 24:29 [*Characterization of Joshua, p. 394*].

Joshua's Victories over Kings West of the Jordan 12:7-24

Whereas verses 1-6 begin with Israelites defeating the kings and end with Moses' giving the land, verses 7-24 emphasize Joshua at the beginning without excluding the Israelites. Twice Joshua is mentioned in verse 7. Now, instead of Moses (v. 6), Joshua *gave their land . . . as a possession according to their allotments* (v. 7; cf. 11:23).

Although verses 1-6 mention only two kings, whose conquest was narrated in Numbers 21:21-35 and Deuteronomy 2–3, verses 7-24 list thirty-one kings whose territory extended from the coastal plain to the Jordan valley and from the area near Mount Hermon in the north to the southern desert (the Negeb; vv. 7-8). The six people groups (v. 8b) are those mentioned elsewhere (see Josh 3:10). Of the thirty-one kings mentioned in verses 9-24, we see sixteen named in chapters 6–10. Conquest accounts naming four of the remaining kings are found in other places outside Joshua: Hormah and Arad (v. 14; Num 21:1-3; Judg 1:16-17); Bethel (Judg 1:22-26); and Taanach (Judg 5:19). All can be identified except for Lasharon (v. 18) and Goiim (v. 23). Although Joshua 12:7-24 asserts that Joshua has conquered all these kings (and presumably their cities as well), the first chapter of the book of Judges indicates that some of these cities were captured after the death of Joshua (Jerusalem, 1:8; Hebron, 1:10; Debir, 1:11; Hormah, 1:17; Bethel, 1:22), and that indigenous inhabitants continue to live in some of those unconquered towns (Jerusalem, 1:21; Taanach, Dor, and Megiddo, 1:27; Gezer, 1:29). Similar notices about remaining population groups also occur in Joshua 13–21. The name Hormah (Josh 12:14) is given an explanation (etiology) in Judges 1:17. According to 2 Samuel 5, Jerusalem is not captured until the time of David. Joshua 12 cannot be harmonized with Judges 1 by suggesting that Joshua 12 lists only the defeat of the kings, and Judges 1 refers to the capture of the towns. Such harmonization diminishes the deliberate idealization of the conquest in Joshua 1–12.

Because of the summarizing function of Joshua 12, it is better to consider the chapter as a conventional generic list that summarizes the totality of the conquest (Younger 1990: 230–32), and that justifies the distribution of the land that follows. What Moses began, Joshua finishes, as though all of this has been done during Joshua's lifetime. The list emphasizes the transition from Moses to Joshua, indicated already in Joshua 1 and finalized in Joshua 24 in the naming of Joshua as *servant of the Lord*. The list also emphasizes the fullness of the divine gift of land, as mediated through Moses and Joshua. The chapter has a literary function in the book that does not reflect the actual events. It signifies completion. It complements *all that land* of Joshua 11:16, 23. And it anticipates the motif of promises fulfilled, found at the end of the book of Joshua (23:14).

Joshua 12, as a hinge between the conquest and the distribution, is best read in anticipation of 13:1. It makes a case for the completeness of the conquest. It comes after the summarizing of 11:16-23 and makes a transition into the next long section that concludes in similar summarizing fashion in 21:43-45. Chapter 12, with its border descriptions, also ties together the first half of Joshua by alluding to the boundary description in 1:4. The mention of as many "kings" as we find in chapter 12 also stands in contrast to the fact that although Joshua is presented as a "royal" figure, he does not reign [*Characterization of Joshua, p. 394*]. In the book of Joshua, Israel is invited to exclusive allegiance to the one Sovereign over all nations, whose active agency in history has given Israel this land, yet has allowed Others to remain among them *to this day*, a motif developed in chapter 13 and following. There, both distribution of land and living with the indigenous population jostles the reader into thinking about the anomaly of having defeated (12:1, 7) and having "occupied" (12:1), yet not dispossessing or driving out earlier inhabitants (13:1). Israel's challenge, in reality, will be to live faithfully, obedient to God, among the peoples.

THE TEXT IN BIBLICAL CONTEXT

Royal Rule Transformed

The fact that these kings are said to have *ruled* is significant to the larger story, in which the one who rules also shapes the character of the community under his dominion. The exercise of kingly rule is usually expressed by the verb *malak*, a cognate of the noun "king" (*melek*). But here the verb "to rule" is *mašal* (in Gen 37:8 both verbs are used as synonyms). This verb has an odd usage, almost never referring to an Israelite king. Only Solomon's rule is described this way, and likely in an ironic or polemical sense, since the noun *mašal* also means "proverb" (1 Kings 4:21). The word is almost always used either of foreign kings who rule over Israel or, by contrast, of God, who rules over Israel (cf. the verb *radah*, "to have dominion," in Gen 1:26, 28 KJV; Isa 14:2, 6; in both texts, as in Joshua, "rest" is the aim [Gen 2:2-3; Isa 14:7]). It seems as though there are only two options for ruler: either God or kings like these. This verb "to rule" (*mašal*) is used only once in Deuteronomy (15:6) and seldom in the DtrH (Judg 8:22, 23; 9:2; 14:4; 15:11; cf. Ps 106:41; Lam 5:8). The verb occurs in a poem about "ruling justly" (2 Sam 23:3), which becomes the benchmark against which Solomon is judged. The Psalms speak of humankind as "ruling," or "having dominion" (8:6), and of the Lord as ruling "over the nations" (22:28), "over Jacob" (59:13), over "the raging sea" (89:9), and "over all" (103:19; cf. 66:7). Zechariah announces a "Branch" who rules alongside the priest Joshua (6:12-13). That "king" who "comes to you . . . on a donkey" will "cut off the chariot . . . and the war-horse, . . . and he shall command peace to the nations; his *dominion* [noun *mošel*] shall be from sea to sea, and from the River to the ends of the earth" (9:9-10; cf. boundary descriptions in Josh 1). Micah anticipates a just ruler on God's behalf (5:2-4), just as Jeremiah looks forward to another "David," ruling with justice (22:30). Isaiah both laments the poor rulers and acknowledges the Lord as the only true ruler (40:10; 63:19; cf. Isa 14:1-6).

All of that is to remind us that the kings mentioned in Joshua 12 are those with *horses and chariots* (11:4). By default, such power cannot bring *rest from war* (11:23). Their rule is inimical to God's intention, however awkwardly we may need to say that as we engage in our conversation with the text *[Horses and Chariots, p. 434]*.

THE TEXT IN THE LIFE OF THE CHURCH

Between the Times

Joshua 12 rarely, if ever, enters the conversation of the church's life. The chapter is best understood as a hinge between the two major sections of the book of Joshua, concluding the first and making a transition into the second. In doing so, the chapter highlights an ironic meditation on the tension between completeness (11:16-24) and incompleteness (13:1). In a figural reading we might suggest a similarly analogous way of being for the church that lives, as it were, in the meantime. In his death on the cross, Christ has conquered the powers and all that is antagonistic to the divine rule in the world. Yet the church awaits the time when God will transform Christ's resurrection, which is yet only a harbinger of the life to come, into a transformation of all things *[Figural Reading, p. 426]*.

Without denigrating the terrifying carnage associated with the defeat of the kings mentioned in Joshua 12, and in the context of the already/not yet tension in the book of Joshua, we see a similar analogy of experience in the life of faith. Many readers of Joshua will find such an analogy either absurd or offensive. Still, one may point out that the literary-theological structure of the book of Joshua resonates with the NT emphasis on living between cross and new creation. Even more radically, we may read this text as completely transformed by Jesus' beatitude "Blessed are the meek, for they will inherit the earth" (Matt 5:5). Although Jesus is likely transposing Psalm 37:11, his eschatological imagination also draws on the hopefulness of the psalmist who writes that in waiting for the Lord, one is assured that the "wicked will be no more" (Ps 37:9-10) *[Conquest and Land in the NT, p. 411]*.

Part 2

Distributing the Land

Joshua 13–24

OVERVIEW

Joshua 13:1 marks the beginning of the second main section of the book of Joshua. Chapter 13 begins the distribution of the land, setting up the mirror image of the book in which the last twelve chapters mirror the first twelve in a roughly chiastic pattern. The division of the land, beginning in chapter 13, mirrors the conquest of the land in the previous chapters (Winther-Nielsen: 264).

Although the distribution of the land has often been perceived as a sequence of boundary lists and city lists in chapters 13–21 (Hess 2005), the narrator has actually incorporated the distribution lists into an interactive narrative that begins with divine instruction in 13:1-7a. The mixture of lists and interactions allows the reader to place the lists into a narrative sequence and gives the distribution a realistic point of view. As with Joshua 1–12, chapters 13 and following offer a perspective we might call telescoped time. Narrative time has collapsed so as to indicate that all the land was distributed, just as all the land was conquered in Joshua 1–12.

Joshua 13:1-7 presents "God's third initiative" (after 1:1-9 and 5:13–6:5; Koorevaar: 288). According to Koorevaar, chapters 13–21 are one long unit, introduced by 13:1-7 and drawn to a conclusion in 21:43-45. The first initiative focuses on the crossing, the second on the taking, and now the third on dividing, which is reflected in the verb *halak*, "to divide, allot, apportion," in 13:7. Although 21:43-45 is a summary paragraph, it is more like the summary at 11:16-23. Joshua 19:49-51 brings a more likely conclusion to the distribution of the land, with its concluding statement, *So they finished dividing the land.* Still, Koorevaar's suggestion is intriguing if we also consider his suggestion of a chiastic structure between 13:1-7 and

21:43-45. If 21:43-45 reflects an overarching synthesis that parallels 11:16-23, then 13:1-7 forms a fitting introduction to a sequence that has, as its middle segment, the episode set at Shiloh's tent of meeting in 18:1-10. That episode stands in the middle since everything before it concerns the two and a half Transjordan tribes (Reuben, Gad, and half the tribe of Manasseh), Judah (including Caleb), and the Joseph tribes (Manasseh and Ephraim) *[Transjordan Tribes, p. 464]*. After the Shiloh episode in 18:1-10, only seven tribes remain, beginning with Benjamin, the youngest of Jacob's sons. According to Koorevaar, "the Tent of Meeting at Shiloh is situated in the center of the third main section and expresses the structural purpose of the whole book of Joshua. The erection of the Tent of Meeting at Shiloh is the fulfillment of an important promise in the Pentateuch: 'I will put my dwelling place among you, and I will not abhor you. I will walk among you and be your God, and you will be my people,' Lev 26:11-12." (Koorevaar's suggestion is linked to his thesis that the book of Joshua includes twenty-eight sections, the sum of numbers one to seven [Koorevaar: 290].)

Another way of seeing the place of 13:1-7 is to notice how the sequence that follows in 13:8-33 deals with the two and a half tribes. The final episode that deals with those tribes is 22:1-34. Although 21:43-45 draws the distribution to a close, chapter 22 rounds out the story line of the distribution by resolving the tension between east and west, between inside and outside *[Plot Tensions in Joshua, p. 452]*. And chapter 22 draws the whole book together by connecting not only the beginning and end of the distribution section (chs. 13–22), but also by connecting the distribution to Joshua's first encounter with the Transjordan tribes in 1:12-18. Moreover, 13:1 begins with a mention of Joshua's old age, which is repeated as the introduction to the final segments of the book in 23:1.

On the surface, chapters 1–12 tell the story of how Israel enters the land and, against all odds, takes the land from the indigenous population. The second section of the book (chs. 13–21), on the surface, suggests that Israel allotted the land to tribal and family groups. I use the phrase "on the surface" because a closer look reveals more complexity in the story as a whole. The text reveals tensions between the total conquest depicted in chapters 1–12 (and summarized in 11:16-23) and the partial conquest depicted in chapters 13 and following. From a flat reading of the book, a reader might ask, "Were all the inhabitants dispossessed (chs. 1–12), or did some remain (chs. 13–21)?" In spite of the hyperbolic statements of 11:16-23, other notations in chapters 13 and following suggest that the resulting situation was more complex than a thoroughgoing conquest. Thus the summary statements of Joshua 21:43-45 and 23:14-15 are significantly different from that of 11:16-23, for those later summaries do not depict the utter destruction of the enemy.

Yet already in chapter 2 we have learned of Rahab and her family, who continue to reside in Israel's midst. And chapter 9 tells us of the Gibeonites, even as 8:30-35 hints at indigenous peoples (*aliens*) among them. In chapters 13 and following, we also discover that Geshurites remain (13:13), as do Jebusites (15:63) and Canaanites of Gezer (16:10). On occasion throughout the commentary, we have noticed that the commands in Deuteronomy 7:1-2 and 20:16 specify "not only dispossession of the inhabitants but also their total removal" (Gunn: 108). The tension between the two parts of the book is palpable. Joshua 11:23 states that *Joshua took the whole land*, yet Joshua 13:1 admits, *Very much of the land still remains to be possessed.* Gunn's solution is not the only one possible, but it will help us on our way: "If we observe both the temporal ambiguities fostered by the allotment accounts and the sporadic itemizing of the *remnant* nations, we shall be less surprised to discover by chapter 18 that seven tribes still await even the process of allotment, let alone have taken possession of their inheritance" (108). Thus when we arrive at Joshua 18:3 and hear Joshua ask, *How long will you be slack about going in and taking possession of the land that the* L*ORD*, *the God of your ancestors, has given you?* we may wonder not only about the sequence of events, but also about the way the entire section is structured. Perhaps we are dealing with hyperbole or irony, as Gunn suggests (108). Or perhaps the distribution in chapters 13–17 is deliberately placed so as to provide a contrast to the seven remaining tribes, whose allotment is sketched in chapters 18 and following. Just as the "conquest" itself is incomplete, so also the distribution perhaps remains incomplete. And in the end, even the shape of Israel as a people in a bounded land remains unresolved (as ch. 22 implies). Only chapters 23–24 bring a kind of resolution to both incomplete conquest and incomplete distribution.

Since Joshua 13:1 and 23:1 begin in the same way, chapter 23 takes up where 13:1 left off. Joshua 13:1-7a and 22:1-34 are narrative accounts. Joshua 13:1-7a introduces the distribution narrative that follows, which begins with the distribution of land to the two and a half Transjordan tribes (13:8-33) and ends with a conflict between the Transjordan tribes and the tribes west of the Jordan (22:1-34). Between these framing accounts are both distribution lists (like those of 13:7b-33) and short narrative/action sequences. The first words of chapter 13, *Now Joshua was old and advanced in years*, which are picked up again in 23:1, suggest that the material between the two age notices is a kind of parenthesis. Viewed that way, 13:1 functions "as if formally to declare a halt, a shift from the narrative of action to the rhetoric of listing and ordering" (Gunn: 102).

What is the purpose of this shift, which marks the major transition in the book? Gunn suggests, "As in Numbers (or Chronicles), listing subdues narrative here, building a land and community out of names and connectives, though occasionally narrated speech and activity push through." Such narration interrupts the distribution section in four places, in addition to the beginning and end sequences of 13:1-7a and 22:1-34 (14:6-15; 17:3-6; 17:14-18; 18:2-10). "But we miss something of the book's special texture if we allow our taste for action or character development to deflect us from this more static, administrative prose. For out of it arises a powerful sense of the myriad elements that constitute 'the people.' 'Israel' takes on substance, as does the task at hand; for the challenge to Israel is to translate those lists and allotments into an actual community in actual possession of the Promised Land" (Gunn: 102–3). The distribution of the land is not simple reporting that draws only on official records and lists (although the authors may well have done so). These chapters include stories, as did chapters 1–12, that reflect on peoplehood and promise. Stories like those of Caleb (chs. 14–15), the daughters of Zelophehad (ch. 17), the protests of the Joseph tribes (ch. 17) and the Transjordan tribes (ch. 22)—such accounts are drawn in as though completing the narrative begun in the book of Numbers. Theological reflection in chapters 13–24 also draws on Deuteronomy's covenantal notion of obedience and love (e.g., Josh 22:5-6).

In other words, because of the telescoped time of the narrative, chapters 1–12 do not simply reflect an "easy success," with chapters 13–21 depicting a "scrupulously fulfilled" allotment based on Moses' instructions in Numbers 34 (Gunn: 103). Rather, as Gunn suggests, chapters 13–24 continue with a kind of narrative density that pushes readers to ask, "Are we dealing with the ideal or the actual? And within what time frame—with reference to narrated time, the narrator's time, or the implied reader's time—might that actuality be located? Or do we slide between prescription and fulfillment?" (103). Or, even more likely, the plot of the book of Joshua is on a trajectory that begins with a call to Joshua to Torah faithfulness in chapter 1 and moves through (incomplete) conquest and (incomplete) distribution to completion in covenantal faithfulness of the people in chapters 23–24. That is the real direction of the plot of this complex story.

Joshua 13:1–14:5

Very Much Remains to Be Possessed

PREVIEW

A good conflict story often surprises the reader by apparent endings and incomplete resolutions. Just when we think a conflict has been resolved, a new one emerges. It is as though the story is forever living between problem and resolution. In the last section of J. R. R. Tolkien's *The Lord of the Rings* (1954–55), the hobbits return to the Shire and find ruffians intimidating the locals. They must decide whether or not to live as though there is a new king in the land, a king whose rule has not yet been announced. The hobbits decide to act as the new king's agents and do according to his will. Similarly, readers of Joshua might be surprised to discover that in Joshua's old age much of the land remains to be possessed (13:1), especially after having read the summary of a thoroughgoing conquest in 11:16-23 and the rather complete list of conquered kings in chapter 12. Following up on the narrative resolutions of chapters 11–12, this text unit introduces the ambiguity of an incomplete conquest set over against the incomplete occupation of the land that follows. Moreover, the chapter begins with a divine promise to *drive out* those indigenous inhabitants who remain (13:6). All of that conspires together with Joshua's mention in chapter 23 that under certain conditions the Lord would not drive out the remaining peoples, but that Israel would *perish from this good land* (23:13). Immediately following that announcement, Joshua acknowledges *that not one thing has failed of all the good things that the Lord your God promised* (23:14), although perishing is still a possibility (23:16; cf. Deut 8:20).

Joshua 1–12 also reflects an emphasis on divine-human cooperation based on faithfulness to divine instruction (Torah), whereas this unit places Israel's responsiveness into the context where not everything has been accomplished. Chapters 1–12 appear to present an "idealized world," and chapter 13 presents an introduction to a "realized world," which not only introduces the second half of the book of Joshua but also prepares readers for the drama of both possession and loss of land, of both life in the good land and the possibility of perishing from it.

The text falls into three parts: an opening section (13:1-7a), followed by distribution to the two and a half Transjordan tribes (13:7b-33), and a closing (14:1-5). The introduction closes with God's command to *divide this land* (13:7a), and the unit closes with a confirmation that the Israelites *allotted the land* (14:5). Those two verses are also similar in their reference to the nine and a half tribes. The unit serves as an introduction to the distribution west of the Jordan that begins in 14:6. The flashback to the Transjordan tribes in 13:8-33 provides a context for what follows by linking the distribution to Moses' (and God's) initiative. It also reintroduces the Transjordan tribes, who have prominent places in Joshua 1 and at the end of the distribution in chapter 22. The Transjordan tribes frame chapters 13–22 and provide a point of reference for reflecting on the meaning of boundaries and of peoplehood *[Transjordan Tribes, p. 464]*.

OUTLINE

Setting the Stage, 13:1-7
Transjordan Inheritance, 13:8-33
Summary and Preview, 14:1-5

EXPLANATORY NOTES

Setting the Stage 13:1-7

The second main section of the book begins with a double reference to Joshua's old age, once by the narrator and once by God (v. 1). The same emphasis is repeated in 23:1, reminding the reader of the importance of what lies in between. The point of 13:1 is not simply Joshua's age, but also that God speaks about the fact that *very much of the land still remains to be possessed* (v. 1b) and then maps out the territory. Verses 2-6b chart that territory by listing the outlying areas (not the central hill country of Ephraim and Judah). Verses

1b-7 are a divine speech, which marks the words as having special significance.

The Lord has spoken throughout the first chapters of Joshua. Only 1:2-9 and 6:2-5 compare in length and significance. The speech in chapter 13, however, does more than instruct in the next step of the process: *Divide this land* (v. 7a). It also serves as a midbook interpretive parenthesis, forming a transition between the selective conquest accounts of chapters 6–12 and the distribution accounts, which begin in 13:8. And it forms the follow-up to the divine speech in Joshua 1. There the emphasis is on gift; here it is on receiving.

The Lord's interpretation of the current state of affairs is odd because of the comments that frame the geographic description, especially in the light of previous references to *the whole land* (2:3; 10:40; 11:16, 23): Joshua is said to have *searched out, defeated*, and *taken* the whole land. In 13:1 the fact that land remains to be possessed (or conquered?) seems not to trouble the Lord: as he states in verse 6, *I will myself drive them out from before the Israelites*. The Lord's statement echoes Joshua's in 3:10, where Joshua states that God will *drive out* the indigenous population. The verb *yaraš* appears twenty-nine times in the book of Joshua and is translated variously as *possess, dispossess, occupy*, or *drive out* (depending on the form used and the context; see also 13:12-13; 23:5, 9, 13; 24:8; cf. 24:12). Fishbane translates the word as "wipe out" (203). In Deuteronomy the same verb is used in two different ways in the same sentence ("drive out" and "dispossess," in 11:23). Here the verb appears in Joshua 13:1 and 6, first with the meaning "to possess," and then with the meaning "to drive out/dispossess" followed by the plural pronoun *them* (NRSV). After all, according to 1:11, 15, the Lord is the one *giving* the land.

The book of Joshua reflects a tension between the Lord's and Israel's actions. Even more important is the repetition of the verb throughout the following chapters in contexts where the narrator makes a point of saying that Israel did not or could not *drive out* the indigenous inhabitants (e.g., 13:13; 15:63; 16:10; 17:13). And then in Joshua 23:12-13 we read the ominous note that if Israel should *turn back and join* the people remaining, then *the* Lord *your God will not continue to drive out these nations before you* (emph. added). These nations that remain will become *a snare and a trap for you, a scourge on your sides, and thorns in your eyes, until you perish from this good land that the* Lord *your God has given you*. Thus the driving out is not a simple matter. First, it is the Lord who says he will do it. Then Israel is not able to do it. And finally, should certain conditions prevail, the Lord will cease doing it (as Judg 2:21 confirms).

But for now, according to Joshua 13:6, the matter is in God's hands. Joshua is to do next only what God commands him to do: *Allot the land to Israel for an inheritance.* The instruction is punctuated with *as I have commanded you.* Moses seems no longer to be the mediator of the divine word. Joshua is to *divide this land*, or apportion or allot it, to nine and a half tribes (including half the tribe of Manasseh) west of the Jordan.

Every mention of *inheritance* from chapter 13 onward refers to the portion of the land determined by Joshua to be the *hereditary portions* (13:7 NJPS) of each group. Yet there are significant exceptions: Caleb (14:13-14), Joshua (19:49-50), the daughters of Zelophehad (17:3-6), and Levites (21:3). Even territory not conquered is considered *inheritance* (23:4), which corresponds to the *very much* that *remains to be possessed* of 13:1. Although 11:23 identifies Joshua as the one who gives Israel their inheritance by tribal allotments, in the second section of the book, both Joshua and Eleazar together distribute the inheritance (14:1; 17:4; 19:51; 21:1). The distribution to the tribal groups ends with the summary in 19:51 (note esp. the expression *finished dividing the land*, with its echoes of Gen 2:1-3). At the end of the book, Joshua alone sends *the people away to their* respective *inheritances* (24:28).

Having given the command, the text turns immediately to a recap of the land distributed by Moses to the Transjordan tribes. Why Manasseh is divided into two parts is not explained here or elsewhere in the book of Joshua (see also 13:29-31; 17:1-6) *[Transjordan Tribes, p. 464]*.

Transjordan Inheritance 13:8-33

The narrator moves from the divine command to *divide this land* (v. 7), referring presumably to the land west of the Jordan, to a flashback summary of the land that the two and a half tribes *received*, and which *Moses . . . gave them* to the east of the Jordan (v. 8). The giving is mentioned twice in verse 8, the second time emphasizing Moses' role as *servant of the Lord*. Moses is referred to as *servant of the Lord* only in Deuteronomy 34:5, then fourteen times in Joshua (see ch. 1), and again in 2 Kings 18:12. Joshua is named *servant of the Lord* only in Joshua 24:29 and Judges 2:8. The emphasis in Joshua serves to highlight the importance of covenantal faithfulness through the mediated divine word, an emphasis that is tragically recalled in 2 Kings 18:12 where Israel "did not obey the voice of the Lord."

The summary of Joshua 13:8 mirrors 12:1-5 and reflects Deuteronomy 3:8-10. The boundaries and districts are classified generally in Joshua 13:9-12. Verse 13 introduces the first of several statements that highlight the limits of Israel's conquest: like Rahab and the Gibeonites, *Geshur and Maacath live within Israel to this day* (cf. 15:63; 16:10; 17:13). In spite of the thoroughness of the conquest highlighted in 11:16-23, Israel's conquest does not cleanse the land of Canaanites.

Verse 14 highlights the fact that the tribe of Levi received no inheritance from Moses (repeated in 13:33; 14:3, 4; 18:7), which will be confirmed and modified slightly in chapter 21, when the Levites are given towns and pastureland throughout the various tribes (cf. Deut 18:1-2 on the Levites' inheritance of *offerings by fire* [Josh 13:14]). Thus 13:8-14 introduces the flashback sequence of allotments east of the Jordan and forms an introduction for the later chapters that deal with the Levites (ch. 21) and the Transjordan tribes (ch. 22). So also mention of the Levites in verse 14, with its recurrence in 13:33, frames the entire unit of Transjordan distribution.

Verses 15-23 summarize the territory of Reuben, Jacob's firstborn son, highlighting again Moses' action (v. 15). The distribution is *according to their clans* (v. 15), which is a social grouping between tribe and household, even though the NRSV sometimes translates the same Hebrew word as "families" (for a clear distinction among the three social groups, see 7:14). The word *clans* occurs throughout the distribution in chapters 13–19. In the mention of Moses' defeating Sihon and his allies (v. 21), the word *with* (NRSV) means "along with," not "with the help of." In a strange aside, verse 22 identifies one of Israel's victims as *Balaam*, whom Israelites killed because he *practiced divination*. He is known from the stories of Numbers 22–24 and in extrabiblical texts found at Tell Deir 'Allā (in Jordan) in 1967. The aside here highlights the supposed danger that, despite God's using him as a mediator of the divine word, Balaam represents practices that (in the Deuteronomic worldview) are considered inimical to exclusive worship of God.

Balaam's death, along with that of the coalition leaders, is also reported in parallel statements in Numbers 31:8, 16. There he is accused of having "made the Israelites act treacherously against the Lord in the affair of Peor" (31:16). These intertextual allusions remind us of the significance of the Transjordan tribes in Joshua 1:12-17 and of the irony implied in the setting of Shittim in Joshua 2:1 (cf. Num 25:1). Balaam is an ambiguous figure who represents the Lord's instrument (in Numbers), but who is also perceived as representing the threat of pagan divination. Hence the book of Joshua notes Balaam's death to suggest that with the removal of such divination, Israel might be prevented from being unfaithful in its allegiance to God. Yet even the book of Joshua (esp. in chs. 23–24) offers hints that such unstinting obedience will not (or cannot) last.

The description of the territories of Gad and Manasseh in Transjordan proceeds in the same way, with a listing of towns and borders (vv. 24-27, 29-31). Half the tribe of Manasseh receives land in Transjordan, and the other half west of the Jordan (see Josh 17:1-13). Verse 31 seems to identify the half-tribe of Manasseh with *half the Machirites* (cf. 17:1; Judg 5:14).

The Levites are mentioned again in verses 32-33, but this time without mention of sacrifices, as in verse 14. Here *the LORD God of Israel is their inheritance*, which is a clear echo of Deuteronomy 18:2. Are the Levites symbolically significant in the distribution? Are they a paradigm of life without possession of land? For further reflection on the place of Levites in Joshua, see chapter 21.

Summary and Preview 14:1-5

A summary preview of the west-of-Jordan inheritances rounds out the episode. The subunit is a bridge between chapter 13 and the distribution to the remaining tribes, beginning in 14:6. Verses 3-4 refer back to the two and a half tribes and the Levites of 13:8-33. Verses 1-2 reiterate the introduction of 13:7 and link that action to a procedure that the Lord has commanded to Moses (cf. Num 34:16-29). And verse 5 confirms the Israelites' obedience to the Lord's instructions mediated through Moses.

The key motifs of 13:7a are repeated in this section, including mention of the nine and a half tribes (14:2) and the use of the word *divide/allot* (14:5). Moses is mentioned three times, which seems to place Joshua and Eleazar, the agents of distribution in 14:1, in a secondary position. Joshua and Eleazar stand in continuity with Moses: like Moses, they act on the Lord's command (13:7; 14:2). The continuity is brought to its rightful conclusion when 14:5 has the Israelites allotting the land *as the LORD commanded Moses*. This does not take away from the action of Joshua and Eleazar, but it puts the emphasis where it ought to be, on the work of the people and their faithfulness to the Lord's instruction as mediated through Moses. Moses too is only an agent. The Lord is the one to be obeyed.

The phrase *in the land of Canaan* in verse 1, which occurs here for the first time in the book, is peculiar. The phrase never appears in Deuteronomy, but it does occur three more times in the book of Joshua and once in Judges. Three of those occurrences refer to Shiloh (Josh 21:2; 22:9; Judg 21:12), and one specifies the location of the altar built by the two and a half Transjordan tribes (Josh 22:10). *In the land of Canaan* stipulates in all of those occasions a location west of the Jordan (see also Num 32:30; 34:29; esp. confirmed in 35:14, which refers to both sides of the Jordan). The phrase is used often in Genesis to locate the residence of Israel's ancestors. In Genesis, "the land of Canaan" is the destination of Abram, where the narrator clarifies that "the Canaanites were in the land" (12:6). The settlement and sojourn of the ancestors is exclusively "in Canaan," even though the stereotypical descriptions of the promised land extend further (see Josh 1:4 and its parallel in Gen 15:18-21; cf. 17:8; Exod 6:4). The occurrence of *in the land of Canaan* in Joshua 14:1 as well as in chapters 21–22 raises several questions concerning both the importance of the distribution of the land in Transjordan that has been summarized in 13:8-31 and the status of the two and a half tribes as reflected in the conflict story of chapter 22 (Josh 24:3 connects ancestors and land of Canaan explicitly). The fact that the Transjordan tribes frame the entire sequence from chapters 13 to 22 suggests either that their status is in question or that the narrative seeks to recover their status.

The subunit also answers the question of how there remains a twelve-tribe distribution if Levites are not given a portion. Verse 4 specifies that the allotment of Joseph (one of the twelve brothers) be distributed to his two sons, Manasseh and Ephraim, who are here called *two tribes*. This absorption of Joseph's sons into the tribal structure is reflected in Jacob's blessing of Genesis 48:5, where Jacob names Ephraim and Manasseh as his own sons, "just as Reuben and Simeon are mine." There too Ephraim is given greater status than Manasseh (48:14-22).

Mention of Moses' mediation serves both to highlight his role east of the Jordan, as in 13:8-33, and to suggest that Moses' words continue to guide the actions of *the Israelites* (v. 5). Joshua and Eleazar are key figures indeed, with Joshua as Moses' successor and Eleazar as keeper of the lot. Eleazar is the third son of Aaron (Exod 6:23) and becomes the high priest after him (Num 20:25-28). Their distribution is facilitated by *the heads of the families of the tribes* (v. 1, though with a different word for *families* than what is found in 13:15, 23, 24, 28, 29, 31). The NJPS's *heads of the ancestral houses of the Israelite tribes* is a better translation.

Thus, even though Joshua is given the instructions by the Lord (13:7), this subunit nuances the process, which is grounded in Moses' authority and Eleazar's expertise. The obedience motif in 14:5 punctuates the entire sequence, which looks back on Moses' faithful distribution of the land east of the Jordan and looks forward to a similar distribution west of the Jordan. Verse 5 summarizes, therefore, what 14:6 begins to spell out in detail.

This overview serves therefore to provide a bridge of continuity between Moses, Joshua, and the Israelites; in so doing, it draws upon the anticipatory statements in 11:23 and 13:7. All of 13:7b–14:5 fills out the introduction in 13:1-7a. And the sequencing of Moses and Joshua in this unit mirrors the parallel of Moses and Joshua at the end of the conquest section in chapter 12 (Moses in 12:1-6; Joshua in 12:7-24; Winther-Nielsen: 254).

THE TEXT IN BIBLICAL CONTEXT

Land and Inheritance

The odd statement *Very much of the land still remains to be possessed* (13:1) stands out as the most striking feature of the unit. It does not seem to be a criticism of the conquest narratives in chapters 6–12, which the divine promise of 13:6 confirms. Still, when read in the light of the whole book of Joshua as well as Deuteronomy and Judges, a point of tension emerges since Joshua 3:10 already has Joshua state that God *will drive out* the indigenous population.

The tension between the Lord's action and Israel's action is expressed throughout Joshua and reflects the same tension as is found in the book of Deuteronomy, where the same verb is used in two different ways in the same sentence: "The LORD will *drive out* all these nations before you, and you will *dispossess* nations larger and mightier than yourselves" (11:23; cf. 7:22-23). Even more important is the repetition of the verb throughout the following chapters in the book of Joshua in contexts where the narrator makes a point to say that Israel did not or could not *drive out* the indigenous inhabitants of the land (e.g., 13:13; 15:63; 16:10; 17:13). Similarly, the book of Judges echoes the "could not" statements of Joshua (Judg 1:19, 21, 27, 29, 30, 31, 33). These "could not" statements can be read in the context of the final chapters of Joshua, where we read (in thoroughly Deuteronomic language) that Israel is to *love the LORD your God* (23:11). And that, remarkably, is followed by the ominous note of 23:12-13, in which Joshua declares that *God will not continue <u>to drive out</u> these nations before you* (emph. added).

In Joshua, therefore, there is a difference between the Israelites' inability to drive out the inhabitants, as reported in chapters 13–17, and the Lord's potential decision to stop driving out these people groups (cf. 13:6; 23:12-13). Judges, however, makes a transition from "could not" to "did not." Beginning in Judges 1 with similar "could not" statements (1:19, 21, 27-33), Judges 2:3, 21 declares a response to Joshua 23:11-13. In Judges 2 the "angel of the Lord" rehearses Israel's liberation, declares God's covenant commitment, and gives his command that Israel not make covenants with the people of the land. But Israel has not obeyed, and so the angel reports that God now announces, "I will not drive them out before you; but they shall become adversaries to you, and their gods shall be a snare to you" (2:3). According to the narrator, Israel has been "following other gods, worshiping them and bowing down to them" (2:19). As a result, God declares that Israel has violated "my covenant" (2:20) and concludes, "I will no longer drive out before them any of the nations that Joshua left when he died" (2:21).

Judges goes further by adding an interpretation, imputing another motive to the Lord's decision: "In order to test Israel, whether or not they would take care to walk in the way of the Lord as their ancestors did, the Lord had left those nations, not driving them out at once, and had not handed them over to Joshua" (2:22-23). Judges 3:1-6, in a transitional aside between the declaration of purpose and the story about the first judge, is an elaboration that "the nations that the Lord left to test all those in Israel who had no experience of any war in Canaan"—presumably, the text goes on to say—"to teach those who had no experience of it [war]" (3:1-2). But after naming the peoples (Philistines and others), the narrator nuances the reason for the testing, "to know whether Israel would obey the commandments of the Lord" (3:4). It is for those motives (mixed though they are) that "the Israelites lived among the Canaanites" with the traditional six people groups. The damning conclusion to this narrative in Judges is that the Israelites "worshiped their gods" (3:5-6b).

Moreover, Deuteronomy's use of the motif that God "will drive out all these nations" is linked to Israel's faithfulness (Deut 11:22-23; cf. 11:25, 32) even though Deuteronomy's explanations are not entirely consistent (cf. 7:22-23, where different verbs are used in the enigmatic line "You will not be allowed to eliminate them all at once, or the wild animals will multiply around you."). The land grant in Joshua, linked in this way to Deuteronomy, remains a gift but with strings attached. The gift bears its own temptations and threats of loss.

Similar language is used in the instructions for conquest in Numbers 33:50-55, which echoes Joshua's "drive out," "take possession," "I have given you the land to possess," "apportion the land," "inheritance," and "those who remain." The last verse of that instruction includes the warning: "But if you do not drive out the inhabitants of the land from before you, then those whom you let remain shall be as barbs in your eyes and thorns in your sides; they shall trouble you in the land where you are settling. And I will do to you as I thought to do to them" (33:55-36). The repeated emphasis in that text on "you shall drive out" (v. 52) and "if you do not drive out" (v. 55) seems to be transformed by Joshua's *the Lord has driven out* (Josh 23:9).

It is not necessary to harmonize these intrabiblical echoes. The tradition understands that Israel's joining up with the indigenous population in their worship, or through intermarriage, is a risky prospect. The book of Judges may well reflect the most realistic portrait of all. Israel is mixed up with the peoples. Israel's worship is syncretistic. The "real world" of Judges, therefore, balances the ideal world of Joshua, where God's initial *will drive out* of chapter 13 becomes the hypothetical *will not continue to drive out* of chapter 23, and which finally becomes a narrator's explanation of why God "did not drive them out at once" of Judges 2. As noted in the Explanatory Notes (13:1-7), the "driving out" is not a simple matter. Although the Lord says he will do it, Israel either cannot or will not do so. It could be that the book of Joshua highlights the fact that these Others, already included in the *alien as well as citizen* of 8:33 and represented by Rahab, the Gibeonites, among others, become part of the fabric of life and worship in Israel.

Finally, the instructions for dividing the land resonate with the book of Numbers, where the Transjordan tribes are allotted their territory by Moses. As with the "could not drive out" motif, the link with Numbers is explicit. The content of Numbers 32–36 corresponds in several ways to emphases within Joshua 13–21. Numbers 32 reports on the conquest of the Transjordan and the distribution of the land to the two and a half tribes. The end of Numbers 33 focuses on the "driving out" motif. Numbers 34 presents a boundary list that corresponds to the extent of the ancient Egyptian province of Canaan (mid to late second millennium BC), along with instructions for how Joshua and Eleazar are to divide the land. Numbers 35:1-8 includes instructions about cities for the Levites (cf. Josh 21), and Numbers 35:9-15 instructs about cities of refuge (cf. Josh 20). Even the daughters of Zelophehad, who have a significant place in the narrative of inclusion in Numbers 27 and 36, are offered a space in the distribution narrative of Joshua 17:3-6.

The distribution narrative beginning in Joshua 13 is therefore bound up with the narratives of Numbers and Judges in such a way that one senses that the narrator has tried to link, although not harmonize, the entire story. Numbers and Judges include ominous interpretations of the "driving out" motif, and the book of Joshua stands "between" them. This suggests that Joshua is being presented as a paradigm of possibility against reality. The reality of exile, in other words, has overwhelmed the possibility of Joshua; in so doing, it has either undermined it or offered hope for emergence of a new faithfulness after the exile.

Ezekiel 47:13-23 draws on that hopefulness. Ezekiel states, however, "You shall divide it equally" (47:14). The allotment of Ezekiel also appeals to the grant to the ancestors, as does Joshua. This is to be an "inheritance" for Israel as well as for "the aliens who reside among you and have begotten children among you" (47:22). There is no sense in which the failure to drive them out has become a snare and a trap. These aliens "shall be to you as citizens of Israel" (47:22). Wherever and with whatever tribe they are associated, "you shall assign them their inheritance" (47:23). After all, immediately prior to the new and equal boundaries list, Ezekiel has described the water flowing from the temple, and the trees, whose "fruit will be for food, and their leaves for healing" (47:12).

The book of Revelation takes Ezekiel's transposition further by identifying those leaves as "for the healing of the nations" (Rev 22:1-2). Among those in God's kingdom, Revelation includes people "from every tribe and language" (5:9; 13:7; 14:6). Revelation also exhibits the tension between the already and the not yet, which we find in the distribution texts of Joshua. The Lamb has conquered, and those who follow the Lamb will also conquer if they remain faithful. "Those who conquer will inherit," but that inheritance concerns not land nor the territory of others, but relationship with God (Rev 21:7). In the sentences in the letters of Revelation that begin, "To everyone who conquers," the conquering is based on the prior conquest of Jesus (3:21). The means of conquest is "by the blood of the Lamb and by the word of their testimony" (12:11). The book of Revelation issues "a call for the endurance and faith of the saints" (13:10b) to "those who keep the commandments of God and hold fast to the faith of Jesus" (14:12). Yet it is the Lamb, not they, who conquers (17:14). Revelation includes a synthesis of symbolic representation. The dark powers, as well as the kings of the earth, represent the oppressive and evil powers who wage war against the faithful, who will conquer as they follow the one who conquers. Their conquest does not involve warfare, but intimacy with God and martyrdom/witness by the sword/word of their testimony. That process will end as the nations and kings of the earth come into the city of God. Revelation's conquest both appropriates and reverses Joshua's conquest narrative. And as it does so, it draws on the inheritance motif and the now/not yet eschatological interpretation of the book of Joshua.

THE TEXT IN THE LIFE OF THE CHURCH

Already and Not Yet

This section, and the entire sequence of distribution lists and short narrative interludes that follow, can only be read in the context of a bundle of intersecting topics, including the larger canonical perspective on land, occupation of land, and loss of land. As noted in the TBC, the loss of land is in the background, which shapes our understanding of the distribution narratives.

Churchly interpretation has often found ways of dismissing these chapters as irrelevant to the larger story. Yet if we allow the textures of the narrative to guide us, it might be possible to read the text within a larger conversation, and to recognize at the same time how easily we import our motivations into the text. And in doing so, we might avoid Calvin's conclusion that the Israelites "turned backwards to indulge in sloth and cowardice" (xx). This, for Calvin, explains why they couldn't take the whole land. "The dominion of the land, which had been divinely offered, they, with flagrant ingratitude, rejected, by taking possession of only a part" (xx–xxi).

But the text does not say that they rejected the opportunity to take it all. More likely, the text reflects a historiographical and even eschatological "already/not yet." For Jesus, the kingdom is both here among you *and* yet to come. For Paul similarly, the new age has dawned *and* is yet to come (Zerbe 1991).

Although this text in Joshua does not say all of that, those ideas belong to the larger conversation that continues beyond the NT. Origen participates in that conversation as he wrestles with the tension between the affirmations in Joshua 13:1 and 11:23. He asks, "Do you think the Scripture would contain things contrary to itself?" (153). Drawing on typology already within the NT, Origen considers Jesus' coming into the world and his mission to be one of taking "possession of all the earth by the casting of seed alone; he put to flight the hostile powers and fugitive angels that had dominated the minds of the nations; and, at the same time, he sowed the word and propagated the churches" (153). To deal with the full possession alongside "very much remains to be possessed," Origen refers to Paul's citation of Ps 110:1, where he writes, "For he must reign until he has put all his enemies under his feet" (1 Cor 15:25). That, claims Origen, is "the land that remains."

Living in the "already/not yet" draws us into the hopeful transformation of the Spirit's work in the struggle that is not against flesh and blood and that anticipates the transformation of earthly enemies into friends in the presence of God. In the meantime, we like Israel live in the midst of the world, and the world lives in our midst *to this day*. Such living requires us to recognize the dynamics of a metaphorical, figural, and conversational hermeneutic that is open and responsive to intrabiblical allusion and conversation among all texts and across all times.

Joshua 14:6–17:18

The Distribution from Caleb to Joseph

PREVIEW

One of the ironies related to this textual unit is the text's explanation of the name of Hebron, which was formerly called Kiriath-arba. Although this is an indigenous Canaanite name (14:15), in the present it is the name of a Jewish settlement adjacent to the historic town of Hebron. Baruch Goldstein, who on February 26, 1994, killed twenty-nine Palestinians in the mosque at the Tomb of the Ancestors in Hebron, came from Kiriath-arba. That contemporary story is a sad caricature of Caleb's hope that through his strength he might one day drive out the Anakim (14:12).

The narrative introduction of the distribution of the land west of the Jordan (13:1–14:5) has set the stage for this new unit. The command to divide the land (13:7a) and its execution (14:5) signal the completion of the task as a response of obedience to divine instruction. Now in 14:6 the narrative continues to do what 14:5 states has already been done.

The distribution begins with a long sequence pertaining to the most historically significant tribes, Judah and Ephraim, along with half the tribe of Manasseh. Judah and Ephraim later became the kingdoms of Judah and Israel (often called Ephraim) after the division of Solomon's kingdom into two parts (1 Kings 11). In the distribution that follows, these three tribes are allotted most of the land, which was situated in the central hill country.

The structure of the distribution lists appears to fall into two parts, a distribution for Judah (14:6–15:63) and a distribution for Joseph (16:1–17:18). But since Joseph is represented by his two sons, Ephraim and Manasseh (thus making twelve landed tribes plus the Levites), there are three sequences, each concluding with a mention of the Canaanites that were not driven out (15:63; 16:10; 17:12-13). The distribution to these three groups is framed by two narrative sequences involving Caleb (14:6-14) and the Joseph tribes (17:14-18). These two stories are linked by the reiteration of the motif of blessing (14:13; 17:14). In between is another narrative sequence involving the daughters of Zelophehad (17:3-6). In the first two cases, the characters' requests are based on a previous memory of divine promise or decision that was articulated through Moses. In each of those cases, Joshua concedes to the request. In the third, Joshua has to mediate the demand by assuring the Joseph tribes not only that they are numerous and strong enough to survive, but also that their allotment is adequate. They will be successful in spite of superior Canaanite military technology.

Together the sequences of three narratives and the lists keep the story going by integrating action sequences into the distribution, giving the impression that the narrative is sequential even when it offers clues that it is not. The distribution, as we have observed in chapter 13, folds back onto the first half of the book. Both halves reflect a narrative tradition that has both collapsed and telescoped the story so as to stylize it through generic, structural, and thematic patterning.

OUTLINE

Caleb's Request, 14:6-15
Distribution to Judah, 15:1-63
Distribution to Ephraim, 16:1-10
Distribution to Manasseh, 17:1-13
Joseph's Request, 17:14-18

EXPLANATORY NOTES

Caleb's Request 14:6-15

Although in the first narrative section (14:6-15) *the people of Judah* approach Joshua at Gilgal (v. 6), Caleb is the key figure in the episode. This subsequent section focuses on his request for Joshua to act on the promise that he should inherit some of the land. In the Numbers account, God promises Caleb's entry (Num 14:24, 30). Caleb now appeals to the Lord's word to Moses (Josh 14:6b). He then quotes a promise concerning himself that he attributes to Moses (v. 9); yet this promise is actually a quotation (by Moses) of God's words in Deuteronomy 1:36. At the center of Caleb's speech is the phrase *wholeheartedly followed the Lord* (Josh 14:8; cf. Num 14:24), which he repeats and punctuates in verse 9b with the phrase *my God*, and which the narrator repeats and supplements with *the God of Israel* (v. 14; cf. Num 14:24; 32:11-12; Deut 1:36; 1 Kings 11:6). In Deuteronomy 1:36 the NRSV translates Caleb's stance as "complete fidelity" (cf. 1 Kings 11:6). The mention of Joshua as a partner in this loyalty to God in Numbers 32:12 makes Caleb's request in Joshua 14:6-15 significant as the first act of distribution to fulfill the Lord's commands. It is also significant, therefore, that the last action here is the allotment to Joshua (19:49-50). In that way Caleb and Joshua become bookends to the distribution. Caleb also sets himself apart in his testimonial by stating that he, unlike his compatriots, has not *made the heart of the people melt* but committed himself to following the Lord (v. 8).

Besides his loyalty, Caleb also mentions his physical fitness, which qualifies him for the continuing task of conquering the hill country (vv. 11-12). He refers to the Anakim, who are also noted in Numbers as gigantic people (see Num 13:22, 28, 33; Gen 6:4). His wish in verse 12b, that he may drive out the Anakim with the Lord's help, overlaps with the note in 11:21-22 that Joshua thoroughly defeated the Anakim in that region. This is a good example of the mirror effect of the book of Joshua. What we are reading in this narrative folds back on the previous sections of the book so that Joshua's conquest and Caleb's wish overlap when the book is "folded" in half. In other words, we are not reading a sequential account but a stylized narrative. Although Caleb and the tribe of Judah continue to struggle against the Anakim for some time, the first part of the book of Joshua presents matters as though Joshua is the director throughout the entire process. In terms of structure, "The stage for the first distribution episode then begins where the closure of the conquest ended. Joshua defeated the Anakites [=Anakim] and won peace—Caleb was allotted the Anakite Hebron and the land had peace" (Winther-Nielsen: 254–55).

Caleb's sweeping request for land on the basis of Moses' promise (v. 9) is not based on an actual promise made by Moses in the Numbers narrative. There we read only that "his descendants shall possess it" (14:24), which refers not to Hebron but to "the land." The reiteration in Deuteronomy 1:36 cites the Lord's promise, now mediated by Moses' reporting concerning Caleb: "He shall see it, and to him and to his descendants I will give *the land on which he set foot*, because of his complete fidelity to the LORD" (emph. added). Deuteronomy mentions Joshua as well, "who will secure Israel's possession of it" (1:38). Caleb's appeal in Joshua 14:9 relies, therefore, on a particular (and rather literal) interpretation of the Lord's promise in Deuteronomy. There is no reference in Numbers or in Deuteronomy to *this hill country of which the LORD spoke on that day* (Josh 14:12). Caleb improvises on the tradition of Deuteronomy and applies the promise to himself in this particular place.

In response, Joshua blesses Caleb and gives him Hebron, whose conquest by Joshua was reported in Joshua 10:36 (14:13-14). The prominence of Caleb and Hebron in the book of Joshua is significant. Hebron is a site of peaceful sojourn in the ancestral stories (Gen 13:18; 18:1; 23:19). And it is the place where David first became king (2 Sam 2:1-5). That Caleb is a Kenizzite (vv. 6, 14) could well raise eyebrows. According to the genealogy of Genesis 36:9-11, Kenizzites are linked with Esau. By the time of the Chronicler, Caleb has been thoroughly integrated into Judah (1 Chron 4:13). Genesis 15:19 includes the land of the Kenizzites with Abraham's inheritance, along with that of the traditional six or seven people groups in Canaan. Caleb is, therefore, another example of an outsider become insider. Although the book of Joshua includes no story about him, as it does about Rahab and the Gibeonites, the double mention of his Kenizzite affiliation testifies to the inclusion of either Caleb or his group at an indeterminate time. And that Caleb should be singled out in the book of Joshua as one who was completely loyal to the Lord, who is both *my God* (v. 9) and *the God of Israel* (v. 14) is a significant indicator of this inclusion.

The puzzling conclusion to this subsection (v. 15) allows readers to make connections between Hebron and its earlier history. The name Kiriath-arba means "city of four," although the identity of the four is unknown. Verse 15 explains *Arba* as the name of an important person among the Anakim (the words *this Arba* do not occur in MT). Puzzling also is how Hebron becomes a city of refuge (Josh 20:7) as well as a Levitical city (21:11). There we find a harmonizing explanation that whereas the Levites were given Hebron and its pasturelands, Caleb was given *the fields of the town and its villages* (21:12).

Joshua 14:15 cites 11:21-23 not only in its reference to the Anakim, but also in its comments about the land as having *rest from war* (see Explanatory Notes for 11:23 and the essay *Rest, p. 455*). The difference is that in 14:6-16 the main character is Caleb, whereas in

11:21-23 the main character is Joshua. The reader is to understand, based on their positive participation in the spy episode reported in Numbers, that Joshua and Caleb are partners in the enterprise of the book of Joshua. That partnership is literally represented in the parallels between these two passages, as well as in the framing device of placing Caleb and Joshua at opposite ends of the distribution of land to the Transjordan tribes (13:6-15; 19:49-51).

Distribution to Judah 15:1-63

Since Judah is the most prominent tribal group, home of the Davidic dynasty, and favored in Jacob's blessing (Gen 49:8-12), it is telling that the book of Joshua has Judah as the first to receive its allotment west of the Jordan. Having heard from Caleb, the archetypal faithful (non-Judean) Judean, the book of Joshua interweaves his story (15:13-19) with that of his tribal group between the boundary list (15:1-12) and the town list (15:20-61).

The boundaries and the towns in those lists encompass a large territory, not all of which are mentioned as having been captured in chapter 12. The picture is of a complete distribution, resonant of the complete conquest of chapters 11–12. Only Jerusalem is singled out as the town from which the Judahites could not drive out the Jebusites (15:63; cf. 13:13; 16:10; 17:13). This too is telling, for readers who know the whole story understand that there are two other reports about the conquest of Jerusalem. Judges 1:8 reports that "the people of Judah" conquered and burned the city. And again, David was the one who first conquered Jerusalem (2 Sam 5:6-10). Oddly, the first chapter of Judges refers to Judah's occupation of the hill country, but adds that they "could not drive out the inhabitants of the plain, because they had chariots of iron" (Judg 1:19). The "chariots of iron" become the complaint of the Joseph tribes in the last episode of this text unit (Josh 17:16). Moreover, in Judges it is the Benjaminites who are said not to be able to drive out the Jebusites of Jerusalem, who "have lived in Jerusalem among the Benjaminites to this day" (1:21). The intertextual referencing here is hard to unravel. Perhaps this is a subtle allusion to a conflict over Jerusalem between Judah and Benjamin.

The mystery of Jerusalem is grounded in the biblical tradition. It may be the home of priest Melchizedek ("of Salem," Gen 14:18). In later prophetic imagination, it becomes the place of peace among the nations (Isa 2:2-4). But the Jerusalem of Josiah's time (and its central position in the Israelite cult) is not reflected in the book of Joshua. As Koorevaar states, "Jerusalem is the city where Israel

(Judah) failed" (292). In the book of Joshua, "Jerusalem is a foreign place for Israel and Judah. . . . There is absolutely no evidence that Jerusalem possessed a special theological position or that Israel had a special theological task in regard to Jerusalem. The editor has neither openly nor in veiled terms placed such a message in the book of Joshua" (292–93). The book of Joshua is far more interested in paradigmatic characters like Caleb and Joshua.

The Caleb incident at the center of this chapter (15:13-19) develops the Caleb story of 14:6-15. Now *the commandment of the* L*ORD* *to Joshua* is the operational term, instead of the commandment to Moses. Although Caleb's defeat of three *sons of Anak* (v. 14) develops the motif from 14:12, it appears to contradict the note about Joshua's complete eradication of the Anakim in 11:21-22 (cf. Judah's defeat of these three men: Judg 1:10). The additional report about Caleb's venture to Debir (Josh 15:15) folds into Joshua's defeat of Debir (12:13) and adds an anecdote about Caleb's daughter Achsah being given as wife to Caleb's brother Othniel, the first judge of Israel (repeated in Judg 1:12-15; cf. Judg 3:7-11). Achsah takes initiative to ask Othniel to ask Caleb for a field. In the end she is the one who asks Caleb for the field that has *springs of water as well* (15:19). She is unhappy because the allotment has placed her in the semiarid south (Negeb). Since that is unacceptable, she asks for a field with springs of water. The syntax is awkward in verse 18. The verse begins with *When she came* but does not stipulate an indirect object (to whom). The next verb is *she incited/urged*, followed by an object pronoun *him* and an infinitive *to ask*. The NIV translates that she asks Othniel. Three observations suggest it is Caleb: first, Caleb is the main actor in verse 17 as well as verse 18b. Second, he is the one to whom she speaks in verse 19. And third, the syntax of verse 18 allows us to read *She urged him to ask*, with the infinitive *to ask* being read as a gerund, and as an explanation of the urging: *she incited him by asking her father for a field* (cf. Winther-Nielsen: 255). The text alludes to an argument in which she bargains with her father as a kind of compensation for his having given her away to Othniel (an arrangement prohibited by Lev 18:6-18). This is confirmed by the NJPS translation of Caleb's question, which is not *What can I do for you?* (NIV) or *What do you wish?* (NRSV), but *What is the matter?* What is the matter is at least the matter of her family's inadequate land in the Negeb. It may also be his unilateral action to give her to Othniel. This initiative on Achsah's part finds a parallel, or analogy, in the request of the daughters of Zelophehad in the section on Manasseh's distribution (17:3-6).

Distribution to Ephraim 16:1-10

The distribution to the Joseph tribes is introduced by 16:1-4, with the explanation that Joseph includes Joseph's two sons, Manasseh and Ephraim (v. 4). This presumably accounts for Levi's exclusion from the tribal distribution. Although Manasseh is mentioned first, Ephraim, the younger, is the one whose allotment is described first (cf. Jacob's blessing in Gen 48:13-14). The Ephraimite territory is summarized in verses 5-9. The distribution concludes with a reference to *the Canaanites who lived in Gezer* and who continue to live *within Ephraim to this day* (v. 10). Unlike the Jebusites, the people of Gezer *have been made to do forced labor* (cf. 17:13; on *forced labor* see Josh 9). The same expression is used in Jacob's blessing to describe the tribe of Issachar, which became subject to forced labor (Gen 49:15; cf. Deut 20:11; Judg 1:28, 30, 33, 35).

Distribution to Manasseh 17:1-13

The distribution to the half-tribe of Manasseh (see 13:29-31 for the Transjordan half of Manasseh) begins with a notice concerning his firstborn status. In verse 1 the reference to Machir, another firstborn, is odd since he is described as *father of Gilead* and since he is *allotted Gilead and Bashan*, both of which are the names of Transjordan territories, not Israelite personal names (cf. Machir's status as a tribe in Judg 5:14). In Joshua 13:31 Machir is described as *son of Manasseh*. In these texts geographic territories become names of individuals, and those names become included in genealogies (cf. Num 26:28-34; 1 Chron 7:14-19). Gilead and Bashan are geographic territories in Transjordan, as assumed in Joshua 17:5 and explicitly stated in 12:2, 5; 13:11, 25, 31. This note in Joshua 17:1 is another flashback to the Transjordan distribution, which has already been made. The remaining groups within the tribe of Manasseh receive their territory as reported in verses 2, 7-11. And even there, Shechem and Hepher are Canaanite entities that have been drawn into Israel's genealogy.

Verses 3-6 also include names of Canaanite towns within the genealogy of Israel. These verses interrupt the distribution with the story of Zelophehad's daughters, who are named and their situation is described as in Numbers (26:33; 27:1; 36:11). Now in verse 4 these daughters, like Caleb, request their inheritance by appealing to the Lord's command to Moses (v. 4; cf. Josh 14:6). Even the names of the daughters may have geographical referents; one of the five, Tirzah (identified with a significant site now known as Tell el-Far'ah, north of Shechem), was the capital of the northern kingdom (Israel) before Samaria was built (1 Kings 14:17; 15:21, 33; 16:6-23). Now that the daughters have spoken up, the distribution to Manasseh includes *ten portions* (17:5), not quite corresponding to six sons (v. 2) and five daughters (v. 3). These daughters are more important than the distribution, for they represent, like Caleb, another marginal group who claim their inheritance according to the instruction of Moses, but whose heritage includes indigenous peoples (e.g., Tirzah; cf. Machir, Shechem, Hepher of vv. 1-2). In other words, Canaanite towns are drawn into "the tribal structure of Israel as 'kin group' names (e.g., Shechem, Tirzah, and Hepher, which were Canaanite cities [Gen 34; Josh 12:17, 24], and later listed among the 'kin groups' of Manasseh [Josh 17:2-6])" (C. Wright 1990: 50).

The episode closes by mentioning that Manasseh's distribution includes several significant towns *within Issachar and Asher* (v. 11), including Beth-shean, Taanach, and Megiddo—all three of which were fortified and controlled trade routes through the region, from the Jordan and the coastal plain to the Jezreel Valley in the north. Of the six towns mentioned here, Taanach, Megiddo, and Dor are mentioned in the list of conquered kings, in 12:21, 23. This bit of information suggests a long history of usurpation in which Manasseh takes over significant portions of other tribal areas, which otherwise diminish and eventually disappear. Even so, the text concludes with another note about how Manasseh does not take *possession of those towns* (v. 12) and that they *put the Canaanites to forced labor* (v. 13). That is echoed in Judges 1:27-28, but the assignment of these significant towns in Joshua 17:11 and the failure to possess them in 17:12 is disconcerting. Even when *the Israelites grew strong* (v. 13), they *did not utterly drive them out*. The text seems to reflect clear knowledge of Israel's actual historical reality, that Israel has always lived in a mixed population. These narratives explain how Israel later comes to control these towns, but they remain strongly Canaanite enclaves at the same time.

Joseph's Request 17:14-18

The sequence ends with a third request, this time of the Joseph tribes, here named *the tribe of Joseph*. The section is strangely placed since the tribes speak as one group, and since the Joseph tribes represented by Joseph's two sons have already been allotted their land. It could be that their complaint concerning *one lot and one portion* is the explanation for why they came to be treated as two groups (cf. Gen 48:5, 13-22). First, although they are blessed by the Lord and become numerous, they have been given only one portion. Joshua acknowledges their problem by telling them both to spread out into the forested regions of the hill country. Second, they cannot spread out into the valleys, which are dominated by Canaanites who have access to iron technology for chariot building. Joshua acknowledges their problem and tells them to clear the forested hills. The chapter concludes with Joshua's assurance that they will actually *drive out the Canaanites* in spite of their chariots and their strength (v. 18b).

Some interpreters think that the Joseph tribes, along with Rahab, Achan, Caleb, and daughter Achsah, daughters of Zelophehad, Levites, and the Transjordan tribes constitute a significant contrast to the "all Israel" portrait of the entrance into the land narratives as a whole *["All Israel," p. 385]*. Polzin identifies them as "exceptional outsiders." Hawk thinks, however, that they represent a "negative image" in the book, in contrast to "the united, obedient, and victorious Israel" (2000: xxii), thereby interpreting the contrast as characteristic of discontinuity in the book. These outsiders represent "an ambivalent status and an energetic determination to secure a place in the land" (xxii). He rightly observes that "these characters stand at the center of most of the stories in Joshua, offering yet another indication of the book's fundamental preoccupation with issues of identity" (xxiii). Yet they are never presented as disobedient. Since issues of identity are paramount in Joshua, outsiders actually illustrate the complexity that arises when peoplehood is defined by being centered on either ethnic or geographic reality.

The complaints of the Joseph tribes and Joshua's responses highlight Joshua's role as mediator and arbiter. He acquiesces to the concerns of Caleb and the daughters of Zelophehad, but he does not give in to the complaints of the Joseph tribes. Although it seems out of place, this incident rounds out the three narrative segments that break apart the distribution accounts in this unit. Although the first two special requests are clearly linked to a command of Moses (even though in Caleb's case that is not literally applied), the third request has no connection to Moses. As it turns out, Ephraim much later will swallow up all the other northern tribes, including Manasseh, and become a large, almost undifferentiated Ephraim/Israel after the death of Solomon.

The Caleb and the Joseph sections offer opposite examples. Caleb, a paradigm of loyalty, continues in the tradition of hopeful expectation. He is able to see the possibilities of the future and to imagine himself as participating in the Lord's promise (Josh 14:12). Although "Joseph" recognizes the Lord's blessing (17:14), "he" can only see the negative in the current situation. The Josephites need

Joshua's assurance that in spite of their failure to *drive out* the indigenous population (16:10; 17:12), they are indeed strong enough to do so (17:17-18). Caleb is sure of his strength; Joseph is not. Caleb takes initiative; Joseph does not. Caleb confronts Joshua; Joshua confronts Joseph. The portrait painted by the narrative is not one-dimensional. An outsider presents a positive paradigm, and insiders behave contrary to expectation.

THE TEXT IN BIBLICAL CONTEXT

Judah's Primacy

The reports about the distribution to the tribe of Judah and to the two Joseph tribes, Ephraim and Manasseh, participate in a larger biblical conversation that spans the entire OT narrative tradition. Jacob's blessing of his sons includes clues to later social and political realities, or predicts such realities. When Jacob blesses Joseph's sons (Gen 48), he follows the trajectory already established of blessing the youngest before the oldest. Although Joseph protests, Jacob asserts that the younger will be greater than the elder and "shall become a multitude of nations" (48:19).

Jacob's blessing includes other connections to Joshua's distribution. Levi, mentioned several times here, is grouped with Simeon and receives an inheritance within the confines of Judah (Josh 19:1-9). Levi and Simeon are scattered (Gen 49:7) and disappear as political or social entities in the Israelite story. Jacob's blessing and Joshua's distribution reflect that reality. In Jacob's blessing, Judah becomes a ruler to whom the brothers bow and to whom the nations are subservient (Gen 49:8-12). Although the book of Joshua does not explicitly link Judah with the Davidic dynasty, the tradition of Davidic rule could well have influenced placing Judah first in the distribution. Judah is also mentioned first in the book of Judges (1:2); is home of the first judge, Othniel (Josh 15:17; Judg 3:7-11); and is the first that is directed to engage his "brother" Benjamin in battle (Judg 20:18). The primacy of Judah, which may be a hopeful theme in Joshua, seems to be tragically reversed by the end of Judges. Chronicles maintains Judah's primacy in placing his genealogy first in the sequence of the sons of Jacob (1 Chron 2:2–4:23).

Faithful Caleb

I have already mentioned Caleb's relationship to the spy story of Numbers 13–14; 26:65; 32:12 (Explanatory Notes on Josh 14:6-15). In Numbers 32:12, Caleb and Joshua are singled out as having "unreservedly followed the LORD." The same Hebrew expression occurs in Deuteronomy 1:36, depicting "his complete fidelity to the LORD." Although that is the only appearance of Caleb in Deuteronomy, both the narratives of Numbers and the recap in Deuteronomy extol Caleb as a paradigm of faithfulness. The book of Sirach (Ecclesiasticus) includes Caleb along with its praise of Joshua as examples of loyalty (46:7), whom the Lord blessed, "so that all the Israelites might see how good it is to follow the Lord" (46:10). Although Caleb does not appear in the OT as a character in a narrative beyond Judges and the genealogies of Chronicles, he reflects the faithfulness of God (cf. 1 Maccabees 2:56). In the story he is a character who imagines that the promise, although received in part, is yet to be fulfilled. He could well have been included in the list of faithful heroes in Hebrews 11:32 who "were commended for their faith" (11:39).

The prominence of Caleb in the texts suggests that the most important dimension of the text is the characters whose stories punctuate both the conquest and distribution sections of the book of Joshua.

The Daughters of Zelophehad

The inclusion of the daughters of Zelophehad in the distribution account confirms the notion that the text is not merely a distribution report. Identifying towns and boundaries would have been adequate for that. The story of Zelophehad's daughters takes up a conversation that begins in the book of Numbers when these women boldly appear not only before Moses, but also before the whole congregation, and complain that neither their father nor they should bear the consequence of his not having sons. Concerned for their father's reputation and their own survival, they ask for "a possession among our father's brothers" (Num 27:4; cf. Gen 31:14; Job 42:15). Moses, upon consulting the Lord, decrees that when anyone dies without sons, his inheritance shall be passed on to his daughter (27:8). Set in the time after the departure from Sinai, whose laws did not include provisions for inheritance, the story illustrates how legal decisions governing the everyday life of the people were understood. Torah—divine instruction—was dynamic, not static. It makes sense, therefore, that the story also illustrates how one divine decision (Num 27:11b) could give rise to a complexity that requires another decision to counteract its misuse or misapplication (for a dynamic understanding of law, see Fretheim 2003) *[Torah, p. 462]*).

The story in Numbers 36 tells of the elders of other tribes who worry about the implications of the earlier decision. These elders are specifically concerned about distribution and inheritance of *land*, which was to have been distributed by lot (36:2). What should happen to that notion of "gift" or "inheritance" by "lot" to specific tribal groups if the daughter who inherits should marry outside the clan/tribe? They presume that the "*inheritance* will be taken from the *inheritance* of our ancestors and added to the *inheritance* of the tribe into which they marry; so it will be taken away from the *allotted portion* of our *inheritance*" (36:3, emph. added). The emphasized words also occur throughout the distribution stories of Joshua. Moses again responds with another divine word, limiting their marriage to men from within their father's clan, and adding that inheritance could not be transferred from one tribe to another (36:7). The Numbers 36 story concludes by saying that the daughters do what the Lord has commanded.

The fact that these daughters appear in Joshua and are not "left behind" in the ancient memory suggests their importance. Even the genealogy of Chronicles does not bypass them, but it does omit their names (1 Chron 7:15). These daughters are paradigms of faithfulness in two ways. They have a long memory of the promises and decrees of the Lord. And they are bold both in their youth and in their old age to bring about that which was promised. They are able to live within the strictures of a developing tradition concerning marriage, but they do not allow that tradition to hinder their appropriation of what is theirs by gift, by lot, by decree, and therefore also by inheritance.

THE TEXT IN THE LIFE OF THE CHURCH

Paradigms of Faithfulness

Caleb is singled out as a paradigm of complete faithfulness. Both Caleb and the daughters of Zelophehad are given pride of place for their insistence on claiming what has been promised by the Lord through Moses. In continuity with the Torah tradition to which the book of Joshua seeks faithful conversation, we see Caleb, the daughters of Zelophehad, and the Joseph tribes as paradigmatic in order to see ourselves, hopefully, in them. The memory of Caleb's reminder, the daughters' demands, and the Joseph tribes' complaints allows us also to recall the importance of memory and resistance. As we enter the story, however tentatively, we find places to recognize ourselves:

- in the claiming of promise and identity (as Caleb the *Kenizzite* outsider finds his place inside Israel's story, he applies God's promises to himself by improvising on and extending God's promises in Num 14:24 and Deut 1:36),

- or in the persistence and perseverance of hope (as the daughters of Zelophehad counted on God's wisdom in assuring a place for them in spite of patriarchal inheritance customs),
- or in the complaints about blessing gone awry or rendered inadequate (as the Joseph tribes, who face insurmountable odds, need to be encouraged along the way).

Does all of that mean we bypass the violence of "drive out" and "conquer"? Or do we rather identify with the reality of the Jebusites' living with Judah *to this day*? Perhaps colonizers and indigenous peoples must find ways to live together. Perhaps Israeli Jews and Palestinians must learn to live together *to this day*. And so the conversation continues. It continues into the NT and beyond insofar as the now and the not yet of the kingdom of God both echoes and transforms the victory of Joshua 6–12 and the reality of *could not drive out* of Joshua 13–17.

Joshua 18:1–19:51

The Territories of the Remaining Tribes

PREVIEW

Getting to the end of a satisfying story is always a good experience. Although we have not yet reached the end of the book of Joshua, these two chapters provide a penultimate ending in words that are among the most significant in the book. At the end of the distribution to the remaining tribes, the narrator tells us that *they finished dividing the land* (19:51). Most remarkably, we find the same verb here as is used of God's completing the work of creation (Gen 2:1-2) and of the completion of the work of building the tabernacle (Exod 39:32; 40:33). These texts participate in the ordering of space as gifted land.

Joshua 18 begins with a change of context from Gilgal to Shiloh (cf. 14:6), where *the tent of meeting* is located (twenty miles north of Jerusalem). The unit opens with a brief note about the context and the status of the conquered land (18:1-2), a speech by Joshua about the remaining land to be apportioned to the remaining seven tribes (18:3-7), and a narrator's summary of the proceedings to carry out Joshua's instructions to describe and distribute the land. The lots apportioned to the seven tribes are, for the most part, like surveyors' notes, briefly noted in 18:11–19:49a. The narrator comments on two of the tribes with additional information (Simeon, 19:9; Dan, 19:47-48). The listing of the seven allotments concludes by noting that the distribution has been completed (19:49a). The concluding section reports on the Israelites' gift of inheritance to Joshua

(19:49b-50; cf. Num 14:30-31) and summarizes the entire distribution from chapters 14–19 by referring again to both Joshua and Eleazar (19:51; cf. 14:1).

OUTLINE

Instructions for the Distribution, 18:1-10
Distribution to the Seven Tribes, 18:11–19:49a
Gift to Joshua and Summary of the Distribution, 19:49b-51

EXPLANATORY NOTES

Instructions for the Distribution 18:1-10

The Shiloh episode of 18:1-10 forms the centerpiece in the distribution section of Joshua from 13:8 to 21:42. Even if we do not treat that section as a chiasm, as Koorevaar does (289), it is still possible to suggest correspondences among the various sections and to appreciate the centrality of the Shiloh episode.

Verse 1 highlights three things. First, whether or not it forms a structural center, this unit is important since it reflects a communal gathering like that at Shechem in Joshua 8:30-35 (cf. 22:12). The significance of the tent of meeting and of its location in Shiloh is new to the book of Joshua. The *tent of meeting* appears in verse 1 and at the end of the unit in 19:51, thereby framing the text. It appears everywhere in Exodus, Leviticus, and Numbers, but only once in Deuteronomy (31:14), and there in relation to the commissioning of Joshua. The tent of meeting makes an appearance during the time of Eli's tenure (1 Sam 2:22) and again under David (2 Sam 6:17), after which it disappears upon Solomon's founding of the temple.

Second, Shiloh becomes a cultic center (this is its first appearance in the OT; cf. Judg 18:31; 21:19, with an "annual festival"). Although Shiloh is such a center during Samuel's time, it seems also to be a center of dissident priests descended from Abiathar, who was expelled by Solomon (1 Kings 2:27), and a prophetic center (1 Kings 14:2). Shiloh comes to have a bad reputation by the time of Jeremiah, who cites the Lord as saying that Shiloh is the place "where I made my name dwell at first" but which has been destroyed under divine judgment (Jer 7:12, 14; 26:6, 9). The psalmist puts Shiloh's demise starkly: "He abandoned his dwelling at Shiloh, the tent where he dwelt among mortals" (78:60). In the book of Joshua, then, Shiloh stands for a moment of clarity, a place of intimacy with God as though it is Israel's Eden (Gen 2). It stands for communion with God who, according to the Deuteronomic tradition, made the divine name dwell "in that place" (cf. Deut 12:5). Exodus understands the tabernacle to be the place of instruction and discernment in the presence of God. But that presence is not limited to one place; it is "every place" (Exod 20:24). In Leviticus the tent of meeting is the relational center where Israel's God not only dwells, but also promises to "walk among you and be your God, and you will be my people" (Lev 26:11-12). If Joshua's meeting at Shiloh belongs to this tradition of divine presence, then Joshua 18:1 represents a significant moment in the Joshua story, which all readers would recognize as a fulfillment of the divine promise (cf. Koorevaar: 290).

Third, the note about the land being *subdued* (18:1) reiterates the summary statements on *rest* in 11:23 and 14:15b. Ironically, the word *subdued* is the same as in Genesis 1:28 in the so-called mandate to "fill the earth and subdue it." The only other place where the verb is used prior to Joshua 18:1 is in the related text in Numbers, where the Transjordan tribes are to go over the Jordan "until the land is subdued before the LORD" (Num 32:22; cf. 32:29, "before you"). The verb is also used elsewhere with this meaning only of David's subjugation of the land (2 Sam 8:11; 1 Chron 22:18; cf. 2 Chron 28:9-10). In spite of suggestions by contemporary interpreters that the word in Genesis 1:28 is not a "conquest" word in that context, it seems as though both Joshua and the David story appropriate the word in a militaristic sense. Israel subdues the earth/land as it enters the land of Canaan and begins to have dominion over it. The irony is that Israel's experience of being conquered and exiled also mirrors the expulsion from the garden in Genesis 3.

Joshua 18:2 sets up the scenario that governs the distribution that follows, identifying seven tribes who have not received their allotment. Joshua delivers a speech that begins by chastising the people for their apparent failure of *going in and taking possession* of the land given to them by God (v. 3). Have the people snubbed the gift of God? Or is this part of an idealized description of an "unconquered" land (Assis)? The criticism seems out of place given the scenario set up in 13:7. It is almost as though 18:1 were itself a flashback to the hinge between chapters 12 and 13. Joshua's further instruction about a reconnaissance mission, which entails *writing a description* (v. 4), was not part of previous distribution reports. Presumably for the narrative to be internally consistent, the distribution by lot would require a "map" of the land. This *writing a description* is a kind of mapmaking, which makes us wonder about the function of the distribution section of Joshua. Is it really an allotment, or is it a literary map? Does it hint at a reality or at an ideal? The fact that the remaining seven tribes do not figure prominently in later Israelite stories suggests that this literary map is part of the historical memory intended to preserve (or invent) a past that no longer exists. It does not justify an occupation, it re-members parts of the body that have been lost to the passage of time.

The seven tribes then become part of the lot-casting procedure (Josh 18:6). The Levites, we are reminded, do not have a portion *for the priesthood of the* L*ORD* *is their heritage* (v. 7; cf. 13:14, 33). This is the first time their priestly function is noted alongside the earlier relational inheritance (13:33). Verses 8-10 round out the introductory section by reporting on the fulfillment of Joshua's instructions to *write the description of the land* (v. 8). The casting of lots takes place *before the* L*ORD* (v. 10), who is present at the tent of meeting (v. 1).

Distribution to the Seven Tribes 18:11–19:49a

The distribution to the seven tribes follows the pattern of reporting found in the review of the distribution to the Transjordan tribes. The seven are Benjamin (18:11-27), Simeon (19:1-9), Zebulun (19:10-16), Issachar (19:17-23), Asher (19:24-31), Naphtali (19:32-39), and Dan (19:40-48). Several features stand out as significant variations from a similar pattern.

First, Benjamin receives a much more detailed listing, including both borders and towns. Its boundary list is punctuated with *boundary by boundary all around* (18:20b). That Benjamin, the youngest brother, should be mentioned first is suggestive. The list begins uniquely by stating that Benjamin's territory *fell between* Judah and Joseph. In the larger story of Israel, Benjamin is both culprit and victim (which is ironic given his status as youngest and favored in the Genesis narratives). According to the stories at the end of the book of Judges, however, Benjamin perpetrates an atrocity against a Levite's concubine, the result of which is Israel's devastation of Benjamin (Judg 19–21), and so the narrator writes, "The LORD defeated Benjamin before Israel" (with thousands killed, 20:35). The irony in the report about the vindictive attack is its parallel to the story of Ai in the book of Joshua (thirty Israelites are killed: Judg 20:39; cf. Josh 7:5; there are two battles, one a failure, another a victory: 20:19-35; there is an ambush scenario: 20:36-48). The story ends with an abduction of women dancers in Shiloh (Judg 21:12, 19-23). Benjamin is questionable, therefore, because of its marginal status in the official memory of moral atrocity. Moreover, Benjamin falls between Judah and Joseph, an untenable situation since, according to the larger story, Ephraim (one of Joseph's two sons) becomes the Northern Kingdom under Jeroboam I, and Judah becomes the Southern Kingdom under Rehoboam. Benjamin disappears and, according to the corporate memory, rightly so. Benjamin is both culprit and scapegoat (Pattison; Matties 2000).

The distribution to Simeon is unique as well. Its placement as first in the list after Benjamin reverts back to birth order, with Reuben's territory as eldest assigned in Transjordan. The order in Jacob's blessing is Reuben, Simeon, Levi, Judah, Zebulun, Issachar, Dan, Gad, Asher, Naphtali, Joseph, Benjamin (Gen 49; cf. Gen 29:31–30:24; 35:16-18). Since Reuben, Gad, Judah, and Joseph have already been assigned, and since Levi receives no allotment, the seven remaining are listed by birth order except for Benjamin's being first and Dan's being last. This shifting of the birth order makes the first and last especially important (perhaps because of their connection to the stories at the end of Judges). Simeon, although the oldest of the seven, is remarkable since his territory is allotted within the tribe of Judah (Josh 19:1, 9). In other words, the distribution accounts for Simeon's disappearance from historical memory. The explanation of 19:9 that Judah's territory *was too large for them* implies an error in the lot-taking process reported in chapter 15. It is more likely a narrative strategy that accounts for the disappearance of Simeon or its absorption into the tribe of Judah. The distribution list reflects a later political reality in which Judah is the only (remaining) tribe of the south with an independent identity.

The highlighting of Dan at the end of the distribution list (19:40-48) corresponds to the placement of Benjamin at the beginning of this list (18:11-28). In the Dan distribution, we see an anomaly in the inclusion not only of a brief boundary list (along the coastal plain), but also of an explicit reference to the migration of Dan to the north, to a place called Leshem. The story in Judges 18 tells of that migration in greater detail.

And since Dan represents one of the places where Jeroboam I sets up his cult site (1 Kings 12:29), it may be that the narrator wishes to highlight both Benjamin, at the beginning of the distribution, and Dan at the end. Benjamin's lot includes Jebus/Jerusalem (Josh 18:28), which becomes the center of power for David and the kingdom called Judah. Hence Benjamin and Judah are rivals, and Benjamin loses to Judah. In place of Jerusalem, Jeroboam chooses Bethel (also in Benjamin, according to 18:13) as his southern cultic site. Judah is the one who intercedes with the brothers on Joseph's behalf (Gen 37:26-27) and who pleads for Benjamin before Joseph (44:18-34). And Judah is the spokesperson for the brothers before

Joseph (43:3, 8; 44:14, 16, 18). Thus this juxtaposition of Benjamin and Dan is best read against the backdrop of Judah's preeminence in distribution lists earlier, in chapter 15.

Gift to Joshua and Summary of the Distribution 19:49b-51

The beginning of verse 49 has usually been read as the introduction to the concluding section, so that the verb "to finish" would both begin and end the section. Syntactically, however, the first "to finish" can serve as a summary conclusion of what has gone before: *So they finished distributing* (Winther-Nielsen: 257). The new section begins with a new action and a newly specified subject: *The Israelites gave*. Since the text specifies that Joshua *asked for Timnath-serah*, and since that town had been granted within the inheritance of the tribe of Ephraim (19:50), the gift needs to be clarified. Moreover, this gift confirms that Joshua as well as Caleb will "settle" in the land (Num 14:30, though its verb for "settle" is different from the one in Josh 19:50). It is a fitting ending. Just as Joshua has distributed God's gifted land to the tribes, now the Israelites should offer a gift to Joshua as his own inheritance. And, as is characteristic of the way Israel ought always to act, they would do so *by command of the Lord* (19:50).

The concluding verse in chapter 19 returns the reader to Joshua and Eleazar, who are mentioned together in 14:1, at the beginning of the distribution west of the Jordan (see also 17:4; 21:1; Num 27:22; 32:28; 34:17). Here all the motifs of Joshua 18:1 and 14:1 are brought together into one verse (19:51): Eleazar and Joshua, the heads of the families, Shiloh, the tent of meeting, the tribes of the Israelites. Thus the text sets the stage for the next phase of the distribution: that of the cities of refuge (ch. 20) and the Levites (ch. 21).

The division of lots by tribe ends with the freighted word *finished*, which echoes the conclusion of God's creative work (Gen 2:1-2) and the completion of the work of building the tabernacle (Exod 39:32; 40:33). This work of distributing is a creation of an environment that brings together the two previous "works," one in which humans can dwell, and the other in which God can dwell. Thus it is appropriate that this unit—which begins and ends with a reference to the tent of meeting and refers to distributing the land ("earth" in Genesis, but same Heb. word) by lot to "seven" tribes—should be completed. Now, as Israel's theologians understand it, both God and human beings (Israel) may dwell together. Ezekiel treasures this cooperative interdependence and indwelling, both lamenting its loss and reimagining its restoration.

The distribution to the seven tribes also concerns the shaping of identity and memory. It does not so much authorize a reconquest as account for transformations in later Israelite communal memory, intertribal relationships, and changing patterns of landholding and land loss by various groups within Israel.

THE TEXT IN BIBLICAL CONTEXT

The Distribution Trajectory

I have already highlighted several motifs in this unit that reverberate throughout the intrabiblical conversation: the significance of Shiloh in later tradition, the subjugation of the land as echo of Genesis 1:28, the placement of Benjamin and Dan in the sequence, and the echoes of Genesis and Exodus in "finishing" God's work. The historical questions raised by this text about the enduring future of the tribes remain hypothetical. We can presume that the distribution lists seek to account for the relationships among the tribes at a later date, just as Jacob's blessing of the sons also bears some resemblance to the later story (e.g., Judah as having the scepter; Simeon and Levi as scattered in Israel). That Benjamin and Dan are highlighted as first and last in the sequence of seven is likely reminiscent of events of victimizing/scapegoating and apostasy that are reported in other biblical texts.

Shiloh eventually disappears, yet it retains a residency of dissident priests and prophets. That story hints at the power of memory in keeping a tradition of protest and alternative theopolitics alive. Shiloh becomes symbolic of divine judgment just as it represents the divine presence experienced and then lost. Since Jeremiah refers to Shiloh as the place where the name dwells, and since Psalm 78:60 refers to Shiloh as the dwelling place of God, this configuration of Shiloh/tent of meeting and the "finishing" of the division allow us to imagine that Joshua's distribution of the land is the final stage in God's work of creation. The distribution, in other words, is a creation story: it is the creation of a habitable home for the particular people claimed by God as God's people (just as the creation of the earth is the creation of a habitable home for humans and animals). Genesis and Joshua, the universal and the particular, resonate as participants in the creation of humankind and of God's people in the land. In this way, Deuteronomy's (and Joshua's) notion of a "good land" resonates with the goodness of the earth in Genesis 1 (cf. Exod 3:8; Num 14:7; and ten times in Deut 1–11, as in 1:25). In Joshua, however, the *good land* appears only in Joshua 23, after the distribution, functioning as a declaration of a deed accomplished (23:13, 15, 16).

Ezekiel's distribution is worth noting again (see TBC for 11:16-23; 13:1–14:5). He imagines an allotment by equal portions so that all, including aliens and Levites, have a place to be. For Ezekiel, the distribution is an imaginary construct, like that of his unrealistic model of the temple. It symbolizes reality more than it represents reality (e.g., note that Benjamin is south of Jerusalem in Ezek 47–48 whereas in Josh 18 it is north of Jerusalem). Like Ezekiel, the Joshua story, although couched in realistic narrative and list formulas, may well symbolize more than it represents.

The apostolic sermon in Acts 13 mentions that the Lord "destroyed seven nations in the land of Canaan" and "gave them their land as an inheritance" (13:19). Yet that sermon is set in the context of the apostles' mission to the Gentiles (13:46-52). Thus, according to the NT writers, "inheritance" in Christ is now available to all, even those who were enemies of God (Gal 3:18; 4:30; Eph 1:11, 14, 18; 5:5; Col 1:12; 3:24; Heb 9:15; 11:8; 1 Pet 1:4).

THE TEXT IN THE LIFE OF THE CHURCH

A Theology of Distribution

These distribution accounts have not fared well in the life of the church. Like genealogies, they have been either avoided or relegated to filler. Because of that, it is important to acknowledge that the function of such reports had more to do with identity than with record keeping. That some of these reports include allusions to disasters and failures says as much about the entire story of Israel as it says about the settlement period. The stylized character of the reports suggests that the narrative shapes the memory more than the memory shapes the narrative. The narrator seems to be saying, "We know the fate of Simeon, Levi, Dan, and Benjamin and Joseph. Now we shall give an account of it so that we all understand that our present reality is both rooted in the past and is part of a long and complex story of promise, fulfillment, failure, and nonfulfillment that continues on into the future."

After the Babylonian conquest of Judah, Ezekiel picks up the distribution and transforms it by providing equal segments for each tribe, and that sequesters the land available for the "prince" and limits his power to confiscate land (Ezek 46:18; 47:14; 48:21). That tells us that the distribution in the book of Joshua was not sacrosanct, nor was it understood as a pattern for future settlement and reconquest. Land was a gift that could be gained or lost. It shares the interplay of promise and responsibility, as well as misfortune, misadventure, and moral failure *[Land: Gifted and Lost, p. 440]*.

That is the way historians now tell the story of the church's expansion into uncharted territory, not in order to fix a specific sequence of historical events, but to understand a shifting identity over time, accounting for gains and losses within the gifts of time and place. Each generation needs to tell the story with nuances that could not be told by previous generations. Distribution of land could be reimagined by Ezekiel not as a way of denying or falsifying the past, but as a reimagining of an alternative future without the roadblocks of the past. Ezekiel was aware that Joshua's distribution was not perfect, even though it was carried out by (divine) lot. The church's story, its inheritances throughout the world, is not set in stone. The center of the church's life is now identified to be Africa and Latin America. Simeon disappears. Joseph complains. The tribe of Benjamin is a culprit and becomes disenfranchised through its violence. I will not resort to typology by comparing Western Christianity to Benjamin or Dan (e.g., the church's complicity in crimes against humanity in Nazi Germany and Rwanda). But it is telling that past realities do give way to new realities, and that actions of the past have consequences that reverberate well into an indeterminate future.

Origen ran out of either time or imagination, for he says that "there is not enough time for us to discuss all the things we read, we shall lightly touch at least a few things, as the Lord grants" (178). As a result, he does not deal with details in the latter chapters of Joshua, not even in the very important chapters 23–24. His apology for the distribution lists is explicit: "Do not read these things with distaste and think Scripture is something worthless because many proper names have been planted in it" (201–2). Joshua contains many "ineffable things" and things that "cannot be explained worthily and wholly," even by the apostles. "I did not say that they may not be fully known, but that they may not be fully explained" (202). What a wonderful disclaimer that we too might wish to appropriate.

Still, Origen remains firmly rooted in the intrabiblical conversation. On the motif of inheritance, Origen appeals to the book of Hebrews, which refers to the heavenly inheritance (200–201). For Origen, the way Joshua received a city as a gift and built it up is like Jesus being given the gift of his people's loyalty along with permission to build them into appropriate "tents of meeting" for the divine presence of Christ, who is our inheritance (203).

Joshua 20:1–21:45

Cities of Refuge and Cities for Levites

PREVIEW

The notion of sanctuary or asylum has survived to our own time. Political refugees seek sanctuary. Safe houses in Nazi Germany provided refuge for dissidents and Jews. Urban shelters provide safety for abused women and children. In ancient Israel, in a context where retributive justice flourished all too easily and erupted into clan vengeance, refuge for perpetrators of unintentional killing became an integral part of maintaining justice. Civil society must, however, be shaped through education in the obligations and responsibilities of communal life. Levites, while resident in towns scattered throughout the land, served as teachers. These two chapters highlight the rudimentary practices necessary for maintaining order and for formation of a just society.

These chapters therefore make it abundantly clear that the *book* of Joshua is not a conquest narrative. The ordering of space that began in 13:1 also includes a designation of cities as refuge for involuntary manslaughter and identification of cities that belong to the Levites. These form a geographic pair. The first establishes geographic centers for maintaining justice, and the second establishes centers for those who would later become teachers of the Torah and representatives of the covenant tradition. These two are necessary for maintenance of right order and right living in the land. Thus the distribution-of-land sequence finds its moral focus here after *they finished dividing the land* (19:51). Dividing the land, the creation story of Israelite identity in the land, requires structures that give order (justice) and people to instruct in the practices of Torah [*Torah*, p. 462].

Like chapter 13, this unit begins with a divine initiative (20:2-6). This speech instructs Joshua to tell the Israelites to set apart *cities of refuge*, to which those who kill another unintentionally may flee for asylum. The following verses explain the need for asylum (20:7-9). The second episode (21:1-42), set in Shiloh, introduces an initiative by the Levites, who appeal to Moses' instruction that they be granted both cities and pasturelands (cf. Num 35:1-8). The Israelites respond by giving them *towns and pasture lands out of their inheritance* (Josh 21:3). The section ends with a summary of the distribution (21:43-45), which includes motifs found in earlier summaries (11:16-23; 19:49b-51) and looks forward to similar motifs in Joshua's final speeches of chapter 23. In particular, the narrator now emphasizes that it is *the Lord* who *gave to Israel all the land* so that all the *good promises . . . came to pass* (21:43, 45). The trajectory initiated in the ancestral stories is now coming to its theological focal point.

OUTLINE

The Lord's Initiative: Cities of Refuge, 20:1-9
The Levites' Initiative, the Israelites' Gift, 21:1-42
Summary: The Lord's Gift, the Promise Fulfilled, 21:43-45

EXPLANATORY NOTES

The Lord's Initiative: Cities of Refuge 20:1-9

The transition from the notice about having *finished dividing the land* (19:51) to the next unit comes via the Lord's initiative. God speaks to Joshua, telling him to tell the Israelites to *appoint cities of refuge* (v. 2). The technical word translated *refuge* is found only in references to cities of refuge.

Even God appeals to Moses here by including a reminder that Moses has been the agent of God's word about this very topic (cf. Exod 21:12-14; Num 35:9-34; Deut 4:41-43; 19:1-13). The cities are *cities of refuge*, places of asylum for the person who has killed another person *without intent or by mistake* (Josh 20:3). The contemporary word is "manslaughter." The "refuge," or "asylum," is to protect the person from *the avenger of blood* (v. 3).

The *avenger of blood* is the nearest relative who takes on responsibility for assuring that the process of justice prevails. Although *avenger* seems to imply a practice of retributive justice, the concern here is to limit inappropriate retribution. Terms related to the

Hebrew word *go'el*, translated here as *avenger*, are used elsewhere in the OT to refer to God's and others' redeeming activity (Exod 6:6; 15:13; Pss 69:18; 72:14; 74:2; throughout Isa 40–66; Jer 31:11; Ruth 2:20; 3:9, 12; Lev 25:25-54). The *go'el* is also the next of kin responsible for "redeeming" the assets of the relative who has found himself in economic trouble (Lev 25:24, 25, 29, 48). In the case of murder, the person, now described as a *redeemer of blood* (AT), becomes responsible for assuring that justice is done. The implication is that the *avenger of blood* could exact retribution if the killer were to leave the city.

Although that concern does not include restorative justice practices, the "refuge" allows for a kind of "redeeming," a limit on vengeance. The text assumes some kind of court or *trial before the congregation*, but the legal procedures are not spelled out here. There are not two different words for "manslaughter" and "murder" as there are in English. Here the word in verse 3 for *kills* is the same as that used in the Ten Commandments to signify murder (*raṣaḥ*, Exod 20:13). The practice of blood vengeance has a long history that continues into our own time (cf. 2 Sam 14:11).

Whereas verse 3 states the reason for the practice of asylum, verses 4-6 explain the practice. The explanation takes place *at the entrance of the gate of the city* (v. 4), which is the traditional place of jurisprudence. Lawcourts were convened there by the elders of the city. Such gates were large structures that included antechambers for meetings. The duration of the asylum is unclear. The NRSV implies two conditions that (in 20:6 MT) are not joined by a conjunction: *until there is a trial before the congregation, until the death of the one who is high priest at the time* (NIV adds *and* between conditions). The text seems to reflect the instructions in Numbers 35:25, 28. It could be that the death of the high priest could signal an amnesty, so that the killer would be free to leave the city after his death.

Verses 7-8 describe the designation of cities, distributed evenly throughout the land, three on each side of the Jordan (see Deut 4:41-43 for the distribution that had already occurred in Transjordan). These cities also appear in chapter 21 as Levitical cities, which suggests that the cities, and the Levites, may have been administrative centers.

A summary statement (v. 9) notes that these cities are *designated* not only *for all the Israelites*, but also *for the aliens residing among them*. The last words sum up the initial instruction of verses 3-6 by giving the motive, *so as not to die by the hand of the avenger of blood*. Thus the designation of cities of refuge serves to curb the cultural tradition of retributive justice.

Both Numbers and Deuteronomy mention the cities of refuge within both divine and Mosaic speeches. It may well be that the narrator wishes the book of Joshua to present a "complete" picture of the distribution and settlement in the land. For that to happen, this distribution must take place. The narrator is presenting, as it were, a narrative in which all has been made ready for full and faithful life in the land. This is the goal toward which the book of Joshua aims. By the time we reach the end of the distribution, including chapters 20–21, it is time to say that all has been accomplished of God's good promises (21:43-45). Thus all the structures of life in the land must be established before the narrative about ongoing life in the land can proceed. Yet even then, chapter 22, which frames the distribution with its parallels to the Transjordan distribution summarized in chapter 13, rounds out the cleanness of the distribution by introducing a motif of disharmony. The juxtaposition of the full readiness for faithfulness and its threat in chapter 22 foreshadows the tragedies told in the book of Judges. Still, Joshua stands paradigmatically at the beginning, either to say that it need not have been that way, or that it may again be possible to live as Israel if certain conditions are met. Yet even then, there are no guarantees, especially when rivalries and desires (as well as other allegiances/gods) threaten to undermine the fragile peace.

Finally, it is important to notice that here, as in other places in Joshua, *the aliens* are included in the life in the land (cf. 8:30-35).

The Levites' Initiative, the Israelites' Gift 21:1-42

After a number of references to the Levites' not receiving an inheritance among the tribes (see 13:14, 32; 14:3; 18:7), the text now makes a concession to the Levites based on Moses' words in Numbers 35. This inheritance comes as the last act of distribution that, together with assigning cities of refuge, forms a geographic pair concerned with maintaining justice and preserving the covenant (Torah) tradition. These are necessary for maintaining right order and right living in the land. Although that is not explicit in chapters 20–21, the summary at the end of chapter 21 implies the necessity of these distributions as a way of representing the fulfillment of Moses' vision of a people in a land under one God. The text therefore continues to present a theogeographical understanding of the land, a kind of ideal drawn into the narration of the past. Archaeological findings indicate that only in the eighth century BC were the towns in this list completely occupied *[Archaeology and Joshua, p. 389].*

Chapter 21 follows seamlessly upon chapter 20 just as the cities of refuge and the Levitical cities belong to the same divine speech of Numbers 35. Only there the Levitical cities are mentioned first (35:1-8) and the cities of refuge second (35:9-15). Reversal of order is typical of intertextual citation. The chapter begins by having the Levites approach Eleazar, Joshua, and the elders in Shiloh (cf. Josh 14:1) and remind them of what the Lord has said through Moses. Thus chapter 20 includes direct divine speech, and chapter 21 resorts to reported speech. The resulting "dialogue" between the two voices suggests a synergism. Verse 8 implies that God's speaking directly and God's speaking indirectly through the remembered words of Moses are equally valid. It is *by command of the LORD* that the Israelites obey (21:3, 8; cf. 19:50).

Shiloh is again cited as being *in the land of Canaan* (21:2; cf. 18:1; 22:9; Judg 21:12), as though that needed clarification (see commentary on Josh 18:1). The reference point of the narrator seems to be outside that geographic area. Perhaps the reference to *the land of Canaan* already implies such "abandonment," as Psalm 78:60 suggests.

The bulk of the chapter describes the selection of forty-eight cities by lot, one for each of the clans of the Levites (vv. 4-40). Most of the reports are straightforward, although one does need some familiarity with the Levitical line (see Boling 1983). According to Genesis 46:11, the children of Levi are Gershon, Kohath, and Merari. The list beginning in Joshua 21:4 deviates from that order by beginning, not surprisingly, with Kohath, who is the grandfather of Moses and Aaron (Exod 6:16-20). Aaron's descendants are first in the distribution (v. 4). Again, it is not surprising that they receive their towns in the central hill country surrounding Jerusalem and within the tribes of *Judah, Simeon, and Benjamin* (21:4). Since Judah eventually absorbs the other two tribes, this lot most likely reflects the status of the Aaronide priesthood in both the (southern) kingdom of Judah and in the Jerusalem cult.

Verses 5-7 summarize the distribution according to the allotment to the three sons of Levi in each of the twelve tribal areas. Verse 8 provides a narrative transition between verses 4-7 (lists by family) and verses 9-40 (lists by tribe). Verses 9-40 list the cities given within each of those tribal areas, beginning with the family of Aaron in the tribe of Judah, into which Simeon is again folded as one unit (21:9-19); following with the remaining Kohathite families according to their tribes (21:20-26); the Gershonites (21:27-33); and the Merarites, called *the rest of the Levites* (21:34-40). The Aaron group is first, and the text makes it clear that *the lot fell to them first* (v. 10).

The complications involved are not avoided. One of the towns, Kiriath-arba, had been given to Caleb (14:6-15; 15:13-19). Now, since Kiriath-arba (Hebron) is to be given to Aaron's group, the text clarifies the extent of Caleb's inheritance, which is now limited to *the fields of the town and its villages*, but presumably does not include the town of Hebron itself (21:11-12). Hebron is also a city of refuge within the tribes of Judah, Simeon, and Benjamin (20:7; 21:13). Together these assignments suggest that Hebron is a key administrative center for the southern region, where David is first designated as king (2 Sam 2:4), and from where he ruled for seven years (2 Sam 2:11; 1 Kings 2:11).

The two sequences each end with a summary statement: the towns given to the three families ends with a summary in verse 8, and the distribution by tribe ends with a summary in verses 41-42. The list reflects a hierarchy of Levitical families, with Aaron's family taking the prominent place, and Judah's being first of the tribal groups. The political realities of Levitical history have likely shaped this text as much as, or more than, an original divine plan (see Boling 1983, 1985).

Summary: The Lord's Gift, the Promise Fulfilled 21:43-45

The narrator has given the conquest story a theocentric overlay by adding this synthetic conclusion. The final distribution sequence ends with a statement reminiscent of 11:16-23 and looks forward to Joshua's speech in chapter 23. In addition, this summary draws together motifs from various places in the book of Joshua. The first words underscore that *the Lord* is the main actor in this narrative of distribution (v. 43). The motif of divine gift of land echoes the divine speech at the beginning of the book, which also includes the motif of rest (v. 44; cf. 1:15). Joshua's speech in Shiloh includes reference both to the divine gift and to the oath to the ancestors (18:3). The giving of *rest* provides a link to chapters 21–22 (21:44; 22:4). *All the land* (v. 43) reiterates the emphasis on the full conquest of the land, beginning with the command to spy out *the whole land* (2:3) and the report of the spies (2:24), the extent of Joshua's fame (6:27), the confession of the Gibeonites (9:24), and the summaries of Joshua's complete conquest (11:16, 23; 23:14). The overlap of those motifs along with the motif of *rest on every side* (v. 44) echoes the earlier statements on rest (1:13, 15; 11:23; 14:15). *Rest* recurs again in 22:4 and 23:1, but the full phrase is repeated within the DtrH only in Solomon's speech to King Hiram in 1 Kings 5:3-4. God has acted through David to give Solomon "rest on every side" *[Rest, p. 455]*. The oath to the ancestors (Josh 21:43-44) reflects a motif that also reverberates throughout Joshua, beginning in the first chapter (1:6; 5:6; 18:3) and culminating in the appeal to the ancestors in the covenant speech of chapter 24. Joshua 24 describes the ancestors as worshiping other gods (24:2, 14, 15), God as the one who "gave" land to Esau (24:4), and God as leading the ancestors out of Egypt (24:6, 17).

The summary at the end of chapter 21 also reiterates the completeness of the conquest by claiming that *not one of all their enemies* had been able to stand against them (v. 44; cf. 11:23; 21:45). Similarly, the motif of *all the land* in 21:43 reflects not only the completeness emphasized in 11:16, 23, but also that Deuteronomy 34:1-4's "all the land" or "the whole land" is only west of the Jordan, and Moses will "not cross over there" (cf. Deut 19:8; Josh 1:4).

The summary of 21:43-45 seems to bypass the chronological ambiguity inherent in the *very much of the land still remains to be possessed* of 13:1 and the several statements of *could/did not drive out* (13:13; 15:63; 16:10; 17:12-13), which are only picked up again in chapter 23. The emphasis here is rather on the completeness of the conquest, the gift of rest, and the fulfillment of the divine promises. Verse 45 adds a motif of promise: *all the good promises*, which *all came to pass*. The expression *good promises that the* Lord *had made* may be translated literally, "any good thing/word that the Lord had spoken," with "thing/word" and "spoken" deriving from the same Hebrew root (*dbr*). This is the same promise with which the book of Joshua begins (1:3), *as . . . promised to Moses* (cf. 22:4; 23:5, 10, 14, 15). The motif of *good things* and *promise* occur again in Joshua's speech of 23:14-15. But there Joshua also introduces the ominous *bad things*.

The summary of 21:43-35 does not fully prepare the reader for what follows in chapter 22. Yet the transition in 22:1-6 suggests a reciprocity between the Lord's actions in 21:43-45 and Joshua's commendation and blessing of the Transjordan tribes in 22:1-6. And the echo of part of 21:43-45 in 23:14b is important because the latter text continues by emphasizing not only the *good things* but also the *bad things* that will/may happen in the future. This raises the question of whether the book of Joshua is simply about the "good things" or whether it also anticipates the "bad things," even as do texts like Deuteronomy 29.

THE TEXT IN BIBLICAL CONTEXT

Cities of Refuge

Joshua 20 echoes the instruction to appoint cities of refuge in Numbers 35. If the *go'el* meets that person outside the city, the fugitive could be killed. The fugitive is allowed to stay in the city until the death of the high priest. It could be that the high priest's death limits the time the fugitive needs to stay under "city arrest," as it were. No ransom is allowed in such cases of blood polluting the land (Num 35:32-33). The priest's death does not propitiate for the offense, as some claim. Rather, as the text states, ransom cannot be paid for any pollution of the land except by the one who shed blood (35:33). This instruction is theologically grounded in the divine presence: "You shall not defile the land in which you live, in which I also dwell; for I the LORD dwell among the Israelites" (35:34). Although 35:31 affirms death for the guilty (cf. Gen 9:5-7), it creates a space for ambiguity in interpretation of such crimes, which are an affront to the presence of God.

The word "sanctuary" bears its double meaning in current English usage from an early reference to asylum at the altar (Exod 21:12-14). Joshua's designation of cities of refuge reflects an interpretation of the Exodus text, with its explicit reference to "my altar" and the cryptic "place to which the killer may flee." That interpretive tradition reflected in Joshua echoes prescriptions by Moses in both Deuteronomy and Numbers. In Deuteronomy 4:41-43 Moses sets apart three cities in Transjordan: "Bezer in the wilderness, . . . Ramoth in Gilead, . . . and Golan in Bashan." These three are mentioned in Joshua 20:8, where it appears that the Israelites are designating these cities. There is no mention of an earlier act by Moses. Part of the puzzle may be resolved by noting what Deuteronomy 19 teaches about the cities of refuge. The chapter begins by assuming a time in the future when God has given them the land and they are living in it. At that time they are to "set apart three cities" in the "three regions" of the land (19:2-3).

Joshua 21 draws on Deuteronomy 4:41-43 and 19:1-7 but does not copy Deuteronomy's explanation for the need for cities of refuge. Indeed, Joshua's explanation is more detailed than the one in Deuteronomy. As in Numbers 35:9-12, Joshua explains the procedure of flight, protection, and trial, which Deuteronomy does not. Even the example of deliberate homicide in Deuteronomy 19:11-13 does not stipulate a trial but is concerned simply that Israel "purge the guilt of innocent blood." Further, in Deuteronomy 19:8-10, while elaborating the two cases presented (unintentional and intentional homicide), Moses gives instructions concerning three additional cities that are to be added, but stipulates that this may only happen "if the LORD your God enlarges your territory" (19:8a). This qualification is linked to God's oath to the ancestors that Israel should receive as a gift "all the land," an oath contingent upon Israel's faithfulness

(Deut 19:8-9). This is the same qualification used in Deuteronomy 11:22-23 of God's "driving out" the nations (cf. Josh 13:1-7).

Thus the designation of three cities in Joshua 20 does not consider the problem that Deuteronomy raises, that of the distance between the cities being too great to guarantee the fugitive's safety (Deut 19:6). Although the criterion for setting up three more cities—that God has given "all the land"—seems to have been fulfilled in the *all the land* emphasis of the book of Joshua (1:4; 2:24; 9:24; 11:16, 23; 21:43; 24:3; cf. 18:1), Joshua does not designate "three more cities to these three" (Deut 19:9). The book of Joshua seems to follow the patterns and stipulations of Numbers 35 of three plus three cities, the trial before the community, the death of the high priest. According to the explanation in Numbers, the cities of refuge are not only a sanctuary for the person who kills someone unintentionally; they are also a way of preserving the sanctity of the land, thereby preserving a place free of blood defilement in which the Lord may "dwell among the Israelites" (Num 35:34). Although Joshua does not pick up that aspect of the Numbers explanation, it may be implied because of the proximity of cities of refuge and Levitical cities in both Joshua 20–21 and Numbers 35.

One further way of engaging the conversation of Joshua 20 with Numbers 35 and Deuteronomy 19 is to note that the LXX translation of Joshua does not include Joshua 20:4-6. Those verses include supplementary material from Deuteronomy 19:1-13. Most likely, as Emanuel Tov suggests, an earlier edition of the book of Joshua (the basis of the LXX) reflects engagement with Num 35:9-34 but not with Deuteronomy. A later and longer edition of Joshua incorporates the Deuteronomic source material (Tov 1986: 325).

These observations suggest that Joshua 21 is part of a long process in the development of the tradition of asylum cities, which is reflected in different texts and manuscript traditions. The texts reflect a process of theological-ethical discernment that is not a static tradition or abstract principle of "biblical justice." Such discernment is a growing practice undergirded by a theological vision (Fretheim 2003). That practice makes an important distinction between premeditated murder and involuntary manslaughter, a distinction in both motivation and consequence. The cities of refuge create a crack in the cycle generated by the tradition of blood vengeance as it was practiced in the ancient world (e.g., Gen 4:23-24; Judg 15:7; 2 Kings 9:7). Although the tradition of asylum cities mentions the death of the high priest, in the NT only the book of Hebrews identifies the death of the high priest (Jesus) as the typological fulfillment that frees not only those who have committed involuntary manslaughter, but also all who violate the personhood of others (Heb 7:26-28; 10:10). Yet even there divine mercy and divine justice live in tension with each other (10:21-22, 30-31).

Levitical Cities

Levi and Simeon are responsible for the killing and pillaging of Shechem (Gen 34). Because of that, according to the Genesis text, Jacob's blessing has them dispossessed, divided, and scattered in Israel (49:7). The Levites are also agents of the bloodbath after the episode of the golden calf (Exod 32:25-29). As Brisman puts it, there is irony because these "butchers" are, in 32:25-29, called on to "become God's butchers." It is not clear how their violent past and their religious vocation intersect, even though one may discern some kind of "poetic justice" (180). But is that something greater or less than a share in the land? That irony is enhanced in Joshua where the Levites are indeed not given an inheritance in the land since *the LORD God of Israel is their inheritance* (13:33) or *the offerings by fire . . . are their inheritance* (13:14). But the echoes of Genesis 34 and Exodus 32 remain for readers of Joshua who know those stories. As Jacob puts it, out of his fear of being "destroyed," "You have brought trouble on me by making me odious to the inhabitants of the land, the Canaanites and the Perizzites" (Gen 34:30). In the next episode, Jacob returns to Bethel and calls on all the people in his household and those with him to "put away the foreign gods that are among you, and purify yourselves" (35:2). They do so, and "as they journeyed, a terror from God fell upon the cities all around them, so that no one pursued them" (35:5).

Ironically the Levites, with their history of "sacred" violence (Gen 34; Exod 32), receive cities of refuge *[Levitical Cities, p. 447]*. Thus Joshua offers a "rehabilitation" of the Levites. They are responsible for the ark (Deut 10:8-9) and for ministering to the Lord, blessing his name "to this day," which is why "Levi has no allotment or inheritance with his kindred; the LORD is his inheritance, as the LORD your God promised him" (Deut 10:9). Although Deuteronomy invents the interpretation "the LORD is his inheritance" (reflected in Josh 13:33), it is important to remember that Jacob has said of Levi and Simeon that "weapons of violence are their swords. May I never come into their council" (Gen 49:5-6). According to Brisman, irony comes through the voice of Jacob, "the perturbed ancestor," which is "a voice of moral reservation that comes like the voice of God" (180–81).

The Levites, perpetrators of violence, judged by their father, appropriated by Moses for sacred violence, and assigned to the sacrificial cult (in Leviticus), now become guardians of the cities of refuge for those accused of murder. Their responsibilities are to become ameliorators of human violence even as they are consigned to permanent refugee status themselves. Even so, they become caretakers of Israel's theological traditions and cultic practices.

If that is so, then the emphasis on faithfulness to Torah in the book of Joshua (including the emphasis on idolatry and pagan practices in chs. 22–24) strengthens the placement of the Levites throughout the land. The list in Joshua 21 therefore is not simply a geographical allotment, but also a theological and moral punctuation mark at the end of the distribution sequence. The last allotments create a context for ongoing instruction in Mosaic Torah. The community is formed, finds it locus in the land, and is now ready to be guided and instructed by the Levitical teachers that Deuteronomy says "reside in your towns" (12:12). Unfortunately, Josiah's so-called reform robs the land of those very agents of justice and instruction that Joshua's narrative assumes will provide the moral structure for life together in the land (2 Kings 23:4-5, 8-9). Josiah's action of disenfranchising the Levites in the Levitical cities is an attempt to purge Israel of its idolatry (also a concern of Joshua); yet he also undermines those who have the task of encouraging covenant loyalty. Perhaps the DtrH wants to show that even the ideal presented in the book of Joshua is unable to sustain a people who are faithful during Joshua's time (Josh 24:31), but who in the end cannot serve the Lord (24:19) *[Levitical Cities, p. 447]*.

The Good Promises and Rest

In the Explanatory Notes I have already observed that the summary in Joshua 21:43-45 echoes numerous texts in both Joshua and Deuteronomy. It asserts that all of the Lord's *good promises* have been fulfilled. The emphatic tone, coupled with intrabiblical allusions of promises to the ancestors, take us as far back as Gen 12:1-3 and other divine promise texts (e.g., 12:7; 13:15-17; 15:7, 18). In addition, the ancestors are said to be living in the land of "promise" as "aliens" (17:8; 20:1; 21:23; 21:34; 23:4; 26:3; 28:4; 35:27; 37:1), which is a sign of both fulfillment and nonfulfillment (Clines 1997). And the motif of "rest" becomes a transformation from alien status to resident status.

But the *good promises* or *good things* of Joshua 21:45 are mirrored ominously in 23:15, where Joshua juxtaposes the *good things* with the *bad things*, leading to a tragic line: *until he has destroyed you from this good land that the Lord your God has given you.* This is not a good development, for it reaches both back to the covenant curses of Deuteronomy and forward to the loss of land at the end of the books of Kings. Only Jeremiah takes up the motif of "good promises" (with the exact Heb. phrase as in Josh 21:45; 23:15). Jeremiah announces that the Lord will fulfill the "good promise" to Israel and Judah by raising up a "righteous branch . . . for David" (33:14-15). Concerning the ancestral promise of "sands of the sea," Jeremiah now imagines that God will "increase the offspring of my servant David, and the Levites who minister to me" (33:22).

Still, Joshua's narrator affirms the divine gift of rest *[Rest, p. 455]*. This gift is rooted in the divine promise, where God tells Moses, "My presence will go with you, and I will give you rest" (Exod 33:14). "Rest" in Deuteronomy is related to "rest from enemies" (3:20; 12:9-10; 25:19), or "rest from his/their/your enemies on every side" (Deut 12:10; 25:19; Josh 23:1; 2 Sam 7:1, 11; cf. 2 Chron 14:6; Neh 9:28; Esther 9:16, 22; Isa 14:3). The rest may well include the extermination of the enemy (Deut 25:19). In the DtrH the Lord "gives rest." The expression occurs in Joshua 1:13, 15 and 21:44 in such a way that those two sections provide a framing device within the book. Joshua 1:15 is Joshua's address to the Transjordan tribes, whom he instructs to continue until the Lord gives rest to the remaining tribes as well. Now that Joshua 21:43-45 draws that rest into its summary statement, the Transjordan tribes are free to return, which is exactly what occurs next in chapter 22. Thus 22:4 echoes 21:44, which ties the two chapters together explicitly. The motif occurs again in 23:1 as part of the transition to the final sequence of episodes in the book of Joshua.

The Lord's gift of rest recurs later only with David and Solomon in the DtrH (2 Sam 7:1, 11; 1 Kings 5:4). The final occurrence of the motif is in Solomon's blessing of the assembly after his dedicatory prayer. In that speech he uses language drawn explicitly from Joshua 21:43-45, with these words and phrases: "given rest," "not. . . failed," "good promise," "ancestors" (1 Kings 8:56-57). By making these explicit connections with Joshua 21, Solomon speaks words that tie his experience of God's goodness to that of God's goodness during Joshua's time. Joshua's era becomes paradigmatic in the DtrH. But on closer inspection, this is an ironic paradigm, for although Solomon experiences imperial success, he ultimately loses his kingdom because of idolatry *[Idolatry, p. 438]*. Joshua is a faithful successor to Moses, but Solomon proves to be an unfaithful successor to David (see Schäfer-Lichtenberger). For the larger biblical context of the "rest" motif, see the essay *Rest, p. 455*.

THE TEXT IN THE LIFE OF THE CHURCH

Cities of Refuge, Criminal Justice, and Community

Although we have no literal parallel in our time to cities of refuge, for the most part democratic societies have been influenced by biblical traditions pertaining to murder and unintentional homicide. Joshua 20 provides an ancient model for dealing with discerning the difference between premeditated murder and unintentional manslaughter. Contemporary legislation (in ideal contexts) presumes innocence until proof of guilt. This seems also to be the case in the laws concerning unintentional homicide, which lie behind the establishment of cities of refuge. Certainly one can imagine that anyone who has killed another person might flee to one of these cities, even if guilty of premeditated murder. The law stipulates that someone can only be found guilty on the basis of several witnesses (Num 35:30; Deut 17:6; 19:15). If there are no witnesses, as often there are not, any murderer could well find protection in a city of refuge. Thus the legal system, including cities of refuge, is not without its loopholes. Still, this ancient tradition calls for a trial, a period of asylum (until the death of the high priest), and eventual freedom. The system curbs another tradition, that of blood vengeance. Again, no one can guarantee that the avenger of blood will not strike even after the death of the high priest. But the ideal scenario allows for a vision of due process and a kind of protective justice.

Perhaps people of God's kingdom can create spaces where wrongdoers and others who are accused and discriminated against can be safe. Churches have offered sanctuary for runaway slaves and refugees of various kinds. We sometimes hear stories of individuals who have taken up residence in church buildings as a way of avoiding deportation or government extradition orders. The situation of refugees seeking sanctuary in churches arose because of a perceived injustice in the refugee claims process. Sanctuary, either in ancient Israel or in Canada, is not an attempt to circumvent the law but is an attempt to honor the principle of justice in evaluating persons' claims to innocence or recognizing their legitimate claims to refugee status. In other words, none should be denied a just and public process to substantiate their claims. In the United States of America, runaway slaves were protected on the Underground Railroad. Some churches sheltered Jews during the Nazi regime's Holocaust in Europe. Many churches provided shelter for Latin American refugees fleeing conflict and persecution. Recently a group called Circles of Concern has begun working at providing a safe place for sex offenders by walking alongside them after their return to the community.

The fact that cities of refuge and Levitical cities are mentioned in similar contexts in both Numbers and Joshua, and that all of the cities of refuge are also Levitical cities, suggests that these cities are within the administrative jurisdiction of the Levites, whose tasks include instructing the community in the way of Torah and, probably, administering the justice system. We have separated the legal realm from the religious realm in Western culture. Any analogous role for the church cannot be directly related to the role of Levites or the function of Levitical cities. Still, today's "Levites" may well be advocates for marginalized people and victims; they may accompany or visit offenders and may be conflict mediation practitioners who seek alternatives to the retributive justice system that often operates in an adversarial mode. Any action, therefore, that reduces the *enmity between them* (Josh 20:5) and seeks to restore relationships may be offering an analogous service.

Levites and Church Workers

Since the sixteenth century many church groups have adopted the notion of the priesthood of all believers. Even those groups that do not use the label "priest" often continue to employ paid pastoral staff. Yet we do not actually believe that pastors have a special "inheritance," with the Lord as their inheritance. On the other hand, they do have a special privilege of attending to the life and well-being of the people.

Even though all believers share the work of ministry, pastoral staff often carry a significant intercessory role and find themselves coming alongside those in need. The text pictures Israelites giving of their own portion/inheritance so that the Levites might have places to live, along with enough land to pasture their flocks. Although the Levites receive a portion of the tithes and offerings, they also live off the land. Thus Paul's encouragement that the church support its workers (1 Cor 9:1-12) seems to be a rightful extension of the care for priests and Levites.

Rest and the Good Promises of God

If the *good promises* of God culminate in a place of safety and security (21:43-45), then it is fitting that the motif of land as place of rest and security from enemies becomes a vital point for conversation in our times, when security issues have become a vital part of the international agenda. Part of that vitality may well involve the church in imagining how this divine rest has both been given to us and yet remains to be entered. It may be possible to imagine ourselves as Israel, or as Canaanites, without stretching the text too far or changing the topic of the conversation. Rahab and the Gibeonites recognize the need for their own security in the face of an invading force. The Joseph and Dan tribes encounter hostility from more heavily armed indigenous populations and either ask for more secure territory (Joseph), or flee to a place where they can settle more easily (Dan; see Judg 18).

Those options are no longer available to us even though Anabaptists and others in the past have fled for their own safety, whether or not their interpretations of their situations were correct. It will not do any longer to make a blanket claim that we are the ones who must defend ourselves against incursions from the outside, and that we must flee to a land safe from the dangers of this one. Without defending Israel's conquest accounts, it is possible to suggest that the final verses of chapter 21 make it quite clear that it is the Lord who gives land, who gives rest, and who generates fulfillment of the divine promises. Since writers like the author of the book of Hebrews transpose the rest/land motif into a spiritual vision of rest in the present and hope for the future, but one unrelated to actual conquest or occupation of land, we can affirm that the intrabiblical conversation also transposes the physical other, the dispossessed Canaanites, into another key *[Rest, p. 455]*.

Joshua 22:1-34

Othering the Insider

PREVIEW

Here is a classic case for conflict resolution studies, although it may illustrate how *not* to practice such efforts. The actions of one party have consequences that affect a second party. The second party infers the intentions of the first party and prepares immediately for out-and-out war. As it turns out, the intentions are honorable (or so they seem), and the second party must revise its presupposed assumptions about the first party. The problem for readers, however, is whether we should read the surface of the text and assume that this is actually such a conflict story, or whether we should assume that a more complex reality lies inside this story, which reverberates into the larger biblical story of Israel's intertribal relations and identities.

As we might expect, after the *good things* had *all come to pass* (21:45 NJPS/NRSV), Joshua sends the two and a half tribes back to their allotted territory east of the Jordan. This text rounds out the distribution section of the book, which begins in chapter 13 with the reiteration of Moses' distribution to the Transjordan tribes (see 13:8-33; Deut 3:8-22) [*Transjordan Tribes, p. 464*]. The chapter also recalls Joshua's first address in chapter 1, which calls for the faithful service of these tribes *until the Lord gives rest to your kindred as well as to you* (Josh 1:15). The motif of *rest* occurs in both chapters (1:13, 15; 22:4), which echoes Moses' instructions to the Transjordan tribes in Deuteronomy 3:20. Thus, with their service completed and their vow of obedience fulfilled (Josh 1:16), we expect the narrative to be rounded out neatly by the return of the Transjordan tribes to the land that Moses has allotted to them (cf. Deut 3:8-22). But that is not to be.

The transitional introduction of Joshua 13:1, which begins the distribution section of the book, recurs in 23:1, which suggests that 23:1 is the marker for the final section of the book of Joshua and that chapter 22 forms a conclusion to the distribution section of chapters 13–22. Similarly, chapter 22 begins with *at that time* (lit.), using the same term as in 8:30a, which closes the sequence of chapters 5–8 (Winther-Nielsen: 260–61). And the final confession of the Transjordan tribes (22:34) "is a befitting ending to the years of conquest and distribution" (262; cf. the confession and commitment at the end of ch. 1). Chapter 22 is therefore an appropriate conclusion to the distribution narrative begun in 13:1–14:5.

The narrative begins with Joshua's affirming the Transjordan tribes, reminding them in good Deuteronomic language to observe the commandments and love the Lord (22:5; cf. Deut 6:5; 7:9; 10:12; 11:1) and sending them off with a blessing (Josh 22:7). On their way these tribes build *an altar of great size* (v. 10), which troubles the other tribes so much that they assemble *to make war against them* (v. 12). That these other tribes (west of the Jordan) are called *the Israelites* (v. 9) already makes us wonder what the narrative is up to. The ensuing hostile conversation finds the western tribes accusing the eastern tribes of treachery and rebellion, which leaves the eastern tribes backpedaling to explain their motives and requires a rapprochement between the two groups. Still, the reader has an uneasy feeling. Is this an authentic peace, or does it foreshadow other conflicts and raise other questions? Moreover, what is the significance of the altar's construction in the light of the two texts reporting other cultic events, the circumcision and Passover in 5:2-12 and the altar building and Torah reading in 8:30-35?

OUTLINE

Joshua's Exhortation, Blessing, and Dismissal of Transjordan Tribes, 22:1-8

The Return Home, 22:9

The Altar and Its Consequences: War? 22:10-12

The Conflict Mediators Sent Out, 22:13-31

The Mediators' Report and the Israelites' Affirmation, 22:32-34

EXPLANATORY NOTES

Joshua's Exhortation, Blessing, and Dismissal of Transjordan Tribes 22:1-8

Now that all the *good promises* have *come to pass* (21:45), Joshua is free to send the Transjordan tribes home. As readers expect (from Deut 3:20-22 and Josh 1:12-15), this "summoning" marks the close of both the conquest and the distribution. The Transjordan tribes have proved themselves true to their word (Josh 1:16-17), which is exactly what Joshua confirms (22:2). And the Lord *has given rest* (v. 4). Joshua's speech reiterates 1:15. The narrative comes full circle with an ending that mirrors its beginning. The interest in the Transjordan tribes frames the entire story thus far. But there will be a complication, which means that chapter 22 cannot be the end of the book. That complication is hinted at in Joshua's comment that this *Lord* who has *given rest to your kindred* is *<u>your God</u>* (v. 4, emph. added). But that hint sits silently until later in the story.

Joshua simply informs the Transjordan tribes that they have been faithful to *Moses the servant of the Lord* (vv. 2, 4, 5). This threefold repetition is significant because it reminds the reader of the priority of Moses' instructions as the norm by which the community shapes its life. They have *observed* all that Moses *commanded* (v. 2; cf. 1:16-17). Moses figures as the prominent character in this chapter, with his name appearing five times in the first nine verses (vv. 2, 4, 5, 7, 9). The threefold emphasis on Moses as *servant of the Lord* is also important because it begins to mark a significant transition between Moses and Joshua. When Joshua dies, the narrator, for the first time in the book, will name him *servant of the Lord* (24:29).

After affirming their faithfulness, telling them that they may return home, and before sending them away with a blessing (v. 6), Joshua offers an exhortation (v. 5) that sounds much like Moses' exhortations in Deuteronomy 6:5 and other places in Deuteronomy. Joshua's use of the Deuteronomic tradition not only emphasizes Joshua's continuity with Moses, but also highlights the heart of the story, which calls for a loving covenant loyalty to God alone (cf. Deut 5:10; 7:9; 11:1).

The opening sequence in chapter 22 ends in verses 7-8. Verse 7 summarizes the distribution narrative, states Joshua's blessing (the word *blessed* occurs in vv. 6 and 7) and his sending them away *to their tents*. Verse 8 adds a permission to return with much spoil to their families in Transjordan.

The expression *to your tents* means something like *go home*, as translated in Judges 19:9 (see also 2 Sam 20:1; 1 Kings 8:66; 12:16). These *tents* (vv. 4, 6, 7, 8) are *where your possession lies* (v. 4; cf. v. 9). Is this *possession* a reflection of the divine promise to the ancestors (Gen 17:8), where the same word is used (cf. Gen 23:4, 9, 20; 48:4)? It is certainly a possession granted by Moses, a grant that is implicitly linked to their subsequent obedience to Moses' commands (Josh 22:2). Readers will be alerted to the use of this word here (and in vv. 4, 9) when later reading the West Jordan tribes' intimation that the *possession* of the Transjordan tribes might be considered unclean (22:19, with the word *possession* used twice in the Hebrew text).

Joshua's affirmation of the Transjordan tribes' faithfulness (vv. 2-3), his exhortation (v. 5), and his blessing/sending (vv. 4, 7-8)—all give no explicit indication that a conflict is brewing. Readers can only assume that this introduction to the story is an affirmation of the commitment made by the Transjordan tribes in Joshua 1:16-17. Given the Deuteronomic language of Joshua's exhortation (v. 5), these tribes are as bound to the covenant commitments as are the tribes west of the Jordan. That the conflict emerges in the next episode illustrates the fragility, not of the Transjordan tribes' covenant loyalty, but of the bonds formed within the community called "Israel" as a whole. If the conflict had not emerged, we would assume that the Transjordan tribes would naturally be part of the congregation gathered to hear Joshua's farewell address and to participate in the covenant renewal event (chs. 23–24). But the events to follow turn our expectations around and highlight the fragility of the communal bond. Not only is covenant with the Lord called into question, but the very constitution and identity of "Israel" are also threatened.

The Return Home 22:9

The summary of the Transjordan tribes' return home (v. 9) includes the first hint of a perceived difference between the groups on either side of the Jordan. Although Moses appears as a figure who has addressed them specifically, and now who continues to authorize their separate identity in a distinct territory (vv. 2, 4, 5, 7, 9), this specialness also hints at a parting and a separation. The narrator makes an important distinction between the Transjordan tribes, who have *the land of Gilead*, and *the Israelites* who are *in the land of Canaan* (v. 9). The land belonging to the Transjordan tribes is called *their own land* (v. 9). The narrator makes a point of identifying *the land of Canaan* four times (vv. 9, 10, 11, 32; cf. four other occurrences, in Josh 5:12; 14:1; 21:2; 24:3), which may suggest a location outside that land as the point of view from which the narrator is telling the story. Alternatively, it may suggest that boundary issues are or will be at stake in chapter 22 and that the identity and relational integrity of the two groups may be called into question.

The Altar and Its Consequences: War? 22:10-12

The journey home is interrupted at the Jordan, where the movement stops when the Transjordan tribes build *an altar of great size* (v. 10; lit., *great in appearance*). The location of this altar is a puzzle for translators. The Hebrew term *gelilot* may be a place name, Geliloth (so NIV; cf. Josh 18:17), or it may be Gilgal, as reflected in the LXX, a site about five miles west of the Jordan. More likely the word means *district/ region* (as in Josh 13:2), which derives its extended meaning from the Hebrew root word meaning "circle" (bounded region). Verse 10 states clearly that this altar is built *in the land of Canaan*. Verse 11 adds to the complexity by stating that they have built this altar *at the frontier of the land of Canaan, in the region near the Jordan, on the side that belongs to the Israelites*. Three geographic terms are ambiguous: *frontier*, *region*, and *on the side*. The NJPS translation illustrates a different understanding: *opposite the land of Canaan, in the region of the Jordan, across from the Israelites*. Whereas the second of the three terms, *region* (NRSV), is ambiguous, the first can mean "in front of," and the third can mean "region across or beyond" (*HALOT*). The NJPS reading is preferable not only because of that, but more so because when *the Israelites* send their representatives to meet with the Transjordan tribes for their apparent breach, they send them *to the Reubenites . . . in the land of Gilead* (v. 13). And when they return to report *to the Israelites*, they *returned from the Reubenites . . . in the land of Gilead to the land of Canaan, to the Israelites* (v. 32). Although the location of the altar may be ambiguous in verse 10, the use of prepositions, as well as the entire context, suggests that the Transjordan tribes have built the altar on the eastern side of the Jordan.

This altar construction leads *the Israelites* to gather at Shiloh, *to make war against them* (v. 12; cf. *Shiloh* in 18:1; 19:51; 21:2). The stakes are immense. The narrator identifies *the Israelites* as dwelling *in the land of Canaan*. The altar creates a problem large enough for the Israelites to treat their *brothers* (22:4, 7, 8 NASB) as enemies. Either the altar is outside *the land* or in a place that has not been designated as a legitimate site for an altar. If outside the land, as I have suggested above, then the altar raises questions about how far God's jurisdiction applies. If inside the land, then this altar may violate a Deuteronomic prescription about where altars are allowed, restricted to the place where the Lord "will choose" (12:5-6; etc.; cf. Josh 9:27). Most important of all, the altar represents a threat to the relational unity of the people of God. After all, the altar that Joshua built (Josh 8:30-35) was built according to Moses' instructions. That altar is the gathering place of *all Israel* (8:33), an identity called into question by this act reported in chapter 22 *["All Israel," p. 385]*. That the narrator calls the tribes west of the Jordan *the Israelites* is telling. It seems to represent a later designation that has come to be associated with the geographic region west of the Jordan. To be "outside" the land is to be "outside" Israel. Yet the Transjordan tribes do not see themselves that way. Thus the narrative raises questions about the relationship between land and identity.

Who is "in" and who is "out"? And who determines that? It is fitting that just as Rahab, an "ethnic outsider" become covenant partner, is the key figure in the first main story in the book, so now the Transjordan tribes, "ethnic insiders" at the end of the book become questionable covenant partners through exclusion by their own compatriots (cf. Polzin; Mitchell). They are excluded as "outside the land" by those who presume that the Lord's presence must remain "inside the land." The narrative gives us no indication that the Transjordan tribes are concerned about negative implications or effects of their altar building. The Israelites appear to interpret the action as apostasy and, as a result, prepare to wage war on the Transjordan tribes. But before they do so, they (wisely?) send out mediation practitioners.

The Conflict Mediators Sent Out 22:13-31

The priest Phinehas and a group of ten representatives set out to meet the Transjordan tribes *in the land of Gilead* (v. 13, 15). These leaders are *from each of the tribal families of Israel* (twice in v. 14). Using a messenger speech form, they come as delegates who speak on behalf of the entire community, which they call *the whole congregation of the* L*ORD* (v. 16). "All Israel," so it seems, has by default already excluded the Transjordan tribes. That exclusion is confirmed in their accusation, in which they use the word translated as *treachery*, as also used of Achan (*ma'al*, in 7:1, *broke faith*). These leaders even cite Achan as a case in point (v. 20), which the representatives use to justify their fear that the treachery might have consequences for more than only the Transjordan tribes (the Heb. word is also in vv. 16, 22, 31). Since *wrath fell upon all the congregation of Israel* and Achan *did not* *perish alone for his iniquity* (v. 20), then the tribes west of Jordan have good reason to fear for their safety. In the seduction of Baal of Peor (Num 25), Phinehas kills a cohabiting Israelite man and Midianite woman and is honored for the deed; hence we wonder about the outcome of sending Phinehas as leader of the delegation (Josh 22:13). This man even mentions the Baal of Peor incident. Phinehas is a "true believer" (even a "militant fundamentalist") in the sense that he is willing to go to any lengths to preserve notions of purity of the faith and peoplehood (note the divine sanction for such actions, Num 25:3-5).

Instead of mediating, the representatives accuse the eastern tribes of *treachery* and *rebellion against the* Lord (v. 16). *Rebellion/rebel* is used six times in five verses (22:16, 18, 19, 22, 29). Rebellion is a breach of covenant/treaty loyalty (the term is used later in DtrH only in 2 Kings 18:7, 20; 24:1, 20). The admonition not to rebel also occurs in Joshua and Caleb's speech in the dispute that arises after the spies' report (Num 14:9). The leaders of Israel similarly use the verbal expression *turning away* (v. 16), which bears a twofold irony. First, this is the same word that Moses has used in granting them the right to "return" after helping their kindred (Deut 3:20). Second, at both the beginning and end of Deuteronomy, Moses speaks of a time to come after their scattering and exile when there will be hope for a "return" to the Lord after apostasy (e.g., 4:30; 30:2, 10). Deuteronomy 30:2 even uses the expression "with all your heart and with all your soul" that we find in Joshua 22:5. Only now the Israelite representatives reapply the word, commonly appearing in contexts calling for repentance (turning around), as a designation for the Transjordan tribes' presumed apostasy (22:16, 18). They do not even allow the Transjordan tribes honor for having redeemed themselves and for having made good their promises made to Joshua by helping the western tribes get their land (1:16). They liken this altar building to the *sin at Peor from which even yet we have not cleansed ourselves* (22:17). As it turns out, these are accusers. They harbor memories of past wrongs and continue to accuse. The contagion of that act at Peor has not been eradicated. Their accusation has been a ploy. It is they who will not let go, and so the contagion continues to undermine their unity.

Phinehas and his delegation are interested in purity. They would rather sacrifice members of their community than risk the safety of the entire congregation (v. 18). It may not be the Lord's anger that they fear, which has not yet been established as a serious factor in this conflict. The Lord appears in the accusations as a convenient instrument of their own paranoia about the supposed purity of the land. Thus the accusers raise an issue in verse 19 that seems quite unrelated to the matter at hand: the altar. They introduce a motive that no one has credibly established: *if your land is unclean* (v. 19). Then they suggest that these Transjordan tribes should consider crossing over *into the LORD's land.* Why is it the Lord's land? Is it because they all recognize the Jordan as the boundary of the Lord's jurisdiction? Or is it because the Lord is localized only at the place of the tabernacle, as they think (v. 19)? In the book of Joshua, *tabernacle* occurs only here and in verse 29. Or is it because the Lord can have only one altar, which could be inferred from verses 19 and 29 (but cf. the altar on Mount Ebal, 8:30-35)? Since the matter remains unclear in the book of Joshua, those are all possible inferences that the accusers might draw from the altar-building action. These assumptions rely in part on the Deuteronomic worldview. They cannot be sure the argument will work. So they draw on the Achan story to cast the final stone in the accusation. They even use the same vocabulary: *break faith* (v. 20; cf. 7:1; 22:22). The connection between Joshua 7 and 22 is not accidental. There is great danger in "apostasy and the terrible corporate culpability that it entails" (Hubbard: 17).

Every point in the argument, however, is inferential and is based on their interpretation of an action that has not yet been explained. The Transjordan tribes have been accused of treachery and rebellion and of turning away from the Lord, the land has been labeled unclean, and the action has been named a contagion that threatens the very life of Israel. This interpretation could be undermined by suggesting that the accusers are really afraid of a repeat incident like that of Peor (Num 25). But even if that is the case, and there is no evidence in the story that it is, the accusers in this conflict scenario act entirely out of their own interpretation, and they allow the old stories to govern their interpretation of this ambiguous incident.

Fortunately the Transjordan tribes do have an opportunity to respond (vv. 21-29). But even then, it is not altogether clear that we should trust their answer. It seems to be in keeping with their earlier confession and commitment to obedience in Joshua 1:16, yet it also seems fabricated to suit the needs and dangers of the moment. Their first statement in defense of their position is a cry of theological affirmation: *The LORD, God of gods! The LORD, God of gods!* (22:22a). The Hebrew text offers only three juxtaposed names for God (repeated twice): *'el 'elohim yhwh*, which could be simply translated as "God, God, Yahweh" (elsewhere only Ps 50:1).

By including three divine names, their affirmation indicates that they consider themselves to be united in faith with the other Israelites. No Israelite has made such a confession before in the book of Joshua. Like Rahab (2:11), the Transjordan tribes exclude all other allegiances in heaven or on earth. After their appeal to God's sovereignty, they turn to the accusation at hand by repeating the very words they have heard from their accusers. Using the same words—*rebellion, breach of faith* (treachery), and *turn away* (vv. 22b-23a; cf. v. 16)—they cast themselves on the mercy of the other Israelites (v. 22b). If they have done this wrong, and moreover if they have built the altar to offer any kind of offerings on it, they even suggest, *may the Lord himself take vengeance* (v. 23b). The word used here means "to seek"; when used without a direct object, it means something like "require a reckoning" (cf. *call us to account*, NIV, though "us" is not in MT; or *demand [a reckoning]*, NJPS).

I trust their theological confession because, in the context of the characterization of the Transjordan tribes in the book of Joshua, it seems believable. But their confession about not making offerings on the altar seems forced, like a ploy to divert attention from the real problem. Why would anyone build an altar except for offerings (vv. 26-27)? We could interpret their statement as a reflection of authentic Deuteronomic conviction, that there ought not to be any altar but the one at the place where the Lord should choose. But then why build one in the first place? Or, we might say, because of Phinehas's reputation for extremism, the Transjordan tribes are forced to fabricate a bogus reason for building their altar, a reason that reveals a truth about communal identity, a legitimate fear about loss of belonging, and a longing for inclusion.

Having cast themselves on the mercy of the Israelites and on divine reckoning, they now redefine the problem in terms of the real conflict, which is not about altars. Nor is it about perceived theological orthodoxy. The real conflict (and fear) concerns the possibility of exclusion and marginalization from the peoplehood of God. And it has to do with the future. It concerns what *your children might say to our children* (v. 24). First generations in a family conflict may well manage to muddle through and come out survivors. But often the second and third generations, who have heard the stories and whose picture of the world and of familial relationships has so shaped their perspective, no longer feel connected to the first generation. In this situation, the danger is rooted in a theology that has the potential for ideological exclusion. *The Israelites* (the tribes west of the Jordan: vv. 11-13) will, in time to come, have the power to exclude. The hypothetical question, *What have you to do with the LORD, the God of Israel?* (v. 24b), says more than any threat of war. If the Transjordan tribes are not "Israel," then does the Lord not have to do with them? Here the real named fear concerns human exclusion from the community of the Lord (v. 24).

What's more, the next generation of so-called *Israelites* might appeal to a fabricated ruling by the Lord to set the boundary at the Jordan River. Half of the hypothetical statement is correct (v. 25a) since the Jordan *is* a natural boundary. But the conclusion *You have no portion in the LORD* (v. 25b) runs against the grain of the entire narrative of distribution (cf. 13:7 uses the verb form of "portion," which means *divide*). All were given their portion. Moses himself has distributed their portion to the Transjordan tribes. Although their hypothetical response overstates the case, the nub of the matter again concerns not the Lord's making the Jordan a boundary, but *your children, who might make our children cease to worship the LORD* (v. 25c). The hypothetical scenario makes the *Israelites* of the next generations the real danger.

Having named *your children* twice as the source of their fear (vv. 24, 25), the Transjordan tribes are now able to name their own motivations and deliberations. They claim, in a confession about why the altar was built, to have built it as *a witness between us and you, and between the generations after us* (v. 27a). The altar becomes a means of generating a story and keeping it alive into the future. The notion of *witness* (Josh 22:27, 28, 34; 24:22) redefines the entire episode in terms that cannot be contained by either land or cult (altars and sacrifices). The fear of exclusion from the community of the Lord must be ameliorated by means of a story that passes from generation to generation, and that reminder must stand at the point of meeting, at the point of crossing the Jordan. The story, and the altar before it, must assure all *that we do perform the service of the LORD in his presence* (v. 27b). Is it God's presence discerned at this altar or another one? The next phrase *with our burnt offerings* is odd in relation to that question. Are these offerings on this altar, or on the one on Mount Ebal (8:30-35), or on one at the tent of meeting in Shiloh (cf. 1 Sam 1:3)? And what if the divine *presence* is where the ark rests, and where the tabernacle has been set up? Then that must be in Shiloh (even though we do not hear of the ark again in Joshua after 8:33). The Transjordan tribes reiterate an earlier fear about *your children* (v. 27c), and then they clarify an even more hard-to-believe statement that the *descendants in time to come* could call on their kindred to observe *this copy of the altar of the LORD* (v. 28). Their final appeal returns to a denial of any motive to *rebel* or *turn away* (v. 29a; cf. vv. 16, 19, 22-23). Now at the end of their defense, they claim that their cultic activity is directed only to *the altar of the LORD our God that stands before his tabernacle* (v. 29b, emph. added; cf. v. 19).

The response of the negotiating team (v. 30) suggests that the Transjordan tribes' explanation is more than adequate. They are pleased with the explanation; it is *good in their eyes* (lit.). Phinehas's response, however, returns to a "this side/that side" perspective (v. 31). It is not clear where he perceives the location of the Lord's presence. What does his affirmation *The LORD is among us* mean (v. 31)? Does his final assurance that *you have saved the Israelites from the hand of the LORD* suggest that the Lord continues to be present only with the *Israelite* tribes west of the Jordan River? Or does the *us* and *our* include the Transjordan tribes? Phinehas perceives that the Transjordan tribes' explanation has *saved* them. Is it a salvation from taking unwarranted vengeance and then being punished by God? The declaration that the Transjordan tribes have *not committed this treachery against the LORD* (22:31) takes us back to the earlier accusation, to their fear of the Lord's anger, and their likening this act to Achan's act (vv. 16-20). Even at the end of the story (v. 33), they continue to focus on themselves. They are interested in self-preservation, not in the unity of Israel as the Lord's people. They continue to exhibit an us-against-them way of thinking.

The Mediators' Report and the Israelites' Affirmation 22:32-34

The narrative draws to a close by reporting the return of the negotiating team (v. 32) and the effect of the news that they bring (v. 33). The *Israelites* were pleased with the report, they *blessed God*, and they *spoke no more of making war* (ceased their warmongering rhetoric) or of destroying their land.

The final confession of the Reubenites and Gadites (v. 34b) bears noting (although it is odd that Manasseh is not included: cf. vv. 25, 32, 33, 34; Num 32:1, 6, 25, 31; Deut 3:12, 16; but with Manasseh: Josh 22:30, 31; Num 32:33; Deut 3:13; 29:8). Only the Reubenites and Gadites name the altar *Witness* (Josh 22:34). The narrator has inserted this summary statement so as to confirm the integrity of the Transjordan tribes' commitment (1:16-18) *that the LORD is God* (v. 34b; cf. vv. 27-28). The confession seems to be a final rounding out of the negotiations, like a closing ceremony. But the two groups have been talking past each other.

Each has demonstrated distinct interests that the other group has not heard and understood. The western tribes are interested in boundaries and in preserving the hegemony of the cult on their side of the Jordan. The Transjordan tribes are interested in preserving their identity as a people of God. The narrative does not reflect a mutual understanding or a coming together of disparate interests through negotiation. Either the Transjordan tribes have pulled the wool over the eyes of the tribes west of the Jordan, or they have spoken truthfully and the other tribes have not heard. There is "peace," but it is a pseudo peace. We are reminded again of how precarious the Transjordan tribes' situation has become through their one act of altar building. The narrative is ironic: as the story of Israel unfolds, we discover that a rift eventually opens and the Transjordan tribes eventually disappear from the scene and lose their status as part of Israel—a tragic reflection on the very fears of these Transjordan tribes. Their situation is tragic because they have affirmed their exclusive allegiance to God, and they have clarified their fear, but that has not been enough to hinder the exclusionary practices of future generations (or the odd turns of history) that led them to become both marginalized and forgotten.

THE TEXT IN BIBLICAL CONTEXT

Where to Sacrifice? A Question of Community

The conflict of chapter 22 reverberates throughout Scripture both explicitly and implicitly. The clearest intrabiblical correspondences may be the explicit connections in Deuteronomy about the altar to be built at the place the Lord will choose (Deut 12:5-6). Although Exodus seems to allow for an altar at "every place where I cause my name to be remembered" (20:24), and Leviticus allows for slaughter of animals only if brought as an offering to the tent of meeting (17:2-9), Deuteronomy seems to limit the altar to one place, but allows slaughter of animals for eating in any place (12:5, 11, 15, 21; 14:23-24; 16:2, 6, 11; 26:2). The relationship of ideas among these three texts is complex.

The idea of one place of sacrifice is reiterated in Solomon's prayer at the dedication of the temple (1 Kings 8:29), but even there God's residence is not located at or limited to the temple (8:43). Even foreigners, according to Solomon, might be welcome at this place (8:41-43). Isaiah imagines nations coming with gifts for the Lord to "the place of the name" (18:7; cf. 57:15). Jeremiah speaks disparagingly of Shiloh as a place where the Lord's name dwelt "at first" (7:12, 14). Malachi imagines that incense and offerings may even be offered "in every place . . . among the nations" (1:11).

Deuteronomy seems to limit the location of the altar, and Josiah carries out a purge that disenfranchises the priests who serve at altars throughout the countryside because he supposes that they are idolatrous (2 Kings 23). Yet the Deuteronomistic historians do not assume a single location for the altar prior to Hezekiah's or Josiah's time (e.g., Judg 6:24; 1 Sam 7:17; 14:35; 1 Kings 3:4; cf. 2 Kings 18:22; 23:15, 19).

Joshua 22 may not, however, be concerned only with the place of the altar. As Weinfeld notes, "The conflict as such has nothing to do with the centralization of the cult—as some used to argue—but with the acceptance of the Tabernacle in Shiloh as the legitimate *central* shrine" (1983: 62). And since *tabernacle* appears only in Joshua 22:19 and 29, it seems as though the Israelites of Joshua 22 do not hold an exclusively Deuteronomic perspective. Joshua 22:19, with its notion of unclean land and location of the tabernacle, reflects more of the priestly notions of Leviticus 17, in which "the Tabernacle is the only legitimate place for sacrifice" (63).

Questions about altars and worship places echo prominently in the story of Jesus' encounter with the woman of Samaria. She assumes her ancestral tradition of worship on the mountain at Shechem (Ebal or Gerizim, where the Samaritans continue to worship to this day). She assumes that Jesus affirms the legitimacy of Jerusalem. Yet he affirms an altogether different "place," the place that can be found at the intersection of "spirit and truth" (John 4:19-24).

Paul transforms the "every place" motif by referring to all who "call on the name" of the Lord Jesus (1 Cor 1:2). The book of Hebrews speaks of "an altar" from which the temple servants cannot eat, which is "outside the camp," referring to Jesus' death. Therefore the author names two kinds of sacrifices not located in a place, but in actions: to "offer a sacrifice of praise," "to do good and to share what you have." These "sacrifices are pleasing to God" (13:10-16). The vision of Revelation has the altar in the presence of God, not the presence of God at the altar (6:9; 8:3, 5; 9:13; 11:1; 14:18; 16:7).

Land Boundaries

The question of land boundaries in Joshua 22 reflects the priestly concern for purity (v. 19). Although Leviticus offers various reasons for defilement of the land, abhorrent behavior can lead to the land's "vomiting out its inhabitants," whether Israelites or the indigenous inhabitants (cf. Lev 18:25-28; 20:22-23). The Jordan serves as a convenient geographic boundary for the territory that ought to be protected from violation. Since the *Israelites* interpret the altar as a violation, the altar could be understood, according to Joshua 22:19, as an attempt to cleanse the land east of the Jordan, thereby linking the Transjordan tribes to the purity of the land on the west. But the twice-repeated emphasis of *other than the altar of the LORD our God* (22:19, 29) suggests that the very act of building an unauthorized altar is cause for pollution and therefore for extermination of the offense and the offender. Even the broad-ranging boundary descriptions of Joshua 1:4 cannot check the limiting language of the *Israelites*, who believe that only the land west of the Jordan belongs to the Lord and that only one altar qualifies as a legitimate place of sacrifice (cf. Naaman, who took "two mule-loads of earth" home so that he could worship God in his own land yet on Israelite soil; 2 Kings 5:17). See further the essay *Extent of the Land, p. 424.*

Community Integrity

Chapter 22 illustrates the multiple challenges to unity and peoplehood and opens the way to interpret the book of Joshua not simply as a narrative of a golden age but also as a story that illustrates both personal (Achan) and corporate (Transjordan tribes) threats to communal integrity. In the first of those stories, the threat is handled by the sacrifice of one for the sake of the whole. In the second, the threat of sacrificing the part for the whole is resolved through negotiation (even though the reasons for the peaceful settlement remain somewhat unclear). Still, the story of Joshua 22 casts ripples into the story that follows. The Transjordan tribes are not able to settle into their "rest." The book of Judges illustrates ongoing conflict between groups on either side of the Jordan (including Jephthah, a Gileadite, and the Transjordan tribe of Ephraim in 12:1-7; and the attack on Jabesh-Gilead in 21:1-14).

Boundary issues are also a concern within the NT. We have already mentioned Jesus' encounter with the Samaritan woman (John 4). Cities of the Decapolis may have been considered out of bounds for many Jews (Mark 5:20; 7:31). Paul is concerned about the inclusion of Gentiles into the story of God's redemptive purposes. This comes through most clearly in his statements about eradication of boundaries between Jews and Gentiles (Gal 3:28; Col 3:11; Rom 10:12). At the heart of that concern is the application of Torah faithfulness to inclusion or exclusion from God's redemptive community. Paul argues that law is a gift of God, but it ought not to restrict God (or the Jesus community) from welcoming Gentiles who ought not be bound by the law. The letter to the Ephesians addresses boundary issues not as geographical, but as ethnic/political. Jews and Gentiles have experienced peace after the breaking down of the dividing wall of hostility between them (Eph 2:14). The vision of the book of Revelation has peoples receiving the good news and worshiping God from every "tribe and language and people and nation" (Rev 5:9; 14:6). Does this shed light on Joshua's conflict among the tribes? Although NT texts do not have Joshua 22 in the background, they reject ethnicity and geographical boundaries as criteria for inclusion or exclusion among the people of God.

Still, if we listen to Joshua 22 in the light of Scripture, we hear a concern for singleness of worship, for one ultimate allegiance (to be clarified further in Josh 23–24), and for transgenerational faithfulness (see further Josh 24:15). None of these are automatic outcomes of identifying with a community of faith that wrestles toward its identity, its place in the world, and its hope for generations to come. The Transjordan tribes take up the identity-shaping significance of the altar as witness, as a reminder of the kind of people they are and ought to be. It reminds them of the story that shapes their lives. Altar building is a symbolic act that reverberates through the generations in the hope that each generation will retell the story. This altar would aid such retelling, just as the altar upon first crossing the Jordan was such a memorial (8:30-35).

THE TEXT IN THE LIFE OF THE CHURCH

Who Is Other (Again)?

The book of Joshua testifies to the fact that each generation both tells and interprets the story of God's redemptive purposes in history. The telling, like the event about which it tells, may also generate conflict. As that story is told and retold, others will misinterpret the intentions of the retelling. The conversation of interpretation works at sorting out the intentions and effects of biblical stories. And the process of discernment, however honest or misguided, either bears fruit in the creation of a peoplehood that together celebrates the unifying and redemptive work of God, or disintegrates into exclusion, marginalization, or silencing. Othering continues today in all kinds of ways. It can only be overcome by acknowledging our common humanity and our common calling into God's redemptive purposes. Acknowledging our propensity to be othering Others, we may discover the resources for continuing to retell our stories for one another (see also the stories about Rahab [ch. 2], Achan [ch. 7], and the Gibeonites [ch. 9] that also concern relationship to "the other").

Joshua 22 reveals the dynamic of difficult conversations as part of the plot structure of the entire book. This story both affirms the need for having difficult conversations and offers insights into how those conversations may allow us either to flourish or to live in debilitating alienation from one another. The book emphasizes the commitment of the Transjordan tribes to the entire community (ch. 1) and then shows how part of that community—a majority—misunderstands, misinterprets, and misbehaves. Chapter 22 also depicts the process of conflict mediation, but it does so by depicting an example to avoid *[Difficult Conversations, p. 421]*.

Although it is risky to assume that analogies alone are adequate avenues for appropriation, I will make three such offerings. First, we have seen that identity issues spill over into outright ethnic conflict throughout the world. Is it also possible that boundary issues (turf wars) continue in the church today? Whose honest actions do we interpret as threatening both to our identity as followers of Jesus wishing to be faithful to Scripture and to our understanding of what it means to be committed only to God as God has come to be known in Christ? We fairly easily assume we know what constitutes "otherness," and we are often willing to exclude those Others from God's redemptive care by identifying ourselves as the true or only people of God.

Second, building altars in border regions of faith (geographical or not) is necessary for fruitful passing on of stories and commitments to the next generation. And it is also necessary for those who happen to be in charge to take time to live with those altars for some time and to listen to those who have built them, before making judgments about the intentions of those actions. We are still in the process of what some have called "the worship wars." One group wishes to appropriate contemporary media (film, music, drama) and alternative worship genres to communicate the good news story to the next generation. Another group seeks to maintain the traditions of the past. The differences between the two groups cannot be easily classified or described. No matter who the majority happens to be, the tendency toward othering is always present. People tend to act before having a conversation, to interpret the other before asking them to tell their story, and to assume the worst before letting them have their say.

Third, beware of religious and theological zealots who are mainly concerned about guarding the boundaries. It may well be more important for us to guide people toward the center than to mark out who is in danger of crossing the boundaries, or to identify who is in and who is out (Hiebert). Although the liberated covenant community needs to be shaped by the boundaries of God's instruction, an orientation toward the center of God's dynamic presence is always a priority. The boundaries only serve the center, loyalty to God. They are not an end in themselves.

The apostle Paul also wrestles with boundaries in his argument with respect to the law in Romans. And Jesus is concerned about those who quibbled with his redemptive actions on the Sabbath (e.g., Mark 2:24, 27; 3:2). But the balance between the appropriate function of the boundaries and the necessary focus on the center can become skewed by overzealous leaders like Phinehas. His story in Numbers 25, which is grounded in divine warrant (25:3-5), alerts us to his tendency toward violence as a way of resolving disputes. Leaders like Phinehas can become fine gatekeepers; they often appear, however, as obsessive guardians of the gates to the center. Certainly this appropriation of the text and Phinehas's place in the story could be questioned. I am simply offering a warning.

Finally, the concern to protect *our children* from *your children* suggests that conflict proceeds across generations. In spite of divine blessing and presence, their life together invariably proceeds toward some kind of conflict or another. This story and its twin, the story of Achan (Josh 7), hint that the community of blessing is not immune from trouble that has tragic consequences. In both cases the solution (execution or warfare) is not what followers of Jesus should advocate or imitate. Exclusion, including shunning, is often practiced unwittingly and through a process of misinterpretation and failure to listen to the story of the other. No matter how it is practiced, othering continues to have devastating effects on the maturing faith of our children. Often generations are lost to the church because they have seen through the sham dialogue involved in maintaining our side as separate from the other side.

In all the conflicts we encounter within our families, among neighboring religious communities, and in the church, we do well to honor the altars of the other, to listen to their stories, and to participate in sharing the "witness" of one to the other. The altar building in Joshua 22 is indeed a way of preserving faith. It represents a commitment to act for the vitality of the next generations. If God is Sovereign over the cosmos, as Rahab confesses (Josh 2:11) and Joshua asserts (3:11, 13), shall not even those whose altars are a threat to us be welcomed by God? Is it any longer possible, therefore, to utter the word "anathema" as it was used during the Reformation of the sixteenth century against the Anabaptists and others, or to call anyone Antichrist, as Menno Simons identified Catholicism and the state churches? The same could be said about other labels we place on people with other "altars" than the ones we recognize.

Joshua 23:1–24:33

Covenant Exhortations, Covenant Making, and Coda

PREVIEW

I have visited several homes in which a wall plaque announces prominently, *As for me and my house, we will serve the* Lord (Josh 24:15b KJV). Through such tangible reminders, Joshua's speeches here and God's words in Joshua 1 (*Be strong and courageous*) have filtered down through the ages and lodged themselves in the imaginations of many. The calls to faithfulness at the book's beginning and end tell us much and provide the framework for understanding the middle. Even so, Joshua's call to commitment in chapters 23–24 shares in the difficult conversation, not only because the nations continue to be marginalized and othered but also because Joshua does not minimize the challenges involved in faithful living, nor deny the reality of violating life-giving relationship with the promise-keeping God.

The book of Joshua closes with three covenant-related episodes (23:1-16; 24:1-24; 24:25-28), followed by a final summary recounting Joshua's death, Israel's faithfulness, and the burial of Joseph's bones (24:29-33). The last two chapters, and especially chapter 23, are full of Deuteronomic themes and language that emphasize promise and fulfillment, obedient faithfulness, *other gods*, and the dangers of covenant disloyalty. The most significant word in the section is the verb "to serve," which occurs eighteen times in chapters 23–24 (and before this only in 22:5 and 27 in the sending of the Transjordan tribes; a nontheological use only in 16:10). Much is said about what God has done for Israel. Above all, as God has been faithful to Israel, so Israel does well to be faithful to God *[Idolatry, p. 438]*.

These chapters resonate with chapter 1, and together they form a fitting framework for the narrative of the book as a whole. Like the final speech of Moses in Deuteronomy 29–31, God's words and Samuel's speeches at the founding of the monarchy (1 Sam 8:7-18; 12:1-25), and the speech of David near the time of his death (1 Kings 2:1-9), Joshua's speech marks a transition and a reminder of covenant loyalty.

Chapter 23 begin like chapter 13 with a double statement on Joshua's old age. The section closes with Joshua's sending the people *away to their inheritances* (24:28), which ties this closing sequence of episodes to Joshua's summoning speech (23:2) and the covenant gathering (24:1). Although 21:43 states that after the distribution the tribes *settled* in the land, it is not until 24:28 that Joshua sends them all away. Like a number of other sequences in the book, a speech (ch. 23) introduces a single main episode following it (24:1-24; cf. 13:1-7; 14:6-12; 18:1-7; 20:1-6). The covenant report closes off the three-part sequence (Winther-Nielsen: 263).

The concluding coda (24:29-33) is a separate section within the narrative structure of the book. I include it here even though it has its own function as a frame unit paired with Joshua 1. Whereas chapter 1 identifies Joshua as *Moses' assistant* and Moses as *my servant* (1:1-2) and *servant of the Lord* (1:13), the concluding frame now names Joshua as *servant of the Lord* (24:29). Although these verses appear to be an unimportant epilogue, they round out the narrative structure in a meaningful and telling way, reemphasize covenant loyalty, and connect this story to the larger canonical setting of the end of Genesis.

OUTLINE

Theological Summary and Covenant Commitments, 23:1–24:28

23:1-16	Joshua's Covenant Monologue
24:1-24	Covenant Dialogue
24:25-28	Report of Covenant Making

Coda for the Book of Joshua, 24:29-33

EXPLANATORY NOTES

Theological Summary and Covenant Commitments 23:1–24:28

23:1-16 Joshua's Covenant Monologue: The Battle of Prepositions/Clauses

Joshua 23 begins the last section of the book with a series of notations introducing a monologue that resonates with Deuteronomic themes. The speech hinges on its use of connecting words: *therefore* (vv. 6, 11) and *if* (vv. 12, 16). The emphasis on *all* in verses 1-2 (*all their enemies* and *all Israel*) echoes similar statements earlier in the book (10:25; 11:16, 23; 21:44; etc.) [*"All Israel," p. 385*]. The Lord's giving *rest* echoes other occurrences of the rest motif (1:13, 15; 11:23; 14:15; 22:4). The combination of *rest* and *enemies all around* is an allusion to Deuteronomy 12:10.

The monologue's introduction indicates the passing of much time, emphasizes the Lord's action and its consequences, notes Joshua's old age, and identifies the summoned audience (vv. 1-2a). The passing of time (*a long time afterward*) suggests not only the final act in the book, but also in Joshua's life (cf. 24:29). This *long time* is highlighted by the comment about Joshua's old age. The same expression about Joshua's age occurs in 13:1, which suggests a narrative folding back, which is characteristic of the book of Joshua. These two identical time indicators imply parallel narrative threads, like two branches of a *Y* emerging from a common point. The common point is Joshua's old age (13:1; 23:1), and the two branches are: (1) the speech of 13:1-7 followed by the distribution narrative of 13:8–22:34, and (2) the speech of chapter 23 followed by the covenant narrative of chapter 24. The parallel between the two sections, as indicated by the age-of-Joshua formula, implies further that these two sections are not to be understood as in chronological sequence. They are two narrative events that occur in narrative time at the end of Joshua's life. This is another indication that the book of Joshua is not a sequential account (see also the note about *a long time* in 11:18).

Although the narrator's introduction to Joshua's speech emphasizes the Lord's participation in Israel's newly experienced *rest*, Joshua develops that emphasis further. His speech repeats the narrator's note about his old age (v. 2a) and then makes his bifocal theological claim: *You have seen* and *the LORD your God has done*. What *you have seen* is nothing other than God's having *fought for you* (v. 3), which introduces a motif firmly rooted in the tradition (Exod 14:14; Deut 1:30; 20:4; also in Josh 10:14, 42). The motif of the Lord's driving out the nations (23:5, 9) also echoes other texts in Joshua (3:10; 13:6).

But Joshua's speech poses an ominous warning that God, under certain conditions, *will not continue to drive out these nations* (23:13). Thus the speech is like that of Moses in Deuteronomy 28–31 with its promises of blessing upon obedience and warning of dire consequences upon disloyalty and disobedience.

Having stated his theological claim, Joshua acknowledges that Israel has been allotted the territory of both *those nations that remain* and *the nations that I have already cut off* (v. 4). Although Joshua is the speaker, the "I" could as well be understood as God who has *cut off* these nations (as the expression is used in Deut 12:29; 19:1). Joshua emphasizes that these experiences are rooted in divine promise (v. 5b) before introducing the expected *therefore* in verse 6, which clarifies the expectation that Israel must be faithful to *all that is written in the book of the law of Moses* (v. 6; cf. *book of the law* in 1:8; 8:31, 34). Now Joshua exhorts the people not to deviate from this book, *neither to the right nor to the left* (v. 6). These are the same words Joshua spoke to the Transjordan tribes (1:7). This exhortation to unswerving obedience is rooted in Deuteronomic language (cf. Deut 5:32; 17:11, 20; 28:14). The narrator of Josiah's story uses the same expression to describe his faithfulness (2 Kings 22:2), but in the context of the whole story, Josiah's faithfulness is tragically ironic *[Characterization of Joshua, p. 394]*.

Joshua gives two reasons for such unwavering faithfulness to the instructions of Moses' book: a negative avoidance (v. 7) and a positive exhortation (v. 8). Obedience will prevent Israel from being *mixed with these nations*, which could be expressed in Israel's worship of *their gods*. Joshua uses four expressions of allegiance related to those gods: mentioning their names, swearing by them, serving them, and bowing down to them. The verb "to serve" is used throughout the OT as a word that can mean either "worship" or "work." That ironic contrast is especially evident in the book of Exodus, where "serving" Yahweh and "serving" Pharaoh are set up as opposing allegiances (e.g., Exod 1:13-14; 4:23; 9:1; 14:5, 12). Israel is called to change allegiances and thereby to change masters. Deuteronomy focuses the contrast more sharply between "other gods" and Yahweh (Deut 4:28-29; 5:7-9; 6:13-14; 7:4, 16; 8:19; 10:12, 20; etc.). Joshua, like Moses in Deuteronomy, exhorts Israel not to *serve* these gods, but rather to *hold fast to the* L*ORD* *your God* (23:7-8). His encouragement regarding their faithfulness *to this day* is significant for two reasons: it echoes what he has said to the Transjordan tribes (22:3), and it is used eleven times in the book before that to describe something that remains (stones, name of a place) up to the narrator's time (not the time of the events). Thus, just as inanimate objects and places remain *to this day*, so also does Israel *hold fast*. Perhaps they, like these others, will prove as enduring (cf. "hold fast" in Deut 10:20; 11:22; 13:4; 30:20; Josh 22:5).

Joshua both affirms and demands loyalty and obedience to God, which he reiterates in a second explanatory section, beginning in verse 9. Taking up motifs from earlier in the speech, he shifts attention from *to this day* to a hypothetical future time that requires *careful* attention (vv. 11-16). Now, as in 22:5, Joshua exhorts Israel to *love the* LORD *your God* (23:11; cf. Deut 6:5; 7:9; 10:12; 11:1, 13, 22; 13:4; 19:9; 30:6, 16, 20). The covenant word *love* is also used in Deuteronomy of God's love for Israel (4:37; 7:13; 10:15; 23:5). "Love" is covenant loyalty; it is not primarily an emotional word. Therefore Joshua's exhortation to love, to be constant in one's loyalty to God alone and forsaking all others, is said in the context of a large rhetorical *if* (v. 12).

The problem is Israel's "turning back," characterized here as intermarriage. The result will be catastrophic. The indigenous peoples will become *a snare and a trap for you*, which will lead to the Lord's ceasing to *drive out* these nations (v. 13; see 24:12 below; cf. Num 33:55; Deut 7:16; Judg 2:3; 8:27). The real problem is not only that state of affairs, which the book of Judges characterizes so well (cf. allusions to Josh 23 throughout Judg 2), but also the ultimate horror, mentioned here for the first time in the book of Joshua, of the prospect that Israel might *perish from this good land that the* LORD *your God has given you* (vv. 13, 16; cf. Deut 4:26; 8:19-20; *11:17*; 28:20, 22, 51, 63; 30:18: underlined references have both "perish/ruin" and "land"; italicized reference has "perish" and "good land").

After mentioning the danger of perishing from the *good land* as the ultimate consequence of disloyalty, Joshua faces his impending death (Josh 23:14a) and articulates the agenda even more starkly (vv. 14b-16). All the *good things* that God has *promised* have been fulfilled; *not one thing has failed*. The *good things* (vv. 14, 15) and the *good land* (vv. 13, 15, 16) are juxtaposed with the not-so-hypothetical *bad things* (v. 15) that will take place if Israel should *transgress the covenant* and *serve other gods and bow down to them* (v. 16): God will destroy *you from this good land* (v. 15). God's *anger* will be the agent of that destruction (v. 16; see 7:1, 26) *[Anger of the Lord, p. 386]*. As Moses has already said, Israel would perish "like the nations" (Deut 8:19-20; ch. 28).

The specific warning not to *transgress the covenant* (v. 16), which punctuates the end of Joshua's speech, is a key Deuteronomic idea even though the two words occur together in Deuteronomy only once, and that also in the context of serving or worshiping other gods (17:2-3). *Transgressed the covenant* occurs in Joshua as a narrative judgment about Israel's/Achan's disloyalty (7:11, 15), which creates a specific link to Deuteronomy 17:2-3 by implicating Achan's action as a transfer of allegiance, hence idolatry *[Idolatry, p. 438]*. The only other reference in Joshua to *covenant* with God apart from *ark of the covenant* is in the report about the events at the Shechem gathering (24:25; cf. "covenant/treaty" with the Gibeonites, 9:6, 7, 11, 15, 16) *[Covenant and Treaty, p. 416]*. Using the word *transgress* in relation to *the covenant* is telling here and in Joshua 7 because the Hebrew word *'abar* is also used with its more common meaning in Joshua, "to cross" (the Jordan). Hence, more than one kind of "crossing" can be imagined: one is a crossing into a good land, which is a fulfillment of the good promises of God; the other is a crossing out of covenant loyalty, which violates the character of the relationship between Israel and its promise-making God. Joshua underlines this latter kind of crossing with his large *if* that could result in another, this time eastward, crossing of the Jordan. In other words, exile is in view in this nearly predictive warning.

24:1-24 Covenant Dialogue

With his "sermon" in the background (ch. 23), Joshua again gathers *all the tribes of Israel* to a specific location, *Shechem*, in the very presence of God (v. 1). Apart from its appearance in the distribution lists, *Shechem* is mentioned here as a gathering place for the first time in the book (even though it is the settlement nearest to the altar at Mount Ebal; 8:30-35). Shechem is well known from Genesis narratives (beginning in 12:6), and infamous for Jacob's sons' violation of the Shechemites (ch. 34). The book of Joshua records no conquest of Shechem. Within the distribution, Shechem seems already to have been absorbed into Manasseh (17:2), and it is both a city of refuge and a Levitical city (20:7; 21:21).

This covenant-making narrative begins with a speech, becomes a dialogue, and ends with a commitment. In the speech (vv. 2-13) Joshua rehearses Israel's story, to which he has alluded in the *good promises* motif of chapter 23. There he has mentioned *other gods* (23:16), but here he links the motif to the *ancestors*, who have *served other gods* (24:2; cf. Deut 29:25-26, where serving other gods is the reason for Israel's exile). This is a shocking presentation of the *ancestors*, whose stories in Genesis touch that topic only tangentially. The ancestors' worship of other gods is juxtaposed here with God's initiative, indicated in the verbs of Joshua 24:3-13: God *took*, *led, made many, gave* children, *sent* Moses and Aaron, *plagued Egypt, brought* [*them/you*] *out, handed over, blessed, rescued, sent the hornet, gave you a land.* God's purpose and direction are confirmed. In spite of their worship of other gods, Yahweh has called them into a relationship and acted on their behalf against Egypt, Balak, Balaam, and the Canaanites. Here at the end of Joshua's story, we have the result of God's initiative: God has *given* the land to Israel.

In Joshua's speech the ancestors are said to have *lived beyond the river* (v. 2 AT). Since the text does not actually name the river as Euphrates, *beyond the river* is allusive. It may imply the other side of the Jordan, even as far as Babylon. Serving *other gods* there is as likely as in Canaan (23:16; cf. Deut 29:25). God's initiative of "taking" and "leading" Abraham is set over against God's "giving" Esau the *hill country of Seir* in Transjordan southeast of the Dead Sea and Jacob's migration to Egypt (vv. 3-4). God's initiative continues from "sending" Moses and Aaron through to defeating the Egyptian military force (though they had *chariots and horsemen*; vv. 5-6). Joshua makes a point of noting that *your eyes saw* (v. 7b) their defeat; in other words, you did not participate in it (cf. v. 12). Narrating the entire story, Joshua characterizes God's action as *rescue* (v. 10). The survey of God's initiative makes no mention of Sinai. When the speech surveys the experience west of the Jordan, Joshua mentions the traditional seven people groups (v. 11) and concludes with the most dramatic metaphor (*the hornet*) and bold theological assertion in the whole book (v. 12), which is tempered by the assertion that Israel occupies that for which it has *not labored* or *built* or *plant*[*ed*] (v. 13).

Verses 12-13 deserve a closer look. Verse 12 introduces two significant words that highlight the Lord's action. The verb *drove out* (*grš*) is used only in this context in the book of Joshua (repeated in v. 18). Chapter 23 uses another more common cognate word (*yrš*) to highlight the Lord's dispossessing the indigenous peoples (vv. 5, 9, 13; the verb is translated variously as *drive out, take possession*, or *dispossess*; cf. 3:10; 13:1, 6, 12-13; 23:5; 24:8). The word *hornet* (NRSV note "Meaning of Heb. uncertain") is found elsewhere in the OT only in Exodus 23:28 and Deuteronomy 7:20. In those two occurrences the NRSV translates the word as "pestilence," the NIV as "hornet" (a tradition stemming from the LXX), and the NLT as "terror." The NJPS translates all three occurrences as "plague."

Whatever it was that the Lord sent ahead of the Israelites (a confounding and confusing terror?), the victory was accomplished by the Lord and *not by your sword or your bow*. There may be an allusion to Jacob's gift to Joseph, which he claims he took from the Amorites "with my sword and with my bow" (Gen 48:22). The only other close parallel to the use of this phrase in the OT is in the prophet Elisha's response to the king of Israel's wish to kill the Aramean captives by saying, "No! Did you capture with your sword and your bow?" Elisha's suggestion of feeding the captives instead of killing them has remarkable consequences (2 Kings 6:22).

The rhetoric of ancient warfare reaches a crescendo here as it ascribes to the Lord the complete victory against the Amorites. As Lind puts it, "Yahweh alone—not their own military might—is the source of their deliverance and protection. In the end, their earthly battles were not really theirs at all: the battle, rather, belonged to the Lord" (135). This is not to say (contra Lind) that Israel did not actually need to fight. Rather, Israel's historians want to emphasize that whatever victories *Israel* has accomplished have been nothing other than *God's* doing. In other words, Joshua emphasizes that the physical benefits that Israel now enjoys are a gift from God. The allusions in verse 13 to Deuteronomy 6:10-12 are explicit. There Moses offers a warning to "take care that you do not forget the LORD," a warning that concludes in Deuteronomy 6:15 with the dire consequence that forgetting will result in God's "destroy[ing] you from the face of the earth."

After having reiterated what God has done for Israel (Josh 24:2-13), Joshua introduces a large *therefore* (v. 14). Here now, he says, are the implications of God's initiative. The indicative of verses 2-13 leads to the imperative of verses 14-15. Similar to 23:7-8, Joshua's requirement includes three responses: *revere the LORD* (often translated *fear the LORD* (NIV; cf. Josh 4:24; Deut 6:2, 24; 10:12, 20; 31:12-13), *put away the gods*, and *serve the LORD* (v. 14). These three motifs are hallmarks of Deuteronomic theology and of the book of Joshua (cf. Deut 6:13-14). In chapter 23 the motif of service to Yahweh or to the gods stands out as central (23:7, 16), just as it stands out in Deuteronomy (cf. 4:28; 7:4, 16; 8:19; 13:2; 17:3; 28:14, 36, 64; 29:18; 30:17; 31:20). Reverence for and serving the Lord is first and foremost expressed in an exclusive loyalty that says no to the gods and yes to Yahweh. "Service" is the response that is required as an act of loyalty because of what God has done for Israel. Therefore Joshua's invitation includes both a negative (*put away the gods*) and a positive (*serve the LORD*).

Joshua slyly introduces a negative condition by suggesting that they might be *unwilling to serve the LORD* (v. 15). If such were the case, there would be three options. The first two offer the choice of gods: gods of the old country, or gods of the new country (v. 15). The language of the pronoun clause is strange in the second option: *in whose land you are living*. Verse 13 states that God has given this land to Israel. Perhaps the Amorites are named as former inhabitants, not as current inhabitants of the land. Still, the juxtaposition in verse 15 seems to allow for an Israel that lives as a sojourner in another's land. The point is not where they live, but in whose land they live, and which god/God they serve. The hinge is the choice, which Joshua makes clear by identifying a third option in his famous line, *As for me and my household, we will serve the LORD* (v. 15). Neither the gods of the old or the new land are adequate. Joshua models a commitment to a new God, the one who took Abraham out of the old land, and the one who took Israel out of Egypt. This is the God to whom Joshua will be loyal. Joshua sets the bar high in order to provoke a response.

And the response comes as one might expect (vv. 16-18). Joshua's audience rejects the option *that we should forsake the LORD to serve other gods*. They also reiterate the basis of their loyalty by restating the story of God's initiatives on their behalf. They too use active verbs for God's work. Each of their three verbal clauses reflects the three stages in the journey: exodus, wilderness, encounter with the indigenous population. As in Joshua's narrative of God's initiatives, Sinai is not singled out as a separate place. It belongs to the wilderness, for there God drew the people into covenant relationship. The people's response concludes with a strong affirmation. They too understand that the divine initiative invites human response. *Therefore we also* [i.e., along with you] *will serve the LORD, for he is our God*. A translation of verse 18 implying that the Israelites are willing to serve *the Lord* in addition to other gods is not possible (cf. KJV: *Therefore will we also serve the Lord*). The word *also* (*gam*) refers to the subject, *we*, not the verb. The Israelites identify fully with this liberating, leading God. Other gods are not *our God [Idolatry, p. 438]*.

Joshua raises the stakes in a ploy that is either a tease or a taunt (vv. 19-20). Apart from the Achan incident, the book does not suggest that Israel is unable to serve this God. Yet Joshua claims that they *cannot* do so, *for he is a holy God*. What is Joshua's point? Although God is often identified as holy, God is not often called "a holy God" in the OT (cf. 1 Sam 6:20; Isa 5:16; 6:3; 8:13; 47:4; 54:5). Joshua's hyperbolic statement that God's jealousy does not include forgiveness seems designed to provoke and scare rather than to make a theological statement. Joshua's provocation continues in verse 20 with another *if* statement about the possibility that they might *forsake and serve foreign gods*. In what some might consider a cruel theological turn, he suggests that the Lord would then *turn and do you harm*, and may even *consume you, after having done you good*. These are hard words that reflect either an odd, even perverse, view of God's fickleness, or a view of divine justice that will not tolerate human sinfulness and disloyalty. In the light of Deuteronomy's sure conviction that Yahweh "is a merciful God" who "will neither abandon you nor destroy you," and who "will not forget the covenant with your ancestors" (Deut 4:31), it seems odd that Joshua should hint at just the opposite possibility here (but cf. Moses in Deut 31:27). Either Joshua's provocation is just a rhetorical ploy to test the conviction of Israel's earlier statement (Josh 24:18b), or he is suggesting that God remains free to honor their choices. The irony is that from the vantage point of exile, and through the lens of the Deuteronomistic worldview, Joshua's statement has proved all too true. Israel was not capable of serving the Lord without duplicity. Still, the point of the Deuteronomistic perspective is not only a question of justifying God's behavior (theodicy) or of explaining Israel's failure, but also of offering an alternative vision that transcends hopelessness. That alternative can be found in the hope of divine faithfulness and mercy (Deut 4:31), in the possibility of choosing God (Deut 30), and in the transformation of the heart that empowers faithfulness (Jer 31:31-34; Ezek 11:19; 18:31; 36:26).

Whatever Joshua means by his rhetorical challenge, the people deny his hypothetical option and affirm that they *will serve the Lord* (v. 21). Joshua has accomplished what he has set out to do. So he seals their commitment with his response: *You have chosen the Lord, to serve him*. The verb "to choose" in Deuteronomy is found mostly in phrases depicting the Lord's "choosing" of Israel on account of love, or a place for God's name to dwell. Almost all uses of the verb "choose" have God as the subject. Here, however, Joshua assumes that the divine choice also requires a corresponding human choice. And in that assumption he echoes the rare Deuteronomic call to "choose life" (Deut 30:19). The people respond by affirming that they are both testifiers and witnesses (Josh 24:22). They will vouch for their own word. "Let your yes be yes" (cf. Matt 5:37).

Joshua counsels two actions as a consequence (v. 23). The first comes as a shock: *put away the foreign gods that are among you*. The expression *foreign gods* (vv. 20, 23) has not been used before in the book. Could the people have been worshiping them? The phrase is reminiscent of Jacob's instructions to his household where he too tells his people to "put away the foreign gods that are among you" (Gen 35:2, 4; cf. Josh 24:14; Judg 10:16; 1 Sam 7:3; Jer 5:19; 2 Chron 33:15). The irony is not only that Joshua uses the same words as those of Jacob, but also that that narrative is likewise set in Shechem.

Deuteronomy favors the expression "other gods" (4:28; 5:7; 6:14; etc.), which is used only three times in Joshua, in the last two chapters (23:16; 24:2, 16). Deuteronomy 6:14 even assumes that these "other gods" are "gods of the peoples who are all around you." As we know by now, the book of Joshua assumes that these peoples continue to reside in Israel's midst. The only use of "foreign gods" in Deuteronomy (31:16) recalls Jacob's instructions and is couched within a speech by God to Moses that seems to predict Israel's apostasy after Moses' death, "prostituting themselves . . . to the gods of the land into which they are going." Joshua's words in 24:23 echo both Jacob's words and God's words.

Joshua counsels a second action: *Incline your hearts to the LORD*, who is *the God of Israel* (v. 23). To *incline your hearts* is to be receptive in such a way that one's will leans in the direction of the divine instruction. That "inclination" is confirmed in yet another response by the people, stating not only that they *will serve* the Lord but also that they *will obey* (v. 24). The word *obey* also means "listen to" or "heed," a motif that set the tone for the book in the first chapter, in the commitment of the Transjordan tribes (1:17). That final word rounds out the covenantal banter in which Joshua goads the people into a fourfold commitment to serve and to obey God (vv. 16-18, 21, 22b, 24). They have declared their intention to be an obedient people, devoted only to one God, in spite of all the warnings about their likely apostasy.

But readers may remain somewhat hesitant to accept the testimony. After all, it was provoked, like the cajoling of a parent who might tell a child not to eat something because it tastes bad, which upon hearing the child immediately downs the food to prove the parent wrong. Is Israel simply trying to prove Joshua wrong? Or is Joshua's *You cannot serve the LORD* (v. 19) more of a premonition of what is to come (e.g., in the book of Judges)?

24:25-28 Report of Covenant Making

After the final confession of commitment to *serve* and to *obey* (v. 24), the narrator summarizes the proceedings. *Shechem* forms a frame around the episode (vv. 1, 25). Joshua is said to have *made statutes and ordinances* (v. 25), to have written *these words in the book of the law of God* (v. 26), and to have set up *a large stone . . . in the sanctuary* (v. 26). Joshua then declares the stone to be a *witness* to the integrity of Israel's commitment in word and in life. With that the narrator reports Joshua's sending *the people away to their inheritances* (v. 28).

This short report is not simply a summary of the preceding speech and dialogue sections. It offers new insight by what it adds and omits. First, in a fine bit of narrative detail, the mention of Shechem, together with the notice of *the oak in the sanctuary of the* Lord (likely in an open courtyard), confirms the hunch that this text echoes the episode of Jacob's return to Bethel, in which he buries "all the foreign gods . . . under the oak that was near Shechem" (Gen 35:4; cf. Gen 12:5; Judg 9:6). Covenant making in Joshua 24 highlights saying no to the gods, as in the Jacob story, and seems to forestall the apostasy about which God warned Moses before his death.

Second, the *statutes and ordinances* that Joshua made could be divine instructions, like those instituted by Moses at Sinai. Even though the English translation is plural for both words, the Hebrew text uses the singular form of both words, which occur exactly this way in only two other places (Exod 15:25; Ezra 7:10). The Marah event illustrates what the text may be suggesting (Exod 15:22-26). There Moses makes bitter water sweet, and "he [NRSV: 'the LORD'] made for them a statute and an ordinance and there he put them to the test" (Exod 15:25b). The "statute and ordinance" is a condition: "If you will listen carefully to the voice of the LORD your God, and do what is right in his sight, and give heed to his commandments and keep all his statutes" (15:26). Although the content of Joshua's *statute(s) and ordinance(s)* (cf. NJPS, *a fixed rule*) is not named in Joshua 24:25, the words used to describe them are identical to those of Exod 15:25. The only other place where the two words occur in this form and combination is Ezra 7:10, where study of Torah, doing the Torah, and teaching the "statutes and ordinances" are the focus of Ezra's attention. Thus, it seems, Joshua's *statutes and ordinances* are shorthand for the terms of the covenant requirements as negotiated in the covenant dialogue of verses 14-24.

Third, Joshua's writing *in the book of the law of God* departs from the expected (elsewhere only in Neh 8:18; cf. "book of the law" in Deut 29:21; 30:10; 31:26; Josh 1:8; 8:34; 2 Kings 22:8, 11). Joshua also uses the more nuanced *book of the law of Moses* (8:31; 23:6; cf. 2 Kings 14:6; Neh 8:1). That the narrator of Joshua 24:26 should omit "of Moses" and add "of God" implies a turning point in the narrative plot concerning the character of Joshua. Most remarkably, Joshua "adds to the written Torah" even though Moses' prohibitions in Deuteronomy 4:2 and 12:32 imply that such ought not to be done (Kissling: 93–94). Joshua is poised to resume the role of Moses, which will be confirmed in the conclusion of the book where Joshua, rather than Moses, comes to be called *servant of the LORD* (24:29) *[Torah, p. 462].*

Fourth, the *stone* set up as *a witness against us* ties this final report to the "witness" language of chapter 22 (vv. 27, 34). There may be a connection to the tradition of setting up memorial stones (*maṣṣebah*, as in Gen 28:22; 31:45; 35:14; Exod 24:4), the calling of heaven and earth as witnesses in the ominous "prediction" of Moses that Israel would soon perish from the good land (Deut 4:26; cf. 30:19), and the "book of the law" as a "witness against you" (31:26). Generally, however, a standing stone is a witness on behalf of what God has done. The altar built by the Transjordan tribes is such a witness. This stone in Joshua 24:26 is a marker of the covenant, unlike the prohibited stones of Deuteronomy 16:22. The narrator avoids the similarity by calling this *a large stone* rather than use the Deuteronomic word *maṣṣebah*. Still, an ambiguity remains (on the significance of "stones" in Joshua, see Hubbard).

The prepositional phrase *against you* (24:27) could be read as *for you*. Shall the stone testify *against* Israel after indiscretion has taken place? Or might it speak *for* Israel, thereby averting the catastrophe of dealing *falsely* with God? The NJPS allows the ambiguity to remain with its translation of the last clause of the verse. Instead of *if you deal falsely*, it reads *<u>lest</u> you break faith with your God* (emph. added). The Hebrew word for *break faith* or *deal falsely* means "to act deceptively." The same word is used in the Achan story about Israel's *deceitful action* (Josh 7:11). That allusion makes this *witness* an ominous one, even though it is tinged with hopefulness. The memory evoked by the stone leaves the future truly open. Will Israel continue to allow the stone to have its say and evoke faithfulness in Israel? Or will the stone need to have its say in the legal proceedings that follow Israel's deceitfulness in violating its allegiance to Yahweh by opting for alternative allegiances to *foreign gods*?

The narrative about covenant proceedings ends with sending the people away to their inheritances (v. 28). The story is complete except for notices about deaths, burials, and Israel's true servitude. Even so, the story remains open-ended, like a movie destined to have a sequel.

Conclusion: Coda for the Book Of Joshua 24:29-33

Deuteronomy ends with the death of Moses, and Joshua begins with *After the death of Moses*. Similarly Joshua ends with the death of Joshua, and Judges begins with "After the death of Joshua." Joshua's ending, therefore, makes an explicit link forward to the book of Judges and rounds out the narrative by referring back to the transition between the books of Deuteronomy and Joshua.

After these things begins the announcement not only of Joshua's death but also introduces *Joshua son of Nun* in a new way as *servant of the Lord* (v. 29). In Joshua 1:1 it is Moses who is *servant of the Lord* and *Joshua son of Nun* is *Moses' assistant*. This transformation occurs here for the first time in the book, suggesting that Joshua has now become a worthy successor to Moses. Moses is identified as servant of the Lord thirteen times in the book of Joshua (only once in Deuteronomy—34:5). Of those occurrences, six concern obedience to Moses' commandments (1:13; 8:31, 33; 11:12; 22:2, 5), and five concern Moses' "giving" the land to the Transjordan tribes (1:15; 12:6; 13:8; 18:7; 22:4). Joshua has been, above all, a servant of the Lord through his careful and discerning attention to the divine word/book of the law. He has not slavishly held to its precepts. Rather, he has been an agent of its ongoing vitality as he has both read, reinterpreted, and written some of that *book* (8:30-35; 24:26). Above all, he has been obedient to God even as he has followed the example of Moses. He is a true and worthy disciple.

After reporting Joshua's burial (v. 30), the coda continues by emphasizing the formation of Israel's character: *Israel served the Lord* for the duration of Joshua's life and the lives of those *elders who outlived Joshua* (v. 31). Their faithful service is rooted somehow in the fact that they *had known all the work that the Lord did for Israel* (v. 31). This sentence provides additional rationale for why keeping the story alive remains a significant assignment for coming generations. Yet one cannot help but wonder: Did Israel indeed serve the Lord that whole time? What about Joshua's exhortations to put away foreign gods? And what about Joshua's cryptic *You cannot serve the Lord* (24:19)? Does the final statement in verse 31 gloss over a more complex reality? Or is it an idealization of Israel during the golden age of Joshua?

More particularly, however, the final clause describing the generation that *had known all the work that the Lord did for Israel* speaks not only of the past but also introduces a criterion for judgment on the future. Even though future generations may well have *known* the story of God's work, they did not serve him. Even though, in the light of Deuteronomic theology, Israel of the next generation(s) failed to hold knowledge and commitment together, it might still be possible to serve the Lord (e.g., Deut 30:10, 19-20).

The final two notices about the burials of Joseph and Eleazar (vv. 32-33) round out the book. They connect this generation (Joseph and Eleazar) to the ancestors through Joseph, the oddly favored and excluded son of Jacob whose own descendants comprise the future body of the Northern Kingdom, Israel/Ephraim, and whose tomb at Shechem is in the plot purchased by Jacob *from the children of Hamor, the father of Shechem.* This purchase *became an inheritance of the descendants of Joseph* (v. 32b). Although we ought not make too much of this purchase (Gen 33:18-20), it stands in sharp contrast to the "taking" and the plundering of land, houses, and vineyards that they had not built, labored for, or planted (Josh 24:13).

Most important, the mention of the burial of Joseph's bones (24:32) takes the reader back to the promise theme of the larger ancestral narrative, which alludes to "Israel's" exile in Egypt before their return when the "iniquity of the Amorites" is "complete" (Gen 15:13-21, esp. v. 16). The story of Joseph's death (Gen 50:22-26) reports that he was 110 years old when he died, and that he made the Israelites promise to carry his bones up from there "when God comes to you" (50:25). The only other biblical character dying at that age is Joshua (Josh 24:29; Judg 2:8). Hauch expresses well the significance of the parallel. "The death of Joseph, on the one hand, concludes the patriarchal narratives which articulate the promise and anticipates its fulfillment in the land. The death of Joshua, on the other, concludes the story of this fulfillment and foreshadows the loss of the land to follow" (64–65). Both deaths are followed by a loss of "knowing." Pharaoh "did not know Joseph" (Exod 1:6-8) and did "not know" the LORD" (5:2), and a new generation after Joshua "did not know the LORD or the work he had done for Israel" (Judg 2:8-10). "The period extending from the exodus through the conquest is thus marked off as constituting a 'single' whole, framed as it is by identical comments regarding the age of a hero at death and by similar statements concerning the faulty memory of those who follow." In Exodus, Yahweh fights for Israel; in Judges, he fights against them (Judg 2:3, 14-15; cf. Num 33:56) (Hauch: 67).

THE TEXT IN BIBLICAL CONTEXT

Covenant Begins with God

Joshua 23–24 are the most theologically dense chapters in the book. The covenant that is reestablished here (24:25) is grounded in divine initiative. God has fought for Israel (23:3, 10; 24:12). Such action is couched as a "rescue" (24:10) of Israel from the dangers represented by indigenous peoples and their gods. Even more, God's initiative is a fulfillment of the *good things . . . promised concerning you* (23:14). The divine word has not gone out without accomplishing its purpose (cf. Isa 55:11). Joshua challenges Israel not to be mixed with the indigenous peoples or to worship their gods (Josh 23:7, 12, 16; 24:14-15, 20, 23). Instead, they are above all *to observe and to do all that is written in the book of the law of Moses/of God* (23:6; 24:26). In spite of Joshua's threats and even apparent predictions of failure (23:12-13, 15-16; 24:19-20, 27), both Joshua and the people commit themselves to serve Yahweh. They *choose this day* whom they will serve (24:15, 18, 21). The narrator's concluding coda affirms, in the end, that Joshua is now designated *servant of the* LORD (24:29), and the people are affirmed as having *served the* LORD in Joshua's time (24:31). Yet even these affirmations are ominous; they remind us of the threats embedded in the speeches and dialogue of the previous chapters. All is well—so far.

The emphasis in the last two chapters of Joshua comes to a focus in the report about covenant making, the association of *statutes and ordinances* as shaping the parameters of that covenant, the writing of the proceedings *in the book of the law of God*, and the symbolic action establishing a tangible memorial of that action (24:25-27) *[Covenant and Treaty, p. 416].*

Joshua's covenant making draws its theological resources from Deuteronomy. In Deuteronomy's theological refraction of "covenant" (twenty-seven times in Deuteronomy), "love" characterizes all aspects of the relationship between God and Israel (Deut 4:37; 6:5; 7:9, 13; 10:12, 15; 11:1, 13, 22; 13:4; 19:9; 23:5; 30:6, 16, 20). Love, in the political metaphor of covenant, is the choice for exclusive allegiance made by both God and Israel (Deut 6:4-5; 7:7, 9). Joshua's covenant reflects Deuteronomy's interest in affirming each generation as the locus of covenant as though each generation is the first generation (Deut 5:3; 29:14-15; cf. the dramatic "us" in 26:5-11). Each generation becomes responsible for recalling, reenacting, and living out this covenant. If they "abandon" the covenant, they will find themselves in exile (Deut 29:24-25; Josh 23:13, 16). The Lord's final words to Moses are not heartening. God predicts that the people will follow other gods and break the covenant with God (Deut 31:16, 20). Yet even those words need to be heard alongside Deuteronomy's awareness of the transience of Israel's love, especially in the tension-filled reflection on the possibility of apostasy in Deuteronomy 30. There, reflecting on God's faithfulness in the face of Israel's waywardness (and subsequent exile), Moses anticipates that God will make Israel capable of loving "with all your heart" (30:6). And that is possible only because, according to Deuteronomy's understanding of God's covenant loyalty, God will never abandon nor destroy Israel (4:31). This is the same hope with which we read the ending of the book of Joshua.

The narrator assumes that in spite of their covenants with the indigenous people (Rahab and the Gibeonites), Israel *served the Lord* (Josh 24:31). Thus the warning (even that by God) in Deuteronomy and the explicit failures recounted in the book of Judges (2:2) do not figure prominently in the book of Joshua. If it can be imagined that the book of Joshua implies failure, the narrative does not make that judgment explicit. The book of Joshua reflects authentic covenant, mediated, interpreted, and embodied by Joshua and his people. The dynamics of obedience are at times ambiguous, but the commitment of the people, in spite of Joshua's cajoling in the dialogue of chapter 24, remains firm.

The underlying and recurring voice in the intrabiblical covenantal conversation continues to sound about the undying faithfulness of God against all odds. Although the DtrH ends without resolution or restoration, the reader is always drawn back to hopefulness in spite of Deuteronomy's tragic foreshadowing of dark days ahead. That hopefulness generates a prophetic vision for a renewed covenant (Jer 31:31-34), which is reflected in the NT writers' interpretation of Jesus' life, death, and resurrection *[Covenant and Treaty, p. 416]*. Such renewal is understood by Deuteronomy, and implied in the prophetic tradition in which the book of Joshua stands, as inaugurated by divine initiative.

The Deuteronomic notion of God's initiative in covenant relationship underlies Joshua's understanding of divine action. It is the Lord *who has fought for you* (Josh 23:3, 10; 24:12). It was not your sword or your bow (24:12). Those affirmations reverberate in the story of Elisha and the king of Aram (2 Kings 6:8-23; cf. 6:15 with Josh 11:4; and 2 Kings 6:22 with Josh 24:12).

The psalmist also testifies to God's action on Israel's behalf in a rejection of bow and sword as instruments of salvation (44:3, 6). The poet mourns the loss of God's presence and help even though "we have not forgotten you, or been false to your covenant" (44:17). This psalm testifies against a simplistic formula for the Lord's protection. Faithfulness to covenant may not always be calculated through moral arithmetic. The prophet Hosea affirms similarly that the Lord will not save Judah by conventional means: "by bow, or by sword, or by war, or by horses, or by horsemen" (1:7; cf. 10:13). The prophet goes on to announce that the Lord "will abolish the bow, the sword, and war from the land" (2:18). Joshua's speech taps into a minority report in the OT that is significant for its shock value. Neither *sword* nor *bow* can assure salvation or the liberation of Israel from oppression *[Horses and Chariots, p. 434]*.

Sometimes Israel experiences the gift of land through divine initiative and protection even though a tension remains between "I will" and "I will not" drive them out (Josh 23:5, 9, 13; 24:12, 18). The promise and the gift lead to good things and good land (23:14-16) even though there are also *bad things*, including perishing from the good land (Josh 23:13-16; cf. Deut 29). Even so, Joshua can assert, *Not one thing has failed* (Josh 23:14) *[Plot Tensions in Joshua, p. 452]*. The narrator monotheizes the story by affirming that "all things work together" within the sovereign purposes of God (cf. Rom 8:28), even when not all will be as it seems to be or ought to be. Joshua therefore becomes a paradigmatic figure who, like Moses, speaks an effective word into the ambiguities of life. The only time Moses is so mentioned in a similar manner is in Solomon's blessing on the people after his prayer of dedication of the temple: "Blessed be the Lord, who has given rest to his people Israel according to all that he promised; not one word has failed of all his good promise, which he spoke through his servant Moses" (1 Kings 8:56, which echoes almost exactly Josh 23:14; cf. 21:45) *[Rest, p. 455]*.

The key to Joshua's (and Deuteronomy's) understanding of the potential failure of Israel's covenant relationship is the serving of other gods (Josh 23:7, 16; 24:2, 14-15, 16, 20), which is counteracted by calls to commitment or to serving the Lord (Josh 24:19-22; 24:31). Idolatry and apostasy turn out to be Israel's demise, according to the books of Kings. As in Deuteronomy, the main danger in Joshua is the gods of Canaan (see Deut 6:14; 7:1-6, 16, 20-26; 18:9-14; 20:17-18; 31:16-20; esp. 12:2-4; cf. Exod 23:23-24; 34:11-16; Num 33:50-56; Halpern 1988: 220, 239n34) *[Idolatry, p. 438]*.

Yet the rhetorical strategy of the book of Joshua gets in the way of outright pessimism. Only divine instruction, which is the heart of God's speech in Joshua 1 (as it is in 8:30-35; 23:6-8; 24:14-15, 19-20), will prevent Israel from being "taught" to do what the other peoples do at the request of their gods (Deut 20:17-18). According to Deuteronomy 20, the heart of that instruction concerns compromising covenant stipulations (sparing Rahab, Gibeonites; Achan's violation; failure to dispossess inhabitants completely; etc.). The covenant (with God's commitment to it) is itself "an expression of optimism, as is the promise that gives shape to our story. Of central interest, therefore, is how this optimistic God will confront the realization of his pessimism" (Gunn: 109).

"Choose This Day"

Joshua's call to *choose this day* (24:15) invites participation in that optimism (echoing the "us" of Deut 5:2-3; 29:14-15). The *today* of Joshua confirms Moses' hope that Israel would continue from generation to generation to choose loyalty to God and God's way. Deuteronomy's "today" is also a covenant not merely with the past and not merely with the future, but also with all of us, as well as with them. As Paul puts it, "Now is the day of salvation" (2 Cor 6:2). Such urgency also grasps the Philippian jailer who asks, "What must I do to be saved?" (Acts 16:30), and who, together with his "household," affirms a new loyalty to "the Lord Jesus" (16:31-34).

The book of Joshua ends with the affirmation that both Joshua and Israel participate in God's salvation and have chosen to live as recipients of God's grace. Israel has *served the LORD*, and Joshua is called *servant of the LORD*. Only Moses and Joshua are called "servant of the LORD" in the DtrH (Deut 34:5; Josh 1:1; Judg 2:8; 2 Kings 18:12; cf. David as "my servant," 2 Sam 7:5; Ps 89:3). Isaiah's "Servant," chosen by God to bring justice to the nations, also calls for obedience to divine instruction (50:4, 10). Although Jeremiah and Ezekiel do not highlight the language of Servant as does Isaiah, the blending of Davidic obedient servanthood and the people's obedience comes through clearly in Ezekiel's vision of a renewed and unified Israel under the leadership of "David," which will result in obedience to the Lord's statutes and ordinances, intergenerational faithfulness forever, and "a covenant of peace between them." Yahweh will be present as their God forever (37:24-28). Like Jeremiah's "new covenant" (31:31), Ezekiel's "heart of flesh" will become the organ of obedience in a renewed covenantal relationship in the land gifted to the ancestors (11:19; 36:26-28).

That Joshua is a disciple of Moses, therefore, is confirmed. But Solomon does not measure up as disciple of David, who submits to the divine/prophetic word of judgment (Schäfer-Lichtenberger). The Gospel of John picks up the imitation motif ("Do what I command you"; 15:14), which is expressed through imitative love (14:23-24; 15:12). The first letter of John, like Deuteronomy, also highlights responsive obedience grounded in God's prior love (1 John 4:19 and context).

In keeping with the intrabiblical conversation, the narrative of Joshua is rooted in what we might call a "spirituality of the book." Observing or obeying the book of the law of Moses (Josh 1:8; 23:6; 24:26; etc.) is living the divine instruction (Torah) as the source of life. As the psalmists affirm, there are two paths (Pss 1; 19; 119). The book is a guide and source for critical discernment and instruction (2 Tim 3:16). Yet as the book of Joshua implies, obedience is a dynamic transposition rather than a flat adherence to a set of rules *[Torah, p. 462]*.

The Servant and the Nations

One prominent area in which such dynamism is most evident is in the intrabiblical conversation about the place of the nations in the divine economy. Hamlin's observations about Isaiah's use of the conquest-of-the-nations tradition deserves attention (1982). Hamlin discusses phrases and word usages in Joshua and Isaiah 40–55 to suggest that Isaiah is reinterpreting the "conquest" tradition, the Exodus narrative, and other traditions for the exiles in need of hope after Cyrus's takeover of the Babylonian imperial world. For example, the Hebrew word *yaraš* in Isaiah 54:3 should be translated as "inherit," which is the same word used in Joshua to mean "to possess," "to dispossess," or "to drive out" (see Explanatory Notes for Josh 13:1-7; 24:12-13). According to Isaiah 57:13, "whoever takes refuge (trusts, NJPS) in me shall possess the land." Israel and the nations, which are exterminated *and* continue to live among Israel in the book of Joshua, are both transformed by Isaiah. Similarly, the verbs "to succeed" and "to prosper" in Joshua 1:7-8 and Isa 52:13 and 53:10 suggest that the figure of Joshua, faithful to divine instruction, has been transposed into the "suffering Servant" of Isaiah. Covenant teaching (Torah) for Israel in the book of Joshua becomes the good news of justice for the nations in Isaiah. In Joshua, *You are witnesses* (24:22) is in service of the people having "chosen," whereas in Isaiah it is the nations who become the witnesses to the fact that *God* has chosen "my servant" (Isa 43:10, 12). The word "land" is also universalized to mean the whole earth in Isaiah. We find such universalizing in Rahab's affirmation of the cosmic sovereignty of God (Josh 2:11) and in Joshua's affirmation that Yahweh is *Lord of all the earth* (3:11, 13).

This cosmic Sovereign is the author of Israel's future and the nations' future. *The work that the Lord did* (Josh 24:31) has become evident to Israel. Variations of this phrase are found four other times in the OT (Exod 34:10; Deut 11:7; Judg 2:7; Jer 51:9-11). In Exodus, the covenant initiative of God, after the first set of tablets has been broken, initiates a divine work that will be visible to the peoples among whom the Israelites live (34:10). The following verses refer to God's "driving out" the traditional list of six people groups (v. 11); warn about not making a covenant with the inhabitants of the land, which would become a "snare to you" (v. 12); and command to destroy their altars (v. 13) and to "worship no other god" because Yahweh is "a jealous God" (v. 14). Most of these motifs occur in Joshua 23–24. Judges 2:7 repeats the motif exactly in a quotation of Joshua 24:31, which makes a literary connection between the two books and highlights the contrast between the former generation's faithfulness and that of the generations after Joshua's death. All distinct occurrences of the phrase *work/deeds of the* LORD (Josh 24:31, lit.) concern divine initiative against the nations. Jeremiah's usage applies the phrase to divine judgment of Babylon's imperial oppression (51:10). God is Sovereign over all peoples and is acting on behalf of this particular people in such a way that they will be given the land that had earlier been given to others (Deut 2; cf. Jer 27:5). Even so, both Exodus 34 and Joshua 23–24 assume that this is not a simple transaction. Everything could backfire. All depends on whether Israel continues to live its life oriented toward only one loyalty: Yahweh. All of that surely assumes at times that, according to Isaiah, God's work among the nations is "strange" indeed (Isa 28:21).

Such strangeness is evident in the way the book of Joshua, with its incorporation of Shechem into Israelite genealogical and geographical identity, echoes and reverses the ominous and ironic narrative of Genesis 34. In that story trickery and violence characterize the relationship. The deception arises as the sons of Jacob offer to "live among you and become one people" (34:16). The Shechemites consider the offer, thinking that "the land is large enough for them" (v. 21). They repeat the assumption that they would "become one people" (v. 22), thinking that everything the sons of Jacob possess will "be ours" if they "agree" that they "live among us" (v. 23). But everything backfires. The ironic inclusion of Shechem into Israel (Josh 17:2, 7; 20:7; 21:21) and of Shechem as a site of covenant renewal (Josh 24:1) implies that Joshua parallels Jacob. Although "living among" is a ploy in Genesis 34, it is an assumed reality in Joshua, even though Shechem is never conquered. The problem noted by Jacob in the following story in Genesis 35, however, is that of "foreign gods" (35:2, 4). This is the very expression that Joshua uses here (Josh 24:20, 23; elsewhere only in Judg 10:16; 1 Sam 7:3; Jer 5:19; 2 Chron 33:15). Moreover, Joshua also uses the verb *put away* (Josh 24:23), which Jacob also uses (Gen 35:2; also in Judg 10:16; 1 Sam 7:3). The overwhelming interest in the gods submerges the threat of Shechem, which has already become, with Israel, "one people" (Gen 34:16, 22) and "live among" each other (Gen 34:16, 23).

THE TEXT IN THE LIFE OF THE CHURCH

A Commitment for Today

I grew up with the positive effects of a strong call to commitment and an awareness of the dangers of the world and its "gods." Those practices work themselves out in both positive and negative ways. They are rooted first in the larger biblical invitation to respond to God's grace and Jesus' call to follow, as narrated in the Anabaptist tradition, and second in the pietist and evangelical movements of the nineteenth and twentieth centuries.

Although those affirmations of faith are rarely, if ever, linked explicitly to the final chapters of Joshua, they are rooted in a worldview that draws some of its resources from the Deuteronomic perspectives embedded in Joshua 23 and 24. For example, the Mennonite evangelist George Brunk (and a good number of others) was traveling throughout North America and calling people to commitment. He held "campaigns" in tents and in church buildings. It is not clear whether these events were designed to welcome outsiders; they certainly were focused on giving the people of the church an opportunity to renounce harmful ways and to recommit themselves to the Lord. "Recommitment" was often the hallmark of such events. The assumption was that people could "backslide," or turn away, from living the life of a true disciple. The "gods of the ancestors" were probably not mentioned, but the invitation was clear: *Choose this day whom you will serve* (Josh 24:15a). Although one may have strayed in one's past, the present offered an opportunity that must not be passed by. For a generation before mine, such commitments also involved saying no to certain practices associated with the world. In some baptismal vows it was common to commit oneself not to attend public places of entertainment of various sorts. Unfortunately the spirituality of that kind of call to commitment was often grounded in unfounded fear, or in guilt that generated an inability to see the good in God's creation. Like aspects of the book of Joshua, calls to separate from the world worked best by stigmatizing the Other(s) and labeling it (or them) as dangerous.

When loosed from such negative stereotyping and rooted in the deep and abiding love of God and the good things God has done in the past, such commitment and response can be a joyful and liberating experience. It can permeate one's entire life and create a community that lives out of a single-hearted and single-minded loyalty to the God who promises, who gives, who rescues, who leads, and who even "fights" on our behalf. If the "therefore" of commitment is rooted in fear, or in false guilt, it is usually counterproductive. I have known many people who have rejected that fear-based spirituality, not because they do not want to be told that they are bad people and therefore need to turn their lives around, but because the call to commitment did not foster life and hope, nor did it generate authentic, honest, and loving community. Joshua 23 and 24 by itself may not generate life and hope either. It may be that Joshua is also cajoling the people into making their commitment under false pretenses. It may be that Joshua has an insight into the human predisposition not to be faithful to one ultimate loyalty. Maybe Joshua knows that, in the end, human beings are duplicitous anyway. In spite of those uncertainties, the narrator seems to know that at the heart of things is intimate awareness of *all the work that the* L*ORD* *did for Israel* (24:31).

Covenants for Today

The communal act of covenant making is even more significant than an emphasis on individual obedience and responsibility. Some congregations now practice an annual service of covenant renewal as a way of distinguishing membership in a congregation from the popular notion of "membership" that is more like an expression of consumer culture. How is church membership different from membership in a health club, service organization, or discount retailer? Could the covenant in Joshua 24 offer an analogy for what might be helpful in our time? Covenant in Joshua 23–24 is rooted in awareness of the narrative of divine initiative (what God has done in the past); it is characterized by a dialogue that demonstrates awareness of the risks and challenges involved in the covenant relationship; and it invites commitment to a single loyalty in and through which all of life will be lived in devotion and obedience to that one God.

Covenant is an act that forms a community in relationship with God and with others. Covenant has community-forming power because of its ritual, or liturgical, heart. As a liturgical act, covenant making "puts something into practice. It is not a verbal commentary on an action external to itself; in and of itself liturgical language is an action" (Connerton: 57). As such, covenant making is formational. As a performative utterance, community is created when "we" make commitments together (Connerton: 59). Such is the power of Joshua's covenantal conversation in Joshua 23–24, and such is the tragedy of its demise beginning in Judges 1 and ending with the exile at the end of 2 Kings.

In the light of that demise, covenantal faithfulness in the book of Joshua is presented as both *prototypical* and *exemplary* (Connerton: 64–65). It is the first expression of Deuteronomy's ambiguity regarding God's unwavering commitment, the possibility of human response, and the inevitability of human failure. And it is an example of human commitment in the face of a realistic appraisal of the human condition. Read that way, the ending of the book of Joshua implies that the renewal of covenant from generation to generation will find a way of transforming enemies even as Joshua's story begins to unravel its own fear of otherness in the welcome of Rahab, the Gibeonites, and Others (*aliens*) among them.

The real danger, which continues to elude us, is the risk of *foreign gods*. And the problem with that danger is our inability to discern the gods. Paul equates idolatry with greed (Col 3:5). Jesus says, "No one can serve two masters." Choose either God or wealth (Matt 6:24; cf. Luke 16:13; 18:24). The place of one's treasure is the location of the heart (Matt 6:21; Luke 12:34). Paul exhorts, "Flee from the worship of idols" (1 Cor 10:14; cf. 1 John 5:21), and admonishes churches to turn from idols to serve the living God (1 Thess 1:9; echoes of Joshua). And the book of Revelation associates judgment with worshiping idols (9:20) *[Idolatry, p. 438]*.

The Conversation Continues

Having said all that about the value of calls to covenant commitment and the community-forming power of covenant renewal, and a saying no to the gods of our time, Joshua 23–24 continues to elicit the need for a difficult conversation. The story of Joshua's call to commitment and the people's response continues to reflect a dualistic worldview in which God favors "us" and disempowers "them." We do well to distinguish between the danger of "foreign gods" of various stripes and the people who are often dispossessed or exterminated because "we" have deemed their gods worthy of the pronouncement of anathema. In the conflict between Israelis and Palestinians today, Jews are living in the homes once occupied by Palestinians before they either fled or were expelled in 1948 and 1967. Since the book of Joshua is read by Israeli school children in their history curriculum (Greenberg 1995), it is not surprising that they should read *towns that you had not built* (Josh 24:13) as analogous to Israeli dispossession of Palestinians in the twentieth century (see Naim Ateek's story about visiting his own home in Beisan [1989: 7–17]). Although the situation is analogous, it is as unacceptable now as biblical Israel's displacement of the indigenous population was then. Coexistence and inheritance need not be mutually exclusive. But they require complex political solutions.

The conversation initiated by Joshua with Israel has not ended. The book continues to invite discernment about the places where we either hear or mishear the divine word, where we welcome or exclude and marginalize the Others, and where we say "yes" to the gods of our time and disregard the One who chooses us and loves us first. We, who were at one time enemies of God and alienated from the commonwealth of Israel (Rom 5:10; Eph 2:12), are the nations, the *peoples of the earth*, who have come to know *that the hand of the Lord is mighty* (Josh 4:24). Unlike the kings of the book of Joshua, we no longer fear, for perfect love drives away fear (1 John 4:18). Those who live in the light of the incarnate Word know that their swords are of no consequence against the principalities and powers of the world. And those who serve this One are free to let go of grasping for the promise in order to receive the gift of the kingdom of God (Luke 12:32), which brings "righteousness and peace and joy in the Holy Spirit" (Rom 14:17).

Outline of Joshua

PART 1: ENTERING THE LAND	**1:1–12:24**
The Promise and the Preparation	**1:1-18**
A Joshua Commissioned for the Task	1:1-9
God's Promise to Joshua	1:1-5
God's Charge to Joshua	1:6-9
B Joshua's Preparation of the People	1:10-11
B' Joshua's Preparation of the Transjordan Tribes	1:12-15
A' Response of the People	1:16-18
Testing the Water: The Story of the Spies	**2:1-24**
Setting the Stage	2:1
A Royal Search	2:2-7
Confession and Covenant	2:8-14
The Escape Plan and Counterconcessions	2:15-21
Return and Report of Findings	2:22-24
Crossing into the Promise: Holy Lord and Holy People	**3:1–4:24**
Setting the Stage: Camping at the Jordan	3:1
Instructions for Preparation	3:2-5
Instructions for Crossing the Jordan	3:6-13
The Crossing	3:14-17
Memorial of the Stones	4:1-10
Conclusion of the Crossing	4:11-14
Coming Up out of the Jordan	4:15-18
Encampment at Gilgal	4:19-24

From Preparation to Passover to Produce	**5:1-12**
Introduction	5:1
Remembering in the Gifted Land	5:2-12
Circumcision and Covenant Commitment	5:2-9
Passover and Covenant Fulfillment	5:10-12
Holy Ground, Holy Presence	**5:13-15**
The Setting	5:13a
The Question	5:13b
The Answer	5:14a
The Response	5:14b
The Command	5:15a
The Response	5:15b
A Battle like No Other: Transforming Otherness	**6:1-27**
God's Instructions: God to Joshua	6:1-5
Joshua Instructs and the People Comply	6:6-11
Action on Days 2 Through 6	6:12-14
Action on the Seventh Day	6:15-20b
The Walls Collapse and the People Act	6:20c-21
The Rescue of Rahab	6:22-25
Joshua's Oath Against Jericho	6:26
Hinge to Chapter 7	6:27
Ai and Achan	**7:1–8:29**
Narrative Introduction: Israel and Achan	7:1
The Defeat at Ai	7:2-5
The Problem with Ai and Achan	7:6-26
Joshua's Cry to the Lord	7:6-9
The Lord's Response	7:10-15
Joshua's Action	7:16-23
The Consequences	7:24-26
Divine Initiative and Command	8:1-2
Joshua's Strategy	8:3-9
The Action	8:10-13
The Ruse Works	8:14-17
Divine Intervention and Victory	8:18-23
Summary and Flashback	8:24-27
Death of the King	8:28-29
The Altar on Mount Ebal: People of the Book	**8:30-35**
Narrative Setup: Building the Altar	8:30-31

The Distribution from Caleb to Joseph	**14:6–17:18**
Caleb's Request	14:6-15
Distribution to Judah	15:1-63
Distribution to Ephraim	16:1-10
Distribution to Manasseh	17:1-13
Joseph's Request	17:14-18
The Territories of the Remaining Tribes	**18:1–19:51**
Instructions for the Distribution	18:1-10
Distribution to the Seven Tribes	18:11–19:49a
Gift to Joshua and Summary of the Distribution	19:49b-51
Cities of Refuge and Cities for Levites	**20:1–21:45**
The Lord's Initiative: Cities of Refuge	20:1-9
The Levites' Initiative, the Israelites' Gift	21:1-42
Summary: The Lord's Gift, the Promise Fulfilled	21:43-45
Othering the Insider	**22:1-34**
Joshua's Exhortation, Blessing, and Dismissal of Transjordan Tribes	22:1-8
The Return Home	22:9
The Altar and Its Consequences: War?	22:10-12
The Conflict Mediators Sent Out	22:13-31
The Mediators' Report and the Israelites' Affirmation	22:32-34
Covenant Exhortations, Covenant Making, and Coda	**23:1–24:33**
Theological Summary and Covenant Commitments	23:1–24:28
Joshua's Covenant Monologue	23:1-16
Covenant Dialogue	24:1-24
Report of Covenant Making	24:25-28
Coda for the Book of Joshua	24:29-33

Essays

"ALL ISRAEL" Joshua's leadership in the book of Joshua is over a united Israel. The book presents "all Israel" as the focus of attention even when there is trouble (Josh 7) or threat of civil war (Josh 22). The phrase *all Israel* occurs seventeen times in Joshua, and in the Pentateuch only twice outside of Deuteronomy (Exod 18:25; Num 16:34; fourteen times in Deuteronomy, twice in Judges, thirty-six times in Samuel, twenty-six times in Kings; and seldom elsewhere in the OT).

Beginning in Joshua 1:2, the Lord's address to Joshua as *you* is inseparably linked to *all this people* and *the Israelites*, who are recipients of the gift of land. The notion of "all Israel" appears in various expressions throughout the book (3:1, 7, 17; 4:1, 11, 14; 6:5; 7:3, 23, 24, 25; 8:15, 21, 24, 33; ten times in ch. 10; eight times in ch. 20; 23:2; 24:2, 27). The twelve representatives of the tribes who pick up twelve stones (Josh 3–4) underscore this unity through a common symbolic action *[Twelve Stones, p. 465]*. The unity of Israel is important because it resonates with several other motifs in the book, including the gathering of *all the tribes* (24:1), the people who are in covenant relationship with *the Lord of all the earth* (3:11), who has made it possible for Joshua to take *all that land* (11:16) and *the whole land* (2:3; 10:40; 11:23; cf. Deut 34:1). The "all" in each of these examples highlights a unifying motif that disintegrates in the book of Judges and culminates in exile at the end of the books of Kings, all presumably because Israel fails to attend to God's instruction (Torah). In this way the narrator takes up the characteristic hyperbole of ancient conquest accounts, normally associated with the assertion of political sovereignty, and applies it to the unity of God's people under divine instruction. Such rhetoric is part of a countercultural agenda in the text that stresses Yahweh's sovereignty over against that of the gods and the imperial powers aligned with them (see McConville 2006: 19–29).

Although "all Israel" represents an ideal unity, a closer look reveals a "mixed multitude" (as in Exod 12:38 KJV). By including a variety of traditional outsiders, the book of Joshua redefines what constitutes "all Israel." The gathering reported in Joshua 8:30-35 involves *all the assembly of Israel, and the women, and the little ones, and the aliens who resided among them* (8:35). Presumably this also accounts for the inclusion of Rahab (ch. 2), the

Gibeonites (ch. 9), those who continue to *live within Israel to this day* (13:13; 15:63; 16:10; 17:12), and Caleb and Othniel, among others (14:6-15; 15:13-19).

ANGER OF THE LORD A number of OT texts characterize the Lord as "slow to anger" (Exod 34:6; Num 14:18; Neh 9:17; Pss 86:15; 103:8; 145:8; Joel 2:13; Jon 4:2; Nah 1:3). That slowness seems not to diminish the occurrences of divine anger in the Bible. The motif appears in three chapters in Joshua (7:1, 26; 22:18, 20; 23:16). The expression *anger of the Lord* is used forty times in the OT, including five times in Deuteronomy (6:15; 7:4; 11:17; 29:20, 27) and ten times in the DtrH (Josh 7:1; 23:16; Judg 2:14; 2:20; 3:8; 10:7; 2 Sam 6:7; 24:1; 2 Kings 13:3; 24:20). A variety of Hebrew words are used to express divine anger (Deuteronomy: *'np* in 1:37; 4:21; 7:4; 9:20; 11:17; 13:17; 29:23, 26, 27; *k's* in 4:25; 9:18; 32:16; *ḥrh* in 7:4; 11:17; 13:17; 29:27; 31:17; *qṣp* in 1:34; 9:7, 8, 19; *ḥmh* in 9:19; 29:27; Joshua: *ḥrh* in 7:1, 26; 23:16; *qṣp* in 22:18, 20; for a full list, see Latvus: 25–26). In Deuteronomy and the DtrH, God's anger highlights Yahweh's role as "the real ruler of the world (instead of political powers or other gods)" and initiates a response of divine justice that corresponds to the violation of the relationship between God and Israel (Latvus: 90).

"Why are the gods angry?" is a question common to many ancient cultures and texts. In the ninth century BC Mesha Inscription (Moabite Stone), a commonly cited example with a similar worldview (*ANET* 320–21; see the essay *Mesha Inscription, p. 447*), King Mesha of Moab looks back on Moab's recent past and on how Israel, under Omri, has colonized Moab for many years, "for Chemosh was angry at his land." The Mesha Inscription offers no rationale for Chemosh's anger. Joshua 7 makes it clear, however, that God's anger is not arbitrary: it derives from a violation of a divine command, which has ruptured the relationship (*my covenant*, 7:11; cf. 7:15). Failure to rectify the violation results in divine abandonment (7:12). Restoration requires that the proscribed objects be returned to God and the one who has taken the objects be *devoted to destruction* (*ḥerem*; 6:18, 21). Achan is a scapegoat: he represents all Israel. He takes the fall for the community. God's response is not merely a reaction to being disobeyed, nor simply an example of retributive justice, but derives from the violation of the covenant relationship.

The covenant concerns God's choice (election) of Israel to mediate God's blessing to the nations (Gen 12:3; 22:18; Exod 19:6). Israel's faithfulness to that relationship is an active participation "in God's world-sustaining activity" (Kaminsky 1995: 92). The covenantal dimension of Joshua 7, therefore, provides the context for having the whole community experience the consequences of Achan's action (Kaminsky 1995: 94). Most remarkably, in the light of the community's covenantal rootedness, Joshua complains to God at the first point of experiencing those consequences (7:6-9). This introduces an opportunity to read this text against the grain, not only by siding temporarily with Joshua in his having taken offense at God, but also by recognizing that Joshua, too, is concerned for Israel's survival *and* for the survival of God's reputation.

Many of the divine anger texts are rooted in God's jealousy for Israel's exclusive loyalty. When Israel forsakes the Lord and serves other gods, the consequences include some kind of retributive justice (e.g., punishment, exile). But when Israel loves and serves only the Lord, Israel will experience blessing and enjoy the fruits of the land (Latvus: 76). These emphases are particularly evident in Deuteronomy, where love between God and Israel is depicted (the Lord as subject: Deut 4:37; 7:8, 13; 10:15, 18; 15:16; 23:5; people as subject: 5:10; 6:5; 7:9; 10:12; 11:1, 13, 22; 13:3; 19:9; 30:6, 16, 20). It should be noted, however, that in all twenty-seven passages in Deuteronomy where the divine anger motif occurs, only 29:23 refers to the destruction of non-Israelites (cf. Deut 1:37; 4:21, 25; 6:15; 7:4; 9:7, 8, 18, 19, 20, 22; 11:17; 13:17; 29:20, 23, 24, 27, 28; 31:17, 29; 32:16, 19, 21, 22; Latvus: 73). None of the warfare against the indigenous population in Joshua is linked with divine anger. That is reserved only for Achan and for potentially recalcitrant Israelites, whose apostasy will result in exile from the land.

Although God can exercise anger or wrath against those who violate Israel (Ezek 25:14; Nah 1:2, 6), most occurrences of divine anger concern Israel (e.g., Ps 106:40; Jer 4:8; 12:13; 23:20; 25:37; 30:24; 51:45; Lam 1:12; 2:1; Ezek 5:13, 15; 7:3; 16:26; 43:8). Similarly, Joshua's references to divine anger must be read in the light of Deuteronomy's use of divine anger—in the context of the people's being threatened with destruction or perishing from the land (6:15; 7:4; 11:17; 29:27). Joshua 23:16 echoes Deuteronomy 11:17, where the Deuteronomic context is shaped by the priority of covenant commitment ("love") and obedience (Deut 11:1; cf. 11:8, 13, 18, 22). The motif of "perishing off the good land" reverberates throughout Deuteronomy both as a threat and also a reality in retrospect (4:26-27; 28:63-64; 29:27-28). In 29:27-28 the "anger of the LORD" is occasioned by Israel's having "abandoned the covenant" and having "turned and served other gods" (29:25-26; cf. Josh 23:16). In consequence, "The LORD uprooted them from their land in anger, fury and great wrath, and cast them into another land, as is now the case" (Deut 29:27-28). Deuteronomy 6:15 is even stronger, with its consequence that the Lord will "destroy you from the face of the earth."

The clearest Deuteronomic allusion to the Achan story is Deuteronomy 13:12-18, which concerns the discovery of "scoundrels" who have enticed a town's inhabitants to "worship other gods" (13:13), which is "an abhorrent thing." (Two different words are used: "outrageous thing," root *nbl* in Josh 7:15 and Deut 22:21, which states that they must "purge the evil from your midst"; and "abhorrent thing," *to'ebah* in Deut 13:14; 17:4.) If such persons are found, then all the inhabitants of that town shall be put "to the sword, utterly destroying it and everything in it" (Deut 13:15). The remainder of the text reflects a scenario similar to that of Joshua 7 (except that Achan, his family, and his livestock are stoned; v. 25). The town is "devoted to destruction" and is to be burned (Deut 13:15-16; so is Achan's household). Moreover, explicit instruction is worth noting: "Do not let anything devoted to destruction stick to your hand, so that the LORD may turn from his fierce anger and show you compassion" (13:17). All of that depends on "obey[ing] the voice of the LORD" (13:18a; cf. Josh 5:6). Achan, like these "scoundrels" (Deut 13:13), is a threat to the well-being of the community because of his disobedient grasping. Although covetousness (Josh 7:21) is a serious problem, the "far more compelling demand" hinted at is "the danger of idolatry and alien cult" (Clements 2000: 117). What endangers the community most are not things themselves, but the threat of alien religious practices (cf. Deut 7:25). One way of reading Joshua 7–8, along with Deuteronomy, is to understand it as a fearful response to the Other, characterized by a "violent anti-Canaanite, anti-idolatry stratum of Deuteronomic thinking" (Clements 2000: 119). Achan's story warns all of the link between greed and idolatry (cf. Col 3:5) *[Idolatry, p. 438]*.

Yet Joshua 7 may offer another image. The chapter ends with the note that *the Lord turned from his burning anger* (v. 26). The restoration of the holiness of God's space also restores God's presence. This final note also resonates with the warning against idolatry in Deuteronomy 13. There the admonition not to let any of the proscribed things "stick to your hand" is "so that the LORD may turn from his fierce anger and show you compassion, and in his compassion multiply you, as he swore to your ancestors" (Deut 13:17). Anger masks a relational disruption. Authentic relationship works toward compassion. Israel's love for God marks God's deepest desire for the relationship (Deut 6:5; Josh 22:5). Unfortunately, the DtrH (and Deuteronomy itself) is also marked by a tragic awareness that God's compassion has not yet run its course. Perhaps exile will open a way.

Joshua 23 reflects the exilic reality that is only hinted at in Joshua 7. In chapter 23 all of the Deuteronomic motifs come together: *perish from this good land . . . given you* (v. 13); *all the bad things . . . destroyed you from this good land* (v. 15); *If you transgress the covenant . . . and serve other gods, . . . the anger of the LORD . . . ; you shall perish quickly from the good land that he has given to you* (v. 16). The only difference between those motifs and Deuteronomy is the assumption in Deuteronomy 29:28 that this has already occurred: "as is now the case." Deuteronomy 29:28 anticipates the expression of that anger in 2 Kings 22:16-17, an anger that brings about "disaster on this place." Joshua, standing between Deuteronomy and Kings, can be read as a "flashback" to a time before "as is now the case." The reader knows from Joshua's speech in chapter 23 that the warning of Deuteronomy 29:28 has already become a reality. Therefore Achan's story in Joshua 7 is a telling tale of how such things tend to come about, through simple acts of "coveting" and "taking." In a sense, the story of Achan is the story of the fall of Israel, even as the seeing, delighting, and taking in the garden is humankind's fall from relational dependence on God (cf. Gen 3:6). And as Adam and Eve are representative humans, so Achan represents Israel. That may be why Joshua 7 emphasizes the plural, and why God accuses *Israel* of having sinned, taken, and stolen (7:11).

Though the parallels between Deuteronomy and Joshua 7 are inexact, the bundle of theological intersections is almost identical. In Deuteronomy, things devoted to destruction are equivalent to "other gods." Hence Achan's act is Israel's first departure from covenant loyalty in the land (Josh 7:11, 15), as it is perhaps remembered in Hosea 2:15 (cf. Josh 7:26). It is an act that allows the reader to move from chapter 7 to Joshua's speech in chapter 23, to the exilic reality at the end of the books of Kings. Ezra 10:1-17 reflects a similar reality: the people have also been unfaithful (*ma'al*, 10:2, 10; cf. Josh 7:1). After the people repent and confess (*todah*, Ezra 10:11; cf. Josh 7:19), the anger of the Lord is averted (Ezra 10:14; cf. 9:14; Josh 7:26). In addition, the property of the unfaithful people has to be devoted to destruction (*ḥerem*, Ezra 10:8; NRSV: "forfeited"; NJPS: "confiscated"). These two passages share a common worldview (Latvus: 50). Yet Ezra, though dealing with a different kind of taking (wives), has transformed the notion of *ḥerem*.

The paradigmatic self-confession of God in Exodus 34:6-7, which is echoed throughout the OT, suggests that although divine mercy does not cancel the consequential justice of divine anger, mercy is by far the more enduring and relationally motivating (cf. Pss 30:5; 78:38; 103:8-9; Isa 12:1; 48:9; Hos 11:9; 14:4; Jon 3:9; Mic 7:18; Zech 10:3). Thus the full biblical conversation transforms divine anger by severing the assumed link between God's anger and human mediation of that anger. Divine slowness to anger provides a check on human retributive justice without precluding that divine justice allows human beings to experience the consequences of their actions.

For further exploration of divine anger, see Baloian; Kaminsky 1995; Latvus.

ARCHAEOLOGY AND JOSHUA Correlating archaeological research with the testimony of the book of Joshua has been one of the most vexing problems in historical research on the OT. We may simply not know enough to be able to affirm how the archaeological evidence and the narrative presentation in the book of Joshua have a bearing on one another. As Meier puts it, "The biblical text preserves remarkable memories of second millennium realities at the same time that it raises major questions on topics where archaeologists disagree with archaeologists, biblical scholars with biblical scholars, historians with historians. . . . The fissures of the discussion are neither easily predictable nor readily resolvable, and inevitably subject to revision in the near future if the history of the interpretation of this subject is any guide" (433). This perspective is corroborated by Mazani: "Different investigators use the same data on the evidence for early Israel but draw contradictory and irreconcilable conclusions" (96).

For that reason, this commentary does not provide readers with explanations about archaeological evidence pertaining to specific biblical sites. Nor does the commentary posit a specific date either for the conquest or the settlement of the land. The focus is on the literary and theological dimensions of the narrative as a whole. Still, it may be helpful to know a little about why a choice must be made one way or another. The main choice governing this commentary concerns the genre of the text of Joshua. The following awkward question puts it clearly: "As what genre should the book of Joshua be read?" An essay below *[Composition of Joshua]* provides a guide to that question. In short, Joshua is not a modern history book. Rather than reflecting modern criteria for historical authenticity, Joshua presents a paradigmatic narrative, an exemplary story grounded in authentic historical memory, yet whose aim is to elicit a response from Israel of exclusive loyalty to their liberating and gift-giving God.

Trying to add the modern penchant for historical accuracy through correlation with elusive archaeological evidence places a burden on the text that takes away from the real conversation the book seeks to elicit. It may be helpful to sketch the problem briefly. With the rise of archaeological research and its interpretation, five issues have surfaced:

Evidence for Destruction of Canaanite Cities Several biblical descriptions of the cities and peoples of Canaan lead readers to imagine huge fortified cities with massive populations (Num 13:28, 30-33; Deut 1:28; 9:1-2). In Joshua, a description resembling those hyperbolic statements appears only in 14:12 in the distribution report to Caleb. Otherwise the only fortifications mentioned are in 10:20 and 19:29, 35. Joshua 7:2-3 reports minimal defenses at Ai. Only the Jericho story mentions walls (2:15; 6:5, 20), although other cities like Hazor also had fortifications.

The book of Joshua, moreover, highlights the destruction of three cities: Jericho, Ai, and Hazor (6:24; 8:28; 11:11, 13). Joshua 11:13 states clearly that, apart from Hazor, Joshua did not burn (and hence destroy) any of *the towns that stood on mounds*. Thus Makkedah (10:28) and Hebron (10:39), although reported as having been conquered and *devoted to destruction*, were not destroyed. And a site like Shechem seems not to have been conquered at all.

In relation to such biblical texts, the archaeological evidence concerns the destruction of Canaanite towns in the thirteenth century BC. The biblical text does not require massive destruction throughout the land. Archaeological evidence for sites mentioned in Joshua suggests that there were Late Bronze Age (1550–1200 BC) settlements in a good number of sites (Merling 1997: 153, listing twelve out of seventeen possible sites). Of these sites, only two have evidence of Late Bronze I destruction (Debir [Tell Beit Mirsim] and Hazor [Tel el-Qedah]), and five have evidence of Late Bronze II destructions (Lachish [Del ed-Duweir], Debir [Tell Beit Mirsim], Hazor [Tell el-Qedah], Madon [perhaps near Tell Qarnei Hittin], and Achshaph [Tell Keisan]). Moreover, excavations at some of the main sites show that they were not inhabited in the Late Bronze Age (Jericho, Ai, Gibeon, Heshbon, Arad).

Comparing the very limited biblical descriptions and the sparse archaeological evidence, "it becomes clear that neither the Bible nor archaeology has produced much information about the conquest events of the Book of Joshua. Yet, our ignorance of the whole, and the specifics of what we do know, have driven the archaeological discussions" (Merling 1997: 152). Moreover, archaeologists continue to debate the location of a good number of biblical sites. Bryant Wood's recent analysis of options regarding the location of Ai, Bethel, and Beth-aven is a good example of the problem. According to Wood (2008), Ai should be located at Khirbet el-Maqatir, not at the traditional et-Tell (which means Ruin). Such debates could be multiplied with respect to other sites as well. Even more significant are debates having to do with what counts as evidence and how to interpret the evidence. Thus Amihai Mazar summarizes:

> We may conclude that in some cases there is an outright conflict between the archaeological findings and the biblical narratives, while in others,

> the archaeological data do not contradict the Conquest stories. Archaeology cannot confirm that Israelite tribes were responsible for the destruction of certain Canaanite cities. The devastation of Canaan did not take place in one sweeping, single military campaign. Rather, the destruction of Canaanite cities resulted from a long-drawn-out process of regional conflicts, the nature of which cannot be identified at the present time. . . . The Conquest tradition may be understood as a telescoped reflection of a lengthy, complex historical process in which many of the Canaanite city-states, weakened and impoverished by three hundred years of Egyptian domination, were demolished during the thirteenth and twelfth centuries BCE. (Finkelstein and Mazar: 64)

The Merneptah Stela In his victory stela, Pharaoh Merneptah (1213–1203 BC) boasts "Israel is laid waste, his seed is not." Of the eight groups of names mentioned on the stela, three are city-states and four are lands or territories. Only Israel is mentioned as a "people" or "socioethnic entity" (Hasel 2008a: 53). Given the names of other cities and areas listed, it is most likely that the Israel referred to by Merneptah was a people group at home in the central hill country (52–53). Like other conquest accounts, Merneptah's description is hyperbolic. Still, it testifies that by 1209 BC (59), a people named Israel existed in the land alongside others like the city-state of Gezer. Yet even that raises an interesting question. What might the relationship be to Merneptah's conquest of Gezer and the victory over Gezer reported in the book of Joshua (10:33), where the king and his people are all said to have been killed? Not only that, but the book of Judges also reports a failure of Ephraim to drive out the inhabitants of Gezer (1:29). That these various references cannot be harmonized should not be surprising.

Artifacts and Material Culture Archaeologists have tried to identify the ethnicity of people groups based on material remains found at various sites, but that has proved to be difficult. First, pottery items like collared-rim storage jars have been found in traditional Israelite areas (hill country) as well as in other areas. These are certainly storage containers that would have been used by any ethnic group. Some suggest that the Canaanite jars are decorated, whereas Israelite ones are not (Mazani: 100; Mazar, in Finkelstein and Mazar: 89–90). It is likely that Israelites and Canaanites shared the technology available at the time, and that such evidence cannot tell us much about whether or when Israelites emerged on the scene (Mazani: 99–100; Finkelstein, in Finkelstein and Mazar: 77–78). Second, pig bones have been found in some urban centers in the early Iron Age (1200–1000 BC), especially in Philistine areas west of the central hill country and along the coast, but not in areas traditionally associated with Israelite settlement in the hill country. Settlers in the hill country were likely pastoralists, a location where it would be difficult to raise animals that cannot be easily herded—such as pigs. Thus the absence of pigs does not prove that these hill country settlers were Israelites, though biblical connections make this a tempting association: the biblical instruction to avoid pork (Lev 11:7-8; Deut 14:8), and the biblical association of Israelites in hill country sites. Unfortunately for this theory, few pig bones have been found in major Canaanite sites of the lowlands (Mazar, in Finkelstein and Mazar: 93). Hess (1993: 507) reports that no pig bones were found at Lachish, a Canaanite site.

Architecture Excavations have uncovered the remains of typical four-room houses in the central hill country at what have been assumed to be Israelite Iron Age sites. Yet such houses have been found elsewhere, as have similar three-room houses in Canaanite sites of Late Bronze Age II. The architecture bears witness to significant settlement activity in the hill country of the Iron Age, reflecting a "transition from a pastoral to a sedentary way of life" (Finkelstein: 237). Although some consider these houses one of the Israelite "ethnic markers" (Mazani: 101–2), the architectural remains of the houses do not identify the ethnicity of their inhabitants.

Cultic Centers The excavations at Mount Ebal have uncovered a thirteenth-century altar similar to that described in Joshua 5:30-35. Archaeologists dispute whether this is an Israelite altar and whether it comes from the time of Joshua (Hess 1993: 135–37).

Conclusion As the Merneptah Stela indicates, a people known as "Israel" inhabited part of Canaan in the thirteenth century BC. Other evidence from the Late Bronze Age and Iron Age I does not provide unambiguous evidence for the origin of Israel, even though it can be discerned that Israelites participated, along with others, in the (re)settlement of the central highlands of Canaan in the Iron Age (beginning ca. 1200 BC). But ethnic distinctions based on artifacts and material culture continue to be disputed. Even so, the archaeological evidence does not disprove the possibility that a group of Israelites entered the land as escaped slaves from Egypt; that in the process of settling down, they and other migratory groups engaged in conflict with Canaanites; and that those who came to be identified as Israelites (including "aliens" who identified with Israel) worshiped a god known as Yahweh (Hess 1993: 139).

As presented in the book of Joshua, the cities of Jericho and Ai, the subjects of the first stories in the book, are not so much actual cities (although there may well be authentic historical memory underlying the stories), but paradigmatic stories that hint at the purpose of the entire book. Ai means "ruin," and this story explains how it got that way. And Jericho, sometimes called the oldest city on earth, is a "legendary symbol of Canaanite might" (McKenzie: 421). But even more, these stories represent both divine participation and human response. Rahab (in the Jericho story) and Achan (in the Ai story) stand as paradigmatic figures who respond to the situation in instructive ways. The historian is interested in the people and their actions, not simply in what happened in the past.

It is possible to suggest that because Joshua's conquest accounts are similar to other ancient conquest accounts, they are not historically accurate; yet that is not a necessary conclusion. The accounts of Joshua are hyperbolic and schematic. They may not present a straightforward chronological narrative. Even so, the conquest *as it is told* in the book of Joshua may reflect "memories of actual situations and events rooted in the second millennium BCE," along with "early aetiological [explanatory] and invented stories" that have a primarily didactic purpose even though they have been presented in a history-like narrative (Mazar, in Finkelstein and Mazar: 65).

It is most likely that the settlement period "spanned as many as several centuries" and involved peoples entering the land from the south, east, and north, who joined indigenous groups within the land and together later "would become known as Israel" (Meier: 430). It may also be possible that the books of Joshua and Judges do not represent two distinct historical periods, but two ways of looking at the reality of Israel: one in which Israel was more or less faithful to God's instruction (Joshua; cf. 24:31), and the other in which Israel was unfaithful (Judges). These two paradigms remain the options available for God's people, as schematically presented in these two books. Questions of historical origins, therefore, might be notoriously difficult to discern.

The archaeology of Israel's origins in the land, together with the correlation of archaeology with the book of Joshua, continues to be relevant today. It is particularly significant for those who seek either to justify or to diminish Israel's claim on the central hill country, which encompasses most of what is currently named Palestine, Occupied Territories, or Judea and Samaria. Especially in Israeli Jewish society, archaeology and the book of Joshua provide the ideological basis for claiming these disputed territories (see esp. Greenberg 1995; Abu El-Haj: 99–105; also Whitelam; Blenkinsopp 2002; Masalha). Emek Shaveh is an organization of archaeologists and community activists focusing on the role of archaeology in Israeli society and in the contemporary Israeli-Palestinian conflict. They view archaeology as a resource for building bridges and strengthening bonds between different peoples and cultures, and they seek to transform politicized archaeological practice so as to have a positive impact on the dynamics of the Israeli-Palestinian conflict (www.alt-arch.org).

The following recent resources provide excellent overviews of the issues involved in bringing archaeological research into conversation with the book of Joshua: Ortiz; Merling 1997, 2004; Hess 1993, 2008a; Younger 1999; Dever 1990, 1992, 2001; Provan, Long, and Longman: ch. 7; B. Wood 1990, 2008; Coogan 1990; Silberman and Small 1997. For comprehensive, although slightly dated, overviews of all the relevant archaeological data, see Finkelstein 1988 and Mazar 1990. The book by Finkelstein and Mazar presents a state-of-the-art debate about the contribution of archaeology to the reconstruction of early Israelite history. Perdue, Toombs, and Johnson (1987) and Merling (1997: 111–55) provide detailed summaries of the major sites in relation to the book of Joshua. Besides its article on "Archaeology" by Ortiz, the *Dictionary of the Old Testament: Historical Books*, edited by Arnold and Williamson, has articles on most of the sites relevant to and named in the book of Joshua.

CHARACTERIZATION OF JOSHUA Major characters in biblical texts are often portrayed as ambiguous and complex figures. Joshua proves to be an exception. On the basis of the choices he makes and the motives attributed to him, the narrator depicts him as relying completely on God and trusting God's capacity to do what God intends. Through the unfolding of the narrative, Joshua takes up Moses' mantle and becomes *servant of the Lord* (24:25-26). As a leader, he encourages others, even though in his prophetic role he either cajoles or warns about the dangers of easy promises of faithfulness (24:19). And he fulfills God's instructions (Torah) even as he bends the rules by including outsiders like Rahab and the Gibeonites. In his role as covenant-making leader, he even *wrote . . . words in the book of the law of God* (24:26). In a certain respect, the book of Joshua is about the gift and challenge of Joshua as a character in the story. Not only is he the paradigmatic Israelite who receives the gifts of God's active presence and who responds in faithful obedience, he is also the prototype of the ideal royal leader who is faithful to divine instruction. Joshua's royal persona resonates with a number of biblical texts and characters, not least of which is Jesus, whose name he shares.

Moses and Joshua Joshua 1 establishes a pattern of reliability in its juxtaposition of Joshua and Moses. The Moses-Joshua typology can be described in terms of imitation or discipleship (Schäfer-Lichtenberger).

The notice about the death of Moses in Joshua 1:1 links the book of Joshua explicitly to the end of Deuteronomy just as the reference to Joshua and the Israelites in Deuteronomy 34:9 links that book to the narrative that follows. Deuteronomy 34:9 takes the reader not only to Joshua 1, where the transition in leadership from Moses to Joshua is explicitly introduced, but also to the last verses of the book of Joshua, where Joshua's death is announced and he is named *servant of the Lord*, and the Israelites are said to have *served the Lord* (24:29-31), just as they are said in Deuteronomy 34:9 to have "obeyed" Joshua. Thus Joshua carries on the tradition of leadership, which fosters faithfulness in the community of Yahweh. It could be said that where Moses failed because of disobedience, Joshua succeeded. Yet that would be saying too much, for the point of Joshua's success is his faithfulness to Yahweh's word as mediated through God's servant Moses. And it is that instruction, particularly as it is reflected in Deuteronomy, that infuses all of Joshua through Kings (excluding Ruth), books that map out the journey into and out of the land. From this perspective the book of Joshua is not simply a narrative that justifies Israel's taking possession of the land; it is especially a narrative that explores how Torah, or divine instruction, takes possession of Israel.

Moses is mentioned five times in Joshua 8:30-35, twice as *servant of the Lord* (8:31, 33) and the first such mention since the three occurrences in chapter 1. Moses is mentioned exactly this way fourteen times in the book of Joshua (1:1, 13, 15; 8:31, 33; 11:12; 12:6 twice; 13:8; 14:7; 18:7; 22:2, 4, 5; cf. *my servant Moses* in 1:2, 7; 2 Kings 21:8). Even more important than his designation as *servant* is his role as one who commands, which is captured in the repetition of the *book of the law* (Josh 8:31, 34), *law of Moses* (8:32), or *words of the law* (8:34), which correspond to what Moses has commanded (8:31, 33, 35; cf. Deut 34:9). This is the second time after chapter 1 that events take place as Moses has commanded (Josh 4:10; cf. 1:7, 13).

This way of describing Moses appears once in Deuteronomy (34:9). Joshua is *servant of the Lord* only at the end of the book of Joshua (24:29; so also Judg 2:8). Moses is mentioned again as servant in Solomon's prayer of dedication (1 Kings 8:53, 56), where Moses is the mediator of election and announcer of God's promises. The expression "servant of the LORD" does not appear again until 2 Kings 18:12, where the narrator declares that Samaria fell "because they did not obey the voice of the LORD their God but transgressed his covenant—all that Moses the servant of the LORD had commanded; they neither listened nor obeyed" (cf. also 2 Kings 17:7-23; 21:8).

Although David is also named "servant" (2 Sam 3:18; 7:5, 8; 1 Kings 11:13, 32, 34, 36, 38; 14:8; 2 Kings 19:34; 20:6), only Moses is mediator of the divine word. Joshua is the ideal follower of Moses (cf. Num 27:18; Josh 8:30-31), even as Solomon is the failed follower of David (cf. David's imitation of Joshua in 1 Kings 2:2-4; see Schäfer-Lichtenberger). "My servant Moses" takes priority over "my servant David" because David is an exemplar only in how he is said to obey Moses' commandments.

Joshua as Royal Figure and Keeper of Torah The book of Joshua also presents Joshua as the prototype of the Deuteronomic royal ideal. Joshua's covenant-renewal ceremony (Josh 8:30-35) is an example of his embodiment of a royal obligation. In particular, his producing *a copy of the law* (Josh 8:32) indicates that he has fulfilled the obligation set upon him by Moses (Deut 27:3), which, according to Deut 17:18, is an obligation of the king. Actually, "Deut 17:18 and Josh 8:32 are the only two occurrences of the expression *mišnēh tôrâ* [a copy of the law] in the OT" (Nelson 1981b: 533). Joshua is not literally a royal figure. Rather, he represents the first of those in the DtrH who embodies the royal ideal and becomes the one to whom later generations of readers must look for the prototypical *servant of the LORD* (Josh 24:29).

As in the instruction for the king's reading of Torah in Deuteronomy 17:18-19, Joshua is told to meditate on the Torah day and night (Josh 1:8; cf. Ps 1:2). Both Joshua and the king are to turn from it neither right nor left (Deut 17:20; Josh 1:7; 23:6; cf. Deut 5:32; 17:11; 28:14). The emphasis in Joshua 1 on *this book of the law*, as in Deuteronomy 31:26 and Joshua 1:8, also appears as "this law" in Deuteronomy 17:18-19 (cf. "this law" also in Deut 1:5; 27:3, 8, 26; 28:58, 61; 29:29; 31:9, 11, 12, 24; 32:46). Joshua's commissioning places him squarely into Deuteronomy's ideal of one who is faithful to God's instruction (Torah) mediated through Moses and written down in a book or scroll (Deut 1:5; 4:8, 44; 29:20, 29; 30:10; 31:9-12, 24-26; 32:46; 33:4, 10; Josh 1; 8:81-35; chs. 23–24; 1 Kings 2:3; 2 Kings 10:31; 14:6; 17:13, 34, 37; 22:8, 11; 23:24, 25; see Nelson 1981b: 531).

God's (and Moses') commissioning of Joshua and David's commissioning of Solomon are strikingly similar, confirming Joshua's characterization as the standard against which kings are to be evaluated (Deut 31:7-8; Josh 1:1-9; 1 Kings 2:2-4). Joshua and Solomon are followers, disciples of the one who has gone before (Schäfer-Lichtenberger). The similarity highlights Joshua's paradigmatic character as faithful disciple of Moses and emphasizes the tragedy of Solomon's failure to follow God's instructions. And the reasons for Solomon's failure lead ultimately to the demise of both Israel and Judah. Notice how David's speech in these verses echoes Deuteronomy (4:29, 40; 6:5; 8:6; 10:12; 11:1, 22) and Joshua (23:14), with their emphasis on keeping faithful to divine instruction. The narrative draws on motifs from Deuteronomy and Joshua, but makes it quite clear that Solomon's following in the footsteps of David will escalate the violence in ways that betray the symbolism of Solomon's own name (e.g., 1 Kings 2:6, 9). As with the death of Moses, the death of David signals a new era. At each transition point, the successor must choose whether to be faithful to the divine instruction.

There are two paths: the path of Joshua and the path of Solomon. Joshua takes the path prescribed by the laws governing kings (Deut 17:14-20). He does not build a standing army with horses and chariots. He reads the Torah to the people. Solomon builds an army and imports horses (1 Kings 10:26-29). If he reads the Torah, the text does not say so (in contrast to strong affirmations of David in this regard) but recounts ways in which he has disobeyed it (cf. 1 Kings 2:3; 11:33-34). More important, Solomon does not follow the path of Joshua in refusing the *foreign gods* (Josh 24:23; cf. vv. 14-15), but builds shrines to other gods (1 Kings 11:4, 10, 33). Although Solomon is a deeply ambiguous character as he is portrayed in 1 Kings, it is clear that the narrative as a whole makes Solomon both the first cause of Israel's potential demise and the first in the books of Kings to announce exile (as seen in his dedicatory prayer in 1 Kings 8:46; cf. Deut 4:25-30; 28:36, 49, 63-64; Josh 23:13-16). Even the Lord announces to Solomon that if he does not keep divine Torah and serves other gods, the Lord "will cut Israel off from the land that I have given them" (1 Kings 9:6-7, 9; cf. Josh 23:13, 16). Solomon's assertions of "rest" and that "not one word has failed of all his good promise" (8:56) are deeply ironic fulfillments in the transition from David to Solomon (cf. "rest" in 5:4; and the affirmation of the fulfillment of promise in Josh 23:14, where the promise fulfilled is set in the context of threat of land revoked in 23:16). Solomon's "dominion" is over all the territory "west of the Euphrates" (1 Kings 4:21, 24; cf. Josh 1:4), and his concern is for "all the nations," "all the kings of the earth" (1 Kings 4:34), and "all the peoples of the earth" who might come to "know your name" (8:43). Such hopeful assertions are countered by the king's embrace of imperial grandeur and the worship of foreign gods.

The Chronicler's history develops even more strikingly the portrayal of David as a second Moses and Solomon as a second Joshua (Dillard; Williamson). Specifically, Solomon, like Joshua, is charged to "be strong and of good courage" (1 Chron 22:13; cf. Deut 31:6, 23; Josh 1:7, 9). Remarkably, the charge to Solomon also includes the notion of prospering by obeying the instruction of the Lord (1 Chron 22:13). The parallel is strengthened by the nearly word-for-word repetition of the themes of divine presence (1 Chron 22:11, 16; cf. Deut 31:6, 8, 23; Josh 1:5, 9), encouragement not to fear or be dismayed (1 Chron 22:13; cf. Deut 3:22; 31:6; Josh 1:9), the promise that God will not fail or forsake (1 Chron 28:20; cf. Deut

31:6, 8; Josh 1:5, 9), and "rest on every side" (1 Chron 22:18 NIV; cf. Josh 1:13, 15; 21:44; 22:4; 23:1). In 1 Chronicles 22 those charges have been transformed from their original context in 1 Kings 2 and have been made part of the charge for Solomon to build the temple and seek the presence of the Lord.

Joshua and Josiah The model of Joshua as leader and prototype is also reflected in the story of King Josiah in 2 Kings 22–23 (Nelson 1981b). First, Josiah's model obedience is described in the same terms as Joshua's (note esp. the motif of not turning to the right or to the left: 2 Kings 22:2; cf. Josh 1:7; 23:6; and the law of the king in Deut 17:20). Second, and related to that, the "book of the law" is mentioned eleven times in 2 Kings 22–23. Similar emphasis is found only in the book of Joshua (Josh 1:8; 8:31, 34; 23:6; 24:26; cf. 22:5). Only when Josiah's priests recover the lawbook does such an emphasis return in the history. Only Deuteronomy, Joshua, and the narrative about Josiah in 2 Kings use the expression "this law." Both Joshua and Josiah are intimately aware of the importance of the book of the law (Josh 8:31; 24:26; 2 Kings 22:8, 11). Third, both Joshua and Josiah are mediators of the covenant (see Josh 8:30-35; ch. 24; cf. 2 Kings 23:1-3). In both Joshua 24 and 2 Kings 23:1-3 the people are drawn into the covenant renewal. The covenantal (and Deuteronomic) language of both texts is almost identical. Fourth, both Joshua and Josiah are the only ones in the DtrH who celebrate the Passover (Josh 5:10-12; 2 Kings 23:21-23; cf. 2 Chron 30, with Hezekiah also celebrating a great Passover festival). Although other Passovers would have been observed, the narrator notes that "no such passover had been kept since the days of the judges" (2 Kings 23:22). Fifth, Joshua 1 presents the entry into the land as more of a "triumphal procession" than a violent invasion (1:3; cf. Deut 11:24). The nonmilitaristic tone of the chapter seems to suggest comparison with the peaceful expansion of territory under Josiah's rule, which was caused by Assyrian withdrawal (Nelson 1981b: 537–38).

Through faithful adherence to the Mosaic law, as presented in Deuteronomy, and through assertion of political rule over the larger territory of Judah and Samaria, Josiah becomes a "second Joshua" in the Deuteronomistic narrator's figural reading (or typological interpretation) of history. Josiah, like Joshua, is faithful to Torah and to exclusive worship of Yahweh. Although his "reform" is clearly politically motivated, the narrative draws on Moses' authority (Deuteronomy) and Joshua's paradigmatic obedience to present Josiah as the Davidic ideal. The narrator concludes with hyperbole: "Before him there was no king like him, who turned to the LORD with all his heart, with all his soul, and with all his might, according to all the law of Moses" (2 Kings 23:25). The combination of the three words "heart, soul, might" is found elsewhere only in Deuteronomy 6:5. "Heart" and "soul" are found ten times throughout Deuteronomy, mostly to refer to faithful obedience to divine instruction (4:29; 6:5; 10:12; 11:13, 18; 13:3; 26:16; 30:2, 6) and once in Joshua 22:5 (cf. also 1 Kings 2:4; 8:48; 2 Kings 23:3, 25).

In drawing the analogy between Joshua and Josiah, the historian has presented a typology of obedience rooted in faithfulness to Yahweh, mediated through the instructions of God to Moses, and embodied in a characteristic royal figure (Joshua, David, Josiah). The tragedy of the history is that it ends in Babylonian exile. The hope of the DtrH is for a turning away from all other ultimate loyalties (cf. Josh 23:16; 2 Kings 22:17) and for embracing again the hope of return "with all your heart and soul" to the Lord (Deut 30:1-10, esp. v. 6; Josh 22:5; 1 Kings 8:46-53).

Although Joshua is a paradigmatic royal figure, he does not set up a monarchy or the accoutrements of kingship such as a standing military, a temple, or a central administration. Rather, Joshua is more of a prophetic/royal figure who models faithfulness to the Lord and to his Torah and who exhorts the people to do the same (Habel 1995: 63, 67). Although one might have expected Joshua to have been mentioned as Josiah's pattern in 2 Kings, he is not because, as McConville suggests, Israel is a Torah community, not a community centered around a leader (2006: 107–9). Although McConville dismisses the typology between the two, it can be argued that the figural relationship between Joshua and Josiah is even more significant for the reason he suggests. The point is not the leader, but the instruction of God (Torah). Ultimately kingship fails to be Torah's steward whereas the priests and prophets, among whom Joshua is the first, remain the primary model.

Although this Joshua is mentioned in the DtrH outside the book of Joshua only at the beginning of the book of Judges (1:1; 2:6, 7, 8; 2:21) and in 1 Kings 16:34, he remains a paradigmatic figure whose faithfulness belongs to the key signature of the entire story. The story as a whole is a tragedy (with its end in exile) only if readers do not consider how they might model their lives in keeping with the one who brought them across the Jordan River into the gifted land.

COMPOSITION OF JOSHUA The book of Joshua is an historical document, the product of a writer or writers who were trying to give an account of Israel's past. Their narrative presents a prophetic perspective on Israel's origins, as one might expect from a book that stands at the beginning of "the Prophets" in the Hebrew canon (MT).

Historiography Historiography is the act of history writing, as the word itself suggests. The study of historiography is the disciplined attempt to explain the perspectives and practices reflected in particular historical accounts. If we identify Joshua's genre as historical writing, it is important to distinguish between ancient and modern conventions of the genre. Many today assume that history writing is first of all interested in setting out what actually happened in the past. Readers working with that assumption may seek confirmation of historical accuracy, or exact correlation of biblical testimony and archaeological evidence. More helpful for reading any historical text, ancient or modern, is an awareness that historical writing is itself an interpretive task. What we assume or expect to glean from a text may not have been the historian's point in the first place.

Modern historians, although concerned with complex causes and effects in the past, work with materialistic assumptions. Biblical writers, like other ancient writers, assumed the active presence of God, or the gods.

The Mesha Inscription from Moab, Israel's neighbor, ascribes causes in historical events to a synergy between Mesha, the king, and Chemosh, his god. Both are said to be historical agents, actors on the stage of space and time *[Mesha Inscription, p. 447]*. The biblical writers, likewise, were not primarily interested in political causes, but in the ways they might understand the paradigmatic presence and activity of God in the past. As Halpern puts it, "Precisely because [the biblical historian] conceived of divine intervention as transcending human agencies, as converging with them in effect, but not intention, he enjoyed the utmost latitude in the interpretation of recorded events. . . . [The writer] did not need to fabricate facts: nothing in his historical philosophy discouraged antiquarian research. . . . Human history was a key to unlock—by a logical analysis . . .—a deeper, truer causality, where human behavior touched on divine" (1988: 234).

In addition, Israel's historians were interested in telling the story in such a way as to describe or shape the identity of the people as it was grounded in the past (McKenzie: 419). Even more, however, the historians of ancient Israel wrote to invite readers to perceive their present as an occasion in which to reimagine their identity and their relationship with God in ever-new contexts so as to discern patterns of divine activity and cooperation with God's ways for an uncertain future.

Deuteronomistic History (DtrH) As noted in the Introduction (p. 17), this commentary assumes that the book of Joshua belongs to a larger work that biblical scholars since Martin Noth in the early to mid-twentieth century have called the Deuteronomistic History (DtrH), which is shorthand for the books of Joshua, Judges, Samuel, and Kings. Each of those books relates in one way or another to Deuteronomy, which provides an overarching theological prism through which the narrative is refracted. These books are called "Former Prophets" in the Jewish tradition because they appear in the second section (Prophets/*Nebi'im*) of the Hebrew Bible in the Jewish canonical ordering (MT) and because the prophetic word is one of the main themes connecting these books. They tell the story of Israel from its entry into the land to its demise as a nation-state in Babylonian exile. They are infused with the phraseology and worldview of the book of Deuteronomy (see Weinfeld 1972: 320–65 for a comprehensive index of all Deuteronomic phraseology).

This working hypothesis must allow for the book of Joshua to have its own integrity and to make its own contribution to the larger whole. The theory assumes that the compositional history of the DtrH is complex. We do not know who wrote the book of Joshua. The best we can do is draw on implicit clues. Joshua, as part of the larger DtrH, stands as a hinge between Deuteronomy and the other three books (Judges, Samuel, Kings). It marks the beginning of the narrative's plot in the land just as the end of the books of Kings marks the departure from the land.

In 1943 Martin Noth developed the hypothesis of a DtrH to explain the overall compositional history of the books Deuteronomy, Joshua, Judges, Samuel, and Kings (1981). He suggested that a single editor working during the exilic period (after 587 BC in Babylon) compiled preexisting sources into a single, unified historical narrative. He organized the material according to eras corresponding to major figures or developments in the story: Moses, Joshua, the judges, Samuel, and monarchy. This editor, working with the theological worldview of the book of Deuteronomy, added interpretive speeches and explanations throughout the history that linked those books explicitly to wording and themes found in the book of Deuteronomy.

Scholars have built on the legacy of Noth in a variety of ways. Most notable has been the thesis that the DtrH was composed in two stages, one during the reign of King Josiah (see 2 Kings 22–23), and one during the exile (Cross; Nelson 1981a). The first edition, it is suggested, ends with 2 Kings 23:25 (including perhaps vv. 28-30), which puts Josiah in the most positive light possible. A second edition compiled during the exile (ca. 550 BC) would have been preoccupied with the fact that Josiah's actions were not adequate to save the kingdom of Judah from its demise at the hands of the Babylonians. So 2 Kings 23:26-27 takes up an alternative explanatory reality: Manasseh's provocation prior to the time of Josiah. Exile, according to this reading of the past, was inevitable even though Josiah displayed exemplary behavior.

Both of those hypotheses have difficulties. More promising is the view that the book is part of a growing tradition rooted in what might be called the "Deuteronomic school" (Weinfeld 1972; Person; see further below).

Because of the possibility of hope for the future, Deuteronomy and the history have been written as an educational tool (e.g., Deut 4:9; 6:20; 11:18; Josh 4:21). When your children ask, the historian writes, tell them this story, which centers on the faithfulness of the covenant-keeping God but has been marred by an unfaithful people. Tell them this story so they might move into the future with confidence that failure is not the last word, but that the word of God's new possibilities may open avenues beyond what is humanly possible.

Even as it leaves the future open to the grace of God, the history also asks the question "Why?" The why question has even been placed in the mouths of foreign nations (Deut 29:24-28; 1 Kings 9:6-9). The risk of "perishing" is real (Josh 23:13, 16; Deut 4:26; 8:19-20; 30:18). Starting from the assumption of the covenant, the historian inquires about the consequences of Israel's infidelity. And starting from the promise of land, he asks why the people have lost it. The entire history is therefore a theopolitical, and therefore a prophetic, evaluation of Israel's past based on the authority of Deuteronomic preaching.

We do well to explore two aspects of Joshua's relationship with the DtrH. First, because of Joshua's striking thematic and textual correspondences with the book of Deuteronomy, Joshua must have been composed with deliberate dependence on that book or in conversation with it. Second, two specific connections between Joshua and the books of Kings imply a close relationship between the two books and suggest implications for the composition of the book of Joshua.

Deuteronomy and Joshua From its first verse, Joshua bears marked thematic and linguistic resemblances to Deuteronomy. Echoes and reverberations between the books have led interpreters to consider Joshua to be either part of a developing theological-literary tradition tied to what has been called the Deuteronomic tradition or school (Weinfeld 1972; Person), or part of a longer historical work, which scholars call the Deuteronomistic History (Noth 1981; Cross). Since Joshua refers both implicitly and explicitly to the book of Deuteronomy, we do well to consider some of the relationships and try to make sense of their significance.

Joshua and Deuteronomy share a large common vocabulary, which implies that the two books derive from a similar milieu and share aspects of a similar worldview (see Weinfeld 1972: 320–65). At the heart of that worldview is a relational focus. The Lord has initiated a relationship with Israel that Israel has not earned nor deserved and that is rooted in God's covenant loyalty and love. That loyalty harks back as far as Israel's ancestors Abraham and Sarah. In Deuteronomy, Moses announces God's saving intention for Israel and calls Israel to responsive obedience to the divine word, now articulated by Moses as God's instruction (Torah) and then recorded in *the book of the law* (Deut 29:21; 30:10; 31:26; Josh 1:7-8; 8:31, 34; 23:6; 24:26). And like the ideal king, Joshua attends to divine instruction (Deut 17:18). As he does so, he prefigures David, whose instructions to his son Solomon follow almost exactly God's words to Joshua (1 Kings 2:1-3; Josh 1:6-9; cf. Deut 17:20; 31:6-8).

The book of Joshua finds Israel beginning to receive the fruits of the divine promises, all of which are mentioned in Deuteronomy. Specifically, God is giving the land to Israel (Deut 1:20, 25; 2:29; 3:20; 4:1, 21, 40; 5:16, 31; 11:17, 31; 12:9; 13:12; 15:4, 7; 16:5, 18, 20; 17:2, 14; 18:9; 19:2, 10, 14; 20:16; 21:1, 23; 24:4; 25:15, 19; 26:1-2; 27:2-3; 28:8; Josh 1:11, 15; see also 1:13; 5:6; 9:24; 11:23; 18:3; 21:43; 23:5; Chaney: 108). The gift of land is emphasized in both books as the land that they are entering, or crossing over, to possess/occupy (Josh 1:11; Deut 4:5, 14, 22, 26; 6:1; 7:1; 9:1, 5; 11:8, 10-11, 29, 31; 23:20; 28:21, 63; 30:16, 18; 31:13; 32:47).

Parts of God's first speech in Joshua 1:3-5 closely echo Moses' words in Deuteronomy 11:24-25. There the phrases "every place on which you set your foot," along with the description of the boundaries of the land and "no one will be able to stand against you" (with Josh 1:5 changing the "you" from pl. to sg.), are repeated in Joshua 1. Joshua 1:5 adds *all the days of your life*. Clearly God's speech to Joshua takes Deuteronomic motifs and language that Moses has used in addressing the people and applies them specifically to Joshua. This suggests that the book of Joshua is as much about Joshua as it is about the people. Joshua, at the end of the book, becomes *servant of the* Lord, just as Moses was *servant of the* Lord (Josh 1:1; 24:29; see commentary there). In this way Joshua takes up the Deuteronomic leadership ideal and brings together both Mosaic and Davidic paradigms. Like David, Joshua obeys divine instruction, which qualifies him for the title *servant of the* Lord.

In Joshua 1:5-7, 9, 18, we find a parallel to Deuteronomy's motif "be strong and bold" (Deut 31:6-8; cf. 1:21; 3:28; Josh 8:1; 10:8; 10:25; 11:6). The actions of Joshua's entering the land and putting the people in possession of it are therefore rooted in that speech in Deuteronomy 31, where Moses tells Israel that the Lord is the one "who goes with you" and who "will not fail you or forsake you" (see Josh 1:5, where the same expression occurs, and 11:23, which reports the fulfillment of that promise). In Deuteronomy, Joshua is already a prominent figure, and distribution of the land is also mentioned (see 1:38; 3:28; 12:10; 19:3; 31:7).

Emphasis on Mosaic Torah in Joshua 1:7-8 picks up the task of the king in Deuteronomy 17:18-20 (see also the emphasis on Torah in 1:5; 4:8, 44; 27:3, 8, 26; 28:58, 61; 29:21, 29; 31:9, 11-12, 24, 26; 32:46). For the book of Joshua, the law of Moses is the criterion by which Joshua is evaluated and to which the people are called to faithfulness (1:7, 8; 8:31, 32, 34, 35; 22:5; 23:6; 24:26). Torah is not mentioned again until David's commissioning of Solomon, where David uses the same language as in Joshua 1 (1 Kings 2:3), and then again in the Josiah story (2 Kings 22:8, 11; 23:24-25). Joshua is counseled not to *turn from it to the right hand or to the left*, just as we find in Deuteronomy 5:32; 17:11, 20; 28:14 (cf. Josh 23:6; 2 Kings 22:2) *[Torah, p. 462]*.

Deuteronomy's instructions concerning warfare (20:16-18; cf. 7:1-5) also echo throughout Joshua, particularly the instructions to *utterly destroy* the enemy (2:10; 6:17-18, 21; 7:1, 11-13, 15; 8:26; 10:1, 28, 35, 37, 39-40; 11:11-12, 20-21; 22:20). Specific people groups are to be "utterly destroyed" (*ḥerem*; Deut 7:2; 20:17). These named groups are listed again in Joshua 3:10; 9:1; 11:3; and 12:8. Rahab, the Gibeonites, other resident aliens, and the Transjordan tribes serve the narrative's goal of questioning rigid application of Deuteronomic laws of warfare (Polzin; Hubbard).

Even so, Deuteronomy's declaration that it is God "who will fight for you" (1:30; 20:4) is confirmed midway through Joshua in the affirmation *for the Lord fought for Israel* (10:14, 42), and again at the end of the book (23:3, 10). In the end, readers of Joshua are to recognize what Israel has experienced: *It was not by your sword or by your bow* (24:12). Yet this surely is not the whole truth. In the book of Joshua, Israel fought its wars. It is a *way of speaking* that draws readers to the heart of the matter: Yahweh alone is God, and Israel is to live in covenant relationship with this God alone (Deut 5:6-7; 6:4-5; Josh 24:14-15).

Those linguistic and thematic correspondences confirm the view that the narrative of Joshua lives within the colors refracted by Deuteronomy's theological prism. That metaphor, however, opens another way to consider the relationship between Deuteronomy and Joshua. Joshua offers a profoundly different perspective on the occupation of the land and on how to treat outsiders (Polzin; Chaney: 110). The book reflects a "tension between strict and 'creative' application of Deuteronomic law to specific cases" (Chaney: 111, summarizing Polzin). In this commentary I argue that the deviation from strict application of Deuteronomic law with respect to outsiders and boundaries serves to raise questions about strict definitions of what "inside" and "outside" mean, both ethnically and geographically.

Other prominent examples of correspondences between Deuteronomy and Joshua can be found throughout the commentary, particularly in the sections on Joshua 1; 8:30-35; and chapters 22–24.

Joshua and Kings The first of the connections between the books of Joshua and Kings concerns Joshua's oath regarding the rebuilding of the walls of

Jericho (Josh 6:26), which is drawn to its tragic conclusion in the announcement that Hiel's two sons died in the endeavor "according to the word of the LORD" (1 Kings 16:34). This motif reinforces the larger perspective of the books of Kings that events unfold not at the sole initiative of human beings, or even kings and empires, but by the agency of the prophetic word. The focus of the Deuteronomic theology of history within the period of the kings is on the prophets, whom God has sent to warn the people. The overarching theme of the impact of Yahweh's word reaches back all the way to Deuteronomy (8:3). The tension between prophetic word and the failure of kings and people to uphold their covenant obligations comes through most clearly in the Deuteronomist's analysis of the fall of Samaria in 2 Kings 17:7-23. By contrast, the books of Kings tell Israel's story through the lens of the prophetic word's power to shape history. It is not so much that the narrative highlights the theme of prophecy-fulfillment, but of divine agency in history through the prophetic word. The books of Kings highlight twelve such "moments" that the narrator evaluates as having occurred by the agency of the prophetic word (1 Kings 11:29-40 and 12:15b; 1 Kings 13:3 and 2 Kings 23:16-18; 1 Kings 14:6-16 and 15:29; 1 Kings 14:12 and 14:17-18; 1 Kings 16:1, 3, 7 and 16:12; Josh 6:26 and 1 Kings 16:34; 1 Kings 21:21-29 and 2 Kings 9:36; 2 Kings 1:2, 16 and 1:17; 2 Kings 7:1-3 and 7:16-18; 2 Kings 10:30 and 15:12; 2 Kings 21:10-16 and 24:2; 2 Kings 22:15-20 and 23:30).

The second connection between the books of Joshua and Kings is the figural relationship between Joshua and King Josiah *[Characterization of Joshua, p. 394]*. The correspondence between the two figures has led some scholars to suggest that an early edition of the book of Joshua may have been composed during Josiah's reign. Of course this suggestion is conjectural. But it corresponds rather neatly with the view (promoted first by Cross) that the first edition of the DtrH ended on the high note that praises Josiah: "Before him there was no king like him, who turned to the LORD with all his heart, with all his soul, and with all his might, according to all the law of Moses; nor did any like him arise after him" (2 Kings 23:25). It could be, however, that a Deuteronomic school was at work much earlier, around the time of Hezekiah, which began to narrate the history of the monarchy. Such a work would have been supplemented along the way, particularly during the time of Josiah and then again after the exile (Provan 1988: 169; Person).

It is most likely that a "Deuteronomic School" viewed both Joshua and Josiah as paradigmatic for the restoration project being imagined after the exile. The two and a half chapters following 2 Kings 23:25 suggest that the covenantal relationship had been violated and that an immediate repair, however well intentioned by Josiah, was ineffectual. Although Josiah alone could not save Judah, Josiah and Joshua remain examples, along with King David (2 Kings 22:2), of those who heeded the prophetic word. Such observations—leading to the perspective that the books of Kings end in exile and that the primary readers of both Joshua and Kings were reading after the destruction of Jerusalem (587 BC)—make it possible to see both books as taking up both the tragic and hopeful dimensions of the book of Deuteronomy.

Both Deuteronomy and Joshua assume the reality of exile (Deut 4:25-30; 29:28; Josh 23:13-16). Deuteronomy even uses the expression "as is now the case" (29:28) to depict the reality experienced by Deuteronomy's exilic readers. On the other hand, both Deuteronomy and Joshua are grounded in the faithfulness of God who "will neither abandon you nor destroy you; he will not forget the covenant with your ancestors" (4:31). This God "will not fail you or forsake you" (Deut 31:6, 8). This is the affirmation of the book of Joshua as a whole in spite of Joshua's sinister announcement, *You cannot serve the Lord* (Josh 24:19). Readers in the postexilic era already know. Their own faithfulness—although modeled in Joshua, David, and Josiah—is not the ground of their relationship with God. God's faithfulness grounds them in the hope that their own success or failure lies in the creative and saving word of God (Deut 4:30-31). *Participation* in that salvation entails attentiveness to the Torah, for that is the way of life (Deut 8:3; 30:19-20; Josh 23:6; 24:15). And such attentiveness will result in exclusive loyalty to God, the giver of life, and rejection of other loyalties, *other gods* whom they *served . . . beyond the Euphrates* (Josh 24:2, 15).

This commentary builds on the assumption that the book of Joshua is a product of a kind of "Deuteronomic school" (Weinfeld 1972), constituted as a guild that grew out of the "bureaucracy of the royal palace and temple in Jerusalem." Scribes who belonged to that group "collected, preserved, and redacted the preexilic sources that they and others brought to Babylon as well as additional material concerning the period following the destruction of Jerusalem" (Person: 28). The commentary also assumes that it is not possible to identify multiple redactions or editions of the DtrH with much clarity "since all Deuteronomic redactors use Deuteronomic language" (Person: 17–18). Changes and additions such as might have been made over time occurred throughout several centuries, culminating in the postexilic, Persian period.

Thus, whenever it was written, the book of Joshua is clearly "in dialogue with the Deuteronomic tradition" (McConville 1993: 98). The text evokes responses based on patterns and paradigms that resonate through time. In postexilic contexts, for example, readers may discover that the narrative authorizes and constitutes a community that has lost its identity, and that through the narrative the community seeks to reconstitute that identity. Yet the narrative itself does not authorize reenacting its own plot through a violent conquest from the outside. Rahab, the Gibeonites, the tribes in Transjordan, and Others participating in Israel offer models for reconstituting the identity of peoplehood. This is not an "ethnic" or "national" reconstitution (contra Mullen) for the revitalization movement during and after the exile. In addition, this commentary assumes that the book of Joshua presents a thoroughly ritualized literary enactment/telling of the settlement/conquest, together with a centralizing function of Torah, which serves as the organizational or structural element that makes sense of the whole.

The book of Joshua is about beginning again after the devastation of exile. It does not simply retell the story, but encourages recommitment to a God whose initiative both creates and sustains the relationship within the mutuality of covenant loyalty. As Person puts it, the Deuteronomic school would have supported the Persian-sponsored mission to return under Zerubbabel because, "from their theological perspective, this was not simply a Persian policy to gain the loyalty of the empire's subjects and maintain control over the empire; it was the beginning of the Lord's plan to restore Israel" (105). But this hope in restoration did not mean that the Deuteronomic school supported Zerubbabel entirely, since the Deuteronomic school placed its hope "in the Lord's promise to restore Israel and was not necessarily tied to one particular human endeavor. This cautious hope is evident in the overall tenor of the DtrH for even the best of the Lord's chosen leaders—Moses, Joshua, David, Solomon, Hezekiah, Josiah—ultimately failed to establish Israel according to the Lord's command" (105). In other words, "a mission like Zerubbabel's may have the potential to restore obedience to the law of God and as such deserved the Deuteronomic school's support, but many similar past possibilities did not reach their potential. This is why the Deuteronomic school placed its hope on the Lord's promise and the divine initiative to restore Israel, a hope that led to the development of a Deuteronomic eschatology" (105–6).

As noted above, such an eschatology imagines that "after all these things" (cf. Deut 30:1-14) refers to "all of the events narrated in the rest of the Deuteronomic history" (Person: 106). Even though this restoration has begun, the work is not finished. According to Deuteronomy 30:6, the Lord will "circumcise your heart." Restoration "can come only at the Lord's initiative" (107). And that is exactly where Joshua 1:1-11 begins. By repeating some of Deuteronomy 34, and from the perspective of the postexilic reader, Joshua 1 implies that "the entrance into the land not only occurred under Joshua, but also under Zerubbabel." Moreover, "now that the temple has been rebuilt and reconsecrated under Zerubbabel, the people will be more likely to obey the law as the Lord has commanded the people through Moses and Joshua" (Person: 108). Although it is not necessary to be as precise about a reading context as Person is, the approach illustrates exactly what the biblical text itself is doing by creating patterns and paradigms that may be appropriated in various historical moments.

Conclusion The history of composition of Joshua through Kings is complex. Certainly older sources were used by the biblical historians. And those sources have been integrated into a coherent narrative while preserving the distinctives of each of those blocks of literature. And it seems likely that such history writing was sponsored by the royal court, perhaps beginning with Solomon and continuing on through the reigns of kings whose stories receive prominence in the narrative, especially Hezekiah (Provan 1988) and Josiah (Cross; Nelson 1981a). But it is not possible to be confident that certain editorial layers or themes can be pinpointed to specific times and places. It is more likely that these books represent a growing body of literature shaped by a "school" or "tradition" that was generally shaped by the book of Deuteronomy. Such an approach accounts well for general thematic echoes (e.g., obedience to the divine word, not worshiping other gods), as well as figural connections (e.g., Moses, Joshua, Solomon, Josiah).

An edition of the book of Joshua could well have been read (or even written) during the time of Josiah, in which case it would have served to highlight the parallels between Joshua and Josiah. But read (or written/edited) during the exile, or even after the return from exile, the book may exemplify a call for renewed leadership, renewed obedience, and thoroughgoing trust in God's capacity to bring his people into a hoped-for future in which all peoples live together within the orbit of the Lord's sovereignty.

This commentary assumes a long tradition of storytelling and history writing in ancient Israel. It could be that an edition of the DtrH existed from the time of Hezekiah (Provan) or Josiah (Cross), but it depended on narratives that had been handed on through the royal courts since the reign of David. The strongly Deuteronomic tone of the final form of the book of Joshua can be ascribed to a Deuteronomistic tradition that had a long association with the royal court before the exile, and with scribal schools that maintained the tradition during and after the exile.

Locating the entire history in the context of exile (as already in Deut 28:36, 49, 63-64; 29:22-28), to where they have "perished" (a common Deuteronomic term found also in Josh 23:13, 16), allows readers of any later time identify with the tragic end of the story. The universal hope of the DtrH is for a turning away from all other ultimate loyalties (cf. Josh 23:16; 2 Kings 22:17) and for embracing again the hope of return "with all your heart and soul" "to the Lord" (Deut 30:1-10; 1 Kings 8:46-53).

For further reading on biblical historiography, see Long 1994, 1999; McKenzie; Provan 1995, 2002; Brettler; Halpern 1988, 2000; Hess, Klingbeil, and Ray. For an excellent survey of the history and state of DtrH research, including a comprehensive bibliography, see Richter. For more on the "Deuteronomic school" approach, see Person.

CONQUEST ACCOUNTS Readers often misinterpret the conquest accounts in the book of Joshua because they do not understand the "cultural encoding nature of ancient Near Eastern and biblical narrative" (Younger 1990: 38). Biblical history writing, like all history writing, reflects a point of view shaped by cultural, theological, or ideological impulses (44). The point is not that history writing is always a deliberate falsifying of the facts, but that all history writing is artistically and ideologically constructed within the possibilities available to the authors, including genre, use of sources, stylistic and literary devices, and ideological and theological perspectives. Thus the style and content of the conquest accounts in the book of Joshua are not unique to the biblical authors.

That fact has been conclusively demonstrated in comparative studies of Egyptian, Hittite, Moabite, Ugaritic, and Mesopotamian war texts. Younger, by comparing ancient conquest accounts, concludes that the same "transmission code" undergirds all ancient conquest accounts (1990: 255). A straightforward example of similar use of conventional language can be seen by comparing Joshua's conquest accounts with the Mesha Inscription *[Mesha Inscription, p. 447]*. In that inscription, dating from the late ninth century BC, we find the following similarities with biblical conquest accounts:

1. Chemosh, the Moabite god, is angry with his land.
2. Chemosh commands, King Mesha obeys.
3. Mesha kills the entire population: they are devoted to destruction, a sacrificial act for Chemosh.
4. Holy objects are taken to Chemosh.
5. Chemosh is depicted as an active agent in warfare.
6. Integral relationship exists between people, god, and land.

This simple comparison could be multiplied many times over with other ancient conquest accounts, as demonstrated by Younger (1990), Rowlett (1996), and others. The book of Joshua depicts the wars of Israel in language similar to that of all ancient Near Eastern conquest accounts. So-called holy war is not an Israelite invention, nor does some special "ideology of holy war" color the narratives in Joshua so as to make them impossible to consider as historical documents. They do, however, share the literary conventions of all known ancient conquest accounts, including so-called divine interventions. This fact ought to inform our interpretation of Joshua. But by itself such a comparison cannot help us to date the original composition of Joshua's accounts, since the transmission code of ancient conquest accounts spans 1300–600 BC (Younger 1990: 262–63). It is possible to suggest, however, that the Deuteronomistic Historians used older accounts as they were available, or imitated the accounts in the light of common generic conventions (Younger 1990: 266).

Those common conventions suggest several specific points of comparison that help to make sense of the way the conquest is depicted in the book of Joshua as an "artificial or simulated account" (Younger 1990: 252):

1. In many ancient conquest accounts, the gods are said to take an active role in the battle. Trusting in the help of the gods rather than on military might is characteristic of most such accounts, including the book of Joshua (Rowlett 1996: 120).
2. The gods are said to participate in the battle by using cosmic agents like the sun, moon, stars, meteors, hailstones, and so forth (cf. Explanatory Notes for Josh 10:7-15; Rowlett 1996: 92; Younger 1990: 208–20).
3. Oracles encouraging combatants not to fear occur in both biblical and neo-Assyrian accounts (cf. Explanatory Notes for Josh 10:7-15; Rowlett 1996: 116–19).
4. Conquest accounts typically include hyperbole and figurative expressions. Expressions like "all the land," "all Israel," "all the kings," "no survivors," and so forth are common to ancient conquest accounts. Such usage suggests that the book of Joshua does not so much contradict the sporadic and partial nature of the conquest as it is presented in Judges 1, but serves rather to highlight the figurative or hyperbolic nature of the narrative in the book of Joshua (Younger 1990: 242–49).
5. Conquests are often perceived as judgment of the gods (e.g., Josh 10:12-14; Mesha Inscription, line 5; Younger 1990: 236–37).

6. The destruction of all humankind or of all living things (*ḥerem*) is common in many ancient conquest accounts (Mesha Inscription, lines 16–17; Stern; Rowlett 1996: 75–76; Younger 1990: 227–28, 234–36). Conquest accounts are intended to generate a kind of "calculated frightfulness" (Younger 1990: 233–24) *[Ḥerem, p. 433].*
7. Conquest accounts tend to depict the "enemy" similarly. They provide an us-them, either-or portrayal of the situation. The Other represents a "Common Threat" (Younger 1990: 233).
8. A stress on retributive justice, even a desire for retributive justice, is common in warfare texts. The god, and that god's people, have been wronged. That wrong must be avenged (e.g., Josh 10:13; Younger 1990: 234–35).

Those similarities suggest that because of the common conventional language of warfare, including hyperbolic and figurative expressions, it is not possible to argue that the biblical accounts present a uniquely Israelite or "Yahweh war" understanding and practice of warfare. Even in Assyrian battle reports, for example, we read that Ishtar "stood at my side breaking their bows, scattering their orderly battle array" (*ANET* 289). The Hymn to the Ishtars of Nineveh and Arbela (attributed to Ashurbanipal, (668–627 BC) states: "Not [with] my [own strength], not with the strength of my bow, but with the power [. . . and] strength of my goddesses, I made the lands disobedient to me submit to the yoke of Aššur" (http://oracc.museum.upenn.edu/saa/P336306). As Rowlett writes, "Therefore, while statements like those of Lind that 'Yahweh as a God of war fought for his people by miracle, not by sword and spear' are true, Lind's argument, that there was something distinctive about God's intervention by means of miracle when compared with the other ancient Near Eastern literatures, is proven false. The [DtrH] must be read with the awareness of the Assyrian uses of rhetoric" (1996: 110).

Rowlett notes a text of Esarhaddon (680–669 BC): "They put their trust upon their own force while I trusted Ashur, my lord" (*ANET* 290–91). We thus must ask a question of texts like that: "To what use might such rhetoric be put?" It could well be, as Lind suggests, that the Exodus story (exemplified in Exod 14:25) and Deuteronomy's distillation of it (Deut 1:30; 20:4) present a theological and ethical paradigm that places warfare in divine hands alone, that the guiding agency in Israel's historical experience is the prophetic word (Lind: 34). Lind's main point, however, is not the uniqueness of "miracle," which is attested in most ancient conquest accounts, but that Yahweh related to Israel's warfare primarily through prophetic rather than royal leadership, and through "Torah and prophetic word" rather than "the coercive structures of kingship law and military power" (Lind: 32–33). As stated in the commentary, Torah faithfulness is an essential feature of the overall presentation of the book of Joshua. Even though other ancient conquest accounts testify to divine messages (a kind of prophetic word) to the king, none present a longer narrative of a *peoplehood* formed by attentiveness to the divine word such as we see in the book of Joshua.

In practice, however, theological warfare rhetoric also carries ideological and political freight. Younger suggests rather generally that "imperialistic" ideology governs all conquest accounts, including those in Joshua (1990: 255). Rowlett locates the specific ideology of Joshua's conquest accounts in Josiah's attempts to consolidate and expand his imperial control over the region contested by Assyrian imperial power (1996: 63 and passim). According to Rowlett, who assumes that Joshua is a product of King Josiah's political agenda in the seventh century BC, the writer uses the conventional language of warfare, borrowing its style from the neo-Assyrian conquest accounts, in order to reassert, against the "colonial oppression" imposed by Assyria, a reconstituted identity for Israel (181–83). For both Assyria and Israel, "a pious-sounding rhetoric of divine control is employed in the service of a hierarchy that is simultaneously political and religious" (111). Therefore, "the folly of putting trust in merely human military might rather than depending on divine strength for victory in battle is joined with the idea that the gods help and intervene on Assyria's behalf" (112). A consequence is that the king "rules the territories by divine will—the gods have given him the land (cf. Josh 1:3)" (114; see other parallels on 115–16). That is exactly the assumption of Jephthah's messengers in their speech to the Ammonite king: "Should you not possess what your god Chemosh gives you to possess? And should we not be the ones to possess everything that the Lord our God has conquered for our benefit?" (Judg 11:23-24).

There are questions left unanswered by both comparative study and ideological interpretation as sketched above. From their analysis of ancient conquest accounts, both Younger and Rowlett extrapolate to the ideological uses of those accounts in political rhetoric. Rowlett assumes that the comparative study of conquest accounts provides the interpretive key for reading the book of Joshua in an imperial context, like that of King Josiah, who sought autonomy from Assyrian control. I have concluded that the book of Joshua as a whole is itself a more sustained historical and theological argument than any of the ancient texts cited. This commentary therefore acknowledges that parts of the book share the generic conventions of warfare language and theology. But the book of Joshua is itself not a conquest account. The book of Joshua incorporates conventional conquest accounts and phraseology for richer and more nuanced purposes than for promoting a simple ideological agenda. For example, comparative and ideological reading does not take into account the possibility that the "exceptional outsiders" in the book of Joshua (Polzin) may be more than "good foreigners" who are "essential to the regime" (Chaney: 110). As argued in this commentary, following the lead of Polzin and others, foreigners like Rahab, the Gibeonites, and other resident aliens are critical to Joshua's challenge to Deuteronomy's somewhat simplistic distinction between insiders and outsiders.

Even so, such careful comparative analysis leads me to conclude, with McConville, that "the stylized features of the narrative" suggest that the biblical ancient conquest accounts "are not factual accounts, but symbolic of loyalty to Yahweh" (2006: 26). Moreover, within the larger context of the DtrH, and the larger canonical context, the conquest accounts in the book of Joshua become incorporated into a larger conversation about peoplehood, attentiveness to God's instruction, idolatry, and the ultimate transformation of imperial power and the militarism by which it is sustained.

For additional resources on ancient conquest accounts, see Hoffmeier; Kang; Niehaus; Rowlett 1996; Weinfeld 1986; Van Seters; Younger 1990 *[Theology of Warfare, p. 458; Torah, p. 462; Idolatry, p. 438]*.

CONQUEST AND COLONIALISM Nowhere in the Bible is there a scenario of repeated conquests modeled on the book of Joshua except as the narrative is transposed into other keys. For example, notice the following: justice to the Gentiles in Isaiah; the exodus-conquest journey of Jesus; the battle against spiritual powers in Paul; the conquest of both oppressors and cosmic forces through death and resurrection in Revelation *[Conquest and Land in the NT, p. 411]*.

Still, it is helpful to know how Joshua has been received and interpreted by those with colonizing and imperial aims. Even conquest of the Americas has been undergirded by a reading of the Joshua story. Both the Puritans in the seventeenth century and the revolutionary preachers of the eighteenth affirmed that the American people and their experience were analogous to Joshua's conquest of Canaan's indigenous people and of God's favor on Israel (Hay). John Wesley, in his sermon "A Caution Against Bigotry," criticizes the colonists: "Even in cruelty and bloodshed, how little have the Christians come behind them! And not the Spaniards or the Portuguese alone, butchering thousands in South America; not the Dutch only in the East Indies, or the French in North America, following the Spaniards step by step: our own countrymen, too, have wantoned in blood, and exterminated whole nations; plainly proving thereby what spirit it is that dwells and works in the children of disobedience." But as Hay puts it, "Tragically few listened to Wesley."

Elsa Támez writes about a similar reality in Latin America: "The story of the conquest of Canaan is the most often used biblical foundation for the conquest of this continent. Juan Ginés de Sepúlveda [a prominent and influential Spanish philosopher of the sixteenth century] used this biblical theme to legitimate the war against its inhabitants. . . . He justified the conquest in order to punish blasphemy, but also because the continent was a special donation by God, as the promised land. . . . God chose the Spanish to carry out this divine judgment against the infidels, and to conquer their lands" ("Biblia y 500 años," in *Revista de interpretación bíblica latino-americana* 16 [1993]: 12; cited by Hay).

Even relatively recently, white South African rhetoric has included citation of the biblical story. Akenson (1992: 16) cites speeches, like the one by Paul Kruger, president of the Transvaal Republic, on December 16, 1989: "When we think of the former emigrants, the Voortrekkers of yore, it is then revealed unto us how God, in his divine providence, dealt with them, even as He dealt with the Israelite nation of old. . . . He summoned them to the same task: Canaan was inhabited by heathen alienated from God. . . . Israel was bidden make it the Lord's dwelling place."

Knowing some of this history of interpretation, or history of application, allows us to ask whether it might be possible to read Joshua as a warning to all who might appropriate the name of God for their own imperial or colonialist goals. Can Joshua be read as we might watch war movies, like *Apocalypse Now* (1979), as depictions of warfare that offer a judgment on the viewers themselves? Could it be that Joshua teaches the opposite of what Joshua tells? It tells of violent conquest, but it teaches trust and dependence on God alone. Covenant with this God in Joshua is on the way to becoming the hospitable community that welcomes rather than excludes, and invites all to attend to the divine word, which shapes its identity in bringing justice to the Gentiles, like Rahab and like those tricksters the Gibeonites. But to read Joshua that way is uncomfortable: it goes against the grain of the narrative. Yet even that narrative contains within it seeds of discontent, as observed throughout the commentary.

And so we live with a biblical theology of land that is "saturated with violence in which even Yahweh is implicated. . . . The ideology of the land of promise shows up in all kinds of imperialisms, never more compellingly than in U.S. political history, which from the outset took North America to be a land of promise for Europeans, willing to displace Native Americans by violence, even as the Canaanites were routed. Belatedly and in a much lesser way, the same ideology feeds the militarism of contemporary Israel" (Birch et al.: 211). Although obedience to divine instruction permeates the book of Joshua, the end of the story in exile adds the grim reminder that possession bolstered by the grasping of imperial ideology and the delusion of self as master lead to an ignominious end.

Although the book of Joshua has been used for justifying colonial occupation and manifest destiny, fortunately others are transforming those uses by imagining new futures for all, including those who continue to be marginalized by mainstream society (see esp. The Promised Land Project: www.thepromisedland.org). For reflections on religion and nationalism, see O'Brien; Hall and Ruether. For a history of interpretation of Joshua to justify colonial expansion and conquest, see Auld 1999; Akenson; Prior 1997, 1999; Warrior; Wilcken. For the use of Joshua's conquest accounts to support the American master narrative of Manifest Destiny, see Hawk 2010. For the appropriation of Joshua in modern Israel, see Greenberg 1995.

CONQUEST AND LAND IN THE NEW TESTAMENT Something odd has happened to the conquest/land motif on its journey through the ancient world into postbiblical Judaism and the NT writings. Joshua's conquest could be said to be completely transformed by Jesus' beatitude "Blessed are the meek, for they will inherit the earth" (Matt 5:5). Although Jesus is likely transposing Psalm 37:11, his eschatological imagination also draws on the hopefulness of the psalmist, who writes that it is in waiting for the Lord that one is assured that the "wicked will be no more" (37:9-10). By the time we arrive at the Johannine writings, among the latest in the NT, we find that Jesus has conquered the entire world (*kosmos*, John 16:33) and that conquest itself has been transformed, being accomplished through suffering and martyrdom (Rev 2:7, 11, 17, 26, 28; 3:5, 12, 21; 5:5; 6:2; 12:11; 15:2; 17:14; 21:7). Clearly the conquest motif has taken on a completely different significance from straightforward ancient conquest accounts.

As this commentary has recognized, even the book of Joshua does not appropriate the conquest accounts uncritically, or for woodenly literal purposes. Cosmic, or worldwide, conquest comes to be associated hyperbolically with Davidic theology as expressed in Psalm 2:7-9. There, the decree "You are my son" is linked with the divine gift of "the nations [as] your heritage" and "the ends of the earth [as] your possession." In the accounts of Jesus' baptism, the sonship declaration of Psalm 2:7 is reiterated (Mark 1:11; Luke 3:22), but without the particularity of the "heritage" and "possession" of Psalm 2:8. The Gospel accounts themselves will spell out how the particularity of Jesus transforms the landedness of royal conquest into the landlessness of kingdom citizens. Similarly the Gospel accounts draw on the exodus tradition for its language of sonship as well, where God calls Israel, the enslaved people, as "my firstborn son" (Exod 4:22). Perhaps the book of Hebrews takes this motif the furthest, with its notion that this "son" has been "appointed heir of all things" (1:2).

Such a sampling as noted here serves to highlight the cosmic scope of the NT's appropriation of exodus and royal traditions, including those of conquest. Since Joshua represents an archetypal royal figure, it is not surprising that the correspondence between the names of Joshua and Jesus, which are identical in Greek, should also be drawn into the symbolic naming of the NT's divine royal son. For a rich and complex analysis of the transformation of the conquest tradition in the synoptic Gospels, see Swartley 1994 (esp. ch. 4).

For example, in Mark's Gospel the conquest tradition has been transformed through redefining greatness as servanthood (Mark 8–10). As such, in Mark "God's victory comes in a most unsuspecting way: the way of self-denial, humble service, and the very giving of one's life for others. . . . For Jesus and his disciples, the way of faithful warfare was and is that of humble service, even unto death" (Swartley 1994: 115). Matthew's Gospel includes a variety of uses of the conquest tradition. In Matthew the church conquers the gates of Hades, or the realm of death (16:18; cf. John 5:25-29; 11:25; Rev 1:18; see Swartley 1994: 120–21); the meek inherit the earth (5:5); Gentile outsiders are welcomed rather than conquered (8:11; 12:15-21; 28:19); those who have left everything receive everything (19:29-30); and all nations are judged at the bar of justice on behalf the marginalized rather than entitlement (25:31-46). In Luke, "inheriting the land" is transformed into "inheriting eternal life" (Swartley 1994: 132). Luke transforms "the Deuteronomic 'land entrance' and conquest traditions" by presenting Jesus both as a "journeying guest" as well as the host of the banquet (134). More particularly, in the great banquet parable (Luke 14:15-24), Jesus invites "the poor, the crippled, and the lame—precisely those who, in the Qumran literature (1QM 7:4-6; 1QSa 2:5-10), were excluded from the expected messianic banquet" (Swartley 1994: 137). Jesus' journey to Jerusalem in Luke is a deliberate transformation of the OT conquest narrative. In Luke, Jesus welcomes all to his table.

But that journey is also a conflicted journey, in which Satan is being conquered, not the Canaanites (Luke 10:18; cf. John 12:31; 1 Cor 15:24-28; Rev 12:7-12). In fact, in the same chapter it is the Samaritan who is exemplified as a neighbor rather than as an enemy, a poignant transformation since Samaritans lived in the territory first conquered by Israel in the early chapters of Joshua. For Luke, "the peace of the kingdom and the conquest of evil are developed in the narrative by actions that are located squarely in the territory of the religious and sociopolitical enemy, the despised Samaritans" (Swartley 1994: 141).

Paul has also transformed the conquest tradition. In light of the apocalyptic cosmic creation and redemption pattern in Paul's thinking, the conquest story becomes Jesus' victory for salvation. And Christian discipleship is both a contest and a victory over evil and adversity (Rom 8:37). As Toews writes, "Because God has acted decisively in Messiah Jesus to effect salvation for the world, Paul asserts that (a) Sin [as a power that enslaves] has been defeated (Gal 1:4; 1 Cor 15:3; Rom 4:25); (b) death has been condemned (1 Cor 15:54-57; Rom 8:31-39); (c) creation itself has been reclaimed by God, although the battle goes on toward God's final victory (1 Cor 15:2-28; Rom 8:18-25); (d) God's sovereignty has been established (Rom 8:31-39)" (35). Human beings are no longer the object of the struggle. That is left in the hands of God (Rom 12:21). Paul even transposes the hyperbolic conquest of Joshua into the experience of becoming "more than conquerors through him who loved us" (Rom 8:37). In Ephesians, the battle/conquest is transformed even further into a spiritual conflict: the opposing coalition is not a human military force but "principalities and powers," cosmic forces, against whom believers are to dress in the armor of God (Eph 6:11-17; for a thorough analysis of conquest in Ephesians, see Yoder Neufeld 1997: 290–316).

Apocalyptic literature has also drawn on the conquest motif in the Bible. And there too, conquest is transformed in the context of persecution and martyrdom. "Those who conquer will inherit these things," we read in Revelation 21:7a. "These things" refers to "a new heaven and a new earth" (21:1). Moreover, that inheritance is linked to a covenant relationship: "I will be their God and they will be my children" (21:7b). As the notion of inheritance is thus transformed from the particular (land) to the universal (cosmos), this change reverses the notion of conquest. Now, instead of conquering the nations, "The nations will walk by its light [the light of God's glory], and the kings of the earth will bring their glory into it [the heavenly city]" (Rev 21:24; cf. similar motifs in Isa 60:5, 11; 61:6; 66:12). The tree of life in that city will produce leaves "for the healing of the nations" (Rev 22:2). Certainly the kings of the earth and the merchants, who are depicted as having done evil, will be judged for their indiscriminate oppression and slaughter (Rev 18). The adversaries in Revelation are depicted as enemies of God, who is represented by the rider on the white horse, who "in righteousness . . . judges and makes war" (19:11). The Lamb makes war on those who initiate war against him and "will conquer them, for he is Lord of lords and King of kings" (17:14). We learn, however, that his weapon is the "sharp sword" that comes from his mouth (19:15). This sword is the same as the one coming from the mouth of the "one like the Son of Man" (1:13, 16). In other battle texts in Revelation 16:14; 13:7, kings of the earth and the beast are "allowed to make war on the saints and to conquer them."

Although that implies martyrdom, Revelation is mostly concerned about "those who had conquered" (e.g., 15:2). The call of Revelation is to follow the Lamb wherever he goes (14:4). Even those who die "have conquered him by the blood of the Lamb and by the word of their testimony" (12:11). Those who follow bear the same weapon, the weapon of truthful testimony (which is *martyria*). It is in the context of their threatened martyrdom that they bear witness in "patient endurance" (1:9; 3:10) and without fear (1:17) and thereby "conquer" (2:7, 11, 17, 26, 28; 3:5, 12, 21). The assurance is that those to whom the letter is addressed may "conquer" not a human enemy but death itself, because "the faithful and true witness, the origin of God's creation" (3:14), the Lamb (17:14), has conquered and will conquer. In the face of such hope, the saints, "those who keep the commandments of God and hold fast to the faith of Jesus" (14:12), are called to endurance. The irony of Revelation, however, is that the kings/nations who have been conquered and judged are also the ones who are healed and restored in the cosmic restoration of all things (for further exploration of these motifs, see Johns).

It is also possible that Revelation 1:12-18, with its image of a man with a sword coming from his mouth, is reinterpreting the image of the commander in Joshua 5:13 (see Rev 1:16; 2:16; 19:15, 21). This "sword" is analogous to nothing other than the "word of their testimony" (12:11). Such reappropriation, or "traditioning," suggests that the writers of Scripture understand the old stories in a dynamic way. In the process, the shock of the imagery may be maintained, but the image is given a new significance in a new context. In Revelation, the adversary is primarily a cosmic enemy, even though there is also a judgment against human powers that participate in injustice and violence against both people and the earth (e.g., 11:18).

In John's Gospel, Jesus even says, "I have conquered the world!" (16:33; cf. 1 John 2:13; 4:4; 5:4-5). Such a conquest theme is not about land or human enemies but about the cosmic darkness that has launched a guerrilla movement against God's reign (cf. Rev 3:21; 5:5; 12:11; 15:2; 17:14; 21:7). The *world* is that which is aligned against the rule of God. The Johannine epistles affirm that believers have conquered the evil one (1 John 2:13; cf. 4:4; 5:4-5).

Thus Ezekiel's hope for a people faithful to God's instruction remains alive in the NT, even as God's people continue to wait for the Spirit's freedom and transformation (Ezek 36:26-28; Rom 8:19-25). The hope for an inherited homeland, as interpreted by Hebrews 11:8-16, has been realized in Jesus, in whose Spirit the NT writers rested and waited for the fullness of the promise. Such waiting is characteristic of the meek as they inherit the earth (Matt 5:5), Jesus' offer of rest to those who desire to learn from him (Matt 11:28-30), the eschatological "rest" of the book of Hebrews (4:11), and the "inheritance" motif in Paul's theology (Rom 4:13; 1 Cor 6:9-10; 15:50; Gal 3:18) *[Rest, p. 455]*.

Postbiblical Jewish literature develops a similar trajectory as that of the NT. Halpern-Amaru explores the way four texts "rewrite" the tradition, including the conquest: *Jubilees*, *Testament of Moses*, *Pseudo-Philo*, and Josephus's *Jewish Antiquities*. "All four authors who rewrite biblical Land theology reconstruct the narrative such that the Land no longer functions as the key signature of covenantal history." These "new narratives . . .

deemphasize the theological significance of the land" (116). For example, in *Jubilees*: "From the perspective of the past, Land promise, acquisition, and retention are the markers of Israel's history. From the author's present, purity of heart and fidelity to the covenant become the new eschatological markers" (51). Summarizing, Halpern-Amaru writes, "Landedness is part of the theological and historical heritages of all the writers. However, it is as troublesome to them as it will become to the later rabbinic tradition which, in the light of destruction and exile, placed people and Torah over Land in the heart of its own system" (127). Such a "downgrade" of land theology is "not because possession of the Land is insignificant, but because it is so significant that it stands in the way of a contemporary reading of Scriptures. Indeed the same can be said of those who currently struggle with the theological significance of the modern return to the Land" (127). For similar reasons, conquest theology has been transformed in the NT. Even the book of Joshua, as noticed in this commentary, highlights faithfulness to covenant peoplehood through attentiveness to the divine word (Torah) over conquest and acquisition of land.

Land in the NT takes on a rather distinct significance as the theme is filtered through a figural imagination *[Figural Reading, p. 426]*. First, although the gift of land appears not to be prominent, NT writers *do* appropriate the promise of land in creative ways, many of which are consistent with the vision of the OT in general, and perhaps even with the book of Joshua *[Land: Gifted and Lost, p. 440]*. In the beatitude of Matthew 5:5, Jesus offers an alternative way of inheriting the earth: the way of meekness. Gardner suggests that the word *meek* "points to a style of relating to others, a style in which we eschew the proud and violent ways of the mighty" (95).

In Jesus' teaching, the theme of the kingdom of God/heaven absorbs but does not eradicate the promises and reality of life on the land. In the NT, Jesus speaks of the gift of the kingdom. In Luke's Gospel, Jesus tells his "little flock" not to be afraid (cf. Josh 1:9), for "it is your Father's good pleasure to give you the kingdom" (Luke 12:32). And although the kingdom is a gift, in Matthew's Gospel it is also specially prepared for those who do the will of God (Matt 7:21, 24; 12:49-50). These are the ones who come to a place of rest and whose obedience is "light" and not burdensome (Matt 11:28-30). People from every "nation" become recipients of eschatological blessing and will "inherit the kingdom" (Matt 25:34). The Gospel language continues the lively intrabiblical conversation about the gifts of God. Paul transposes gift language to describe the work of the Spirit (1 Cor 2:12; 4:7).

Second, Jesus' followers become a transnational peoplehood. God's "Emmanuel" (Matt 1:23) is now the motivation for mission, making disciples of all nations, incorporating them into God's community by baptism, and teaching them the importance of obedience (28:18-20). The group gathered after Jesus' death asks whether he will "restore the kingdom to Israel" (Acts 1:6). The response is an expansive declaration that they will, by God's own power, be his witnesses "to the ends of the earth" (1:8). But this world-embracing perspective is not unique to NT teaching. Even the book of Joshua, as we have begun to see, raises questions about the identity, boundaries, and definition of the community of promise.

Third, the call for obedience is reflected in numerous ways in the NT. The motif of hearing and doing Jesus' teachings in the Gospels sets the stage for reflection on the character of obedience (Matt 7:24; Luke 6:46; John 3:21; 8:31; 14:15). In various ways the Gospels present Jesus as affirming the law or as highlighting a core of instruction. In answering the question about what good deed would bring eternal life, Jesus responds, "If you wish to enter into life, keep the commandments" (Matt 19:17b; cf. Deut 5:33; 8:1; 32:46-47). John's Gospel transposes life in the land to "eternal life" (3:15; 10:28), which is experienced as "abundant life" (cf. 10:10). The book of Hebrews affirms the need for diligent obedience in faith. The author refers specifically to Joshua's incomplete rest as a motive for continuing to strive to enter God's rest (4:8-10). Only now the weapons are not military, but the word of God (Heb 4:12; cf. Eph 6:10-17). Joshua 1 already affirms the priority of heeding the word. Thus, with the prophets Isaiah and Micah (Isa 2:2-4; Mic 4:1-5), the violence of the book of Joshua stands under the judgment of the word of the Lord, which ultimately undermines all human weapons and violent means of acquisition. The heart of this "word" theology is expressed in Deuteronomy 8:3b: "One does not live by bread alone, but by every word that comes from the mouth of the LORD."

This notion of victory achieved through obedience to the word of God stands out as one of the ways the NT writers reinterpret the conquest theme. That victory motif is rooted in the model of Jesus, as he is presented in the Gospels as Victor. Swartley suggests that Jesus is depicted as Victor in at least three ways: "(1) Jesus continues to battle with evil; (2) Jesus himself is the divine Warrior who gives his life instead of taking the lives of others; and (3) the victory of Jesus is appropriated to Jesus' followers, in their authority over evil and in the shape of their life together" (1994: 146).

On exodus, conquest, conflict, and warfare in the NT, see McDonald; Swartley 1994, 2003b; Yoder Neufeld 1997, 2011; Zerbe 1993. See also the following for thoughtful reflection on the biblical theology of land in general, and land in the NT in particular: Brueggemann 2002; Burge 2003, 2010; Jeschke 2005; March; Gordon; Weaver 2007.

COVENANT AND TREATY The book of Joshua draws its life from the worldview and practices inherent in covenantal relationships (7:11, 15; 23:16; 24:25). The Hebrew word for *covenant* (*berit*) is both a political and a theological word in the OT. We can know its significance by studying two contexts: covenantal practices and texts in the ancient Near East, and use of the term *covenant* within the Bible. In ordinary usage *berit* describes the establishment or maintenance of relationships sealed with a "treaty." Within the OT, treaties seal and describe the terms of a relationship (a friendship, an alliance) that has been established between two parties. Abraham, for example, makes a covenant with Abimelech (Gen 21:27), Jonathan makes a covenant with David (1 Sam 18:3), and David makes a covenant with the elders of Israel at Hebron (2 Sam 5:3). In the book of Joshua, Israel makes a covenant with the Gibeonites (ch. 9). Israel's theologians have "borrowed" the political notion of treaty and used it as a way of sketching the character of the relationship between Yahweh, Israel's God, and Israel as a people.

Ancient Near Eastern political treaties provide some background for understanding the notion of covenant in the OT (McCarthy 1978). In the ancient world, when a king conquered a territory, he would usually set the terms of future relationship by means of a treaty, often called a "vassal treaty." For example, Hittite vassal treaties of the second millennium include "(1) an introduction to the parties; (2) historical prologue (rehearsing their past relations); (3) stipulations; (4) document clause (requiring the preservation of the document in a temple and its regular reading); (5) god list (i.e., witnesses to the treaty); and (6) blessings and curses invoked for keeping or violating the treaty" (McConville 1997: 747–48).

Israel makes a bold theological move in borrowing the practice of treaty making from the political sphere. Politics and the identity of the community now become imagined in a completely different way. God, not imperial politics, becomes the center of this relationship. Four points may be recognized:

1. Covenant is the establishment of a relationship in which one party pledges to be loyal to the other party. Sometimes the relationship is unilateral (obligations impressed on one party); sometimes it is bilateral (reciprocal obligations).
2. Within the theological appropriation of the OT, covenant is a relational initiative taken by God to restore harmony and well-being (*šalom*) to humankind and to creation.
3. Covenant is a political metaphor that, used theologically, invites a reimagining of ultimate loyalties, allegiances, commitments, and power structures.
4. Covenant implies a new community that is energized by the relational practice of loyalty and is embodied in alternative social and political practices.

Within the OT, covenant appears first in the Noah story, where God makes a covenant with Noah and his descendants (Gen 6:18; 9:9). Covenant with Israel's ancestors in Genesis 15 and 17 is a covenant of promise that includes descendants and land. Covenant as binding relationship begins in Genesis 12:1-3 with the purpose of bringing blessing to the nations through Abram. The bilateral dimension of this relationship is exemplified in the interesting monologue in Genesis 18, in which God affirms Abraham's vocation of "doing righteousness and justice" (vv. 17-18). After this, Abraham negotiates with God on Sodom's behalf, assuming his right to challenge God to "do what is just" (18:25).

The liberated Israelite slaves make a covenant with God at Mount Sinai (Exod 24). The covenant-making ritual includes sacrifice, reading of stipulations, and a response by the people (v. 7; cf. Josh 24:18). Covenant involves both divine initiative and human response (Exod 2:23-25; 3:7-8; 19:4-6; 20:1-3). God's intent is that Israel as a people becomes "my people" (6:7). God's desire is to "dwell among the Israelites" (25:8; 29:45). The disobedience of the people (the golden calf episode) does not nullify the covenant with the ancestors (33:1). In the sequence of events that follow in chapters 33–34, Moses intercedes, God declares his character (34:6-9), and God renews the covenant (34:10-28). There is a relationship between the character of God and the pattern of covenant making (34:6-7). The Exodus covenant includes a prohibition against "covenants" with other peoples or their gods (23:23; 34:12; cf. Josh 9:15; 24:15).

God also makes a covenant with David. A new historical situation has called for a reshaping of the relationship with God. A new promise from God results in a commitment to a permanent reign by David and his descendants. It is a new covenant (2 Sam 7:11b-16), even though the word "covenant" does not appear in the text. The commitment of God to David is expressed in an exemplary way in Psalm 89 ("covenant," vv. 3, 28, 34). Although God sustains the relationship, there remains a tension between the unilateral and the conditional dimensions of God's relationship with David (cf. Pss 89:27-34; 132:12; 1 Kings 2:4; 8:25; 9:4-5).

Although covenant with David is not mentioned explicitly in Joshua, there is an analogy that can be seen in three ways: in the charge to Joshua in chapter 1, in the dynamic mirroring of Joshua and Josiah (2 Kings 22–23), and in the discipleship/imitation motif reflected in the parallels between Moses/Joshua and David/Solomon (Josh 1:6-9/1 Kings 2:1-3; Schäfer-Lichtenberger). In the context of those covenantal moments, it is important to place Joshua's notion of covenant firmly in Deuteronomy's invitation to communal faithfulness (7:9, 12). The covenant loyalty of God is linked with the love and obedience of the people. Deuteronomy highlights the reciprocal character of the relationship by adding another covenant in Moab that emphasizes the timelessness of covenant making. Deuteronomy suggests that the past generation, the present community in Moab, and future generations are all part of the ongoing covenant-keeping community (Deut 4:9; 5:2-3; 6:2, 20; 29:14-15, 29). The covenant reported in Joshua 24 shares in that ongoing covenant making in which each generation participates (cf. 1 Sam 12; 2 Kings 23:1-3; Neh 9:6–10:39; Ps 78).

Such an ongoing covenant making is drawn from Deuteronomy's developed sense of "covenant" (twenty-seven times in the book), where "love" characterizes all aspects of the relationship between God and Israel (4:37; 6:5; 7:9, 13; 10:12, 15; 11:1, 13, 22; 13:4; 19:9; 23:5; 30:6, 16, 20). Linking covenant relationship with the Ten Commandments (4:13), Moses admonishes Israel "not to forget the covenant" and not to make idols (4:23). Characteristic of Deuteronomy's covenant theology is the assurance that because God is a "merciful God, he will neither abandon you nor destroy you; he will not forget the covenant with your ancestors that he swore to them" (4:31). In reflecting back on the covenant at Horeb, Moses assures the people that God did not make "this covenant" with our ancestors, "but with us, who are all of us here alive today" (5:3). Moses understands the covenant as a continually present event, one that each generation may experience as though it were the first (cf. 26:5-11). Yet that covenant is conditioned upon the loyalty of both parties (7:9). Since God will not forget (4:31), it remains for the people to give attention to their part (7:9, 12).

Although this second covenant on the plains of Moab is a re-presentation of the one in Horeb (Deut 29:1), it is also a covenant with the future generations: "not only with you . . . but also with those who are not here with us today" (29:14-15). Thus the covenant in Deuteronomy becomes timeless (5:3; 29:14-15). Each generation becomes responsible for recalling, reenacting, and living out this covenant. If they "abandon" the covenant, they will find themselves in exile (29:25). The Lord's final words to Moses are not heartening. God predicts that the people will follow other gods and break the covenant with God (31:16, 20). Yet even those words need to be heard alongside Deuteronomy's awareness of the transience of Israel's love, especially in the tension-filled reflection on the possibility of apostasy in Deuteronomy 30. There, in reflecting on God's faithfulness in the face of Israel's waywardness (and subsequent exile), Moses anticipates that God will make Israel capable of loving "the LORD your God with all your heart" (30:6).

The book of Judges continues the motif of covenant by emphasizing God's commitment to the relationship (2:1) and then noticing how the Israelites have violated the relationship by making covenants with the inhabitants of the land (2:2), which has resulted in divine judgment (2:20). The covenant making in Joshua includes covenants made with the inhabitants of the land (e.g., Rahab and the Gibeonites) and with God. The narrator assumes that in spite of their covenants with the indigenous people, Israel *served the LORD* (Josh 24:31). Thus the warning (even from God) in Deuteronomy and the explicit failures recounted in the book of Judges do not figure prominently in the book of Joshua. If there is an implied failure in Joshua, the narrative does not make that judgment explicit. The book of Joshua reflects authentic covenant, mediated, interpreted, and embodied by Joshua and his people. The dynamics of obedience are at times ambiguous, but the commitment of the people, in spite of Joshua's cajoling in the dialogue of chapter 24, remains firm.

In light of that affirmative ending, tinged with tragedy through warnings of exile by Moses and by Joshua, we can best understand Josiah's reading from the book of the covenant as part of the "reform" that he initiates upon finding the book in the temple. Josiah, like Joshua, holds a Passover festival in keeping with the instructions of that book (2 Kings 23:2, 21). From the theological assurance of Deuteronomy (e.g., 4:31), the introduction to Judges (2:1), and Solomon's appropriation of that assurance (1 Kings 8:23-24), we know that God keeps covenant relationships. According to the larger narrative that extends from Judges through Kings, however, Israel repeatedly violates covenant (Judg 2:20; 2 Kings 17:15, 35, 38; 18:12). Broken covenant, according to the DtrH, was the main reason for the fall of the Northern Kingdom. That is what makes the people's joining Josiah "in the covenant" (2 Kings 23:3) a tragically ironic episode in the sequence of events leading to the fall of Judah. In spite of Josiah's mirroring of Joshua, and in spite of the renewed covenant, Judah did not stand.

The prophets also indict Israel for covenant violation (e.g., Isa 24:5; Jer 11:10; 22:9; Ezek 16:59; Hos 6:7; 8:1; Amos). Yet these same prophets also envision a covenant not abrogated by God (Isa 54:10; Jer 33:20-21; 33:25-26), or implore God not to break covenant (Jer 14:21), or imagine a renewed covenant (Isa 55:3; 59:21; 61:8; Jer 31:31-33; 32:40; Jer 50:5; Ezek 16:60; 34:25-26). Renewed covenant will result in a "new heart" that empowers the people to live truly in the light of divine instruction, which will not be forgotten (Ezek 36:22-28). Hosea even imagines a covenant of peace with animals that will include abolishing weapons of war (2:18).

Those prophets imagine a covenant not marked by disobedience, alienation, and hostility. It will be grounded in forgiveness, involving a community committed to Torah obedience. There is not an end to the law, but a readiness and capability for obedience. The result will be a joyful commitment to justice, mercy, and compassion, with righteousness characterizing all relationships, in contrast to the pursuit of knowledge, power, and wealth (Jer 9:23-24). The new community will be marked by knowledge of Yahweh (cf. 22:15-16), which, grounded in the ancient tradition, is attentive to the poor and the needy.

In both its historical and eschatological modes, covenant therefore offers a subversive understanding of a God who liberates in order to create a community that is loyal to an alternative way of being in the world. This is a God who enters the human fray, waits to see how things will turn out, and responds to the human situation even when no way forward seems possible. God's covenanting represents God's relational initiative on behalf of the powerless and the marginalized. As Brueggemann puts it, a covenant-making, covenant-keeping God is concerned about "human justice and human dignity," is primarily known in "relational, political categories," and stands over against other gods that legitimate "imperial power of one kind or another" (1994: 56–57).

Although the NT moves into a new place for a new time, the essence of covenant remains the same (Luke 22:20; 1 Cor 11:25). The NT texts testify to God's creating a community whose calling is to embody an alternative way of being in the world, and to point to God's dream of restoring, reconciling, and healing all of creation. That way is embodied in Jesus and will be brought to its fullness in him, in God's time. We continue to be part of that journey, living in the meantime, discerning what this place and time requires in the light of God's vision for peace and healing in the world.

The NT writers interpret Jesus' life, death, and resurrection as a renewal of the ancient covenant. Descriptions of Jesus' death are particularly reminiscent of Passover theology in their use of language like "blood of the covenant" (Matt 26:28; Mark 14:24; Luke 22:20). Luke mentions covenant from the beginning of his Gospel (1:72) and in Acts identifies the covenant with Israel as a means for blessing the nations (Acts 3:25). Paul speaks of covenant as forgiveness of sins (Rom 11:27) and as blood of the new covenant (1 Cor 11:25). Paul contrasts "old covenant" and "new covenant" (2 Cor 3:14, 17). God's covenant with God's people is not limited to the Sinai event but extends before and after that (Gal 3:17). The author of Hebrews speaks of a "better covenant" (7:22; 8:6) and a "new covenant" (8:8), which is exactly that of Jeremiah's and Ezekiel's announcement (Heb 8:10; 10:16). The notion of making the first covenant "obsolete" (8:13) stands in contrast to Paul's notion that God's relationship with Israel is ongoing (Rom 9–11). Hebrews' new covenant may be more like a redemption from the failures of the first covenant (9:15), of which Jesus is the mediator (12:24). (But cf. Shillington, who suggests that for Paul, in 2 Corinthians, "the effective function of the Mosaic covenant was rendered inoperative," and this "theme reached its fullest Christian expression in . . . Hebrews" [1997: 71–72].)

When Jesus announces a "new covenant in my blood" (Luke 22:20; 1 Cor 11:25), he offers a new vision of relationality: Jesus' life, death, and resurrection is superimposed on all covenant making, all sacrifices undergirding such covenants, so that no one need any longer be sacrificed for the covenant to be effective. Jesus' death inaugurates a new covenant and in so doing abrogates any further requirement of death to seal the relationship established by the covenant.

DIFFICULT CONVERSATIONS This commentary draws part of its inspiration from an unlikely source, the book *Difficult Conversations: How to Discuss What Matters Most* (Stone et al.). The book breaks down a difficult conversation into three components: (1) The "What Happened?" Conversation: exploring both views from a third-party perspective; (2) The Feelings Conversation: unraveling the complexity of emotions of both parties and diffusing any negative effects; and (3) The Identity Conversation: recognizing how our perception of ourselves may affect our position. The process needs adaptation for a conversation with a biblical text. The first step could, for example, involve learning to understand the narrative of the book of Joshua in the context of other ancient Near Eastern warfare narratives. The second component of the conversation could include being honest about the emotional impact of the text and our emotional response to it, and then understanding how those emotional responses came to be. The third aspect of the conversation would be to acknowledge that because we understand Scripture as an identity-forming and community-forming document, the hostility between readers and the book of Joshua needs clarification. One way of gaining access to that process is to recognize, as with any relationship, that the text is Other.

Buber's book *I and Thou* (1970) sets the stage for a conversation between readers and the book of Joshua by suggesting a stance of respect and an awareness of "otherness" in the relationship between persons. Steven Kepnes (in a book called *The Text as Thou*) has shown that Buber's perspectives on relational "otherness" also characterize his understanding of the reader's relationship to a text. In other words, just as in human relationships we do well not to avoid or ignore the other, healthy relationships with texts can be nurtured by attentiveness to the Other—the text in this case—and to the transcendence that is mediated to us through such attentiveness. Such relational interpretation implies not only that readers try to uncover the meaning or significance of a text (or of what a narrator might have been trying to communicate), but also that readers enter a dialogue with the text. If the engagement involves more than two voices (reader and text), the metaphor of a conversation might be more appropriate. A number of interpreters of the book of Joshua have incorporated a conversational or dialogical approach to the book of Joshua (Polzin; Hauch; Matties 2009) and to biblical theology (Claassens; Green; Kittredge; Newsom).

Thiselton names the virtues that accompany such attentiveness to the voices of Others: "Hermeneutics demands patience, tolerance, and a willingness to understand the Other as something more than a projection of one's own prior assumptions. The Other is not an object to be manipulated in accordance with one's own stereotypes and interests" (53). If we are willing to move beyond hearing what we want to hear, we do well to practice attentiveness to the text as Thou, as Other. Thiselton continues: "Biblical exposition which does not do justice to the otherness of biblical texts reduces everything to the bland, dull, and predictable. The cutting edge of the text is assimilated into some repeated hobbyhorse of the preacher" (54). Even more sharply, Thiselton writes: "Only understanding texts and selfhood in their otherness and alienness can make it possible for them to address us in ways that avoid readings already domesticated and made bland by our construing them as products of our own world" (56). The kind of "otherness" that I am inviting us to respect is not the detached observer-analyst status often attempted by biblical interpreters, but the Otherness that acknowledges interpretation as a relational activity.

Hospitable hermeneutics allows all the voices to be heard around the table without predetermining what those voices must say. Hospitable hermeneutics, unlike a hermeneutics of suspicion, also gives us a place to be honest with our understandings (right or wrong though they may be), our feelings, and our identities as interpretive communities. For if the conversation with the book of Joshua is a "difficult conversation," it will require vulnerability from all sides, including the text, which has already become vulnerable to misuse and misappropriation. Such "dialogism," as Green puts it, recognizes "voices intensively engaged with each other, simultaneously listening and responding as well as [being] influenced and shaped" (35). With such attentiveness as the relational basis for our reading, we, as individual readers embedded in a community of interpreters, become open to being changed by what we read. Interpretation becomes transposition and ultimately transformation. In the process both text and readers become vulnerable, since even our "translation" of the text imposes our choices, which ends up changing the text into our language and idioms.

Because the commentary engages in such transposition, I include here a brief summary of the commitments and assumptions underlying this commentary's engagement with the book of Joshua.

Confessional Conversation Set in the context of genocide and ethnic cleansing—Germany, Armenia, Cambodia, Rwanda, the Balkans, Sudan, and other places—the book of Joshua should not surprise us. Perhaps this book exposes, within a scriptural context, what human beings are capable of doing. We do well to confess our tendencies to be like Israel the conqueror, especially where Western colonial enterprises have banked on the biblical text as justification for its assaults on indigenous populations in the Americas and Africa. Rahab and the Gibeonites, as well as all the assembled resident aliens and those peoples left among Israel, stand as witness to what happened and what continues to happen.

Community Conversation Reading in such a global community will empower the church to identify with others who have welcomed strangers, who have lived by trusting God rather than by grasping for treasures. It will be a community that knows how to discern the gods of the time. And it will be a community that heeds the voice of God and knows how to distinguish the god-language of culture from the words of the living God.

Constructive Conversation Reading with a hospitable hermeneutic will be reading in conversation with and among texts. As in any conversation, the flow will not always be linear. One voice responds to another, sometimes to develop, argue with, challenge, question, introduce new ideas, or return to traditional answers. Each section of the commentary, particularly the sections TBC and TLC, will introduce the main topics of conversation or voices in the conversation. Interpretation is not simply explaining what the author meant, or the historical context of the text, or the historical veracity of the events narrated in the text. It is theological conversation with this particular text and its effects in the lives and communities of those who read it. The narrative lives inside the particularity of Israel against the peoples, but it reaches toward a larger vision that extends to *all the earth* (Josh 3:11, 13; cf. 2:11) and to *all the peoples of the earth* (4:24).

Critical Conversation The OT contains a longing for peace. That longing may be generated by an ideal that God fights for Israel and Israel need not participate (Exod 14; Deut 1:30; Josh 6). Clements offers a second reason for such longings: "It is not the miracles of God-given victories that nourish the Old Testament's longing for peace, but the terrifying descriptions given by such prophets as Jeremiah and Ezekiel of the pain of war, the miseries of widowhood, and the degradation of once fertile lands into a wilderness" (125). McEntire thinks that "violence is the issue with which the whole of the Hebrew canon, not just certain traditions within it, grapples" (125). If that is so, then critical conversation with the book of Joshua takes us to the very heart of Scripture, which, as Girard has suggested, is a "text in travail" (1987a: 141). Scripture's authority is best perceived as its ability to transform and shape a community that trusts and obeys, yet that attends to the counterfeit voices calling for alternative allegiances, that seek to assure us that true trust (like the voice of the Rabshakeh in 2 Kings 18) is a trust in imperial and military power.

Commentary as Conversation Every narrative invites readers to negotiate their relationship with the world depicted in the story. Because of that, interpretations of the book of Joshua have largely focused on questions posed by readers. Interrogation of the book of Joshua has been like a war-crimes trial, in which everyone already knows the outcome. The questions of the book of Joshua to us, however, have hardly been addressed. The challenge of commentary on Joshua is to pay attention, to let the text have its say, and to engage in the difficult conversation that will inevitably follow. We will not always find it easy to be open and patient enough to exchange ideas and feelings. In order for the conversation not to be one-sided, readers will have to assume that everything is open to negotiation. This does not mean that the text may say anything we want it to say. As much as we might be tempted to judge Joshua for the apparent effects of that book in the history of interpretation (and that will certainly come up in the conversation), we may also find ourselves taking or assigning responsibility for the interpretive failure of the reading community throughout history. My hope is that we will find a way of moving into a hopeful future that does not easily dismiss or naively embrace the book without attentive, critical, and respectful conversation.

DISPOSSESSED PEOPLES The list of six/seven people groups, mentioned throughout the book of Joshua, belongs to a somewhat fluid tradition (Josh 3:10; 24:11; Deut 7:1). There is no satisfactory explanation for this fluidity. Six peoples, with the Girgashites missing, are mentioned in Deuteronomy 20:17 and Joshua 9:1; 11:3; 12:8, although the Girgashites also appear in the Samaritan Pentateuch and LXX of Deuteronomy 20:17. All the six-nation lists in the OT include the peoples mentioned here. The covenant with Abraham lists ten peoples (Gen 15:18-21). Six are listed throughout Exodus (3:8, 17; 13:5, with Perizzites missing; 23:23; 33:2; 34:11). In Exodus, when those lists speak of dispossessing the indigenous inhabitants, the text identifies God as the one who will "blot out" or "send an angel" or "drive out" (23:23; 33:2; 34:11).

In the context of these lists, Deuteronomy 7 mentions serving other gods, whereas Deuteronomy 20 includes an additional warning about not being taught to do what these nations do. Deuteronomy's concern is for Israel to be taught only by God. Such attentiveness to divine instruction is part and parcel of the exhortation to single-hearted allegiance to one God (6:4). In both of those Deuteronomy texts, the divine action is muted and the focus falls on Israel's actions. Both mention Israel's responsibility to destroy them completely (7:1-2; 20:16-17), which does not happen in Joshua 9. There is an expansive reference to five of the groups (Canaanites are missing) in the story of Solomon's empire. As "slave labor" (1 Kings 9:20-21) or "forced labor" (9:15), he engages those "who were not of the people of Israel . . . who were still left in the land, whom the Israelites were unable to destroy completely" (9:20-21; cf. Josh 23:7; *could not drive out*: 15:63; 17:12; *did not drive out*: 13:13; 16:10; 17:13).

For reflection on election and otherness in the Bible, see Cohn 1994; Kaminsky 2003, 2007; Lohr 2009; Spina 2005.

EXTENT OF THE LAND God's expansive declaration of the grant of land to Joshua personally at the beginning of Joshua (1:3-4) echoes the promise texts in the Pentateuch. The tradition that includes Transjordan extends the boundaries as far as the Euphrates (Gen 12:1-7; 15:18-21; 17:8; Exod 23:31; Num 34:1-12; Deut 1:7-8; 11:24; Pss 72:8; 80:11; 89:25; Zech 9:10) and sets the stage for the unfulfilled idealism of Joshua 13:1-7, the distribution lists in Joshua 13:8–19:51, and the ongoing tradition reflected in Kings and Chronicles (1 Kings 4:21, 24; 8:65; 1 Chron 13:5). These texts reflect fluid boundaries that correspond roughly to traditional Egyptian descriptions of the land of Canaan during the fourteenth and thirteenth centuries BC (Weinfeld 1983: 65–66). The area between Egypt and Mesopotamia was considered, in the ancient world, "one geopolitical unit" (Mabie: 316). Within that larger expanse from Egypt to the Euphrates, "the geographical extent of Israel ebbed and flowed throughout the different periods of Israel's history" (316).

The first six chapters of Joshua depict a limited range of land acquisition within the traditional boundaries of the tribe of Benjamin in the central hill country. The engagement with the Gibeonites and their adversaries (Josh 9–10) gives Israel a slightly wider range, including part of the low rolling hills of the Shephelah (between the coastal plain and the hill country). This limited incursion into the land of Canaan becomes much more expansive in the victories reported in the south (Josh 10:16-43) and north (11:1-22). In these two chapters, the narrative summarizes Israel's having acquired *the whole land* (10:40-43; 11:23) and *all that land* (11:16). Summaries are given in each of those places:

- *the hill country and the Negeb and the lowland and the slopes (10:40)*
- *the hill country and all the Negeb and all the land of Goshen and the lowland and the Arabah and the hill country of Israel and its lowland, from Mount Halak, which rises toward Seir, as far as Baal-gad in the valley of Lebanon below Mount Hermon (11:16-17)*

These victories, however, do not reflect occupation. There is no narrative of occupation in the first half of Joshua. Israel always returns to Gilgal. The point of the narrative seems to be *rest from war* (11:16, 23). Although many kings are said to have been conquered by Moses and Joshua (in ch. 12), chapter 13 reports that *very much of the land still remains to be possessed* (13:1; cf. 13:1-6, 13; 15:63; 16:10; 17:11-16; 18:1-3). Even so, the land is given and distributed by lot, as determined by the Lord (13:6-7; 21:43-45). Even in Joshua's final speeches, he acknowledges *nations that remain* (23:4) along with the promise that the Lord will *drive them out* (23:5). Joshua's speech (ch. 23) "helps to clarify the theological nuances surrounding the parallel realities of *completely given land* and *incomplete conquest* (cf. Num 33:53; Deut 8:1; 11:22-23)" (Mabie: 318). The book of Joshua reflects an occupation in the central hill country and parts of Transjordan, with limited excursions into areas traditionally controlled by Egypt for its trade routes in the Late Bronze Age (Galilee, Negev, coastal plain, and the Shephelah).

The distribution lists of Joshua 13–19 seem to reflect the gift in anticipation even though, as Hess puts it, "the text of Joshua does not promise something. Rather, like the [ancient Near Eastern] royal grants, it claims to record the actual deeding of land to the tribes of Israel, whose vassal status in relation to God is undeniable." Even so, the gift of land in Joshua remains conditional on Israel's faithfulness (8:30-35; 23:12-13; 24:1-28) (2002: 496). Moreover, the extent of the land is not somehow predetermined or inviolable. The story of Joshua 22 implies some dispute about the extent of the land. In Joshua the crossing of the Jordan River represents a crossing into the promised land, and the Transjordan represents an ambiguous land that was taken, as it were, "by accident" (Weinfeld 1983: 59). After all, not all descriptions of the extent of the land include Transjordan (Num 34:1-12).

Moreover, Deuteronomy states that parts of Transjordan, particularly the lands of Edom, Moab, and Ammon, are not part of the land of promise (2:5, 9, 19). Ezekiel's new peoplehood is constituted in land distributed only west of the Jordan. The conflict by the Jordan River, therefore, raises the question of the status of Transjordan. The question posed by Joshua 22 is not whether the land is unclean or not: Jacob encounters God in Transjordan and beyond (Gen 31:3-16; 32:1-3, 28-30; 33:17); the ark located in Transjordan ("at Sukkoth"; 2 Sam 11:11 NJPS; cf. Gen 33:17); and David's census involves Transjordan (2 Sam 24:5-6). The issue concerns whether or not the people "outside" the land are able to *love the Lord* and serve him fully (Josh 22:5, 22-23). In an exilic or postexilic context, such a question is remarkably relevant. The book of Joshua calls for the creation of a people loyal to God and to God's ways. Wherever that happens, the Lord rules.

For a fuller exploration of the topic, see Mabie; Havrelock; Hess 2005; Jobling; Weinfeld 1983, 1993. On the transformation of Joshua's boundary descriptions in Chronicles, see Japhet: 207–10.

FIGURAL READING For most of the history of interpretation, the book of Joshua has been a source of reflection on the character of the Christian life. Apart from a few commentators, like Calvin, it was not until the modern era that the book of Joshua came to be interpreted in the light of literary and historical analysis. Figural reading is not allegorical. It works with typological clues within the text, discerning echoes and reverberations of that text throughout Scripture. As the book of Hebrews puts it, past events were reported in Scripture for the benefit of later readers (Heb 11:39-40; cf. 1 Cor 10:6, 11). For example, Hebrews 4:1-11 describes a trajectory of significance around the motif of "rest" in the land (see Josh 1:13, 15; 21:44; 22:4; 23:1), linking it to Sabbath rest (including Gen 2:2-3) and the warning of Psalm 95:11. In doing so, Hebrews presents the case that Joshua's "rest" remains available as a present and eschatological reality.

Figural reading of Joshua is also highlighted within Joshua and the DtrH with analogies between Moses and Joshua, Joshua and Josiah, and David's commission to Solomon echoing God's commissioning Joshua (1 Kings 2:2-3; cf. Josh 1). Similarly, the crossing of the Jordan River becomes a reiteration of the crossing of the Red Sea, and Joshua's encounter with the man holding a drawn sword mirrors Moses' encounter with God at the burning bush. Such examples suggest that the book of Joshua participates in a larger intrabiblical conversation (Schniedewind). Commentators through the ages have drawn on the impulse to recognize patterns and figural relationships that encourage readers to imagine that similar relationships might also hold true for them.

Origen (b. AD 185) is a master of such discernment. He is clear that his reading does not annul the original text, or rewrite it, but finds in it a way of overlaying the present experience of the church so that what that narrative was telling then is what it is possible to affirm as happening today. And since Origen also reads in conversation with all of Scripture, he knows that Jesus (as well as others) could not affirm the kind of ethnic violence described in the text. Even so, he is aware that Jesus is also Joshua (the names are from the same Heb. root and are identical in the Greek). Since Origen assumes that Jesus makes all things new, he discerns in the book of Joshua hints of that coming transformation. Dawson writes concerning Origen's work: the "fundamental aim of the project was to show how former things were spiritually transformed, not rejected" (215). Origen's notion of transformation is that "things increasingly become what they are. Paradoxically, becoming what they are means changing the way they are" (215).

Origen's approach does not simply repeat the text, as though in a conversation he were to say, "I hear you saying . . ." Rather, Origen interprets Joshua by saying, "That is what you say, and in order for me to appropriate that into my context, this is what I must say in the light of how I understand other Scriptures resonating with motifs that I hear in your words." It is not the words of the book of Joshua that are authoritative for Origen, but the words as they resonate with the Scriptures as a whole. But because of his conviction that Scripture is a life-giving word for all time, Origen gives the book of Joshua a hearing against all its detractors. He wishes it to be "useful," suggesting that it "benefits the soul even if our perception at the present does not understand why" (177, citing 2 Tim 3:16).

Origen is intent on rescuing the story for Christian faith rather than leaving it as it is in the realm of historical interpretation. Citing Hebrews 8:5 and Ephesians 6:12, Origen suggests that Joshua's wars are "a shadow and type of heavenly things," namely, the fight of Jesus "against the Devil and his angels" and "against spiritual forces of wickedness in heavenly places" (120). And since the believers are not promised "kingdoms of earth" but "kingdoms of heaven," therefore "we shall not fight in the same manner as the ancients fought" nor against the same kind of enemy (121).

That was Origen's answer to those who were disturbed by the violence of the OT. He addresses them by name: "Marcion and Valentinus and Basilides and the other heretics with them" (123). Origen used a figural reading to offer an alternative to those who would have discarded these texts entirely. So I pay attention to Origen not because his figural reading is the only model available for our own interpretation but because his transposition addresses the integrity of the canon and also the matter of theodicy, the justice of God. The battle is internalized, teaching us "to trample on the demon of avarice, . . . boasting, . . . arrogance" (123). To express the hope that this is possible through the cross of Christ (123), Origen draws from Joshua's exhortation in Joshua 10:25 and writes, "If we understand these things spiritually and manage wars of this type spiritually, . . . then we shall be able at last to receive from Jesus as a share of the inheritance even those places and kingdoms that are the kingdoms of heaven, bestowed by our Lord and Savior Jesus Christ" (123–24). In his final homily on Joshua 10, Origen transforms the wars of that chapter into a wish, even a prayer: "Would that the Lord might thus cast out and extinguish all former evils from the souls who believe in him" (127).

Although contemporary interpreters of Joshua might balk at some of Origen's analogies between the book of Joshua and his own time, he is clearly interested in how the plot of the story might have a transforming and shaping impact on his community of readers. Working with the best tools of insight available to him, he crafts a conversation with the book of Joshua. Dawson summarizes Origen's approach:

> Figural reading in the Christian tradition seeks to express the dynamic process of spiritual transformation in ways that respect the practitioners' commitment to both past and future, both old identity and newly refashioned identity. Imbedded in figural practice is all the drama of discerning the point of existence and identifying one's place in it, figured as a journey from a former mode of existence through various states of transformation toward some ultimate end. There are, of course, other ways of imagining existence and one's place in it, many of which are profoundly unrelated to the journey motif, or its literary analog, narrative. But the Christian imagination, at least as it expresses itself in the tradition of figural reading, is structured in just that way. (216)

That activity of finding oneself in the journey (or in the plot) is what the church has always done. And in every generation readers have been both limited and empowered by that practice. Origen is limited by his Neoplatonic worldview when he looks for analogies with what we might consider insignificant details, yet he strives to enter the story and find himself interpreted by it. So every generation of interpreters who approach the conversation with the book of Joshua have worked similarly even though the interpreter's ideology all too often gets in the way (e.g., Crusaders, colonizing Western powers, Israeli settlements in the West Bank). The process of faithful reading, suggests N. T. Wright, might be called "improvisation" (ch. 5; taken up and modified by Middleton and Walsh: 182–95; and again by Wells 2004; for a summary discussion, see Matties 2009).

Interpretation through time is a testimony to countless improvisations of the text, in which communities of faith seek to embody the sovereign rule of God in their lives. Middleton and Walsh (building on N. T. Wright) suggest our imagining that a previously unknown Shakespeare play has been found, but this play has been broken off in the middle of the fifth and final act. Their analogy with Scripture suggests that Acts 1–4 includes creation, fall, the story of Israel, the story of Jesus, with Act 5 beginning but not ending the story of the church. Suppose a director considers the new Shakespeare play and decides, rather than writing a final act and staging the play, to give the unfinished piece to a group of seasoned actors whose task it will be to immerse themselves in the script so deeply that they are able to make out where the final act would take them if Shakespeare actually wrote it. These actors discern clues in the text that lead them to sketch the outline of a plot development beyond the middle of the fifth act and all the way to a final resolution. After this immersion in the story, the actors are invited, not to write the fifth act (which would fix it into one form), but to improvise the whole of the fifth act in the light of what they know of the unfinished work. Samuel Wells suggests a slight modification of the image of a five-act play (creation, Israel, Jesus, church, and eschaton). The church lives in the fourth act, improvising in the light of the first three acts and in anticipation of the fifth. The outcome of the drama is not the church's to produce, which sets the church free from the compulsion to get everything right the first time. The church need not replicate one of the first three acts, nor attempt to bring about the consummation of the fifth act on its own terms and by its own performance (Wells: 55–57).

The usefulness of the analogy, which I seek to embody in this commentary, is that the biblical narrative provides the unfinished drama, and that the life of the church in the world is the improvisation toward the completion of the drama. In this scenario, the book of Revelation is not the end of the story; it both narrates the life of the church and intimates how the drama might end. Similarly, other biblical texts also point to that end. In a sense, the many biblical writers and texts each contribute to that testimony upon which improvisation might be based. The end is discerned, the journey glimpsed, and the means to that end exemplified throughout the story in various ways; hence the church lives its life by improvising on the narrative in which it has been immersed. Because the life of the church is an improvisation of the whole story, it cannot be an improvisation merely of the book of Joshua. This is liberating for the interpreter and for the community of faith because it allows those who read the book of Joshua to read it in conversation with others who are also reading (or who have also read) the same Scriptures. There may well be many improvisations, many readings. Are all correct? Is any interpretation right? Or should we think, rather, of a discernment of the *telos*, the goal of Scripture, and improvise in the light of that goal as it is hinted at throughout the text, including the book of Joshua? In this way it is possible to see interpretation as "the church's praxis or 'performance,' [which] must be faithful to the thrust, momentum and direction of the biblical story" (Middleton and Walsh: 183).

The book of Joshua does not disappear once that momentum is discerned. The church continues to argue with and attend to it in a variety of ways. We might even decide that some of what we hear in Joshua, although "guided by God's overarching purposes," also belongs to a larger story that "is full of dead ends, plot conflict, and narrative tension, which are not normative but interrupt plot fulfillment and go against God's purposes. Faithful improvisation does not mean blind submission to every text of Scripture but the enactment of God's redemptive purposes through discernment of the thrust of the entire metanarrative" (Middleton and Walsh: 185). It is precisely through such honesty that we are able to approach disagreements without abandoning the text. Instead, we are readers committed "to maintain the relationship" because our "dissent [is] in the service of faithfulness" (Middleton and Walsh: 186). Since the book of Joshua is rooted in covenantal relationship, and since covenant is essentially dialogical (cf. Abraham's argument with God in Gen 18), we are able "to wrestle trustingly with God—and with the text of Scripture—as we seek to discern and embody the Author's will and enact his purposes in our lives" (Middleton and Walsh: 186). Such reading is open to "counter-conventional" insight because, like the voices within the Bible itself, our reading is part and parcel of an "interpretive struggle" (Fowl: 135). We wrestle with the text even as the Scripture itself, as Girard puts it, is a "text in travail" (1987a: 141), longing for a redemptive ending to the story it tells.

There may well be a distinction between intrabiblical interpretation (the play of allusion, repetition, and interpretation among texts within the canon) and figural interpretation (the discernment of typological patterns that resonate through Scripture and that become paradigmatic for the life of the people of God). Even so, the line is blurred since the former leads effectively into the latter.

For a solid defense of Origen's interpretation of Scripture, see Reno. And for a rich exploration of figural interpretation, see Dawson. Since figural reading was practiced by ancient Christian interpreters, readers may wish to consult Franke's volume of the Ancient Christian Commentary on Scripture. And for a summary of intrabiblical interpretation, see Schniedewind. For a history of Christian figural interpretation of Joshua, see Auld (1999).

GENOCIDE AND SACRED VIOLENCE Genocide, according to the United Convention, "is a crime under international law." Under Resolution 260, "genocide means any of the following acts committed with intent to destroy, in whole or in part, a national, ethnical, racial or religious group, such as: (a) Killing members of the group; (b) Causing serious bodily or mental harm to members of the group; (c) Deliberately inflicting on the group conditions of life calculated to bring about its physical destruction in whole or in part; (d) Imposing measures intended to prevent births within the group; (e) Forcibly transferring children of the group to another group" (Resolution 260 [III] A, Dec. 9, 1948). Since the Holocaust, we know all too well the terror of ethnic violence, ideologies of racial purity, and desire for land giving birth to rivalry that leads to communal violence.

The problem of genocide is exacerbated by the god-language that often accompanies the rhetoric of both smaller-scale communal violence and the so-called clash of civilizations. The conquest accounts within the book of Joshua share the same god-language as other ancient conquest accounts. The Mesha Inscription offers a prime example, in which King Mesha receives instructions from his god to destroy the enemy, which in this case happens to be Israel *[Conquest Accounts, p. 406; Mesha Inscription, p. 447]*.

Ever since Gerhard von Rad published his book *Holy War in Ancient Israel* (1991 [1958]), the sacred violence of these texts has been labeled either "holy war" or "divine warfare," with some specifying the OT warfare as "Yahweh war." All labels are inadequate. The problem with "sacred warfare" and other such terms is that warfare in the ancient world was not simply a war that the gods fight, nor a war that is particularly "holy," as though one might contrast it to "secular" warfare. The point of recognizing warfare in the ancient world as *genocide* and as *sacred warfare* is to expose the rhetoric of warfare by exploring its roots. Three explanations of the origin of such language illustrate the point. Each of these makes a contribution: none is adequate on its own.

One explanation, which helpfully draws conclusions based on comparing biblical texts with other ancient conquest accounts, is that conquest accounts in which genocide is reported belong to the rhetoric of political ideology. Such rhetoric is rooted in a worldview in which the cosmos (including the gods) has its origin in violence. The cosmos is considered to be fundamentally violent from the beginning, and violence is inscribed in the myths of origin, which justify the ideology of military power and imperial expansion (Younger 1990; Rowlett 1996). Sharing in a contextually rooted worldview, the biblical conquest accounts plunder the genre available, along with the common ways of speaking about divine-human engagement with enemy peoples on the ground. In other words, Israel does not invent the god-language rhetoric of the conquest accounts. The genre, however, allows Israel's theologians a way of writing history (using the literary conventions available at the time) while at the same time beginning to undermine the worldview that undergirds such conquest accounts *[Conquest Accounts, p. 406]*.

A second explanation builds on the argument from genre by positing a theological conflict between reality and vision—between life in the world that requires political legitimation, and its necessary ideological justification disguised as theological vision. Birch and his coauthors suggest that Joshua reflects a tension between "real land" and "promised land." Joshua 1 seems to present a "pure theological ideal and is completely unbothered by economic-political-military realities that are yet to come" (180). Yet the realities of the following chapters are not as neat as the "promised land" theology has suggested.

> The reason is that real land, unlike theologically promised land, is always contested, disputed, and conflictual. That is, there are already other people there who do not yield easily to Israel's theological claim. And therefore to receive the promise, Israel must either engage in military conflict with other contestants for the land or accommodate and compromise. Either strategy turns out to be a far remove from the simplicity of the Torah promise. Thus it may be suggested that the burden of Joshua and Judges is to adjudicate between the simple normative claims of the Torah promises and the lived ambiguities of life in the world. (180)

Genocide, in other words, belongs to a theological argument; it concerns "a quarrel among the gods. . . . Yahweh the king is here reassigning land for the benefit of Israel." Thus "Israel, like every such land-seeking community, does not want to base its claim to land on the sheer act of violence but on a respected, credible legitimacy that reaches to the intention of the gods" (186). Moreover, "the land is only available to Israel as Israel obeys the Torah . . . and reorders life in the land according to the requirements of Deuteronomic Torah. That is, this is a land revolution that is driven by a social vision with a particular interest" (187).

A third explanation, perhaps the most satisfying of the three, supplements the previous two without denying their explanatory power. It suggests that warfare and sacrifice belong to the phenomenon of mimetic desire, an explanation articulated most profoundly in René Girard's various writings. Warfare is the result of two people groups wanting the same thing. The god-language of ancient texts simply reflects the fact that human desire is often ascribed to divine desire. Mimetic desire, therefore, is a human reality, not simply an aspect of an outmoded ancient worldview. It is expressed in the practices of victimage and scapegoating in which a sacrificial victim becomes the means through which conflict is diminished and order is restored to society.

> Mimetic or mediated desire inevitably leads to rivalry. We humans will fight over everything whether honor or money, ideology or relationships, and we do so to the death. This is the curse of mimesis. If you posit something as desirable (gold, diamonds, that new SUV, power, etc.), and I imitate your desire, we have a problem because we cannot both possess the same object. Someone will lose. Taken to its extremes, this rivalry often leads to some sort of violent behavior in order to possess the object desired. (Hardin, 2010)

According to mimetic theory, the Bible testifies to the complex process of the revelation of victimage. As Girard puts it, the Bible is "a process under way, a text in travail; it is not a chronologically progressive process, but a struggle that advances and retreats" (1987a: 141). Thus our reading of Joshua within the entire canon of Scripture suggests that the Bible bears witness not to a duplicitous God, but to two paradigms, one that reflects the mimetic desire implicit in ethnic nationalism, and the other a critique and even renunciation of violence and sacrifice. These two paradigms become interpretive options that debate one another within the Bible, a debate that is ultimately transformed by the vision of the peaceful reign of God (in the OT) and the kingdom of God (in Jesus' teaching).

This transformation is not an example of some texts trumping other texts. Rather, to appeal to mimetic theory is a way of recognizing that in some way all biblical texts share in the struggle toward transformation. Even the book of Joshua—with its explicit evidence of mimetic desire (e.g., in the Achan story of Josh 7 and in the intertribal conflict of Josh 22), and with its struggle to include the outsider, the one devoted to destruction (e.g., in Rahab of Josh 2 and 6, and the Gibeonites in Josh 9)—there is evidence of a "text in travail, . . . a struggle that advances and retreats." (For excellent explanations of mimetic theory applied to conflict, see Redekop; www.preachingpeace.org.)

The insight of mimetic theory suggests that because Israel's acquisition of land is founded on violence, it will ultimately fail. It represents an imitation of the pagan worldview grounded as it is in irreconcilable conflict at the heart of the cosmos. The gods are violent, and so are humans. The narrative of Joshua, viewed from that perspective, is a mirror of humankind's propensity to absolutize and grasp rather than trust and receive. In the light of that kind of worldview analysis, it is possible to suggest that the prohibition against "serving the gods," and the exhortation to exclusive loyalty to and trust in the Lord alone, amounts to the beginning of Israel's struggle with and against the warfare worldview. The Bible never fully escapes that worldview, but it struggles, in its overarching narrative, to transform it within a larger conversation about the purposes of God in the world.

Even if the violence in the book of Joshua can be explained in one of these three ways, the particularity of the association of God, people, and land remains a stumbling block that cannot altogether be removed. Perhaps the offense of particularity is the path that God treads on the way to restoration of all things.

***ḤEREM*, "DEVOTED TO DESTRUCTION"** There is hardly an idea more problematic to contemporary readers than the notion that God might command one people group to annihilate another people group. That notion of divinely sanctioned genocide or ethnic cleansing is reflected in the Hebrew noun *ḥerem* (and its related verb), which in the cognate Moabite language is the same word as is found in the Mesha Inscription *[Mesha Inscription, p. 447]*. The verb has been translated in a variety of ways: devote to destruction, utterly destroy, annihilate, exterminate, proscribe. The noun and its related verb form occur twenty-seven times in Joshua. Although the word is primarily associated with warfare in Deuteronomy and Joshua, it is also associated with other contexts (e.g., Exod 22:20; Lev 27:21, 28-29; Num 18:14) where it applies to matters from capital punishment to handing over ownership of things to the Lord or to his priestly representatives. Most often, however, *ḥerem* is concerned with the annihilation of the Other, those perceived either as enemies or as a hindrance to the fulfillment of the Lord's promise of land to Israel (Num 21:2-8; Deut 2:34; 3:6; 7:2, 26; 13:15-17; 20:17; 1 Sam 15:3).

Drawing on a number of earlier studies, Lohr offers this succinct summary of the meaning of the word *ḥerem*: "Whether used in the context of war or in the sanctuary, the word evokes the idea of an 'irrevocable surrender to God.' This separating or devoting something to God is absolute, irrevocable, permanent, complete. Once something is devoted, it cannot be redeemed. The thing devoted is taken from profane or common use and is given over or dedicated to be something set apart or sacred. A connection to the idea of holiness, whether positive or negative, is inevitable" (208).

Most explanations of *ḥerem* that try to justify the command to annihilate the enemy run aground on the objection that they bypass the biblical text. Lohr summarizes a number of such solutions, ranging from "the idea that the *ḥerem* never happened to the idea that God did not really command it to the idea that God commanded it because he is a God that gets his hands dirty. All of the above suggestions seem to read something into the text that is not present" (225). Lohr proposes that the biblical texts are primarily concerned with "the fulfillment of God's blessings to Abraham, one of which included a land that his descendants were to possess but that was populated" (225). From this perspective, Lohr suggests that *ḥerem*, "though repugnant to the contemporary reader, shows YHWH's absolute loyalty to his oath made to Israel's foreparents" (161). Although Lohr states that the Canaanites were simply "in the wrong place at the wrong time" (225), the promise to the ancestors does include a reference to "the iniquity of the Amorites," which, according to Genesis 15:16, will form the basis for their dispossession.

Lohr does not consider the fact that *ḥerem* also stands at the heart of the Mesha Inscription, where the god Chemosh promises to give victory to Mesha, king of Moab, who is to devote Israelites—men, women, children, and livestock—to destruction for the god Chemosh. The Mesha Inscription and the biblical text assume an integral relationship among god, land, and people. Both texts reflect the theology of Jephthah's messengers (Judg 11:23-24). Like the Mesha Inscription, biblical texts that use the word *ḥerem* appropriate the conventional language of the conquest-account genre. And when Deuteronomy commands *ḥerem*, it shares the same theological perspective on that relationship as does the Mesha Inscription: that the god (Yahweh or Chemosh) has a right to rid an "alien people" from the land designated for the deity's special people.

The "solution" to the *ḥerem* problem, therefore, cannot be derived simply from within the text of the OT. Although Lohr is correct in linking *ḥerem* to the Lord's loyalty to the ancestors, the book of Joshua itself subordinates *ḥerem* to divine instruction (Torah), even though it is clear that not all divine instruction in Deuteronomy is to be obeyed in perpetuity. Moreover, as Seibert points out, "Even the most theologically troubling texts contain other insights, ideas, and perspectives that can, and should, be explored" (213). For further development of that idea, see Matties (2009).

See the related essays *[Mesha Inscription, p. 447; Theology of Warfare, p. 458]* and Nelson 1997b; Niditch; Stern; Earl 2010a: ch. 6, 2010b; Lohr: Appendix 2.

HORSES AND CHARIOTS In 1 Kings the biblical historian describes Solomon's military and offers an ironic critique of his "horses and chariots" (1 Kings 4:26; 10:26). First, the implicit critique mirrors Deuteronomy's prohibition of acquiring horses and chariots from Egypt (17:16; cf. 20:1-4). Second, Solomon's speech to Hiram, king of Tyre, presents an ironic echo of Joshua's motif "rest on every side," where it highlights God's exclusive victory (1 Kings 5:4; cf. Josh 11:23; 21:44). Solomon's blessing to his people takes up the theme again (1 Kings 8:56). To Hiram he says, "There is neither adversary nor misfortune," as though clueless about the future implications of acquiring horses (1 Kings 5:4; cf. 4:26; 10:26-28). And third, the list of provisions in 1 Kings 4:20-28 is loaded with intrabiblical allusions that lead the reader to infer that the entire description is tongue in cheek, if not thoroughly ironic, especially given that Solomon ultimately loses the empire precisely because of what "going to Egypt" has brought him: the worship of other gods (11:2-8). Thus horses and chariots are not altogether unrelated to the worship of other gods that support his militaristic endeavors.

Several motifs stand out in the list of provisions in 1 Kings 4 (Brueggemann 1981). First, the text mentions that Judah and Israel (the distinction is a premonition of division) "were as numerous as the sand by the sea" (4:20). This reminds us of the size of Jabin's coalition forces (Josh 11:4) and of the ancestral promise of Genesis (22:17; 32:12). Second, Solomon "had dominion" and "peace on all sides" (*šalom* in 1 Kings 4:24 [with its wordplay on Solomon's name; cf. 1 Chron 22:9], but "rest" in 1 Kings 5:4; as in Josh 11:23; 21:44; cf. 1 Chron 22:9-10, 18; 2 Chron 14:7; 32:22). These texts provide more evidence that Chronicles transforms the warfare/rest theme initiated in

Joshua. The "dominion" language of 1 Kings 4 echoes Genesis 1:28, but militarizes the human vocation and subordinates it to Solomon's imperial policy. Third, 1 Kings 4:25 states that Israel is living "in safety." The Hebrew word is "trust," (Heb. *baṭaḥ*), which is the same word used in 2 Kings 18 by the Rabshakeh, who wishes to subvert Judah's "trust" in both God and Pharaoh's chariots and horsemen (2 Kings 18:21-22, 24). Fourth, everyone in Solomon's "Judah and Israel" sit "under their vines and fig trees." In this expression we can hear an allusion to several biblical texts. It is again the Rabshakeh who invites Judah to "make your peace [lit., "blessing"] with me" so that "every one of you will eat from your own vine and your own fig tree" (2 Kings 18:31). This is nothing other than a promise of "blessing" through compromise that, according to Jeremiah, ends in reverse conquest and devastation as the foreign army destroys vines and fig trees (5:17; cf. Hos 2:12; Joel 1:7).

Two groups of texts offer alternative perspectives on vines and fig trees. One group faces the reality of devastation and offers hope in spite of the loss of vines and fig trees (Joel 2:22; Hab 3:17; Hag 2:19). Another text offers the most remarkable transformation of all: when the nations heed the instruction of the Lord, and when the Lord will "arbitrate between strong nations far away," they will "beat their swords into plowshares, and their spears into pruning hooks; nation shall not lift up sword against nation, neither shall they learn war any more" (Mic 4:2-3). Only then will they "all sit under their own vines and under their own fig trees, and no one shall make them afraid" (Mic 4:4). Although this textual affinity suggests that 1 Kings 4 is deeply ironic, there are other clues within the DtrH that lead to a rich understanding of "horses and chariots" in Joshua 11.

It has become clear that horses and chariots are normally associated with royal power and oppression (Exod 14:9, 23; 15:9; Deut 20:1; 2 Sam 15:1; 1 Kings 18:5; 22:4; 2 Kings 3:7; 18:23; 23:11). Five texts in the books of Kings in particular offer a critique of royal power via horses and chariots and present a vision of another kind of power. First, in an encounter with Israel, the Syrians are sure of their strength in horses and chariots (1 Kings 20:23-25). God defeats them through a prophetic word, a brutal military encounter, and a wall falling on the rest (20:28-30), which leads to a sparing of King Ben-hadad and a treaty with Israel. Second, in another encounter the perturbed Aramean king surrounds Elisha with "horses and chariots . . . and a great army" (2 Kings 6:14). Although Elisha's servant sees many of the king's "horses and chariots" (6:15), the Lord opens the servant's eyes to see that "the mountain was full of horses and chariots of fire all around Elisha" (6:17). The Lord strikes the army blind, and Elisha leads them into the heart of Israel's capital city. The king of Israel wants to kill them, but Elisha responds, "No! Did you capture with your sword and your bow those whom you want to kill? Set food and water before them so that they may eat and drink; and let them go to their master" (6:22; on the motif "not by your sword and bow," see Josh 24:12). Third, four lepers enter the Syrian camp safely because the Syrians have been scared off by the sound of horses and chariots (2 Kings 7:3-8). A cosmic or hidden army is at work. Fourth, in a text to which I have already referred, the Assyrians mock Israelite weakness and offer two thousand horses if Israel has riders (which they do not; 2 Kings 18:23). The outcome of the story is a victory wrought by an angel (19:35). Fifth, all of those examples reflect the transcendent perspective of the prophetic word. As highlighted in the Explanatory Notes for Joshua 3:17 (and 3:1–4:24 TBC), Elijah and Elisha reverse the journey of the Joshua story when they cross the Jordan on dry ground (2 Kings 2:8). Moreover, in the story as a whole, "the real chariot of Israel is not that on the field of battle, . . . but the fiery chariot [sic] that carries away Elijah. . . . It is Elijah, rather than any king, who encapsulates Israel's true power. . . . The implication: true kingly power resides not with kings but with the word of God" (2 Kings 2:11-12; Brodie: 73–74) *[Torah, p. 462]*.

Prophetic and psalm texts offer additional insight. Hosea announces that God "will not save them by bow, or by sword, or by war, or by horses, or by horsemen" (Hos 1:7; cf. Josh 24:12). Isaiah levels a critique of "those who go down to Egypt for help and who rely on horses and trust in chariots because they are many" (31:1). Instead of fleeing on horses, salvation will come "in quietness and in trust," (30:15). In a judgment speech, Micah announces, "In that day . . . I will cut off your horses from among you and will destroy your chariots" (5:10). Concerning Israel's release from Babylonian captivity, Isaiah speaks of the action of the Lord "who brings out chariot and horse, army and warrior; they lie down, they cannot rise, they are extinguished, quenched like a wick" because "I am about to do a new thing" (43:17, 19). And Zechariah announces, "Not by might, nor by power, but by my spirit, says the Lord of hosts" (4:6). In another place Zechariah announces that the coming one "will cut off the chariot from Ephraim and the war-horse from Jerusalem," and in the process the "battle bow" will be "cut off," and "his dominion shall be from sea to sea, and from the River to the ends of the earth" (9:9-10). The prophetic imagination here modifies the boundary description from Joshua 1 and rejects the bow (weapons) of Joshua 24:12.

Finally, psalm texts testify to the contrast between conventional weapons and the power of God. "Some take pride in chariots, and some in horses, but our pride is in the name of the Lord our God" (Ps 20:7; cf. Pss 33:16-17; 147:10-11). One psalm even proclaims that God "broke the flashing arrows, the shield, the sword, and the weapons of war" and that "both rider and horse lay stunned" (76:3, 6). And perhaps most provocatively, Psalm 46 announces in hope that God "makes wars cease to the end of the earth; he breaks the bow, and shatters the spear; he burns the shields with fire" (v. 9; cf. Josh 11:6, 9). This is what makes it possible to "Be still, and know that I am God! I am exalted among the nations, I am exalted in the earth" (Ps 46:9-10). Yet selectivity is always a danger: Psalm 149:6-9 exhorts worshipers to "execute vengeance on the nations" with the "two-edged swords in their hands." These contrasts emphasize the need not only to acknowledge the intrabiblical conversation, but also to keep that difficult conversation alive in an ongoing and dynamic interpretive process in the church.

Horses and chariots come to represent, therefore, the grasping kind of power that prevents trust in the Lord (Ps 20:7; cf. Deut 20:1-4). Isaiah presents them in various contexts alongside gold, silver, and idols, all of which are sources of pride that prevent Israel from trusting God (2:7; 31:1; 36:9). It is God alone who is sovereign over horses and chariots, who calls them to fulfill his purposes, and who brings them to nothing (Isa 43:17; Jer 50:37; 51:21; Ezek 39:20; Hag 2:22).

HYPERBOLE The conquest accounts embedded in the book of Joshua, like other ancient conquest accounts, resort to hyperbole as a rhetorical device: exaggeration not intended to be taken literally.

Totality The most well known of such ancient Near Eastern texts is the Mesha Inscription, in which King Mesha of Moab writes about his god Chemosh, who "saved me from *all* the kings and caused me to triumph over *all* my adversaries" (emph. added). Not only is the hyperbolic language ("all") typical of such conquest accounts; Mesha also claims to have slain "all," just as does the biblical text. Similarly, reports of taking "the whole region" or "all these kings and their lands" or "left none that breathed" are not unique to the DtrH. These rhetorical statements can be accounted for by the figurative nature of the conquest-account genre. Younger's analysis of ancient conquest accounts demonstrates widespread use of such hyperbole in the narratives. "Once one admits this element into the interpretive process, there is no reason to maintain that the account in Joshua 9–12 portrays a *complete* conquest" (1990: 243). He refers to Shalmaneser's accounts of having "conquered" and suggests that "conquest" may not be complete subjugation of the land (as admitted in, e.g., Josh 11:18; 13:1-2; 15:63; 16:10; 17:12). "The phrase 'all the land' must be understood as hyperbole. The claims to conquest have been overstated. This is a very similar situation in the vast majority of ancient Near Eastern conquest accounts" (Younger 1990: 244). Understanding the genre of the text, therefore, helps to avoid misinterpretation. As Younger points out, "Summary reports in ancient Near Eastern conquest accounts . . . were often hyperbolic—they clearly overstated matters to emphasize the text's ideological aims" (2008: 24).

Conquest accounts therefore are generically hyperbolic statements with respect to geographic completeness of the conquest and total populations killed. Recognizing hyperbole confirms that the biblical accounts are not verbatim reports. Israel's settlement in the land must have involved military engagements, but not at all on the scale suggested by a flat reading of the text *[Conquest Accounts, p. 406; Ḥerem, p. 433]*.

Large Numbers Large numbers are found in several places in the book of Joshua. Joshua 4:13 reports that *about forty thousand armed for war* crossed the Jordan River. In 7:3-4, Joshua is said to have sent three thousand people to attack Ai, out of which thirty-six are said to have been killed. In the next chapter, Joshua sends thirty thousand warriors in the second strategic assault (8:3), with another five thousand in hiding (8:12). The final report states that twelve thousand inhabitants of Ai were killed that day (8:25). This story, with its concrete numbers, parallels the Jericho story, which reports that *all in the city* were killed (6:21).

Scholars have proposed two approaches to large numbers in the Bible (see Fouts). The first approach treats the Hebrew word *'elep* as either "thousand" or "clan, troop, or squad," depending on the context. Accordingly, some of the numbers above would be reduced considerably to, for example, thirty fighting groups in Joshua 8:3. According to a second approach, more consistent with ancient Near Eastern scribal techniques, the large numbers are hyperbolic. In similar historical reports of conquests, scribes employed "numerical hyperbole to glorify a given king; the writers of Israel's history did the same to glorify the King of kings (or one of his theocratic rulers)" (Fouts: 753). According to Fouts, such "numerical hyperbole may be seen as both polemical and theological," reflecting the "common literary convention of purposeful embellishment" (752–53). A clear example of such hyperbole can be seen in the Mesha Inscription (line 16), where the text reports that seven thousand Israelites were killed in one battle (see *Mesha Inscription, p. 447*).

IDOLATRY Almost nothing in the book of Joshua makes sense without setting it in the context of Deuteronomy's exhortations to worship and serve only one God (e.g., Deut 5:6-10; 6:4-5). The covenantal framework of Deuteronomy assumes that allegiance to God alone also means saying no to all other gods, all other claims to ultimate religious and political loyalty (6:14). Other gods are a chief concern of Deuteronomy, being mentioned more than forty times. Yet this one God rescued Israel from slavery; this One has made a claim on this people; and this One calls Israel to a life governed by God's word. The Deuteronomic appeal to exclusive allegiance to Yahweh and the call to reject other gods find echoes throughout the OT, from Elijah's contest with the prophets of Baal (1 Kings 18) to the accounting for Israel's defeat (2 Kings 17:7, 33, 35-38), and on to the prophetic proclamation to the exiles in Babylon that the gods of empire are no gods at all (Isa 43:10; 44:6; 45:5, 14, 18, 21, 22; 46:9).

In the book of Joshua, the word *gods* appears only in the final three chapters of the book, chapters laden with Deuteronomic language (22:22; 23:7, 16; 24:2, 14-16, 20, 23). Israel's God is called *God of gods!* (22:22). Choosing to serve the Lord, and not other gods, is Joshua's plea: *Put away the gods that are among you* (24:23). These chapters mention *other gods* three times, each time in language reminiscent of Deuteronomy (Josh 23:16; 24:2, 16). Each of those occurrences is in the context of covenantal monotheism, in which other gods may be worshiped/served, as did the ancestors (24:2), but serving other gods constitutes a violation of the exclusive covenant relationship (23:16). Covenant commitment involves saying "no" to the gods and saying "yes" to exclusive allegiance to Yahweh (24:16). Violation of that exclusivity leads to perishing quickly from the good land given to Israel by God (23:16).

Oddly, the name Baal, the most frequently mentioned Canaanite deity in the books of Kings, is not mentioned in Joshua except in place names (thirty-five times after 1 Kings 16:31; otherwise in the Pentateuch only in Num 23:3, 5; Deut 4:3 and in the DtrH in Judg 2:13; 6:25-32; 8:33; 9:4). The particulars are not important for Joshua. The generic temptation is the main concern of the book, which sets up the paradigmatic concerns emerging from the book of Deuteronomy (cf. Judg 6:10).

The temptation for Israel was to "polytheize"—to trust in other nations that were more powerful and numerous and to trust in their great gods. The biblical call, beginning with Deuteronomy, is an invitation, amid competing ideologies and worldviews, to pledge allegiance to only one. This press toward single-minded and exclusive worship of Yahweh is borne through the centuries as a monotheizing impulse (James Sanders: 43–44). Deuteronomy therefore includes an anti-idolatry polemic—a vigorous argument against the gods (4:16, 23, 25; 5:8) that includes destruction of pagan shrines and images (7:5; 12:3). Although Joshua does not include the words "idol" or "idolatry," it bears Deuteronomy's confessional polemic. The aniconic (without idols or images) tradition exists, according to Deuteronomy's explanation, because Israel "saw no form" (4:12). This gave rise to the emphasis, in Deuteronomy, on the priority of the divine word (4:10, 12, 15; 8:3) and divine name (5:11; 12:5, 11) as mediators of God's presence. Israel's relationship to Yahweh was an exclusive relationship that did not deny the reality of other gods, even of other gods that have been assigned by Yahweh (29:26; 32:8-9). Deuteronomy vigorously calls Israel not to worship those gods. Even so, Deuteronomy seems to assume that Israel in exile will do so (4:28).

Deuteronomy takes up the concern about "other gods" and makes it into a leitmotif that runs through the book (4:28; 5:7; 6:14; 7:4; 8:19; 11:16, 28; 13:2-3, 6, 13; 17:3; 18:20; 28:14, 36, 64; 29:25-26; 30:17-18; 31:18, 20). Even more telling is the notion that these gods are a danger to Israel's exclusive allegiance (covenant) with Yahweh (31:16), which mirrors the earlier statements in Deuteronomy about Yahweh's exclusive choice of Israel from among the nations in 7:1-26, a text that also includes statements about God's clearing away many nations (7:1, 22) and a prohibition against covenant making (7:2). Rather, Israel is to live as a people chosen and loved by God (7:6-8).

The polemic against "other gods" in Deuteronomy and the DtrH must also be understood as part and parcel of Israel's perception of itself as over against dangerous "other peoples." The book of Joshua not only participates in the struggle toward monotheism, but also in the related conflict against the people groups associated with the worship of other deities. In rather mythic language, Deuteronomy 33 depicts the conquest as a divine ride through the heavens, subduing "ancient gods" and "forces of old" even as he "drove out the enemy before you" (33:27). The defeat of the historical (Canaanite) and the cosmic (gods) enemies are linked in one and the same divine act. Deuteronomy advocates exterminating the Canaanites "so that they may not teach you to do all the abhorrent things that they do for their gods" (20:18). In these books it is both the gods of the nations and the peoples that are dangerous to Israel. Israel's *ḥerem* laws (Deut 20) find their meaning in this context. The command to annihilate the enemy in Deuteronomy and Joshua is intimately linked to a worldview in which the peoples and their gods are inextricable *[Conquest Accounts, p. 406]*. Thus 2 Samuel 7:23 even asserts the incomparability of Yahweh because of his "driving out before his people nations *and their gods*" (emph. added; cf. Judg 11:24).

The NT writers all live within the world of Jewish covenantal monotheism. Yet that monotheism is not defined over against idolatry as a single practice. Idolatry, or worship of other gods, extends from Jesus' warning about the impossibility of serving two masters, "God and wealth" (Matt 6:24), to Paul's definition of "greed" as "idolatry" (Col 3:5). In both cases the disloyalty to one's covenantal allegiance is not technically a worship of a specific deity (in the traditional sense of that word), but wealth/greed has become the "consuming passion" (see book by that title edited by Clapp). Where the NT reflects engagement with those who revere other gods, the apostles sometimes exhibit respect, as though the idolaters' understanding is but a partial truth that might lead them to embrace Jesus as the embodiment of God (e.g., Acts 17:22-31). Where there is polemic, it is in the context of debate, not warfare (Acts 19:26; 1 Cor 8:5). Thus the debate in which Paul is accused of speaking about "foreign divinities" (Acts 17:18) in Athens actually allows for affirmation rather than othering of his human opponents (Acts 17).

More insidious than the gods themselves, therefore, are those social and political arrangements and spiritual powers that claim our allegiance and worship without being labeled divine (see works by Wink and Boyd, who explore those ideas more fully). Just as Isaiah was quite aware of the danger of imperial idolatry, so also the book of Revelation warns of such allegiances that vie for human loyalty (Rev 13; ch. 18) and asserts that only the slain Lamb is worthy to receive human worship. Reflecting on the dangers of subtle deception, J. H. Yoder writes: "In the politics of rebellious mankind, we are ready to sacrifice persons to causes, even to ideas. General labels like 'freedom' or 'justice,' 'socialism' or 'capitalism,' 'order' or 'humanism' become positive or negative values in their own right, causes to combat for or to destroy. The modern word for this is 'ideology.' The biblical word that fits best is probably 'idol'" (1997: 232). In a provocative conclusion to his reflection on worshiping other gods in the context of Christian nationalism, Lee Camp writes, "The most important question about our pledge of allegiance is not whether we pledge allegiance to a flag under 'one God,' but to *what* god we are pledging our allegiance. Perhaps it is, after all, not the God revealed in Jesus Christ we are worshiping, but the god of the nation-state, the god of power and might and wealth" (130).

For further reflection on idolatry, see Beale; Miller 2004; Meadors; Middleton; Rosner 1999, 2007; Ramachandra; Shenk; and the spring 2011 issue of *Vision: A Journal for Theology and the Church*.

LAND: GIFTED AND LOST

The Gift of Land The book of Joshua begins with the Lord about to give the land, as promised to the ancestors (Gen 12:7; 13:15, 17; 15:7, 18; 17:8; 24:7; 26:3; 28:4, 13; 35:12; Exod 6:4, 8), a promise that is reiterated throughout Deuteronomy (1:8; 4:1; 6:10, 18, 23; 7:13; 10:11; 11:9, 21; 19:8; 26:3; 28:11; 30:20; 31:7; 34:4). The motif of "giving" occurs eight times in Joshua 1 alone (see also 2:9, 14, 24; 5:6; 8:1; 9:24; 13:6; 18:3; 22:4; 23:13, 15, 16; 24:13).

The gift of land to Israel, along with the hints of exile in Deuteronomy, must be viewed in relation to Deuteronomy's notion that God has also given land to other people groups, and in doing so has dispossessed other indigenous peoples as well (Deut 2:8-23). Deuteronomy also announces that "the Most High apportioned the nations [and] . . . fixed the boundaries of the peoples." Just as "Jacob" is the Lord's "allotted share," these peoples each have their own gods (Deut 32:8-9), and their apportionment is "according to the number of the gods" (NRSV, as in the Qumran manuscripts, a thousand years older than the MT, which has "according to the number of the sons of Israel"; LXX has "according to the number of the messengers/ angels of God"). A monotheizing tendency is evident in the tradition, in which, over time, "the gods" disappear from the text (cf. Ps 82). Jephthah negotiates with the King of the Ammonites, who states his right to his own land (Judg 11:13), to which Jephthah responds by saying, "So now the LORD, the God of Israel, has conquered the Amorites for the benefit of his people Israel. Do you intend to take their place? Should you not possess what your god Chemosh gives you to possess? And should we not be the ones to possess everything that the LORD our God has conquered for our benefit?" (11:23-24).

According to Deuteronomic theology, the story of dispossession in Joshua is in continuity with God's direct involvement in the dispossession of people groups in times past. Amos testifies to a similar all-encompassing divine sovereignty among the nations, giving each of them their own "exodus" (9:7-8). In Amos it is "the sinful kingdom" that God will destroy. God's sovereignty, in other words, allows him both to give and to take, but not to act arbitrarily, apart from a moral compass. The rise and fall of nations is viewed, at least by some in the prophetic tradition, as God's governance in the face of evil. God has "made the earth" and therefore asserts, "I give it to whomever I please" (Jer 27:5), even Nebuchadnezzar (27:6). Yet his "time" will also come (27:7). In the case of the indigenous Canaanite population, Deuteronomy ascribes their defeat by God to "the wickedness of these nations" (9:4; cf. their "iniquity" in Gen 15:16). Joshua, however, nowhere mentions their wickedness or their iniquity, but warns about the dangers of their gods. That emphasis, however, can only be seen in Joshua if we assume the perspective of Genesis 15:16 and the prophetic judgment on the nations for crimes against humanity (Amos 1–2). But that critique is not explicit in Joshua, where *Israel's* covenantal relationship with God is the primary concern.

Prior to such obligation, however, the book of Joshua affirms that the gift of land is grounded in the assurance of God's presence: *I will not fail you or forsake you* (1:5b). Israel's entry into the land across the Jordan will be like Israel's exit from Egypt across the Red Sea. Only now, instead of wilderness, God is giving them a place of *rest* (cf. Exod 33:14; Num 32:20-22; Deut 3:18-20; 12:10; 25:19; 2 Sam 7:1, 11; 1 Kings 5:4; 8:56) *[Rest, p. 455]*. Those who might *stand against you* (Josh 1:5) are like Pharaoh and his army. By inference, they cannot stand (cf. Pss 2:1-2; 110:1, 5-6).

In Joshua 1 obedience is also associated with "rest," which is rooted in Deuteronomy's notion of faithfulness to God's instruction (Josh 1:7-8). In a number of places, Deuteronomy affirms that obedience is a condition for entry into the land (6:18; 8:1; 11:8-9) and for remaining in the land (11:8-9,

18-21). Deuteronomy 16:20 distills the criterion further to "justice" as a prerequisite, "so that you may live and occupy the land that the Lord your God is giving you."

Accountability to the Gift The *gift* of land, therefore, invites (renewed) obedience to covenantal instruction. We do well to remember that even in some of the ancestral promises, the gift is provisional. As the Lord reflects concerning Abraham, "I have chosen him . . . to keep the way of the Lord by doing righteousness and justice; so that the Lord may bring about for Abraham what he has promised him" (Gen 18:19; cf. 26:5). The connection between obedience and acquisition of the land is especially stressed in Deuteronomy, along with the threat of land loss (Deut 11; ch. 28). In the light of Israel's covenant violation, the promise of God's presence affirms that God's compassionate presence transcends human rebellion but does not cancel the consequences of disobedience (cf. Deut 4:31 in context).

Even so, the tension between divine commitment and human obligation (with the implied condition of keeping/losing the land) underscores the theme of divine presence in Joshua 1 and throughout the book. The assured presence of God echoes both the promise of presence to the ancestors (Gen 26:3; 31:3) and to Moses (Exod 3:12). Both Moses and God reiterate the promise in Deuteronomy (31:8, 23). The theme appears again in the call of Jeremiah (Jer 1:8). In both Moses' and Jeremiah's situations, the fear of failure stands out in their response to God (cf. Deut 31:6, 8). The Lord is "with" the community; the Lord will not fail or forsake.

The book of Joshua therefore shares in the larger biblical thematic of land, which according to Brueggemann is "gift, promise, and challenge in biblical faith" (from the subtitle of his book of 2002). It is a "prism for biblical faith," for it is "a central, if not *the central theme* of biblical faith" (3). Right relationship with the land begins with the Lord's affirmation to the ancestors that land is above all gifted land. Such gift is contingent on responding to a prior call to leave known land (Mesopotamia for the ancestors, slavery for Israel in Egypt) and to embrace homelessness and exile/wilderness in order to receive the gift. Only such obedience and trust in the Lord's promissory word creates the possibility of receiving the gift of land. And only such trust empowers Israel to live in the Lord's presence in the context of exile.

In particular, the book of Joshua is grounded in the promise of land to Israel's landless ancestors (1:2, 6; 5:6; 18:3; 21:43-44; 24:2) and the liberation of Israel's ancestors from Egypt (24:6, 17). Those ancient traditions serve not only to highlight God's gift of land, but more importantly to buttress the call to covenant loyalty, the rejection of idolatry, and the attentiveness to God's instruction (Torah: 1:7-8; 24:14-24). Above all, the book of Joshua highlights the presence of God (1:9; 22:31; 23:10; 24:8-13). The divine "I" takes initiative to give the land and to invite covenant loyalty in response. The reality of land is the context for relationship, disloyalty the occasion for loss of land (23:13, 15-16). Such disloyalty is expressed primarily in lack of attention to God's Torah (1:7-9; 23:3-13). Even so, the book of Joshua is preeminently grounded in Deuteronomy's notion of God's gift (*milk and honey*, Josh 5:6/Deut 6:3; 11:9; *good land*, Josh 23:13-16/Deut 1:25; *perish . . . from the good land*, Josh 23:16/Deut 11:17; towns not built by Israel, Josh 24:13/Deut 6:10; etc.).

Since the land belongs to the Lord (Lev 25:23; Josh 22:19), the land is to be considered a divine grant to the clan groups in Joshua even though ownership remains in God's hands. The gift confers both permission and responsibility. The gift assumes that God is the primary historical actor, not Israel (Josh 24:11-13). But to remain in the land requires obedience to God's instruction (Torah), not military defense strategies or political alliances. It is faithfulness to Torah that consolidates the gift, and disloyalty that presents the threat of loss and exile. The tragedy of the larger story is that Joshua's dire warning proves true: Israel *cannot serve the Lord* (24:19). The temptations of landedness, even the very gifts of the land itself, can become the occasion for "perishing" (Deut 8; Josh 23:16; 24:13, 20).

Hence the grasping of Achan is a prelude to loss, and Joshua's nearly cynical jibe about Israel's inability to be loyal (24:19-20) hints at what may yet come to pass. Even so, the book of Joshua remains firmly grounded in promise and trust, which Joshua affirms over and over (e.g., 24:12). The taking and the receiving live in tension with each other in the book of Joshua. Yet land, God, and peoplehood remain inextricably bound together, even in the transpositions required by exile and by longing for the kingdom to come in its fullness.

It is as though the book of Joshua embraces the entire story of land promised, covenant disloyalty, and land lost. Deuteronomy assumes the reality of exile, which Joshua anticipates. The notion of being plucked up off the land (Deut 28:63-65) and of perishing from the land (4:26; 29:28), "as is now the case" (29:28), hovers in the background. Only the notion of God's loyalty beyond human waywardness is a stronger presence in Deuteronomy (e.g., 4:31; 30:6). Although Deuteronomy's hopefulness assumes a reciprocal choice of "life" (30:1-20), as does Joshua's call to *choose this day whom you will serve* (Josh 24:15), the divine "I" stands ever present even among those whom Joshua provokes with his *You cannot serve the Lord* (24:19).

Although a theology of land grounds and frames the book of Joshua, it is not the conquest of land that stands out as its signal contribution to biblical theology. The book of Joshua participates in a long intrabiblical conversation that remains "in travail" (Girard 1987a: 141) between the particular and the universal. For example, a biblical theology of land is rooted in the gift of land to Israel (the particular, expressed in the promises to the ancestors in Genesis and reinforced in Deuteronomy), and flowers into an inheritance of the whole earth by the meek (the universal, expressed in Jesus' beatitude of Matt 5:5). Moreover, theology of land often seems to live hand in hand with ideology of land. It is as though the particulars of landless anticipation (ancestral promise), possession (conquest and royal governance), loss (exile), and restoration (return to land) must also be negotiated in historical moments where power, oppression, and life under colonial rule require retellings, reinterpretations, and reimagining of the tradition over time.

It is this dynamism that gives birth to a variety of perspectives on land in the Bible. Norman Habel (1995) has sketched six such "ideologies": (1)

land as source of wealth (royal ideology, as reflected in 1 Kings 3–10 and royal psalms); (2) land as conditional grant (theocratic ideology, as in Deuteronomy); (3) land as family lots (ancestral household ideology, as in Joshua); (4) the land as the Lord's personal entitlement and rightful property (prophetic ideology, as in Jeremiah); (5) land as Sabbath bound (agrarian ideology, as in Lev 25–27); (6) land as host country (immigrant ideology, as in the Abraham narratives). Although there is a tendency to isolate these ideologies in particular texts, it is more likely that various texts share aspects of these ideologies. A holistic approach to texts recognizes emphases or thematic elements within texts but does not restrict a particular text to a single "ideology." Texts are far too porous and cross too many historical boundaries for that to be the case. For example, Joshua participates in Deuteronomy's notion of land as gift and conditional grant (ideology 2), and is grounded in the notion of land as host country (ideology 6) in both the ancestral promises (Genesis) and in the practice of negotiation (Rahab, Gibeonites) reflected in the Abraham narrative. Joshua draws from royal ideology (ideology 1) in its parallels between Joshua and Josiah, but transforms the royal metaphor into a prophetic call to loyalty of family units to God and to God's instruction, Torah (ideology 3: Josh 1:8; 8:34-35; 23:6; 24:26). And throughout the narrative of Joshua is the undercurrent of Sabbath rest (ideology 5: Josh 1:13; 11:23; 22:4), which relies on the notion of land as God's own possession (ideology 4: Josh 22:19).

The Gift and the Scandal of Particularity The promise and possession of land has created a scandal of particularity. How is it that one (particular) people can be granted their own land to the exclusion of Others? The particularity of election, and therefore of the promise and reality of land, continues as "joy and burden" for the Jewish community (Blumenthal: 20; on election, see Kaminsky 2007; Lohr). That burden is particularly evident in the modern state of Israel and in the West Bank (occupied territories), where Palestinians have been marginalized and excluded for decades in a land that had been their home. Although the Jewish community is divided on whether life in the land or life in Diaspora are equally viable ways of being Jewish, the political and military solutions to the conflict in Israel/Palestine draws primarily on the particularity of the biblical texts, yet without always finding ways to live toward the vision of blessing promised and commanded, and shalom implied, by the call of Abraham (Gen 12:1-3).

But that is not necessarily the perspective of the book of Joshua. Those who enter into the covenant with Yahweh are those who trust in the God who has liberated slaves from captivity, including Rahab and other "resident aliens." Certainly the indigenous population continues to offer tempting options that run counter to Yahweh's call to exclusive allegiance. But the concern of the book of Joshua is to show that, however tenuous such faithfulness might be, it is possible even in the midst of those people groups that Israel is unable to dispossess.

The particularity and burden of land creates problems for both Jews and Christians. From a political studies perspective, Tony Judt argues in his controversial article in *The New York Review of Books*:

> The problem with Israel, in short, is not—as is sometimes suggested—that it is a European "enclave" in the Arab world; but rather that it arrived too late. It has imported a characteristically late-nineteenth-century separatist project into a world that has moved on, a world of individual rights, open frontiers, and international law. The very idea of a "Jewish state"—a state in which Jews and the Jewish religion have exclusive privileges from which non-Jewish citizens are forever excluded—is rooted in another time and place. Israel, in short, is an anachronism. . . . Israel itself is a multicultural society in all but name; yet it remains distinctive among democratic states in its resort to ethnoreligious criteria with which to denominate and rank its citizens. It is an oddity among modern nations not—as its more paranoid supporters assert—because it is a Jewish state and no one wants the Jews to have a state; but because it is a Jewish state in which one community—Jews—is set above others, in an age when that sort of state has no place.

That argument is dismissed out of hand by those who believe political control of the land was always destined to be in Jewish hands. Jews who currently live near Jericho (since 1993) argue that

> Jericho reflects the Israeli reality. There is a grave injustice. The heart of the Land, Jericho and the Temple Mount, have been handed over to the enemy. The People fight for the gates of the body—the border—yet they disregard the heart.
>
> Just as in the time of Joshua, Jericho is the peak of defilement. This defilement guards the holiness that must soon be revealed in Jericho. "Remove your shoes from your feet," the angel in Jericho told Joshua. "This place is holy." We must return to the area by Torah-guided activities, effort to bond with the land, and Torah-based creativity. (www.jewishjericho.org.il/english/thoughts/hashkafa.html)

Similarly, Wyschogrod argues that the conquest of the land is necessary (220): "If Israel is not sovereign in the political realm, then the redemption has not yet occurred. Israel is meant to be ruled by Hashem, who is its only real king" (219; Hashem is Heb. for "the name," meaning God). Because conquest is necessary, "the potential for conflict with the ethical arises" (220). The solution, he thinks, is in the retained memory of conquest. "The land had to be conquered. The result has been that Jewish consciousness has vividly retained the memory of the land as having belonged to others before it came to belong to Israel. Other nations do not retain such memories" (220). Other nations have land-bound identities, whereas Israel came into being on the basis of promise before having land and continues to exist even after losing land. "The radical novelty of Hashem's teaching was that his jurisdiction extended everywhere. He was therefore not the God of only one territory but rather of a people who were subject to him wherever they were" (221). Yet God wants a bond to land: God dwells on the earth and not just in heaven. God's authority "permeates somewhat more sharply the land of Israel, which is holy because he dwells on it" (222). Because of that, according to Wyschogrod, "Judaism is the religion of the land of Israel. It is a religion that is inconceivable without the land of Israel. The land is not simply a locale in which, it so happens, Judaism developed. It is an essential component of the faith because it is the location of God's preeminent dwelling, both past and present. Thus the God of Israel is identified primarily in two ways: as the God of the Jewish people and as the God who dwells in Jerusalem" (245).

Segal offers a different perspective, which highlights Israel's obligation rather than its claim to a divine right to land: "Never could the Jews cite a 'natural right,' nor could their claim, no matter how phrased, be absolute. Neither could the obligation of possession ever be understood to be fulfilled through achievement of control; possession implied further duties. Unlike the medieval Western doctrine of the Divine Right of Kings, which was meant to stifle questions and to guarantee power, the view of Israel as a divine gift led to a universe of obligation, duty, and a tenuous hold on the Land" (31).

Those modern voices affirming Israel's connection to the land (whether focusing on gift or responsibility) seem as much derived from modern notions of the nation-state as from biblical interpretation. Halpern-Amaru's reflection on the reinterpretation of biblical land/covenant texts in postbiblical Jewish literature suggests that return to the land was not necessarily construed in political terms. Rather, the biblical narratives of exodus and entry into the land became experiences valid for all time, not necessarily paradigms guaranteeing political control. For example, in the writer known as Pseudo-Philo, according to Halpern-Amaru, "the covenant assures eternal peoplehood, not everlasting possession of the Land, for in historical fact, once achieved[,] Israelite possession was not eternal. Within Israel's history possession was lost, and the fact of that loss—the Babylonian exile—negates any statement of the patriarchal covenant that would include divine assurance of everlasting possession" (80). Such paradigmatic events as the exodus, conquest, and exile become figural events that have become transposed into new settings over time.

Today Jews and Palestinians (both Christians and Muslims) share the inheritance of land. The State of Israel was born in the confluence of Zionism and nineteenth-century nationalisms. The twenty-first century will likely see ongoing challenges as all residents of that troubled land continue to find ways to live together in peace. Israeli Jews and Palestinians (both Israeli citizens and those in the Palestinian territories) will need to let go of their particularity in order to embrace the other.

For concise summaries on land in the Bible, see P. Williamson; W. Janzen (1992). For various explorations, including land theology and the Israeli-Palestinian conflict, see Brueggemann 2002; Burge 2003, 2010; Chapman; Davies 1991, 1992; Gordon; Greenberg 1995; Habel 1995; L. Hoffman; Orlinsky; March; Miller 1969; Sizer; Weaver 2007; Weinfeld 1993. On Jewish and Christian responses to the scandal of particularity, see Bader-Saye; Ellis; Kaminsky 2007; Kinzer; Lohr; Novak; Weaver 2008; Wyschogrod; J. H. Yoder 2003. See also the essay *Conquest and Land in the NT, p. 411.*

LEVITICAL CITIES The book of Numbers does not name the cities of refuge and forty-eight Levitical towns (35:6-7). The Levitical cities are named only in the distribution lists and well before the actual settlement of these cities. Once in the land, the Levites begin to function as Deuteronomy specifies. They are responsible for the ark and the Torah. Over time they become teachers and interpreters of the law (Deut 33:8-11).

The identification of cities for the Levites (Josh 21:1-42) ends the distribution of the land to the tribes of Israel. The summary statement of 21:43-45 highlights all the stereotypical expressions reflecting completeness that were first expressed earlier in the book. As such, the distribution list is ideal, having been implemented during the monarchy. Not all the towns were always in Israelite possession, as can be seen in the Mesha Inscription, where Jahaz (= Jahzah, Josh 21:36), one of the towns in Transjordan, falls into Moabite control. As the last act of distribution, remarkably at the Levites' own initiative, the identification of Levitical cities fills out the enactment of Moses' instructions to Joshua in Numbers 35 to establish cities for the Levites and cities of refuge (see Explanatory Notes on Josh 21).

A similar list of Levitical cities occurs in 1 Chronicles 6:54-81, where the list has been placed immediately after King David's appointments of musicians (6:31-53). Chronicles does not mention the allotments within the tribe of Dan, perhaps because the Chronicler knows that Dan never actually settled in the territory allotted in the book of Joshua (Josh 19:40-48; Judg 1:34-36; 18:1-31). The same could be said for other cities listed in Joshua 21. A good number of the cities were not in Israelite possession until much later (e.g., Judg 1:27, 29, 31; 1 Kings 9:16). It is most likely that Chronicles depends on the list in Joshua, although the Chronicler includes a listing of the Aaron priests first, perhaps to highlight their relative importance (1 Chron 6:54-60; cf. Josh 21:13-20).

Ezekiel rearranges the tradition significantly. He identifies the "levitical priests, the descendants of Zadok," as those who attend to the sacrifices (44:15). Their task in Ezekiel's vision is to "teach my people the difference between the holy and the common, and show them how to distinguish between the unclean and the clean. In a controversy they shall act as judges" (44:23-24). Ezekiel reports that these Zadokite priests do not receive an inheritance, since "I am their holding" (44:28). In Ezekiel's visionary provision, the priests and the Levites live in separately designated areas within the "holy portion [district]" surrounding the temple (45:4-5; 48:10-14). The LXX interprets this small area designated by Ezekiel with the language of the old tradition, a wording reflected in the NRSV: "cities to live in" (45:5b).

For a more comprehensive survey, see Hartley.

MESHA INSCRIPTION This inscription, also known as the Moabite Stone or Mesha Stela, is an account in which King Mesha (late ninth century BC), with the help of his god Chemosh (Kemosh), conquers part of the Transjordan area (Medeba), thereby recovering it from Israelite control. The inscription is discussed in several essays [*Conquest Accounts, p. 406; Anger of the Lord, p. 386; Genocide and Sacred Violence, p. 430; Ḥerem, p. 433; Hyperbole,* *p. 437; Theology of Warfare, p. 458].* W. F. Albright's translation is in *ANET* 320–21. A more recent translation is in Hallo, 2:137–38. K. C. Hanson's adaptation of Albright's translation is at http://www.kchanson.com/ANCDOCS/westsem/mesha.html.

For interpreting the book of Joshua, the following are the most important lines from the original inscription:

> Omri was the king of Israel, and he oppressed Moab for many days, for Kemosh was angry at his land. . . . And Omri took possession of the whole land of Medeba, and he lived there in his days and half the days of his son: forty years. But Kemosh restored it in my days. . . . And the men of Gad lived in the land of Atarot from ancient times; and the king of Israel built Atarot for himself, and I fought against the city and captured it. And I killed all the people of the city as a sacrifice for Kemosh and for Moab. . . . And Kemosh said to me, "Go, take Nebo from Israel." And I went in the night and fought against it from the daybreak until midday, and I took it and I killed the whole population: seven thousand male subjects and aliens, and female subjects, aliens, and servant girls. For I had put it to the ban [*ḥerem*] for Ashtar Kemosh. And from there I took the vessels of Yahweh, and I presented them before the face of Kemosh. . . . Kemosh drove him [the king of Israel] away before my face. (Hanson's translation, from lines 4–19)

MODELS OF THE SETTLEMENT The book of Joshua seems to present both a unified total conquest of the land of Canaan (e.g., 10:40-42; 11:16, 23) and an incomplete partial conquest (13:1, 13; 15:63; 16:10; 17:12-13) *[Plot Tensions in Joshua, p. 452].* Moreover, the book of Judges seems to confirm not a quick and thorough conquest, but a settlement that emerged over a long period of time, even after the death of Joshua. Some of those events are described in Judges as taking place after the death of Joshua even though they have already been narrated in Joshua (Josh 15:14b-19/Judg 1:10b-15; Josh 15:13-14/Judg 1:20; Josh 15:63 and 18:28/Judg 1:21, where Judah and Benjamin are assigned the same inheritance; Josh 17:11-13/Judg 1:27-28; Josh 16:10/Judg 1:29). Moreover, the LXX version of the book of Joshua contains a good many rearranged textual units, additions, and divergent readings (it is four-to-five percent shorter than the MT), which makes it difficult to know how to evaluate texts for historical reconstruction (for a summary of these difficulties, see Meier: 426).

Archaeological research has also demonstrated a complexity in the material remains that cannot easily be correlated with the ambiguous evidence of the biblical accounts *[Archaeology and Joshua, p. 389].* These ambiguities have given rise to various hypotheses, or models, of conquest and/or settlement by Israel in the land of Canaan, none of which are adequate in and of themselves. As the following four proposed models will imply, establishing a fixed date for the settlement of the land is impossible. Hypotheses range from the fifteenth to twelfth centuries BC (see Ortiz; Meier).

Unified Conquest According to W. F. Albright (in the 1930s), archaeological evidence supports the view that Israel gained the land as a result of military conquest at the end of the Late Bronze Age (thirteenth century BC), thereby confirming the broad outline of events as reported in the book of Joshua. Albright acknowledged that the military campaign occurred in the late thirteenth century BC, but that ongoing struggle with the existing population continued for centuries. The Conquest Model affirms the basic historicity of reported events and tries to correlate the text with archaeological evidence. Discrepancies between the text and archaeological evidence are often ascribed to inadequate knowledge, misinterpretation of archaeological evidence, or the etiological (explanatory) character of biblical texts.

Peaceful Infiltration Based on correlation of social transitions within specific geographical areas, Albrecht Alt and Martin Noth (1960) championed the hypothesis—modified by others since then—that various pastoral nomadic and/or farming groups entered the land and settled in unoccupied areas in the hill country, eventually merging with existing Canaanite groups and coalescing around the worship of Yahweh. There was no massive exodus from Egypt. Rather, settlement of pastoralists in the hill country was made possible primarily by the introduction of terracing and cisterns cut from limestone and sealed with lime plaster. According to this view, the biblical narrators invented the entrance-into-the-land narrative (as etiological/ explanatory) in order to promote the view that Israel originated from a common ancestor outside the land. According to early proponents of this model, neither archaeology nor the Bible provides a complete or adequate picture of the complexity of social movement and geographical settlement during the period. More recent analysis of archaeological evidence leads some archaeologists to support this model (Ray: 82). And evidence from the book of Joshua supports the model: the lack of conquest accounts for some areas (e.g., Shechem, Josh 8:30-35; 24:1, 32), incorporation of the Gibeonites (Josh 9), inclusion of so-called non-Israelites (Rahab, Caleb), and incorporation of Canaanite towns into biblical kinship lists (Machir, Shechem, Tirzah, Hepher in 17:1-6).

Peasant Revolt / Internal Revolution Later and in a more nuanced way, George Mendenhall (1970, 1973) and Norman Gottwald suggested that Israel emerged in Canaan through a complex combination of social revolt by oppressed indigenous landless peasants who rallied against oppressive Canaanite city-states. These peasants then joined small groups of escaped Egyptian slaves, who brought with them the worship of Yahweh. This creation of a covenantal unity around commitment to Yahweh reflected the religious ideals of the new social revolution, which imagined an alternative to the feudal society of statist Canaan. The model has been modified by others who reject the notion of a peasant revolt and suggest, rather, a more complex social process involving both pastoralists and agriculturalists (see Ray: 85–88).

Transition: Late Bronze Age to Iron Age I Based on complex technological, social, economic, and political changes occurring at the transition between the Late Bronze Age and the Iron Age, this model affirms that Israel emerged in Canaan as a people not determined primarily by ethnicity or religion, but by the land itself and the political and economic climate of the time. The model affirms a long process of settlement and symbiosis. Yet it also allows for conquest accounts that report hill-country settlers engaging with lowland inhabitants. This process would have taken centuries, crystallizing during Israel's monarchic era (see Ray: 88–90).

Each of the models is an attempt to make sense of either textual or archaeological data or both. Hess has suggested, "To accept all the models to at least some degree is not simply to opt for a 'middle of the road' position but to affirm the diversity of human motivations and social action involved in the process of becoming a people" (1993: 132–33). Archaeological research is ongoing and incomplete. "None of the models, by itself, fully does justice to the archaeological evidence or the textual data (both biblical and extrabiblical). Although each of these schools has developed some compelling points, the emergence of Israel is very complex" (Ray: 91). It is very likely that Israel emerged in Canaan through a settlement process that took several centuries, and that Israel was constituted by various groups coming from Egypt, Transjordan, and from within Canaan itself, as the commentary points out (see Meier: 429–30, 433). At least some form of Israel as a peoplehood existed in the land at the time of Egyptian Pharaoh Merneptah (1213–1203 BC), whose stela refers to Israel as a people, or population group, but not as a nation (for a full exploration, see Hasel 2008a).

As will be obvious to readers, this commentary has not focused on historical reconstruction of the Israelite conquest and settlement in Canaan. Various historical reconstructions of how Israel emerged in Canaan help us to understand that the book of Joshua is not modern historiography *[Composition of Joshua, p. 398]*. Instead, the book of Joshua presents us with a schematic theological and literary historiography that is riddled with a theological point of view, even though much of the source material in the book may well be grounded in authentic historical memory (as the essays in the volume edited by Hess, Klingbeil, and Ray clearly demonstrate).

The book presents us not so much with the *how* of the conquest, but the *who*. Yahweh is in the process of shaping a people in a land. That land is a gift that invites faithfulness as a condition of retaining the land and that risks the loss of land as the cost of unfaithfulness. Nevertheless, set within the larger contours of the DtrH, the book of Joshua suggests that Yahweh is ultimately faithful and can be trusted with Israel's future. The testimony of the book of Joshua is essentially that it was not Israel that emerged, but Israel whom God created in the land. This testimony cannot be confirmed or denied by archaeology or by historical models. Coote states that "no author yet can be in a position to claim knowledge of exactly how Israel originated" (1990: 6). Or as Halpern observes, "Extrinsic models always do violence to local particularities" (1992: 65). Thus, as Hess affirms, "The conclusions which the evidence suggests is that the biblical evidence does not perfectly coincide with any of the models proposed. In itself this neither 'proves' nor 'disproves' these accounts. The biblical material serves purposes other than those which the modern historian may seek" (1993: 133).

For survey and discussion of the issues, see articles by Ray and Mazani; Dever 2003: ch. 4; Halpern 1983; Hess 1993; Meier; Merling 1997; Ortiz; Provan, Long, and Longman: 138–49; Rasmussen; Younger 1999.

NARRATIVE THEOLOGY AND COMMUNAL IDENTITY Because we live by the stories we tell, attentiveness to the figural and transformative dynamics of the biblical drama is significant, especially so because narratives like Joshua are not straightforwardly didactic. A description of an event does not automatically endorse the assumptions underlying that description. Wise readers will not be fooled by the surface of a narrative. They will listen to the gaps, the voices that speak around the fringes, and the intrabiblical interpretation that refocuses attention away from the violence and toward the cosmic purposes of God for the nations. In other words, a story may open up to more than it tells.

For example, J. H. Yoder begins his chapter "God Will Fight for Us" in *The Politics of Jesus* by suggesting that the approach of harmonizing two generalizations—that God sanctions war in the OT and that war is contrary to the will of God—is not an appropriate way of dealing with the biblical texts. "For the believing Israelite, the Scriptures would not have been read with this kind of question in mind. Rather than reading with the modern question in mind, whether it confirms certain moral generalizations or not, the Israelite read it as his or her own story, as the account of his or her own past throwing light on who he or she was. A story may include a moral implication or presuppose moral judgments, but it does not necessarily begin at that point" (1994: 76). Nor, we might add, are those moral judgments or implications necessarily normative for later communities of faith. What matters for later readers has more to do with the discernment of God's purposes through time than with discerning normative truths from any particular narrative.

Throughout the commentary and in various essays, I have recognized that the Gospel writers interpret the Jesus story through the lens of the ancient biblical narrative plot of exodus, conquest, land, and exile (Swartley 1994). If we include creation and renewal of creation as central to the biblical plot, and if we set the divine action within the context of God's cosmic sovereignty, then even the violent moments of the story can be drawn into God's redemptive transformation of the world—without assuming either that God is inherently violent or that human beings must also be violent. The point I am making here concerns whether the cosmos (and the Creator) are inherently violent, and whether human beings are therefore also imitators of a violent God (see the fine exploration of this point by Middleton 2005: ch. 6, "Created in the Image of a Violent God?"). Saying that the narrative shapes the community's self-understanding, however, must be grounded, not in the particularities of individual texts, but in the scope and direction of the narrative as a whole, beginning with a nonviolent creation, through to a blessing for the nations, and eventually a reconstitution of God's hope for cosmic transformation.

That way of positioning Joshua allows our reading to resonate with the way writers of the NT read their Scriptures. For them the narrative is not a static entity from which moral principles are to be mined and then applied. Nor is such a reading thwarted or threatened by other ways of reading that are not interested in the formation of a community in covenantal relationship with God. As Yoder writes, our goal is "not to seek to reconstruct in just what way whatever happened did happen when YHWH saved Israel, or whether in each case any of the Israelites used weapons or not. Our present concern is rather with what it meant for Jesus and his contemporaries and his disciples to read this kind of story in their Bible" (1994: 83). But this is slightly different from reading it as its authors intended (78). Yoder, whose reading is in continuity with Origen in this regard, works at a hermeneutic of dynamic analogy rather than a strictly historical reading that seeks to locate meaning in the original context or in the intention of the author (see *Figural Reading, p. 426*).

Questions certainly arise from such a dynamic reading of biblical narrative. How is it that misreadings occur? Or further, how is it possible that the conquest of indigenous peoples ever came to be justified from a reading of the book of Joshua? Habel states that Joshua was a charter document for the Crusades and that "such a position can no longer be tolerated" (1991: 91). Michael Prior documents how the book of Joshua authorized colonial enterprises in Latin America, South Africa, and Israel/Palestine (1997). Akenson traces a similar appropriation of the biblical notion of covenant (also central to Joshua) in nationalist movements in South Africa, Israel, and Ulster. Habel juxtaposes the use of Joshua with the dispossession of Australian aboriginal peoples (1991): "The ideology of Joshua, from a post-New Testament perspective of social justice, must be acknowledged as alien and superseded. This raises afresh the role of the Book of Joshua in the canon and the criteria by which it can be interpreted as a 'word of God.' Does the New Testament gospel, in fact, judge the Book of Joshua as alien just as a contemporary justice reading would?" (91).

The short answer to Habel's question is "Yes." But to claim a later confessional supersession of Joshua raises further questions and complicates matters even more. Since the promise of land is at the heart of Jewish identity, a narrative theology also needs to acknowledge that the biblical narrative constructs identities in various ways, including landedness and exile. A truly dialogical interpretation will attend to the voices that resist either-or solutions: either the transformation of landedness into a colony of the kingdom, or into permanent exilic existence (Schlabach).

PLOT TENSIONS IN JOSHUA The first and most often cited thematic tension in the book concerns Joshua's supposed obedience to the law code of Deuteronomy. In particular, obedience to Moses' instructions (so highly valued in the book of Joshua) are more of a dynamic transposition than a literal fulfillment of the letter of the law. Polzin has shown how the book of Joshua modifies its application of Mosaic Torah. Covenants with indigenous peoples seem to violate Deuteronomic instructions (Deut 7 and 20). Polzin points out how the narrative opens the way for outsiders to become insiders (Rahab and the Gibeonites), and warns that insiders can become outsiders (Achan). In some respects, Deuteronomy's openness to the alien, sojourner, and marginalized person seems to distinguish between the lesser principle and the greater principle (*qal we-homer*, a tradition long practiced in Jewish circles). The greater concern for the resident alien takes precedence over the lesser concern to marginalize and expel and exterminate the indigenous population. It is as though the book of Joshua was written from the vantage point of full awareness of a significant resident alien population. More particularly, the narrative questions both ethnicity and geography as criteria for defining insider and outsider. Although Deuteronomy clearly makes the indigenous population an Other to be exterminated, the book of Joshua finds various ways of including these same Others into the community called *all Israel, alien as well as citizen* (Josh 8:33). It seems as though Joshua takes up Deuteronomy's concern for the alien, while calling into question Deuteronomy's aversion to the indigenous population.

A second and related thematic tension within Joshua concerns the contrast between the command to exterminate the enemy (*ḥerem*) and the affirmation that God is the one who has fought for Israel (10:14, 42; 23:3, 10). Like other ancient conquest accounts, the book testifies to the memory of theologically sanctioned human violence on the one hand, and a theological confession that minimizes human military activity. Although the conquest accounts in Joshua share many of the generic conventions and theological vocabulary of those accounts, the book of Joshua uses this genre as a "special effect" in the context of a more comprehensive goal *[Conquest Accounts, p. 406]*. The contrast between the conquest genre and the openness to outsiders opens the way to the larger Deuteronomistic interest in exclusive loyalty to one God rather than the exclusion of other peoples. Covenant loyalty and idolatry become the main interest of the plot. The fact that the book of Judges refers to the gods of the remaining people groups as a snare suggests that it is the gods and not simply the people that become the problem, as is highlighted in the demise of both Israel and Judah in 2 Kings (Josh 23:13; Judg 2:3; 2 Kings 17:7-12, 33-38; 22:17).

A third tension in the book is the contrast between the completeness and the incompleteness of the conquest. According to Joshua 11:23, everything was accomplished, all the land was taken, all the indigenous population was conquered. Yet chapters 13 and following state explicitly that the Israelites did not conquer all the peoples (cf. 13:1, 13; 15:63; 16:10). Not only that, but by chapter 18 we discover that seven tribes "still await even the process of allotment, let alone have taken possession of their inheritance" (Gunn: 108). Perhaps just as the "conquest" itself is incomplete, so also the distribution remains incomplete. And in the end, even the shape of Israel as a people in a bounded land remains unresolved (as ch. 22 implies). There are different ways of interpreting this tension. According to one view, the failure to drive out the indigenous inhabitants should be interpreted negatively (Nelson 1997a; Hawk 1991; Hauch). According to Nelson, for example, both the total conquest and the partial conquest reflect Deuteronomic perspectives. One "glorifies the faithfulness of Yahweh and looks back to the promises of Deuteronomy, and the second explores the theme of disobedience and penalty and looks forward to the story told in Judges and Kings" (1997a: 19). A second view suggests a tension between ideal and reality (Assis). And a third view understands the tension positively as a way of accounting for the inclusion of outsiders into the fabric of Israelite peoplehood (Polzin). Each of those explanations tries to account for the ambiguity within the text; each is partly correct.

It is also possible that the problem of not driving out the indigenous inhabitants (the third tension) has to do with a larger intrabiblical dialogue that encompasses a variety of other texts. For example, in Exodus 23:20-33 God announces that an "angel" will go ahead of them (23:20), and that "I will send my terror" and "pestilence in front of you" (23:27-28), but "I will not drive them out from before you in one year" lest the "wild animals . . . multiply against you" (23:29). Rather, "little by little I will drive them out from before you" (23:30), "and you shall drive them out before you" (23:31). Deuteronomy 7 states that "the LORD your God will clear away these nations before you little by little; you will not be able to make a quick end of them, otherwise the wild animals would become too numerous for you" (7:22). The opening of the book of Judges implies that the Israelites deliberately did not dispossess the indigenous population (1:19, 21, 27-33), with the exception of 1:19, where superior weaponry is the reason. Joshua 13–18, however, suggests that they *could not drive out* (cf. Josh 15:63 with Judg 1:21; Josh 17:12 with Judg 1:27). In Joshua's narrative setting, the inability of Israel reflects the phraseology of Deuteronomy 7:22 (Fishbane: 203) and therefore does not carry a negative judgment on Israelite inability to dispossess the Canaanites. The final speeches of Joshua continue to elaborate on the theme by asserting that the LORD will continue to do what he has been doing all along (23:3, 5, 10). If Israel should *turn back, however, the LORD your God will not continue to drive out these nations before you* (23:12-13). Maintaining the gift, in other words, now depends on Israel (cf. Gen 18:19). Otherwise they will *perish quickly from the good land that he has given you* (Josh 23:16; cf. 23:13; similar statements in Deut 11:17; 28:20). Joshua foregrounds the gift and backgrounds the responsibility, whereas Judges foregrounds the responsibility/failure. Both are integral to the narrative's worldview, but Joshua sets the parameters of divine favor to Israel and only hints at the dark days to come.

The study of narrative technique demonstrates that the juxtaposition of contrasting ideas is integral to the story, which in unexpected ways tends to surprise the reader. It may help also to recognize ambiguity in the story: the tensions in a narrative act to undermine and at other times to supplement the vision or perspective within the text. That complex notion of ambiguity allows Mitchell to suggest that the narrative as a whole moves between "dream" and "reality" (190). Similarly, Hauch describes the tensions as belonging to the "apparent" and the "submerged" stories (75). With its tensions, the story presents a way for a powerless people in exile or under colonial rule to live with the unresolved tension of wishing for an impossible but hoped-for future.

The interwoven tensions in the narrative confirm the hypothesis that there is a conversational hermeneutic at work within the story itself. According to the Deuteronomistic tradition, for example, although disobedience has dire consequences, the historical process of covenantal relationship between Yahweh and Israel is grounded in God's attentiveness to his own promises, which results in the formation of a people in a land, committed to the cosmic sovereignty of God. The book of Joshua cannot answer all the questions that arise precisely because the narrative of Joshua lives in the middle of time. It provides "an interpretive history of one slice of Israel's life as a people" (Howard 1998: 30). It is not so much that God is "in control of the events of history," as Howard puts it, but that the gift of land is part of Yahweh's sovereignty over all nations. Even in Deuteronomic perspective, Israel is not unique as a recipient of Yahweh's sovereign gifting of land (see Deut 2 and 32:8-9). But the narrative of Joshua begins the particular story of a particular people in a particular land—the story that ends tragically outside the land hundreds of years later. In the meantime, the narrative tells of Israel's improvisation in the light of the gift, in view of the covenant, through the empowerment of Torah-centered leadership, toward the goal of rest and peace and an end to war.

Although the gift of land leads to rest from war, the tensions between gift and responsibility, between fulfillment and nonfulfillment—all are woven together with profound reflections on the relationship between divine justice and mercy. Mercy for some is the flip side of retributive justice for others. Is the submerged story of Joshua a testimony to God's concern for the marginal characters in the narrative? Are they incidental to the story? Could it be that the Joseph tribes—along with Rahab, Achan, the Gibeonites and other indigenous "aliens," Caleb and his daughter Achsah, the daughters of Zelophehad, Levites, and the Transjordan tribes—form a significant contrast to the unified "all Israel" portrait of the entrance-into-the-land narrative as a whole (Polzin)? Or do they represent, as Hawk thinks, a "negative image" in the book, in contrast to "the united, obedient, and victorious Israel" (2000: xxii)? According to Hawk, these outsiders represent "an ambivalent status and an energetic determination to secure a place in the land" (xxii). Yet never in the narrative of Joshua is there an explicit judgment on their presence, or even a critique of Israel's welcoming them into their peoplehood. The indigenous population represents a threat only because mixing with the peoples that remain might tempt Israel to worship their gods (Josh 24:2, 14-16). And the threat of exile comes not from the peoples but from God (23:16).

For further resources on plot tensions in the book of Joshua, see Gunn; Hauch; Hawk 1991; Hubbard; Mitchell; Polzin.

REST The Deuteronomic motif of rest reverberates from the beginning to the end of the book of Joshua (*nwḥ*, *rest*, 1:13, 15; 21:44; 22:4; 23:1; cf. 3:13; 4:3, 8; 6:23 with the meaning "to set foot," "to set down," or "to place"; cf. Deut 3:20; 5:14; 12:9-10; 25:19; 2 Sam 7:1, 11; *šqṭ*, *rest from war*, Josh 11:23; 14:15). What is most significant about the "rest" in Deuteronomy and the DtrH is that it is rest for a purpose: it "is not so much 'rest from' . . . as it is 'rest for'" (Roth: 10). In Deuteronomy 12:9-10, "The divine gift of rest calls for the response of the recipients" (10–11) in worship at the place where God should "choose as a dwelling for his name" (Deut 12:11). Although that emphasis does not become explicit in the book of Joshua, it does become clear later in the narrative during the reigns of David and Solomon.

In Deuteronomy "rest" (3:20; 12:9-10; 25:19) results in an "inheritance," which "is a rightful share or allotment, an approved entitlement to land, property, or people" (Habel 1995: 35). "Inheritance" refers either to Israel the people as God's inheritance (Deut 4:20; 9:26, 29; 32:9), or to the land as Israel's inheritance (often "possession" in NRSV; e.g., Deut 4:21, 38; 15:4, where inheritance, giving, and land appear together). Land is therefore a "conditional grant" by God to Israel (Habel 1995: 36–53). This land had been granted, as it were, at the foundation of the world, just as land has been granted to all the peoples of the world (Deut 32:7-9). But the emphasis in Deuteronomy 32 is on relationship with a people, not land. In Deuteronomy, land is subordinate to people, with whom God has a special relationship (Habel 1995: 53). Moreover, in Deuteronomy the land as inheritance (possession) serves to make sure no one is in need (15:4). Boundary markers of this inheritance are to be protected (19:14). The inheritance must not be defiled through inappropriate actions, even in cases of capital punishment (21:23) or abuse of divorce legislation in marriage relationships (24:4). And the fruit of the inheritance is to be given to God (26:1-2).

In 1 Kings 8:56-61 the noun "rest" "receives its fullest interpretation" in Solomon's blessing, which is reminiscent of Joshua's speeches at the end of Joshua. Rest here is not security or "physical settlement in Canaan, nor a period of time characterized as rest" (Roth: 11). Roth argues that 1 Kings 8:56-61 does not mention temple or its building. "Rather, it equates with 'rest' Israel's certainty that its God is day by day, day and night, accessible and sees to it that justice is done to his people among the nations, that is, his people in exile" (11–12). Rest is "a situation in which, wherever it may be, the Lord is graciously turned to his people and they wholly toward him. Israel's rest has become a relational term!" (12).

Even for readers of Joshua, whether in exile or after the return from Babylon, "rest" may still be gained through loving and loyal service to the Lord. And that loving service, rooted in Torah faithfulness, stems first and foremost from a deep and abiding love for the Lord and God's word (cf. Pss 1; 19; 119; see esp. Pss 119:47, 48, 127; Neh 1:5; Dan 9:4; John 14:15, 21; 15:10; 1 John 5:2, 3; 2 John 1:6).

Outside of Deuteronomy and the DtrH, the motif of rest takes on even more sharply focused relational and even eschatological significance. In Leviticus, when land and rest are mentioned in the same context, it is about the Sabbath rest for the land in the Sabbatical Year (Lev 25:4-5). When the people are exiled from their land, the land will again rest (Lev 26:34-35; cf. 2 Chron 36:21). Although the book of Joshua does not speak of this kind of rest, if the book of Joshua is read in exile, that Levitical "rest," although quite different in origin and purpose, could well find readers wondering whether rest from war is a prerequisite to renewed Sabbath rest. This juxtaposition may be possible if one considers the rather striking approach to possession or even inheritance of land in the famous line "The land is mine; with me you are but aliens and tenants" (Lev 25:23).

Chronicles echoes Joshua's motif of "rest" (2 Chron 20:30). In Joshua *rest* is promised to the Transjordan tribes (1:13, 15). The *land had rest from war* (11:23; 14:15). The speeches at the end of the book assert that God has given them *rest . . . all around* (Josh 21:44; 23:1; cf. Deut 12:10; 25:19; on "rest" in Chronicles, see 1 Chron 22:9, 18; 2 Chron 14:6-7; 15:15). In 2 Chronicles 15:15 we find the motif of "rest" associated in the same context as "seeking" the Lord, a motif that appears characteristically throughout Chronicles to indicate turning to the Lord in worship and supplication. Chronicles takes up and transforms the motifs of warfare and rest. In Chronicles, David speaks of rest to the people in the same breath as stating that the Lord "resides in Jerusalem forever," and that occurs immediately within the context of listing the Levites and their functions (1 Chron 23:25), "to assist the descendants of Aaron for the service of the house of the LORD" (23:28).

Yet the prophetic perspective on the Lord's activity of "giving rest" is larger even than all of that. Isaiah anticipates the rest that will come with the downfall of Babylon's oppressive regime (14:3, 7), such that "the whole earth" will be "at rest and quiet." Isaiah 28 depicts the people's refusal to accept the divine rest (28:12; cf. 63:14). Jeremiah picks up a similar motif in recognizing the Babylonian oppression that extends beyond Israel's experience to other nations, such that the Lord of hosts will act to "give rest to the earth, but unrest to the inhabitants of Babylon" (50:34).

Joshua's rest is therefore only the beginning of the journey of God's people. Jesus reuses the motif by offering, "Come to me, . . . and I will give you rest" (Matt 11:28-29). The author of the book of Hebrews makes explicit use of the rest motif, but turns it around by claiming that it was an incomplete rest, requires a further fulfillment, and may also be forfeited through disobedience (4:11). The book of Hebrews, beginning with a citation of Psalm 95:11 (in both Heb 3:11 and 4:3), interprets both the promise and the rest as an experience that can be resisted through hardening the heart (3:8, 15) or being "hardened by the deceitfulness of sin" (3:13). Taking the wilderness generation's failure to enter the land (or to enter "rest") as an example of those who continue to rebel, or to sin, or to exercise unbelief (3:16-19), the writer shifts to a "therefore" in 4:1, claiming that "the promise of entering his rest is still open" and encouraging readers to "take care that none of you should seem to have failed to reach it." The similarity in the analogy with the wilderness generation is that both "they" and "we" have heard the "good news," but only "we who have believed enter that rest" (4:2-3a).

The author of Hebrews also thinks typologically when he links Scripture texts together based on common motifs and vocabulary. He cites Psalm 95:11 a third time, then takes up the divine rest motif from Genesis 2:2, concluding by saying, "Therefore it remains open for some to enter it" (Heb 4:6) because David, in the same psalm, speaks of a "today" in which one may still "hear his voice" and not harden one's heart (Ps 95:7). If David offered a new "today," then the author of Hebrews may do so as well by suggesting, "For if Joshua had given them rest, God would not speak later about another day" (Heb 4:8). This new "day" becomes a new "Sabbath," linked to the divine rest of Genesis 2:2: "A sabbath rest still remains for the people of God; for those who enter God's rest also cease from their labors as God did from his. Let us therefore make every effort to enter that rest, so that no one may fall through such disobedience as theirs" (Heb 4:10-11). The exegesis of the author of Hebrews reminds us that the church of the first three centuries was working with an interpretive approach to Scripture like that of Jewish midrash, which is based on typological analogies and rooted in finding similar motifs across the spectrum of Scripture *[Figural Reading, p. 426]*.

For the author of Hebrews, the problem (of no rest) is caused by unfaithfulness, sin, and rebellion against the Lord. Rest, on the other hand, comes by trusting and through obedience (Heb 4:11). It comes by allowing the "word of God" to become the sword that conquers the very "intentions of the heart" (4:12b). Hebrews transposes the motif of rest into a different key because the original key can no longer be sung.

THEOLOGY OF WARFARE The starting point for reflection on a theology of warfare in the Bible, and in the book of Joshua in particular, must be the answer to this awkwardly phrased question: "What should the book of Joshua (or the Bible for that matter) be read *as*?" And a second question is like it: "How do we make sense of Joshua's contribution to the diversity of expression on the topic of warfare in the Bible?" I began this commentary by resolving that this project would not set out to solve the "problem" of warfare in the book of Joshua. Although I have resisted the urge to attempt partial answers time and again, it is important here to make my response clear. I have read the book of Joshua against the grain for I have called into question the notion that its depiction of warfare ought to be understood as a normative resource for theological reflection. In other words, I have tried to demonstrate, in a close reading of the text, that the book of Joshua is not a conquest account and that its theological center is not warfare but the faithfulness of Yahweh, the one who invites committed attentiveness to divine instruction (Torah). I have also tried to show that those central interests have been the focus of the book of Joshua's echoes within Scripture itself and the focus of the book's theological interpretation through time.

Are those interests diminished or clouded by the book's having been shrouded in the clothing of its ancient conceptualities? Yes and no. We are not reading *The Lord of the Rings*. We are reading of a geographic location (often called the Holy Land) to which many of us have traveled. For many of those reading Joshua, the book continues to provide the grounding for their claim to the land (Greenberg 1995). For others, because of its use to justify their own marginalization in their own land, the book remains virtually unreadable. Yet we are not reading *history* in the modern sense of that term. We are reading a theologically informed adaptation, somewhat like historical fiction *[Conquest Accounts, p. 406]*. I make such an overstatement here in order that we might not miss the point that this writing must be read extremely carefully, with both its cultural context and its rhetorical aim in mind.

Still, we find ourselves drawn to the conquest accounts as though somehow through those texts we will either vilify or exonerate the book of Joshua. After all, as Chris Hedges has stated so well, "War is a drug. . . . It dominates culture, distorts memory, corrupts language, and infects everything around it." It raises "fundamental questions about the meaning, or meaninglessness, of our place on the planet" and "exposes the capacity for evil that lurks not far below the surface within all of us." Not only that, but also war "can give us what we long for in life. It can give us purpose, meaning, a reason for living" (3). If only, therefore, we could put warfare in its theological place. Even better would be for us to be able to justify our understandings and our practices based on biblical precedent.

Unfortunately, the problem of warfare in the book of Joshua raises much the same kind of question as Joshua asks the man with the sword in his hand (Josh 5:13). Is war legitimate or is it not? The answer could well be, "Neither" (NRSV), or better, "No. That's the wrong question." That is not to deny that the Bible offers guidance about questions concerning "national loyalty and the outsider, about God and our enemies" (J. H. Yoder 2010: 73). But that guidance cannot come by weighing texts against one another or by rejecting some in favor of others. It must come through a more nuanced understanding of what's going on in the Bible as a whole (even in the book of Joshua itself!).

Throughout this commentary I have argued that the Bible is a "text in travail," borrowing a phrase from René Girard (1987a: 141). The book of Joshua is given literary birth in an ancient world that was familiar with the genre and idiom of conquest stories *[Conquest Accounts, p. 406]*. The Deuteronomic school, the authorial context for the book of Joshua, drew on that fund of cultural awareness in shaping the conquest accounts within the book of Joshua. In fact, biblical writers lived in a context informed by a "warfare worldview" that assumed divine involvement in earthly warfare. The God of Israel as well as the gods of the nations were warrior gods who were involved in the lives of their peoples (Exod 15:3; Zeph 3:17; Albrektson; Younger 1990). Land was part of the "divine estate": the god was the king of the estate, and the king granted land to whom he pleased (see Judg 11:23-24; Block; Hess 2002). In the OT, Israel's primary role is to trust that the Lord will defend and give victory (Exod 14:13-14; Deut 1:30; 20:1-4; Isa 31:1).

Conquest stories also become part of Israel's memory of reversal as Assyrian and later Babylonian armies conquer Israel and then Judah. The prophets announce Israel's and Judah's defeat by Assyria and Babylon (Jer 5–6; esp. Isa 7:17; 9:11-12; Jer 21:5-7; Ezek 5:8-9). God becomes Israel's enemy as the warrior God, who through these imperial powers turns the *ḥerem* on Israel (e.g., Judg 2:14-15; Isa 43:28; Jer 25:8-9). Such reversals are not unique to Israel's warfare ideology. We find the same principle applied to Moab in the Mesha Inscription *[Mesha Inscription, p. 447; Conquest Accounts, p. 406; Ḥerem, p. 433]*.

Alongside that transformation, however, is another tradition about warfare in which Israel's God alone defeats the cosmic powers Gog and Magog (Ezek 38–39), and where weapons are transformed into agents of peace (Isa 2:2-4) or are destroyed (Isa 9; 11). Israel's writers and poets present God as one who vanquishes the cosmic and historical forces of chaos (Pss 29; 68; 89:7-18) and maintains order by seeing that justice is done (Pss 82; 96; 97; 99). This One is greater than all the gods: he is Lord of hosts (lit., Lord of armies), who is beholden to no one. That tradition is developed and transformed in the NT, where Jesus becomes the divine warrior who makes peace by defeating the demonic powers, evil, injustice, and death itself *[Conquest and Land in the NT, p. 411]*.

The point of setting the conquest account into the framework of faithfulness depicted at the beginning and end of the book of Joshua is to nurture a trust in Yahweh, the God of Israel. The point is not whether God alone fights the battle (à la Lind), or whether God participates synergistically with Israel (Craigie: 41), or whether God works within the "political realism" of ancient Israelite life (McConville 2006: 104), or whether Israel fights alone and only thinks they hear God tell them to fight (Eller). Warfare is placed without reservation within the sovereignty of God. Yahweh sets the boundaries of the nations, not only of Israel (Deut 32:3-9). Yahweh creates an exodus for Israel as for the Philistines (Amos 9:7). Yahweh becomes warrior who fights against Israel as he did against Egypt (Jer 21:1-5), even as he uses Nebuchadnezzar to fight against Judah and all the kingdoms of the earth (25:9, 15-38). This God is not *simply* on one side or another.

What then might be said theologically about God and warfare in the OT? Biblical writers were seeking to articulate a theopolitical vision, a vision that is metahistorical in scope, a vision that places all human strife and striving under the sovereign purposes and care of God. These writers are indeed realists because they write about real events. In using the available language of the day, the book of Joshua along with other OT writings seek to elicit trust in the God who will not be reduced to being a god of the nation, a tribal deity. In the prophetic tradition, this God's representatives advocated against trust in militaristic modes of nation building (Isa 31:1). They saw salvation as having its ultimate means and end in God, not "by bow, or by sword, or by war, or by horses, or by horsemen" (Hos 1:7). The prophets imagined an alternative way for humankind, one that encompasses all of creation, one in which "the bow, the sword, and war" would be abolished (2:18). Isaiah even imagines a time when God's arbitration will result in an unprecedented action on the part of the nations: "They shall beat their swords into plowshares; . . . nation shall not lift up sword against nation, neither shall they learn war any more" (2:4).

The writers of the book of Joshua, by depicting Joshua as one called to trust divine instruction (Torah) and to let God's word live inside him fully (1:8-9), are positing a source of life outside the autonomous self and nation (Deut 8:3). And by confirming that *it was not by your sword or by your bow* that Israel finds itself where it is, the narrator presents God saying, *I gave you a land on which you had not labored* (Josh 24:12-13). All of this, in other words, is in the service of the embodied call to *choose this day whom you will serve*, either the gods or Yahweh (24:14-15, 21-24). Of course we know that the book of Joshua sets up what amounts to an impossible scenario that anticipates a nearly tragic end when Joshua announces, *You cannot serve the Lord* (24:19). Whether cajoling or prescient, the book of Joshua ends with the affirmation that life may flourish only because of *all the work that the LORD did for Israel* (24:31). The warfare theme has been thoroughly subordinated into the larger project that will, hopefully, reconcile all things into God's redemptive purpose, a purposeful and peaceful future that God himself has embodied and inaugurated in the life, death, and resurrection of Jesus Christ (Col 1:19-20). It is this trajectory on which Jesus draws when he says, "Love your enemies" (Matt 5:43). And if the heart of that vision is to break down the dividing wall between peoples and to end "the hostility between us" (Eph 2:14), then even the warfare texts of Joshua begin to participate in the undoing of the tradition that has assumed, rightly or wrongly, that the Canaanite is to be eliminated from the land. For the narrator of Joshua, Rahab and the Gibeonites on the one hand, and the Transjordan tribes on the other—both become signs that the boundaries of ethnicity and geography cannot limit the sovereignty of God nor the covenant loyalty of the people.

To narrate such a trajectory of divine purpose, and Joshua's participation in it, allows disparate biblical texts to stand side by side without forcing a choice between war-affirming and war-denying stances. A biblical theology of warfare is one that places God's sovereignty at the center, that creates space for human freedom to engage in warfare, yet that invites participation in a vision of cosmic salvation and transformation that the Bible calls *šalom* (P. Yoder). This hopeful biblical theology encompasses ancient Near Eastern warfare genres without requiring those genres to become the warrant for warfare as a normative human endeavor. Such a theology is also grounded in a purposeful hope characterized by *šalom* among the nations, whom God invites and instructs and yet who must, in the end, also participate in the transformation by choosing to beat swords into plowshares.

The book of Joshua is testimony to the fact that God gives birth to a people whose life is shaped by the word of God (Deut 8:3; Josh 1:8; Ps 1:1) and whose tragedies are embraced within the gracious loyalty of God (Deut 4:31), even when they are scattered among the peoples (4:26-27). The book of Joshua does not offer a warrant for ongoing conquests of "our home and native land" (Canada's national anthem). It offers a crack through which a little light might shine, through which to perceive, in small measure, a vision of the good life in a good land.

What I have sketched above is not a thorough exploration of a theology of warfare in the Bible. It certainly assumes that individual warfare texts are not autonomous, nor can they be read as somehow independently authoritative without considering how they participate in a larger cultural and canonical setting.

The following resources provide a more diverse exploration of these matters: Barrett; Cowles et al.; Craigie; Eller; Hanson 1984, 1987; Hess 2008b; Hess and Martens; Knierim; Lind; Longman and Reid; McDonald; Nelson 2003; Ollenburger 1988, 1994; Rad 1991; Rofé; Schwager; Seibert; Swartley 1983, 2003b; Walzer; Winn; J. Wood; C. Wright 2008, ch. 4, "The Canaanites: Three Dead Ends" and ch. 5, "The Canaanites: Three Frameworks"; Yoder Neufeld 2011; J. H. Yoder 1994, 2010; *Conquest Accounts, p. 406; Conquest and Land in the NT, p. 411; Genocide and Sacred Violence, p. 430.*

TORAH

The Instruction of God According to the Psalms, Torah gives light and life, is a joy and delight, invites commitment, and elicits a life characterized by justice and righteousness. Psalms 1, 19, and 119 give classic poetic expression to what might be called a Torah-shaped life. Such a description goes far beyond the English word *law*, which normally translates the Hebrew word *torah* in contemporary Bible translations. The word is often rendered as *instruction*, or *teaching*, as it is commonly in the NJPS version. The Jewish tradition has applied the term "Torah" to the first five books of the Bible. In this commentary, the word will most often be presented as Torah, except where the specific Hebrew word is under discussion. Then it will appear as *torah*.

Torah is the most common word used for God's instruction or teaching in the book of Deuteronomy, occurring there as a noun twenty-two times (Deut 1:5; 4:8, 44; 17:11, 18-19; 27:3, 8, 26; 28:58, 61; 29:21, 29; 30:10; 31:9, 11-12, 24, 26; 32:46; 33:4, 10; and only thirty-four times in all of Genesis through Numbers). The emphasis on God's teaching preoccupies Deuteronomy; within the DtrH, it is picked up prominently only in Joshua (1:7-8; 8:31, 32, 34 twice; 22:5; 23:6; 24:26) and Kings (1 Kings 2:3; 2 Kings 10:31; 14:6; 17:13, 34, 37; 21:8; 22:8, 11; 23:24-25). The focus of the Torah theme in the books of Kings is on the responsibility to attend to God's instruction. Beginning in David's instruction to Solomon in 1 Kings 2:3-4, which echoes Deuteronomy 6:5 in the Shema (*šemaʿ*: 6:4-6), David calls on Solomon to live by the law/instruction of Moses, which will bring him success (echoing Josh 1:7-8). By drawing on those allusions, the books of Kings draw a figural relationship between Moses and Joshua, and between David and Solomon. In 2 Kings 17 the narrator draws on the tradition of the written Torah, which was mediated through "my servants the prophets" (17:13). Moses is the servant par excellence, named as such once in Deuteronomy (34:5), eighteen times in Joshua (1:1-2, 7, 13, 15; 8:31, 33; 9:24; 11:12, 15; 12:6 twice; 13:8; 14:7; 18:7; 22:2, 4-5), and four times in Kings (1 Kings 8:53, 56; 2 Kings 18:12; 21:8). Joshua happens to be named *servant of the Lord* once at the end of the book of Joshua (24:29; cf. Josh 5:14; Judg 2:8).

This combined concentration on *torah* and *servant* is striking in the book of Joshua. The word *torah* in Joshua pertains either to the teaching of Moses or to the scroll of the teaching. The motif becomes the key signature of the book in 1:7-8, where Joshua is instructed not to deviate from the Torah (cf. the echo here of Moses' words in Deut 17:11, and David's words to Solomon in 1 Kings 2:3). It is crystallized in the covenant ceremony on Mount Ebal reported in Joshua 8:30-35. There it is the *book of the law of Moses* (8:31) that becomes the focus of attention, just as it was in 1:7-8. Only here it involves all Israel, *alien as well as citizen, . . . the women, and the little ones, and the aliens who resided among them* (8:33, 35). This event is depicted as a reenactment of the instructions of Deuteronomy to attend to the Torah. Joshua seems to be enacting the public performance of Torah as instructed in Deuteronomy 31:10-13. The motif of not turning from the *torah . . . to the right hand or to the left* (Josh 1:7) mirrors the teaching on kingship in Deuteronomy 17:14-20 (also 5:32; 28:14; Josh 23:6). There the emphasis falls on having "come into the land" and having "taken possession" (Deut 17:14) and on the temptations of landedness (17:16-17).

Given that scenario, Deuteronomy speaks of attending to "this law written for him" (17:18) and of not turning from it "to the right or to the left" (17:20). These words are also the words of God to Joshua in 1:7-8. Joshua therefore becomes both *servant of the Lord* (24:29) and faithful follower of Moses, who mediates God's Torah to the people. He is the one who, in Joshua 23:6, repeats the admonition of not turning aside to the right or to the left. Moreover, in chapter 24 Joshua *made statutes and ordinances for them at Shechem* (24:25) and then becomes an "author" of Torah, writing *these words in the book of the law of God* (24:26). In a remarkable way, therefore, Joshua becomes both a royal and a prophetic figure since his words and actions echo the instructions for kingship in Deuteronomy 17; and in his new role as "servant," he becomes a prophetic mediator of the divine instruction to the people in calling them to faithfulness (chs. 23–24). Joshua therefore becomes the prototype for Josiah in 2 Kings 22–23 *[Characterization of Joshua, p. 394]*.

Although faithfulness to God's teaching is the means for keeping the gift of land, such faithfulness is nothing other than single-minded loyalty to God (Josh 23:6; 24:14-16). *Other gods* are the real danger (Josh 24:14) *[Idolatry, p. 438]*. Although Joshua, in a rhetorical cajoling, announces the impossibility of Israel's success (24:19), the testimony of Deuteronomy 4:29-31 is that even in exile, even after the loss of land, God's mercy is overwhelming. Torah faithfulness (or failure) will not diminish God's intention: "He will neither abandon you nor destroy you" (Deut 4:31). This surely is the word that needs to be heard again by the exiles, whose story begins at the end of 2 Kings. For them, the book of Joshua is the place from which to begin again, not so that Israel can enact a new conquest of land, but so that a renewed covenant might give birth again to a people who attend to the teaching of God and whose lives are oriented toward God alone.

Living Torah in the Book of Joshua and Beyond The case of the daughters of Zelophehad offers an example of how legal traditions grow as needs arise in Israel's experience (Num 27:1-11; 36:1-12; Josh 17:3-6). Law is dynamic, flexible, and adaptable, although with a firm center in the character and purposes of God. Rahab's story is an example of how the narrative of Israel's experience shapes its understanding, interpretation, and practice of Deuteronomic law in creative directions even as Israel discerns that the Deuteronomic laws about exterminating the Other (Deut 20) are not written in stone. The intention of Deuteronomic law is to protect Israel's exclusive loyalty to God. One of the ways of trying to assure such loyalty is to frame the problem as a danger arising from the indigenous Canaanite population.

When the first such Canaanite actually appears on the scene in the person of Rahab, the law loses its cutting edge. The wedge has been inserted, and the narrative can proceed with the assumption that even those so-called outsiders can have a place at the table. Rahab's story, coming immediately after the intense exhortation to keep Torah, suggests that God is not always constrained by God's own commands. Moreover, divine instructions are not comprehensive: they grow out of Israel's ongoing dialogue with God about life in the land. Openness to Rahab is a greater good than keeping the letter of the commandments. For readers at a later time, including our own, the story serves to awaken the conversation about how a community might go about being faithful to Torah.

Deuteronomy, for example, modifies and adds to the laws of Exodus. Ezekiel draws from both and introduces changes. And the apostolic community of the first century works hard at discerning which biblical laws continue to be valid for the community of Jesus' followers. Of particular concern within the NT are the requirements of keeping Torah for both Gentile and Jewish followers of Jesus. As the book of Acts reports, after much debate, Gentile followers come to be welcomed into the fellowship (Acts 11:1-18) and are required to observe a limited range of laws (15:19-20). Of particular interest to the Rahab story (and later to that of Achan in Josh 7) is the encouragement "to abstain . . . from things polluted by idols" (Acts 15:20). The apparent xenophobia of Deuteronomy can be distilled into a concern for exclusive loyalty to God, along with the danger that outsiders (with their worship practices) pose for Israel. Achan, the first Israelite to violate the instructions explicitly, took some of the things dedicated to God alone (Josh 6:19; ch. 7), an act that might otherwise be associated with greed, which the apostle Paul calls idolatry (Col 3:5).

The OT itself also bears witness to various attitudes toward foreigners. Even the book of Deuteronomy offers both exclusive and inclusive perspectives. No compromise with foreigners is allowed. Yet Deuteronomy encourages care for aliens "in your midst" (1:16; 5:14; 23:16; 24:14-21). In Deuteronomy the radical rejection of the religion of Canaan is presented as rejection and extermination of the inhabitants. Radical hospitality to strangers offers an alternative. That model is rarely demonstrated but is seen clearly in Rahab's story, as well as in Elisha's advice to the king of Israel about offering hospitality to the enemy army (2 Kings 6:20-23) *[Theology of Warfare, p. 458]*.

On theologies of law, instruction, and commandment, see Fretheim 2003; Greenberg 1990; Levenson; Vogt.

TRANSJORDAN TRIBES The Transjordan tribes, Reuben, Gad, and half the tribe of Manasseh, play a prominent role in Joshua 1 and 22. Chapter 22 is a hinge between the distribution section of Joshua and the final events narrated in chapters 23–24. The chapter looks back all the way to chapter 1, where the Transjordan tribes are key figures in Joshua's initial conversation with the people. They affirm their loyalty to Joshua even as they were loyal to Moses (1:16-17). They even assure Joshua that those who rebel and disobey his orders "shall be put to death" (1:18). Ironically, in chapter 22 the entire community of Transjordan tribes is threatened with death by the so-called *Israelites*. The irony is doubly significant because Joshua's exhortation to the Transjordan tribes in his speech in 22:2-6 both affirms their faithfulness to Moses and Joshua (v. 2) and confirms that the promised *rest* has been achieved (v. 4; cf. 1:15).

This second speech to the Transjordan tribes builds on that first one in Joshua 1 by adding two exhortations, to *observe the commandment and instruction* of Moses, as well as to *love the Lord* and *serve him* (v. 5). Both of those expressions are thoroughly Deuteronomic in tone and usage. The same motifs recur in chapters 23–24, where Joshua addresses *all Israel* (23:2) and *all the tribes of Israel* (24:1), but it is not clear whether that *all* includes the Transjordan tribes. Are the Transjordan tribes part of the covenant-making event of chapter 24, or have they departed to their territory with Joshua's exhortation and the other tribes' challenges ringing in their ears? Likely the *all Israel* perspective of chapters 23–24 intends to embrace even the Transjordan tribes by illustrating that the conflict of chapter 22 has indeed been overcome *["All Israel," p. 385]*. The chapter also looks ahead to the exhortations to faithfulness and to the "witness" motif of the covenant making (24:14-27).

The distribution to the Transjordan tribes follows the tradition reflected in the book of Numbers, where Moses grants land to Reuben, Gad, and half the tribe of Manasseh (32:33-40). The half-tribe of Manasseh in Transjordan is represented by the descendants of Machir, son of Manasseh (32:39-40). In Joshua 17:1, Machir, the father of Gilead, is said to have received *Gilead and Bashan*, Transjordan territories, *because he was a warrior* (cf. Num 32:39-40). Moreover, in Numbers 26 and 36—the stories about the daughters of Zelophehad—Manasseh's son Machir is named as the father of Gilead (26:29-30; 36:1). As stated in the Explanatory Notes for Joshua 17:1-13, *Machir* and *Gilead* are indigenous names that have been incorporated into the genealogy of Israel.

Although Genesis 48 forms the basis for treating Joseph's sons as two tribes (48:5, 13-22), Jacob's blessing seems to allude only to distribution to the other half-tribe of Manasseh west of the Jordan River (with the Heb. word for "portion" in 48:22 being a play on the name of the town Shechem).

The Transjordan tribes are not prominent in the DtrH, although the books of Chronicles mention them much more often (Reuben, Judg 5:15-16; Gadites and Reubenites, 1 Sam 10:27; all three, 2 Kings 10:33; Gad, 1 Sam 13:7; 2 Sam 24:5; Jer 49:1).

On the tribes and tribal territories, see Hess 2005.

TWELVE STONES Although following the ark and heeding the words is the focus of the preparation for the crossing, the commemoration after the crossing contributes toward making the narrative itself a pattern rooted in memory. The twelve stones taken from the river (Josh 4:3-9) are set up in Gilgal (4:19-20). These are to have instructional value (4:6, 21). The motif of the children's question is based on Deuteronomy 6:20 (cf. Exod 12:26-27). The children's question in Deuteronomy 6:20 concerns the meaning of the divine instructions, which are to be written on the stones of the altar, according to 27:2-8. Joshua 3–4 and 8:30-35 are therefore linked to the instruction to set up a stone altar on which are written words of the Torah, as explicitly spelled out in Deuteronomy 27:2-8: "On the day that you cross over the Jordan, . . . you shall set up large stones and cover them with plaster. . . . [And] you shall write on the stones all the words of this law very clearly." Moreover, these stones shall be set up "on Mount Ebal" (27:4). All of that happens and is reported in Joshua 8:30-35. Therefore these stones in Joshua 3–4 are not those stones of Mount Ebal. Yet Joshua 3–4 demonstrates obedience to the Deuteronomic instruction for these stones are set up "on the day that you cross over." Here is another example of how the narrative of Joshua builds on the instructional base of Deuteronomy, but does not conform to the letter of the law. Two separate incidents in Joshua reverberate out of Deuteronomy 27:2-8. Yes, the stones are set up at the camp in Gilgal (4:8) immediately after coming out of the river. And the (other) stones are also set up on Mount Ebal (8:30-31). The double occurrence of the stones in Joshua does not so much create a problem as draw attention to the importance of memory and obedience as twin motifs in the shaping of identity and mission. Israel is called to remember so as to be empowered to act in accordance with divine instruction. Such concrete embodiments of memory are integral to the task of heeding the words of the Lord. The stones are a memorial to the past that gives shape to the future. The *story* about the stones becomes a way of remembering and, therefore, of reimagining identity. We are who we are because of this story, this God, this memory, this wonder.

For a rich exploration of the motif of "stones" in Joshua, see Hubbard.

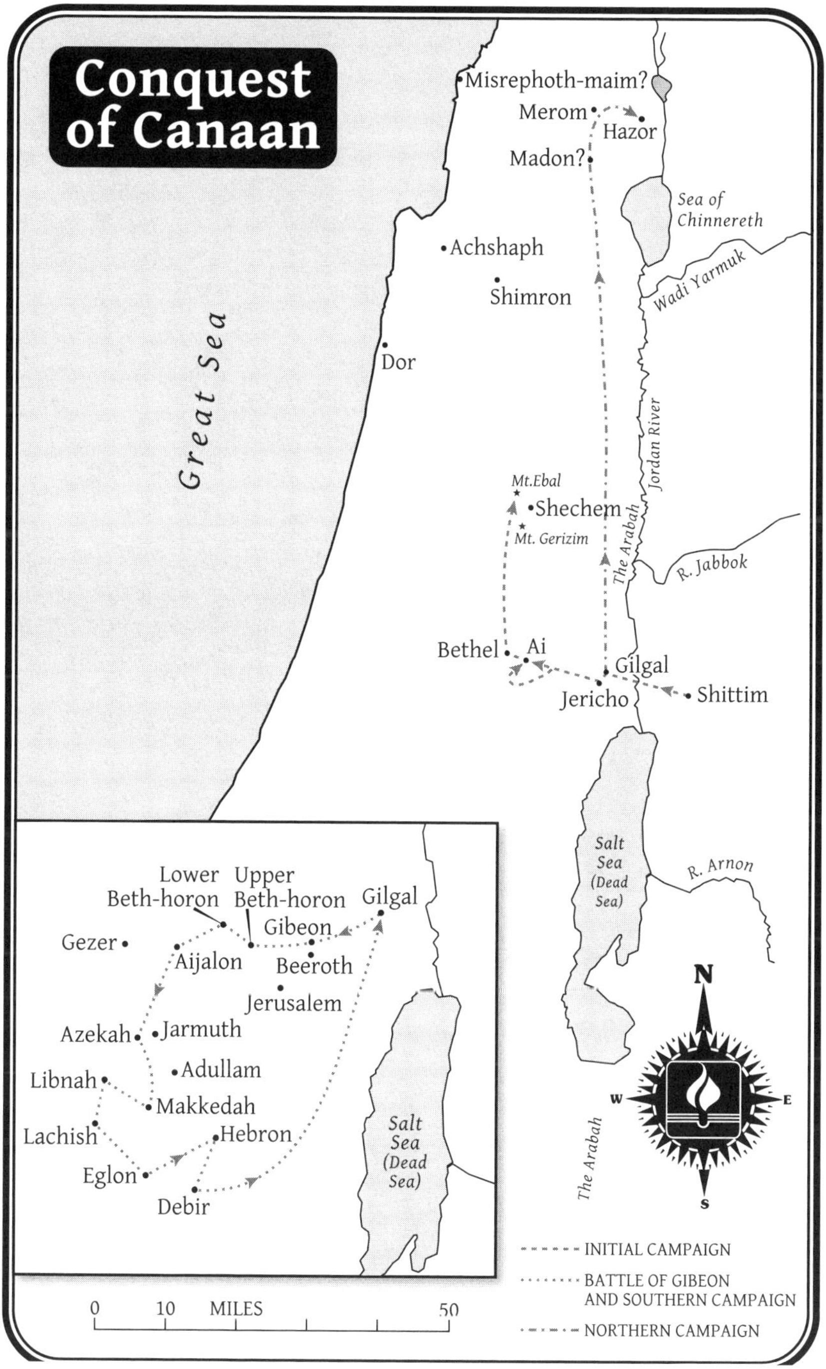
Conquest of Canaan
Misrephoth-maim?
Merom
Hazor
Madon?
Sea of Chinnereth
Achshaph
Shimron
Wadi Yarmuk
Great Sea
Dor
Jordan River
Mt.Ebal
Shechem
Mt. Gerizim
The Arabah
R. Jabbok
Bethel
Ai
Gilgal
Jericho
Shittim
Lower Beth-horon
Upper Beth-horon
Gilgal
Gibeon
Gezer
Aijalon
Beeroth
Jerusalem
Azekah
Jarmuth
Adullam
Libnah
Makkedah
Lachish
Hebron
Eglon
Debir
Salt Sea (Dead Sea)
Salt Sea (Dead Sea)
R. Arnon
N
W
E
S
The Arabah
0 10 MILES 50
INITIAL CAMPAIGN
BATTLE OF GIBEON AND SOUTHERN CAMPAIGN
NORTHERN CAMPAIGN

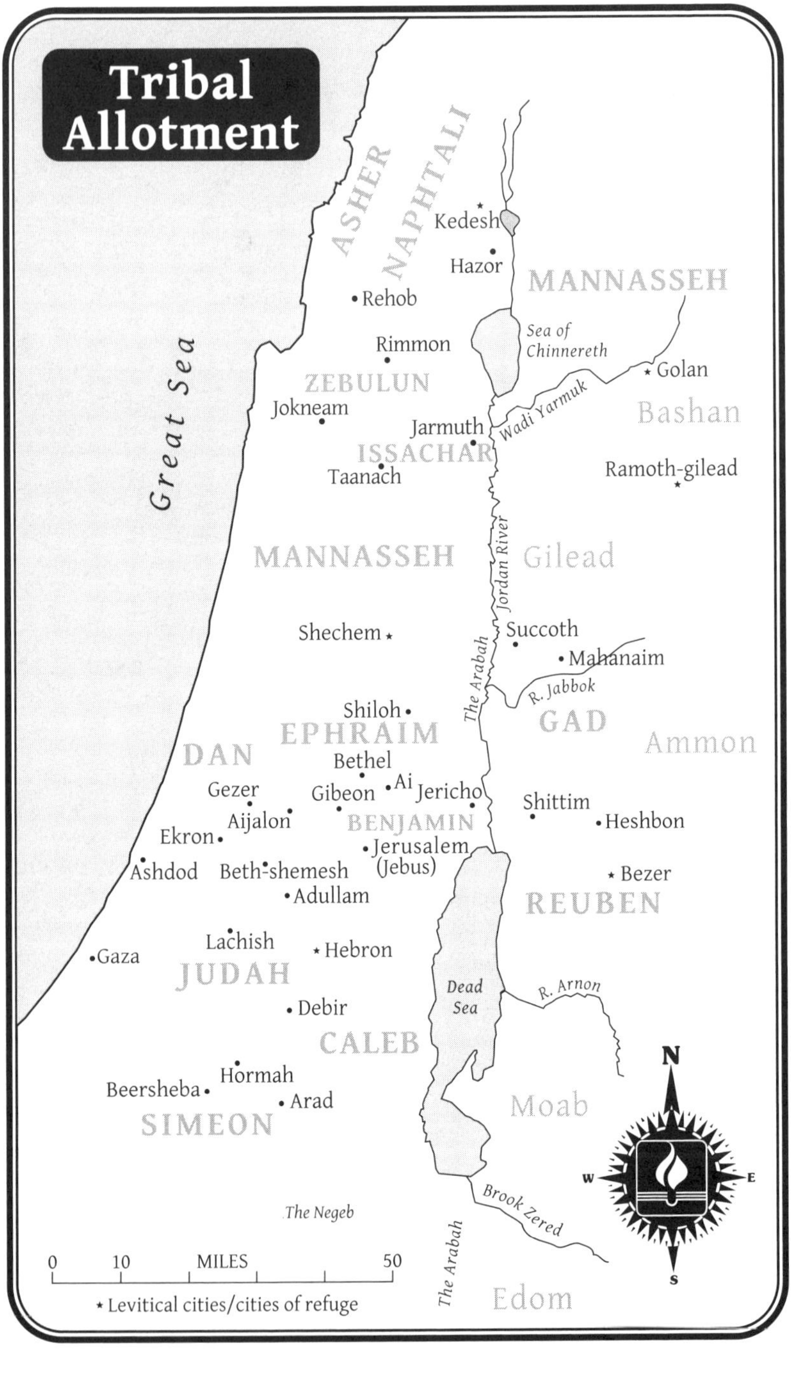

Tribal Allotment
ASHER
NAPHTALI
Kedesh
Hazor
MANNASSEH
Rehob
Sea of Chinnereth
Rimmon
Golan
ZEBULUN
Great Sea
Jokneam
Wadi Yarmuk
Bashan
Jarmuth
ISSACHAR
Taanach
Ramoth-gilead
MANNASSEH
Jordan River
Gilead
Shechem
Succoth
Mahanaim
The Arabah
R. Jabbok
Shiloh
GAD
EPHRAIM
Ammon
DAN
Bethel
Gezer
Ai
Gibeon
Jericho
Shittim
Aijalon
Heshbon
BENJAMIN
Ekron
Jerusalem (Jebus)
Ashdod
Beth-shemesh
Bezer
Adullam
REUBEN
Lachish
Hebron
Gaza
JUDAH
Dead Sea
R. Arnon
Debir
CALEB
N
Hormah
Beersheba
Arad
Moab
SIMEON
W
E
Brook Zered
The Negeb
0
10
MILES
50
The Arabah
S
Levitical cities/cities of refuge
Edom

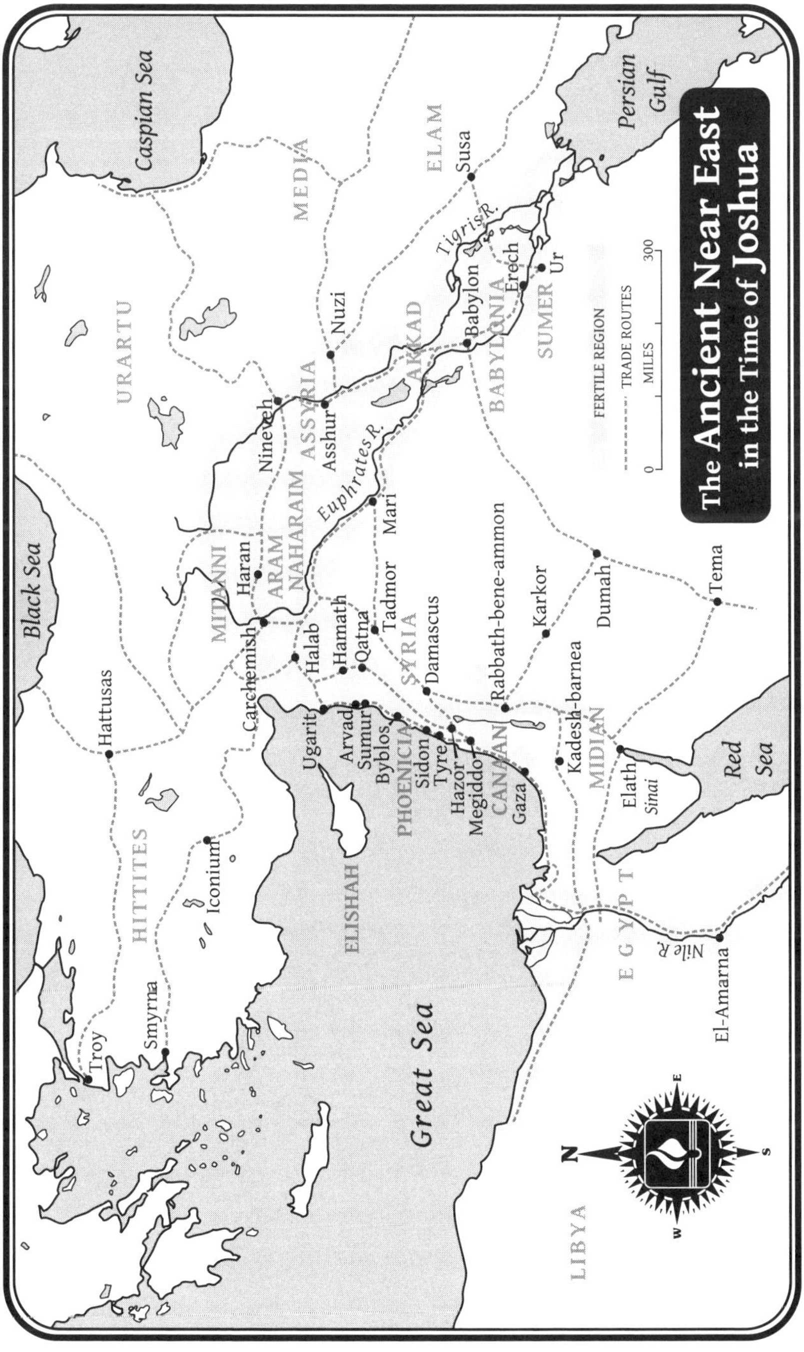
The Ancient Near East
in the Time of Joshua
FERTILE REGION
TRADE ROUTES
MILES
0
300
Caspian Sea
Black Sea
Persian Gulf
Great Sea
Red Sea
URARTU
MEDIA
ELAM
ASSYRIA
AKKAD
BABYLONIA
SUMER
MITANNI
ARAM NAHARAIM
HITTITES
SYRIA
PHOENICIA
CANAAN
MIDIAN
ELISHAH
EGYPT
LIBYA
Sinai
Tigris R.
Euphrates R.
Nile R.
Susa
Nuzi
Nineveh
Asshur
Babylon
Erech
Ur
Mari
Haran
Carchemish
Halab
Hamath
Qatna
Tadmor
Damascus
Rabbath-bene-ammon
Karkor
Dumah
Tema
Hattusas
Ugarit
Arvad
Sumur
Byblos
Sidon
Tyre
Hazor
Megiddo
Gaza
Kadesh-barnea
Elath
Iconium
Smyrna
Troy
El-Amarna
N
E
S
W

Bibliography

Abu El-Haj, Nadia
2002 *Facts on the Ground: Archaeological Practice and Territorial Self-Fashioning in Israeli Society*. Chicago: University of Chicago Press.

Akenson, Donald Harman
1992 *God's Peoples: Covenant and Land in South Africa, Israel, and Ulster*. Ithaca and London: Cornell University Press.

Albrektson, B.
1967 *History and the Gods: An Essay on the Idea of Historical Events as Divine Manifestations in the Ancient Near East and in Israel*. Lund: C. W. K. Gleerup.

Albright, William F.
1935 "Archaeology and the Date of the Hebrew Conquest of Palestine." *Bulletin of the American Schools of Oriental Research* 58:10–18.
1939 "The Israelite Conquest of Canaan in the Light of Archaeology." *Bulletin of the American Schools of Oriental Research* 74:11–23.

Alt, Albrecht
1966 *Essays on Old Testament History and Religion*. Translated by R. A. Wilson. Oxford: Blackwell.

Alter, Robert
1992 *The World of Biblical Literature*. New York: Basic Books.

Arnold, Bill T., and H. G. M. Williamson, eds.
2005 *Dictionary of the Old Testament: Historical Books*. Downers Grove, IL: InterVarsity; Leicester: Inter-Varsity.

Assis, Elie
2003 "'How Long Are You Slack to Go to Possess the Land?' (Jos. xviii 3): Ideal and Reality in the Distribution Descriptions in Joshua XIII–XIX." *Vetus Testamentum* 53/1:1–25.

Ateek, Naim Stifan
1989 *Justice and Only Justice: A Palestinian Theology of Liberation*. Maryknoll, NY: Orbis Books.
1995 "A Palestinian Perspective: Biblical Perspectives on the Land." In *Voices from the Margin: Interpreting the Bible in the Third World*,

edited by R. S. Sugirtharajah, 267–76. 2nd ed. Maryknoll, NY: Orbis Books; London: SPCK.

Auld, A. Graeme

1980 *Joshua, Moses and the Land: Tetrateuch-Pentateuch-Hexateuch in a Generation Since 1938*. Edinburgh: T&T Clark.

1990 "The Cities in Joshua 21: The Contribution of Textual Criticism." In *Textus: Studies of the Hebrew University Bible Project* 15:141–52. Reprinted in Auld 1998a: 49–57.

1995 "Reading Joshua After Kings." In *Words Remembered, Texts Renewed: Essays in Honour of John F. A. Sawyer*, edited by Jon Davies, Graham Harvey, and Wilfred G. E. Watson, 167–81. Journal for the Study of the Old Testament: Supplement Series 195. Reprinted in Auld 1998a: 102–12.

1998a *Joshua Retold: Synoptic Perspectives*. Old Testament Studies. Edinburgh: T&T Clark.

1998b "The Former Prophets: Joshua, Judges, 1-2 Samuel, 1-2 Kings." In *The Hebrew Bible Today: An Introduction to Critical Issues*, edited by Steven L. McKenzie and M. Patrick Graham, 53–68. Louisville: Westminster John Knox.

1999 "Joshua, Book of." In *Dictionary of Biblical Interpretation*, edited by John H. Hayes, 1:625–32. Nashville: Abingdon. Also printed in Auld 1998a: 129–39.

Bader-Saye, Scott

1999 *Church and Israel After Christendom: The Politics of Election*. Eugene, OR: Wipf & Stock.

Bailie, Gil

1995 *Violence Unveiled: Humanity at the Crossroads*. New York: Crossroad.

Balentine, Samuel E.

1999 *The Torah's Vision of Worship*. Minneapolis: Fortress.

Baloian, Bruce

1997 "Anger." In *New International Dictionary of Old Testament Theology and Exegesis*, edited by William VanGemeren, 4:377–85. Grand Rapids: Zondervan.

Barrett, Lois

1987 *The Way God Fights: War and Peace in the Old Testament*. Scottdale, PA, and Kitchener, ON: Herald Press.

Barstad, Hans M.

1989 "The Old Testament Feminine Personal Name *Rāḥāb*: An Onomastic Note." *Svensk exegetisk årsbok* 54:43–49.

Beale, G. K.

2008 *We Become What We Worship: A Biblical Theology of Idolatry*. Downers Grove, IL: InterVarsity; Nottingham: Apollos.

Beek, Martin van

1994 "Joshua the Savior." In *Voices from Amsterdam: A Modern Tradition of Reading Biblical Narrative*, edited by Martin Kessler, 145–53. Society of Biblical Literature Semeia Studies. Atlanta: Scholars Press.

Bergant, Diane

1994 "Yahweh: A Warrior God?" In *The Church's Peace Witness*, edited by Marlin E. Miller and Barbara Nelson Gingerich, 89–103. Grand Rapids: Eerdmans.

Billman, Kathleen D., and Daniel L. Migliore

1999 *Rachel's Cry: Prayer of Lament and Rebirth of Hope.* Cleveland: Pilgrim / United Church Press. Reprinted, Wipf & Stock, 2007.

Birch, Bruce C., Walter Bruggemann, Terence E. Fretheim, and David L. Peterson

1999 *A Theological Introduction to the Old Testament.* Nashville: Abingdon.

Bird, Phyllis A.

1989 "The Harlot as Heroine: Narrative Art and Social Presupposition in Three Old Testament Texts." *Semeia* 46:119–39.

Blenkinsopp, Joseph

1972 *Gibeon and Israel: The Role of Gibeon and the Gibeonites in the Political and Religious History of Early Israel.* Society for Old Testament Study: Monograph Series 2. Cambridge: Cambridge University Press.

2002 "The Bible, Archaeology and Politics; or The Empty Land Revisited." *Journal for the Study of the Old Testament* 27/2:169–87.

Block, Daniel I.

2000 *The Gods of the Nations: Studies in Ancient Near Eastern National Theology.* 2nd ed. Evangelical Theological Society Studies 2. Grand Rapids: Baker Academic; Leicester: Apollos.

Blumenthal, David R.

1993 *Facing the Abusing God: A Theology of Protest.* Louisville: Westminster John Knox.

Boling, Robert G.

1982 *Joshua: A New Translation with Notes and Commentary.* Anchor Bible 6. New York: Doubleday.

1983 "Levitical History and the Role of Joshua." In *The Word of the Lord Shall Go Forth: Essays in Honor of David Noel Freedman in Celebration of His Sixtieth Birthday*, edited by Carol L Meyers and M. O'Connor, 241–61. Winona Lake, IN: Eisenbrauns.

1985 "Levitical Cities: Archaeology and Texts." In *Biblical and Related Studies Presented to Samuel Iwry*, edited by Ann Kort and Scott Morschauser, 23–32. Winona Lake, IN: Eisenbrauns.

Boris, Walter John

1999 [Baptismal Sermon:] "The Waters of Our Past." http://www.kccucc.org/sermons/1999/1999-01-10.htm.

Bosch, David J.

1980 *Witness to the World: The Christian Mission in Theological Perspective.* London: Marshall, Morgan & Scott.

Boyd, Gregory A.

1997 *God at War: The Bible and Spiritual Conflict.* Downers Grove, IL: InterVarsity.

Brettler, Marc

1995 *The Creation of History in Ancient Israel.* London and New York: Routledge.

Brisman, Leslie

1999 "Sacred Butchery: Exodus 32:25-29." In *Theological Exegesis: Essays in Honor of Brevard S. Childs*, edited by Christopher Seitz and Kathryn Greene-McCreight, 162–81. Grand Rapids and Cambridge: Eerdmans.

Brodie, Thomas L.

1999 *The Crucial Bridge: The Elijah-Elisha Narrative as an Interpretive Synthesis of Genesis-Kings and a Literary Model for the Gospels.* Collegeville, MN: Liturgical Press.

Brueggemann, Walter

1981 "'Vine and Fig Tree': A Case Study in Imagination and Criticism." *Catholic Biblical Quarterly* 43:188–204.

1982 *The Creative Word: Canon as a Model for Biblical Education.* Philadelphia: Fortress.

1986 *Revelation and Violence: A Study in Contextualization.* The 1986 Père Marquette Theology Lecture. Milwaukee: Marquette University Press.

1994 "Covenant and Social Possibility." In *A Social Reading of the Old Testament*, edited by Patrick D. Miller, 54–69. Minneapolis: Fortress.

2002 *The Land: Place as Gift, Promise, and Challenge in Biblical Faith.* 2nd ed. Philadelphia: Fortress.

Buber, Martin

1967 *Kingship of God.* 3rd ed. New York: Harper & Row.

1970 *I and Thou.* Translated by W. Kaufmann. New York: Charles Scribner's Sons.

Burge, Gary M.

2003 *Whose Land? Whose Promise? What Christians Are Not Being Told About Israel and the Palestinians.* Cleveland: Pilgrim.

2010 *Jesus and the Land: The New Testament Challenge to "Holy Land" Theology.* Grand Rapids: Baker Academic.

Butler, Trent C.

1983 *Joshua.* Word Biblical Commentary 7. Waco: Word.

1991 *Understanding the Basic Themes of Joshua.* Dallas: Word.

Calvin, John

1949 *Commentaries on the Book of Joshua.* Translated by Henry Beveridge. Grand Rapids: Eerdmans.

Camp, Lee

2003 *Mere Discipleship: Radical Christianity in a Rebellious World.* Grand Rapids: Brazos.

Campbell, K. M.

1972 "Rahab's Covenant: A Short Note on Joshua ii 9-21." *Vetus Testamentum* 22:243–44.

Chaney, Marvin L.

2001 "Joshua." In *The Blackwell Companion to the Hebrew Bible*, edited by Leo G. Perdue, 103–12. Oxford and Malden, MA: Blackwell, 2001.

Chapman, Colin

2002 *Whose Promised Land? The Continuing Crisis over Israel and Palestine.* Grand Rapids: Baker Academic.

Childs, Brevard S.
1962 *Memory and Tradition in Israel*. London: SCM Press.
1963 "A Study of the Formula 'Until This Day.'" *Journal of Biblical Literature* 82:279–92.
1979 *Introduction to the Old Testament as Scripture*. Philadelphia: Fortress.
1992 *Biblical Theology of the Old and New Testaments: Theological Reflection on the Christian Bible*. Minneapolis: Fortress.

Claassens, L. Juliana M.
2003 "Biblical Theology as Dialogue: Continuing the Conversation on Mikhail Bakhtin and Biblical Theology." *Journal of Biblical Literature* 122/1:127–44.

Clapp, Rodney, ed.
1998 *The Consuming Passion: Christianity and the Consumer Culture*. Downers Grove, IL: InterVarsity.

Clements, Ronald E.
2000 "Achan's Sin: Warfare and Holiness." In *Shall Not the Judge of All the Earth Do What Is Right? Studies on the Nature of God in Tribute to James L. Crenshaw*, edited by David Penchansky and Paul L. Redditt, 113–26. Winona Lake, IN: Eisenbrauns.

Clines, David J. A.
1997 *The Theme of the Pentateuch*. 2nd ed. Sheffield: Department of Biblical Studies, University of Sheffield.

Cohn, Robert L.
1994 "Before Israel: The Canaanites as Other in Biblical Tradition." In *The Other in Jewish Thought and History: Constructions of Jewish Culture and Identity*, edited by Laurence J. Silberstein and Robert L. Cohn, 74–90. New York: New York University Press.

Collins, John
2003 "The Zeal of Phineas: The Bible and the Legitimation of Violence." *Journal of Biblical Literature* 122/1: 3–21.

Connerton, Paul
1989 *How Societies Remember*. Themes in the Social Sciences. Cambridge: Cambridge University Press.

Conrad, Edgar W.
1985 *Fear Not Warrior: A Study of 'al tîrā' Pericopes in the Hebrew Scriptures*. Brown Judaic Studies 75. Chico, CA: Scholars Press.

Coogan, Michael David
1990 "Archaeology and Biblical Studies: The Book of Joshua." In *The Hebrew Bible and Its Interpreters*, edited by W. H. Propp, B. Halpern, and D. N. Freedman, 19–32. Biblical and Judaic Studies from the University of California, San Diego, 1. Winona Lake, IN: Eisenbrauns.

Coote, Robert B.
1990 *Early Israel: A New Horizon*. Minneapolis: Fortress.

Cowles, C. S., Eugene H. Merrill, Daniel L. Gard, and Tremper Longman III
2003 *Show Them No Mercy: Four Views on God and Canaanite Genocide*. Grand Rapids: Zondervan.

Craigie, Peter C.
1978 *The Problem of War in the Old Testament*. Grand Rapids: Eerdmans.

Creach, Jerome F. D.
2003 *Joshua*. Interpretation: A Bible Commentary for Teaching and Preaching. Louisville: John Knox.

Cross, Frank Moore
1973 *Canaanite Myth and Hebrew Epic*. Cambridge, MA: Harvard University Press.

Culley, Robert.
1984 "Stories of the Conquest: Joshua 2, 6, 7, and 8." *Harvard Annual Review* 8:25–44.

Daniélou, Jean, SJ.
1960 *From Shadows to Reality: Studies in the Biblical Typology of the Fathers*. Westminster, MD: Newman.

Dauphinais, Michael, and Matthew Levering
2005 *Holy People, Holy Land: A Theological Introduction to the Bible*. Grand Rapids: Brazos.

Davies, W. D.
1991 *The Territorial Dimension of Judaism: With a Symposium and Further Reflections*. Minneapolis: Fortress. First published in 1982 by the University of California Press, Berkeley.
1992 "Reflections on Territory in Judaism." In *"Sha'arei Talmon": Studies in the Bible, Qumran, and the Ancient Near East Presented to Shemaryahu Talmon*, edited by Michael Fishbane and E. Tov, 339–43. Winona Lake, IN: Eisenbrauns.

Davis, Ellen F.
2000 "Critical Traditioning: Seeking an Inner Biblical Hermeneutic." *Anglican Theological Review* 82:733–51.

Davis, Stephen T.
1993 *Risen Indeed: Making Sense of the Resurrection*. Grand Rapids: Eerdmans.

Dawson, John David
2002 *Christian Figural Reading and the Fashioning of Identity*. Berkeley: University of California Press.

Dever, William G.
1990 "The Israelite Settlement in Canaan: New Archaeological Models." In *Recent Archaeological Discoveries and Biblical Research*, 39–84. Seattle: University of Washington Press.
1992 "Israel, History of (Archaeology and the 'Conquest')." In *Anchor Bible Dictionary*, edited by David Noel Freedman, 3:545–58. New York: Doubleday.
2001 *What Did the Biblical Writers Know and When Did They Know It? What Archaeology Can Tell Us about the Reality of Ancient Israel*. Grand Rapids and Cambridge: Eerdmans.
2003 *Who Were the Early Israelites and Where Did They Come From?* Grand Rapids: Eerdmans.

Dillard, R. B.
1981 "The Chronicler's Solomon." *Westminster Theological Journal* 43:207–18.

Dozeman, Thomas B.
1996 *God at War: Power in the Exodus Tradition*. New York and Oxford: Oxford University Press.
Drucker, Rabbi Reuven
1982 *Yehoshua: The Book of Joshua*. Artscroll Tanach Series: A Traditional Commentary on the Books of the Bible. Brooklyn: Mesorah.
Earl, Douglas S.
2010a *Reading Joshua as Christian Scripture*. Journal of Theological Interpretation: Supplement 2. Winona Lake, IN: Eisenbrauns.
2010b *The Joshua Delusion? Rethinking Genocide in the Bible*. Eugene, OR: Cascade.
Eller, Vernard
1981 *War and Peace from Genesis to Revelation*. Scottdale, PA, and Kitchener, ON: Herald Press.
Ellis, Marc H.
1999 *O, Jerusalem! The Contested Future of the Jewish Covenant*. Minneapolis: Fortress.
Eslinger, Lyle
1989 *Into the Hands of the Living God*. Bible and Literature Series 24. Sheffield: Almond.
Finkelstein, Israel
1988 *The Archaeology of the Israelite Settlement*. Jerusalem: Israel Exploration Society.
Finkelstein, Israel, and Amihai Mazar
2007 *The Quest for the Historical Israel: Debating Archaeology and the History of Israel*. Edited by Brian B. Schmidt. Archaeology and Biblical Studies 17. Atlanta: Society of Biblical Literature.
Fishbane, Michael
1986 *Biblical Interpretation in Ancient Israel*. Oxford: Clarendon.
Fouts, D. M.
2005 "Numbers, Large Numbers." In *Dictionary of the Old Testament: Historical Books*, edited by Bill T. Arnold and H. G. M. Williamson, 750–54. Downers Grove, IL: InterVarsity; Leicester: Inter-Varsity.
Fowl, Stephen E.
1998 *Engaging Scripture: A Model for Theological Interpretation*. Oxford and Malden, MA: Blackwell.
Franke, John R., ed.
2005 *Joshua, Judges, Ruth, 1-2 Samuel*. Ancient Christian Commentary on Scripture: Old Testament 4. Downers Grove, IL: InterVarsity.
Fretheim, Terence E.
1983 *The Deuteronomic History*. Nashville: Abingdon.
1997 "The God Who Acts: An Old Testament Perspective." *Theology Today* 54:6–18.
1999 "To Say Something—About God, Evil, and Suffering." *Word and World* 19:339, 346–50.
2003 "Law in the Service of Life: A Dynamic Understanding of Law in Deuteronomy." In *A God So Near: Essays on Old Testament Theology*

in Honor of Patrick D. Miller, edited by Brent A. Strawn and Nancy R. Bowen, 183–200. Winona Lake, IN: Eisenbrauns.

Gardner, Richard B.

1991 *Matthew*. Believers Church Bible Commentary. Scottdale, PA, and Waterloo, ON: Herald Press.

Gilbert, Pierre

2001 "Human Free Will and Divine Determinism: Pharaoh, a Case Study." *Direction* 30/1:76–87.

Girard, René

1977 *Violence and the Sacred*. Baltimore, MD: Johns Hopkins University Press.

1987a *Violent Origins: Walter Burkert, René Girard, and Jonathan Z. Smith on Ritual Killing and Cultural Formation*, edited by Robert G. Hamerton-Kelly. Stanford: Stanford University Press.

1987b *Things Hidden Since the Foundation of the World*. Stanford: Stanford University Press.

Glueck, Nelson

1967 *Ḥesed in the Bible*. Cincinnati: Hebrew Union College Press.

Gordon, Robert P.

2004 *Holy Land, Holy City: Sacred Geography and the Interpretation of the Bible*. Carlisle: Paternoster.

Gottwald, Norman K.

1979 *The Tribes of Yahweh*. Maryknoll, NY: Orbis Books.

Green, Barbara

2000 *Mikhail Bakhtin and Biblical Scholarship: An Introduction*. Society of Biblical Literature Semeia Studies 38. Atlanta: Society of Biblical Literature.

Greenberg, Moshe

1990 "Three Conceptions of the Torah in Hebrew Scriptures." In *Die hebräische Bibel und ihre zweifache Nachgeschichte: Festschrift für Rolf Rendtorff zum 65. Geburtstag*, edited by Erhard Blum, C. Macholz, and E. W. Stegemann, 365–78. Neukirchen-Vluyn: Neukirchener Verlag.

1995 "On the Political Use of the Bible in Modern Israel: An Engaged Critique." In *Pomegranates and Golden Bells: Studies in Biblical, Jewish, and Near Eastern Ritual, Law, and Literature in Honor of Jacob Milgrom*, edited by David P. Wright, David Noel Freedman, and Avi Hurvitz, 461–71. Winona Lake, IN: Eisenbrauns.

Griffiths, Paul J.

2004 *Lying: An Augustinian Theology of Duplicity*. Grand Rapids: Baker Academic.

Gunn, David M.

1987 "Joshua and Judges." In *The Literary Guide to the Bible*, edited by Robert Alter and Frank Kermode, 102–21. Cambridge, MA: Harvard University Press.

Habel, Norman

1991 "Conquest and Dispossession: Justice, Joshua, and Land Rights." *Pacifica: Australian Theological Studies* 4/1:76–92.

1995 *The Land Is Mine: Six Biblical Land Ideologies*. Minneapolis: Fortress.

Hall, Douglas John, and Rosemary Radford Ruether
1995 *God and the Nations.* Minneapolis: Fortress.

Hallo, William W., ed.
1997 *The Context of Scripture.* 2 vols. Leiden: E. J. Brill.

Halpern, Baruch
1983 *The Emergence of Israel in Canaan.* Society of Biblical Literature Monograph Series 29. Chico, CA: Scholars Press.
1988 *The First Historians: The Hebrew Bible and History.* San Francisco: Harper & Row.
1992 "Sociological Comparativism and the Theological Imagination: The Case of the Conquest." In *"Sha'arei Talmon": Studies in the Bible, Qumran, and the Ancient Near East Presented to Shemaryahu Talmon*, edited by M. Fishbane and E. Tov, 53–67. Winona Lake, IN: Eisenbrauns.
2000 "The State of Israelite History." In *Reconsidering Israel and Judah: Recent Studies on the Deuteronomistic History*, edited by Gary N. Knoppers and J. Gordon McConville, 540–65. Winona Lake, IN: Eisenbrauns.

Halpern-Amaru, Betsy
1994 *Rewriting the Bible: Land and Covenant in Post-Biblical Jewish Literature.* Valley Forge, PA: Trinity Press International.

Hamlin, John E.
1982 "The Joshua Tradition Reinterpreted." *South East Asia Journal of Theology* 23/2:103–8.
1983 *Inheriting the Land: A Commentary on the Book of Joshua.* Grand Rapids: Eerdmans; Edinburgh: Handsell.

Hanson, K. C.
n.d. "The Mesha Stele." http://www.kchanson.com/ANCDOCS/westsem/mesha.html.

Hardin, Michael, et al.
2010 "Mimesis, Mimetic Theory." http://www.preachingpeace.org/2010/04/06/mimesis/.

Hanson, Paul D.
1984 "War and Peace in the Hebrew Bible." *Interpretation* 38:341–62.
1986 *The People Called: The Growth of Community in the Bible.* San Francisco: Harper & Row.
1987 "War, Peace and Justice in Early Israel." *Bible Review* 3:32–45.

Hartley, J. E.
2005 "Levitical Cities." In *Dictionary of the Old Testament: Historical Books*, edited by Bill T. Arnold and H. G. M. Williamson, 652–57. Downers Grove, IL: InterVarsity; Leicester: Inter-Varsity.

Hasel, Michael G.
2005 *Military Practice and Polemic: Israel's Laws of Warfare in Near Eastern Perspective.* Berrien Springs, MI: Andrews University Press.
2008a "Merneptah's Reference to Israel: Critical Issues for the Origin of Israel." In *Critical Issues in Early Israelite History*, edited by Richard S. Hess, Gerald A. Klingbeil, and Paul J. Ray, Jr., 47–59. Bulletin for Biblical Research: Supplement 3. Winona Lake, IN: Eisenbrauns.

2008b "Assyrian Military Practices and Deuteronomy's Laws of Warfare." In *Writing and Reading War: Rhetoric, Gender, and Ethics in Biblical and Modern Contexts*, edited by Brad E. Kelle and Frank Richtel Ames, 67–81. Atlanta: Society of Biblical Literature.

Hauch, Gerhard

1991 "Text and Contexts: A Literary Reading of the Conquest Narrative (Joshua 1–11)." PhD diss., Princeton Theological Seminary.

Hauerwas, Stanley, and William Willimon

1989 *Resident Aliens: Life in the Christian Colony*. Nashville: Abingdon.

Havrelock, Rachel

2011 *River Jordan: The Mythology of a Dividing Line*. Chicago: University of Chicago Press.

Hawk, L. Daniel

1991 *Every Promise Fulfilled: Contesting Plots in Joshua*. Literary Currents in Biblical Interpretation. Louisville: Westminster John Knox.

1992 "Strange Houseguests: Rahab, Lot, and the Dynamics of Deliverance." In *Reading Between Texts: Intertextuality and the Hebrew Bible*, edited by Nana Nolan Fewell, 89–97. Literary Currents in Biblical Interpretation. Louisville: Westminster John Knox.

2000 *Joshua*. Berit Olam: Studies in Hebrew Narrative and Poetry. Collegeville, MN: Liturgical Press.

2005 "Joshua, Book of." In *Dictionary of the Old Testament: Historical Books*, edited by Bill T. Arnold and H. G. M. Williamson, 563–75. Downers Grove, IL: InterVarsity; Leicester: Inter-Varsity.

2010 *Joshua in 3-D: A Commentary on Biblical Conquest and Manifest Destiny*. Eugene, OR: Cascade.

Hay, Roy H., Jr.

Joshua and the Promised Land. Nashville: General Board of Global Ministries, United Methodist Church. Excerpted in "Promised Land and Land Theft," http://gbgm-umc.org/umw/joshua/may7180.stm.

Hays, Richard B.

1990 "Scripture Shaped Community: The Problem of Method in New Testament Ethics." *Interpretation* 44:42–55.

Hedges, Chris

2002 *War Is a Force That Gives Us Meaning*. New York: Anchor.

Hellman, Peter

2004 *When Courage Was Stronger than Fear: Stories of Christians and the Jews They Saved from the Holocaust*. 3rd ed. Cambridge, MA: Da Capo.

Heschel, Abraham

1965 *Who Is Man?* Stanford: Stanford University Press.

Hess, Richard S.

1993 "Early Israel in Canaan: A Survey of Recent Evidence and Interpretations." *Palestine Exploration Quarterly* 125:125–42. Reprinted in *Israel's Past in Present Research: Essays on Ancient Israelite Historiography*, edited by V. Philips Long, 492–518. Winona Lake, IN: Eisenbrauns.

1996 *Joshua: An Introduction and Commentary*. Tyndale Old Testament Commentaries. Leicester: Inter-Varsity; Downers Grove, IL: InterVarsity.

1997 "West Semitic Texts and the Book of Joshua." *Bulletin for Biblical Research* 7:63–76.

2002 "The Book of Joshua as a Land Grant." *Biblica* 83:493–506.

2005 "Tribes of Israel and Land Allotments/Borders." In *Dictionary of the Old Testament: Historical Books*, edited by Bill T. Arnold and H. G. M. Williamson, 967–71. Downers Grove, IL: InterVarsity; Leicester: Inter-Varsity.

2008a "The Jericho and Ai of the Book of Joshua." In *Critical Issues in Early Israelite History*, edited by Richard S. Hess, Gerald A. Klingbeil, and Paul J. Ray Jr., 33–46. Bulletin for Biblical Research: Supplement 3. Winona Lake, IN: Eisenbrauns.

2008b "War in the Hebrew Bible: An Overview." In *War in the Bible and Terrorism in the Twenty-First Century*, edited by Richard S. Hess and Elmer A. Martens, 19–32. Bulletin for Biblical Research: Supplement 2. Winona Lake, IN: Eisenbrauns.

Hess, Richard S., Gerald A. Klingbeil, and Paul J. Ray Jr., eds.

2008 *Critical Issues in Early Israelite History*. Bulletin for Biblical Research: Supplement 3. Winona Lake, IN: Eisenbrauns.

Hess, Richard S., and Elmer A. Martens, eds.

2008 *War in the Bible and Terrorism in the Twenty-First Century*. Bulletin for Biblical Research: Supplement 2. Winona Lake, IN: Eisenbrauns.

Hiebert, Paul

1982 "The Flaw of the Excluded Middle." *Missiology* 10/1:35–47.

Hoffman, Lawrence A., ed.

1986 *The Land of Israel: Jewish Perspectives*. University of Notre Dame Center for the Study of Judaism and Christianity in Antiquity 6. Notre Dame, IN: University of Notre Dame Press.

Hoffman, Yair

1999 "The Deuteronomistic Concept of the *Ḥerem*." *Zeitschrift für die alttestamentliche Wissenschaft* 111:196–210.

Hoffmeier, James K.

1994 "The Structure of Joshua 1–11 and the Annals of Thutmose III." In *Faith, Tradition, and History: Old Testament Historiography in Its Near Eastern Context*, edited by A. R. Millard, J. K. Hoffmeier, D. W. Baker, 165–79. Winona Lake, IN: Eisenbrauns.

Holladay, John S., Jr.

1968 "The Day(s) the Moon Stood Still." *Journal of Biblical Literature* 87:166–78.

Hostetter, Edwin C.

1995 *Nations Mightier and More Numerous: The Biblical View of Palestine's Pre-Israelite Peoples*. Bibal Dissertation Series 3. N. Richland Hills, TX: Bibal.

Howard, David M., Jr.

1997 "All Israel's Response to Joshua: A Note on the Narrative Framework of Joshua 1." In *Fortunate the Eyes That See: Essays in*

Honor of David Noel Freedman in Celebration of His Seventieth Birthday, edited by Astrid B. Beck, Andrew Bartelt, and Chris Franke, 81–91. Grand Rapids: Eerdmans.

1998 *Joshua*. The New American Commentary 5. Nashville: Broadman & Holman.

Hubbard, Robert L., Jr.

2001 "'What Do These Stones Mean?' Biblical Theology and a Motif in Joshua." *Bulletin for Biblical Research* 11/1:1–26.

Janzen, David

2003 "The God of the Bible and the Nonviolence of Jesus." In *Teaching Peace: Nonviolence and the Liberal Arts*, edited by J. Denny Weaver and Gerald Biesecker-Mast, 53–63. Lanham, MD: Rowman & Littlefield.

Isaac, Munther

2012 "Reading the Old Testament in the Palestinian Church Today: A Case Study of Joshua 6." In *The Land Cries Out: Theology of the Land in the Israeli-Palestinian Context*, edited by Salim J. Munayer and Lisa Loden, 217–33. Eugene, OR: Cascade.

Janzen, Waldemar

1992 "Land." In *Anchor Bible Dictionary*, edited by David Noel Freedman, 4:143–54. New York: Doubleday.

2000 *Exodus*. Believers Church Bible Commentary. Scottdale, PA, and Waterloo, ON: Herald Press.

Japhet, Sara

1979 "Conquest and Settlement in Chronicles." *Journal of Biblical Literature* 98:205–18.

Jeschke, Marlin

1990 "Discipline, Church." In *The Mennonite Encyclopedia*, edited by Cornelius J. Dyck and Dennis D. Martin, 5:239–40. Scottdale, PA, and Waterloo, ON: Herald Press.

2005 *Rethinking Holy Land: A Study in Salvation Geography*. Scottdale, PA, and Waterloo, ON: Herald Press.

Jobling, David

1986 "'The Jordan a Boundary': Transjordan in Israel's Ideological Geography." In *The Sense of Biblical Narrative: Structural Analyses in the Hebrew Bible*, 2:88–134. Journal for the Study of the Old Testament: Supplement Series 39. Sheffield: JSOT Press.

Johns, Loren L.

2003 *The Lamb Christology of the Apocalypse of John: An Investigation into Its Origins and Rhetorical Force*. Tübingen: Mohr Siebeck.

Judt, Tony

2003 "Israel: The Alternative." In *The New York Review of Books* 50/16 (October 23). http://www.nybooks.com/articles/archives/2003/oct/23/israel-the-alternative/.

Kaminsky, Joel S.

1995 *Corporate Responsibility of the Hebrew Bible*. Journal for the Study of the Old Testament: Supplement Series 196. Sheffield: Sheffield Academic.

2003 "Did Election Imply the Mistreatment of Non-Israelites?" *Harvard Theological Review* 96/4:397–425.

2007 *Yet Jacob I Loved: Reclaiming the Biblical Concept of Election.* Nashville: Abingdon.

Kang, Sa-Moon

1989 *Divine War in the Old Testament and in the Ancient Near East.* Beiheft zur Zeitschrift für die alttestamentliche Wissenschaft 177. Berlin and New York: Walter de Gruyter.

Keel, Othmar

1974 *Wirkmächtige Siegeszeichen im Alten Testament: Ikonographische Studien zu Jos 8,18-26; Ex 17,8-13; 2 Kön 13,14-19 und 1 Kön 22,11.* Orbis biblicus et orientalis 5. Freiburg, Switzerland: Universitätsverlag; Göttingen: Vandenhoeck & Ruprecht.

Keizer, Garret

2002 *The Enigma of Anger: Essays on a Sometimes Deadly Sin.* San Francisco: Jossey-Bass.

Kepnes, Steven

1992 *The Text as Thou: Martin Buber's Dialogical Hermeneutics and Narrative Theology.* Bloomington and Indianapolis: Indiana University Press.

Kinzer, Mark S.

2005 *Post-Missionary Messianic Judaism: Redefining Christian Engagement with the Jewish People.* Grand Rapids: Brazos.

Kissling, Paul J.

1996 *Reliable Characters in the Primary History: Profiles of Moses, Joshua, Elijah and Elisha.* Journal for the Study of the Old Testament: Supplement Series 224. Sheffield: Sheffield Academic.

Kittredge, Cynthia Briggs

2000 "Diverse Voices Reclaim Tradition." *Anglican Theological Review* 82:753–64.

Klaassen, Walter, ed.

1981 *Anabaptism in Outline: Selected Primary Sources.* Scottdale, PA, and Kitchener, ON: Herald Press.

Knierim, Rolf P.

1994 "On the Subject of War in the Old Testament and Biblical Theology." *Horizons in Biblical Theology* 16/1:1–19.

Koorevaar, Hendrik Jakob

1990 *De opbouw van het boek Jozua.* Heverlee: Centrum vor Bijbelse Vorming België.

Kuhn, Karl Allen

2008 *Having Words with God: The Bible as Conversation.* Minneapolis: Fortress.

Latvus, Kari

1998 *God, Anger and Ideology: The Anger of God in Joshua and Judges in Relation to Deuteronomy and the Priestly Writings.* Journal for the Study of the Old Testament: Supplement Series 279. Sheffield: Sheffield Academic.

Leddy, Mary Jo
2002 *Radical Gratitude*. Maryknoll, NY: Orbis Books.

Levenson, Jon D.
1980 "The Theologies of Commandment in Biblical Israel." *Harvard Theological Review* 73:17–33.

Levine, Baruch A.
1974 *In the Presence of the Lord*. Studies in Judaism in Late Antiquity 5. Leiden: E. J. Brill.

Lind, Millard C.
1980 *Yahweh Is a Warrior: The Theology of Warfare in Ancient Israel*. Scottdale, PA, and Kitchener, ON: Herald Press.

Loewen, Harry
1988 *Why I Am a Mennonite: Essays on Mennonite Identity*. Scottdale, PA, and Kitchener, ON: Herald Press.

Lohfink, Norbert
1994 "The Deuteronomistic Picture of the Transfer of Authority from Moses to Joshua: A Contribution to an Old Testament Theology of Office." In *Theology of the Pentateuch: Themes of the Priestly Narrative and Deuteronomy*, 234–47. Minneapolis: Fortress.

Lohr, Joel N.
2009 *Chosen and Unchosen: Conceptions of Election in the Pentateuch and Jewish-Christian Interpretation*. Siphrut: Literature and Theology of the Hebrew Scriptures 2. Winona Lake, IN: Eisenbrauns.

Long, V. Philips
1994 *The Art of Biblical History*. Grand Rapids: Zondervan.
1999 "Historiography of the Old Testament." In *The Face of Old Testament Studies: A Survey of Contemporary Approaches*, edited by David W. Baker and Bill T. Arnold, 145–75. Grand Rapids: Baker Academic; Leicester: Apollos / Inter-Varsity.

Longman, Tremper, III, and Daniel G. Reid
1995 *God Is a Warrior*. Grand Rapids: Zondervan.

Lynch, Joseph H.
2003 "The First Crusade: Some Theological and Historical Context." In *Must Christianity Be Violent? Reflections on History, Practice, and Theology*, edited by Kenneth R. Chase and Alan Jacobs, 23–36. Grand Rapids: Brazos.

Mabie, F. J.
2005 "Geographical Extent of Israel." In *Dictionary of the Old Testament: Historical Books*, edited by Bill T. Arnold and H. G. M. Williamson, 316–28. Downers Grove, IL: InterVarsity; Leicester: Inter-Varsity.

Martens, Elmer A.
1998 *God's Design: A Focus on Old Testament Theology*. N. Richland Hills, TX: BIBAL.

March, W. Eugene
2007 *God's Land on Loan: Israel, Palestine, and the World*. Louisville and London: Westminster John Knox.

Masalha, Nur
2007 *The Bible and Zionism: Invented Traditions, Archaeology and Post-Colonialism in Israel-Palestine*. London and New York: Zed Books.

Matties, Gordon H.

1990 *Ezekiel 18 and the Rhetoric of Moral Discourse*. Society of Biblical Literature Dissertation Series 126. Atlanta: Scholars Press.

2000 "Can Girard Help us to Read Joshua?" In *Violence Renounced: René Girard, Biblical Studies, and Peacemaking*, edited by Willard M. Swartley, 85–102. Telford, PA: Pandora Press U.S.

2003 "God's Reign and the Missional Impulse of the Psalms." In *Beautiful upon the Mountains: Biblical Essays on Mission, Peace, and the Reign of God*, edited by Mary H. Schertz and Ivan Friesen, 17–49. Elkhart: Institute of Mennonite Studies; Scottdale, PA, and Waterloo, ON: Herald Press.

2009 "The Word Made Bitter: At the Table with Joshua, Buber, and Bakhtin." In *The Old Testament in the Life of God's People: Essays in Honor of Elmer A. Martens*, edited by Jon Isaak, 307–32. Winona Lake, IN: Eisenbrauns.

Mazani, Patrick

2008 "The Appearance of Israel in Canaan in Recent Scholarship." In *Critical Issues in Early Israelite History*, edited by Richard S. Hess, Gerald A. Klingbeil, and Paul J. Ray Jr., 95–109. Bulletin for Biblical Research: Supplement 3. Winona Lake, IN: Eisenbrauns.

Mazar, Amihai

1990 *Archaeology of the Land of the Bible, 10,000–586 B.C.E.* Anchor Bible Reference Library 2. New York: Doubleday.

McCarthy, Dennis J.

1971 "The Theology of Leadership in Joshua 1–9." *Biblica* 52:165–75.

1978 *Treaty and Covenant: A Study in Form in the Ancient Oriental Documents and in the Old Testament*. 2nd ed. Analecta biblica 21a. Rome: Biblical Institute Press.

McConville, J. Gordon

1993 *Grace in the End: A Study in Deuteronomic Theology*. Grand Rapids: Zondervan.

1997 *"B^{e}rît." In New International Dictionary of Old Testament Theology and Exegesis*, edited by William VanGemeren, 1:747–55. Grand Rapids: Zondervan.

2006 *God and Earthly Power: An Old Testament Political Theology*. London and New York: T&T Clark.

McConville, J. Gordon, and Stephen N. Williams

2010 *Joshua*. Two Horizons Old Testament Commentary. Grand Rapids and Cambridge: Eerdmans.

McDonald, Patricia M.

2004 *God and Violence: Biblical Resources for Living in a Small World*. Scottdale, PA, and Waterloo, ON: Herald Press.

McEntire, Mark H.

1999 *The Blood of Abel: The Violent Plot in the Hebrew Bible*. Macon, GA: Mercer University Press.

McKenzie, S. L.

2005 "Historiography, Old Testament." In *Dictionary of the Old Testament: Historical Books*, edited by Bill T. Arnold and H. G. M.

Williamson, 418–25. Downers Grove, IL: InterVarsity; Leicester: Inter-Varsity.

Meadors, Edward P.
2006 *Idolatry and the Hardening of the Heart: A Study in Biblical Theology.* London and New York: T&T Clark.

Meier, S. A.
2005 "History of Israel 1: Settlement Period." In *Dictionary of the Old Testament: Historical Books*, edited by Bill T. Arnold and H. G. M. Williamson, 425–34. Downers Grove, IL: InterVarsity; Leicester: Inter-Varsity.

Mendenhall, George E.
1970 "The Hebrew Conquest of Palestine." *Biblical Archaeology Review* 3:100–120.
1973 *The Tenth Generation: The Origins of the Biblical Tradition.* Baltimore: Johns Hopkins University Press.

Menno Simons
1956 *The Complete Writings of Menno Simons, c. 1496–1541.* Translated by Leonard Verduin. Edited by John C. Wenger. Scottdale, PA: Herald Press.

Merling, David, Sr.
1997 *The Book of Joshua: Its Theme and Role in Archaeological Discussions.* Andrews University Seminary Doctoral Dissertation Series 23. Berrien Springs, MI: Andrews University Press.
2004 "The Relationship between Archaeology and the Bible: Expectations and Reality." In *The Future of Biblical Archaeology: Reassessing Methodologies and Assumptions*, edited by J. K Hoffmeier and A. Millard, 29–42. Grand Rapids: Eerdmans.

Middleton, J. Richard
2005 *The Liberating Image: The* Imago Dei *in Genesis 1.* Grand Rapids: Brazos.

Middleton, J. Richard, and Brian J. Walsh
1995 *Truth Is Stranger Than It Used to Be: Biblical Faith in a Postmodern Age.* Downers Grove, IL: InterVarsity.

Miller, Patrick D., Jr.
1969 "The Gift of God: The Deuteronomic Theology of the Land." *Interpretation* 23:451–65.
1973 *The Divine Warrior in Early Israel.* Harvard Semitic Monographs 5. Cambridge, MA: Harvard University Press.
2004 *The God You Have: Politics, Religion, and the First Commandment.* Minneapolis: Fortress.

Mitchell, Gordon
1993 *Together in the Land: A Reading of the Book of Joshua.* Journal for the Study of the Old Testament: Supplement Series 134. Sheffield: Sheffield Academic.

Mulholland, M. Robert, Jr.
2000 *Shaped by the Word: The Power of Scripture in Spiritual Formation.* Rev. ed. Nashville: Upper Room.

Mullen, E. Theodore, Jr.
1993 *Narrative History and Ethnic Boundaries.* Society of Biblical Literature Semeia Studies. Atlanta: Scholars Press.

Murray, Stuart
2000 *Biblical Interpretation in the Anabaptist Tradition.* Studies in the Believers Church Tradition 3. Kitchener, ON: Pandora; Scottdale, PA: Herald Press.

Nelson, Richard D.
1981a *The Double Redaction of the Deuteronomistic History.* Journal for the Study of the Old Testament: Supplement Series 18. Sheffield: JSOT Press.
1981b "Josiah in the Book of Joshua." *Journal of Biblical Literature* 100:531–40.
1997a *Joshua.* Old Testament Library. Louisville: Westminster John Knox.
1997b "*Ḥērem* and the Deuteronomic Social Conscience." *Deuteronomy and Deuteronomistic Literature.* Bibliotheca ephemeridum theologicarum lovaniensium 133. Edited by M. Vervenne and J. Lust, 39–54. Leuven: Leuven University Press.
2003 "Divine Warrior Theology in Deuteronomy." In *A God So Near: Essays on Old Testament Theology in Honor of Patrick D. Miller*, edited by Brent A. Strawn and Nancy R. Bowen, 241–59. Winona Lake, IN: Eisenbrauns.
2005 "Joshua." In *Dictionary of the Old Testament: Historical Books*, edited by Bill T. Arnold and H. G. M. Williamson, 559–62. Downers Grove, IL: InterVarsity; Leicester: Inter-Varsity.

Neufeld, John
2002 "Children and Communion." Board of Faith and Life of the Canadian Conference of Mennonite Brethren Churches. http://mbconf.ca/resource/File/PDFs/Children_and_communion.pdf.

Neufeld, Thomas R. Yoder
1997 *"Put on the Armour of God": The Divine Warrior from Isaiah to Ephesians.* Journal for the Study of the New Testament: Supplement Series 140. Sheffield: Sheffield Academic.

Newsom, Carol A.
1996 "Bakhtin, the Bible, and Dialogic Truth." *Journal of Religion* 76:290–306.

Niditch, Susan
1993 *War in the Hebrew Bible: A Study in the Ethics of Violence.* New York and Oxford: Oxford University Press.

Niehaus, Jeffrey J.
1988 "Joshua and Ancient Near Eastern Warfare." *Journal of the Evangelical Theological Society* 31:37–50.

Noll, Mark A.
"Searching for Christian America." *Crux* 27/2:23–30.

Noth, Martin
1960 *The History of Israel.* 2nd ed. Translated by P. R. Ackroyd. New York: Harper & Row.

1981 *The Deuteronomistic History*. Journal for the Study of the Old Testament: Supplement Series 15. Sheffield: JSOT Press. Translated from the 1957 2nd ed. of *Überlieferungsgeschichtliche Studien*.

Novak, David

1995 *The Election of Israel: The Idea of the Chosen People*. Cambridge: Cambridge University Press.

Nowell, Irene, OSB

2008 "Jesus' Great-Grandmothers: Matthew's Four and More." *Catholic Biblical Quarterly* 70/1:1–15.

O'Brien, Connor Cruise

1988 *God's Land: Reflections on Religion and Nationalism*. Cambridge, MA: Harvard University Press.

Ollenburger, Ben C.

1984 "The Hermeneutics of Obedience: Reflections on Anabaptist Hermeneutics." In *Essays on Biblical Interpretation: Anabaptist-Mennonite Perspectives*, edited by Willard M. Swartley, 45–61. Text-Reader Series 1. Elkhart: Institute of Mennonite Studies.

1987 *Zion, the City of the Great King: A Theological Symbol of the Jerusalem Cult*. Journal for the Study of the Old Testament: Supplement Series 41. Sheffield: JSOT Press.

1988 "The Concept of 'Warrior God' in Peace Theology." In *Essays on Peace Theology and Witness*, edited by Willard M. Swartley, 112–34. Occasional Papers 12. Elkhart: Institute of Mennonite Studies.

1994 "Peace and God's Action against Chaos in the Old Testament." In *The Church's Peace Witness*, edited by Marlin E. Miller and Barbara Nelson Gingerich, 70–88. Grand Rapids: Eerdmans.

Origen

2002 *Homilies on Joshua*. Translated by Barbara J. Bruce. Edited by Cynthia White. Fathers of the Church 105. Washington, DC: Catholic University of America Press.

Orlinsky, Harry M.

1986 "The Biblical Concept of the Land of Israel: Cornerstone of the Covenant between God and Israel." In *The Land of Israel: Jewish Perspectives*, edited by Lawrence A. Hoffman, 27–64. University of Notre Dame Center for the Study of Judaism and Christianity in Antiquity 6. Notre Dame: University of Notre Dame Press.

Ortiz, S. M.

2005 "Archaeology, Syro-Palestinian." In *Dictionary of the Old Testament: Historical Books*, edited by Bill T. Arnold and H. G. M. Williamson, 60–79. Downers Grove, IL: InterVarsity; Leicester: Inter-Varsity.

Ottosson, Magnus

1989 "Rahab and the Spies." In *DUMU-E$_2$-DUB-BA-A: Studies in Honor of Åke W. Sjöberg*, edited by H. Berhrens, D. Loding, and M. T. Roth, 419–27. Occasional Publications of the Samuel Noah Kramer Fund 11. Philadelphia: University of Pennsylvania Museum.

Pattison, George
1991 "Violence, Kingship and Cultus." *Expository Times* 102/5:135–40.
Perdue, Leo G., Lawrence E. Toombs, and Gary L. Johnson, eds.
1987 *Archaeology and Biblical Interpretation: Essays in Memory of D. Glenn Rose.* Atlanta: John Knox.
Person, Raymond F., Jr.
2002 *The Deuteronomic School: History, Social Setting, and Literature.* Studies in Biblical Literature 2. Atlanta: Society of Biblical Literature.
Peterson, Eugene H.
1989 *Answering God: The Psalms as Tools for Prayer.* San Francisco: Harper & Row.
2006 *Eat This Book: A Conversation in the Art of Spiritual Reading.* Grand Rapids and Cambridge: Eerdmans.
Pitkänen, Pekka M. A.
2011 *Joshua.* Apollos Old Testament Commentary. Downers Grove, IL: InterVarsity.
Polzin, Robert
1980 *Moses and the Deuteronomist: A Literary Study of the Deuteronomistic History.* New York: Seabury.
Porter, J. Roy
1983 "The Succession of Joshua." In *Proclamation and Presence: Old Testament Essays in Honour of Gwynne Henton Davies*, edited by John I. Durham and J. R. Porter, 102–32. New corrected ed. Macon: Mercer University Press. Original, 1970.
Prior, Michael, CM
1997 *The Bible and Colonialism: A Moral Critique.* Biblical Seminar 48. Sheffield: Sheffield Academic.
1999 *Zionism and the State of Israel: A Moral Inquiry.* London and New York: Routledge.
Pritchard, James B.
1969 *Ancient Near Eastern Texts Relating to the Old Testament.* 3rd ed. with Supplement. Princeton: Princeton University Press.
Provan, Iain W.
1988 *Hezekiah and the Books of Kings: A Contribution to the Debate about the Composition of the Deuteronomistic History.* Beihefte zur Zeitschrift für die alttestamentliche Wissenschaft 172. Berlin: Walter de Gruyter.
1995 "Ideologies, Literary and Critical: Reflections on Recent Writing on the History of Israel." *Journal of Biblical Literature* 114/4:585–606.
2002 "In the Stable with the Dwarves: Testimony, Interpretation, Faith, and the History of Israel." In *Windows into Old Testament History: Evidence, Argument, and the Crisis of "Biblical Israel,"* edited by V. Philips Long, David W. Baker, and Gordon J. Wenham, 161–97. Grand Rapids: Eerdmans.
Provan, Iain W., V. Philips Long, and Tremper Longman III
2003 *A Biblical History of Israel.* Louisville: Westminster John Knox.

Rad, Gerhard von

1966 "There Remains Still a Rest for the People of God: An Investigation of a Biblical Conception." In *The Problem of the Hexateuch and Other Essays*, 94–102. New York: McGraw-Hill.

1991 *Holy War in Ancient Israel.* Translated by Marva J. Dawn. Grand Rapids: Eerdmans. This ed. has a thirty-three page introduction by Ben C. Ollenburger and a bibliography on "War, Peace, and Justice in the Hebrew Bible," compiled and annotated by Judith E. Sanderson. Original, 1958.

Ramachandra, Vinoth

1996 *Gods That Fail: Modern Idolatry and Christian Mission.* Downers Grove, IL: InterVarsity.

Rasmussen, Carl G.

2003 "Conquest, Infiltration, Revolt, or Resettlement? What Really Happened During the Exodus-Judges Period?" In *Giving the Sense: Understanding and Using Old Testament Historical Texts*, edited by D. M. Howard Jr. and M. A. Grisanti, 138–59. Grand Rapids: Kregel.

Ray, Paul J., Jr.

2008 "Classical Models for the Appearance of Israel in Palestine." In *Critical Issues in Early Israelite History*, edited by Richard S. Hess, Gerald A. Klingbeil, and Paul J. Ray Jr., 79–93. Bulletin for Biblical Research: Supplement 3. Winona Lake, IN: Eisenbrauns.

Redekop, Vern Neufeld

2002 *From Violence to Blessing: How an Understanding of Deep-Rooted Conflict Can Open Paths to Reconciliation.* Ottawa: Novalis.

Reno, R. R.

2006 "Origen and Spiritual Interpretation." *Pro ecclesia* 15/1:108–26.

Richter, Sandra

2005 "Deuteronomistic History." In *Dictionary of the Old Testament: Historical Books*, edited by Bill T. Arnold and H. G. M. Williamson, 219–30. Downers Grove, IL: InterVarsity; Leicester: Inter-Varsity.

Rofé, Alexander

1985 "The Laws of Warfare in the Book of Deuteronomy: Their Origins, Intent and Positivity." *Journal for the Study of the Old Testament* 32:23–44.

Rosner, Brian S.

1999 "The Concept of Idolatry." *Themelios* 24/3:21–30.

2007 *Greed as Idolatry: The Origin and Meaning of a Pauline Metaphor.* Grand Rapids: Eerdmans.

Roth, Wolfgang

1976 "The Deuteronomic Rest Theology: A Redaction-Critical Study." *Biblical Research* 21:4–14.

Rowlett, Lori

1992 "Inclusion, Exclusion and Marginality in the Book of Joshua." *Journal for the Study of the Old Testament* 55:15–23.

1996 *Joshua and the Rhetoric of Violence: A New Historicist Analysis.* Journal for the Study of the Old Testament: Supplement Series 226. Sheffield: Sheffield Academic.

Sanders, James A.
1984 *Canon and Community: A Guide to Canonical Criticism*. Philadelphia: Fortress.

Sanders, John
1992 *No Other Name: An Investigation into the Destiny of the Unevangelized*. Grand Rapids: Eerdmans.

Sawyer, J. F. A.
1972 "Joshua 10:12-14 and the Solar Eclipse of 30 September 1131 B.C." *Palestine Exploration Quarterly* 104:139–46.

Schäfer-Lichtenberger, Christa
1994 *Josua und Salomo: Eine Studie zu Autorität und Legitimität des Nachfolgers im Alten Testament*. Vetus Testamentum Supplements 58. Leiden: E. J. Brill.

Schlabach, Gerald W.
1999 "Deuteronomic or Constantinian: What Is the Most Basic Problem for Christian Ethics?" In *The Wisdom of the Cross: Essays in Honor of John Howard Yoder*, edited by Stanley Hauerwas, Chris K. Huebner, Harry J. Huebner, and Mark Thiessen Nation, 449–71. Grand Rapids: Eerdmans.

Schniedewind, W. M.
2005 "Innerbiblical Exegesis." In *Dictionary of the Old Testament: Historical Books*, edited by Bill T. Arnold and H. G. M. Williamson, 502–9. Downers Grove, IL: InterVarsity; Leicester: Inter-Varsity.

Schwager, Raymund, SJ
1987 *Must There Be Scapegoats? Violence and Redemption in the Bible*. San Francisco: Harper & Row.

Segal, Benjamin J.
1987 *Returning: The Land of Israel as Focus in Jewish History*. Jerusalem: Department of Education and Culture of the World Zionist Organization.

Seibert, Eric A.
2009 *Disturbing Divine Behavior: Troubling Old Testament Images of God*. Minneapolis: Fortress.

Shenk, David W.
1995 *Global Gods: Exploring the Role of Religions in Modern Societies*. Scottdale, PA, and Waterloo, ON: Herald Press.

Shillington, V. George
1997 *2 Corinthians*. Believers Church Bible Commentary. Scottdale, PA and Waterloo, ON: Herald Press.
1998 "Atonement Texture in 1 Cor 5.5." *Journal for the Study of the New Testament* 71:29–50.

Silberman, Neil Asher, and David Small
1997 *The Archaeology of Israel: Constructing the Past, Interpreting the Present*. Sheffield: Sheffield Academic.

Simons, Menno
(*see Menno Simons*)

Sizer, Stephen
2007 *Zion's Christian Soldiers? The Bible, Israel and the Church*. Downers Grove, IL: InterVarsity.

Spina, Frank Anthony
1997 "Rahab." In *New International Dictionary of Old Testament Theology and Exegesis*, edited by William VanGemeren, 4:1123–26. Grand Rapids: Zondervan.
2005 *The Faith of the Outsider: Exclusion and Inclusion in the Biblical Story*. Grand Rapids: Eerdmans.

Stern, Philip D.
1991 *The Biblical Ḥerem: A Window on Israel's Religious Experience*. Brown Judaic Studies 211. Atlanta: Scholars Press.

Stone, Lawson G.
1991 "Ethical and Apologetic Tendencies in the Redaction of the Book of Joshua." *Catholic Biblical Quarterly* 53:25–36.

Stone, Douglas, Bruce Patton, and Sheila Heen
1999 *Difficult Conversations: How to Discuss What Matters Most*. New York: Penguin.

Swartley, Willard M.
1983 *Slavery, Sabbath, War, and Women: Case Issues in Biblical Interpretation*. Scottdale, PA, and Kitchener, ON: Herald Press.
1994 *Israel's Scripture Traditions and the Synoptic Gospels: Story Shaping Story*. Peabody, MA: Hendrickson.
2003a *Homosexuality: Biblical Interpretation and Moral Discernment*. Scottdale, PA, and Waterloo, ON: Herald Press.
2003b "War." In *The Westminster Theological Wordbook of the Bible*, edited by Donald E. Gowan, 524–28. Louisville: Westminster John Knox.

Thiselton, Anthony C.
1995 *Interpreting God and the Postmodern Self: On Meaning, Manipulation, and Promise*. Grand Rapids: Eerdmans.

Thompson, Leonard L.
1981 "The Jordan Crossing: *Ṣidqôt* Yahweh and World Building," *Journal of Biblical Literature* 100:343–358.

Tiessen, Terrance L.
2004 *Who Can Be Saved? Reassessing Salvation in Christ and World Religions*. Downers Grove, IL: InterVarsity.

Toews, John E.
2004 *Romans*. Believers Church Bible Commentary. Scottdale, PA, and Waterloo, ON: Herald Press.

Tov, Emmanuel
1986 "The Growth of the Book of Joshua in the Light of the Evidence of the LXX Translation." In *Studies in Bible*, 1986, edited by S. Japhet, 321–39. Scripta hierosolymitana 31. Jerusalem: Magnes.

Vannoy, J. Robert
1997 "Joshua: Theology of." In *New International Dictionary of Old Testament Theology and Exegesis*, edited by William VanGemeren, 4:810–19. Grand Rapids: Zondervan.

Van Seters, John
1990 "Joshua's Campaign of Canaan and Near Eastern Historiography." *Scandinavian Journal of the Old Testament* 2:1–12.

Vogt, Peter T.
2006 *Deuteronomic Theology and the Significance of* Torah*: A Reappraisal.* Winona Lake, IN: Eisenbrauns.
Volf, Miroslav
1996 *Exclusion and Embrace: A Theological Exploration of Identity, Otherness, and Reconciliation.* Nashville: Abingdon.
Wakely, Robin
1997 "*Mā'al, ma'al* I". In *New International Dictionary of Old Testament Theology and Exegesis*, edited by William VanGemeren, 2:1020–25. Grand Rapids: Zondervan.
Walzer, Michael
1992 "The Idea of Holy War in Ancient Israel." *Journal of Religious Ethics* 20/1:215–28. Followed by a response by John Howard Yoder (229–34) and a reply by Walzer (235).
Warrior, Robert Allen
1995 "A Native American Perspective: Canaanites, Cowboys, and Indians." In *Voices from the Margin: Interpreting the Bible in the Third World*, edited by R. S. Sugirtharajah, 277–85. 2nd ed. Maryknoll, NY: Orbis; London: SPCK.
Weaver, Alain Epp
2008 *States of Exile: Visions of Diaspora, Witness, and Return.* Scottdale, PA, and Waterloo, ON: Herald Press.
Weaver, Alain Epp, ed.
2007 *Under Vine and Fig Tree: Biblical Theologies of Land and the Palestinian-Israeli Conflict.* Telford, PA: Cascadia; Scottdale, PA: Herald Press.
Weinfeld, Moshe
1972 *Deuteronomy and the Deuteronomic School.* Oxford: Oxford University Press.
1983 "The Extent of the Promised Land—the Status of Transjordan." In *Das Land Israel in biblischer Zeit*, edited by Georg Strecker, 59–75. Göttinger theologische Arbeiten 25. Göttingen: Vandenhoeck & Ruprecht.
1986 "Divine Intervention in War in Ancient Israel and in the Ancient Near East." In *History, Historiography and Interpretation: Studies in Biblical and Cuneiform Literatures*, edited by H. Tadmor and M. Weinfeld, 121–47. Jerusalem: Magnes / Hebrew University.
1993 *The Promise of the Land: The Inheritance of the Land of Canaan by the Israelites.* Berkeley and Oxford: University of California Press.
Wells, Samuel
2004 *Improvisation: The Drama of Christian Ethics.* Grand Rapids: Brazos.
Wenham, G. J.
1971 "The Deuteronomic Theology of the Book of Joshua," *Journal of Biblical Literature* 90:140–48.
Whitelam, Keith W.
1996 *The Invention of Ancient Israel: The Silencing of Palestinian History.* New York: Routledge.

Wiebe, Philip
1997 *Visions of Jesus: Direct Encounters from the New Testament to Today.* Oxford: Oxford University Press.
Wilcken, John
1997 "The Biblical Promised Land and Australian Aboriginal Peoples." *The Australian Catholic Record* 74:86–98.
Wilcoxen, Jay A.
1968 "Narrative Structure and Cult Legend: A Study of Joshua 1–6." In *Transitions in Biblical Scholarship*, edited by J. Coert Rylaarsdam, 43–70. Essays in Divinity 6. Chicago and London: University of Chicago Press.
Williamson, H. G. M.
1976 "The Accession of Solomon in the Book of Chronicles." *Vetus Testamentum* 26:351–61.
Williamson, P. R.
2005 "Land." In *Dictionary of the Old Testament: Historical Books*, edited by Bill T. Arnold and H. G. M. Williamson, 638–43. Downers Grove, IL: InterVarsity; Leicester: Inter-Varsity.
Wink, Walter
1992 *Engaging the Powers: Discernment and Resistance in a World of Domination.* Minneapolis: Fortress.
Winn, Albert Curry
1993 *Ain't Gonna Study War No More: Biblical Ambiguity and the Abolition of War.* Louisville: Westminster John Knox.
Winther-Nielsen, Nicolai
1995 *A Functional Discourse Grammar of Joshua: A Computer-Assisted Rhetorical Structure Analysis.* Coniectanea biblica: Old Testament Series 40. Stockholm: Almqvist & Wiksell.
Wiseman, D. J.
1964 "Rahab of Jericho." *Tyndale Bulletin* 14:8–11.
Wood, Bryant G.
1990 "Did the Israelites Conquer Jericho? A New Look at the Archaeological Evidence." *Biblical Archaeology Review* 16/2:44–58.
2008 "The Search for Joshua's Ai." In *Critical Issues in Early Israelite History*, edited by Richard S. Hess, Gerald A. Klingbeil, and Paul J. Ray Jr., 205–40. Bulletin for Biblical Research: Supplement 3. Winona Lake, IN: Eisenbrauns.
Wood, John A.
1998 *Perspectives on War in the Bible.* Macon: Mercer University Press.
Work, Telford
2002 *Living and Active: Scripture in the Economy of Salvation.* Grand Rapids and Cambridge: Eerdmans.
Wright, Christopher J. H.
1990 *God's People in God's Land: Family, Land, and Property in the Old Testament.* Grand Rapids: Eerdmans; Exeter: Paternoster.
2008 *The God I Don't Understand: Reflections on Tough Questions of Faith.* Grand Rapids: Zondervan.

Wright, N. T.
1992 *The New Testament and the People of God. Vol. 1 of Christian Origins and the Question of God.* Minneapolis: Fortress.

Wyschogrod, Michael
1983 *The Body of Faith: Judaism as Corporeal Election.* New York: Seabury.

Yoder, John H.
1984 *The Priestly Kingdom: Social Ethics as Gospel.* Notre Dame, IN: University of Notre Dame Press.
1989 "'To Your Tents, O Israel': The Legacy of Israel's Experience with Holy War." *Studies in Religion* 18:345–62.
1992 "Texts That Serve or Texts That Summon? A Response to Michael Walzer." *Journal of Religious Ethics* 20/1:229–34.
1994 *The Politics of Jesus: Vicit Agnus Noster.* 2nd ed. Grand Rapids: Eerdmans; Carlisle: Paternoster.
1997 "Discerning the Kingdom of God in the World." In *For the Nations: Essays Public and Evangelical*, 237–45. Grand Rapids and Cambridge: Eerdmans.
2003 *The Jewish-Christian Schism Revisited.* Edited by Michael G. Cartwright and Peter Ochs. Grand Rapids and Cambridge: Eerdmans.
2010 *Nonviolence—A Brief History: The Warsaw Lectures.* Edited by Paul Martens, Matthew Porter, and Myles Werntz. Waco: Baylor University Press.

Yoder, Perry B.
1987 *Shalom: The Bible's Word for Salvation, Justice, and Peace.* Institute of Mennonite Studies Series 7. Newton, KS: Faith & Life.

Yoder Neufeld, Thomas
1997 *"Put on the Armour of God": The Divine Warrior from Isaiah to Ephesians.* Journal for the Study of the New Testament: Supplement Series 140. Sheffield: Sheffield Academic.
2011 *Killing Enmity: Violence and the New Testament.* Grand Rapids: Baker.

Younger, K. Lawson, Jr.
1990 *Ancient Conquest Accounts: A Study in Ancient Near Eastern and Biblical History Writing.* Journal for the Study of the Old Testament: Supplement Series 98. Sheffield: JSOT Press.
1999 "Early Israel in Recent Biblical Scholarship." In *The Face of Old Testament Studies: A Survey of Contemporary Approaches*, edited by David W. Baker and Bill T. Arnold, 176–206. Grand Rapids: Baker Academic; Leicester: Apollos / Inter-Varsity.
2008 "The Rhetorical Structuring of the Joshua Conquest Narratives." In *Critical Issues in Early Israelite History*, edited by Richard S. Hess, Gerald A. Klingbeil, and Paul J. Ray, Jr., 3–32. Bulletin for Biblical Research: Supplement 3. Winona Lake, IN: Eisenbrauns.

Zakovitch, Yair
1990 "Humor and Theology or the Successful Failure of Israelite Intelligence: A Literary-Folkloric Approach to Joshua 2." In *Text and Tradition: The Hebrew Bible and Folklore*, edited by Susan

Niditch, 99–104. Society of Biblical Literature Semeia Studies 20. Atlanta: Scholars Press.

Zerbe, Gordon

1991 "The Meaning of the Kingdom of God for the Stewardship of Creation." In *The Environment and the Christian: What Does the New Testament Say About the Environment?* edited by Calvin B. DeWitt, 73–92. Grand Rapids: Baker Books.

1993 *Non-retaliation in Early Jewish and New Testament Texts: Ethical Themes in Social Contexts.* Journal for the Study of the Pseudepigrapha: Supplement Series 13. Sheffield: JSOT Press.

Selected Resources

General Reference

Arnold, Bill T., and H. G. M. Williamson, eds. *Dictionary of the Old Testament: Historical Books*. Downers Grove, IL: InterVarsity; Leicester: Inter-Varsity, 2005. Includes articles on archaeology (Ortiz), many of the sites mentioned in the book of Joshua, Deuteronomistic History (Richter), historiography (McKenzie), history of the settlement period (Meier), the book of Joshua (Hawk), Joshua as a character (Nelson), and much more.

Commentaries

Butler, Trent C. *Joshua*. Word Biblical Commentary 7. Waco: Word, 1983. A traditional academically oriented commentary written prior to focused studies on the literary complexity of the book of Joshua.

Creach, Jerome F. D. *Joshua*. Interpretation: A Bible Commentary for Teaching and Preaching. Louisville: John Knox, 2003. A short, accessible, and theologically focused commentary.

Hawk, L. Daniel. *Joshua*. Berit Olam: Studies in Hebrew Narrative and Poetry. Collegeville, MN: Liturgical Press, 2000. Focuses on the artistry of the biblical narrative and the way Joshua subverts the readers' expectations. A development of his earlier work (1991).

———. *Joshua in 3-D: A Commentary on Biblical Conquest and Manifest Destiny*. Eugene, OR: Cascade, 2010. Juxtaposes the book of Joshua with the American master narrative of Manifest Destiny.

Hess, Richard S. *Joshua: An Introduction and Commentary*. Tyndale Old Testament Commentaries. Leicester: Inter-Varsity; Downers Grove, IL: InterVarsity, 1996. Includes historical and archaeological evidence for the "historicity" of the conquest.

Howard, David M. Jr. *Joshua*. The New American Commentary 5. Nashville: Broadman & Holman, 1998. A thorough traditional commentary with an historical and theological focus.

Hubbard, Robert L. *The NIV Application Commentary: Joshua*. Grand Rapids: Zondervan, 2009. A thoroughly theological commentary that is richly peppered with practical application and lessons that are either gleaned or extrapolated from the book of Joshua.

McConville, J. Gordon, and Stephen N. Williams. *Joshua*. The Two Horizons Old Testament Commentary. Grand Rapids and Cambridge: Eerdmans, 2010. A short commentary followed by long essays and responses on reading Joshua theologically, by McConville (biblical scholar) and Williams (theologian).

Nelson, Richard D. *Joshua*. Old Testament Library. Louisville: Westminster John Knox, 1997. A fine traditional commentary that deals with textual variants, redaction criticism, and literary and theological reflection.

Pitkänen, Pekka M. A. *Joshua*. Apollos Old Testament Commentary. Downers Grove, IL: InterVarsity, 2011. This commentary leaves no stone unturned. Detailed and comprehensive.

Focused Studies

Butler, Trent C. *Understanding the Basic Themes of Joshua*. Dallas: Word, 1991.

Earl, Douglas S. *Reading Joshua as Christian Scripture*. Journal of Theological Interpretation: Supplement 2. Winona Lake, IN: Eisenbrauns, 2010.

———. *The Joshua Delusion? Rethinking Genocide in the Bible*. Eugene, OR: Cascade, 2010. The book includes a response by Christopher J. H. Wright and a reply by the author.

Habel, Norman. *The Land Is Mine: Six Biblical Land Ideologies*. Minneapolis: Fortress, 1995.

Hawk, L. Daniel. *Every Promise Fulfilled: Contesting Plots in Joshua*. Literary Currents in Biblical Interpretation. Louisville: Westminster John Knox, 1991.

Hess, Richard S., Gerald A. Klingbeil, and Paul J. Ray Jr., eds. *Critical Issues in Early Israelite History*. Bulletin for Biblical Research: Supplement 3. Winona Lake, IN: Eisenbrauns, 2008.

Hess, Richard S., and Elmer A. Martens, eds. *War in the Bible and Terrorism in the Twenty-First Century*. Bulletin for Biblical Research: Supplement 2. Winona Lake, IN: Eisenbrauns, 2008.

Mitchell, Gordon. *Together in the Land: A Reading of the Book of Joshua*. Journal for the Study of the Old Testament: Supplement Series 134. Sheffield: Sheffield Academic, 1993.

Niditch, Susan. *War in the Hebrew Bible: A Study in the Ethics of Violence*. New York and Oxford: Oxford, 1993.

Polzin, Robert. *Moses and the Deuteronomist: A Literary Study of the Deuteronomistic History*. New York: Seabury, 1980.

Rowlett, Lori. *Joshua and the Rhetoric of Violence: A New Historicist Analysis*. Journal for the Study of the Old Testament: Supplement Series 226. Sheffield: Sheffield Academic, 1996.

Younger, K. Lawson, Jr. *Ancient Conquest Accounts: A Study in Ancient Near Eastern and Biblical History Writing*. Journal for the Study of the Old Testament: Supplement Series 98. Sheffield: JSOT Press, 1990.

Joshua, Promised Land, and Contemporary Conflict over Israel/Palestine

Burge, Gary M. *Whose Land? Whose Promise? What Christians Are Not Being Told About Israel and the Palestinians.* Cleveland: Pilgrim, 2003.

———. *Jesus and the Land: The New Testament Challenge to "Holy Land" Theology.* Grand Rapids: Baker, 2010.

Chapman, Colin. *Whose Promised Land? The Continuing Crisis over Israel and Palestine.* Grand Rapids: Baker, 2002.

Jeschke, Marlin. *Rethinking Holy Land: A Study in Salvation Geography.* Scottdale, PA, and Waterloo, ON: Herald Press, 1995.

Johnston, Philip, and Peter Walker, eds. *The Land of Promise: Biblical, Theological and Contemporary Perspectives.* Downers Grove, IL: InterVarsity; Leicester: Apollos, 2000.

March, W. Eugene. *God's Land on Loan: Israel, Palestine, and the World.* Louisville and London: Westminster John Knox, 2007.

Munayer, Salim J. and Lisa Loden, eds. *The Land Cries Out: Theology of the Land in the Israeli-Palestinian Context.* Eugene, OR: Cascade, 2012.

Sizer, Stephen. *Zion's Christian Soldiers: The Bible, Israel and the Church.* Downers Grove, IL: InterVarsity, 2007.

Weaver, Alain Epp, ed. *Under Vine and Fig Tree: Biblical Theologies of Land and the Palestinian-Israeli Conflict.* Telford, PA: Cascadia; Scottdale, PA: Herald Press, 2007.

Index of Ancient Sources

Exodus

Deuteronomy

1 Chronicles

2 Chronicles

Ezra

The Author

Gordon Matties is professor of biblical studies at Canadian Mennonite University in Winnipeg, Manitoba, Canada. He has been teaching in Winnipeg since 1984, beginning at Mennonite Brethren Bible College, which became Concord College in 1991. Most recently he served as dean of humanities and sciences at CMU.

Gordon was born and grew up in British Columbia's Fraser Valley. He is a graduate of Briercrest College (Saskatchewan), the University of British Columbia (BA, Classics), Regent College (Vancouver, BC), and Vanderbilt University (Nashville, TN), where he received a PhD in Old Testament. In 1990 the Society of Biblical Literature published his dissertation, *Ezekiel 18 and the Rhetoric of Moral Discourse*. He has published articles in church periodicals and has contributed essays to published collections. He contributed to Abingdon Press's *The New Interpreter's Study Bible*. He currently teaches biblical studies and dabbles in film studies. He has served on several juries at international film festivals. And he has led numerous study tours to Israel/Palestine.

He is married to Lorraine (Nix), whom he met at Regent College. They have two adult children. Gordon is a member of the River East Mennonite Brethren Church in Winnipeg where he currently serves as the congregation's moderator.

Joshua

"Gordon Matties approaches the book of Joshua, which has been used to justify some of the most reprehensible behavior in Western history, precisely the way a peace church scholar should—staring it square in the face. This work brilliantly illustrates why we need a Believers Church Bible Commentary series."—*Daniel Smith-Christopher, professor of theological studies, Loyola Marymount University*

"Matties invites readers to enter a conversation marked by hermeneutical hospitality, giving Joshua its say as well as providing opportunity to listen to other biblical texts. A masterful treatment!"—*Lynn Jost, professor of Old Testament, Fresno Pacific Biblical Seminary*

"Matties engages in theological interpretation of Joshua in ways that make this difficult book relevant to modern readers without anachronistically forcing a peace tradition theology on the text."—*Ray Person, professor of philosophy and religion, Ohio Northern University*

"Be prepared for surprises. While some commentaries offer definitive answers, Matties encourages dialogue—with other biblical texts, with the early Church Fathers, Origen, and with Tolkien and modern films."—*Elmer A. Martens, professor emeritus of Old Testament, Fresno Pacific Biblical Seminary*

"A careful scholar, sound theoretician, and sensitive interpreter, the author brings many years of teaching and research to this rich and evocative volume."—*Keith Bodner, professor of religious studies, Crandall University*

"Attentive to the often negative legacy of Joshua, Matties provides profound insight, and exemplifies a commitment to both Scripture and community that reflects the peace church tradition at its best. Sometimes resources for peace can be found in the most unexpected places."—*W. Derek Suderman, assistant professor of religious studies, Conrad Grebel University College, University of Waterloo*